Advances in Pattern Recognition

Advance in Pattern Recognition is a series of books which brings together current developments in all areas of this multi-disciplinary topic. It covers both theoretical and applied aspects of pattern recognition, and provides texts for students and senior researchers.

Springer also publishes a related journal, **Pattern Analysis and Applications**. For more details see: http://link.springer.de

The book series and journal are both edited by Professor Sameer Singh of Exeter University, UK.

Also in this series:

Principles of Visual Information Retrieval
Michael S. Lew (Ed.)
1-85233-381-2

Statistical and Neural Classifiers: An Integrated Approach to Design
Šarūnas Raudys
1-85233-297-2

Advanced Algorithmic Approaches to Medical Image Segmentation
Jasjit Suri, Kamaledin Setarehdan and Sameer Singh (Eds)
1-85233-389-8

NETLAB: Algorithms for Pattern Recognition
Ian T. Nabney
1-85233-440-1

Object Recognition: Fundamentals and Case Studies
M. Bennamoun and G.J. Mamic
1-85233-398-7

Computer Vision Beyond the Visible Spectrum
Bir Bhanu and Ioannis Pavlidis (Eds)
1-85233-604-8

Hexagonal Image Processing: A Practical Approach
Lee Middleton and Jayanthi Sivaswamy
1-85233-914-4

Support Vector Machines for Pattern Classification
Shigeo Abe
1-85233-929-2

Bidyut B. Chaudhuri (Ed.)

Digital Document Processing

Major Directions and Recent Advances

Bidyut B. Chaudhuri, PhD
Indian Statistical Institute, Kolkata, India

Series editor
Professor Sameer Singh, PhD
Department of Computer Science, University of Exeter, Exeter, EX4 4PT, UK

British Library Cataloguing in Publication Data
A catalogue record for this book is available from the British Library

Advances in Pattern Recognition Series ISSN 1617-7916

ISBN-13: 978-1-84996-614-6   e-ISBN-13: 978-1-84628-726-8
Printed on acid-free paper.

9 8 7 6 5 4 3 2 1

springer.com

Preface

The field of automatic document processing, more than a century old, is quite a mature one. It started with an attempt to automatically read printed text in the era well before the birth of digital computers and has been since continuing on various topics like document image enhancement, document structure and layout analysis, handwritten character recognition, document data compression, graphics recognition, document information retrieval and meta-data extraction. In addition to OCR, applications like tabular form and bank cheque processing or postal mail reading are of great interest to the software industry.

This edited book is a compilation of twenty chapters written by leading experts on the above and several other important topics. These chapters describe the state of the art in these areas, enumerate the research challenges and propose one or more possible solutions in a systematic way. Usually, edited books are compiled on some special area of a general discipline. But this one attempts to cover wider aspects of digital document processing and hence has the flavour of a handbook. Since there is no standard textbook with a wide coverage of the subject, this book will immensely help students taking undergraduate and graduate courses in digital document processing. Also, it is hoped that the researchers in the field will benefit from this book. About 9 years ago, Bunke and Wang edited a useful book of similar nature. However, the activities on document analysis have since advanced much, with newer techniques being invented by the community and younger disciplines like super-resolution text processing, handwriting individuality identification or web document mining gaining importance. Even on older topics like OCR, good work is in progress on challenging problems like the reading of Indian and Tibetan scripts. All these advancements contributed to the need for another edited book.

This book starts with an excellent introduction to the general discipline of document processing, followed by studies on document structure analysis. The next few chapters describe OCR systems for some difficult printed scripts that are followed by advances in on-line and off-line handwritten text recognition, with applications to postal automation and bank cheque processing. Then come the special topics of mathematical expression and graphics recognition, as well as super-resolution text analysis. Other problems like image degradation modelling, meta-data extraction, document information retrieval are addressed in the next few chapters. Some emphasis has been given on web document analysis and data mining problems. The last three chapters of this book are dedicated to these topics.

This book is the outcome of my interaction with the authors over a reasonably long period. In this endeavour, my sincerest thanks go to Professor Horst Bunke with whom I initially made plans to co-edit this book. At the preparatory stage, I received generous help from his vast experience on various issues like framing of book structure, the choice of chapter topics, the choice of potential authors as well as fixing other subtle points. However, because of heavy workload and subsequent illness, he had to discontinue his involvement in the editorial process. Nevertheless, I am grateful for his continuous advice, encouragement and best wishes for the completion of this project.

I express my sincere thanks to all authors for their hard work in preparing their manuscripts. Special mention should be made of Prof. L. Schomaker who not only wrote an introductory chapter but also patiently read all other chapters in order to write critical summaries of them. The readers will get a quick idea of all the topics by reading this chapter alone.

During my work on this book I enjoyed a sabbatical leave as well as a *Jawaharlal Nehru Fellowship*. The support of my institute and of the Jawaharlal Nehru Memorial Fund is gratefully acknowledged. I am thankful to my colleagues, Dr Utpal Garain, Mr Chittaranjan Das and Ms Shamita Ghosh, who helped me in various stages of the editorial work. The understanding and support of my family is also highly appreciated. Finally, I thankfully acknowledge the patience of Ms Catherine Brett of Springer Verlag for replying to my numerous e-mails and other support provided to me during the editing of this book.

Bidyut B. Chaudhuri
Kolkata, India

Contents

**3   OCR Technologies for Machine Printed
     and Hand Printed Japanese Text** 49
Fumitaka Kimura

**7   New Advances and New Challenges in On-Line
Handwriting Recognition and Electronic
Ink Management** 143
Eric Anquetil and Guy Lorette

8   Off-Line Roman Cursive Handwriting Recognition 165
Horst Bunke and Tamás Varga

Contributors

Stefan Agne, German Research Center for Artificial Intelligence (DFKI), 67608 Kaiserslautern, Germany. agne@dfki.de

Y. Al-Ohali, Computer Science Department, King Saud University, Riyadh, KSA. yousef@ccis.ksu.edu.sa

Eric Anquetil, IRISÃ-INSA, Université de Rennes1, Campus de Beaulieu, F-35042 Rennes Cedex, France. anquetil@irisa.fr

Apostolos Antonacopoulos, School of Computing, Science and Engineering, University of Salford, Greater Manchester, United Kingdom. A.Antonacopoulos@primaresearch.org

N. E. Ayat, Laboratory for Imagery, Vision and Artificial Intelligence, École de technologie supérieure / University of Quebec, 1100, Notre-dame W. Montreal (Qc), Canada H3C 1K3. nedjem@livia.etsmtl.ca

Henry S. Baird, Computer Science and Engineering Department, Lehigh University, 19 Memorial Drive West, Bethlehem, PA 18015, USA. baird@cse.lehigh.edu

A. Belaïd, University Nancy 2-LORIA, F-54506 Vandoeuvre-lès-Nancy, France. abelaid@loria.fr

D. Besagni, INIST 2, Allée du Parc de Brabois, F-54514 Vandoeuvre-lès-Nancy, France. besagni@inist.fr

Horst Bunke, Institutät für Informatik und angewandte Mathematik, Universität Bern, Neubrückstrasse 10, CH-3012 Bern, Switzerland. bunke@iam.unibe.ch

B. B. Chaudhuri, Indian Statistical Institute, 203 B. T. Road, Kolkata 700108, India. bbc@isical.ac.in

M. Cheriet, Laboratory for Imagery, Vision and Artificial Intelligence, École de technologie supérieure / University of Quebec, 1100, Notre-dame W. Montreal (Qc), Canada H3C 1K3 mohamed. cheriet@etsmtl.ca.

Sung-Jung Cho, Interaction Lab., Samsung Advanced Institute of Technology, P.O. Box 111, Suwon, 440-600, Korea. sung-jung.cho@samsung.com, sjcho@ai.kaist.ac.kr

Andreas Dengel, German Research Center for Artificial Intelligence (DFKI), 67608 Kaiserslautern, Germany. dengel@dfki.de

Xiaoqing Ding, Department of Electronic Engineering, Tsinghua University, Beijing, 100084, China. dingxq@tsinghua.edu.cn

Hiromichi Fujisawa, Central Research Laboratory, Hitachi, Ltd, Tokyo, Japan. fujisawa@crl.hitachi.co.jp

Utpal Garain, Indian Statistical Institute, 203 B. T. Road, Kolkata 700108, India.

Nikolai Gorski, Artificial Intelligence and Image Analysis (A2iA), 40-bis rue Fabert, 75007 Paris, France. gorski@a2ia.com

Jianying Hu, IBM T. J, Watson Research Center, 1101 Kitchawan Road, Route 134, Yorktown Heights, NY 10598, USA. jyhu@us.ibm.com

Chen Huang, Center of Excellence for Document Analysis and Recognition (CEDAR), University at Buffalo, State University of New York, 520 Lee Entrance, Amherst, NY 14228, USA.

Anil K. Jain, Michigan State University, East Lansing, MI - 48824, USA. jain@cse.msu.edu

Markus Junker, German Research Center for Artificial Intelligence (DFKI), 67608 Kaiserslautern, Germany. junker@dfki.de

Harish Karnick, Department of Computer Science and Engineering, Indian Institute of Technology, Kanpur 208016, India. hk@cse.iitk.ac.in

Jin Hyung Kim, CS Div., EECS, Korea Advanced Institute of Science and Technology (KAIST), Yousong-ku, Daejon 305-701, Korea. jkim@ai.kaist.ac.kr

Fumitaka Kimura, Faculty of Engineering, Mie University, Tsu 514-8507, Japan. kimura@hi.info.mie-u.ac.jp

Koichi Kise, Department of Computer Science and Intelligent Systems, Osaka Prefecture University, 1-1 Gakuencho, Sakai, Osaka 599-8531, Japan. kise@cs.osakafu-u.ac.jp

Stefan Klink, Department of Database and Information Systems (DBIS), University of Trier, 54286 Trier, Germany. klink@uni-trier.de

Josep Lladós, Computer Vision Center, Department Informática. Universitat Autónoma de Barcelona, 08193 Bellaterra (Barcelona), Spain. josep@cvc.uab.es

Guy Lorette, 2IRISÃ, Université de Rennes1, Campus de Beaulieu, F-35042 Rennes Cedex, France. lorette@irisa.fr

Céline Mancas-Thillou, Faculté Polytechnique de Mons, Laboratoire de Théorie des Circuits, et Traitement du Signal, 7000 Mons, Belgium. celine.thillou@tcts.fpms.ac.be

Rupesh R. Mehta, Department of Computer Science and Engineering, Indian Institute of Technology, Kanpur 208016, India. rrmehta@cse. iitk.ac.in

Majid Mirmehdi, Department of Computer Science, University of Bristol, Bristol BS8 1UB, UK. M.Mirmehdi@cs.bris.ac.uk

Pabitra Mitra, Department of Computer Science and Engineering, Indian Institute of Technology, Kharagpur 721302, India. pabitra@cse.iitkgp. ernet.in

Anoop M. Namboodiri, International Institute of Information Technology, Hyderabad, 500 019, India. anoop@iiit.ac.in

Lambert Schomaker, Artificial Intelligence Department, Groningen University, The Netherlands. schomaker@ai.rug.nl

Vivek Shah, Center of Excellence for Document Analysis and Recognition (CEDAR), University at Buffalo, State University of New York, 520 Lee Entrance, Amherst, NY 14228, USA.

Sargur N. Srihari, Center of Excellence for Document Analysis and Recognition (CEDAR), University at Buffalo, State University of New York, 520 Lee Entrance, Amherst, NY 14228, USA. srihari@cedar.buffalo.edu

Harish Srinivasan, Center of Excellence for Document Analysis and Recognition (CEDAR), University at Buffalo, State University of New York, 520 Lee Entrance, Amherst, NY 14228, USA.

C. Y. Suen, CENPARMI, CSE, Concordia University, Suite VE-3.105, 1455 de Maisonneuve Blvd West, Montreal, Quebec H3G 1M8, Canada. suen@cenparmi.concordia.ca

Tamás Varga, Institutät für Informatik und angewandte Mathematik, Universität Bern, Neubrückstrasse 10, CH-3012 Bern, Switzerland. varga@iam.unibe.ch

Hua Wang, Department of Electronic Engineering, Tsinghua University, Beijing, 100084, China.

1

Reading Systems: An Introduction to Digital Document Processing

Lambert Schomaker

1.1 Introduction

Methods for the *creation and persistent storage* of text [10] have existed since the Mesopotamian clay tablets, the Chinese writings on bamboo and silk as well as the Egyptian writings on papyrus. For *search and retrieval*, methods for systematic archiving of complete documents in a library were developed by monks and by the clerks of emperors and kings in several cultures. However, the technology of *editing* an existing document by local addition and correction of text elements has a much younger history. Traditional copying and improvement of text was a painstakingly slow process, sometimes involving many man years for one single document of importance. The invention of the pencil and eraser in 1858 was one of the signs of things to come. The advent of the typing machine by Sholes in 1860 allowed for faster copying and a simultaneous on-the-fly editing of text. The computer, finally, allowed for a very convenient processing of text in digital form. However, even today, methods for generating a new document are still more advanced and mature than are the methods for processing an existing document.

This observation may sound unlikely to the fervent user of a particular common word-processing system, since creation and correction of documents seems to pose little problems. However, such a user has forgotten that his or her favourite word-processor software will only deal with a finite number of digital text formats. The transformation of the image of an existing paper document − without loss of content or layout − into a digital format that can be textually processed is mostly difficult and often impossible. Our user may try to circumvent the problem by using some available software package for optical-character recognition (OCR). Current OCR software packages will do a reasonable job [16] in aiding the user to convert the image into a document format that can be handled by a regular word-processing system, provided that there are optimal conditions with respect to:

- image quality;
- separability of the text from its background image;
- presence of standard character-font types;
- absence of connected-cursive handwritten script;
- simplicity of page layout.

Indeed, in those cases where strict constraints on content, character shape and layout do exist, current methods will even do quite a decent job in faithfully converting the character images to their corresponding strings of digital character codes in ASCII or Unicode. Examples of such applications are postal address reading or digit recognition on bank cheques.

On the other hand, if the user wants to digitally process the handwritten diary of a grandparent or a newspaper snippet from the eighteenth century, the chances of success are still dim. Librarians and humanities researchers worldwide will still prefer to manually type ancient texts into their computer while copying from paper rather than entrusting their material to current text-recognition algorithms. It is not only the word processing of arbitrary-origin text images that is a considerable problem. Even if the goal can be reduced to a mere search and retrieval of relevant text from a large digital archive of heterogeneous text images there are many stumbling blocks. Furthermore, surprisingly, not only are the ancient texts posing problems. Even the processing of modern, digitally created text in various formats such as web pages with their mixed encoded and image-based textual content will require "reverse engineering" before such a digital document can be loaded into the word processor of the recipient.

Indeed, classification of text within an image is so difficult that the presence of human users of a web site is often gauged by presenting them with a text fragment in a distorted rendering, which is easy on the human reading system but an insurmountable stumbling block for current OCR systems. This weakness of the artificial reading system thus can be put to good use. The principle is known as "CAPTCHA: Completely Automated Public Turing Tests to Tell Computers and Humans Apart" [5]. During recent years, yet another exciting challenge has become apparent in pattern-recognition research. The reading of text from natural scenes as recorded by a camera poses many problems, unless we are dealing with a heavily constrained application such as, e.g. the automatic recognition of letters and digits in snapshots of automobile licence plates. Whereas licence-plate recognition has become a "mere" technical problem, the camera-based reading of text in man-made environments, e.g. within support systems for blind persons [8], is only starting to show preliminary results.

Non-technical users will often have difficulties in understanding the problems in digital-document processing (DDP) and in optical character recognition. The human reading process evolves almost effortlessly in the experienced reader. Therefore, it is difficult to explain to users that machine reading of documents involves a wide range of complicated algorithms, which in one way or another must emulate the processing of text by the human brain. Where the human eye samples the text opportunistically from syllable to syllable and from word to word, the algorithms in DDP will scan a complete page image and will need to segment its layout at a number of hierarchical levels. Where the human reader eclectically takes into account several layers of contextual information on language and text topic, systems in DDP are still limited in their analytic and associative capabilities to handle arbitrary textual input. Rather than aiming to develop a *universal reading machine*, most engineering efforts today are aimed at dealing with a structured subset of all possible text-processing problems. In some cases, the machine already outperforms humans. A state-of-the art cheque reading system has been trained on more variants of handwritten digit shapes and styles than most humans will ever encounter during a lifetime. For the first few minutes of reading digits, human and machine will have comparable digit-classification performances. However, after half an hour, the machine would have won, not being distracted by problems of perceptual-cognitive concentration and/or tedium. For other tasks, where the human will prove to be the better reader, the machine still provides an attractive alternative due to the speed of processing and the massive amounts of data that can be processed, albeit in a crude manner. Let us take a look at the differences between human and machine reading. In Table 1.1, a comparison is made between aspects of the human and artificial reading system. We focus on each of the numbered items in this table.

1.2 Text Sensing

Humans are able to read texts easily as flat 2D patterns in orthonormal projection or as filled 3D objects from a wide range of poses. In machine reading, usually flat-bed scanners are used. There is an increased interest in the challenging problem of camera-based text reading from photographs or video recorded in a man-made environment with text patterns embedded within a natural scene. The input consists of an image $I(x, y)$ where the intensity I may be scalar, as in grey-scale images, or vectorial, as in RGB colour images. In some systems and application settings for automatic handwriting recognition such as, e.g. an enhanced mobile phone, recordings of pen-tip movement and writing force (pressure) can be recorded, yielding a signal (x_t, y_t) or (x_t, y_t, p_t).

1.3 Sensor Scope

Although in conflict with our subjective experience, human vision does not function like the camera at all. Cameras and scanning devices are

Table 1.1. A comparison between human and machine reading. Letters in the first column refer to corresponding paragraphs in the text

	Aspect	Human	Machine
(a)	**text sensing**	any visual modality 2D, 3D	− flat-bed scanner − digitizer tablet − camera
(b)	**sensor scope**	opportunistic, limited-field panning sensor	full-page scan
(c)	**sensor grid**	"log polar"	Cartesian
(d)	**pre-processing power**	powerful, flexible and adaptive in hypothesizing "layers" of foreground and background	designed for known ink and background colours and textures, difficulties with touching or overlapping shapes
(e)	**affine invariance**	high	usually some position, size, slant, and perspective sensitivity
(f)	**ink thickness invariance**	high	often some ink-thickness sensitivity
(g)	**shape features**	on-demand, various	prefixed, limited
(h)	**processing type**	analytic and associative power	fixed, probability and/or shape-based models, brute-force computation
(i)	**computing architecture**	open-ended	fixed processing pipeline
(j)	**computing strategy**	satisficing	fixed thresholds and goals
(k)	**knowledge base**	broad	narrow
(l)	**cognitive reliability**	stochastic	deterministic
(m)	**response in case of difficult input**	graceful degradation	counter-intuitive output
(n)	**classification accuracy**		
	− machine print	very high	very high
	− isolated hand print	very high	high
	− cursive handwriting		
	− in context	high	low to medium
	− out of context	medium to high	very low
	− 3D multicolor text	very high	low
(o)	**energy, concentration**	limited	indefatigable
(p)	**speed**	limited	high
(q)	**volume processing**	limited	massive

designed to record images with an even resolution over the whole visual field. The eyes, on the contrary, view a limited part of the visual field and sample the surrounding world in a series of saccades, i.e. eye jumps and fixations. The illusion of a permanent "Ganzfeld" is not in the eye, but is constructed by the occipital part of the brain. The human system has the advantage of not having to compute image transformations over the whole image. There is a price to be paid, naturally. The movements of the sensor must be guided by computed estimates of what is the most informative jump of the eye towards the next particular spot in the text. Additionally, the system must retain, more centrally in the cortex, all information in the image that is pertinent to reading but is not in central, foveated view. Whereas the engineered system is forced to sense the complete field, the biological system uses "opportunistic sampling". This means that in machine reading, there exists a problem of layout analysis and segmentation, which is completely different from the problems that are encountered and solved by the human reader. Figure 1.1 shows a recording of human eye movement during reading.

The top half of Figure 1.1 shows a text fragment from *Hamlet*, with dotted lines depicting the saccadic movements. In the bottom half of Figure 1.1, the eye movements are isolated from the text and the order of the fixation points is represented by their number. The regular reading behaviour is characterized by a focus, which is located mostly just below the text

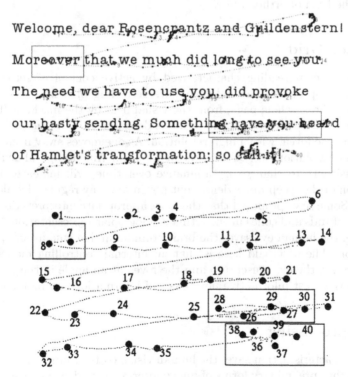

Fig. 1.1. Eye movements in the human reading of a text fragment from Shakespeare's *Hamlet* (Dutch subject). The reader is referred to the text for further details. Data courtesy: H. van Rijn and L. van Maanen.

line. Words and syllables are scanned, usually from left to right. At the end of the line there is an "eyes return" (cf. "carriage return") movement, to a horizontal position corresponding to about the fourth letter, in this font. The exceptions to the rule are informative. The word *"Moreover"* is fixated first in its rightmost half, probably due to a stochastic undershoot of fixation 7, which is compensated by a leftward saccade and fixation 8. Where there are syntactical surprises, the regular pattern is clearly disturbed. The Shakespearean phrasing surprises the Dutch reader, such that the scanning behaviour is characterized by backtracking: fixations 25, 26, 27, leftwards to 28, etc. (in *"Something have you heard"*); and fixations 35, 36, 37 then leftwards to 38 (in *"so call it"*). Such recordings illustrate the purposive nature of reading. Contrary to the intuition in traditional views on human information processing, syntax and semantics are not "late" end stages of a long and unidirectional processing pipeline, they directly influence the low-level sensing behaviour. It can also be observed that the foreign name *"Rosencrantz"* elicits three fixations (2, 3, and 4). In Dutch spelling, the nearest neighbour would be spelled "Rozenkrans". In order to decipher the exact spelling, iterative fixations seem to be required here to solve the reading puzzle at the level of orthography.

1.4 Sensor Grid

Not only is human reading characterized by active control of selective attention, as opposed to the indeterminate recording of a large rectangular portion, i.e. a whole page, from the visual field by the machine. The distribution of receptive cells in the retina is determined by a dense region in the retina, the fovea, with a high resolution. As one moves away from the centre is, the resolution decreases, while at the same time temporal acuity, i.e. the sensitivity to changes in luminance over time, will increase. The organization of the receptors is dense, but not in any way regular, let alone Cartesian. Some have proposed that the most appropriate interpretation of the density of rods and cones in the retina is a log polar representation [28]. In any case, the human eye saves the brain from an undue amount of optic computation. The cost paid here is that an internal controlling model is needed to guide the eye muscles to aim the fovea at an angle in the visual field where the most informative next piece of information can be found.

1.5 Pre-processing

A second characteristic that saves the human visual cortex from undue computation is that preliminary forms of image filtering and edge enhancement already take place within the eye itself. What is more, the biological system in primates makes a distinction between "Where" and "What" channels for processing optical information. These two pathways start within the eye, i.e. a slow, parvocellular system representing the "What" information for pattern classification in area "V4"[1] [3] of the visual cortex and a fast magno-cellular system representing information to solve "Where" questions from motor control in area "MT" of the cortex [33]. Within area "V1", with its early projections coming from the optic nerve, additional optical pre-processing takes place on the basis of a distribution of centre-surround kernels that are optimal for adaptive foreground–background separation and orientation detection by "grating" neurons [18].

Although many improvements have been made in scanner and camera technology over the last decade, a lot can be improved. The reader is challenged to try to make a scan from a personal, old, coffee-stained, folded, crackled, and lineated page with conference notes and attain a perfect foreground–background separation of the handwritten text. Obviously, local thresholding methods for binarization exist. Methods that are exclusively oriented on local luminance will fail in case complex texture and colours with low luminance-differences are involved. Humans appear to be able to maintain active hypotheses on layers of visual information yielding, subjectively, a solid percept of "hovering layers" each representing paper texture, lineation, stains and, of course, the ink that makes up the shape of a character. In current OCR systems on the contrary, a problem as "simple" as the touching characters will pose a problem. Usually heuristics are applied, which may work in some conditions but will fail miserably elsewhere. While some researchers are interested in biologically motivated methods for textural background removal [18] using Gabor functions, others exploit a combination of mathematical morphology and genetic algorithms [9] for trained foreground–background separation. Figures 1.2 and 1.3 give examples of, difficult and manageable historic material as regards foreground–background separation respectively.

1.6 Invariance to Affine Transforms

Human reading is not completely insensitive [32] to affine transforms of character shape (position, scale, orientation, shear). This indicates that shape normalization in the human vision system might not be as simple as a matrix–vector multiplication: There exists a confounding between geometric processing and the statistics of the common text pose. As an example, reading speed will remain constant for a wide range of orientations, but reading text that is upside down will demand increased cognitive efforts. Similarly, there is a range of an acceptable shear transforms of text,

---

[1] Brodmann (1868–1918) started a systematic analysis of the histology (tissue typing) of the brain, suggesting names for brain areas that usually coincide with a particular function. Modern brain atlases [26] are in use within functional magnetic-resonance imaging (fMRI) research, but reference to Brodmann is still common.

Fig. 1.2. Infeasible foreground−background separation in an eighteenth-century Dutch shipping list. Even a native Dutch historian will have problems reading this material.

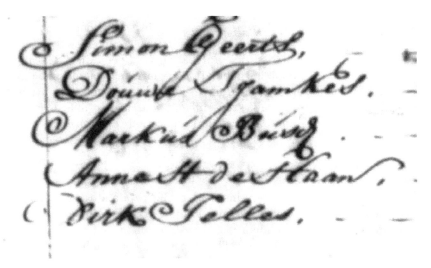

Fig. 1.3. Although not easy, foreground−background separation seems feasible on this eighteenth-century Dutch sample. Both Figures 1.2 and 1.3 are digitized from microfiche of a collection of harbour-tax registers: Paalgeldregisters, selected years 1744–1748, Gemeente Archief Amsterdam, courtesy of Dr. George Welling. Automatic transcription of text and amounts in these financial documents is still impossible.

beyond which it becomes illegible. Position invariance is solved because the eye-movement control will lead to a relative coding of the image information. Notably, it is the output signal of the muscle-control signals that represents the position of a foveated syllable within the text. This demonstrates that perceptual facilities cannot be decoupled from motor facilities [22]. Scale invariance in human vision is very good for characters larger than the lower limit of visual acuity and small enough to be foveated and focused as a complete pattern.

In systems for digital document processing we usually have to be pragmatic in order to realize a tolerance for affine transforms. Algorithm design in the field of pattern recognition is, on the one hand, characterized by the quest for a comprehensive mathematical formulation of an invariant geometric space for relevant shape features that would provide the necessary robustness against natural variation. This appears to be rather difficult. Therefore, there also exists, on the other hand, a quest for automatic geometric normalization tricks. Examples are the methods to estimate baseline pose, character size, and slant, followed by a normalization stage after which non-invariant features may be used. Reasonable results can be obtained in this area, but also here, the flexibility of the machine is limited in comparison to biological vision with its head start of millions of years of evolution in a harsh environment. Here, as in the other levels of processing there is a "chicken and egg problem": we need to have an idea about the content of, e.g. a camera-based snapshot of text to be able to unslant it while we need to unslant the pattern to be able to classify it reliably (Figure 1.4).

1.7 Invariance to Ink-Trace Thickness

In traditional OCR systems, it makes a difference whether one recognizes 12pt Times Roman in normal as compared to bold rendering. To the human reader, boldness in font rendering is an irrelevant superficial property of text. Some multi-font approaches, however, actually require that several rendering styles of a font family and size are represented within the recognition engine. Alternatively, omnifont character-recognition methods may attempt to minimize the influence of ink thickness by the use of thinning and skeletonization techniques. Although the stroke-width variation is reduced, new problems emerge due to thinning. It is especially the case in handwriting that the skeletonization to an ink-trace thickness of only one pixel may complicate recognition rather than facilitating it due to the addition of structural features in the residual trace where the pattern was simple, before. A simple crossing in the digit 8 may be replaced by a forked pattern of unpredictable orientation after thinning. Chapter 11 will contain an example of problematic skeletonization in Arabic script. Historical documents in particular will pose problems. Each time the ink pen or quill

Fig. 1.4. A challenge to camera-based reading systems: perspective deformation, low contrast, and glare make this a difficult sample. The addition of colour would only partly alleviate the pre-processing problems (the text is: "HEMA").

Fig. 1.5. Realistic problems of ink width and grey-level variation. There are black boundaries in the horizontal line, where the metal pen scratched the paper, leading to increased ink absorption, (Kabinet van de Koningin, Nationaal Archief, Den Haag, 1903).

is dipped into the ink bottle, the trace of the subsequently written characters will be wide and dark. As the ink flows into the absorbing paper, the trace usually gets thinner and less satiated. For metal pens that make use of capillary ink flow, the trace may actually consist of two dark lines that are formed by the metal legs pressed apart too widely, the middle part of the trace being less satiated (Figure 1.5). Ink-trace thickness invariance remains an important problem.

1.8 Shape Features

A plethora of feature representations has been developed in our research field to describe the shape of characters or words. The design of, e.g. a character-feature vector is still an art rather than a technology. Successful approaches are usually copied: the evidence for success is often derived from empirical evaluation rather than being obtained through principled design. No amount of mediocre features or classification algorithms is a substitute to an excellent feature. A good feature, i.e. a source of information with generalizing power as regards all instances of a target class together with a discriminative power as regards instances of irrelevant classes, will yield reasonable performances on even simple nearest-neighbour search. There are some general criteria as regards features.

A good shape feature:

- is informative as regards class separation;
- is robust to noise;
- is invariant to affine transforms and ink width;
- is homogeneously scaled with other features in the feature vector;
- can be computed efficiently.

Character-based features are useful but they assume that characters can be segmented out of the input pattern stream. Word-shape features may avoid character segmentation, but they must be powerful enough to give each lexical word its own unique and separable volume in the word-feature space. Unfortunately, little is known about the features that humans use in reading. The informative value of ascenders and descenders is so high [23], that it would be strange if human readers would not use it in reading. In reality, however, it is difficult to detect human usage of word-shape features if the individual characters are clearly separable from the background. There is some support for the notion that human perception is drawn to singularities [25] in the script pattern [23]. A clear disadvantage of many approaches to pattern recognition is the fact that all features must be computed for all classes in a fixed-dimensionality feature vector classification method. Some techniques, such as decision trees, allow for the ad hoc and on-demand computation of feature values, per class. However, tree-based approaches suffer from the "premature commitment" problem: An erroneous decision in the beginning leads to a certain misclassification in the end. Furthermore, while class-specific features may be desirable, the manual design of features per class quickly becomes prohibitive in free-style handwriting or international scripts with many shape classes. In this respect, human perception may be exquisitely equipped with mechanisms for opportunistic feature extraction, i.e. exploiting the presence of features as they are required to obtain a solid decision.

Currently a hot topic in neuro-scientific analysis of the reading process [30] is the question whether and how word-shape analysis plays a separate role next to character-level shape analysis in human reading [17, 23]. Recently, a brain region has been detected, dubbed "Visual Word Form Area" or VWFA. It is located in the left brain hemisphere, where language resides, notably in the left fusiform gyrus. The VWFA area is active while literate subjects are reading [6]. Also, this brain region shows a stronger activation in response to real letters and real words as compared to letter strings or pseudo-fonts of comparable visual complexity. Underscoring the separation between Where and What routes of processing, the activation in the VWFA region is invariant to the spatial location. Furthermore, the specific case or font type that is used to present words has no noticeable effect [6]. It has been suggested that the VWFA region contains orthographic representations of written words [4]. Dehaene et al. [7] recently proposed an explanation for the neural coding scheme of words, which stresses on a gradual transition between low-level features and high-level view-independent features. Rather than committing itself to "symbolic" codes, the neural activity simultaneously represents, from low- to high-level features: local contrast, oriented bars, local contours, case-specific character shapes, case-unspecific letter detectors, local character bigrams upto small words, and recurring ("reusable") substrings or morphemes. Such a model also would explain more easily than the strict left-to-right Markov models why a sequence such as "fsat cempoutr porgarm" can be deciphered as "fast computer program" by human readers mastering the English language [15, 21]. It is argued [7] that a minimalistic, symbolic code for visual words is unlikely. Rather, a diverse and redundant repertoire of reading-related neurons are expected to be involved, which make use of and modify the information delivered by the pre-existing primate visual system. After all, the phenomenon of reading only exists since five to six thousand years. It is unlikely that structural, genetic changes have led to reading-specific modules in the brain, as is the case in speech, in such a short period.

1.9 Processing Type

Human and machine reading are evidently different at the level of implementation, i.e. neural wetware vs. silicon hardware. Within the current context, the functional differences in processing are more relevant. Engineered systems provide a level of reading performance that can be attributed to both (a) massive training with labeled data and (b) the availability of exact, "brute" computations according to heavily structured algorithms. The process of human reading, however, is characterized by a limited amount of training on stylized characters provided by a single teacher and a schoolbook. Punctuated supervision, where character image and its spoken representation are coupled explicitly by the teacher, only lasts a relatively brief period at primary school. Generalization over script styles is realized in an independent manner by the reading child itself. In case of illegible script, human readers activate a number of cognitive facilities. If superficial association fails, the reader may solve the underlying reading puzzle by analytically combining elements from (a) the linguistic context, (b) the shape context [19, 31] as well as (c) the pragmatic context. At the very moment of being handed a handwritten shopping list, the human reader is pre-cued to a very limited subset of the total lexicon, even before having attempted to read the first character. Similarly, the envelope with the logo of the tax department (IRS in the United States) will pre-cue the reader as regards the linguistic context to be expected. Once reading has started, linguistic structure determines the interpretation of the patterns in a top-down manner. At the same time, the shape of characters in flanking words to the current gaze provides cues as regards the peculiarity of a current font or script style. It is the flexible manner in which the human reader actively hunts for the necessary information, which contrasts distinctly with the stereotyped and rigid processing in machine reading.

1.10 Computing Architecture

This brings us to the computing architecture. Although not enough is known about the details of human cognition, its architecture is very different from the architecture of a cheque-reading system or a word recognizer on a hand-held pen-based computer. To a large extent, our artificial systems are still built according to the factory metaphor: A pipeline where raw data come in at the left, being refined in successive stages and dropping a perfect product in the form of a symbolic character string at its output on the right. Feedback processes have been tried, e.g. for the purpose of optimization of a geometric normalization stage. However, the variable response time, which is the result of feedback, is often unacceptable in industrial or interactive applications. Also, the uncertainty that is involved in incremental learning or live adaptation is considered much too large to yield an efficient and stable system behaviour. Indeed, most reading systems implicitly rely on the fact that a human reader is still somewhere in the loop. Modern interactive handwriting-recognition systems – as are in use in the Tablet-PC[2] software by Microsoft – allow for interactive corrections to written words by adding or deleting elements in the input pattern. In such an approach, the design and implementation of the word classifier is heavily determined by considerations of computing architecture.

1.11 Computing Strategy

There is an additional distinction between human and machine computing that needs to be taken into account. This distinction is both related to the intention of the computing process itself and to the way in which purposive computation proceeds, strategically. In machine reading, the designer of the algorithm strives for the perfect response, which is either a correct

---

[2] *Pen Computing Magazine*, July 2001, http://www.pencomputing.com/.

answer or a *Reject* response in case of unknown input material, given constant thresholds on probability or distance values. Human cognition, on the other hand, is more liberal and sloppy in its nature. The usual operating strategy in many aspects of human cognition is called *"satisficing"* [24]. The human brain, much as the electronic computer, has a finite computing power. Perfect rationality requires an undue amount of computation such that a best possible response often cannot be given in a predictable and limited amount of computing time. It is therefore assumed that the human cognizer has adopted the strategy to be content with "bounded rationality", yielding reasonably correct answers with an acceptable time delay. In order to survive, the trick is to apply heuristics in a pre-determined order until a sufficient level of certainty is reached [11]. Such a sloppy strategy may indeed seem irrational if the reading puzzle can be solved in a closed and perfect manner, given the evidence that is present in the patterns. However, if there are many problems of uncertainty due to low pattern quality, computing the perfect answer becomes virtually impossible. Here, a satisficing reader may very well yield an average performance that is higher than that of a well-trained but bare-bones hidden-Markov model (HMM). The latter system has no intrinsic cognitive functionality to take a step aside and conclude, e.g. that it makes no sense to compute the posterior probabilities for all characters due to the bad image quality in the middle zone of the given word pattern. In this matter, natural cognition and practical systems might be closer than one would expect. Where performance counts, a large portion of an *engineered* reading system is devoted exactly to such smart use of heuristics and multiple strategies. It may come as a disappointing surprise to academicians, but as a rough estimate, less than 5% of the source code of reading systems is concerned with (statistical) shape classification, per se, even if the user-interface code is not counted. Of course it is important to strive for the best possible character classifier. However, without a proper embedding in a powerful goal-directed computing strategy, the isolated HMM classifier is as practical as a combustion engine on a shaky test bench.

1.12 Knowledge Base

From the scientific viewpoint, keeping in mind Occam's razor, it is very unfortunate; but the massive amount of parameters representing human knowledge is hard to beat by an artificial reading system. The availability of explicit knowledge allows an address-reading system to take into account diverse information such as word shape or the list of allowable ZIP codes. Unfortunately, the slightest cultural change will require human labour in the form of newly entered knowledge. In licence-plate reading, once the character-classification problems have stabilized, a company will spend a considerable amount of time in manual knowledge engineering if their systems are sold in a new, hitherto unknown country with its own licence-plate formats. One of the reasons why the *universal reading machine* cannot be built, as yet, is that we cannot simply glue together knowledge from different areas and expect to have a more powerful system. With the addition of each new category of text (numbers, licence plates, addresses, traffic-sign text, handwritten material, etc.) current artificial systems will be clogged rather than helped by the growing amount of knowledge. In such a *universal reading machine*, there will be a new problem: How to know which subset of all the available knowledge pertains to the problem at hand?

1.13 Cognitive Reliability

Beside all its strengths, human cognition also has flaws. Apart from its intrinsic "satisficing" sloppiness, there is the ever-present problem of noise. To persons with a mathematical mind and a fondness for logic it may be disconcerting but the basic computing element of the human brain, the neuron, can be viewed as a generator of a stochastic point process in time [29]. By virtue of the population statistics of the firing behaviour of groups of neurons, a behaviour results that is partly deterministic, however, with an intrinsic amount of residual noise that is ever present. This can be observed from the trembling fingers after two cups of coffee or the numerous typing, writing and speaking errors that are made during the day by an average human being. The laser pointer that is used to point at items on the screen during a presentation at a conference relentlessly amplifies such motor noise to a wandering trajectory of the light spot, even in the relaxed speaker. This intrinsic system noise leads to problems as diverse as handwriting variability in writers and typing errors in data-entry operators. In this area, fortunately, we prefer silicon hardware, to yield the same response on the same scanned word, deterministically, regardless of time.

1.14 Response in Case of Difficult Input

For real-life practical systems, a proper response in case of difficult input is highly important. Users and journalists often like to joke about mis-recognitions in reading systems as well as in automatic speech recognition. However, inappropriate system behaviour is a serious problem and still constitutes a major stumbling block to widespread acceptation of document processing systems in the market. Human reading is characterized by graceful degradation [20]. If there is an error, the Levenshtein or edit distance between the response and the input word usually will be low. In artificial reading systems, again, the state of affairs is less fortunate. On the one hand, the use of lexicon-based response improvement may enhance the reading performance. On the other hand, an error in such a system will concern a full wrong word. Full-word errors are hard to accept by human users and difficult to correct if the original document is not present for inspection. Depending on the application and the preferences of the user, a *Reject* response may be most appropriate. However, it depends on the details of the user interface in interactive applications whether a system failure will be accepted by the human users.

1.15 Classification Accuracy

Human reading of machine printed text is near perfect, apart from fatigue problems to be mentioned in the following paragraph. Therefore it is not useful to use recognition error rates. The differences between the regular font types are usually negligible. Reading speed decreases when font size decreases to 10pt and smaller. Legge et al. [13] have compiled a series of chapters on the *Psychophysics of reading*, addressing the legibility of fonts. The conditions in reading of handwritten material are different. Here, human reading has limitations, too (Table 1.2), yielding imperfect recognition of isolated words or words from a small and restricted context window.

As can be observed in Table 1.2, only in handprint does human recognition reach a high recognition rate of 98%, whereas the recognition of cursive words varies from 54 to 88%. The combination of sloppy writing and absence of linguistic and shape context leads to a poor 54%. These and other [2] findings suggest that it is unrealistic to assume that the asymptote for cursive recognition is 100%. This poses an interesting problem concerning the reliability of the ground truth provided for handwritten words in free style. Usually, multiple truthers will be called in to increase the reliability of text labels to the raw handwritten-image data. As regards human reading performances on free-style text in natural scenes, there are currently no reference data. Finally, as regards measuring classification performance, these human-reading results should make us sceptical when considering overly optimistic results published in academic research. Fortunately, system benchmarking has improved from an earlier stage in research where

Table 1.2. Human recognition rates of handwritten words on paper (H.L. Teulings and L. Schomaker, unpublished). Experiments: A: single-word recognition; B−D: three-word sequences, middle-word recognition

Exp.	Context	Style	Writers	Target words	Readers	Words	Recognized
A	frequently used Dutch words	handprint	1	30	12	$N = 360$	98%
	frequently used Dutch words	neat cursive	1	30	12	$N = 360$	88%
B	sentence fragments, same writer	cursive	3	15	12	$N = 180$	85%
C	sentence fragments, same writer	cursive	4	13	20	$N = 260$	85%
	unrelated words, same writer	cursive	4	13	20	$N = 260$	77%
D	unrelated words, same writer	fast cursive	12	12	15	$N = 180$	72%
	unrelated words, different writers	fast cursive	12	12	15	$N = 180$	54%

a PhD student worked for several years on a single training/test set combination. In order to report reliable classification performance values, it is common to use k-fold cross-validation of systems [12], today. It would even be better if thesis advisors would keep back unseen data, for an objective measurement at project conclusion.

1.16 Energy and Mental Concentration

The reading process in human and machine require energy for both (a) document handling, scanning and (b) computing. Both document transport and the physical movement of the sensors require energy and imply wear and tear. Where human and machine differ is in the recognition performance over time, which is constant in the machine. In humans, recognition performance degrades over time due to fatigue. For this reason, data typists and cheque-reading operators are only allowed to work for limited time spans (20−30 min) if the consequences of an error are grave, as is the case in financial applications.

1.17 Processing Speed

Human reading speed from screen varies from 160−200 words per minute (wpm) on average [1]. Fast readers may attain speeds above 200 wpm. Such a speed corresponds to 160 bits per second for a language with an average word length of eight characters. It should be noted that the reading speed from paper is much faster, i.e. 250−300 wpm. The cause of this phenomenon is unknown. The contrast and resolution of printed documents on paper still outperforms current electronic display technologies (CRT or LCD). Typing (keying) speed in transcription is 27−40 wpm, on average. The speed of optical character recognition (OCR) can exceed 1500 words per minute. However, such a rating does not take into account the manual handling, i.e. the scanning process itself, manual annotations and manual image adjustment and finally, the manual correction of recognition errors that may be required. For difficult text images, human typing may often be attractive, especially if the volume in terms of number of pages is small.

1.18 Volume Processing

Indeed, the strongest point for digital document processing and OCR is the ability to process massive amounts of data. Today, several companies refrain from promising perfect text recognition. Since text retrieval is even more important than document editing in many office applications, a product that aims at an acceptable performance on keyword-based retrieval will be more attractive than a product promising veridical transcription that cannot be achieved in practice. If proper text-matching algorithms are used, such a keyword-based search and retrieval system may provide a valuable functionality in allowing access to an otherwise unwieldy archive of digital-text images. As stated earlier, the applications of cheque reading and address reading may provide quite good recognition rates, in addition to volume processing. In these latter applications, routine human labour can be saved.

1.19 Summary of Human Versus Machine Reading

As can be concluded from Table 1.1, both human and machine reading have powerful characteristics and it cannot be denied that the machine has attractive performances in terms of speed and volume, especially in the case of constrained-shape and constrained-content text images. Still, the robustness of the human reading system poses a challenge to system developers. Recent results in human-reading research and brain imaging provide an increasingly detailed picture of the architecture and processes in the human reading system. These findings may provide inspiration for system designers.

Book Overview

This book describes in detail many of the aforementioned topics in digital document processing, and more, by experts from within the difference subfields of our research area.

Chapter 2 *Document Structure and Layout Analysis* by Anoop M. Namboodiri and Anil K. Jain

This chapter gives an overview of layout-analysis methods, mostly concentrating on scanned, off-line, image analysis. Furthermore it describes the case of layout analysis of on-line handwritten text obtained sampling pen-tip coordinates in time. Both traditional methods such as the analysis of ink-density profiles as well as more advanced and recent approaches based on connected-components are handled. Bottom-up and top-down approaches in document-structure analysis are described, also introducing important concepts such as physical versus logical document structure. In order to evaluate hard-coded or trained layout-analysis systems, it is important to use reliable and valid methods for performance evaluation. It is noted that we are still far away from having a truly generic document-layout analysis. Also here, the development of the universal reading system remains an exciting scientific challenge.

Chapter 3 *OCR Technologies for Machine Printed and Hand Printed Japanese Text* by Fumitaka Kimura

This chapter describes the complete processing pipeline for optical character recognition in Japanese text, assuming machine-printed or hand-printed characters. Japanese texts pose interesting problems due to the fact that different scripts (Kanji, Katakana, Hiragana, English and Arabic numerals) are contained in one document. Additionally, the orientation of text lines may be vertical or horizontal. The Asian characters are "monospaced", while the English text contains character boxes of another size, potentially also in a font with a proportional horizontal spacing. The pre-processing stages of deskewing, slant normalization and non-linear size normalization are described. For the feature-extraction phase, directional features are presented. Finally, the chapter compares a number of classification methods and addresses the problem of feature scaling and dimensionality reduction.

Chapter 4 *Multi-Font Printed Tibetan OCR* by Xiaoqing Ding and Hua Wang

The authors introduce a complete system for the recognition of multi-font Tibetan script. By deskewing pages, detecting the base line, which in this script is about at the top of the characters and by a subsequent normalization of the upper and lower parts of the character, statistical classification can be realized on features derived from the segmented character boxes. Feature selection is guided by testing the entropy-based mutual information measure and by using linear-discriminant analysis in order to obtain a compressed feature set. The actual classification method is a modified quadratic discriminant function.

Chapter 5 *On OCR of a Printed Indian Script* by Bidyut Baran Chaudhuri

The diversity of scripts on the global scale is large. Multi-script, international digital encoding of text is a fairly recent development, after a long stage in information-technology that was dominated by the use of the ASCII code, which is only really suitable for a limited number of Western scripts. Not surprisingly, OCR of a multitude of scripts is just starting to develop since the acceptation of Unicode has become widespread. There are a billion people in India, writing in a dozen of scripts. In this chapter, an OCR method for the Bangla script is described. The chapter explains the structure of this alphabetic-syllabic script. The similarities between Bangla and the Devanagari script allow for a use of similar OCR approaches. Based on character-shape knowledge, a distinction can be made between upper, middle and lower zones. The presence of elongated horizontal structures aids in the pre-processing stage. A method for solving touching characters in Bangla is introduced. Words can be represented as a graph where the nodes constitute the basic recognized parts and the edges represent the geometric organization of structural elements. The large number of shape classes for the latter makes it difficult to exploit statistical methods (ANN,HMM,SVM) beyond nearest-neighbour matching. More research in this area is deemed necessary.

Chapter 6 *A Bayesian Network Approach for On-line Handwriting Recognition* by Sung-Jung Cho and Jin Hyung Kim

This chapter presents a novel method in modelling on-line handwriting. It is noted that traditional hidden-Markov modelling misses long-range dependencies between strokes in handwriting. Durational modelling is far from ideal in such models. By using an explicit modelling of inter-stroke relationship using Bayesian nets, assuming conditional Gaussian distributions, the authors are able to show very high recognition rates on three databases as compared to two traditional approaches. The model also allows for a generation of clear character prototypes that are considerably more natural than the HMM-generated patterns.

Chapter 7 *New Advances and New Challenges in On-Line Handwriting Recognition and Electronic Ink Management* by Eric Anquetil and Guy Lorette

On-line handwriting recognition is concerned with the "live" transform of pen-tip movements of handwriting into character codes, as is used on pen-based digital appliances and pen-based notebook computers. This application consequently poses a number of constraints on a handwriting-recognition system that are noted in this chapter. Whereas on-line handwriting recognition usually goes along with higher recognition rates than is the case in off-line handwriting recognition and techniques may even address writer dependence, the on-line field lagged with respect to the aspects of document-layout analysis, which is highly advanced in off-line systems. However, the increased availability of hardware and the emergence of standards for "electronic ink" have provided an impetus for the development of methods for the interpretation of on-line generated document structure. The chapter addresses lazy versus eager interpretation of document structure. Additionally problems of small devices and their consequences for the human—machine interface are addressed.

Chapter 8 *Off-Line Roman Cursive Handwriting Recognition* by Horst Bunke and Tamás Varga

This chapter describes digital document processing with Roman cursive handwriting recognition as its main purpose. It is noted that, while isolated character recognition is a mature field, the recognition of words and word sequences is still a topic of research. After pre-processing and normal-ization stages, such as the removal of the predominant slant in the hand-written patterns (which is jointly determined by pen grip and preferred movement direction [14], LS), a number of classification (reading) strate-gies are possible: isolated character recognition, cursive word recognition, (over)-segmentation-based approaches bridging the gap between grapheme sequences and words, hidden-Markov model based recognition; and, finally cursive word sequence recognition, possibly using statistical language mod-els. As emerging topics, the chapter identifies (1) an ongoing trend towards standardized databases and performance evaluation, (2) the possibilities of solving the data starvation problem of machine learning approaches by using original data with synthetic mixtures based on proper distortion models and (3) the usefulness of using multiple classifiers in handwriting recognition.

Chapter 9 *Robustness Design of Industrial Strength Recognition Systems* by Hiromichi Fujisawa

Fujisawa provides an overview on performance-influencing factors (PIF) in postal-address analysis systems. The general theme of this chapter is "know thy enemy". By an explicit modelling of all hostile factors that in-fluence recognition performer, robust systems can be designed for operation in the real world. A detailed enumeration of noise factors, defects, varia-tions, imperfections and distortions is given. An example of a particular problem class would be the "touching characters". An argument is made for a number of robustness-enhancing techniques. Although the chapter is not explicitly oriented towards agent-based computing, the design philos-ophy is based on a clear encapsulation of document-related expertise in specialized modules that are only activated when needed. An important and useful warning is issued concerning the reliance on posterior proba-bilities for generating rejects on irrelevant or unknown input. Indeed, a good recognizer should ideally first recognize if the input pattern belongs to the classes on which it has been trained. Many systems are flawed in this respect. In real systems in the real world such "meta intelligence" is needed. Theoretical work in this area [27] may be used for defining a single-class classifier, which encompasses all targeted classes on which it is trained.

Chapter 10 *Arabic Cheque Processing System: Issues and Future Trends* by M. Mohamed Cheriet, Y. Al-Ohali, N.E. Ayat and C.Y. Suen

There is a clear trend towards handling more and more international scripts. This chapter deals with the interesting case of reading text on

Arabic cheque. The availability of an Arabic cheque-processing system will have an impact on this application in at least twenty countries. Interestingly, numerals may be written as Indian numerals, not Arabic numerals in some regions. Using a data set of realistic samples from a bank, the study describes processing steps, feature choice and classification technology. The goal is to use discrete-HMM models for sub-words. The ISODATA algorithm is used for searching shape clusters, and vector quantization is used to adopt the discrete model. The chapter illustrates how an analysis of the errors provides insight in the strengths and weaknesses of the approach. For the special case of the Indian numerals, the suitability of the support-vector machine is successfully demonstrated. Finally, the chapter discusses the requirements for future scalable Arabic cheque processing systems.

Chapter 11 *OCR of Printed Mathematical Expressions* by Utpal Garain and Bidyut Baran Chaudhuri

With the success of optical character recognition on general texts, it also becomes clear where there are limitations. In scientific documents, the presence of mathematical expressions will pose a problem to current OCR systems. Such expressions contain a multitude of additional characters and symbols. Additionally, their organization in the plane is vastly different from the regular line structure of normal text. The chapter gives a detailed overview on the detection of page zones containing mathematical expressions, the recognition of symbols, the segmentation of touching symbols and the interpretation of expression structure. Performance evaluation poses problems in this domain, since annotated reference data are hard to obtain and the measurement of correctness in terms of element classification and structure detection is not trivial.

Chapter 12 *The State of the Art of Document Image Degradation Modelling* by Henry S. Baird

In the chapter by Baird, the disconcerting problem of the fragility of many systems for digital document processing is brought to our attention. Small defects in image quality to have detrimental effects on text-recognition performance. Fortunately, however, new methods have evolved that allow for a controlled generation of degraded text images in order to improve recognizer robustness during training or in order to test the sensitivity to image degradation in a given OCR system. The chapter gives an overview of the state of this art in literature. Two basic approaches are introduced (1) physics-based modelling of defects and (2) statistical modelling of text-image defects. Current degradation models are based on bi-level document images. Still, the availability of degradation models allows for an effective enlargement of a given training set. Indeed, two important concluding remarks of this chapter are, (1) "real data is corrupting: it is so expensive that we reuse it repeatedly [...]", and (2) "training on a mixture of real and synthetic data may be, today, the safest [method]".

Chapter 13 *Advances in Graphics Recognition* **by Josep Lladós**

This chapter provides an overview of the sub-domains of digital document processing, which focus mostly on non-textual two-dimensional graphical patterns. Here, the goal is to regularize and abstract images of schematic drawings by means of pixel-to-vector transforms and shape classification. Application examples concern: electrical and logic diagrams, geographic maps, engineering drawings, architectural drawings, musical scores, logo recognition, table and chart recognition. A distinction can be made between off-line analysis of scanned images of graphics and on-line processing of drawing and sketching movement in pen-based systems. Whereas the problem of vectorization of bitmapped images has been solved to a large extent, it is this success itself that has revealed more clearly the residual and fundamental problem of extracting a meaningful structural description from two-dimensional graphic patterns. The field of graphics recognition is particularly evolved in the area of integrating low-level processing modules within a knowledge-based framework for the interpretation of shape. The availability of benchmarks for performance evaluation in graphics recognition has provided a major impetus to the maturity of the field.

Chapter 14 *An Introduction to Super-Resolution Text* **by Céline Mancas-Thillou and Majid Mirmehdi**

The introduction of camera-based OCR has reintroduced an interest in image-processing techniques. While digital document processing has advanced from bitonal 200 dpi scans to 300 dpi and higher-resolution greyscale or colour scanning from paper, camera recordings contain jagged low-resolution text images. The regular structure of characters allows for advanced reconstruction schemes known as super-resolution processing. In still images, local bilinear interpolation can be used. In video recordings, super-resolution can also be obtained using frame-to-frame information. The additional information can be used in order to determine a warping transform in conjunction with a deblurring and denoizing step. The amount of parameters makes this problem ill-posed, still. A number of methods are described. The authors introduce an advanced variant, using filtering, Taylor series and bilinear interpolation in a robust framework. Super-resolution techniques are shown to improve OCR performance from 72 up to 91%.

Chapter 15 *Meta-data Extraction from Bibliographic Documents for Digital Library* **by Abdel Belaïd and D. Besagni**

The authors of this chapter describe knowledge-based methods for the analysis of text representing bibliographic information. By using linguistic and structural constraints, it becomes possible to automatically generate meta-data for bibliometric and retrieval purposes in digital library applications. The modelling methods may use, for instance, linguistic background information as made explicit through part-of speech (POS) tagging. Examples are given of experimental results.

Chapter 16 *Document Information Retrieval* by S. Klink, K. Kise, A. Dengel, M. Junker and S. Agne

This chapter provides an introduction to information retrieval. The field of information retrieval is concerned with the search for documents in large electronic collections (i.e. ASCII or Unicode text) on the basis of keywords. The basic vector-space method (VSM) is explained, as introduced by Salton. Subsequently, the chapter continues to address more advanced topics. Relevance feedback concerns the guided search and improved retrieval on the basis of user feedback on the relevance of found hit lists. A speciality of the authors is *passage retrieval*, where the goal is to find relevant passages rather than whole documents. Collaborative information retrieval (CIR) is introduced: A later user with similar information needs to earlier searchers can profit from automatically acquired knowledge in several ways. A CIR system keeps tracks of queries and the returned documents. This information can be used to adapt a given query to an expanded or more precise format. Methods for textual ASCII/Unicode retrieval of electronic documents can be generalized to retrieval of documents, which are archived as sequences of page images by means of an OCR front-end indexer.

Chapter 17 *Biometric and Forensic Aspects of Digital Document Processing* by Sargur N. Srihari, Chen Huang, Harish Srinivasan and Vivek Shah

The advances in digital document processing not only have an impact on OCR, per se. Using current methods for pre-processing and feature extraction, new applications are possible. In forensic applications, one would like to find the identity of the unknown writer of a given sample of handwriting. Another possible application concerns the verification of a claimed identity for a given sample of handwriting or handwritten signature. In traditional forensic handwriting analysis, human experts perform manual measurements and judgements. Using current techniques, a more objective semi-automatic approach becomes feasible. The chapter introduces a number of interactive processing methods, handwriting features and matching schemes for writer and signature verification, using Bayesian modelling. Explicit statistical modelling allows for the use of probabilities and likelihood ratios, which is essential for the acceptance of this technology by forensic practitioners.

Chapter 18 *Web Document Analysis* by Apostolos Antonacopoulos and Jianying Hu

The chapter by Antonacopoulos and Hu provides an eye opener for those who think that life is easy if a document is already in an encoded electronic format beyond the flat image. Even if a document is decoded at the character level its content must be analysed for repurposing or retrieval. An example is the induction of the structure of tables. Additionally, the image material in web pages that contains text poses new problems that are different both from the problems encountered in scanned document images and problems in camera-based text recognition. Figures 2 and 3 in this chapter provide example of the large difficulties of analysing text of machine-based origin in images on web pages.

Chapter 19 *Semantic Structure Analysis of Web Documents* by Rupesh R. Mehta, Harish Karnick and Pabitra Mitra

Even in cases where a document exists in digitally encoded and enriched form, a reading system must be able to structure the content. Web documents are usually encoded in HTML, representing text with rendering attributes in a particular layout, as well as referring to non-textual page elements such as images. The human reader is well able to direct attention to the textual core content of a web page. Information retrieval systems that aim at finding relevant documents on the basis of key words or example texts will benefit from a thorough analysis of layout for semantically homogeneous text passages. In this chapter, an analysis of visual elements on a page is proposed in order to determine topical text elements. Examples are visual elements of background colour, lines and images used as separators, font changes, and so on. Bayesian modelling can be used to estimate the predictive value of visual page attributes in the determination of semantic categories for a web page.

Chapter 20 *Bank Cheque Data Mining: Integrated Cheque Recognition Technologies* by Nikolai Gorski

A comprehensive view on an actual cheque-reading system is provided in this chapter. Cheque reading started with attempts to read legal and courtesy amounts on cheques. However, the continued use of handwritten and signed cheques and the need for automation necessitated the development of recognition of other fields, as well. The visual content of a cheque contains machine printed and handwritten items: payee name, payer's address, date, cheque number, legal amount, bank name, address and logo, a memo line, a courtesy amount and the field containing the payer's signature. Each of these fields requires a specialized approach. Especially in case of handwritten fields the amount of information is not sufficient to allow for perfect classification. Domain knowledge is needed to segment and recognize the visual content. As a more elaborate example, the handling of name aliases is described. Payee or payer's name often occur in a number of variations ("aliases"). By training a neural network on real and generated name aliases, the resulting alias detector can be used to improve system performance. The chapter also gives an insight into the process of internationalization and the concomitant improvement of the described cheque-reader as a product.

1.20 Conclusion

This book focuses on technological problems of digital-document processing from different angles and at different levels of the document processing pipeline. The motivation for the development of new algorithms in this area is fed by the strong conviction that DDP will not only solve a number of existing problems in the ways we manipulate text, but it will also allow us to develop new methods of working with documents, extracting detailed and often hidden pieces of information. New algorithms will be available to determine writer identity, historical dating of a text and even estimation of the author's age in handwritten documents. New data-mining methods will be able to uncover hidden relations between documents in huge collections, not only in terms of textual content but also in terms of layout and typographic styles. Improved modelling of character shapes will lead to a more general applicability of optical character recognition on artistic or three-dimensional shapes. Even if it is unlikely that we will be able to construct a *universal reading machine* anytime soon within the next decade, it is certain that research in digital document processing will help to pave the road towards understanding perceptual intelligence. At the same time the book shows that an important part of the work devoted to this exciting topic has an actual impact on the ways in which documents are processed in the world of real practical applications.

References

1. Bailey, R.W. (1996). *Human Performance Engineering: Designing High Quality Professional User Interfaces for Computer Products, Applications and Systems*. Upper Saddle River, NJ: Prentice Hall.
2. Barrière, C. and Plamondon, R. (1998). Human identification of letters in mixed-script handwriting: an upper bound on recognition rates. *IEEE Transactions on System, Man and Cybernetics (B), 28(1)*, pp. 78–82.
3. Brodmann, K. (1909). Vergleichende Lokalisationslehre der Grosshirnrinde in ihren Prinzipien dargestellt auf Grund des Zellenbaues. Leipzig: Barth.

4. Booth, J.R., Burman, D.D., Meyer, J.R., Gitelman, D.R., Parrish, T.B., and Mesulam, M.M. (2002). Functional anatomy of intra- and cross-modal lexical tasks. *Neuroimage, 16(1)*, pp. 7–22.

5. Coates, A.L., Baird, H.S., and Fateman, R.J. (2001). *Pessimal Print: A Reverse Turing Test.* Proceedings of the 6th International Conference on Document Analysis and Recognition, Seattle, WA, USA, September 10–13. Los Alamitos: IEEE Computer Society, pp. 1154–1158. ISBN 0-7695-1263-1.

6. Cohen, L., Lehericy, S., Chochon, F., Lemer, C., Rivaud, S., and Dehaene, S. (2002). Language-specific tuning of visual cortex? Functional properties of the Visual Word Form Area. *Brain, 125(5)*, pp. 1054–1069.

7. Dehaene, S., Cohen, L., Sigman, M., and Vinckier, F. (2005). The neural code for written words: a proposal. *Trends in Cognitive Sciences, 9(7)*, pp. 335–341.

8. Ezaki, N., Bulacu, M., and Schomaker, L. (2004). *Text Detection from Natural Scene Images: Towards a System for Visually Impaired Persons.* Proceedings of ICPR 2004. Cambridge, UK: IEEE Computer Society, pp. 683–686. ISBN: 0-7695-2128-2.

9. Franke, K. and Köppen, M. (1999). Towards an universal approach to background removal in images of bank checks. In: S.-W. Lee (Ed.). *Advances in Handwriting Recognition.* Singapore: World Scientific, pp. 91–100.

10. Georges Jean (1997). *Writing: The Story of Alphabets and Scripts.* London: Thames and Hudson Ltd.

11. Gigerenzer, G., Todd, P.M., et al. (2000). *Simple Heuristics That Make Us Smart.* (Evolution and Cognition Series). Oxford: Oxford University Press.

12. Goutte, C. (1997). Note on free lunches and cross-validation. *Neural Computation, 9*, pp. 1211–1215.

13. Mansfield, J.S., Legge, G.E., and Bane, M.C. (1996). Psychophysics of reading. XV. Font effects in normal and low vision. *Investigative Ophthalmology & Visual Science, 37*, 1492–1501.

14. Maarse, F.J. and Thomassen, A.J.W.M. (1983). Produced and perceived writing slant: difference between up and down strokes. *Acta Psychologica, 54*, pp. 131–147.

15. McCusker, L.X., Gough, P.B., and Bias, R.G. (1981). Word recognition inside out and outside in. *Journal of Experimental Psychology: Human Perception and Performance, 7(3)*, pp. 538–551.

16. Nagy, G., Nartker, T.A., and Rice, S.V. (2000). *Optical Character Recognition: An Illustrated Guide to the Frontier.* Invited paper in Proceedings of SPIE: Document Recognition and Retrieval VII, Volume 3967, San Jose, California, 2000.

17. Pammer, K., Hansen, P.C., Kringelbach, M.L., Holliday, I.E., Barnes, G., Hillebrand, A., Singh, K.D., and Cornelissen, P.L. (2004). Visual word recognition: the first half second. *Neuroimage, 22(4)*, pp. 1819–1825.

18. Petkov, N. and Kruizinga, P. (1997). Computational models of visual neurons specialised in the detection of periodic and aperiodic oriented visual stimuli: bar and grating cells, *Biological Cybernetics, 76(2)*, pp. 83–96.

19. Plamondon, R., Lopresti, D.P., Schomaker, L.R.B., and Srihari, R. (1999). On-line handwriting recognition. In: J.G. Webster (Ed.). *Wiley Encyclopedia of Electrical & Electronics Engineering.* New York: Wiley, pp. 123–146.

20. Plaut, D.C. and Shallice, T. (1994). Word reading in damaged connectionist networks: computational and neuropsychological implications. In: R. Mammone (Ed.). *Artificial Neural Networks for Speech and Vision.* London: Chapman & Hall, pp. 294–323.
21. Rawlinson, G. (1999). "Reibadailty" [Letter to the Editor]. *New Scientist, 162(2188)*, p. 55.
22. Schomaker, L.R.B. (2004). *Anticipation in Cybernetic Systems: A Case Against Antirepresentationalism.* The Netherlands: IEEE SMC Delft.
23. Schomaker, L. and Segers, E. (1999). Finding features used in the human reading of cursive handwriting. *International Journal on Document Analysis and Recognition, 2*, pp. 13–18.
24. Simon, H. (1957). *Models of Man.* New York: Wiley.
25. Simon, J.C. and Baret, O. (1990). *Handwriting Recognition as an Application of Regularities and Singularities in Line Pictures.* Proceedings of the International Workshop on Frontiers in Handwriting Recognition (IWFHR). Montreal: CENPARMI Concordia, pp. 23–37.
26. Talairach, J. and Tournoux, P. (1988). *Co-Planar Stereotaxic Atlas of the Human Brain.* New York: Thieme Medical.
27. Tax, D.M.J. and Duin, R.P.W. (2002). Uniform object generation for optimizing one-class classifiers. *Journal of Machine Learning Research, 2*, pp. 155–173.
28. Tistarelli, M. and Sandini, G. (1993). On the advantages of polar and log-polar mapping for direct estimation of time-to-impact from optical flow. *IEEE Transactions on Pattern Analysis and Machine Intelligence archive, 15(4)*, pp. 401–410.
29. Truccolo, W., Eden, U.T, Fellows, M.R., Donoghue, J.P., and Brown, E.N. (2005). A point-process framework for relating neural spiking activity to spiking history, neural ensemble, and extrinsic covariate effects. *Journal of Neurophysiology, 93*, pp. 1074–1089.
30. Turkeltaub, P.E., Weisberg, J., Flowers, D.L., Basu, D., and Eden, G.F. (2004). The neurobiological basis of reading: a special case of skill acquisition. In: Rice and Catts (Eds.). *Developmental Language Disorders: from Phenotypes to Etiologies.* Mahwah, NJ: Lawrence Erlbaum Associates.
31. Veeramachaneni, A. and Nagy, G. (2005). Style context with second-order statistics. *IEEE Transactions on Pattern Analysis and Machine Intelligence, 27(1)*, pp. 14–22.
32. Whitney, C. (2001). An explanation of the length effect for rotated words. In: E. Altmann, A. Cleermans, C. Schunn, and W. Gray (Eds.). *Proceedings of the Fourth International Conference on Cognitive Modeling.* Mahwah, NJ: Lawrence Erlbaum Associates, pp. 217–221.
33. Wilson, F.A.W., Scalaidhe, S.P.O., and Goldmanrakic, P.S. (1993). Dissociation of object and spatial processing domains in primate prefrontal cortex. *Science, 260(5116)*, pp. 1955–1958.

2

Document Structure and Layout Analysis

Anoop M. Namboodiri and Anil K. Jain

2.1 Introduction

A document image is composed of a variety of physical entities or regions such as text blocks, lines, words, figures, tables and background. We could also assign functional or logical labels such as sentences, titles, captions, author names and addresses to some of these regions. The process of *document structure and layout analysis* tries to decompose a given document image into its component regions and understand their functional roles and relationships. The processing is carried out in multiple steps, such as preprocessing, page decomposition, structure understanding, etc. We look into each of these steps in detail in the following sections.

Document images are often generated from physical documents by digitization using scanners or digital cameras. Many documents, such as newspapers, magazines and brochures, contain very complex layout due to the placement of figures, titles and captions, complex backgrounds, artistic text formatting, etc. (see Figure 2.1). A human reader uses a variety of additional cues such as context, conventions and information about language/script, along with a complex reasoning process to decipher the contents of a document. Automatic analysis of an arbitrary document with complex layout is an extremely difficult task and is beyond the capabilities of the state-of-the-art document structure and layout analysis systems. This is interesting since documents are designed to be effective and clear to human interpretation unlike natural images.

As mentioned before, we distinguish between the physical layout of a document and its logical structure [3]. One could also divide the document analysis process into two parts accordingly.

(a)   (b)

Fig. 2.1. Examples of document images with complex layouts.

2.1.1 Physical Layout and Logical Structure

The *physical layout* of a document refers to the physical location and boundaries of various regions in the document image. The process of *document layout analysis* aims to decompose a document image into a hierarchy of homogenous regions, such as figures, background, text blocks, text lines, words, characters, etc. The algorithms for layout analysis could be classified primarily into two groups depending on their approach. Bottom-up algorithms start with the smallest components of a document (pixels or connected components) and repeatedly group them to form larger, homogenous, regions. In contrast, top-down algorithms start with the complete document image and divide it repeatedly to form increasingly smaller regions. Each approach has its own advantage and they work well in specific situations. In addition, one could also employ a hybrid approach that uses a combination of top-down and bottom-up strategies.

In addition to the physical layout, documents contain additional information about its contents, such as titles, paragraphs, captions, etc. Such labels are logical or functional in nature as opposed to the structural labels of regions assigned by layout analysis. Most documents also contain the notion of *reading order*, which is a sequencing of the textual contents that makes comprehension of the document easier. Languages such as Arabic, Chinese, etc. can have different reading directions as well (right-to-left, top-to-bottom). The set of logical or functional entities in a document, along with their inter-relationships, is referred to as the *logical structure* of the document. The analysis of logical structure of a document is usually performed on the results of the layout analysis stage. However, in many complex documents, layout analysis would require some of the logical information about the regions to perform correct segmentation.

Most document images contain noises and artefacts that are introduced during the document generation or scanning phase. In order to make the analysis algorithms more robust to this noise, the layout and structure

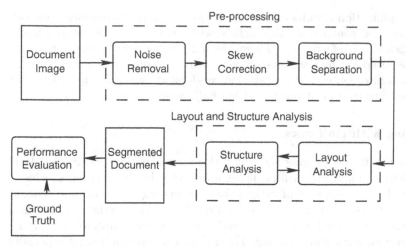

Fig. 2.2. Schematic diagram of a document layout and structure analysis system.

analysis is usually preceded by a pre-processing stage. The pre-processing stage consists of tasks such as noise removal, background separation, skew detection and correction, etc. Figure 2.2 shows a schematic diagram of a document layout and structure analysis system. We discuss each of the modules in detail in the remainder of this chapter.

2.2 Pre-processing

The pre-processing stage in document understanding primarily involves the following processes (i) removal of noise and other artefacts that are introduced during the scanning phase and during the production of the document, (ii) separation of background regions of the document from the foreground and (iii) correction of skew that is introduced in the document image during scanning/acquisition. We look into each of these problems and present commonly used techniques in this section. Some of these pre-processing algorithms could also be implemented as part of other modules during layout and structure analysis. However, pre-processing algorithms that are more specific to other modules of document understanding, such as character recognition, are not studied here. Such methods might include binarization of a grey-level image and scaling of characters to a standard size.

2.2.1 Noise Removal

Noise is a common problem in most of the image understanding problems. These involve white noise that is introduced by interferences in the sensors and amplification circuits of the digitization mechanism (scanner, camera). The common sources of noise include white noise, salt and pepper noise, quantization artefacts, etc. These are well-known noise sources that are compensated for by using techniques such as median filtering, dithering, low-pass filtering, etc. In this section, we look at one of the artefacts that is specific to document images, called *halftones*.

Dealing with Halftones

Halftoning is the process by which documents with smooth grey level or colour changes are printed using fewer grey levels or colours. This is achieved by placing dots of various sizes, depending on the desired tone, at different parts of the image (see Figure 2.3(a)). The method is also used in colour documents when one would like to create continuously varying colours with few-colour printing. This artefact becomes apparent especially in high-resolution scans, which are very common with modern-day sensors. There exist a variety of methods for halftoning depending on the resolution and grey levels available in the printing process [2]. Many algorithms that are designed for processing grey-level images break down in such situations.

One of the most commonly used solutions to overcome this problem is to develop algorithms to detect half-toned areas from a model of the halftoning process. The detected regions are either processed separately or converted to continuous grey scale using an appropriate low-pass filtering, which is often followed by application of a sharpening filter to reduce the blur (see Figure 2.3(b) and (c)).

2.2.2 Foreground Detection

One of the important problems in document structure understanding is that of separating the foreground from the background image. The problem is relatively simple in case of many documents that have a white or

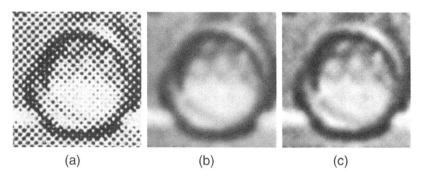

(a)   (b)   (c)

Fig. 2.3. Halftoning: (a) an image printed using halftoning, (b) result of applying gaussian blur to (a) and (c) result of sharpening (b).

plain background. Even in such documents, determining the exact pixels that belong to the foreground is a challenging problem due to sampling and quantization of slant edges and lines. One could take two different approaches to solve this problem. We could assign every pixel to either foreground or background based on a specific criterion, such as a threshold, and assume that the later processing algorithms will accommodate the errors made during foreground detection. A second approach is to assign a probability measure or a fuzzy membership to each pixel for the foreground and background classes. This uncertainty is propagated to the following stages, which will utilize the context to arrive at a final decision. In most applications, the first approach yields useful results and hence a hard classification is used due to its simplicity.

The problem of foreground detection is much more challenging in the case of documents with complex backgrounds [17] (see Figure 2.1(a)). A variety of approaches have been used to decide whether a particular pixel belongs to the foreground or background. A common approach is to compute statistical or spectral properties of image patches and assign them as foreground or background using a classifier trained on labelled samples. Statistical features used for this purpose include the variance and moment features computed in a local neighbourhood. Spectral features such as the responses from a bank of Gabor filters have been used with good success for this purpose [8]. A third approach is to train a classifier such as a neural network that directly accepts the image values in a neighbourhood of a pixel region as input for its classification. Figure 2.4 shows a sample document with complex background and colour-reversed text, along with the foreground and background regions.

The problem of foreground detection could be posed as that of detecting text, since many documents contain only text in the foreground [21]. One of the problems that many text-detection algorithms find difficult to handle is that of reverse colour text, i.e. text of light colour in a dark background. One of the approaches to overcome this difficulty is to run an edge detection

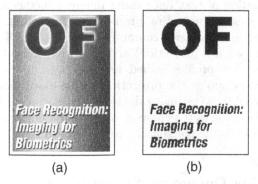

(a)   (b)

Fig. 2.4. (a) a document image with complex background, (b) foreground and background separated from (a).

Fig. 2.5. Example of a document image with a skew of 5 degrees.

algorithm on the document image and use the properties of the edges to determine whether a pixel is part of text (foreground) or not (background). These algorithms use properties of character edges such as the presence of parallel lines and uniformity of colour between them for classification.

2.2.3 Skew Correction

Skew is introduced in a document image when a document is scanned or imaged at an angle with respect to the reference axes (see Figure 2.5). The problem of skew correction plays an important role in the effectiveness of many document analysis algorithms, such as text line estimation, region boundary detection, etc. For example, algorithms based on projection profiles assume an axis-aligned scan. The primary challenge in skew correction is the estimation of the exact skew angle of a document image.

A variety of techniques are used for the detection of skew. Most of them assume the presence of some text component in the document and estimate the orientation of text lines using different methods. The commonly used techniques are projection profiles and line fitting. In the projection profile-based approach, we compute the histogram of text pixels on the vertical axis (vertical projection) and try to maximize the distance between consecutive line profiles, called *line spacing*, while rotating the document image. We examine the projection profile-based method in the next section. One could also estimate the skew of a document by fitting a line to the centroids of connected components within a line and measuring the angle with respect to the horizontal axis, which can then be corrected.

2.3 Representing Document Structure and Layout

A critical component in facilitating the understanding of document structure and layout is its representation in memory. An appropriate representation can encapsulate the prior knowledge about the documents being processed. In addition, the representation can also help to organize the extracted information and guide the analysis algorithm [4, 10].

A document contains multiple regions that are spatially and logically related to each other. Such a model is captured well in the formalism of a *graph*. A graph $\mathcal{G}$ is defined as a set of *vertices*, $\mathcal{V}$, and a set of *edges*, $\mathcal{E}$. Each edge, $e \in \mathcal{E}$, is an ordered pair of vertices, (v_1, v_2), where $v_1, v_2 \in \mathcal{V}$. The regions in a document image correspond to the vertices or nodes in a graph, while a relationship between two regions is denoted by an edge between the corresponding nodes. For a document we need to specify the relationship between two regions, rather than just stating that one exists. For this purpose, we will associate an attribute with each edge that specifies the nature of the relationship. The vertices also have attributes that specify the properties of a region, such as the type, size, location, etc. Such graphs, where the vertices and edges have associated attributes, are called *attributed graphs*.

The graph representation can encapsulate the relationship between regions and their properties. However, in many documents, the attributes are not conclusive during the analysis stage. One needs to handle the ambiguity and estimate the most likely set of values for the attributes. To facilitate this processing and to enable the graphs to model the uncertainties in the knowledge itself, one could describe the attributes in terms of probability distributions. Such graphs are referred to as *attributed random graphs*. In attributed random graphs, each attribute is defined by the parameters of a probability distribution (say Gaussian with specified mean and variance values). Special cases of attributed random graphs, such as first-order Gaussian graphs, have been successfully used in modelling and classifying document images [6].

The graph representation, however, fails to capture the hierarchical nature of a document structure and layout. To accomplish this, one could use a rooted tree for representing document layout and logical structure [1]. The root of the tree will represent the complete document, while each node of the tree will represent a specific region within the document. The set of children of a node will form sub-regions that compose the parent region. For example, consider the business card-recognition application. A child node of the root could represent the address field, and its children in turn could represent fields such as street, city, zip code, etc. A node representing the name field could be another child of the root, and hence a sibling of the address node. Such a representation incorporates the prior information about the logical structure of a business card. Similar to attributed graphs, a tree-based representation, where each node and edge is associated with a set of properties or attributes, is known as *an attributed tree*. The trees could also be implicitly represented in terms of a set of rules [10]. Probabilistic versions of tree representations are quite useful to handle the uncertainties in real-life documents in structure and layout.

One of the most powerful ways to express hierarchical structures is to use formal grammars. The class of *regular* and *context-free* grammars is extremely useful in describing the structure of most documents. A *document* is represented as a sequence of *terminal symbols*, T, which correspond to smallest units that we would like to represent in a document (pixels, character, regions, etc.). A *formal grammar* is defined as a set of rules that transform a starting symbol, corresponding to the complete document, into a set of terminal symbols, each representing a specific primitive. The *primitives* are the smallest units that one needs to address during the document structure and layout analysis. These could be units such as words, characters, pixels or connected components. Note that unlike the generic rule-based representation of trees that we mentioned before, formal grammars restrict the type of rules that can be used, which make their analysis and estimation more tractable. We also define a set of intermediate symbols, called *non-terminals*, which correspond to the different regions in a document layout. The non-terminals could correspond to physical regions such as text regions, columns, paragraphs, lines, etc. or structural units such as headings, captions, footnotes, etc. The grammar transforms the start symbol into a string of non-terminals and terminals. Each non-terminal is in turn replaced with other non-terminals or terminal symbols, according to the rules defined by the grammar. This is repeated until all symbols in the string consists only of terminals.

A specific interpretation of the layout or structure of a document will correspond to a specific sequence of grammar rules (productions) that generate the terminal symbols corresponding to the document. Such a sequence of productions is referred to as *a derivation*. However, there could be multiple derivations corresponding to a particular sequence of terminals. This would mean multiple interpretations of the structure or layout. The process of document analysis is hence to determine the correct derivation for a particular document. (See Figure 2.6 for an example of a grammar and the sequence of derivations that describe a specific document.)

One could associate a probability measure to each of the grammar rules, which represent the probability that the rule would form a part of the interpretation of a document. Such a grammar, where there are probabilities associated with each production, is referred to as a *stochastic grammar*. Stochastic grammars are especially useful to integrate multiple evidences and estimate the most probable parse or interpretation of a given document. One could also attach attributes to each of the nodes in the grammar, such as properties of a region. Such grammars are called *attributed grammars* and are commonly used for layout and structure analysis purposes.

2.4 Document Layout Analysis

The primary purpose of a document layout analysis module is to identify the various physical regions in a document and their characteristics. A *maximal region* in a document image is the maximal homogenous area

```
[0.5] < START >  →  < TITLE >  < COLUMN >  < COLUMN >
[0.5] < START >  →  < TITLE >  < COLUMN >
[1.0] < TITLE >  →  < text_line >
[1.0] < COLUMN >  →  < TEXT_BLOCKS >
[0.8] < TEXT_BLOCKS >  →  < TEXT_BLOCK >  < space >  < TEXT_BLOCKS >
[0.2] < TEXT_BLOCKS >  →  < TEXT_BLOCK >
[1.0] < TEXT_BLOCK >  →  < TEXT_LINES >
[0.9] < TEXT_LINES >  →  < text_line >  < newline >  < TEXT_LINES >
[0.1] < TEXT_LINES >  →  < text_line >
```

(a)

```
< START >  →  < TITLE >  < COLUMN >
→  < text_line >  < COLUMN >
→  < text_line >  < TEXT_BLOCKS >
→  < text_line >  < TEXT_BLOCK >  < space >  < TEXT_BLOCKS >
→  < text_line >  < text_line >  < newline >  < TEXT_BLOCK >  < space >  < TEXT_BLOCKS >
→  < text_line >  < text_line >  < newline >  < text_line >  < space >  < TEXT_BLOCKS >
→  < text_line >  < text_line >  < newline >  < text_line >  < space >  < TEXT_BLOCK >
→  < text_line >  < text_line >  < newline >  < text_line >  < space >  < text_line >
```

(b)

Fig. 2.6. Representing a document in terms of formal grammars. (a) Example of a stochastic context-free grammar that derives a text document with a title. Upper-case symbols refer to non-terminal symbols, while lower-case symbols show terminal symbols. (b) A sample document with a title and three lines, derived using the grammar in (a).

of a document image. The property of homogeneity in the case of layout refers to the type of region, such as text block, image, graphic, text line, word, etc. These regions are not mutually exclusive and one region could contain other region types within it. Before proceeding further, we define a segmentation of an image as follows:

Definition 2.1. *A segmentation of an image is a set of mutually exclusive and collectively exhaustive sub-regions of the image. Given an image, I, a segmentation is defined as* $S = \{R_1, R_2, \cdots, R_n\}$*, such that,* $R_1 \cup R_2 \cup \cdots \cup R_n = I$*, and* $R_i \cap R_j = \phi \ \forall i \neq j$*.*

Based on the above observations one could define layout analysis as follows:

Definition 2.2. *The process of document layout analysis decomposes a document image into a hierarchy of maximally homogeneous regions, where each region is repeatedly segmented into maximal sub-regions of a specific type.*

For a document image, D, the layout is a sequence of segmentations, $S_1, S_2, ..S_n$, where S_1 is a segmentation of the complete document image, and S_i is a segmentation of one of the regions in S_j; $1 \leq j < i$.

Note that the regions of each segmentation are also defined to be homogeneous in addition to being maximal. In fact, there exists a unique segmentation of a document image, given a specific definition of homogeneity of the regions. However, in practice, one could get multiple interpretations due to an ill-defined homogeneity criterion. For example, two text blocks that are close to each other may be considered as a single block if the homogeneity measure used is not able to differentiate between them based on the spacing and alignment between the two blocks.

2.4.1 Approaches to Layout Analysis

Document layout analysis algorithms are primarily divided based on their order of processing into *top-down* approaches and *bottom-up* approaches [5]. Top-down approaches start with the complete document image and repeatedly split them into smaller homogeneous regions. The splitting is stopped when all the resulting regions correspond to the primitives, based on which the document is to be described. The primitives could be pixels, connected components, words, etc. depending on the application. Conversely, bottom-up approaches start with the primitives and repeatedly group them into larger regions such as words, lines, text-blocks, columns, etc. There are also *hybrid* algorithms that combine the above two approaches. The primary challenges in any of the above approaches are:

- Region Segmentation: To split a document image into component regions, we need to decide where the homogeneity criterion is satisfied. The homogeneity is often defined based on a parameter vector, $\boldsymbol{\theta}$, whose value plays a critical role in the success of the algorithm. This is also true for bottom-up approaches, when we try to group smaller components into regions. Computing a parameter vector, $\boldsymbol{\theta}$, that works well for all possible documents is often not possible. Current approaches try to tune the parameters based on feedback from later processing stages such as character recognition. The problem is also present at lower levels of segmentation such as line and word segmentation.
- Region Classification: The second challenge is to decide the type of a particular region, once it is segmented. Typical problems are in text versus image classification and identification of graphics and tables. Region classification is a prerequisite for further processing of many region types.

There are a variety of algorithms that have been proposed to perform layout analysis of documents. We now look into three of the popular algorithms to illustrate the three approaches mentioned above.

Examples of Algorithms

Typical top-down approaches proceed by dividing a document image into smaller regions using the horizontal and vertical projection profiles.

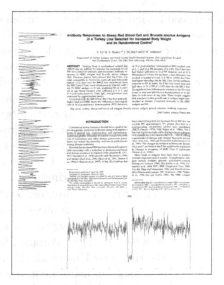

Fig. 2.7. Horizontal and vertical projection profiles of a document image.

The *X–Y Cut* algorithm [12] starts dividing a document image into sections based on valleys in their projection profiles (see Figure 2.7). The algorithm repeatedly partitions the document by alternately projecting the regions of the current segmentation on the horizontal and vertical axes. The splitting is stopped when a particular criterion that decides the atomicity of a region is met. Projection profile-based techniques are extremely sensitive to the skew of the document. A small amount of skew could completely change the nature of the projection, resulting in no clear valleys. Hence extreme care has to be taken while scanning of documents, or a reliable skew correction algorithm has to be applied before the segmentation process.

Efficient and accurate methods have been devised for documents with white background and a manhattan (rectangular) layout of the regions, based on geometric approaches that cover the background. Examples include the shape-directed cover algorithm by Baird et al. [16] and the white streams-based segmentation by Pavlidis and Zhou [19]. These are top-down approaches that divide a document image into smaller regions based on the structure of the background. The primary idea is to detect a set of maximal rectangles that do not contain any foreground pixels. These rectangles divide the document image into regions that may contain text, images or graphics. A region classification algorithm could be applied to them before further processing. The algorithms mentioned above are very complex to implement due to the representation of intermediate results and many special cases that need to be handled. The whitespace cover algorithm by Breuel [18] is an efficient variation of the same idea using geometric principles. The algorithm is simpler due to the lack of special cases and performs very well for this class of documents. Texture based approaches have also been used for document page segmentation [7, 9].

Bottom-up approaches need to define primitive components to start the grouping process. The *Docstrum* algorithm by O'Gorman [14] proceeds by identifying a set of connected components in the document as the primitives. Large noise or non-text components are then removed from this set. *K*-nearest neighbours of each component are identified and text lines are formed based on a threshold of the angle between the component centroids. Histograms of component spacings are used to identify inter-character distance within a word and between words. Transitive closures of neighbouring components using the within-line-distance and between-line-distance are computed to form text lines and text blocks. The algorithm has a set of threshold parameters, which are set by experiments on a set of documents. The algorithm performs well for English language documents with a wide variety in layout. Figure 2.8 shows two examples of document images segmented using Docstrum. As we can see, the algorithm handles fonts of various sizes and styles well, even with relatively complex layouts.

The Voronoi diagram based algorithm by Kise et al. [13] is another effective method that functions by grouping connected components in a page. We start with computing a Voronoi tessellation of the document image.

(a)

(b)

Fig. 2.8. Typical examples of document images segmented using the *Docstrum* algorithm. Detected lines of text are shown in boxes.

The neighbour graph of connected components is a computer from the Voronoi diagram. The algorithm then uses a threshold based on the area and distance between adjacent components in the Voronoi diagram to decide region boundaries. Text lines are identified based on a threshold on the inter-component distance computed from its distribution in the neighbour graph. The results are very reliable and highly accurate on documents with white background, where the connected components can be identified reliably. Figure 2.9 shows two examples of document images segmented using the Voronoi-based algorithm. As in *Docstrum*, the Voronoi-based algorithm is able to handle very complex layouts and performs well on most pages in English.

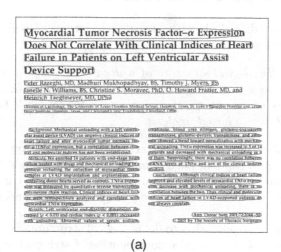

(a)

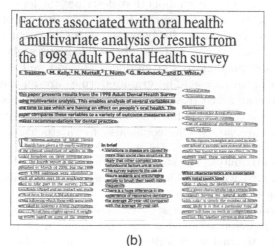

(b)

Fig. 2.9. Typical examples of document images segmented using the *Voronoi* algorithm. Detected lines of text are shown with the boundaries of the Voronoi cells.

The run-length smearing algorithm of Wahl et al. [20] is another example of bottom-up approach. Kopec and Chou [15] describe an algorithm for segmenting a column of text that is modelled using a generative Markov model. However, this model makes the assumption that the connected components are recognizable and belong to a specific vocabulary.

Pavlidis and Zhou [22] proposed a hybrid algorithm using a split-and-merge strategy. Here a top-down approach is used to arrive at an over-segmented document image. Regions that are similar and nearby are then merged to form homogeneous regions.

2.5 Understanding Document Structure

Structure understanding deals with logical descriptions of regions rather than their physical attributes.

Definition 2.3. *The logical structure of a document image is a mapping from the physical regions in the documents to their logical labels. Document structure analysis is the process of assigning the logical labels to physical regions identified during layout analysis.*

The logical labels include title, abstract, sub-title, paragraph, sentence, words, header, footer, caption, page number, etc. Even though the logical layout analysis process is defined to follow the layout analysis, in practice, the two processes could be combined into a single document understanding framework.

One of the popular approaches to define logical structure of a document is to treat the set of regions in a document as a string of symbols. A grammar is defined over these symbols that describes the logical structure of an arbitrary document under consideration. The process of structure analysis then computes the most likely parse (set of grammar rules) that generates the observed string of symbols. The problem arises when there are multiple parses corresponding to a given document and we have to decide which interpretation to choose. The grammar rules are augmented with attributes of regions and their relationships to accommodate this situation. The most likely parse could be defined using a cost function that takes into account, the attribute values. One could also use a stochastic grammar, that could give a likelihood value for a parse, depending on the rules used and the terminal attributes. The stochastic grammar rules also contain a probability associated with it, which can be used to determine the most likely parse, along with the region attributes.

Related methods use other representations of the logical structure, such as tree or graph representations that were discussed in Section 2.3. The approach is similar to what we described for the grammar-based analysis. The domain knowledge is stored as a set of constraints on the structure of the tree or graph, instead of grammar rules. The problem is to identify the variation of the tree, according to the definition, that best matches the observed document [23].

Rule-based systems have also been proposed to determine the logical structure of a document. Note that these are different from the grammar rules that describe, formally, a set of derivations that are permissible. Rules in a rule-based system could denote actions to be taken in a particular situation or encode domain knowledge. The *DeLoS* system proposed by Niyogi and Srihari [25] uses three levels of rules that encode domain knowledge, control information and strategies. The approach works well even for complex documents such as newspaper pages. However, the rules themselves are hard coded and rule-based systems do not have the ability to learn from a set of sample documents.

A second approach is to apply domain knowledge about the layout and structure on the result of OCR and graphics recognition on a given document [24]. This approach assumes that the layout identification stage correctly identifies the text regions, which are then recognized by an OCR. The approach is very powerful, since it can make use of the contents of the text to decide its function. Note that this was not available in the previous methods. For example, the OCR-based approach can use the words in a text line near an image to decide whether it is a caption or not.

2.6 Performance Evaluation

There are many factors that affect the results of evaluation of a document segmentation algorithm. To perform evaluation, one needs to decide on the following points (i) A set of test documents, (ii) ground truth of segmentation of the chosen documents, (iii) an evaluation or performance metric that is unambiguous and meaningful and (iv) a set of statistics over the performance metric to summarize the results over the complete document set.

Algorithms could be compared against each other only when they are tested on a common dataset that has sufficient number and variety of documents. In addition, one should also agree on a common ground truth. This is often difficult as even human experts could assign different ground truths to a specific document. One needs to develop standardized datasets with ground truth to overcome these problems. The University of Washington datasets, the *NIST* document image dataset [29], etc. are among the most commonly used standards of datasets with ground truth that are used for performance evaluation. The data sets need to be updated and expanded or new ones created according to the future requirements. Details about some of the current datasets could be found at [30].

To evaluate the performance of a segmentation algorithm, we need to compare the result of segmentation against a ground truth. However, this is not a trivial task, since the result of a page segmentation algorithm is not a single mathematical quantity or model that can be compared with the ground truth to compute the error. General image segmentation algorithms output a set of regions for an image, which could be compared against the ground truth for overlap. However, document segmentation poses additional problems due to the hierarchical nature of segmentation. The approaches to define a performance metric could be primarily classified into two categories:

- Overlap-based performance metrics: This is similar to image segmentation evaluation measures. The metric is defined based on the overlap area of labelled regions against regions of the same label in the ground truth. We could compute the overlap at the lowest level of the hierarchy or report results at multiple levels. The performance metric could be any function of the overlap area. For example, the accuracy, $\rho(G, S)$, could be measured as:

$$\rho(G, S) = \frac{O_I(G, S) - (M_I(G, S) + S_I(G, S))}{Area(G)}, \quad (2.1)$$

  where I is the document image, G is the ground truth and S is the result of layout and structure analysis. The function O_I measures the overlap area of regions between G and S, where the labels agree, $M_I()$ and $S_I()$ measure the areas of missing and spurious regions in S, compared to G, and $Area(G)$ is the total area of the regions in the image (or G).

- Split-and-Merge-based metrics: Such metrics are defined based on the observation that most errors that are made by a document segmentation algorithms stem from splitting of uniform regions and merging of two different neighbouring regions. We measure the accuracy of a segmentation based on the number of split-and-merge operations that are required to transform the result of segmentation to the ground truth. We could also include missing and spurious regions into the metric. For example, Mao and Kanungo [26] define the accuracy of text line detection, $\rho(G, S)$, as:

$$\rho(G, S) = \frac{\#L - \#\{C_L \cup S_L \cup M_L\}}{\#L}, \quad (2.2)$$

  where $\#$ stand for the cardinality operator; L is the set of all text lines in the document; and C_L, S_L and M_L represents sets of spurious, split and merged lines, respectively.

Common statistical measures that are used for summarization of error results include the mean and variance of the accuracy over the complete test set. Cross-validation accuracy is reported for algorithms that estimate parameters or learn from a dataset.

2.7 Handwritten Document Analysis

The problem of document understanding can be extended to the domain of handwritten documents as well. The problem is to decipher the physical layout and the logical structure of a handwritten page. The problem is much more complicated due to the lack of physical organization in most handwritten documents. Hence, the problem has not been studied in a generic setting. However, handwritten document analysis has been extensively used in specific areas such as postal address recognition and recognition of hand-filled forms. In the case of hand-filled forms, the format of the form is assumed to be known. This helps the algorithms to remove the form background from the document image. In addition, the recognition is also facilitated in many form-filling applications, since the characters are often well separated and printed.

One of the most impressive success stories of handwritten document understanding has been in the field of postal automation. The problem is to recognize the destination of an envelope for automatic routing of mails. The problem of postal address recognition will be discussed in detail, elsewhere in this book. A third successful application area of handwritten document analysis is that of recognition of mathematical equations.

Most of the successful systems that carry out handwritten document analysis have been domain specific with clear and simple document structures. A generic handwritten document analyser is still beyond the reach of the state of the art in the field. We now look into a special case of handwritten documents that have received attention, namely on-line handwritten documents.

2.7.1 On-Line Documents

On-line documents are captured during the writing process using a digitizer such as special pens and pads, touch sensitive screens or vision-based pen tip trackers. They encode the dynamic information of the writing process in addition to the static physical layout. The data in on-line documents are stored as a sequence of strokes.[1] The temporal information regarding the stroke order helps us to reduce the two-dimensional segmentation problem into that of segmenting a linear sequence of strokes. This is true in most documents, where one does not move back and forth between multiple regions. Jain et al. [11] proposed a clustering-based scheme, where the individual strokes are initially classified as belonging to text or non-text regions. The strokes are then clustered based on their spatial and temporal proximities onto various regions. Figure 2.10 shows an on-line document and the result of layout analysis from [11].

---

[1] A stroke is the trace of the pen between a pen-down and the following pen-up.

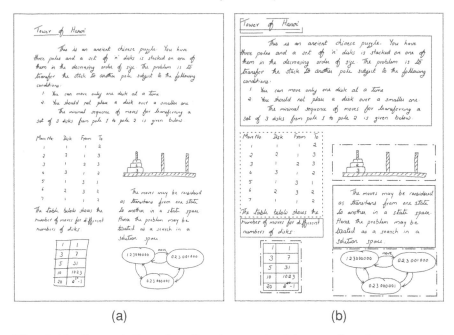

(a)   (b)

Fig. 2.10. Segmentation of on-line documents: (a) an on-line document and (b) result of segmentation [11].

On-line document understanding and handwriting recognition are popular due to the large number of handheld devices that accept pen input. Such data require segmentation algorithms without assuming strict models about the layout. Grammar-based techniques are very promising for this problem, especially those using stochastic formal grammars for modelling document regions [27, 28].

2.8 Summary

Document layout and structure understanding often forms the basis on which many document understanding systems are built. One can reliably segment and decipher the structure of many document images with a regular structure and plain white background, such as technical journals, telephone books, text books, etc. However, a generic document layout and structure understanding system that can deal with complex backgrounds and layout is still an elusive goal. One such application that deals with a large variety of layouts is the document understanding/search module in a digital library. Learning-based approaches have the potential to adapt to such large variations in layout and structure.

A complete understanding of the structure of a document is possible only with information about the contents of the document. Hence, it is important to develop an integrated approach to document layout and structure analysis and various recognition modules. Robust OCR techniques that will work on noisy and degraded documents will go a long way towards structure and layout understanding.

References

1. Nagy, G. and Seth, S.C. (1984). *Hierarchical Representation of Optically Scanned Documents.* Proceedings of the 7th International Conference on Pattern Recognition, Montreal, 1984, pp. 347–349.
2. Ulichney, R. (1987). *Digital Halftoning.* Cambridge, MA: The MIT Press.
3. Haralick, R.M. (1994). *Document* image understanding: geometric and logical layout. *Proceedings of the IEEE International Conference on Computer Vision and Pattern Recognition, Seattle, WA*, pp. 385–390.
4. Jain, A.K. and Yu, B. (1998). Document representation and its application to page decomposition. *IEEE Transactions on Pattern Analysis and Machine Intelligence, 20,* pp. 294–308.
5. Nagy, G. (2000). Twenty years of document image analysis in PAMI. *IEEE Transactions on Pattern Analysis and Machine Intelligence, 22,* pp. 38–62.
6. Bagdanov, A.D. and Worring, M. (2003). First order Gaussian Graphs for efficient structure classification. *Pattern Recognition, 36,* pp. 1311–1324.
7. Etemad, K., Doermann, D.S., and Chellappa, R. (1997). Multiscale document page segmentation using soft decision integration. *IEEE Transactions on Pattern Analysis and Machine Intelligence, 19.* pp. 92–96.
8. Jain, A.K. and Bhattacharjee, S. (1992). Text segmentation using Gabor filters for automatic document processing. *Machine Vision and Applications, 5,* pp. 169–184.
9. Jain, A.K. and Zhong, Y. (1996). Page segmentation using texture analysis. *Pattern Recognition, 29,* pp. 743–770.
10. Fisher, J.L. (1991). Logical structure descriptions of segmented document images. *Proceedings of International Conference on Document Analysis and Recognition, Saint-Malo, France*, pp. 302–310.
11. Jain, A.K., Namboodiri, A.M., and Subrahmonia, J. (2001). Structure in on-line documents. *Proceedings of International Conference on Document Analysis and Recognition, Seattle, WA*, pp. 844–848.
12. Nagy, G., Seth, S., and Viswanathan, M. (1992). A prototype document image-analysis system for technical journals. *Computer, 25,* pp. 10–22.
13. Kise, K., Sato, A., and Iwata, M. (1998). Segmentation of page images using the area Voronoi diagram. *Computer Vision and Image Understanding, 70,* pp. 370–382.
14. O'Gorman, L. (1993). The document spectrum for page layout analysis. *IEEE Transactions on Pattern Analysis and Machine Intelligence, 15,* pp. 1162–1173.

15. Kopec, G.E. and Chou, P.A. (1994). Document image decoding using Markov source models. *IEEE Transactions on Pattern Analysis and Machine Intelligence, 16*, pp. 602–617.
16. Baird, H.S., Jones, S.E., and Fortune, S.J. (1990). Image segmentation by shape-directed covers. *Proceedings of International Conference on Pattern Recognition, Atlantic City, NJ*, pp. 820–825.
17. Baird, H.S. (1994). *Background Structure in Document Images. Document Image Analysis.* Singapore: Word Scientific, pp. 17–34.
18. Breuel, T.M. (2002). Two geometric algorithms for layout analysis. *Proceedings of the Fifth International Workshop on Document Analysis Systems, Princeton, NY, LNCS 2423*, pp. 188–199.
19. Pavlidis, T. and Zhou, J. (1991). Page segmentation by white streams. *Proceedings of International Conference on Document Analysis and Recognition, Saint-Malo, France*, pp. 945–953.
20. Wahl, F., Wong, K., and Casey, R. (1982). Block segmentation and text extraction in mixed text/image documents. *Graphical Models and Image Processing, 20*, pp. 375–390.
21. Wu, V., Manmatha, R., and Riseman, E.M. (1997). Finding text in images. *ACM DL*, pp. 3–12.
22. Pavlidis, T. and Zhou, J. Page segmentation and classifcation. *Graphical Models and Image Processing, 54*, pp. 484–496.
23. Yamashita, A., Amano, T., Takahashi, I., and Toyokawa, K. (1991). A model-based layout understanding method for the document recognition system. *Proceedings of the International Conference on Document Analysis and Recognition, Saint-Malo, France*, pp. 130–138.
24. Kreich, J., Luhn, A., and Maderlechner, G. (1991). An experimental environment for model-based document analysis. *Proceedings of the International Conference on Document Analysis and Recognition, Saint-Malo, France*, pp. 50–58.
25. Niyogi, D. and Srihari, S.N. (1995). Knowledge-based derivation of document logical structure. *Proceedings of the International Conference on Document Analysis and Recognition, Montreal, Canada*, pp. 472–475.
26. Mao, S. and Kanungo, T. (2001). Empirical performance evaluation methodology and its application to page segmentation algorithms. *IEEE Transactions on Pattern Analysis and Machine Intelligence, 23*, pp. 242–256.
27. Artières, T. (2003). Poorly structured handwritten documents segmentation using continuous probabilistic feature grammars. *Workshop on Document Layout Interpretation and its Applications (DLIA2003).*
28. Namboodiri, A.M. and Jain, A.K. (2004). Robust segmentation of unconstrained on-line handwritten documents. *Proceedings of the Fourth Indian Conference on Computer Vision, Graphics and Image Processing, Calcutta, India*, pp. 165–170.
29. NIST. NIST Scientific and Technical Databases, http://www.nist.gov/srd/.
30. LAMP. Documents and Standards Information, http://documents.cfar.umd.edu/resources/database/

3

OCR Technologies for Machine Printed and Hand Printed Japanese Text

Fumitaka Kimura

3.1 Introduction

Commercial products of Japanese OCR are classified into form processing OCR and document OCR. The form processing OCR is mainly aimed at reading handwritten characters filled in a printed form with blank spaces for information. Its implementation is either by hardware device or computer software. Meanwhile the document OCR is mainly aimed at reading machine printed documents such as newspapers, magazines and general documents. Its implementation is by computer software in most cases.

The OCR products are used to save labour and time of keyboard entry in various business tasks including customer support, sales management, financial account, questionnaire survey, etc. The OCR software is also used as built-in OCR applications in word processing, spread sheet processing, full text retrieval, facsimile OCR, filing system and document workstation.

Many technologies relating to image processing, pattern recognition and linguistic processing are employed in Japanese OCR systems. This chapter deals with the OCR technologies for pre-processing, feature extraction, classification, dimension reduction and learning as well as the performance evaluation of those techniques.

3.2 Pre-Processing

Pre-processing for Japanese text recognition includes text line segmentation, character segmentation and relating normalization techniques for skewed documents, slant of characters and size of characters.

3.2.1 Text Line Segmentation and Skew Correction

In text line segmentation, horizontal projection of a document image is most commonly employed, when actual text line orientation is horizontal

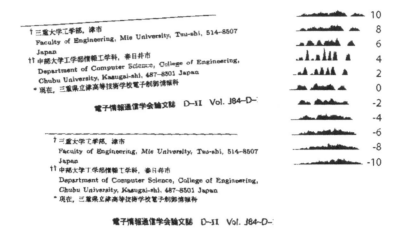

Fig. 3.1. Example of skew correction.

(Figure 3.1). If lines are well separated and are not skewed, the horizontal projection has well separated peaks and valleys. These valleys are easily detected and used to determine the location of boundaries between lines. Main difficulties of this simple strategy are encountered when dealing with skewed lines. The peaks and valleys are not distinctive for skewed document images, and the text lines are not separable by horizontal boundary lines. A typical approach to handle the problem of skew is to estimate and correct the skew preceding the line segmentation.

Crossing Point Method [5]

Skew correction is generally performed in two steps. The skew is estimated in the first step and then a rotation transformation is applied to correct the skew. The basic strategy of the skew estimation is to find the direction in which the projection of the document has maximum separability regarding the peaks and valleys. In the crossing point method, only crossing points are counted to obtain the projection. Where the crossing point is a pixel with value "1" adjacent to its left pixel with value "0". The use of the crossing points rather than entire foreground pixels is advantageous both in improving the separability of the projection and in saving computation time. As a simple measure of the separability, variance of the number of crossing points is used. To find the direction that maximizes the separability measure, multiple projections in slightly different direction by one or two degrees are calculated within the range of expected skew.

It is worth observing that this straightforward enumerative search for maximum separability is more efficient than expected, if it is implemented carefully: all the multiple projections are calculated in a single raster scan. Only the crossing points are projected in multiple directions. The mapping is performed in incremental method without heavy multiplications. If the document image is quite large and has sufficient resolution, the raster scan can be performed for every two pixels for every two scan lines. This inter-leaving is equivalent to work on down sampled image, and is more efficient unless the down sampled image itself is needed in succeeding process.

Once the skew is estimated, the rest of the task is merely the rotation transformation.

In the process of skew estimation, several characteristics of the document image, e.g. the number of lines, the interval and the average height of characters, can be estimated, which are of great use in succeeding process.

Figure 3.1 shows the example of skew correction. In this example, the direction that maximizes the variance of crossing counts was selected in every two interval from −10 to +10 in terms of the single pass algorithm.

Text Line Segmentation

After the skew correction horizontal projection of a document image is calculated, and the valley points are detected and used to determine the location of boundaries between lines. Some valley points may be merged or removed based on heuristics such as expected interval of lines. If two valley points are closer than a given threshold, they are merged. The advantage of the projection method is its robustness for connected lines due to extenders of handwritten documents.

3.2.2 Character Segmentation of Japanese and English Mixed Text

Performance of Japanese OCR is deteriorated when the input Japanese text includes English words, English sentences, computer programs and com-mands. The performance deterioration for such Japanese–English mixed text is mainly caused by the problems of character segmentation and recog-nition of the English region.

The Japanese OCR software always has two reading modes, i.e. Japanese mode and English mode. The English mode is aimed at recognizing charac-ters used in English text (alphanumerals and symbols), while the Japanese mode is aimed at recognizing all characters used in Japanese text, i.e. Kanji (Chinese characters), Hiragana and Katakana as well as alphanumer-als and symbols. Because the English mode is specialized in segmentation and recognition of English characters, it performs better for English region than Japanese mode does. However, the English mode is not available for Japanese–English mixed text, thus the recognition accuracy of the English region is relatively low. A procedure for fixed pitch region detection for improving character segmentation is described below.

The height and width of printed Japanese characters are correlated, and the characters are usually aligned in fixed pitch. This property can be utilized to estimate the pitch of character alignment and to detect the fixed pitch regions. Once the fixed pitch regions are detected, the Japanese region (with fixed pitch) and English region (with variable pitch) are detected and separated.

Estimation of Character Pitch

The pitch of character alignment in each line is estimated by the following procedure:

(1) Given a width of rectangular frame of a character, a ladder of horizontally aligned frames is shifted from left to right (Figure 3.2). The width of the frame ranges from 80 to 125% of the height of characters, and the horizontal displacement of the ladder ranges from 0 to 100% of the width.
(2) The width of the frame that minimizes the number of black pixels on the edges of the ladder found in (1) is defined as the estimated pitch.

The number of black pixels on the edges of the ladder is calculated using vertical pixel projection of the text line.

Detection of Fixed Pitch Region

Shifting the ladder with estimated frame width from left to right on the text line, a region of characters enclosed in five or more successive frames without intersection is detected as a fixed pitch region (Figure 3.3). At both ends of the text line, a region of characters enclosed in three or more successive frames is detected as a fixed pitch region.

Character Segmentation of Japanese–English Mixed Text

Characters in the fixed pitch regions are synchronously segmented with the estimated pitch. This synchronous character segmentation avoids mis-separation of Kanji or Hiragana characters with disconnected left and right

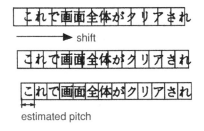

Fig. 3.2. Estimation of character pitch.

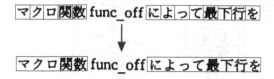

Fig. 3.3. Detection of fixed pitch region.

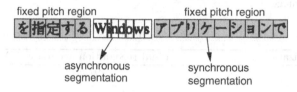

Fig. 3.4. Character segmentation of Japanese–English mixed text.

parts (Figure 3.4). Characters in the variable pitch regions are segmented asynchronously. The asynchronous character segmentation, which is asynchronous in the sense that the ladder parameters for Japanese script are ignored, is suitable for alphanumerals with narrow variable pitch alignment.

3.2.3 Nonlinear Normalization of Character Size

Nonlinear normalization of character size reduces the positional variation of character strokes and hence suppresses the increase of the features with large within-class variance, with poor separability.

The nonlinear normalization is performed as follows:

(1) Smoothing operation with 2×2 mean filter is applied to the input (binary) image. The output is again a binary image.
(2) Density of lines $\rho(i, j)$ [18] is calculated at each pixel point (x_i, y_j) and is projected by

$$h_x(x_i) = \sum_{j=1}^{J} \rho(i, j) + \alpha \qquad (3.1)$$

$$h_y(y) = \sum_{i=1}^{I} \rho(i, j) + \alpha$$

to obtain horizontal and vertical projections h_x and h_y, to which the histogram equalization is applied ($i = 1, 2, \ldots, I$, $j = 1, 2, \ldots, J$).
(3) Mapping functions that equalize the projections h_x and h_y are applied to the smoothed binary image.
(4) Smoothing operation with 3×3 mean filter is applied.

(a)   (b)

Fig. 3.5. Nonlinear normalization: (a) input image with re-sampling grid and
(b) normalized image.

Table 3.1. Comparison on nonlinear normalization (300 categories)

Normalization	Final recognition accuracy (%)
Linear	97.55
Nonlinear	
Method 1	97.81
Method 2	98.07
Method 3	98.17

Figure 3.5 shows a conceptual example of the nonlinear normalization.
The parameter α in (3.1) controls the nonlinearity of the normalization,
e.g. the larger the value of α is, the less the nonlinearity is. Several algorithms for nonlinear normalization which utilize different horizontal and
vertical projections h_x and h_y have been proposed. Three typical methods
are described below. The first method takes the horizontal and vertical
projection of number of lines (crossing counts) [18]. The second method
utilizes density of lines defined by distance between strokes [14]. While the
first method and the second one calculate independently the horizontal and
vertical projections, the third method utilizes two dimensional density of
lines, which is defined by the distance between strokes [18]. The density of
lines $\rho(i, j)$ in step (3) is the one used in the third method.

The nonlinear normalization often enlarges the jags of the input binary
image and gives undesirable side effect on the recognition algorithm employing direction of edge as the primary feature. The smoothing operation
in steps (1) and (4) is aimed to reduce the side effect.

Table 3.1 shows the recognition rates for each method as well as for
linear normalization. The recognition test was performed for 300 character
categories including 71 Hiragana and 229 Kanji characters.

3.2.4 Slant Correction

4-Directional Chain Code Method

Handwritten English words are often sheared horizontally to right or left
direction. Meanwhile, characters in Japanese handwritten documents that
are written vertically are usually sheared vertically to right upper direction
or sometimes to right lower direction.

To estimate effectively the average slant of this type of documents, the 4-directional chain code method [2] for English text was modified directly. Since horizontal and near horizontal chain elements contribute to the slant, the slant estimator is given by

$$\theta = \tan^{-1}\left(\frac{n_1 - n_3}{n_1 + n_0 + n_3}\right), \tag{3.2}$$

where n_1, n_0, n_3 denote the number of chain elements at angles 45, 0, −45, respectively. Figure 3.6 illustrates the calculation of average slant of a chain code sequence.

Because Chinese characters have complex structures, the estimated slant by (3.2) tends to be overestimated, as shown in Figure 3.7(b). In order to solve this problem, an iterative 8-directional method was proposed.

Iterative 8-Directional Chain Code Method

Chain code can be quantized to eight directions by following every two border pixels as shown in Figure 3.8. To avoid the overestimate, 8-directional

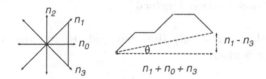

Fig. 3.6. Average slant of a chain code sequence.

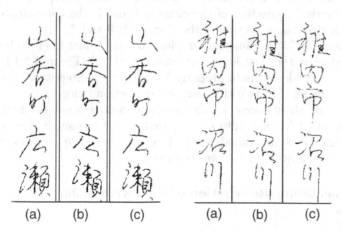

(a)　　(b)　　(c)　　　　(a)　　(b)　　(c)

Fig. 3.7. (a) Original image, (b) overestimated by 4-directional method and (c) slant correction by the modified iterative 8-directional method.

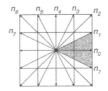

Fig. 3.8. 8-Directional quantization of chain code.

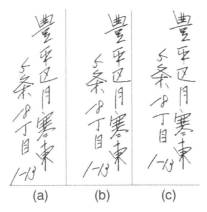

Fig. 3.9. (a) Original image, (b) underestimate by estimator (3.3) and (c) slant correction by iterative 8-directional method.

method is modified to count only the chain code in direction 1, 0 and 7. Then the estimator is given by

$$\theta = \tan^{-1}\left(\frac{n_1 - n_7}{2n_1 + 2n_0 + 2n_7}\right), \tag{3.3}$$

where n_i denotes the number of chain elements at direction i, $(n_1 - n_7)$ is the sum of vertical projection of the element 1 and 7, the denominator is the sum of horizontal projection of the element 1, 0 and 7.

The estimator (3.3) has another problem such that slant tends to be underestimated when the slant is greater than $\tan^{-1}(1/2)$ (Figure 3.9(b)). To compensate the underestimate properly, an iterative 8-directional method repeats the process of slant estimation and correction twice.

Examples of slant correction by iterative 8-directional method are shown in Figures 3.7(c) and 3.9(c). Compared with the 4- and 8-directional method, iterative 8-directional method is obviously superior in slant estimation for handwritten Japanese address.

3.2.5 Segmentation–Recognition of Handwritten Japanese Document

Pre-Segmentation

In document recognition, line detection and character segmentation are important because they have a great influence on all subsequent processes.

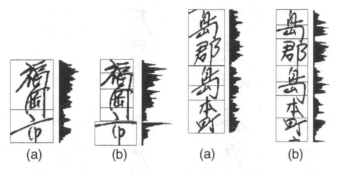

Fig. 3.10. Pre-segmentation for (a) original image and (b) slant corrected image.

For segmentation of lines and characters, one of the typical methods employs pixel projection of a binary image. The other method uses a labeling process to detect character regions and a merging process to merge close regions.

Since text lines in Japanese documents can be vertical or horizontal and sometimes a mixture of the two, segmentation task tends to be difficult. For the sake of simplicity, we focus on examples with vertical lines and the projection method is employed for pre-segmentation.

At first vertical projection of the address image is used to separate each line. Then horizontal projection is employed to determine pre-segmentation points by valley point analysis of the projection. However, when the slanted characters touch or overlap with adjacent characters, valleys are not found between them and determination of the threshold becomes very difficult.

Figure 3.10 shows two examples of pre-segmentation for original image (a) and for slant corrected image (b). It is known by comparison that the separability of overlapping characters can be improved by the slant correction.

The slant of address image is corrected prior to the segmentation to reduce overlapping characters and to make the valley point detection easier.

Lexicon Driven Segmentation–Recognition

Lexicon driven segmentation–recognition is employed in such application as postal address recognition where a lexicon is available. First an addresses lexicon is generated from address database. Each lexicon address consists of EUC code of Japanese characters.

Segments are merged into the characters to match with the characters in the lexicon address. For each lexicon address, the best match is obtained by calculating the minimum total distance between the segments and the lexicon characters by dynamic programming. Each distance is calculated by a classifier described in Section 3.4.

Consider an example which matches N segments with a lexicon address of M characters. While matching the first j segments with the first i

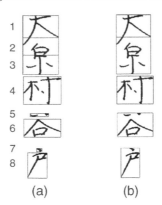

Fig. 3.11. (a) Pre-segmentation and (b) optimum character segmentation.

characters, assuming that up to three segments are possible to merge, the minimum distance between them is given by

$$f(i,j) = \min(f(i-1,j-1) + d_1(i,j), f(i-1,j-2) + d_2(i,j-1),$$
$$f(i-1,j-3) + d_3(i,j-2)), \tag{3.4}$$

where $1 \leq i \leq M$ and $i \leq j \leq N$. The function $d_k(i,j)$ $(1 \leq k \leq 3)$ gives the distance between ith character and jth to $(j+k-1)$th segments, and $f(i,j)$ represents the minimum total distance for the matching first j segments with the first i characters. According to the definition, the initial value of $f(i,j)$ is given by $f(1,1) = d_1(1,1)$, $f(1,2) = d_2(1,1)$, $f(1,3) = d_3(1,1)$. And the final optimal matching is determined by value $f(M,N)$.

For a test address, matching is performed with all lexicon addresses. Then the lexicon address with minimum average distance $f(M,N)/M$ is selected for the best candidate.

The process of address matching is illustrated by the example shown in Figure 3.11. Based on the pre-segmentation result of Figure 3.11(a), minimum total distance $f(i,j)$ is calculated by the dynamic programming as shown in Table 3.2. Then the best matching is obtained with the minimum total distance $f(5,8) = 42.40$, meanwhile the optimum character segmentation is also generated as shown in Figure 3.11(b).

3.3 Feature Extraction

Many character recognition techniques have been proposed and studied for isolated character recognition. Among those techniques those having the following characteristics are desirable for Japanese OCR.

(1) Robustness for wide variation of complex shapes
(2) Automatic learning capability
(3) High speed recognition of large character set
(4) Availability to different character set

Table 3.2. Example of calculating minimum total distance $f(i,j)$

Characters Segments	大	泉	村	谷	戸
1	*4.60*				
2	26.28	33.97			
3	27.19	*19.65*	64.83		
4		33.05	*31.37*	99.79	
5		57.09	35.52	68.04	122.63
6		50.22	54.73	*37.65*	101.78
7			66.20	42.34	54.32
8			79.84	65.40	*42.40*

It is known that these properties are of statistical and neural classification techniques rather than syntactic and structural approach. In this section feature extraction suitable for Japanese OCR is described.

In the statistical and neural classification, a feature vector representing the shape of character is composed in the process of feature extraction. Generally, features of character such as medial axis, contour, cavities and loops are first extracted and then the feature vector is calculated from the features. Among these features the contour (edge) of character is desirable for high speed feature extraction because of relative simplicity of the contour extraction. The shape of contour is easily characterized in a form of feature vector using local chain code histogram. The shape information of character contour is also characterized using gradient of character image. These two basic procedures are described below.

3.3.1 Chain Code Histogram

Simple Chain Code Histogram [6]

Local chain code histograms of character contour are used as a feature vector (Figure 3.12). The rectangular frame enclosing a character is first divided into 7×7 blocks. In each block, a chain code histogram of character contour is calculated. The feature vector is composed of these local histograms. Since contour orientation is quantized to one of four possible values (0, 45, 90 or 135), a histogram in each block has four components. After the histogram calculation, the 7×7 blocks are down sampled with Gaussian filter into 4×4 blocks. Thus the feature vector has 64 elements when all the 16 blocks are included.

The height normalization is simply performed by multiplying each vector component by the ratio of standard height to the actual height of the letter.

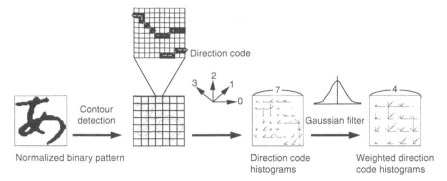

Fig. 3.12. Feature extraction from contour chain code.

The variable transformation is performed by taking the square root of each component. The use of power transformation to obtain Gaussian-like distribution from a distribution of causal (positive valued) features is described in [3].

WDH Feature Vector [9]

The Weighted Direction code Histogram (WDH) feature vector of size 392 is extracted by the following procedure:

(1) The chain coding is applied to the contour pixels of the normalized character image. Vector sum of adjacent two chain elements is taken to produce 16-directional code.
(2) The normalized character image is divided into 169 (13 horizontal × 13 vertical) blocks. The number of the contour pixels in each direction is counted in each block to produce 169 local direction code histograms.
(3) The spatial resolution is reduced from 13×13 to 7×7 by down sampling every two horizontal and every two vertical blocks with 5×5 Gaussian filter. Similarly the directional resolution is reduced from 16 to 8 by down sampling with a weight vector $[1\ 2\ 1]^{\mathrm{T}}$, to produce a feature vector of size 392 (7 horizontal, 7 vertical and 8 directional resolution).
(4) Variable transformation taking square root of each feature element is applied to make the distribution of the features Gaussian-like.

The 5×5 Gaussian filter and the weight vector $[1\ 2\ 1]^{\mathrm{T}}$ in step (3) are the high cut filters to reduce the aliasing due to the down sampling. Their size was empirically determined for this purpose.

3.3.2 Gradient Feature [16]

Steps (1) and (2) for the WDH feature vector are replaced by the following processing that uses gradient of a grey scale image: Gaussian filter and Roberts filter is applied to a character image to obtain a gradient image

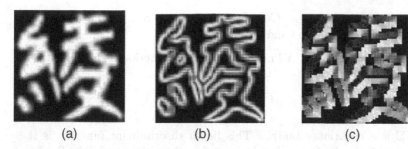

(a)   (b)   (c)

Fig. 3.13. Grey scale image and the gradient: (a) grey scale image after nonlinear normalization and filtering, (b) strength of gradient and (c) direction of gradient (shading representation).

(Figure 3.13). The arctangent of the gradient is quantized into 16 directions and the strength of the gradient is accumulated in each direction in each block. The rest of the steps are the same as steps (3) and (4) for the WDH feature vector.

3.4 Classification

The frequently used classifiers in Japanese OCR are the city-block distance classifier, the Euclidian distance classifier, the linear classifier, the projection distance classifier, the subspace method classifier and the modified quadratic classifier. The modified quadratic classifier is a parametric classifier, which is derived from the Bayes decision rule for the normal distributions [7].

3.4.1 Linear Classifiers for High-Speed Pre-Classification

(1) City-block distance classifier: The city-block distance is defined by

$$g(_jX) = \sum_{i=1}^{n} |x_i - m_i|, \tag{3.5}$$

where x_i and m_{ij} are the ith element of a feature vector X, and the mean vector M_j of the jth class, respectively, and n is the dimensionality of the feature vector. The class ω_{j*} which minimizes $g_j(X)$ is selected as the recognition result. The required computation time and storage is $O(n)$. For notational simplicity the subscript j will be omitted hereafter.

(2) Euclidian distance classifier: The Euclidian distance is defined by

$$g(X) = ||X - M|| = \sqrt{\sum_{i=1}^{n}(x_i - m_i)^2}. \tag{3.6}$$

The class which minimizes $g(X)$ is selected as the recognition result. The required computation time and storage is $O(n)$.

(3) Linear classifier [1,3]: A linear discriminant function is defined by

$$g(X) = M^T \Sigma^{-1} X - \frac{1}{2} M^T \Sigma^{-1} M, \tag{3.7}$$

where Σ is a covariance matrix. This linear discriminant function is the one derived from the Bayes discriminant function (the quadratic discriminant function) for a normal distribution with known parameters under the assumption that the covariance matrix is common to all classes. The covariance matrix is replaced by the within-class sample covariance matrix in practice. The class which maximizes $g(X)$ is selected as the recognition result. The required computation time and storage is $O(n)$.

3.4.2 Quadratic Classifiers

(4) Projection distance classifier [4]: The projection distance is defined by

$$g(X) = ||X - M||^2 - \sum_{i=1}^{k} \{\Phi_i^T (X - M)\}^2, \tag{3.8}$$

where Φ_i is the ith eigenvector of the covariance matrix. The function $g(X)$ gives the distance from the feature vector X to a hyper-plane, which is the minimum mean square error fitting plane to the distribution of the class. The class which minimizes $g(X)$ is selected as the recognition result. The value k determines the dimension of the hyper-plane. The required computation time and storage is $O(kn)$.

(5) Subspace method classifier [11,17]: The discriminant function is defined by

$$g(X) = \sum_{i=1}^{k} \{\Phi_i^T X\}^2, \tag{3.9}$$

where Φ_i is the ith eigenvector of the auto-correlation matrix. The feature vector X is assumed to be normalized so that $||X|| = 1$ prior to the classification. The function $g(X)$ gives the projection of the feature vector X to a hyper-plane passing through the origin. The hyper-plane is the minimum mean square error fitting plane to the distribution which is on the surface of a unit hyper-sphere. The class which maximizes $g(X)$ is selected as the recognition result. The value k determines the dimension of the hyper-plane (subspace). The required computation time and storage is $O(kn)$.

(6) Modified quadratic classifier [7]: The discriminant function is defined by

$$g(X) = \frac{1}{\alpha\sigma^2}\left[||X - M||^2 - \sum_{i=1}^{k}\frac{(1-\alpha)\lambda_i}{(1-\alpha)\lambda_i + \alpha\sigma^2}\{\Phi_i^T(X-M)\}^2\right]$$

$$+ \sum_{i=1}^{k}\ln\{(1-\alpha)\lambda_i + \alpha\sigma^2\} \tag{3.10}$$

where λ_i and Φ_i are the ith eigenvalue and eigenvector of the covariance matrix, respectively, σ^2 and α are an initial estimates of the variance and a confidence constant, respectively. The class which minimizes $g(X)$ is selected as the recognition result. The required computation time and storage is $O(kn)$.

The modified quadratic discriminant function is insensitive to the estimation error of the covariance matrix because it employs only k dominant eigenvectors [7]. The discriminant function is derived from the quadratic discriminant function for Gaussian distributions [1]. The covariance matrix is replaced by a pseudo-Bayes estimate $(1 - \alpha)\Sigma + \alpha\Sigma_0$, where Σ_0 and α are the initial covariance matrix and its confidence constant. When the features are of the same kind on the same scale, e.g. chain code histogram and gradient features, it is reasonable to assume $\Sigma_0 = \sigma^2 I$, where I is the identity matrix.

3.5 Dimension Reduction

While higher dimensional feature vector improves the separability between categories in the feature space, it requires more computation time and storage. To save the computation cost, it is preferable to employ a statistical dimension reduction technique to select smaller number of discriminative features sacrificing as less discriminating power of the feature vector as possible.

3.5.1 Discriminant Analysis

The discriminant analysis extracts an n' feature elements from an n dimensional feature vector as follows $(n' < n)$ [1, 3].

The eigenvalues and eigenvectors satisfying

$$S_b\Phi = S_w\Phi\Lambda \tag{3.11}$$

is calculated, where S_b and S_w are between-class scatter matrix and within-class scatter matrix, respectively. The matrices Λ and Φ are eigenvalue matrices having eigenvalues λ_i $(\lambda_1 > \lambda_2 > \cdots > \lambda_n)$ as their diagonal elements, and eigenvectors Φ_i as their column vectors, respectively. Each of new feature elements is obtained by

$$z_i = \Phi_i^T X \quad (i = 1, 2, \ldots, n'). \tag{3.12}$$

Since the dimension reduction is completed by n' times of the inner products, the computation time is sufficiently small relative to the total computation time of Japanese character recognition. It reduces the required computation time and storage of succeeding process by factor two or more.

3.5.2 Principal Component Analysis

In the principal component analysis, the basis vectors (eigenvectors) are calculated using the total scatter matrix $S_t(= S_w + S_b)$ by

$$S_i \Phi = \Phi \Lambda \tag{3.13}$$

instead of (3.11) for the discriminant analysis. Using the eigenvectors, the new features are calculated by (3.12).

3.6 Performance Evaluation of OCR Technologies

Performance of OCR technologies are evaluated and described through Sections 3.6.2–3.6.4 where the alternative techniques for each and the dimension reduction, pre-classification and the main classification are experimentally tested and compared.

3.6.1 Used Database

All experiments were performed using JIS first level Chinese character database ETL9B [12] collected by the Electrotechnical Laboratory. All samples are binary image of size 64W × 63H. The ETL9B includes 200 sample characters for each of 3036 character categories, 2965 Chinese and 71 Hiragana characters.

3.6.2 Dimension Reduction

Comparison on Dimension Reduction

The efficiency of the dimension reduction by the discriminant analysis and the principal component analysis as well as the reduction of spatial resolution was experimentally compared.

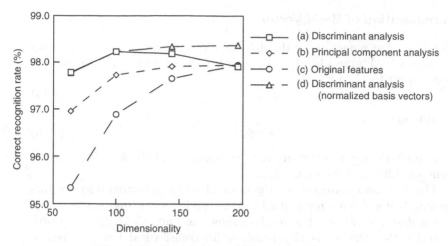

Fig. 3.14. Comparison of dimension reduction.

For the numeral set, which consists of much smaller number of categories than the feature size (dimensionality), it is known that the principal component analysis more effectively reduces the feature size less sacrificing the classification performance than the discriminant analysis [8]. The effectiveness of the discriminant analysis is limited due to the rank deficiency of the between-class scatter matrix S_b in the numeral recognition application. However for the large Japanese character set, the discriminant analysis is free from the rank deficiency problem, and is superior to the principal component analysis.

The WDH feature vector of size 196, which is obtained by employing 4 bi-directional code instead of 8-directional code described in Section 3.3.1 is used as the original feature vector. The recognition accuracy of the modified quadratic discriminant function employing the dimension reduced feature vectors by the discriminant analysis and the principal component analysis is shown in Figure 3.14(a) and (b), respectively. Figure 3.14(c) shows the result for the original features detected with lower spatial resolution. The number of used eigenvectors of the modified quadratic discriminant function is 40. It is shown that the reduction of spatial resolution causes rapid performance deterioration than the dimension reduction. These results are summarized as follows:

(1) Reduced feature vectors are more discriminative than the low resolution original feature vectors.
(2) The discriminant analysis performs better for the large Japanese character set than the principal component analysis.

The dimension reduction by the discriminant analysis achieves higher recognition accuracy at lower dimensionality than the original one.

Normalization of Basis Vector

The dimension reduction by the discriminant analysis causes the peaking phenomenon (Figure 3.14(a)). The eigenvectors of (3.11) is orthonormal with respect to S_w, i.e.

$$\Phi^T S_w \Phi = I \tag{3.14}$$

instead of

$$\Phi^T \Phi = I. \tag{3.15}$$

As a result the eigenvectors are not orthogonal, and the length (norm) of them are different from each other.

The dimension reduction by the normalized basis vectors (eigenvectors the length of which are normalized to 1) is applied and tested in the similar way as described above. The result is shown in Figure 3.14(d). It is worth observing that the recognition accuracy for transformed 196 dimensional feature vector is significantly better than for the original feature vector. The peaking phenomenon disappears.

3.6.3 Comparison on Pre-Classification

Figure 3.15 shows the cumulative recognition rates of the pre-classifiers. While the Euclidian distance classifier and the city-block distance classifier achieve 99.9% cumulative correct classification rate at rank 60 and 50, respectively, the linear classifier does at rank 20, and reduces the processing time of the main classification significantly. The recognition test was performed for 3036 character categories. The original feature vector is the WDH feature vector of size 196.

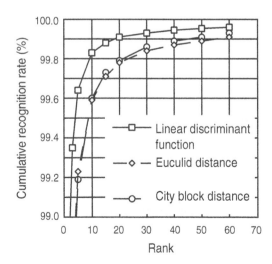

Fig. 3.15. Cumulative recognition rates of pre-classifiers.

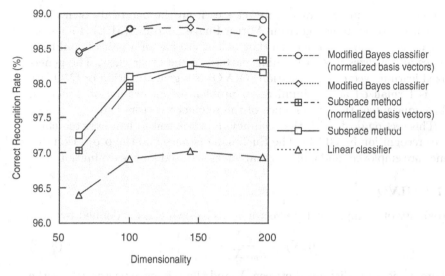

Fig. 3.16. Comparison of classifiers.

3.6.4 Comparison on Main Classification

The performance of the modified quadratic classifier and the subspace method as well as the linear classifier was compared in a similar way as in Section 3.6.2. The dimension reduction was performed by the discriminant analysis. The result is shown in Figure 3.16. The modified quadratic classifier (modified Bayes classifier) achieved better performance than the subspace method. Since Japanese character has a large number of categories, the performance of the subspace method may be deteriorated by subspace sharing with different categories.

The basis vectors for the dimension reduction are normalized in the same way as described in Section 3.6.2. The normalization of the basis vectors resolves the peaking phenomenon. Since linear classifier is invariant under the linear transformation, the performance is not affected by the normalization of the basis vectors.

3.7 Learning Algorithms

Statistical pattern recognition techniques generally assume that the density function and the parameters of each class are only dependent on the sample of the class. To improve the classifier performance beyond the limitation due to the assumption, several learning algorithms that exploit learning patterns of other classes (counter-classes) have been proposed.

The Averaged Learning Subspace Method (ALSM) [11] adaptively modifies the basis vectors of a subspace (hyper-plane) by subtracting the auto-correlation matrix for counter-classes from the one of its own class. The corrective learning algorithm Mirror Image Learning (MIL) [15] generates a mirror image of a pattern that belongs to one of a pair of confusing classes and utilizes it as a learning pattern of the other class. The generalized learning vector quantization (GLVQ) is a generalization of LVQ [10] and is formalized as a minimization problem of an evaluation function, which guarantees the convergence of the reference vectors [13].

This section deals with the accuracy improvement of handwritten character recognition by GLVQ. The Euclidian distance and the projection distance are employed, and Chinese characters are used for the evaluation test.

3.7.1 GLVQ

Proximity of an input feature vector X to its own class is defined by

$$\mu(X) = \frac{d_m(X) - d(_jX)}{d_m(X) + d(_jX)}, \tag{3.16}$$

where d_m is some distance between X and the reference vector R_m of the class to which X belongs, and d_j is the distance between X and the nearest reference vector R_j of the class to which X does not belong. The proximity μ takes the value in $[-1, 1]$ for any X, and leads to correct (incorrect) classification when it is negative (positive).

The purpose of the learning is to reduce the incorrect classification by reducing the value of μ for as many X as possible. The GLVQ is formalized as a minimization problem of an evaluation function Q defined by

$$Q = \sum_{i=0}^{N} (\mu f_i), \tag{3.17}$$

where N is the total number of the input vectors and $f(\mu)$ is a monotonically increasing function of μ. The evaluation function Q can be minimized by iterative modification of the reference vectors,

$$R^m_{k,t+1} = R^m_{k,t} + \alpha \cdot \frac{\partial}{\partial \mu} \frac{f}{(d_m + d)^2_j} \frac{d_j}{}(X_k - R^m_{k,t}), \tag{3.18}$$

$$R^j_{k,t+1} = R_{k,t}{}^j - \alpha \cdot \frac{\partial}{\partial \mu} \frac{f}{(d_m + d)^2_j} d_m (X_k - R_{k,t}{}^j), \tag{3.19}$$

which are derived by the steepest descent method. Generally the first derivative of the function f is defined by

$$\frac{\partial}{\partial \mu} =^f F(\mu, t)(1 - F(\mu, t)), \tag{3.20}$$

where k is the dimensionality, t is the number of iteration and $F(\mu, t)$ is the sigmoid function defined by

$$F(\mu, t) = \frac{1}{1 + e^{-\mu(X)t}}. \tag{3.21}$$

As the initial reference vectors, the mean vector of each class is used.

Table 3.3. Result of handwritten Chinese character recognition

Distance	Transformation and learning	Recognition rate (%)
Euclidian distance	–	94.61
	DA	96.73
	GLVQ	97.22
	DA+GLVQ	97.51
Projection distance	–	97.26
	DA	98.05
	GLVQ	97.83
	DA+GLVQ	98.30

3.7.2 Performance Evaluation

In the performance evaluation test, 3036 classes of handwritten Chinese characters in ETL9B collected by the Electrotechnical Laboratory were used. The WDH feature vector of size 196 was extracted from each character image. The sample size is 200 per class and was divided into learning sample and test sample of size 100 per class, respectively. The performance evaluation of the two classifiers with the reference vectors obtained by the GLVQ as well as the original mean vectors was performed for comparison. The result is shown in Table 3.3. This table implies that

(1) the modification of the reference vectors by the GLVQ improves the recognition accuracy,
(2) the feature transformation by the discriminant analysis (DA) improves the recognition accuracy,
(3) the direct cascading of the DA and the GLVQ further improves the recognition accuracy.

The number of iteration of the GLVQ was about 40 for the Euclidian distance classifier, and is about 20 for the projection distance classifier. When the DA was applied, the size (dimensionality) of the transformed feature vector was 144.

The highest accuracy (98.30%) for the Chinese character recognition was obtained when the DA, GLVQ and the projection distance were employed.

3.8 Conclusion

This chapter deals with Japanese OCR technologies for pre-processing, feature extraction, classification, dimension reduction and learning. The performance of those technologies were experimentally studied and compared for further improvement and development of those technologies.

The results are summarized as follows:

(1) The nonlinear normalization of character image improves the recognition accuracy of the statistical classifier employing the WDH feature vector.
(2) Reduced feature vectors are more discriminative than the original feature vectors. The discriminant analysis performs better for the large Japanese character set than the principal component analysis.
(3) The linear classifier can reduce the size of category set in the main classification more efficiently than the minimum distance classifiers.
(4) The modified quadratic classifier achieved better performance than the subspace method.
(5) The modification of the reference vectors by the GLVQ improves the recognition accuracy.

Further studies on

(1) character segmentation of Japanese and English mixed text,
(2) segmentation–recognition of handwritten Japanese document by lexicon driven and lexicon free segmentation–recognition

are remaining as future research topics.

References

1. Duda, T.O. and Hart, P.E. (1973). *Pattern Classification and Scene Analysis.* New York: John Wiley & Sons, Inc.
2. Kimura, F., Shridhar, M., and Chen, Z. (1993). Improvements of a lexicon directed algorithm for recognition of unconstrained handwritten words. *Proceedings of 2nd ICDAR*, pp. 18–22.
3. Fukunaga, K. (1990). *Introduction to Statistical Pattern Recognition*, 2nd ed. New York: Academic Press.
4. Ikeda, M., Tanaka, H., and Moto-oka, T. (1983). Projection distance method for recognition of hand-written characters. *Transactions of IPS Japan, 24(1)*, pp. 106–112.
5. Ishitani, Y. (1993). Document skew detection based on local region complexity. *Proceedings of 2nd ICDAR*, pp. 49–52.
6. Kimura, F., Miyake, Y., and Shridhar, M. (1995). ZIP code recognition using lexicon free word recognition algorithm. *Proceedings of 3rd ICDAR*, pp. 906–910.
7. Kimura, F., Takashina, K., Tsuruoka, S. and Miyake, Y. (1987). Modified quadratic discriminant functions and the application to Chinese character recognition. *IEEE Transactions on Pattern Analysis and Machine Intelligence, 9(1)*, pp. 149–153.
8. Kimura, F., Wakabayashi, T., and Miyake, Y. (1996). On feature extraction for limited class problem. *Proceedings of 13th ICPR*, pp. 191–194.
9. Kimura, F., Wakabayashi, T., Tsuruoka, S., and Miyake, Y. (1997). Improvement of handwritten Japanese character recognition using weighted direction code histogram. *Pattern Recognition, 30(8)*, pp. 1329–1337.

10. Kohonen, T. (1989). *Self-Organization and Associative Memory*, 3rd ed. Berlin: Springer-Verlag.

11. Oja, E. (1983). *Subspace Methods of Pattern Recognition*. England: Research Studies Press.

12. Saito, T., Yamada, H., and Yamamoto, K. (1985). An analysis of handprinted character database VIII: an estimation of the database ETL9 of handprinted characters in JIS Chinese characters by directional pattern matching approach (in Japanese). *Bulletin of Electrotechnical Laboratory Japan, 49(7)*, pp. 487–525.

13. Sato, A. and Yamada K. (1996). *Generalized learning vector quantization. Advances in Neural Information Processing*. Cambridge, MA: MIT Press, Volume 8, pp. 423–429.

14. Tsukumo, J. and Tanaka, H. (1988). Classification of handprinted Chinese characters using non-linear normalization and correlation methods. *Proceedings of 9th ICPR*, pp. 168–171.

15. Wakabayashi, T., Shi, M., Ohyama, W., and Kimura, F. (2001). Accuracy improvement of handwritten numeral recognition by Mirror Image Learning. *Proceedings of ICDAR'01*, pp. 338–343.

16. Wakabayashi, T., Tsuruoka, S., Kimura, F., and Miyake, Y. (1995). Increasing the feature size in handwritten numeral recognition to improve accuracy. *Systems and Computers in Japan, 26(8)*, pp. 35–44 (English Edition). Scripta Technica, Inc.

17. Watanabe, S. and Pakvasa, N. (1973). Subspace method of pattern recognition. *Proc. of 1st International Joint Conference on Pattern Recognition*. Washington, DC, Oct–Nov. pp. 2–32.

18. Yamada, H., Yamamoto, K., and Saito, T. (1990). A nonlinear normalization method for handprinted Kanji character recognition – line density equalization. *Pattern Recognition, 23(9)*, pp. 1023–1029.

4

Multi-Font Printed Tibetan OCR

Xiaoqing Ding and Hua Wang

4.1 Introduction

Tibetan culture has a very long history and it is a splendid contribution both in China and over the world. As a significant representative of Tibetan culture, Tibetan language is still used by more than six million people in China at present. The Tibetan character set, which records Tibetan language and Tibetan culture, is very special and different in comparison with other character sets in the world, such as Chinese and so on. Therefore, research on Tibetan OCR, which will enable easier modernization of Tibetan culture and digitization of Tibetan document, is very important in theoretical value as well as in extensive application perspective. However, only few research works have been undertaken so far.

Masami et al. created an object-oriented dictionary [16], by combining categorization and character identification procedures to separately recognize basic consonants, combination characters and vowels. Furthermore, Euclidean distance with deferential weights [17] was designed to discriminate similar characters. Ma et al. established an experimental system [?] based on fuzzy line features and Euclidean distance classifier. Overall, the research of Tibetan OCR is still in its infancy and there remain several limitations in previous works. First, the importance of multi-font Tibetan character recognition problem has not been widely thought of. Reported researches are all focused on single font samples. Second, no effective and robust strategy to recognize actual Tibetan scripts has been proposed. Finally, huge dictionaries of Tibetan syllables are indispensable in achieving encouraging recognition results.

In this chapter, a novel and effective method based on statistical pattern recognition approach for multi-font printed Tibetan OCR is proposed. A robust Tibetan character recognition algorithm is designed whose destination character set contains 584 modern Tibetan character categories used commonly in the Tibetan documents.

On the other hand, it is still challenging to develop a character-and-document recognition system, which can achieve extremely high recognition accuracy regardless of the quality of input scripts. Researchers have noted that most recognition errors that occur in an OCR system are due to character segmentation errors [15]. In this chapter, document segmentation, which is divided into two steps, is also discussed: line separation and character segmentation. To the authors' knowledge, no special technique aiming at printed Tibetan scripts' segmentation has been reported. However, many ideas can be borrowed from previous techniques that deal with other scripts [1, 5, 7, 11, 15]. Various algorithms [12] are available for skew detection and correction before text line separation. Histogram of horizontal projection is commonly used to separate text lines. Many segmentation strategies [1, 15] have been proposed to segment words into their character components. However, no exact previous technique can be directly implemented to solve Tibetan text segmentation. A comprehensive text segmentation method for multi-font Tibetan recognition is developed. Its validity is demonstrated by experimental results on a large-scale set.

The organization of this chapter is as follows. A brief introduction to the properties of Tibetan characters and scripts is given in Section 4.2. Section 4.3 describes the details of Tibetan recognition algorithm, including character normalization, statistical feature vector formulation and classifier design. The two-stage document segmentation strategy is discussed in Section 4.4. Experimental results are given in Section 4.5. The final section summarizes the chapter.

4.2 Properties of Tibetan Characters and Scripts

There are totally 34 basic elements (Figure 4.1), which consist of 30 consonants (3 of which have modified forms) and 4 vowels expanding the whole Tibetan character set in modern Tibetan language.

There are two kinds of characters used in written Tibetan language: (1) *consonants*, which serve as valid characters by themselves. We call them

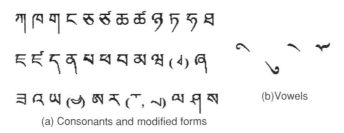

(a) Consonants and modified forms   (b)Vowels

Fig. 4.1. Basic elements of Tibetan character set.

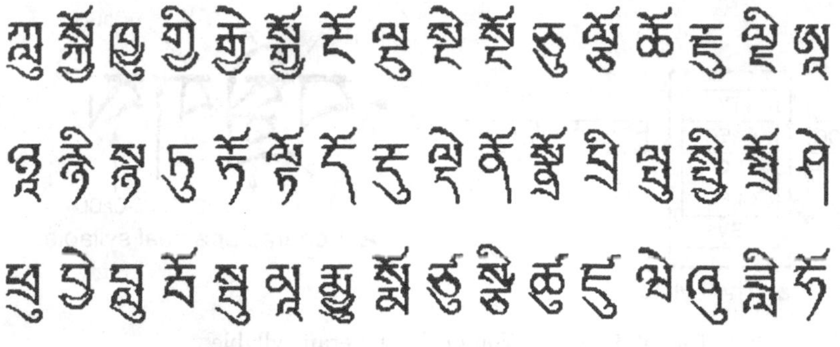

ཀྱ སྐུ ཨེ ཀྱི རྗེ སྐྲ རྡ སྱེ རྭ རུ སྨོ ཚ ཌྷ ཀྱི ཨུ

རུ རྗེ སྙ ཏུ རྟོ སྐོ རྡ ར རྡ སྱེ རྣ སྐྲ ཕ སྐུ སྐྱི སྐྲ ནེ

སུ ཝི སྦ རྟོ སྐུ སྐུ སྐུ སྐོ ཇ རྗི ཚ ཌ རུ ཨེ ཨ རྗི ཌ

Fig. 4.2. Some samples of combined characters.

ཀ ཁ ཙ ཚ ཆ ཆ ཉ ཏ ཌ ཌ བ ཕ སྣ ཉ ཟ ཡ ཤ ཧ ཌ ཟ

(a) EC

ར [ྲ]   ཨ སྐ [ྣ] ཝ [ྭ] ར [ྼ]   ~ ~ ~ ~

(b)   (c) CbEC   (d)TV   (e)BV
CaEC

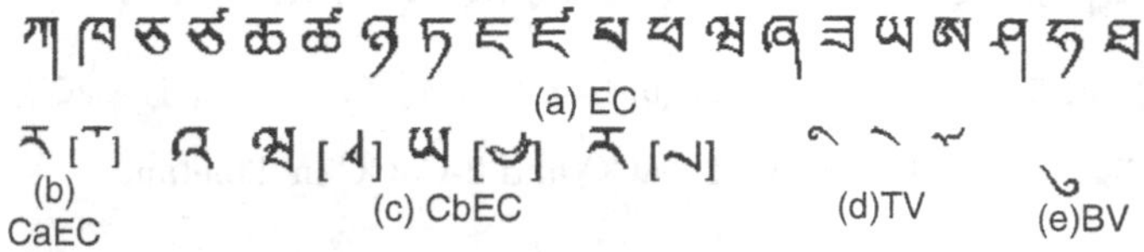

Fig. 4.3. Valid characters for each component of a CC.

single characters (SC) for convenience and (2) *combined characters* (CC), which are composed of a consonant called *essential consonant* (EC), 0–2 other consonant(s) and/or 1 vowel. Some samples of combined characters are shown in Figure 4.2. Arranged from top to bottom, a CC may have the top vowel (TV), the consonant above the essential consonant (CaEC), the consonant below the essential consonant (CbEC) and the bottom vowel (BV). What should be borne in mind is that the TV and the BV cannot appear in the same CC simultaneously. Thus, all possible structures of CCs can be divided into 12 types (x ↓ y means x is on the top of y): EC, EC ↓ CbEC, EC ↓ BV, EC ↓ CbEC ↓ BV, CaEC ↓ EC, CaEC ↓ EC ↓ CbEC, CaEC ↓ EC ↓ BV, CaEC ↓ EC ↓ CbEC ↓ BV, TV ↓ EC, TV ↓ EC ↓ CbEC, TV ↓ CaEC ↓ EC, TV ↓ CaEC ↓ EC ↓ CbEC. Not all vowels can serve as TV and BV; in the same way, not each consonant can play a part as EC, CaEC or CbEC. All legal TV and BV, all valid EC (20 consonants), CaEC (3 consonants and a modified consonant), CbEC (4 consonants and 3 modified consonants) are listed in Figure 4.3. As a result, thousands of CCs may be obtained by combination rules, whereas only about 500 CCs are most frequently used in applications, which hit over 99.95% of all possible CCs according to our statistics on very large language materials containing about 20,000,000 Tibetan characters.

In Tibetan language, syllables are basic spelling units, whose structure is demonstrated in Figure 4.4. Each syllable consists of a centre character (CC) and 0–3 other characters, namely the character before centre character (CbCC), the 1st character after the centre character (1-CaCC) and the 2nd character after the centre character (2-CaCC). Thus, all possible

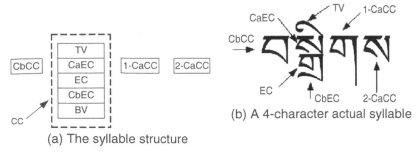

(a) The syllable structure

(b) A 4-character actual syllable

Fig. 4.4. Illustration of the Tibetan syllable.

(a) CbCC   (b) 1-CaCC   (c) 2-CaCC

Fig. 4.5. Valid CbCC, 1-CaCC and 2-CaCC in Tibetan.

character combinations of a syllable are {CC, CC→1-CaCC, CC→1-CaCC→2-CaCC, CbCC→CC, CbCC→CC→1-CaCC, CbCC→CC→1-CaCC→2-CaCC}, where (x→y) indicates x is on the left of y. In a syllable, CC can be either a combined character or a single character, while CbCC, 1-CaCC and 2-CaCC are single characters only, whose possible set (5, 12 and 2 single characters, respectively) are listed in Figure 4.5.

A Tibetan text line, which usually ends with a special mark called *shad*, can be divided into several syllables, which are separated from each other by another special mark called *inter-syllabic tsheg* (Figure 4.6). Each text line has a horizontal baseline at the upper part. Characters in a text line are aligned by their tops at the baseline position except those centre characters with top vowels over the baseline. Particularly, tops of inter-syllabic tshegs are located exactly on the baseline. The distance from the baseline location to the top of the text line occupies about 1/4 of the whole text line height. In Tibetan scripts, the width of characters of the same font and the same font size is comparatively stable, while the character height varies dramatically from each other.

From the view of isolated character recognition, the difficulties for a robust Tibetan OCR algorithm result from:

(1) The number of character categories: It is much larger than the number of numerals or alphabets. Tibetan character set recognition is within the scope of large-set pattern classification.
(2) Font variations: Quite a few fonts are applied in Tibetan publications. Characters in several fonts vary greatly in different shapes and postures (Figure 4.7).

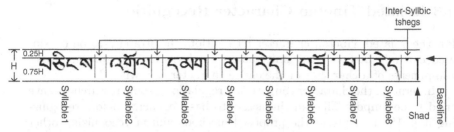

Fig. 4.6. A sample of Tibetan text line.

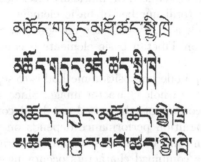

Fig. 4.7. Text of four different fonts in the same font size and style.

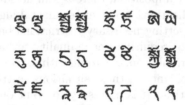

Fig. 4.8. Some similar character pairs.

(3) Similar characters: There are more than 100 similar character pairs in the most commonly used character set (Figure 4.8 shows some samples).

(4) Character structure: Most Tibetan characters, especially combined characters, are composed of many strokes in various styles. Compared with Chinese characters, however, the size variation of Tibetan characters is enormous.

For a character segmentation process, the most important task is to deal with touching characters since Tibetan characters often get connected through the baseline. It should tolerate the variations of character shape and size in multi-font text situations as well.

4.3 Isolated Tibetan Character Recognition

For the isolated Tibetan character recognition, the strategy to be considered carefully first is: what unit should be chosen as recognition target, components of a character or the entire character as a whole?

In terms of the character constitution regulations, some researchers have tried to decompose Tibetan characters to basic elements before recognizing it [8, 18] as many of the proposed methods aim at recognizing other phonemic character sets like Latin. This may be a natural idea because the category number can be reduced dramatically after decomposition. For Tibetan characters, the total number of basic elements (consonants and vowels) is only 34, which is fairly easy for recognition. So design recognition algorithm based on Tibetan basic elements becomes an attractive option.

However, the key step in decomposition method is to separate each consonant and vowel from the whole character image. Since single characters are made up of a sole consonant, they need not be decomposed further. Thus, the eventual recognition performance depends on whether we can obtain isolated consonant and vowel from combined characters accurately and robustly due to the combined characters occupying over 30% in Tibetan documents. Unfortunately, although lots of efforts have been focused on combined character decomposition, there is still no satisfactory method that can be put into applications. Some experimental algorithms reported acceptable results [8] by setting necessary restrictions beforehand such as specifying a certain font or requiring image quality to be perfectly "neat" and scanning with high resolution. Such algorithms cannot meet the demand of real applications, since in those situations restrictions on font or input image are not practical. It is necessary to point out that the failure to get a satisfactory decomposition algorithm comes directly from the intrinsic connection characteristics of components within Tibetan combined characters. Two adjacent components in a character may touch tightly, overlap several pixels or even nest each other, which make their boundary blurred, let alone the quality degeneration of character image.

Based on the above-mentioned reasons, in order to achieve a robust Tibetan character recognition performance, the totally character-based statistical character recognition algorithm has been researched. That is, while processing a recognition task, we treat a combined character as a whole unit instead of decomposing it into components. In this way, we separate isolated characters from text lines and avoid decomposing isolated characters especially combined characters further. There usually exists a small run of blank between two adjacent characters. Even in the situations where a character touches the next one, their boundary can be identified explicitly. Therefore, isolated character separation is feasible and its accuracy can be expected as long as an effective algorithm is developed.

The destination category of our recognition algorithm includes 30 single characters, 534 most frequently used combined characters. To be completely practical, 10 Tibetan digits and 10 Tibetan marks in common use are also involved. Then, the total category number reaches 584.

4.3.1 Character Normalization

In an OCR system, character normalization is a crucial step to eliminate variations in character size and position.

We use a matrix $[B(i,j)]_{H \times W}$ to represent a character image whose height is H and width W and the coordinate system is shown in Figure 4.9

$$[B(i,j)]_{H \times W} = \begin{bmatrix} B(0,0), & B(0,1), & \cdots, B(0,W-1) \\ B(1,0), & B(1,1), & \cdots, B(1,W-1) \\ \vdots & \vdots & \cdots \vdots \\ B(H-1,0), & B(H-1,1), & \cdots, B(H-1,W-1) \end{bmatrix}.$$

(4.1)

Here for convenience, we divide all Tibetan characters into two sub-sets: characters with top vowels belong to set T_1, while set T_2 is made up of characters without top vowels. Based on the analyses in Section 4.2, there exists a baseline across the top of characters belonging to T_2 or across the top vowel bottom of characters in T_1. So, given an input character $[B(i,j)]_{H \times W}$, it can be regarded as two sub-images $[B_1(i,j)]_{H_1 \times W}$ and $[B_2(i,j)]_{H_2 \times W}$, $H_1 + H_2 = H$, splicing in vertical. These two sub-images

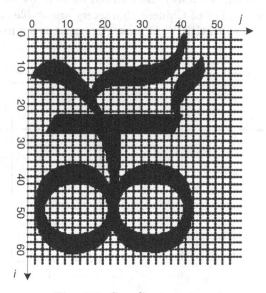

Fig. 4.9. Coordinate system.

are bounded by the baseline and have no inter-section. Therefore, for characters in T_1, $[B_1(i,j)]_{H_1 \times W} \neq \emptyset$ and $[B_2(i,j)]_{H_2 \times W} \neq \emptyset$, while for characters in T_2, $[B_1(i,j)]_{H_1 \times W} = \emptyset$ and $[B_2(i,j)]_{H_2 \times W} \neq \emptyset$, where $\emptyset$ denotes empty set. A natural strategy while normalizing character is to normalize $[B_1(i,j)]_{H_1 \times W}$ and $[B_2(i,j)]_{H_2 \times W}$ to $[G_1(i,j)]_{M_1 \times N}$ and $[G_2(i,j)]_{M_2 \times N}$, respectively. Here $[G_1(i,j)]_{M_1 \times N}$ and $[G_2(i,j)]_{M_2 \times N}$ represent the normalized image over baseline and the normalized image below the baseline, M and N are the height and the width of normalized image, $M_1 + M_2 = M$ and $N_1 = N_2 = N$. Imagine a sequence of input characters that come from the same text line and are aligned with the baseline. After normalization by adopting the above-mentioned strategy, the out characters are aligned with the baseline, too. That is, the baseline position is kept fixed before and after normalization. The following matching process of classification can be considered as two sub-processes, say, matching of features from images over baseline and matching of features from images below baseline, respectively. In this way, local details of two images in different parts are enhanced rather than possibly overwhelmed.

In a Tibetan text line, the baseline of the text line coincides in position with the baseline of characters within the text line. So character baseline location is proven to be fairly accurate and robust. Since the distance from the baseline to the top boundary of the text line occupies about one-quarter of the total height of the text line, we set $M_1 = M/4$ and $M_2 = 3M/4$. Hence, the map from an input character to a normalized one can be demonstrated in Figure 4.10.

The next problem is to select proper target mesh size M and N. In Chinese OCR, characters are always normalized to 48 or 64 both in width and height, because shapes of Chinese characters are stable squares and the ratio of height to width (RHW) of most characters is approximately 1.

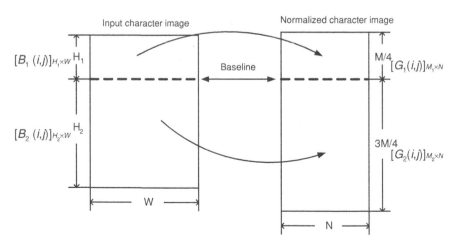

Fig. 4.10. Illustration of Tibetan character normalization strategy.

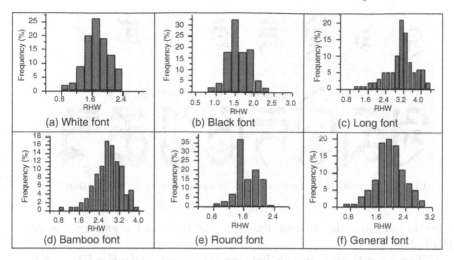

Fig. 4.11. RHW distribution of characters.

Unlike Chinese characters, Tibetan characters of the same text line share almost the same width. However, heights of Tibetan characters vary greatly owing to the different number of components that constitute different characters. Even for single characters, heights differ tremendously from one another. So, we cannot normalize Tibetan characters to squares as we do with Chinese characters. A reasonable RHW M/N should be set first in line with actual conditions of Tibetan character size.

According to the RHW distribution of Tibetan characters of six fonts (Figure 4.11), we can see that (1) character RHW of each font covers a wide range, but there exists an interval in which RHW of over 50% characters is located; (2) RHWs of characters of different fonts vary greatly. Hence, after an all-sided consideration, a trade-off of target RHW is set 2.

We assign 48 to N because in Tibetan/Chinese mixed documents, width of Tibetan characters is nearly the same as that of Chinese characters. So $M = 2N = 96$ and the eventual normalized Tibetan character size is $M \times N = 96 \times 48$. Finally, cubic B-splines [6] are applied to minimize the zigzag effect on the character stroke borders while stretching or shrinking input characters $[B(i,j)]_{H \times W}$ to $[G(i,j)]_{M \times N}$. Several samples to illustrate Tibetan character normalization are shown in Figure 4.12.

4.3.2 Feature Formulation

Features play a crucial role in statistical pattern recognition to achieve excellent performance. Thus, selecting an appropriate kind of feature set becomes a key step in an OCR system. We combine feature extraction and feature compression to generate more efficient feature space subject to

Fig. 4.12. Some Tibetan characters before and after normalization.

a certain optimization criterion based on the information entropy theory (IET) [2, 19].

IET analyses the relationship between the feature space $F = \{X, p(X)|$ $X \in R^d\}$ and the category space $W = \{\omega_i, P(\omega_i)|\omega_i \in \Omega, i = 1, 2, \ldots, c\}$ in the recognition process, where $p(X)$ denotes the observation probability of the feature vector X in a d-dimensional feature space R^d, $P(\omega_i)$ is a priori probability of category ω_i and Ω is the category set of c categories. A basic result is that the recognition error P_e of Bayes classifier is upper bound by the a posteriori conditional entropy $H(W|F)$:

$$P_e \leq H(W|F) = \frac{H(W) - I(F, W)}{2}. \tag{4.2}$$

This bound shows the restriction imposed on the best performance of an ideal Bayes classifier by feature extraction. As $H(W)$ is constant for a given category space, the only way to get lower P_e is to increase $I(F, W)$, the mutual information between the feature space and the category space. Hence it is reasonable to (1) select "good" feature set to maximize $I(F, W)$ as possible; (2) choose $J = I(F, W)$ as the optimization criterion.

It is obvious that the most basic elements of features are stroke border directions of characters. Directional line element features (DLEF) [9], which well describe the stroke edge information of characters in a unified way, are implemented widely in Chinese OCR and have proved to be effective and robust in various applications. As for Tibetan characters, directional features of stroke edges also contain adequately discriminative information that can serve the classification processing well. One of the most significant differences in stroke structures between Chinese characters and Tibetan characters is that the former ones have few arc strokes that occupy a huge proportion of all Tibetan character strokes. Therefore, to represent Tibetan characters as properly as possible, directional arc elements are taken into account besides line elements. Given an input character image, the process of feature formulation includes the following steps in turn.

Feature Extraction

At first, $[Q(i,j)]_{M \times N}$, the contour of the normalized character $[G(i,j)]_{M \times N}$, is extracted by analysing its 8-neighbour connectivity. Four kinds of line elements (vertical line, horizontal line, line slanted at 45 degrees and line slanted at 135 degrees, Figure 4.13(a)–(d)) and eight kinds of arc elements (Figure 4.13(e)–(l)) are assigned to each black pixel in $[Q(i,j)]_{M \times N}$ by mask matching to get 12-directional feature planes $[P(i,j)]_{M \times N}$

$$[P^{(k)}(i,j)]_{M \times N} = \begin{bmatrix} P^{(k)}(0,0), & P^{(k)}(0,1), & \cdots, & P^{(k)}(0,N-1) \\ P^{(k)}(1,0), & P^{(k)}(1,1), & \cdots, & P^{(k)}(1,N-1) \\ \vdots & \vdots & \cdots & \vdots \\ P^{(k)}(M-1,0), & P^{(k)}(M-1,1), & \cdots, & P^{(k)}(M-1,N-1) \end{bmatrix},$$

$$k = 1,2,\ldots,12 \tag{4.3}$$

where

$$P^{(k)}(i,j) = \begin{cases} 1, & \rho^{(k)}(i,j) \geq 3 \\ 0, & \rho^{(k)}(i,j) < 3 \end{cases}, \tag{4.4}$$

$$\rho^{(k)}(i,j) = [R^{(k)}]_{3 \times 3} \otimes [Q'(i,j)]_{M \times N} = \sum_{m=0}^{m=2} \sum_{n=0}^{n=2} R^{(k)}(m,n)Q'(i+m-1,j+n-1),$$
$$\tag{4.5}$$

$$Q'(i,j) = \begin{cases} Q(i,j), & 0 \leq i < M, 0 \leq j < N \\ 0, & \text{otherwise} \end{cases}. \tag{4.6}$$

Next, each feature plane is divided equally into $M' \times N'$ sub-areas of $u_0 \times v_0$ pixels. Each sub-area overlaps u_1 pixels vertically and v_1 pixels horizontally to neighbouring sub-areas, respectively. Thus,

$\begin{smallmatrix}0&0&0\\1&1&1\\0&0&0\end{smallmatrix}$	$\begin{smallmatrix}0&1&0\\0&1&0\\0&1&0\end{smallmatrix}$	$\begin{smallmatrix}0&0&1\\0&1&0\\1&0&0\end{smallmatrix}$	$\begin{smallmatrix}1&0&0\\0&1&0\\0&0&1\end{smallmatrix}$	$\begin{smallmatrix}0&0&1\\1&1&0\\0&0&0\end{smallmatrix}$	$\begin{smallmatrix}0&0&0\\1&1&0\\0&0&1\end{smallmatrix}$
$[R^{(1)}(i,j)]_{3\times3}$	$[R^{(2)}(i,j)]_{3\times3}$	$[R^{(3)}(i,j)]_{3\times3}$	$[R^{(4)}(i,j)]_{3\times3}$	$[R^{(5)}(i,j)]_{3\times3}$	$[R^{(6)}(i,j)]_{3\times3}$
(a)	(b)	(c)	(d)	(e)	(f)
$\begin{smallmatrix}1&0&0\\0&1&1\\0&0&0\end{smallmatrix}$	$\begin{smallmatrix}0&0&0\\0&1&1\\1&0&0\end{smallmatrix}$	$\begin{smallmatrix}0&1&0\\0&1&0\\1&0&0\end{smallmatrix}$	$\begin{smallmatrix}0&1&0\\0&1&0\\0&0&1\end{smallmatrix}$	$\begin{smallmatrix}1&0&0\\0&1&0\\0&1&0\end{smallmatrix}$	$\begin{smallmatrix}0&0&1\\0&1&0\\0&1&0\end{smallmatrix}$
$[R^{(7)}(i,j)]_{3\times3}$	$[R^{(8)}(i,j)]_{3\times3}$	$[R^{(9)}(i,j)]_{3\times3}$	$[R^{(10)}(i,j)]_{3\times3}$	$[R^{(11)}(i,j)]_{3\times3}$	$[R^{(12)}(i,j)]_{3\times3}$
(g)	(h)	(i)	(j)	(k)	(l)

Fig. 4.13. Element masks of directional features.

$$M' = \left(\frac{M - u_0}{u_0 - u_1} + 1\right), \quad N' = \left(\frac{N - v_0}{v_0 - v_1} + 1\right). \tag{4.7}$$

Compressed feature planes $[E^{(k)}(i,j)]_{M' \times N'}$, $k = 1, 2, \ldots, 12$ are obtained by mapping each sub-area to a point

$$E^{(k)}(i,j) = \sum_{m=0}^{u_0-1} \sum_{n=0}^{v_0-1} W^{(k)}(m,n) P^{(k)}((u_0 - u_1)i + m, (v_0 - v_1)j + n),$$

$$i = 0, 1, \ldots, M' - 1, j = 0, 1, \ldots, N' - 1, \tag{4.8}$$

where $[W^{(k)}(m,n)]_{u_0 \times v_0}$ is a weight matrix:

$$W^{(k)}(m,n) = \frac{\exp\left(-\frac{(m-u_0/2)^2}{2\sigma_1{}^2} - \frac{(n-v_0/2)^2}{2\sigma_2{}^2}\right)}{2\pi\sigma_1\sigma_2}, \sigma_1 = \frac{\sqrt{2}}{\pi}u_1,$$

$$\sigma_2 = \frac{\sqrt{2}}{\pi}v_1,$$

$$m = 0, 1, \ldots, u_0 - 1, \quad n = 0, 1, \ldots, v_0 - 1. \tag{4.9}$$

Then, a $d = 12 \times M' \times N'$ dimensional directional feature vector $X = [x_1, x_2, \ldots, x_d]^T$ is obtained by arranging all elements of $[E^{(k)}(i,j)]_{M' \times N'}$, $k = 1, 2, \ldots, 12$, in a certain order.

Feature Vector Compressing

The feature dimension of original feature vectors is too high for practical classifiers compared with the number of collected training sample sizes. The original feature vectors also contain redundancy. To lighten negative effects on classifier parameter estimation caused by high feature dimension and limited sample size, these vectors are compressed before classification. Assuming identical Gaussian feature distribution, linear discriminant analysis (LDA) [4] can be proved by applying optimal linear mapping to the fixed feature detection outputs that maximizes $I(F, W)$ [2]. The r-dimensional output feature space is obtained by applying an $r \times d$ linear transform Φ d-dimensional input feature space ($r \leq d$):

$$Y = \Phi^T X, \tag{4.10}$$

where Φ is the LDA transform matrix with dimensions $r \times d$ and Y is the compact feature vector of X.

4.3.3 Classifier Design

Classifier Description

Since the number of Tibetan character categories is far larger than that of numerals or alphabets, a two-stage classification strategy (Figure 4.14) is designed to lower computation costs.

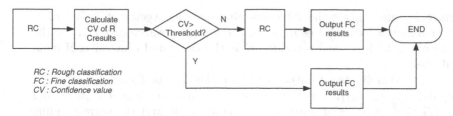

RC : Rough classification
FC : Fine classification
CV : Confidence value

Fig. 4.14. Classification flowchart.

The task of the rough classifier is to select a few candidates from the large number of categories as quickly as possible [9]. Besides speed, a high accumulated accuracy of selected candidates is expected to reduce the eventual recognition error. To meet those requirements, a new discriminant function, Euclidean distance with deviation (EDD), is designed:

$$d_{\mathrm{EDD}}(\boldsymbol{Y}, \boldsymbol{M}_i) = \sum_{k=1}^{d} [t(y_k, m_{ik})]^2, \tag{4.11}$$

where

$$t(y_k, m_{ik}) = \begin{cases} 0, & |y_k - m_{ik}| < \theta_i \cdot \sigma_{ik} \\ \gamma_i \cdot \sigma_{ik} + C, & |y_k - m_{ik}| > \gamma_i \cdot \sigma_{ik} \\ |y_k - m_{ik}|, & else \end{cases} \tag{4.12}$$

$\boldsymbol{Y} = (y_1, y_2, \ldots, y_r)^T$, $\boldsymbol{M}_i = (m_{i1}, m_{i2}, \ldots, m_{ir})^T$ are r-dimensional input vector and the standard vector of category i ($i = 1, 2, \ldots, 584$), respectively. σ_{ik} is the feature standard deviation of kth element of category i. θ_i and γ_i ($\theta_i, \gamma_i > 0$, $\theta_i < \gamma_i$) are parameters related to the category i, which will be obtained during training process. C is a positive constant to measure the distance offset.

The most significant property of EDD is that character feature variations are taken into account in the traditional Euclidean distance measure. As a result, it can provide description of some ability of the pattern distribution in the feature space.

Generally speaking, the quadratic discriminant function (QDF) is optimal in the Bayesian sense for classification. But QDF suffers severely from the performance degradation for estimation errors of the covariance matrix. So, MQDF [11] is applied instead. It employs pseudo-Bayesian in place of commonly used maximum likelihood estimator of the covariance matrix in QDF design, and prevents the performance degradation due to estimation errors in small sample size situations. The discriminant distance of MQDF can be calculated by:

$$g_i(\boldsymbol{Y}, \boldsymbol{M}_i) = \frac{1}{h^2} \left\{ \sum_{j=1}^{r} (y_j - m_{ij})^2 - \sum_{j=1}^{K} \left(1 - \frac{h^2}{\lambda_{ij}}\right) [(\boldsymbol{Y} - \boldsymbol{M}_i)^T \phi_{ij}]^2 \right\}$$

$$+ \ln \left(h^{2(r-K)} \prod_{j=1}^{K} \lambda_{ij} \right), \tag{4.13}$$

where λ_{ij} and ϕ_{ij} are the jth eigenvalue and eigenvector of Σ_i, which is the maximum likelihood estimate of the feature covariance matrix of the category i. h^2 is a small constant. K is the truncated dimension of main sub-space.

Let the candidate set output by rough classifier be $CanSet = \{(c_1, d_1), (c_2, d_2), \ldots, (c_n, d_n)\}$, n is the number of candidates in $CanSet$. c_k and d_k ($d_1 \leq d_2 \leq \cdots \leq d_n$) are kth candidate code and the corresponding classification distance, respectively. The function of fine classifier is to re-sort candidates in $CanSet$ according to their re-calculated discriminant distances. If the first candidate in $CanSet$, say (c_1, d_1), is the correct classification result of the input pattern, it is reasonable to output $CanSet$ directly rather than call fine classification process to save computation costs. Confidence value (CV) of (c_1, d_1), which is calculated by (4.14), is regarded as a measure [14] to decide whether the fine classification is necessary or not

$$f_{cv}(c_1) = \frac{d_2 - d_1}{d_1}. \tag{4.14}$$

If $f_{cv}(c_1)$ is smaller than a threshold that is set beforehand, continue the fine classification. Otherwise, accept $CanSet$ as the eventual recognition results directly.

Classifier Parameters Selecting

So far 1200 sample sets have been collected from the predominant Tibetan publishing system (Founder system, Huaguang system, etc.) in China. Each set contains 584 Tibetan characters. Sample sets cover six widely used Tibetan fonts: white font, black font, long font, round font, bamboo font and general font. Characters are of various qualities. The ratio of normal character number to other character (noisy, blurred or broken) number is about 1:1. The training set is formed by randomly extracting 900 sets from all sample sets and the test set is made up of the rest 300 sets.

The classification dictionary contains 584 character templates so that each character holds only one template. Characters in the training set are picked out to train isolated character classifier.

Experiment 1: LDA compressed dimension (CD) selection

Original 384-dimensional feature vectors are sent to EDD classifier to observe first candidate recognition accuracy (1-ACC) on the test set when CD changes from 8 to 380 (Figure 4.15). CD=176 is selected as the object feature dimension.

Experiment 2: EDD performance

This experiment is carried out to examine the ability of EDD. Two other well-known rough classifiers, say Euclidean distance (ED) classifier and city block distance (CBD) classifier, are also tested. 176-Dimensional

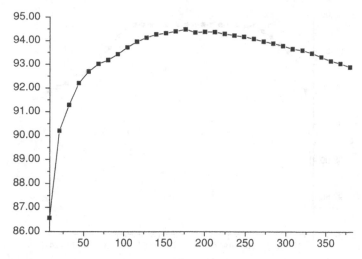

Fig. 4.15. Relationship between 1-ACC and compressed dimension of feature vectors.

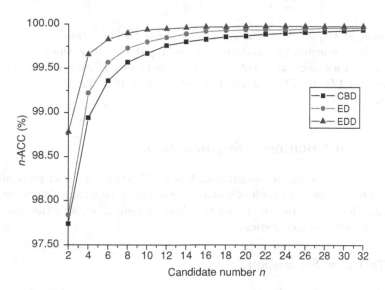

Fig. 4.16. Relationship between n-ACC of rough classifiers and candidate number n.

compressed feature vectors are input to the 3 classifiers, respectively. Top n candidates accuracy (n-ACC) on the test set is taken as evaluation criterion (Figure 4.16). We can see that EDD exceeds ED and CBD at performance. Accordingly, EDD rough classifier is employed to select 14 candidates for an unknown pattern from the total of 584 categories.

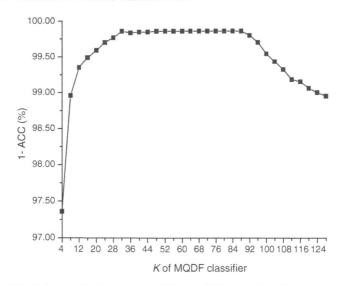

Fig. 4.17. Relationship between 1-ACC and MQDF classifier parameter K.

Experiment 3: MQDF main sub-space dimension (K) selection

Candidates selected by EDD are sent to MQDF classifier, the first candidate recognition accuracy (1-ACC) is recorded when K ranges from 4 to 128 (Figure 4.17). 1-ACC reaches its peak value at $K = 32$, so $K = 32$ is selected.

4.4 Tibetan Document Segmentation

For real Tibetan document recognition, besides Tibetan character recognition the other important problem is character segmentation from document, which includes two steps, one being text line segmentation, and the other Tibetan character segmentation.

4.4.1 Text Line Separation

The skew document image will cause serious problem in character segmentation stage. In Tibetan documents, the slope of baselines can represent the image skew completely. Two efficient skew detection algorithms are presented.

Algorithm 1: Inter-syllabic tshegs-based skew detection (Figure 4.18)
Step 1: Extract inter-syllabic tshegs from selected text image region using connectivity analysis.
Step 2: Fit lines through tops of extracted inter-syllabic tshegs (fitted lines are regarded as baselines of selected text image region).

པོས་གོང་གསལ་མཆིམས་ཀྱི་བསྐུན་རིམ་ཀྱི་ལུགས་ནི་དོར་ནས་
'ཚོས་རྗེའི་' བསྐུན་རིམ་ཀྱི་ལུགས་ཏོ་སྤྲོད་བྱས་ཡོད། དེ་རྗེས་
ཚོམ་པ་པོ་ནེས་ 'ཚོས་རྗེས་' མེ་ཡོས་མོར་(1207)ཧང་ཆེན་དུ་
བསྐུན་ཙོས་གཉིག་བཟོས་གཏང་བ་དང་། ཚོམ་པ་པོ་རང་
ཉིད་ཀྱིས་སྤྱགས་བུ་མོར་(1261)བསྐུན་ཙོས་གཉིག་བཙམས་
པའི་སྐོར་བརྗོད་ཡོད། དེང་སྐབས་དེར་འཁོར་པའི་'ཚོས་
རྗེ'' ནི་ཀ་ནི་རྒྱ་རིའི་ཡུལ་ནས་བྱོན་པའི་མཁས་པ་
Sakyasribhadra ལ་གོ་དགོས་ཤིང་། ཧང་ཆེན་ཞེས་པ་དེ་
ནི་'1017ཡོར་བཞིངས་པའི་འབྱོངས་རྒྱས་ཡུལ་ཀྱི་སོལ་ནག་
ཧང་པོ་ཆེ་དགོན་ཞེས་པ་དེ་ཡིན། བསྐུན་ཙོས་དེ་ཡང་ཀ་ནི་མེ་
རིའི་སྨུཁས་པ་ནེས་ཧང་པོ་ཆེ་དགོན་ན་བཙམས་པ་ཞིག་ཡིན་
པ་ལས། ཚག་མོ་རུ་བ་ཚོས་རྗེ་དཔལ་(1197—1264)ཕྱུ་བ་
དེས་བཙམས་པ་ཞིག་མ་ཡིན། ཁ་པོས་དེ་སྟོན་

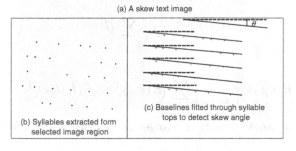

(a) A skew text image

(b) Syllables extracted form selected image region

(c) Baselines fitted through syllable tops to detect skew angle

Selected Image Region to perform skew detection

པོས་གོང་གསལ་མཆིམས་ཀྱི་བསྐུན་ཙོས་ཀྱི་ལུགས་ནི་དོར་ནས་
'ཚོས་རྗེའི་' བསྐུན་ཙོས་ཀྱི་ལུགས་ཏོ་སྤྲོད་བྱས་ཡོད། དེ་རྗེས་
ཚོམ་པ་པོ་ནེས་ 'ཚོས་རྗེས་' མེ་ཡོས་མོར་(1207)ཧང་ཆེན་དུ་
བསྐུན་ཙོས་གཉིག་བཟོས་གཏང་བ་དང་། ཚོམ་པ་པོ་རང་
ཉིད་ཀྱིས་སྤྱགས་བུ་མོར་(1261)བསྐུན་ཙོས་གཉིག་བཙམས་
པའི་སྐོར་བརྗོད་ཡོད། དེང་སྐབས་དེར་འཁོར་པའི་'ཚོས་
རྗེ'' ནི་ཀ་ནི་རྒྱ་རིའི་ཡུལ་ནས་བྱོན་པའི་མཁས་པ་
Sakyasribhadra ལ་གོ་དགོས་ཤིང་། ཧང་ཆེན་ཞེས་པ་དེ་
ནི་'1017ཡོར་བཞིངས་པའི་འབྱོངས་རྒྱས་ཡུལ་ཀྱི་སོལ་ནག་
ཧང་པོ་ཆེ་དགོན་ཞེས་པ་དེ་ཡིན། བསྐུན་ཙོས་དེ་ཡང་ཀ་ནི་མེ་
རིའི་སྨུཁས་པ་ནེས་ཧང་པོ་ཆེ་དགོན་ན་བཙམས་པ་ཞིག་ཡིན་
པ་ལས། ཚག་མོ་རུ་བ་ཚོས་རྗེ་དཔལ་(1197—1264)ཕྱུ་བ་
དེས་བཙམས་པ་ཞིག་མ་ཡིན། ཁ་པོས་དེ་སྟོན་

(d) Text image after skew correction

Fig. 4.18. A sample of skew detection and correction.

Step 3: Detect optimal slant angle of fitted lines by dynamic clustering or Hough transform (the detected angle is expected to be the very skew angle of the entire text image).

Algorithm 2: Discriminant function-based skew detection

It is observed that with the increase of $|\theta|$ (θ is the skew angle), the horizontal pixel projection $H(k|\theta)$ ($i_t \leq k \leq i_b$, i_t and i_b are vertical coordinate values of the top and bottom of the image, respectively) of text image is uniform. A discriminant function is then defined:

$$f(\theta) = \frac{\sqrt{D(H(k|\theta))}}{E(H(k|\theta))},\qquad(4.15)$$

where

$$E(H(k|\theta)) = \frac{1}{i_b - i_t} \sum_{k=i_t}^{i_b} H(k|\theta)\qquad(4.16)$$

and

$$D(H(k|\theta)) = \frac{1}{i_b - i_t} \sum_{k=i_t}^{i_b} [H(k|\theta)]^2 - [E(H(k|\theta))]^2.\qquad(4.17)$$

Thus the skew angle detection changes to an optimization process:

$$\theta_{opt} = \arg \max_{|\theta| \leq \theta_{TH}} f(\theta),\qquad(4.18)$$

where θ_{opt} is the exact skew angle of the text image and θ_{TH} is a constant set beforehand to limit the likely maximum skew angle. Practically, a series of discrete values are chosen to obtain an approximation of θ_{opt}.

Generally, algorithm 1 is fit for clean scripts where inter-syllabic tsheg extraction is available. When dealing with text images that are too severely blurred to extract inter-syllabic tshegs, algorithm 2 is more effective. In both algorithms, to save computation costs, sub-image, which should be guaranteed to cover at least one baseline area, is selected instead of the whole image.

After the skew angle θ is detected, Pixel (i, j) in the original image is mapped to (i', j') in the corrected image by:

$$\begin{bmatrix} i' \\ j' \end{bmatrix} = \begin{bmatrix} 1, & -\tan\theta \\ 0, & 1 \end{bmatrix} \begin{bmatrix} i \\ j \end{bmatrix} + \begin{bmatrix} 0, & \tan\theta \\ 0, & 0 \end{bmatrix} \begin{bmatrix} i_0 \\ j_0 \end{bmatrix},\qquad(4.19)$$

where (i_0, j_0) is the left-top pixel coordinates of the original image.

After skew correction, the histogram of the horizontal pixel projection is applied to separate text lines. Width of lines is analysed to determine whether lines are normal, touching or broken, by dynamic clustering. Consecutive narrow lines are merged to a regular line, while touching lines are further split.

4.4.2 Character Segmentation

Segmentation Process Description

Character segmentation is regarded as one of the decisions processed in an OCR system. It is inter-dependent with local decisions regarding shape similarity and contextual acceptability [6]. A reliability-based character segmentation model is proposed to take the place of commonly used rules- and thresholds-based model.

Given a text line image X, let $P = \{x_1, x_2, \ldots, x_n\}$ be a certain partition of X (n is the number of partitioned units), $R = \{c_1, c_2, \ldots, c_n\}$ be the recognition result of P, the purpose of character segmentation is to find the optimal P to maximize the confidence of R. On the other hand, information feedback from R may be greatly beneficial to obtain the optimal P. Thus the character segmentation is a dynamic process interactive with character classification process. To measure its performance, both the validity of P, $f_{Vad}(P)$ and the recognition confidence value of R, $f_{Cof}(R)$ are taken into account. In this chapter, the evaluation function of segmentation, S, can be described as:

$$S(P, R) = \alpha f_{Vad}(P) + (1 - \alpha)f_{Cof}(R), \qquad (4.20)$$

where $a(0 < a < 1)$ is a constant, and

$$f_{Vad}(P) = \sum_{k=1}^{n} f_{Vad}(x_k), \qquad (4.21)$$

$$f_{Cof}(R) = \sum_{k=1}^{n} f_{Cof}(c_k). \qquad (4.22)$$

Usually, c_k is a candidate set containing several candidates with corresponding classification distances. Let d_{k1} and d_{k2} denote classification distances of the 1st and the 2nd candidates in c_k; $f_{Cof}(c_k)$ can be calculated with reference to (4.14).

However, it is difficult to express $f_{Vad}(x_k)$ by a uniform equation. Its appropriate form should be taken with reference to actual situations.

Thus, the whole segmentation process can be described as an optimization process

$$(P_{opt}, R_{opt}) = \arg \max_{P \in \Psi(X)} [S(P, R)], \qquad (4.23)$$

where (P_{opt}, R_{opt}) is the optimal combination of P and R, $\Psi(X)$ represents the set in terms of possible partitions of X.

Based on the above character segmentation model, multi-level information is arranged hierarchically:

Level 1: Edge spot information in image pixels (projection valley, bounding box of connected components, etc.)

Level 2: Character shape information (average character size, blank size, baseline information, etc.)
Level 3: Validity feedback from recognition kernel
Level 4: Priori knowledge (Size continuity for nearby characters, spelling regulations, etc.)

Coarse Segmentation

The flowchart of coarse segmentation is demonstrated in Figure 4.19. Firstly, the input text line is cut into a sequence of coarse blocks (CB) by a histogram of vertical pixel projection. Each CB may be a normal isolated character, a part of a broken character or touching characters. Recognition module is called to determine whether the current text line is Tibetan-dominant by analysing recognition results. For a Tibetan-dominant text line, the baseline location L_B is detected by

$$L_B = \arg \max_{i_t < k \leq i_b} [H(k) - H(k-1)], \qquad (4.24)$$

where $H(k)$ is the horizontal pixel projection of the text line, and i_t, i_b are vertical coordinates of the text line top and bottom, respectively. Moreover, character parameters (Tibetan character width, inter-syllabic tshegs width and height, pixel mask of inter-syllabic tshegs) are analysed from recognition results of CBs. All parameters, as well as recognition results of CBs, derived from coarse segmentation are saved in a global dynamic parameter library (GDPL), which is preserved during the whole segmentation process.

Fine Segmentation

The input of the fine segmentation (Figure 4.20) is the CB sequence produced by the coarse segmentation. While cutting touching characters, a

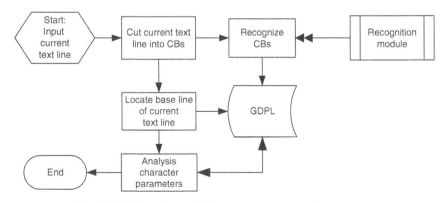

Fig. 4.19. Flowchart of the coarse segmentation process.

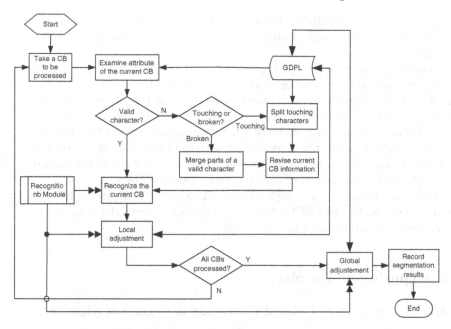

Fig. 4.20. Flowchart of the fine segmentation process.

modified discrimination function $g(m)$ is employed to determine the optimal cut position [13]

$$g(m) = \left[\max\left(\frac{|V(m-1) + V(m+1) - 2V(m)|}{V(m) + 1}, \frac{|P(m-1) + P(m+1) - 2P(m)|}{P(m) + 1} \right) \right]^{\beta},$$

(4.25)

where $V(m)$ and $P(m)$ denote the vertical pixel projection and the vertical profile projection in terms of the variable m in the horizontal direction, respectively. Parameter β brings the 2nd-order non-linearity into $g(m)$ to make it more distinguishable.

The local adjustment step performs local check on the segmentation result (within the range of one CB). Different segmentation attempts will be tried to test whether there are characters that are erroneously split or merged.

The segmentation results for the whole line go through the global adjustment step (in the range of the whole text line), where an advanced checking algorithm based on high-level information and rules is performed to correct errors that are missed by the former steps. Here an important operation, say spell check, is designed to provide recognition module with context information and a priori knowledge.

We focus on spell check for Tibetan syllables to verify the segmentation and the recognition results in terms of syllable constitution rules introduced in Section 4.4.2. Basically, it includes three inter-dependent operations.

Extracting object syllable: Characters between an inter-syllabic tsheg and its very adjacent inter-syllabic tsheg are included to compose an object syllable.

Searching missed inter-syllabic tsheg(s): An inter-syllabic tsheg goes connected with its previous or next characters at the baseline area frequently. So the object syllable possibly contains more than four characters, or more than one valid centre character, which are not allowed by spelling rules. There must be some inter-syllabic tshegs missed within the range of the object syllables selected. That is, the current object syllable consists of at least two syllables. Hence, it is necessary to examine and find the missed inter-syllable tshegs to further divide it into single syllables.

Verifying characters in a single syllable: The centre character is located firstly, then validity of CbCC, 1-CaCC, 2-CaCC is verified by matching them with characters listed in Figure 4.5.

4.5 Experiment Results

4.5.1 Performance of Isolated Character Recognition Algorithm

The first candidate recognition accuracies of different fonts on the isolated character test set described in "Classifier Parameters Selecting" under Section 4.3.3 are listed in Table 4.1.

The average accuracy reaches 99.79% and the highest error rate is lower than 0.5%, which shows the validity of our algorithm in recognizing characters from Tibetan character set with a very large category number. Though characters of different fonts vary considerably, the recognition results by our method differ minutely. This indicates that our method can tolerate character variations caused by font effectively. In Tibetan character set, about 100 pairs of categories are very similar out of the total 584 categories, and discriminating them from each other is very difficult. Let us take long font characters as an example. There about 3000 pairs of characters that are pretty similar out of 17,520 characters. Recognition error rate is 0.42%, i.e. 73 characters are incorrectly recognized. That means our method fails to distinguish not more than 37 pairs of similar characters, that is, more than 98.7% of similar character pairs is discriminated from each other successfully. Hence, it can be concluded that our method behaves satisfactorily while coping with similar characters.

Table 4.1. Recognition accuracy on the test set

Font	White	Black	General	Round	Long	Bamboo	Aver. ACC (%)
Char Num	46,720	29,200	35,040	29,200	17,520	17,520	
Recog Acc (%)	99.87	99.76	99.82	99.85	99.58	99.70	99.79

4.5.2 Performance of Segmentation Algorithm

Experiments were carried out on the test set comprising actual documents from Tibetan magazines. All documents were scanned at a resolution of 150–300 dpi. The test set contained about 520,000 characters of six different fonts (white, black, long, round, bamboo and general).

Documents in the test set can be manually divided into 14,365 text lines, 14,278 of which are obtained by the proposed line separation algorithm. The separation accuracy achieves 99.39%. The failure to separate the remaining 87 lines is mainly caused by extreme noises and blur.

Incorporating the isolated character recognition engine discussed in Section 4.4.3, the recognition accuracy on the test set is 95.06%. According to the recognition error analysis by applying Fang's automatic OCR performance evaluation system [3], assured segmentation error (ASE), assured classification error (ACE) and unsure type's error (UTE) are 1.92%, 2.06% and 0.96%, respectively. Figure 4.21 shows the character segmentation process of an actual text line.

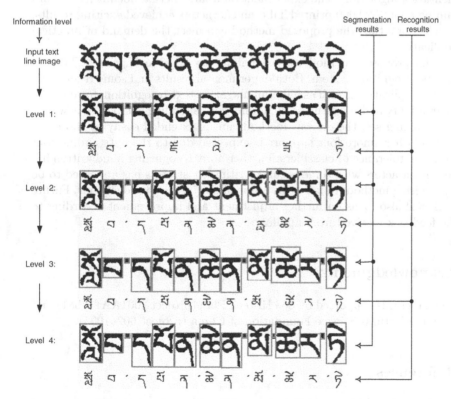

Fig. 4.21. A sample of character segmentation.

4.6 Summary

After a brief introduction of the characteristics of Tibetan characters and scripts, a comprehensive printed Tibetan OCR approach based on statistical pattern recognition was presented. Our emphases focused on two aspects: isolated Tibetan character recognition algorithm and Tibetan text segmentation method.

To recognize isolated characters, the input image was firstly normalized in a special way. Then directional line and arc element features were extracted from its contour. After feature dimension reduction by LDA, a two-stage classification strategy was applied. A new discriminant function, EDD, was designed to produce coarse classification results, while MQDF was introduced to perform fine classification. By selecting appropriate classifier parameters by experiments, 99.79% encouraging recognition results on the test set had been achieved.

While dealing with the text segmentation task, the process included skew detection and correction, text line separation, dynamic recursive segmentation algorithm. The experiment on a large actual document set containing about 520,000 printed Tibetan characters achieved exciting results, which shows that the proposed method can meet the demand of practical applications.

The proposed method can contribute to multi-font printed Tibetan scripts recognition system. Both experimental results and some recent successful applications, such as Tibetan magazine text recognition, have shown their validity and robustness. By adding corresponding samples of new font to a training set, the current method can be extended easily to those situations where more font support is expected due to the outstanding font variation tolerance of classifiers. Furthermore, recognizing handwritten Tibetan characters with some regular writing constraints has appeared to be a promising method. In fact, this is one of our future considerations. Future work will also focus on further adjustment and improvement according to the feedback received from applications.

Acknowledgments

The paper was supported by 863 Hi-tech Plan (project 2001AA114081) and National Natural Science Foundation of China (project 60241005).

References

1. Fang, C. and Liu, C. (2002). Automatic performance evaluation of printed Chinese character recognition systems. *IJDAR, 4(3)*, pp. 177–182.

2. Ding, X.Q. (2002). Information entropy theory in pattern recognition. *Acta Electronica Sinica, 21(8)*, pp. 2–8.
3. Liang, S., Ahmadi, M., and Shridhar, M. (1993). Segmentation of touching characters in printed document recognition. *Proceedings of 2nd ICDAR, IEEE, Tsukuba, Japan*, pp. 569–572.
4. Wang, H., Zhao, N., and Deng, G. (2001) A stroke segmentation extraction algorithm for Tibetan character recognition (in Chinese). *Journal of Chinese Information Processing, 15(4)*, pp. 41–46.
5. Kato, N., Suzuki, M., Omachi, S., et al. (1999). A handwritten character recognition system using directional element feature and asymmetric Mahalanobis distance. *IEEE Transactions on PAMI, 21(3)*, pp. 258–262.
6. Lin, X., Ding, X., Chen, M., et al. (1998). Adaptive confidence transform based classifier combination for Chinese character recognition. *Pattern Recognition Letters, 19(10)*, pp. 975–988.
7. Wu, Z. and Ding, X. (2001). Implement of robust multi-font printed English character recognition system (in Chinese). *Journal of Computer Engineering and Application, 20*, pp. 120–122.
8. Lu, Y. (1995). Machine printed character segmentation – an overview. *Pattern Recognition, 28(1)*, pp. 67–80.
9. Kahan, S., Pavlidis, T., and Baird, H.S. (1987). On the recognition of printed characters of any font and any size. *PAMI, 9(2)*, pp. 274–287.
10. Le, D.S., Thoma, D.R., and Wechsler, H. (1994). Automated page orientation and skew angle detection for binary document image. *Pattern Recognition, 27(10)*, pp. 1325–1344.
11. Masami, K., Chikako, N., Takanobu, K., Yoko, A., and Yoshiyuki, K. (1995). Recognition of similar characters by using object oriented design printed Tibetan dictionary. *Transactions of IPSJ, 36(11)*, pp. 2611–2621.
12. Casey, R.G. and Lecolinet, E. (1996). A survey of methods and strategies in character segmentation. *PAMI, 18(7)*, pp. 690–706.
13. Hou, H. and Andrews, H. (1978). Cubic splines for image interpolation and digital filtering. *IEEE Transactions on Acoustics, Speech, and Signal Processing, 26(6)*, 508–517.
14. Fukunaga, K. (1990). *Introduction to Statistical Pattern Recognition*, 2nd ed. New York: Academic Press, pp. 460–465.
15. Kuo, H.H. and Wang, J.F. (1999). A new method for the segmentation of mixed handprinted Chinese/English characters. *Proc. of 5th ICDAR, Bangalore, India*, pp. 810–813.
16. Ma, S., Jin, Y., Jiang, Z., et al. (2002). A method of printing Tibetan character recognition. *Proceedings of 4th World Congress on Intelligent Control and Automation, IEEE, Shanghai, China, 3*, pp. 2304–2307.
17. Masami, K., Yoshiyuki, K., and Masayuki, K. (1996). Character recognition of wooden blocked Tibetan similar manuscripts by using Euclidean distance with deferential weight. *IPSJ SIGNotes Computer and Humanities, 30*, pp. 13–18.
18. Kimura, F., Takashina, K., and Tsuruoka, S. (1987). Modified quadratic discriminant functions and the application to Chinese character recognition. *IEEE Transactions on PAMI, 9(1)*, pp. 149–153.

19. Kang, C., Jiang, D., and Dai, Y. (2004). A recognition algorithm of Tibetan based on components (in Chinese). *Proceedings of Symposium on Chinese Minority Language Information Processing and Language Resource Construction*, pp. 290–295.

5

On OCR of a Printed Indian Script

Bidyut B. Chaudhuri

5.1 Introduction

One of the earliest practical problems solved successfully by the pattern recognition community is the optical character recognition (OCR) whereby text in a document is automatically converted into electronic format [16]. The application potentials of OCR have been soundly established over the past thirty years and many commercial products are available in the market for business letter reading, table form processing, postal address reading, signature verification and reading aid for the blind. Excellent surveys on the OCR research are available in [12–14, 21].

For recognition tasks, we can distinguish between machine-printed and handwritten texts. The latter can be further subdivided into on-line or off-line handwritten text recognition. We are concerned here on the OCR of machine-printed Indian text only. The problem is very important since it is largely unsolved, although Indian languages have a following of more than one billion people and there are more than a dozen of major Indian scripts used in this country. Here the problem is challenging because Indian scripts consist of large collection of compound characters, and as described in section 5.2 next section, there may be more than one thousand different shapes to be recognized by the OCR system.

Till 1990, recognition studies on Indian scripts were concentrated on a small subset of manually segmented basic characters only [24–26]. The development of a complete OCR system from real documents with good accuracy was first reported for single font printed Bangla and Devanagari text in the middle of 1990s [5, 17–19]. The work has since been extended to other major Indian scripts like Oriya, Punjabi, Telugu and Tamil [1, 6–8, 11, 15, 17, 18, 22] with various degrees of success. Work on handwritten character recognition was also attempted [2, 3, 20].

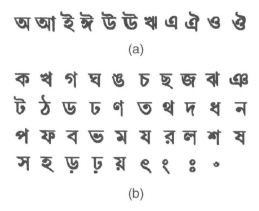

Fig. 5.1. Basic Bangla characters: (a) vowel, (b) consonant and (c) vowel allograph.

This chapter will describe briefly the problem of printed Indian script OCR and concentrate on the Bangla Script. The basic alphabet of Bangla script is shown in Figure 5.1. Bangla and Devanagari are the most popular scripts used for writing the languages of more than half of Indian sub-continent. The choice of Bangla is made by the fact that it is one of the most difficult Indian scripts from OCR point of view and it will shed light on different problems that may be encountered in Indian script OCR effort. Moreover, Devanagari script is quite similar, but somewhat simpler than Bangla. So, techniques of Bangla OCR could be used for Devanagari with little modification.

The rest of this chapter is organized as follow. The origin and properties of Indian Scripts are described in Section 5.2. Section 5.3 deals with document pre-processing approaches. Feature extraction and recognition of characters are described in Section 5.4. Section 5.5 treats the performance analysis of such an OCR system. Concluding remarks are given in Section 5.6.

5.2 Origin and Properties of Indian Scripts

Scholars agree that most alphabetic scripts are derived from the ancient Semitic alphabet that originated in the second millennium BC in and around Palestine and Syria. The root of most modern Indian scripts is Brahmi. It is likely that the ancient Aramic script alphabet brought to India by Semitic merchants was the prototype for Brahmi script. However, it was only the idea of alphabetic writing that was transmitted through Aramic and the fully developed Brahmi writing system was the outcome of brilliant philological and phonological research of Indian scholars. Over the next three millennia, Brahmi has slowly transformed into popular modern scripts namely Bangla, Devanagari, Gujarati, Oriya, Kannada, Malayalam, Punjabi and Telugu. Another script, named Tamil has somewhat independent origin while Kashmiri and Urdu have descended from Arabic script.

Most Indian languages also descended from ancient Sanskrit language. Because of single origin, the character names in many scripts remained almost the same and the shapes of characters have visible similarities. For example, ka is the name of the first consonant in most Indian scripts and it looks quite similar in Bangla and Devanagari. In fact, Bangla, Devanagari, Gujarati and Punjabi scripts have some shape similarity. Among the south Indian scripts, Kannada has some similarity with Telugu and Malayalam has similarity with Tamil, respectively. There is no upper/lower case distinction in Indian scripts. But there are many shapes other than the basic alphabets like allographs and compound characters describe below.

These similarities may be helpful in developing a general OCR engine encompassing all scripts. On the other hand, the similarities create more difficulty in script identification tasks. If a single document contains mixture of Bangla and Devanagari, script identification may need analysis at the level as low as characters. Tamil and Gurmukhi scripts have no compound characters, hence higher recognition rate are achievable for these scripts.

Although Indian writing is alphabet based, it is not as alphabetic as the Roman system. It should be mentioned that within a word, the vowels in Indian scripts become simplified allographs to be combined with consonants (see Figure 5.1(c)). These allographs can sit to the left, right, partly right and partly left (with the consonant in between) as well as touching below the basic consonant to generate a different shape. Combination of consonant and vowel represents something like a syllable. For example, in the word of Figure 5.2, character 1 is a vowel, 2 is a consonant, 3 is a vowel modifier, 4 is a consonant, 5 is a vowel modifier, 6 is a consonant marker, 7 is a consonant, 8 is a vowel modifier and 9 is a compound character, described below. Clearly, the left–right sequence is not maintained at the character level. If the consonant–vowel combination is considered as a syllable then the left-to-right sequence of the syllables is more or less maintained. In a few cases, the vowels may cling to the consonant at positions other than those shown in Figures 5.1 and 5.2. Moreover, two, three and even four consonants can make a combined shape, which we call here as *compound character*. In Figure 5.2 the character 9 is a compound of two

Fig. 5.2. Irregular positioning of characters and allographs in a Bangla word.

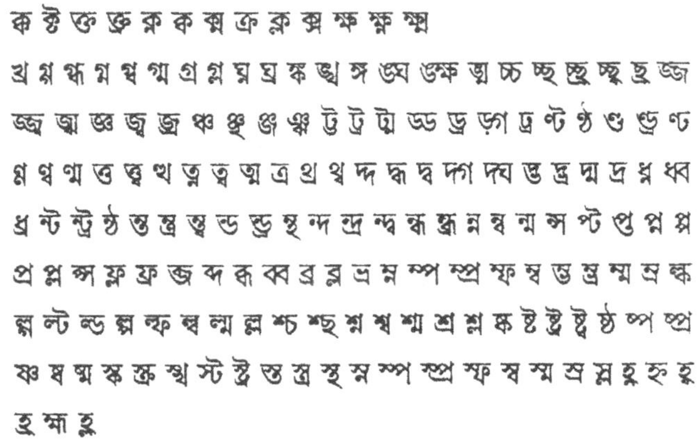

ক ঈ ঊ ঊ ক্র ক্র ক ক্ষ ক্র ক্র ক্ম ক্ষ ক্ষু ক্ষ্ম

থ য ধ্ব গ্ম ঘ য গ্ল গ্ল ঘ ঘ্ন ক ঝ্ম স জ্ঞ ঞ্ক ভ্য চ ছ ছ্ৰ ছ্ব ছ্ন ছ জ্ঞ

জ্ব জ্ঞ জ্ব জ্ঞ জ্ঞ ঞ্চ ঞ্ছ ঞ্জ ঞ্ঝ ট্ট ট্ব ট্ম ড্ড ড্ৰ ড্ৰ গ্ৰ ত্ৰ ণ্ট ণ্ঠ ণ্ড ণ্ড ণ্ট

ণ্ব থ্ম ত ত্ব থ ত্র ত্র ত্ম ত্র থ থ দ্দ দ্ৰ দ্ব দ্গ দ্ঘ ভ ত্ৰ দ্ম দ্র ধ ধ্ব

ধ ন্ট ন্ট ঠ ন্ত ন্ত্র ন্থ ড ন্ডু হ ন্দ ন্দ্র ন্ধ ন্ধ্র ন্ন ন্স ন্ম ন্স প্ট প্ত প্ল প্ল

প্র প্ল শ্ম ফ্র ফ্ল জ্ব ব্দ ব্ক ব্ব র্ব র্ল ভ ম্প ম্প প্র ফ্য ব্র ভ্র ভ্র ম্ম ম্ব ক্ক

ল্ল ল্ট ল্ড ল্ল ল্ফ ল্ব ল্ম ল্ল শ্চ শ্ছ ষ্ব ষ শ্য শ্র শ্ল ষ্ক ষ্ট ষ্ট ষ্ট ঠ শ্প প্র

ষ্ণ ষ্ব ষ্ম ষ্ক ষ্ক ষ্ম স্ট স্ট স্ত স্ত্র স্থ স্ম স্প স্প্র স্ফ স্ব স্ম স্ম স্ম হ্ন হ্ন

হ্ম হ্ম হ্ম

Fig. 5.3. A subset of Bangla consonant cluster shapes.

consonants. In some compound consonants, partial shape of individual consonants can be visualized, but they cannot be easily segmented for the benefit of OCR work. A subset of compound consonants is shown in Figure 5.3. These facts indicate that the Indian scripts are hybrid alphabetic–syllabic scripts.

Because of a large character set, as well as the alphabetic–syllabic nature and 2D irregular positioning of characters in a running text, OCR system development and error analysis in Indian script is a challenging problem. Also, more care is needed for ground-truth generation for testing the software under development. These problems are addressed in Section 5.5.

For some Indian scripts (like Devanagari, Bangla, Punjabi, etc.) many characters have a horizontal line at the upper part. In this paper, we call this line as *head-line*. When two or more characters form a word, the head-line portions touch one another and generate a longer head-line (see Figures 5.2

and 5.4) making the characters topologically connected. So, character segmentation is necessary in non-holistic OCR models. An advantage of having head-line is that it can also be used as a shape feature at the recognition stage. In some scripts (like Gujarati, Oriya, etc.), however, the head-line is absent, and the characters are already isolated in running text.

In Bangla and Devanagari script, a text-line may be partitioned into three zones. The upper-zone denotes the portion above the head-line, the middle zone covers the portion of basic (and compound) characters below head-line and the lower-zone is the portion below the lowermost point of basic characters in a word, where some vowel allograph like 5 in Figure 5.2 can reside. Examples of zoning are shown in Figure 5.4. Automatic zone division is also helpful in the OCR problem of Bangla and Devanagari.

Many Bangla and Devanagari characters have a vertical line stroke, which is also a useful shape feature. For characters having no vertical line stroke, a structure having convexity from below is observed (e.g. fifth and sixth character in first row of Figure 5.1(a)). Also, the strokes of many characters begin or end with a circular dot-like shape (e.g. first four characters of first row of Figure 5.1(a)). Moreover, four Bangla characters have distinct dots at the lower region (three characters of last row in Figure 5.1(b) are distinguished by this dot only). The last character of Figure 5.1(b) is a nasalisation sign for vowel that may appear only with other consonant characters at the upper zone. See component numbered 7 and 8 in Figure 5.4(b), for example.

Fig. 5.4. (a) Original image and (b) the components after headline deletion.

5.3 Document Pre-Processing

Traditionally, the document pre-processing steps involve skew detection/ correction, noise cleaning and binarization, text region identification, text line, word and character segmentation, etc. Of them, steps like noise cleaning and binarization as well as text region identification are almost script independent.

5.3.1 Binarization

For clear to moderate quality documents, Otsu's histogram-based global thresholding approach is good for text binarization. But for noisy document with uneven background, the threshold should be local. Among many useful alternatives, Sauvola's modification of Niblack's local threshold may be employed. Here the threshold $T(i, j)$ for pixel (i, j) is given by

$$T(i,j) = \mu(i,j)[1 + k(\sigma(i,j)/R - 1)], \tag{5.1}$$

where R is the dynamic range of grey value in the image, $k = 0.5$ while $\mu(i,j)$ and $\sigma(i,j)$ are mean and standard deviation of grey values in 15×15 or 17×17 neighbourhood of (i,j).

But the equation will return a threshold even on a uniformly white region where no text is present. As a remedy, Sauvola and Pietikainen [23] crudely classified a page into background, picture and text region and applied the above threshold at the text regions only. Instead of crude partitioning, our approach is to check if the ratio $\sigma(i,j)/\mu(i,j)$ is less than a threshold $t(i,j)$ which is decided on the basis of *just noticeable difference* of grey value. If the ratio is less than $t(i,j)$, then Otsu's global approach is used. Otherwise, Niblack threshold is chosen. This approach provides good binarization for moderately bad quality paper and print of the document.

5.3.2 Skew Detection/Correction

A wide variety of techniques are available in the literature for document skew detection and correction. A script specific technique suitable for Devanagari and Bangla proposed by Chaudhuri and Pal [4] attempts to find the head-lines of printed words and considers the slant of these lines as the skew of the document. The idea is to choose the big connected components (so that dots, dashes and comma are ignored) and find the upper profile. On the upper profile of each component, digital straight line segments depicting head-lines are detected. The slope of these line segments, when aggregated, gives an accurate estimate of the skew angle. This approach works equally well for Assamese and Punjabi scripts.

5.3.3 Text Region Detection

For structurally complex document, e.g. a newspaper/magazine page, the geometric and logical layout is complicated and the basic task is to separate text region from non-text region. We developed a new text detection method based on the property that (a) almost all text region components are elongated and (b) the lower parts of these elongated components are nicely aligned along a line called *baseline*. Our algorithm finds and chooses the *elongated* connected components as first approximation to the text region. Then from these components we finally choose those having neighbouring components aligned in horizontal direction. Finally, the text columns are identified by detecting a cluster of long white vertical runs. The approach works well for documents of varied types. However, it gives unsatisfactory results in detecting text embedded within complex texture or half-tone images.

5.3.4 Text Line and Word Identification

To identify individual text lines, a text column is partitioned into strips by imaginary vertical lines of separation 500 pixels. Over each strip, the product of (i) horizontal grey value sum and (ii) the number of white-to-black transition count on horizontal scans are computed and plotted like a histogram. In the plot, the position of local minima less than T(l) are noted. The region between two successive minima is deemed as the position of a text line on that strip provided the difference between the minima is more than 15 pixels (correspond to the character height of 6 pt font at 300 dpi. Indian scripts are rarely printed below 8 point size). Regions having height less than 16 pixels are merged into the nearest neighbouring text lines. Next, the lines found in each vertical strip are combined to form a full text line by a simple clustering approach. This strip-wise line detection is helpful in stopping any error propagation in line detection beyond one strip. Also, it helps in geometrically locating the position of lines and stanza. Moreover, this approach is effective even if the image is skewed by a small angle, up to $5°$.

For poor or closely packed documents, error may occur due to inter-line touching, where a word of upper text line may touch that of a lower line and form a single connected component in say, Kth strip. If the horizontal projection histogram minimum does not go below T(l), then these two touching text lines can be identified as a single line of nearly double height, as compared to the text line segments in $(K - 1)$ and/or $(K + 1)$th strip. This near-doubling of height is used as a clue to re-examine the relevant line segment in Kth strip and initiate corrective measures.

5.3.5 Zone Separation and Character Segmentation

The detection of head-line and identification of upper zone is also done during the line detection phase. However, in this case the grey value projection profile alone is employed and maxima, rather than minima, signify the head-line positions on each strip are detected. In this way, the upper zone of the text is separated from the rest of the part. The lower zone is approximately found from black–white transition count. If we start from the bottom of a text line, the transition count makes a sudden jump at the transition region between lower and middle zone. This jump is used to locate the beginning of middle zone [5].

Isolation of words from text lines precedes the character segmentation task. In a text line, individual word positions are found by looking at the width of local minima in the vertical grey value projection profile of each isolated text line. The threshold on width is chosen as a fraction of the text line height (i.e. approximate point size of the text). Since in Bangla or Devanagari, the characters are mostly connected by head-line, there is little chance (about 0.2%) of over-segmentation of words. Also, such over-segmentation can be tackled at the recognition phase.

The final pre-processing is the identification/segmentation of characters, numerals, punctuation signs, etc. in all three zones. For a clear good quality document, the easiest way for character segmentation is to delete the head-line portion (i.e. convert all pixel along that horizontal strip into white) and then do the component labelling. Most characters are segmented out as labelled components. The character parts in the upper zone can also be distinctly labelled and separated out. However, some characters in the middle zone are union of two or more components. The situation is shown in Figure 5.2 (see two components of character no. 8).

When the head-line is deleted from Figure 5.4(a), we get several distinct components, as shown in Figure 5.4(b). Of them, some characters (denoted by component numbered 6, 9 and 12) are correctly separated, but the first character is fragmented into three components (numbered 1, 2 and 3). Now, the two distinct components (numbered 1 and 2) should be combined into one. To combine them, the software uses the information that Bangla characters do extend up to the lower zone which is violated by the component above it. So, it must be a part of its nearest character. The vowel allographs are also separated as two components (numbered 4, 5 and 10, 11) lying in two different zones. They are combined at the post-processing stage. Also, very small component like (number 3) are treated as part of initial signature in the middle zone, or ignored, depending on its size.

For noisy, blurred and old documents, the neighbouring characters may touch at some unauthorized positions. In our scheme, the separation of touched neighbouring characters are tackled in the character recognition phase, described in Section 4.5.

5.4 Character Recognition

Because the number of shapes to be recognized is reduced if the signatures at upper, middle and lower zones are segmented, we use this approach in our recognition engine. Later on, the recognition results from different zones are combined to make the character recognition. The contagious characters are put into words and then some word level error correction is done.

5.4.1 Recognition of Upper Zone Shapes

The set of shapes that may lie above the head-line is shown in Figure 5.5. In addition to these, there may be apostrophe sign partly above and partly below the head-line. For the recognition of these shapes, we used black–white transition count as well as structural and topological information in a combined recognition module. The transition or crossing count feature based matching is explained in Section 5.4.2. The structural features are described below.

From Figure 5.5 we note that a few of the strokes in this region are continuation of the shapes in the middle zone, e.g. the third shape in the first row of Figure 5.5. So, continuity is a clue for recognition of these strokes. Next, some strokes touch the head-line while some do not, like fourth shape of first row. This moon-and-star-like structure is called *chandravindu*. Some shapes touch the head-line at two and even three positions. This number, easily found by transition count, is also useful for classification of shapes. At least one of the head-lines touching part has a smooth continuation in the middle zone, normally in the form of a vertical line. If we start from these touching positions and go up, then they normally meet at a point. The meeting point may lie to the left of both touching positions, in between, or to the right of both touching positions. Also, starting from the head-line, most strokes move to the left direction, but a few go to the right direction as well. These characteristics can be utilized for the recognition of the strokes above the head-line.

So, we have employed the following structural and topological features in detecting these shapes: (a) number of connected components, (b) number of black runs where the strokes touch the head-line, (c) head-line touching position (left/middle/right) of the strokes with respect to the character

Fig. 5.5. Shapes that may appear in the upper zone of Bangla text (shown darker).

below them in the middle zone, (d) for the strokes touching the head-line at two positions, whether their extension meet each other, (e) if the extension meet somewhere, whether it is to the right/left of both touching position or in between, (f) the number of holes formed in the upper zone and (g) the number of upper zone signatures that have continuity in slope with any shape in the middle zone.

For example, consider the first element of the first row in Figure 5.5. Here the value of features (a) is 1, (b) is 1, (c) is *right*, (d) is *do not care*, (e) is *do not care*, (f) is 0 and (g) is 0. Computation of these features is not very difficult and they are reasonably robust and reliable for clear document.

However, the interpretation of strokes does not end in their successful recognition only. Correct detection of continuity as well as recognition of the signature at the middle zone is important in the final recognition of the vowel allographs and other diacritical marks. That is why in the software implementation, the module for upper zone recognition comes after recognition in the middle zone of one text line is over.

5.4.2 Middle and Lower Zone Character Recognition

Recognition of middle and lower zone character is the most difficult and challenging problem. Though demarcation of lower zone is possible, the segmentation of lower zone diacritical signs cannot be made very accurate. So, we considered the signature in the combined mid-lower zone for initial recognition, but employ the information of lower zone at post-processing stage to improve the accuracy of results.

The number of shapes in the mid-lower zone is about a thousand, because of vowel diacritical markers that may be attached below each basic and compound character. We use a two-stage classifier where in the first stage weighted value of some robust stroke features like full vertical line, head-line, concavity at the lower part, presence of dot structure below the mid-zone shape, etc. are employed. Moreover, among those having predominant vertical line, some do have significant stroke to its right, but others do not. With such features, the character set is partitioned into smaller subsets, using a tree classifier.

Now, a second level classifier is used on each subset of characters. For designing this classifier, the characters are normalized in height to 50 pixels and width is normalized to this proportion. Then several features are considered for classifier design. These are (i) white–black transition or crossing count in horizontal and vertical scan direction, (ii) left, right and bottom profile projection (iii) left, right and bottom pixel projection and (iv) local slope, etc. The first three features can be computed by scanning along horizontal/vertical direction. The fourth one is computed over 4×4 pixel blocks in the bounding rectangle of the character image.

The feature vector defined by horizontal and vertical crossing count is less sensitive to expanded, contracted and bold versions of characters. It shows less dependence on font shape variation as well. Let C be scanned along each row from top to bottom and let N be the total number of scan lines. For each scan line, we count the number of distinct black runs, called here as crossing count. A black run is a sequence of black pixels with a white pixel at either end of the sequence. Figure 5.6 shows the run numbers for horizontal and vertical scans for a Bangla compound character. For the ith scan line, let $R_c[i]$ be the number of distinct black runs. The sequence $\{R_c[i]; i = 1, \ldots, N\}$ may be considered as a vector of N integer components. We can call it the horizontal crossing count vector of C.

The crossing count vector may be given an abbreviated notation by observing that the count normally remains unaltered over a sequence of several scan lines. Noise and binarization error can be partially tackled using this clue. Now, each such sequence may be represented as a pair like (m_k, n_k), where m_k denotes the number of scan lines for which the crossing count is a constant n_k. Note that $\sum_k m_k = N$. To normalize the sum, we can divide the individual m_ks by N. Let $w_k = m_k/N$. Clearly, $\sum w_k = 1$. Hence, the character C is represented by a normalized horizontal run count vector defined as

$$V_H(C) = \{w_k, n_k; k = 1, 2, \ldots, K\} \text{ where } \sum_{k=1}^{K} w_k = 1. \quad (5.2)$$

Similarly, a vertical crossing count vector $V_V(C)$ can also be computed.

In the classification phase, feature vectors for a target character are computed and matched with the stored prototypes in feature space. Matching is done by defining a distance measure explained below.

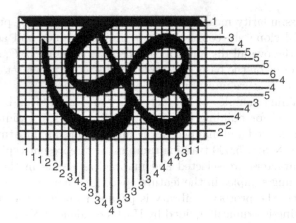

Fig. 5.6. Example of white to black transition or crossing count in horizontal and vertical direction.

Let $V_H(C)$ and $V_H(D)$ be the normalized horizontal crossing count vectors of characters C and D. $V_H(C)$ and $V_H(D)$ are represented as

$$V_H(C) = \{w_k, n_k; k = 1, 2, \ldots, K\} \text{ where } \sum_{k=1}^{K} w_k = 1 \qquad (5.3)$$

$$V_H(D) = \{w_j, n_j; j = 1, 2, \ldots, J\} \text{ where } \sum_{j=1}^{J} w_j = 1 \qquad (5.4)$$

Next, define $W_k(C) = \sum_{i=1}^{k} w_i(C)$ and $W_j(D) = \sum_{i=1}^{j} w_i(D)$. Then the union of $\{W_k(C); k = 1, 2, \ldots, K\}$ and $\{W_j(C); j = 1, 2, \ldots, J\}$ is sorted in increasing sequence. Let this sequence of numbers be $\{W_r ; r = 1, 2, \ldots, R\}$, where $W_R = 1$. It is clear that the crossing count of character C is constant over the range $W_r - W_{r-1}$ for any $r = 1, 2, \ldots, R$. Similarly, the crossing count of character D is also constant over $W_r - W_{r-1}$ for any $r = 1, 2, \ldots, R$. Now, we can re-define the crossing counts of C and D as $\{w_r n_r(C); r = 1, 2, \ldots, R\}$ and $\{w_r n_r(D); r = 1, 2, \ldots, R\}$, respectively. The distance measure is now formulated as

$$J_H(C, D) = \sum_{r=1}^{R} w_r |n_r(C) - n_r(D)| \qquad (5.5)$$

It may be understood that J_H satisfies metric property since $\sum w_r = 1$. In a similar way, we can scan the characters vertically within the bounding box and find the crossing count dissimilarity measure $J_V(C, D)$. The overall dissimilarity measure may be defined as

$$J(C, D) = J_H(C, D) + J_V(C, D) \qquad (5.6)$$

Also, the dissimilarity measures based on profile projection, pixel projection and local slope are computed in a similar manner and added to $J(C, D)$ to get the overall dissimilarity or distance measure $J(C, D)$. The classification is done on the basis of computing distance from a set of training samples in the feature multidimensional feature space.

A set of training samples of characters in various fonts and different styles is considered for building the prototype library. The training samples are size normalized and mapped in the multidimensional feature space described above. Nearly 5,000 training samples that represent typical variation of the characters are selected and mapped as points in the feature space. The training samples in the feature space may not be the optimum choice and hence, the prototype library is pruned to reduce the size. The method of pruning is primarily guided by Hart's condensed Nearest Neighbour (NN) algorithm [10]. However, we have made two modifications to this basic approach. We have taken the centroid of each class in the feature space and its nearest datum for initialization of the pruning process. Also, we have chosen the border data of each class by looking at k-NN of each datum. Those data for which the k-NNs belong to more than one class are on the border of these classes. These data are retained in the condensed set. By executing this approach, the size of original template set is reduced by a factor of nearly 2/3 (from 5,000 to 1,650) without affecting the OCR performance. This module is then ready for classification.

Now, for an unknown input character C, the classifier calculates the distances $Jo(C, X_i)$ from the prototypes and finds the minimum value for the prototype, say X_j. If the minimum is more than a pre-defined threshold θ_1 then the input character is rejected. Otherwise, it is assigned to the class of prototype character X_j. An alternative approach is to take k-NNs according to this distance and take a majority vote. Tie can be broken by examining the sum of distance values of the prototype from the competing neighbours.

5.4.3 Punctuation Mark Recognition

Punctuation marks are small characters and carry very little distinct shape information. Symbols like comma (,), hyphen (-), colon (:), semicolon (;) and single or double quotes are simple in shape and in our system, these shapes are recognized by a tree classifier where at each branch of the node certain feature is tested. For this purpose, the classifier computes features like (i) presence of dot, (ii) presence of horizontal line, (iii) aspect ratio and (iv) position of the character with respect to the word middle zone, etc. Spatial information plays an important role to resolve ambiguities arising during recognition. For example, the shape of *right quote* and *comma* are exactly the same and only difference lies in their position with respect to the word. The quote sign is placed near the *head-line* of a word, whereas comma is placed near the baseline. Also, right quote sometimes act as apostrophe sign. This ambiguity can be resolved by searching for the dual of quote sign. Similarly, vertical alignment of two dot-like shapes is recognized as a *colon* while a dot with a comma below as semicolon. Detection of *full stop* is, however, relatively easy, since in both Devanagari and Bangla scripts, it is denoted by an isolated vertical line.

5.4.4 Recognition of Touching Characters [9]

Normally, two and rarely three consecutive characters touch at the middle of the mid-zone of a word. Unlike English, the touched characters do not look like another valid character. The aspect ratio of these combined characters is often larger than 1.2. At the point of touching, the vertical black run is very short, usually a few pixels only. Also, it makes a sharp change in the slope and look like a corner at the point of touching.

In our approach, touching character identification is done using the character recognition score and aspect ratio of its bounding box. Any character component for which the smallest distance measure from the prototypes computed by (5.5) and (5.6) is more than a pre-defined threshold is suspected to be touching character provided the aspect ratio of its bounding box is also more than a threshold value. These suspected components are then segmented as follows. If the confidence of recognition improves with the segmented version, then they are retained. Else, the original component is rejected as mis-recognized.

Statistically, we have found that about 74% of touching occurs at the middle position, as shown in Figure 5.7. So, to segment the touching characters, three features are computed for each scan-line in vertical direction: (i) degree of middleness (in most cases, the characters touch at the middle region of the middle zone), (ii) crossing counts (the vertical crossing count is normally 1 at the touching position) and (iii) the stroke thickness (the vertical thickness is small at the position of touch). These three features are combined in a quantitative manner as follows.

For a column scan having a single black run, let p be the mid-point of the black run and l_1 and l_2 be the distance of p from the uppermost and lowermost row of the middle zone. See Figure 5.8, for convenience. The degree of middleness is defined as

$$d_m = min(l_1, l_2)/max(l_1, l_2) \qquad (5.7)$$

Let t be the thickness of the single black run. The value of t, in general, is small for a cut position. We combine t and d_m to obtain weights for potential cut positions. For any column X the weight $W_C(X)$ may be written as

$$W_C(X) = d_m(X)/t(X) \qquad (5.8)$$

The cut positions are obtained by finding local maxima in the histogram of $W_C(X)$ computed for $X = 1$ to N where N is the number of columns in the bounding box of the touching character image. In the recognition phase, the segment between the leftmost column and the column marked as the first cut position from the left is tried for recognition. If it is recognized, this part is considered as a single character and the remaining portion is subject to recognition module. On the other hand, if the first segment is

Fig. 5.7. Different types of Bangla touching characters. The touching position is shown encircled. The type of touching shown in the first row is most common.

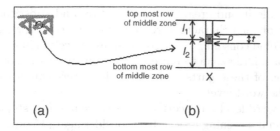

Fig. 5.8. Determination of middleness.

not recognized (i.e. rejected) then the segment defined by the second cut position is subject to the recognition procedure. In this way all the cut positions are considered.

This approach cannot tackle the touching at the bottom of middle zone, as shown by the second row of Figure 5.7. However, such touching occurs mostly in case of two types of allographs. So, for a poor recognition score, we try to identify the shape features of these two allographs. If the shape is detected, we try to segment it at the bottom region and run the recognition engine. In this way, a reasonable percentage of touching can be corrected.

5.4.5 Combination of Results and Post-Processing

The results obtained in the previous steps are to be combined into a meaningful representation of recognized words. These recognized words and punctuation marks would then form meaningful sentence representation. This representation is often used as the final recognized version and stored in electronic format. Some commercial OCR systems also return the character size and style information, as well as the geometric layout such as line end, paragraph end, etc. Our system does not attempt to compute the character size and style information, but detect the line end and paragraph end only.

The combination of recognized parts into word-level representation is not a trivial task for Bangla OCR systems. First, the system should remember that allograph for short i should be associated to its right consonant character while that for long i should be associated to the left one. Second, we noted that parts of some vowel allographs (those of long and short i as well as of oi, ou) may reside in two different zones. Also, the allographs for o and ou have two distinct parts in the middle zone and their associated consonant or compound character sits in between them. The allograph for ou is most complex because it has actually three components in three places (two in the middle zone and one at the upper zone). Now, to recognize the complete allograph, a particular signature at upper zone will expect one or two particular signatures at the middle zone. If there is a mismatch in the recognition of one or other part, then the final word recognizer finds it difficult to handle it and creates more insertion and substitution error than the number of such characters. Also, as mentioned before, in Bangla script there are some consonants allograph signs as well. These signs may reside at upper or middle zone to represent consonant cluster sound. Inadequate association of these parts with other characters can create bizarre mis-spelling in the word level.

A module for word level error correction is there in our system. It works in a two dimensional matching procedure. Consider again Figure 5.2, where the character parts are enclosed by boxes. Let each box be represented by a node of a graph-like structure that can have four types of connections: (a) above (N), (b) right (E), (c) below (S) and (d) above–right (N–E). The name of the nodes are given by the recognized glyph or character name. One node may be connected to the other through these three types of connections. The words of the language are represented in this form and stored in a file. A typical representation of Figure 5.2 is given in Figure 5.9.

The OCR output is also represented in the same structure and the graphical structure of a dictionary word, say W is compared against this OCR output graphical structure V. If they match then V signifies the correctly recognized word corresponding to W. Otherwise, V is tried to be converted into W. To convert V into W, three operations namely deletion, insertion and substitution are permitted for nodes as well as for connections. For insertion of a connection node, the 2D sequence (above, right or below another node) must also be specified. The minimum number of changes required to transform the OCR output representation V into W is the distance between the two. In case of Figure 5.9, the distance is four, since Figure 5.9(b) is converted into Figure 5.9(a) by three substitutions at node 4, 6 and 7 as well as one insertion above node 9.

Now, if the distance is smaller than certain percent of the total number of nodes of W, then the OCR output is converted into the word for W, i.e. the correction is invoked. If the distance is larger, no correction is attempted.

This approach may be called *2D edit distance* based matching since the representation of text here has a 2D graphical structure, compared with conventional edit distance which works on 1D array of sequential characters. Our attempt to try 1D matching has led to inferior error correction for Bangla script.

5.5 Performance Analysis

The performance analysis, done on the basis of recognition error, is necessary for evaluation of an OCR system. For performance evaluation it is always good to create a set of ground-truth data. Using such data, the error can be automatically computed and the OCR system can be improved at the design phase.

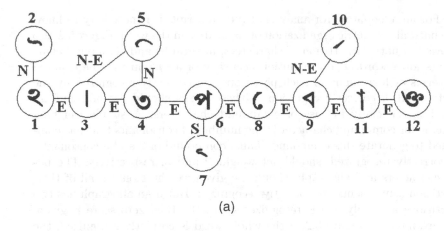

(a)

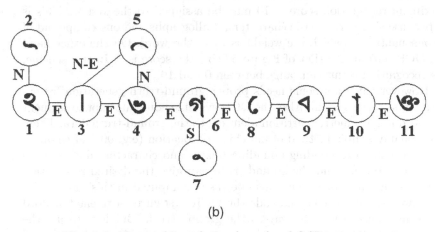

(b)

Fig. 5.9. 2D matching of stored word and OCR output.

The error in OCR system is usually computed in terms of number of recognized characters or words. Most OCR recognition engines have character reject option and because of this two types errors namely rejection and mis-recognition error are possible. At the character level, a good system should have one order of higher rejection rate than mis-recognition rate. At the word level, rejection of a complete word is rare, and the error is commonly counted only in terms of mis-classification. The word level performance measure is a pessimistic one since the whole word is considered mis-recognized even if the system fails to recognize only one character in it.

However, the above framework cannot be easily applied for Indian script like Bangla, since it is not as alphabetic as English script. Indian scripts are more 2D structure and error analysis should incorporate the positional information of the characters. Also, the error analysis here is somewhat dependent on the OCR methodology adopted by the system.

For an adequate error analysis of Indian script, it is necessary to know the natural geometric organization of signatures in the word. Figure 5.2 also shows the natural partition of characters, allographs and compound characters for a word. The recognition accuracy of a system may be counted in terms of how many of such partitions are correctly recognized by the system. Also, correct recognition in these boxes should get non-uniform weights, especially in case of compound characters. A simple weighing scheme for compound character is the number of consonants that has combined to generate this compound. Thus, compound of 2 and 3 consonants, if correctly recognized, should get weight 2 and 3, respectively. The basic characters and allographs should be given weight 1 only if all of their partition components are correctly recognized. But if an allograph has two partitions and only one is recognized correctly, then zero score is given. For example, in Figure 5.2, if the whole word is correctly recognized, the maximum recognition score of 10 may be assigned to the system. This is so because there are 4 basic characters, 4 allographs and one compound of 2 consonants (for which the weight is 2) in the word. On the other hand the OCR output like that of Figure 5.9(b), the score is 7. In this scheme, the recognition count can range between 0 and 10.

However, such a scheme needs proper ground-truth generation for experiments on the system. Also, the OCR system should attempt to segment the word in a geometric partition identical to the ground-truth data. Then, a reasonably simple method of matching of location (e.g. 90% of common area between corresponding bounding boxes) and character label between the system output and the ground-truth can give the desired recognition score. Rejection error rate can also be easily computed in this way.

However, this scheme demands the OCR system to segment the word image in exactly the same way as the ground-truth. But how to use the ground-truth data if the system does segment the word in a different way? For example, our own system does not partition the character 4 and allograph 5 and send them together to the recognition engine. After recognition, it is interpreted as a combined character and a score of 2 is given if recognition is correct. To tackle such problem, we can consider equivalent levels of ground-truth hierarchy. The lowest level is a partition like that of Figure 5.2. An intermediate level may be syllable-like partition of the word where the scores are accordingly modified. The highest level is the whole word in a single box. This level will be useful if the system attempts to recognize the word in a holistic manner, without any character segmentation. Note that the higher level of equivalent structures can be generated from the lowest level automatically if we know the writing rules of Bangla script.

Inclusion of positional information in this way solves several problems for recognition error calculation. First, otherwise, if an over-segmentation or under-segmentation would occur at the first character position of the word, then all the subsequent characters would mismatch in sequence of ground-truth data. In the current scheme, the error at one position will not affect the error computation at the other position. Second, the mismatch in the number of characters between the ground-truth and OCR output will not affect the accuracy of computation. Third, we can combine geometric layout error and mis-classification error into a single entity. A detailed work on the problems of error correction and error analysis of Bangla OCR systems is under preparation and will be reported soon.

On the basis of above analysis, we have computed the accuracy of our Bangla script OCR system. For clear documents and in multi-font environment, the system performs with 96.83% accuracy at character level and 86.12% at the word level. If trained for a single font, the performance goes up to 97.27% at character level and 90.11% at word level. In both cases the experiment was conducted on 50,000 words. The line and paragraph end can be detected with less than 0.1% error. The space between neighbouring words is mistaken in less than 0.5% cases.

5.6 Conclusion

The problems of developing Indian script OCR system have been described in this chapter with one of the difficult but more popular scripts named Bangla. The possible approach to the solution of this problem is also described. It involves classification of an order of thousand classes of characters and allographs. The main recognition engine can be based on artificial neural net (ANN), but tackling such a large number of character classes is a difficult problem. It involves training set of huge size with sufficient variability. Yet additional module is needed for recognizing simple and small shapes of allographs, punctuation marks. An attempt to use ANN classifier for Bangla did not yield better result than the nearest neighbour classifier described here. There are other powerful recognition techniques like Hidden Markov Model (HMM) and Support Vector Machine (SVM). However, no report on using these techniques robustly on any Indian script has yet been published. We invite researchers to take up this challenging problem of recognizing Indian scripts as robustly as the OCR systems available for roman-based scripts.

Acknowledgments

The author would like to thank Dr. U. Pal and Dr. U. Garain for valuable discussions as well as Jawaharlal Nehru Memorial fund, New Delhi for partial support rendered in the form of *Jawaharlal Nehru fellowship*.

References

1. Ashwin, T.V. and Sastry, P.S. (2002). A font and size independent OCR system for printed Kannada documents using support vector machines. *Journal of Sadhana, 27*, pp. 35–58.
2. Bhattacharya, U., Das, T.K., Datta, A., Parui, S.K., and Chaudhuri, B.B. (2002). A hybrid scheme for hand-printed numeral recognition based on a self-organizing network and MLP classifiers. *International Journal of Pattern Recognition and Artificial Intelligence, 16*, pp. 845–864.
3. Bishnu, A. and Chaudhuri, B.B. (1999). Segmentation of Bangla handwritten text into characters by re-cursive contour following. *Proceedings of the Fifth International Conference on Document Analysis and Recognition*, pp. 402–405.
4. Chaudhuri, B.B. and Pal, U. (1997). Skew angle detection of digitised Indian Script documents. *IEEE Transactions on Pattern Analysis and Machine Intelligence, 19*, pp. 182–186.
5. Chaudhuri, B.B. and Pal, U. (1998). A complete printed Bangla OCR system. *Pattern Recognition, 31*, pp. 531–549.
6. Chaudhuri, B.B., Pal, U., and Mitra, M. (2002). Automatic recognition of Printed Oriya Script. *Journal of Sadhana, 27*, pp. 23–34.
7. Dhanya, D., Ramakrishna, A.G., and Pati, P.B. (2002). Script recognition in bilingual documents. *Journal of Sadhana, 27(1)*, pp. 73–82.
8. Garain, U. and Chaudhuri, B.B. (1998). Compound character recognition by run-number-based metric distances. *SPIE Proceedings, 3305*, pp. 90–97.
9. Garain, U. and Chaudhuri, B.B. (2002). Segmentation of touching characters in printed Devnagari and Bangla scripts using fuzzy multifactorial analysis. *IEEE Transactions on Systems, Man, and Cybernetics, Part C, 32*, pp. 449–459.
10. Hart, P.E. (1968). The condensed nearest neighbor rule. *IEEE Transactions on Information Theory, 6(4)*, pp. 515–516.
11. Lehal, G.S. and Singh, C. (1999). Feature extraction and classification for OCR of Gurmukhi script. *Journal of Vivek, 12*, pp. 2–12.
12. Mantas, J. (1986). An overview of character recognition methodologies. *Pattern Recognition 19*, pp. 425–430.
13. Mori, S., Suen, C.Y., and Yamamoto, K. (1992). Historical review of OCR research and development. *Proceedings of IEEE, 80(7)*, pp. 1029–1058.
14. Nagy, G. (1992). At the frontiers of OCR. *Proceedings of IEEE, 80(7)*, pp. 1093–1100.
15. Negi, A., Chakravarthy, B., and Krishna, B. (2001). An OCR system for Telugu. *Proceedings of the Sixth International Conference on Document Analysis and Recognition*, pp. 1110–1114.
16. O'Gorman, L. and Kasturi, R. (1995). *Document Image Analysis*. Los Alamitos, CA: IEEE Computer Society Press.
17. Pal, U. (1997). On the development of an optical character recognition (OCR) system for printed Bangla script. Ph.D. thesis. Kolkata: ISI.
18. Pal, U. and Chaudhuri, B.B. (1997). Printed Devanagari script OCR system. *Journal of Vivek 10*, pp. 12–24.
19. Palit, S. and Chaudhuri, B.B. (1995). A feature-based scheme for the machine recognition of printed Devanagari script. In: P.P. Das, B.N. Chatterjee (Eds.).

Pattern Recognition, Image Processing and Computer Vision. New Delhi, India: Narosa Publishing House, pp. 163–168.

20. Parui, S.K., Chaudhuri, B.B., and Majumder, D.D. (1982). A procedure for recognition of connected hand-written numerals. *International Journal of Systems Science, 13*, pp. 1019–1029.

21. Plamondon, R. and Srihari, S.N. (2000). On-line and off-line handwritten recognition: a comprehensive survey. *IEEE Transactions on Pattern Analysis and Machine Intelligence, 22*, pp. 62–84.

22. Rajasekaran, S.N.S. and Deekshatulu, B.L. (1977). Recognition of printed Telugu characters. *Computer Graphics and Image Processing 6.* pp. 335–360.

23. Sauvola, J. and Pietikainen, M. (2000). Adaptive document image binarization. *Pattern Recognition, 33*, pp. 225–236.

24. Sethi, I. and Chatterjee, B. (1976). Machine recognition of constrained hand-printed Devanagari. *Pattern Recognition, 9*, pp. 69–76.

25. Sinha, R.M.K. and Mahabala, H. (1979). Machine recognition of Devanagari script. *IEEE Transactions on Systems, Man, and Cybernetics, 9*, pp. 435–441.

26. Siromony, G., Chandrasekaran, R., and Chandrasekaran, M. (1978). Computer recognition of printed Tamil characters. *Pattern Recognition, 10*, pp. 243–247.

6

A Bayesian Network Approach for On-line Handwriting Recognition

Sung-Jung Cho and Jin Hyung Kim

6.1 Introduction

On-line handwriting recognition is used to automatically transcribe characters handwritten with electronic devices like tablets and pens. Compared to off-line handwriting recognition, it has the advantage of utilizing time series information of hand movements captured by the electronic devices. Given the widespread use of mobile devices such as cell phones, PDAs and pen computers these days, on-line handwriting recognition has gained large attention again as a convenient and portable input method. Also, its application area has further extended to 3D writing space where a user can draw gestures and characters with inertial sensor-embedded input devices [1].

For highly accurate character recognition, it is necessary to model the structure of characters as realistically as possible. In this Chapter, a character is regarded to have points and basic strokes as its composition structure. The basic strokes are defined as straight or nearly straight traces that have distinct directions from connected traces in writing order. Figure 6.1(a) and (b) shows such examples in numerical and Chinese characters. They are apparently identifiable in the characters with only straight lines like 1, 4 and the Chinese ones. The curvilinear trace, like the lower part of the character 5, can be approximated with several ones.

To describe and identify characters, strokes and their relationships are important (for simplicity, a *stroke* will be used as a shorthand notation of a *basic stroke* in this chapter even though it usually refers to a set of consecutive points from pen-down to pen-up movement). Figure 6.1(b) shows one example. The two Chinese characters have same number and kinds of strokes. However, they belong to different character classes because of difference in stroke relationships; the vertical stroke of the left character is located below the top horizontal stroke. However, that in the right character is located across the top horizontal stroke.

Fig. 6.1. Basic strokes of numerical and Chinese characters. The two Chinese characters belong to different classes because of difference in stroke relationships.

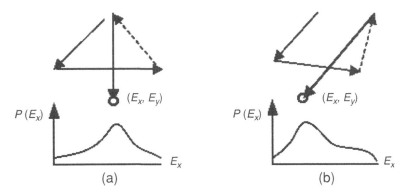

Fig. 6.2. Example of stroke relationship in the character 4. According to positions of other strokes, E_x (X position of the last stroke end point) is likely to be (a) centred in X-axis and (b) in the left-hand side of X-axis.

Relationships between strokes can be statistically defined as dependencies of positions between them; a stroke position gets influence from those of other strokes. For example, when the three strokes of the character 4 are written like Figure 6.2(a), the X position of the end point of the last stroke (E_x) is likely to be centred in X-axis. However, when they are slightly skewed clockwise like Figure 6.2(b), E_x is likely to be located in the left-hand side of X-axis.

To explicitly model strokes and their relationships have the following advantages. First, strokes are conceptual elements and their relationships are conceptually meaningful, especially in characters of oriental languages such as Korean, Chinese and Japanese. Second, their shapes are usually simple and consistently written so that they can be reliably trained with less amount of data compared with holistic character modelling approaches. Last, stroke relationships are robust against geometric variations and important for discriminating characters of similar shapes.

In spite of the advantages, strokes and their relationships have not been actively adopted in on-line handwriting recognition systems because of limitations in their modelling frameworks. The systems have mainly employed hidden Markov models (HMMs) [2–4] and time delay neural networks [5], which are not adequate for explicit modelling of long-range feature dependencies. For instance, a handwriting input, including stroke instances, is usually divided in equal time interval and converted into local feature vectors independent of one another. Thus, strokes and their relationships are ignored by the independence assumption or unrealistically modelled like exponential stroke length distribution in HMMs.

To complement the modelling limitation of the HMMs, several variations are introduced. Duration modelling HMMs [6] and non-stationary HMMs [7] can model the length of feature vectors dwelled at each state explicitly, which can be regarded as lengths of strokes. Segmental HMMs can model trajectory of each state explicitly with trajectory parameters [8, 9]. Even though they can model stroke shapes more realistically, they still have difficulty in modelling stroke relationships.

Another popular but heuristic approach is to post-process HMM's outputs with other external knowledge and classifiers. HMM's outputs are complemented with other classifiers such as neural networks [10], structural classifiers [11] and template matching classifiers [12]. Even though the heuristic methods can incorporate structural knowledge of a character to a certain extent, it has an ad hoc probability (or score) integration problem to the baseline HMM framework.

On the other hand, strokes and their relationships have been modelled in many structural off-line handwritten character recognition systems. Strokes are represented as line primitives [13, 14] or statistical line primitives [15] in which the centre of each point distribution is located along a line. Stroke relationships are also incorporated in various ways. They are encoded as derived features such as distances and angles between strokes [13]. Their symbolic descriptions like intersection and parallel relationships are also incorporated [14]. Joint Gaussian distributions are also adopted for modelling dependencies between strokes [15].

However, those approaches have two limitations when applied to on-line handwriting recognition. First, characters are usually more cursively written in on-line handwriting. Therefore, more flexible stroke models rather than straight lines are required. Second, stroke relationships are not smoothly and probabilistically incorporated into the baseline recognition framework.

Our research goal is to devise a framework in which strokes and their relationships are explicitly modelled and to develop a robust recognition system based on the framework. To achieve the goal, we propose a Bayesian network-based framework with following properties.[1] First, a character is represented in the hierarchy of a character model, stroke models and point models. Second, relationships between strokes and between points are explicitly and statistically modelled as their positional dependencies. Last,

---

[1] This chapter is extended from [16].

Bayesian networks are adopted for representing all the models and relationships, which are useful for modelling dependencies graphically and probabilistically.

The rest of this chapter is organized as follows. Section 6.2 explains the point model, the stroke model and the character model. Section 6.3 describes recognition and training algorithms of the character model. Section 6.4 analyses recognition performance and modelling capacity of the proposed system with handwritten digits. Finally, Section 6.5 summarizes and concludes this chapter.

6.2 Modelling of Character Components and Their Relationships

6.2.1 Bayesian Network Modelling Framework

A Bayesian network [17] is a graphical model that represents probabilistically and graphically random variables and their dependencies at the same time. It can effectively encode the joint probability of random variables by factorizing it into their local conditional probabilities.

The Bayesian network is a directional acyclic graph. Its nodes represent random variables. Its arcs represent their dependency structure. A directional arc from a node Y to X denotes that the random variable X depends on Y. In this case, X is a child of Y, and Y is a parent of X. For example, the Bayesian network S in Figure 6.3 indicates that X_1 and X_2 have no dependent variable, X_3 depends on X_1, and X_4 depends on X_1, X_2 and X_3. Each node encodes the conditional probability of $P(X|pa(X))$, where $pa(X)$ denotes the parent nodes of X. The joint probability distribution $P(X_1, X_2, X_3, X_4)$ is decomposed into the product of conditional probability distributions of all the nodes by probability chain rule and the dependency structure as follows:

$$P(X_1, X_2, X_3, X_4) = \prod_{i=1}^{4} P(X_i|pa(X_i))$$

$$= P(X_1) \cdot P(X_2) \cdot P(X_3|X_1) \cdot P(X_4|X_1, X_2, X_3). \quad (6.1)$$

Conditional probability distributions are very important to represent relationships between variables. However, it is not a simple task to get them exactly when variables have continuous values and high-order dependencies. The conventional approach is to make a conditional probability table for all the possible configurations of random variable values. However, it requires quantization of continuous values. Also, the table size grows exponentially as the order of dependency increases so that required training data grow exponentially to the dependency order.

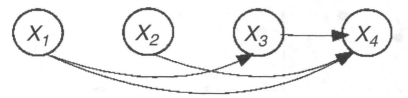

Fig. 6.3. Example of a Bayesian network.

The reasons drive us to adopt conditional Gaussian distributions [18]. The value of a random variable is assumed to be determined by linear weight sum of its dependent variable values with Gaussian estimation error. When a multivariate random variable X depends on $X_1, \ldots, X_n$, the conditional probability distribution is given as follows:

$$P(X = \mathbf{x} | X_1 = \mathbf{x_1}, \ldots, X_n = \mathbf{x_n}) \tag{6.2}$$
$$= (2\pi)^{-\frac{d}{2}} |\mathbf{\Sigma}|^{-\frac{1}{2}} \exp[-\frac{1}{2}(\mathbf{x} - \mu_{X|X_1,\cdots,X_n})^T \mathbf{\Sigma}^{-1}(\mathbf{x} - \mu_{X|X_1,\cdots,X_n})].$$

The mean $\mu_{X|X_1,\cdots,X_n}$ is determined by the dependent variable values:

$$\mu_{X|X_1,\cdots,X_n} = \mathbf{W}[\mathbf{x_1}^T, \ldots, \mathbf{x_n}^T, 1]^T, \tag{6.3}$$

where $\mathbf{W}$ is a $d \times k$ linear regression matrix, d is the dimension of X, and k is the dimension of $[\mathbf{x_1}^T, \ldots, \mathbf{x_n}^T, 1]^T$.

When there is no dependent variable, the conditional mean of (6.3) is reduced to the mean of the conventional Gaussian distribution:

$$\mu_X = mean(X) \cdot 1. \tag{6.4}$$

6.2.2 Point Model

A point instance has the attribute of (x, y) position on the 2D plane. Figure 6.4(a) shows examples of the first starting points in the character 2 instances. Figure 6.4(b) shows the distribution of their positions within character bounding boxes. Small dots denote training data instances.

A point model has 2D Gaussian distribution for modelling 2D point positions (Figure 6.4(c)). The darkest position denotes Gaussian mean and the gradual dim black colour denotes shrinking probability density outside the mean. It is represented by one node in a Bayesian network (Figure 6.4(d)).

The matching probability of a point instance and a point model is obtained from Gaussian distribution. Let $O = (x, y)$ denote the point instance and $P = (X, Y)$ the point model. Then, the matching probability is given as follows:

$$P(P = O) = P(X = x, Y = y)$$
$$= (2\pi)^{-1} |\mathbf{\Sigma}|^{-\frac{1}{2}} \exp[-\frac{1}{2}(O - \mu_P)^T \mathbf{\Sigma}^{-1}(O - \mu_P)], \tag{6.5}$$

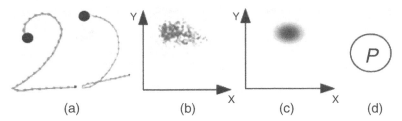

Fig. 6.4. Point instances and a point model. (a) Examples of the starting points of the character 2. (b) Sample distribution of their X–Y positions. (c) Corresponding 2D Gaussian point model. (d) Bayesian network representation of the point model.

where

$$\mu_P = [mean(X)\ mean(Y)]^T. \tag{6.6}$$

When the point P depends on other points $P_1, \ldots, P_n$, its matching probability is given from the conditional Gaussian distribution. By substituting the random variable Ps for Xs of (6.2) and (6.3), it is given as follows:

$$P(P = O|P_1 = O_1, \ldots, P_n = O_n) \tag{6.7}$$
$$= P(x, y|x_1, y_1, \ldots, x_n, y_n)$$
$$= (2\pi)^{-1}|\mathbf{\Sigma}|^{-\frac{1}{2}} \exp[-\frac{1}{2}(O - \mu_{P|P_1,\cdots,P_n})^T \mathbf{\Sigma}^{-1}(O - \mu_{P|P_1,\cdots,P_n})],$$

where

$$\mu_{P|P_1,\cdots,P_n} = \begin{bmatrix} w_{1,1}, w_{1,2}, \ldots, w_{1,2n+1} \\ w_{2,1}, w_{2,2}, \ldots, w_{2,2n+1} \end{bmatrix} [x_1, y_1, \ldots, x_n, y_n, 1]^T. \tag{6.8}$$

6.2.3 Stroke Model

A stroke instance is composed of points. Therefore, a stroke model is composed of point models with their relationships, called *within-stroke relationships* (WSRs).

A WSR is defined as the dependency of a mid-point on two end points of a stroke. The mid-point is the point at which the length of the left partial stroke and that of the right one are equal. In Figure 6.5(a), *ip*s are mid-points, and ep_0s and ep_1s are end points of stroke instances. Figure 6.5(b) is the Bayesian network representation of one WSR, composed of one mid-point model (IP), two end point models (EP_0, EP_1) and dependency arcs from EP_0, EP_1 to IP.

Because a stroke is a nearly straight and smooth trace, it has strong WSRs. Figure 6.6 shows one example in the character 4. In Figure 6.6(a), *ip*, ep_0 and ep_1 are the mid-point and the end points of the first stroke.

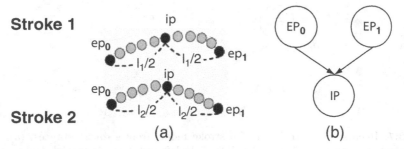

Stroke 1

Stroke 2

(a)   (b)

Fig. 6.5. Within-stroke relationship (WSR). (a) Mid-points ips and two end points ep_0s and ep_1s of stroke instances. (b) Bayesian network representation of one WSR: dependency of the mid-point model IP on two end point models (EP_0, EP_1).

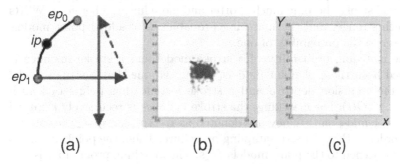

(a)   (b)   (c)

Fig. 6.6. WSR example in a character 4. (a) Mid-point (ip) and end points (ep_0 and ep_1) of the first stroke. (b) Plotting of deviation of ips from their mean in the training data. (c) Plotting of deviation of ips from their expected positions computed with ep_0 and ep_1.

Figure 6.6(b) is the plotting of the differences of ip instances from their mean in the training data. The centre of the figure corresponds to the mean. The ip instances are scattered from the mean with large deviation. However, when ep_0 and ep_1 are given, they have small differences from their expected positions by the WSR as shown in Figure 6.6(c). The greatly reduced variance indicates the strong dependency of IP on EP_0 and EP_1.

A stroke model is constructed by recursively adding mid-point models and specifying WSRs. Figure 17.5 shows the recursive construction example from stroke instances. At the first recursion ($d = 1$), IP_1 is added for modelling mid-points of all the stroke instances. It has the WSR from the end points (the arcs from EP_0 and EP_1 to IP_1). At the second recursion ($d = 2$), IP_2 and IP_3 are added for mid-points of the left and of the right partial strokes, respectively, with WSRs. Figure 17.5(c) is the extended stroke model. With this recursion procedure, a stroke model can have as many point models as necessary. In this chapter, the recursion depth $d = 3$ is chosen for all the stroke models.

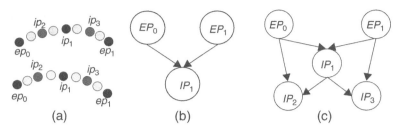

Fig. 6.7. Recursive construction of a stroke model from stroke instances. (a) Stroke instances. ip_2s and ip_3s: mid-points of the left and the right partial strokes. (b) Stroke model of the recursion depth $d = 1$ and (c) that of $d = 2$.

It is worth noting that point models at large recursion depths do not incur the problem of probability value degradation. As the depth gets deeper, the partial strokes become much shorter and more linear. Therefore, WSRs get much stronger and the matching probabilities of added point models get closer to the probability of one.

The matching probability of a stroke model and a stroke instance is obtained from those of point models. Let us assume that a stroke model S has the recursion depth d and a stroke instance has points of length t: $O(1), \ldots, O(t)$. For matching, the stroke instance is recursively sampled into $2^d - 1$ mid-points. They are denoted as $ip_1, ip_2, \ldots, ip_{2^d-1}$ according to the order of the recursive sampling procedure. Then, the point instances ip_is are matched to the point models IP_is. The matching probability is calculated as follows by the local Markov property of conditional probabilities in Bayesian networks [17]:

$$P(S = O(1), \ldots, O(t)) \tag{6.9}$$
$$= P(EP_0 = O(1), EP_1 = O(t), IP_1 = ip_1, \ldots, IP_{2^d-1} = ip_{2^d-1})$$
$$= P(EP_0 = O(1))P(EP_1 = O(t)) \prod_{i=1}^{2^d-1} P(IP_i = ip_i | pa(IP_i))$$

where $pa(IP_i)$ is the configuration of parent nodes of IP_i.

6.2.4 Character Model

A character instance consists of strokes. Also, close relationships exist between them. Therefore, a character model consists of stroke models with their relationships, called *inter-stroke relationships* (ISRs).

ISRs are represented with dependencies of stroke end points. Ideally, a stroke gets influence from all the points of other strokes. Figure 6.8(a) illustrates the situation that the end point of the last stroke of the character 4 has relationships with all the points of other strokes (marked by arrows). However, representing all the relationships is too complex and

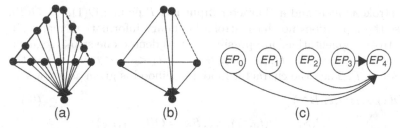

Fig. 6.8. Representation of inter-stroke relationships (ISRs). (a) Relationships of the last stroke of the character 4 with all the points of other strokes. (b) Encapsulation of ISRs as those between stroke end points. (c) Their Bayesian network representation.

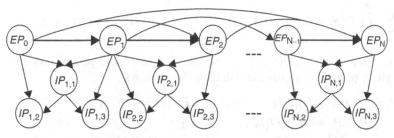

Fig. 6.9. Bayesian network representation of a character model with N strokes and the stroke recursion depth $d = 2$.

redundant. So, we encapsulate them as relationships of stroke end points (Figure 6.8(b)). Then, ISRs are represented as arcs from preceding stroke end points to the current one in Bayesian networks (Figure 6.8(c)).

A character model is constructed by concatenating stroke models according to their writing order and specifying ISRs. Figure 6.9 shows a Bayesian network-based character model with N strokes. EP_is are the stroke end point models and $IP_{i,j}$s are the point models within the ith stroke. The right end point of the preceding stroke is shared with the left one of the following stroke. ISRs are represented by the arcs between EP_is, and WSRs are represented by the incoming arcs to $IP_{i,j}$s. This figure shows that point models, stroke models and their relationships are represented hierarchically in one character model.

The writing order of point models is represented by their left–right positions in the character model; the point models in the left-hand side are written before those in the right-hand side. In Figure 6.9, EP_0 is the first written one. The point models of the first stroke are written in the order of $IP_{1,2}, IP_{1,1}, IP_{1,3}$ and then, the second stroke in the order of $EP_1, IP_{2,2}, IP_{2,1}, IP_{2,3}$. In turn, the following strokes are written. Finally, EP_N is the last one.

The model likelihood of a character is calculated by enumerating all the possible stroke segmentations. Let us assume that a character model BN

has N stroke models and a character input has T points: $O(1), \ldots, O(T)$. Because the input does not have stroke boundary information, many different stroke segmentations are possible. Let us denote one stroke segmentation instance as $\gamma = (t_0, t_1, \ldots, t_N)$, $t_0 = 1 < t_1 < \cdots < t_N = T$, and the whole set as Γ. Then the character model likelihood is given as follows:

$$P(O(1), \ldots, O(t)|BN) \tag{6.10}$$

$$= \sum_{\gamma = (t_0, \ldots, t_N) \in \Gamma} P(S_1 = O(t_0, t_1), \ldots, S_N = O(t_{N-1}, t_N))$$

$$= \sum_{\gamma \in \Gamma} \prod_{i=1}^{N} P(S_i = O(t_{i-1}, t_i)|S_1 = O(t_0, t_1), \ldots, S_{i-1} = O(t_{i-2}, t_{i-1}))$$

$$= \sum_{\gamma \in \Gamma} \prod_{i=1}^{N} P(S_i = O(t_{i-1}, t_i)|EP_0 = O(t_0), \ldots, EP_{i-1} = O(t_{i-1})),$$

where $O(t_i, t_j) = O(t_i), O(t_{i+1}), \ldots, O(t_j)$. The matching probability of a stroke given preceding strokes is calculated as follows:

$$P(S_i = O(t_{i-1}, t_i)|EP_0 = O(t_0), \ldots, EP_{i-1} = O(t_{i-1}))$$

$$= \begin{cases} P(EP_i = O(t_i)|O(t_0), \ldots, O(t_{i-1})) \\ \quad \cdot \prod_{j=1}^{2^d - 1} P(IP_{i,j} = ip_{i,j}(O(t_{i-1}, t_i))|pa(IP_{i,j})) \text{ , if } i > 1 \\ P(EP_0 = O(t_0)) \cdot P(EP_1 = O(t_1)|O(t_0)) \\ \quad \cdot \prod_{j=1}^{2^d - 1} P(IP_{i,j} = ip_{i,j}(O(t_{i-1}, t_i))|pa(IP_{i,j})) \text{ , if } i = 1 \end{cases} \tag{6.11}$$

where $ip_{i,j}(O(t_{i-1}, t_i))$ is the jth recursively sampled point of $O(t_{i-1}, t_i)$.

By substituting (6.11) for (6.10), the model likelihood is given as the product of matching probabilities of EPs and IPs.

$$P(O(1), \ldots, O(t)|BN) \tag{6.12}$$

$$= \sum_{\gamma \in \Gamma} \prod_{i=0}^{N} P(EP_i = O(t_i)|O(t_0), \ldots, O(t_{i-1}))$$

$$\prod_{i=1}^{N} \prod_{j=1}^{2^d - 1} P(IP_{i,j} = ip_{i,j}(O(t_{i-1}, t_i))|pa(IP_{i,j})).$$

The matching probabilities of EPs can be interpreted as the probabilities of global stroke positions and those of IPs as those of local stroke shapes.

6.3 Recognition and Training Algorithms

6.3.1 Recognition Algorithm

A handwritten character is recognized by finding the character model that produces the highest a posteriori probability given the input. When the ith character model is denoted as BN_i and the input points as $O(1), \ldots, O(T)$, then the recognition problem can be formulated as below:

$$argmax_i P(BN_i | O(1), \ldots, O(T)) \qquad (6.13)$$

$$= argmax_i \frac{P(BN_i) P(O(1), \ldots, O(T) | BN_i)}{P(O(1), \ldots, O(T))}$$

$$= argmax_i P(BN_i) P(O(1), \ldots, O(T) | BN_i).$$

The character model likelihood is described in the previous section (Equation (6.12)). For calculating it, all the possible stroke segmentations Γ should be considered. To prevent the exponential time complexity, we assume that it can be approximated by the character matching probability of the most probable stroke segmentation instance γ^* in Γ as follows:

$$P(O(1), \ldots, O(T) | BN_i) \qquad (6.14)$$

$$\approx max_{\gamma \in \Gamma} P(S_1 = O(t_0, t_1), \ldots, S_N = O(t_{N-1}, t_N)).$$

To make the calculation of the model likelihood manageable in time, we need more assumption about the search of γ^*. When matching a stroke, all the possible segmentations of its preceding strokes should be considered because of inter-stroke dependencies. For simplicity of the search, we assume that the matching probability of a stroke is highest with the most probable configuration of its preceding strokes. Then, dynamic programming search algorithm is adopted as follows:

S_i: ith stroke model
$\gamma_i(t)$: the most probable stroke segmentation when $S_1, \ldots, S_i$ and $O(1, t)$ are matched
$\delta_i(t)$: the most probable stroke matching probability given $\gamma_i(t)$
Initialization:
$\delta_0(1) = 1, \gamma_0(1) = \{\}$
Stroke matching:
for t =2 to T
  for i = 1 to N
    $\delta_i(t) = max_{1 \leq b < t} P(S_i = O(b, t) | \gamma_{i-1}(b)) \cdot \delta_{i-1}(b)$
    $b^* = argmax_{1 \leq b < t} P(S_i = O(b, t) | \gamma_{i-1}(b)) \cdot \delta_{i-1}(b)$
    $\gamma_i(t) = \gamma_{i-1}(b^*) \cup \{t\}$
  end
end
Character model likelihood:
$P(O(1), \ldots, O(T) | BN_i) \approx \delta_N(T)$

6.3.2 Training Algorithm

To construct a character model, its dependency structure and conditional probability parameters should be determined. In this chapter, the dependency structure is determined by a model designer from a priori knowledge and experiments. The recursion depth of stroke models is chosen as three. The number of stroke models is determined from the typical stroke number of the character.

The conditional probability parameters are trained from data. They are the linear regression matrices $\mathbf{W}$s ($\mathbf{W} = [w_{i,j}]$) and the covariances Σs from point models (Equations (6.7) and (6.8)). If all the point models are matched to point instances, then they can be estimated from maximum likelihood estimation algorithm [18]. Let us assume that a point P depends on $P_1, \ldots, P_k$ and there are N training samples. Let us denote the ith sample of P as $\mathbf{p}^{(i)}$ and the dependent variable values as $\mathbf{z}^{(i)} = [x_1^{(i)}, y_1^{(i)}, \ldots, x_k^{(i)}, y_k^{(i)}, 1]$. Then, they are estimated as follows:

$$\mathbf{W} = \left(\sum_{i=1}^{N} \mathbf{p}^{(i)} (\mathbf{z}^{(i)})^T \right) \left(\sum_{i=1}^{N} \mathbf{z}^{(i)} (\mathbf{z}^{(i)})^T \right)^{-1}, \qquad (6.15)$$

$$\Sigma = \frac{1}{N} \sum_{i=1}^{N} \mathbf{p}^{(i)} (\mathbf{p}^{(i)})^T - \frac{1}{N} \mathbf{W} \sum_{i=1}^{N} \mathbf{z}^{(i)} (\mathbf{p}^{(i)})^T. \qquad (6.16)$$

During training of the character model, the parameter re-estimation and the search for the most probable stroke segmentation γ^* are repeated alternatively. It is similar to the EM (expectation–maximization) training method. Given the parameters ($\mathbf{W}$s and Σs), γ^* is updated. Then, with the updated γ^*, the parameters are re-estimated. The detailed algorithm is as follows:

Step 1. Initialize the character model with initial data (a small amount of manually stroke-segmented character instances).
Step 2. Find the most probable stroke segmentations (γ^*s) from large amount of unsegmented training characters by the previous search algorithm.
Step 3. Estimate the parameters ($\mathbf{W}$s,Σs) with stroke instances partitioned by γ^*s.
Step 4. Repeat Steps 2 and 3 until the sum of model likelihoods does not change.

6.4 Experimental Results and Analysis

We evaluate the proposed framework with on-line handwritten digit databases (DBs). We analyse the contribution of stroke dependency modelling to the recognition performance in terms of the prediction accuracy of input point positions by the point models and the recognition rates of the proposed system at the different dependency modelling degree. The recognition performance of the proposed system is compared with those of other

Table 6.1. Properties of digit DBs for experiments

DB	# of characters (# of writers)		Degree of writing variation
	Training	Test	
KAIST	4,046 (20)	1,963 (18)	Small
Turkey	7,494 (30)	3,498 (14)	Medium
UNIPEN .	8,734 (150+)	7,157 (60+)	Large

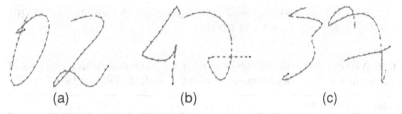

(a)   (b)   (c)

Fig. 6.10. Sample characters from (a) KAIST DB, (b) Turkey DB and (c) UNIPEN DB.

published recognition systems. To intuitively evaluate the modelling capacity, we generate characters from the models and analyse how natural the character shapes look.

6.4.1 Data Set

To test and analyse the proposed system, we use three digit DBs with different degrees of writing variation: KAIST DB, Turkey DB [19] and UNIPEN DB[2] [20]. Table 6.1 summarizes the DB properties. All the writers of the test data are different from those of the training data. Figure 6.10 shows some sample characters from the DBs.

6.4.2 Analysis of Within-Stroke Relationship Modelling

WSRs are dependencies of positions of mid-points on those of stroke end points (Figure 6.5). Their numbers increase when the stroke recursion depth becomes larger (Figure 6.11). When the depth $d = 0$, only stroke end points are modelled and WSRs are not. When $d = 1$, one WSR is modelled. When $d = 2$, three of them are modelled. In this way, a stroke is more finely modelled with increased WSRs.

WSRs increase the accuracy of point models for predicting input point positions. Point models are represented by conditional Gaussian

---

[2] We used train_v01_r07 CD and partitioned it into training and test sets. The training set comes from 1a/aga to 1a/pri directories. The test set comes from 1a/syn0 to 1a/val directories.

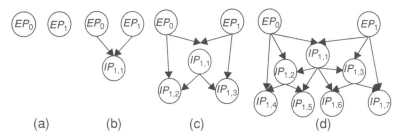

(a)   (b)   (c)   (d)

Fig. 6.11. Control of WSRs of a stroke model. m: the number of WSRs. (a) $m = 0$, (b) $m = 1$, (c) $m = 3$ and (d) $m = 7$.

Table 6.2. Average determinant values of internal point models as a measure of prediction accuracies. *No*: dependencies are not modelled. *Yes*: modelled

Point models	KAIST DB		TURKEY DB		UNIPEN DB	
	No	*Yes*	*No*	*Yes*	*No*	*Yes*
IP_1	1.6×10^{-3}	1.8×10^{-7}	1.4×10^{-4}	4.4×10^{-7}	3.5×10^{-4}	1.1×10^{-6}
IP_2, IP_3	2.7×10^{-3}	4.0×10^{-9}	1.7×10^{-4}	9.3×10^{-9}	4.2×10^{-4}	2.1×10^{-8}
$IP_4, \ldots, IP_7$	3.0×10^{-3}	2.9×10^{-9}	1.7×10^{-4}	1.7×10^{-9}	4.4×10^{-4}	2.2×10^{-9}

distributions that have linear regression matrices and covariances. The determinant of a covariance measures the prediction accuracy. When it is small, the Gaussian distribution is narrowly concentrated around its mean and vice versa. Table 6.2 shows that WSRs reduce the determinant values of point models; when WSRs are not modelled, they range from 10^{-4} to 10^{-3}. However, when modelled, they are reduced to $10^{-7} - 10^{-6}$ when $d = 1$, to $10^{-9} - 10^{-8}$ when $d = 2$, and to 10^{-9} when $d = 3$.

The increased modelling accuracy by WSRs also improves recognition rates of the system. Figure 6.12 shows the recognition rates according to the number of WSRs. Compared to the recognition rates without WSRs, seven WSRs increase recognition rates from 83.1 to 98.5%, thus reducing 93% of relative recognition errors on average. The figure also suggests that three WSRs are sufficient for modelling a stroke, from the saturated recognition rates beyond three.

6.4.3 Analysis of Inter-Stroke Relationship Modelling

The modelling degree of ISRs is controlled by the number of preceding strokes on which a stroke depends (ISR order). Figure 6.13 shows the example of controlling them. When the order $n = 0$, a stroke end point does not have any dependency from other strokes. When $n = 1$, it depends only on the preceding stroke. In this way, a stroke can have relationships with all the preceding ones.

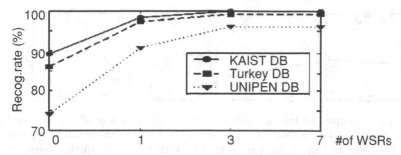

Fig. 6.12. Recognition rates according to the number of WSRs (ISRS: fully modelled).

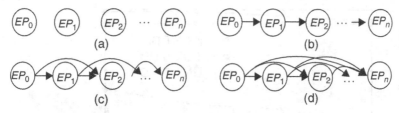

Fig. 6.13. Control of ISR order n. (a) $n = 0$, (b) $n = 1$, (c) $n = 2$ and (d) $n =$ fully modelled.

Table 6.3. Determinant values of stroke end point models with different ISR orders

DB	Order = 0	Order = 1	Order = 2	Fully
KAIST DB	7.1×10^{-5}	5.8×10^{-5}	5.5×10^{-5}	4.9×10^{-5}
Turkey DB	2.8×10^{-4}	2.2×10^{-4}	1.8×10^{-4}	1.6×10^{-4}
UNIPEN DB	8.7×10^{-4}	3.6×10^{-4}	3.1×10^{-4}	2.5×10^{-4}

ISRs also increase the prediction accuracy of stroke end point models. Table 6.3 shows that the determinant values of covariances of stroke end point models are reduced constantly as ISR orders increase. They are reduced by 48% on average when ISRs are fully modelled. It also shows that a stroke depends most strongly on the previous stroke because the determinants are reduced most significantly when the order increases from zero to one.

The proposed ISR models have the capability of successfully learning typical stroke relationships. Figure 6.14 shows examples of trained stroke end point models of characters 4 and 5. In the figure, dark points denote the positions of stroke end points and ellipses denote boundaries within one standard deviation from means of point models in the input space. Figure 6.14(a) shows that it learns the stroke relationship mentioned in Section 6.1; the mean of the last stroke end point model, EP_5, moves from

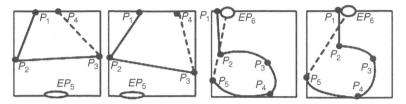

Fig. 6.14. Examples of ISR modelling. Dark point: position of a stroke end point. Ellipse: positions within one standard deviation from the mean of a point model. (a) Relationships of the last point EP_5 with $P_1, \ldots, P_4$ in the character 4. (b) Relationship of the start point of the second pen-down trace, EP_6, with $P_1, \ldots, P_5$ in the character 5.

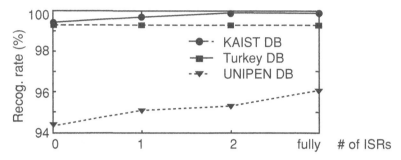

Fig. 6.15. Recognition rates according to the order of ISRs (WSRs: 7).

the centre to the left-hand side when $P_1, \ldots, P_4$ are skewed clockwise. Figure 6.14(b) shows the relationship of the first point P_1 and the start point of the second pen-down trace, EP_6. The mean of EP_6 has the tendency to be located in the right-hand side of P_1. These trained models show relationships coinciding with our concept.

Recognition rates become increased when the ISR order increases in all the DBs (Figure 6.15). When ISRs are fully modelled, they become from 97.7% to 98.5% on average (33% relative recognition errors are reduced).

6.4.4 Comparison to Other Recognition Systems

The performance of the proposed system is compared with other on-line handwriting recognizers. *BN* is the proposed system. WSRs are modelled until the recursion depth is three and ISRs are fully modelled. *HMM1* is the discrete HMM-based recognizer with chain code feature [4]. It post-processes IIMMs outputs with neural network verifiers [10]. The results of *NN* and *HMM2* are from other research groups. *NN* is a recognizer composed of two neural network classifiers [19]; one uses character images and the other uses sequence of points as input features. *HMM2* is based on continuous HMMs and uses various features such as Y coordinate and directions [12]. It has template matching modules for post-processing.

Table 6.4. Comparison of recognition results between recognizers. *BN*: the proposed system

	KAIST DB (%)	Turkey DB (%)	UNIPEN DB (%)	Average (%)
BN	99.9	99.3	96.1	98.5
HMM1	99.2	97.9	94.7	97.3
NN	N/A	97.2	N/A	N/A

Table 6.4 shows that *BN* has a favourably comparable recognition performance to other recognizers, even though it uses only a simple feature-of-point positions. *BN* outperformed *HMM1* over all the DBs. Also, its recognition performance was superior to that of *NN*. For the different partition of training and test sets of UNIPEN DB, *HMM2* showed 96.8%, which cannot be compared directly with ours because the DB is divided into different training and test sets.[3]

In addition to the recognition rate, the recognition speed is also an important measure for real-time interactive response to users. We measured the recognition speeds of *BN* and *HMM1*[4] on IBM ThinkPad T23 with 1.1 GHz CPU. The measurement shows that *BN* and *HMM1* can recognize 84 and 354 characters per second on average, respectively, with less than 100 KB memory size. It suggests that both systems are applicable to many PDAs on the current market even though it is considered that PDAs are usually several times slower than the test computer.

6.4.5 Evaluation of Modelling Capacity by Generation of Characters

To intuitively evaluate the modelling capacity of the proposed system, we generated the most probable characters from the Bayesian network-based character models and compared their shapes with those from HMM-based character models. This is possible because both are generative models. The most probable character can be interpreted as the most representative character pattern that each model has. If a model successfully learns the concept of characters from training data, then it can generate natural shapes and vice versa.

A character is generated from the proposed character model by generating points according to their dependency order. The points without dependencies are generated first. Then, points whose all dependent points are already generated are sequentially generated.

Step 1. Sort all the point models in a character model according to the dependency topology order. Let us denote them as P_is ($i = 1, \ldots, N$).

---

[3] The training and test data set partition information of *HMM2* [12] is not available.

[4] The recognition systems of *NN* and *HMM2* are not available to us.

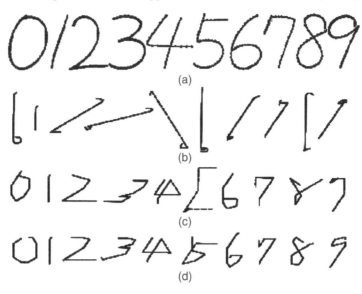

Fig. 6.16. Characters generated from (a) proposed Bayesian network-based models, (b) standard HMMs, (c) duration modelling HMMs and (d) non-stationary HMMs.

Step 2. For $i = 1, \ldots, N$, generate the most probable point instance $O(i)$ from the point model P_i as follows:

$$O(i) = (x, y) = \begin{bmatrix} w_{1,1}, w_{1,2}, \ldots, w_{1,2n+1} \\ w_{2,1}, w_{2,2}, \ldots, w_{2,2n+1} \end{bmatrix} [x_1, y_1, \ldots, x_n, y_n, 1]^T$$

(from (6.8)).

Step 3. Sort $O(i)$s according to their writing order.

The generation algorithms for various kinds of HMMs are found in [21].

Figure 6.16 shows that the proposed character models seem to fit well our concepts of characters. The generated digits have natural shapes; strokes have not only straight but also cursive shapes, and their relationships are natural. On the other hand, digits generated by several kinds of HMMs are not as much natural.[5] In Figure 6.16(b), only one stroke of each character is enlarged unrealistically because stroke lengths are not realistically modelled in standard HMMs. In Figure 6.16(c) and (d), strokes have more realistic lengths but the overall character shapes are not natural because stroke relationships are not explicitly modelled. This result shows the superior modelling capacity of the proposed model.

---

[5] Figure 6.16(b)–(d) are reprinted from [21] with permission of the authors and the publisher.

6.5 Conclusions

In this chapter, we propose a Bayesian network framework for explicitly modelling character components and their relationships. A character model is composed of stroke models with inter-stroke relationships (ISRs). Similarly, a stroke model is composed of point models with within-stroke relationships (WSRs). A point model has a 2D conditional Gaussian distribution for modelling X–Y positions of points. All the models and relationships are represented in a Bayesian network framework, which is useful for modelling dependencies between random variables probabilistically.

WSRs enhance the modelling accuracies of stroke models. A stroke model is composed of point models with covariances. The determinant value of a covariance is a measure of the prediction uncertainty of point positions. It is greatly reduced from the order of 10^{-4} to that of 10^{-9} when seven WSRs are modelled. The enhanced modelling accuracy increases the recognition performance of the system; seven WSRs increase the recognition rates of the system from 83.1% to 98.5% on average, thus reducing 93% relative recognition errors.

ISRs also improve the modelling accuracies of character models. They increase the modelling accuracies of stroke end points; the determinant values of stroke end point models are reduced by 48% on average when ISRs are fully modelled. We also observe that ISR models can learn typical stroke relationships of the characters 4 and 5 by examining a stroke position according to other stroke positions. The fully modelled ISRs improved the recognition rates from 97.7% to 98.5% on average, thus reducing 33% relative recognition errors.

The proposed system shows a favourably comparable recognition performance to other published systems. On three different on-line handwritten digit sets, it shows higher recognition rates than the HMM-based recognizer with chain code features and the neural network-based recognizer with static image and dynamic pen-movement features. From a character generation experiment, we find that it generates characters in more natural shapes than those of various kinds of HMMs; strokes have smooth curvilinear traces with natural stroke relationships. This result comes from the enhanced modelling capacity with WSRs and ISRs.

Our future work is to apply this framework to the recognition of Asian scripts such as Korean and Chinese. The framework is more suitable for them than digits because they are more structural. The scripts have usually straight strokes and strong stroke relationships. One challenging problem is to handle the large number of classes, more than thousands, in those scripts. To remedy the problem, we have studied a hierarchical modelling approach in Korean script by sharing components between characters.

References

1. Cho, S.-J., et al. (2004). Magic wand: a hand-drawn gesture input device in 3-d space with inertial sensors. *Proceedings of the Ninth International Workshop of Frontiers on Handwriting Recognition, Tokyo, Japan*, pp. 106–111.
2. Nathan, K.S., Beigi, H.S.M., Subrahmonia, J., Clary, G.J., and Maruyama, H. (1995). Real-time on-line unconstrained handwriting recognition using statistical methods. *Proceedings of IEEE ICASSP, Detroit, USA, 4*, pp. 2619–2622.
3. Starner, T., Makhoul, J., Schwartz, R., and Chou, G. (1994). On-line cursive handwriting recognition using speech recognition methods. *Proceedings of IEEE ICASSP, Adelaide, Australia, 5*, pp. 125–128.
4. Sin, B.-K. and Kim, J.H. (1997). Ligature modeling for online cursive script recognition. *IEEE Transactions on Pattern Analysis and Machine Intelligence, 19(6)*, pp. 623–633.
5. Jaeger, S., Manke, S., and Waibel, A. (2000). Npen++: an on-line handwriting recognition system. *Proceedings of the Seventh International Workshop of Frontiers on Handwriting Recognition, Amsterdam, The Netherlands*, pp. 249–260.
6. Rabiner, L.R. (1989). A tutorial on hidden markov models and selected applications in speech recognition. *Proceedings of IEEE, 77(2)*, pp. 257–285.
7. Sin, B.-K. and Kim, J.H. (1995). Nonstationary hidden markov model. *Signal Processing, 46(1)*, pp. 31–46.
8. Artieres, T., Marchand, J.-M., Gallinari, P., and Dorizzi, B. (2000). Stroke level modeling of on line handwriting through multi-modal segmental models. *Proceedings of the Seventh International Workshop of Frontiers on Handwriting Recognition, Amsterdam, The Netherlands*, pp. 93–102.
9. Ostendorf, M. (1996). From hmm's to segment models: a unified view of stochastic modeling for speech recognition. *IEEE Transactions on Speech and Audio Processing, 4(5)*, pp. 360–378.
10. Cho, S.-J. and Kim, J.H. (2000). Verification of graphemes using neural networks in hmm-based online Korean handwriting recognition. *Proceedings of the Seventh International Workshop of Frontiers on Handwriting Recognition, Amsterdam, The Netherlands*, pp. 219–228.
11. Kwon, J.O., Sin, B.-K., and Kim, J.H. (1997). Recognition of on-line cursive Korean characters combining statistical and structural method. *Pattern Recognition, 30(8)*, pp. 1255–1263.
12. Hu, J., Lim, S.G., and Brown, M.K. (2000). Writer independent on-line handwriting recognition using an hmm approach. *Pattern Recognition, 33(1)*, pp. 133–147.
13. Kim, H.Y. and Kim, J.H. (2001). Hierarchical random graph representation of handwritten characters and its application to hangul recognition. *Pattern Recognition, 34(2)*, pp. 187–201.
14. Liu, C.-L., Kim, I.J., and Kim, J.H. (2001). Model-based stroke extraction and matching for handwritten Chinese chracter recognition. *Pattern Recognition, 34(12)*, pp. 2339–2352.
15. Kim, I.-J. and Kim, J.H. (2000). Statistical utilization of structural neighborhood information for oriental character recognition. *Proceedings of the Fourth*

International Workshop on Document Analysis Systems, Rio de Janeiro, Brazil, pp. 303–312.

16. Cho, S.-J. and Kim, J.H. (2004). Bayesian network modeling of strokes and their relationships for on-line handwriting recognition. *Pattern Recognition, 37(2)*, pp. 253–264.

17. Jensen, F.V. (1996). *An Introduction to Bayesian Networks.* New York: Springer.

18. Murphy, K.P. (1998). Inference and learning in hybrid bayesian networks. *Technical Report 990, U.C.Berkeley, Department.of Computer Science.*

19. Alimoglu, F. and Alpaydm, E. (1997). Combining multiple representations and classifiers for pen-based handwritten digit recognition. *Proceedings of the Fourth International Conference on Document Analysis and Recognition, Ulm, Germany*, pp. 637–640.

20. Guyon, I., Schomaker, L., Plamondon, R., Liberman, M., and Janet, S. (1994). Unipen project of on-line data exchange and recognizer benchmarks. *Proceedings of the Twelveth International Conference on Pattern Recognition, Jerusalem, Israel*, pp. 29–33.

21. Sin, B.-K. and Kim, J.H. (1998). Network-based approach to Korean handwriting analysis. *International Journal of Pattern Recognition and Artificial Intelligence, 12(2)*, pp. 233–249.

7

New Advances and New Challenges in On-Line Handwriting Recognition and Electronic Ink Management

Eric Anquetil and Guy Lorette

7.1 Introduction

The main goal of this chapter is to make an overview of new advances in on-line handwriting recognition systems, electronic ink management systems, open problems, new challenges and new perspectives.

In the recent years, several papers dealing with surveys or states of the art in on-line handwriting recognition have been published; namely:

- for western languages by Faure and Lecolinet [29], Guyon and Warwick [37], Plamondon [74], Guyon, Schenkel and Denker [36], Plamondon, Lopresti, Schomaker and Srihari [75], Plamondon and Srihari [76]; a study on the question of "handwriting recognition or reading?" has also been proposed by Lorette [54];
- for Chinese by Liu, Jaeger and Nakagawa [51];
- for Japanese by Jaeger, Liu and Nakagawa [41].

During the last years the main new trends in on-line pen-based digital devices were:

- extension of on-line handwriting recognition to the recognition of large or very large vocabularies;
- widening of the domain from on-line handwriting recognition systems to the composition of on-line composite documents containing handwriting, graphics, drawings and symbols;
- ink management in documents, i.e. edition of documents by graphic gestures, annotation of documents;
- more involvement of the HCI community in the domain of pen-based systems.

This chapter is organized as follows. In the first section, the generic architecture of on-line handwriting systems is presented. In the second section, new advances for each module of the recognition process are described more in details. In the third section, electronic ink management systems are highlighted. New pen interface systems, graphic gesture recognition and electronic ink processing are investigated.

7.2 On-Line Handwriting Recognition Systems

7.2.1 Main Features

The use of an on-line handwriting recognition system (HRS) must not be tedious or cumbersome since they are mostly used as part of mobile pervasive computing and facilitate ubiquity. The quality and usability of on-line handwriting recognition systems are conditioned by some main characteristics and constraints:

- the usability of the user interface and its acceptability by the user;
- the necessity of a sufficient value of the initial recognition rate of a writer-independent system. Otherwise, the system would be rejected by any new user;
- an efficient adaptability to each new user;
- the use of a limited amount of data needed to learn a new handwriting style;
- a fast recognition, i.e. a small running time to recognize a character or a cursive word;
- the use of limited computing resources for on-line HRS embedded in handheld or mobile devices.

To date, these features have not always been considered altogether for designing every new device.

7.2.2 General System Architecture

Classically, the general architecture of an on-line HRS consists in a linear succession of stages or modules: acquisition, pre-processing, character and cursive word segmentation, feature extraction, classification and linguistic post processing. The reader interested in it can refer to the previous papers [41,52,75,76] to get more details on the different approaches, methods and processing techniques.

7.3 New Trends in On-Line Handwriting Recognition

7.3.1 Classical vs. New Acquisition Devices

For a wide part, progress in on-line HRS was conditioned by the quality of the input signal acquisition issued from the handwriting. This improvement was achieved through successive advances in hardware equipment. To date, the genealogy tree of on-line handwriting input devices seems to have four branches: digitizing tablets, pen-based systems, digital pen and paper, 3-D devices.

Digitizing Tablets

This is the most important branch of the tree due to the frequency of its uses. At the beginning, the first generation of on-line handwriting acquisition devices was digitizing tablets mainly dedicated to CAD (e.g. Summagraphics). A first progress was accomplished by the suppression of the connecting wire between the pen and the tablet (e.g. Wacom). This enables easier movements of the pen, more natural and thus convenient for handwriting. So, a second generation of input devices was born. But, there was still a problem: the decoupling between the handwriting surface area and the view area on the screen. This forces the user to look alternatively to both of them. Then, a new progress in user interface was the apparition of transparent digitizing tablets, superposed with screen displaying an *electronic ink*. This was a third generation of devices. And to date, *smart displays* and *interactive pen displays* (e.g. Cintiq from Wacom) are examples of such devices with large sizes.

Recently new devices were put on the market to create wide *electronic whiteboards*. These devices are able to detect the pen tip position of a stylus used on a whiteboard and to send these coordinates to a computer. They can also be interactive by the use of a digital projector projecting on the whiteboard an image issued from the computer. Some of them are equipped with an on-line HRS.

Pen-Based Systems

These systems derived from the concept of *Dynabook* first proposed by Kay [45]. The new progress was to associate the previous pen displays with embedded computers leading to pen-based devices of small size such as PDAs (Personal Digital Assistants) or of A4 size such as Tablet PCs. More recently, new devices of A5 format, with a lot of possibilities of communication have been put on the market such as *internet tablets* (e.g. Nokia 770), *webpads* (Tatung), *handtops* (e.g. Dialogue's flybook) and also new *smartphones* (e.g. Ericsson P910, Motorola A728, Nokia 7710, Purplelabs, etc.).

Digital Pen and Paper

Recently another progress consists in re-creating the well known and daily used *pen and paper*. This was done thanks to a digital pen with an embedded camera and a digital paper with invisible small dots printed on it (e.g. Anoto). This new system allows an accurate location of the successive positions of the pen tip.

3D Devices

Only a very few of these devices exists and are still in an experimental state. The handwriting is deduced from the 3D trajectory of the extremity of the input device. For that, a video camera can observe the movement of the pen-tip [18]. Another idea is to enter handwriting by recognizing virtual one-stroke characters directly traced in the air. Cho et al. proposed the Magic Wand, a gesture input device [23,70]. Long et al. proposed a camera based system for detecting the position of the fingertip of the user [53].

What can be observed from these different branches and successive generations of devices is manifold. The on-line handwriting input devices:

- are specifically dedicated to handwriting input;
- permit a more and more natural way of writing;
- are more powerful in terms of computing resources and communication capabilities;
- allow also the input of command orders (pointing, selecting, etc.); drawings and more generally on-line composite documents.

7.3.2 Modelling

Berthilsson proposed to describe characters by parametrized planar curves and their corresponding affine geometric invariants and to use a proximity measurement between invariants for the recognition [10]. This technique is behind the Decuma handwriting recognizer systems. Sternby and Friberg used a graph representation for handwriting [92].

In the case of the HMM paradigm, Artières et al. proposed a stroke level modelling of on-line handwriting [8].

7.3.3 Classification

To improve the performance of handwriting recognizers, it has been proposed to use hybrid recognition systems, e.g. HMM and NN. Systems which reduce the error rate such as SVM have also been used [9,62]. Another approach consists in using soft computing techniques able to make soft decisions instead of crisp decisions. The use of fuzzy recognition systems [6,30], fuzzy NN and Bayesian networks [24,39] occurred.

7.3.4 System Architecture

Instead of a linear succession of modules it has been proposed to use 2-stage [1, 102] or multi-stage recognition systems, either a pre-recognizer and a recognizer stage followed by a discriminating stage [77, 81]. To increase the recognition rate, one possibility is to combine the results of classifier ensembles [99]. The basic assumption at the origin of this approach is that different classifiers will make different kinds of errors and then the combination of their results will decrease the error number.

7.3.5 Linguistic Post-Processing

To date, linguistic post-processing is frequently used [73]. On-line handwriting recognition systems are able to work with large or very large vocabulary [16, 88]. They are able to work in a *close or open vocabulary* mode, depending on their capability to recognize only words appearing in a lexicon or words based on coherent sequences of letters. To overcome the recognizer errors it has been proposed to use linguistic post-processing, i.e. to use lexical, syntactical and semantic context. The simplest way to do lexical post-processing is to use a lexicon and to extract, in a ranked order, the words of the lexicon which are closer to those issued from the recognizer. This is done by string matching between the input word and the lexicon words using a modified Levenshtein distance. New kinds of distance have been proposed, which are much more adapted to the variations observed in handwriting [19, 87]. Compact data structure for representing lexicons has been suggested [50]. Statistical post-processing can be carried out using language models based on N-grams statistics [72, 80].

7.3.6 User Adaptation

Even if writer-independent recognizers are more and more accurate for unconstrained handwriting, they remain error prone. In fact, in the context of real world applications, they have to deal with many different writing styles, and the error rate is still too high for many users. One solution to overcome this limitation is to design adaptation techniques to optimize a writer-independent system by using writer-dependent specialization [93]. The challenge is to produce an *accurate* and *robust* optimization of the system which should be as *fast* and *transparent* as possible for the user, i.e. without requiring a too large amount of training data from the writer. Moreover the adaptation should induce only a little additional memory requirement. Adaptation techniques are strongly connected to the classifier type. We can thus report adaptation works on Time Delay Neural Network (TDNN) [63], on HMM [26], on prototype-based classifier [71, 101] and on Fuzzy Inference System [67].

Two different strategies can be considered. The first one consists in an off-line adaptation using a labelled database [16, 26, 63]. The second one is rather based on a continuous on-line adaptation using characters inputted by the user [67, 71, 101]. The adaptations are carried out either in a supervised or in self-supervised interaction with the user. In the first case, the user labels explicitly the input character. In the second case, the approach is more user-friendly since the labels are automatically deduced by the adaptation system according to the recognition results and the user's actions. From this point of view, adaptation strategies based on prototype-based classifier [71, 101] and on Fuzzy Inference System [67] are really interesting approaches: they offer first solutions to develop adaptation methodologies that are fast, accurate and transparent for the user.

Finally, it is important to mention the key role of user-centered design to develop a graphical user interface to solicit appropriate user feedback during the adaptation cycles [27].

7.3.7 From Off-Line to On-Line and from On-Line to Off-Line Handwriting Recognition

Some attempts have been made to recover a coherent pen trajectory from off-line handwriting [42, 47, 48, 79, 84] allowing the use of an on-line handwriting recognition system to recognize off-line handwritten words. On the reverse side, off-line data issued from a small local image matrix have been used to overcome ambiguities, on t crosses for example, due to variations in the stroke order sequence [40, 100]. Spatial information representation can also be used [61]. Moreover, the use of simultaneous on-line (signal) and off-line (image) data has been proposed to improve the recognition process like in the Quickstroke system [64].

7.4 New Trends in Electronic Ink Management Systems

7.4.1 Pen-Based Applications

In recent years, computer applications that accept pen-based written input have gained attention. Two main elements lead to the development of digital inking systems using pen-based interfaces.

The first one is associated to the mobility and the wireless aspects. Many people need to work away from a desk. This induces the growth of mobile devices like digital assistants (PDAs) and mobile phones (smartphones) that have become widely used consumer products. They must be easy-to-transport and to decrease their size and to fit to the mobility situations, these systems have abandoned the traditional keyboard–mouse couple to a pen-based interaction. Tablet PC and digital pens represent the latest pen-based mobile devices.

There is a growing interest in incorporating all these new mobile devices coupled with a wireless communication into many real applications. Moreover, the mobile, wireless communication aspect of these new devices is enforced by the convenience of pen-based interaction which constitutes the second element that leads to the growing interest of the digital inking system. Pen-based human computer interaction appears to be a very attractive input modality. For many computer applications this interaction is more intuitive and easy-to-use because it is adapted to the application purpose: sketch diagrams design, mathematical formula edition, musical score creation, handwritten note taking, digital document annotation, etc. It reproduces the metaphor of the paper–pen, a medium known by everybody. It makes it possible to use computer systems the way we do with a sheet of paper, drawing on a tactile screen. Such an interaction can increase the applications' user-friendliness and offer an access to these new technologies to a larger public.

Today, pen-based human–computer interfaces are subjected to a strong expansion. Nevertheless to ensure user acceptance of these new digital inking systems and their pen-based interfaces, all recognition and interpretation processes must be enough accurate and robust. Moreover, many industrial feedback have shown the importance of the interface quality even if the associated recognizer reaches good recognition rates. The pen-based interface must be user-friendly, adapted in terms of user cognitive capacities and in terms of acceptability. These conditions allow an optimal use of the system and favor its long-term acceptance. Recognition, interpretation and reading pen-generated input coupled with the design of pen-based interaction and user interface constitute the current and future research challenge to explore all the possibilities of digital inking system.

The three next sections focus on the current research activities on pen-based input techniques and digital inking system.

7.4.2 Digital Ink Annotations of Documents

Paper–pen media is always widely used because of its interesting properties [38]. One of the goals of digital ink systems is to exploit all the good properties of the classical paper–pen medium by also providing new functionalities such as user-friendly editing capabilities, archiving, indexing and retrieval possibilities.

Ink annotations offer facilities to highlight text and to add handwritten notes without necessarily involving a complex handwriting recognition process. Many contexts are studying the advantages of using digital ink to annotate their documents: university classroom to integrate digital ink in lecture presentation [2, 3], web documents [82], digital libraries [59], data visualization [28], etc.

Works on this area are focussing on the ink rendering, storage, retrieval (on-line word spotting) and understanding. About the storage, it is important to mention the emerging Digital Ink Mark-up Language (InkML) standard from W3C. But one of the most important issues is ink understanding in order to semantically associate the ink annotations with the underlying document structure. The topic of these researches is strongly connected with the next two sections.

7.4.3 Interpretation of On-Line Structured Documents

Most of the researches in document analysis have been done for off-line documents (scanned documents): table identification [14], handwriting layout analysis [103, 104], etc. To date, in parallel with the strong expansion of digital inking systems, the first experiences with pen-based applications show that added value to them requires some degree of ink understanding. Therefore, one of the most important research challenges for digital inking systems is the analysis, the recognition, the interpretation and the composition of highly structured handwritten documents. In this context, the interpretation of handwritten drawings is a complex problem. Indeed, such handwritten documents are composed by many elements of various natures: text, graphics, tables, mathematical formulae, diagrams, etc. Moreover a same drawing can have different meanings according to the context in which it has been done, and as a consequence it is necessary to take into account the knowledge of the document in order to interpret it.

To date, we can distinguish several research sub-topics on this complex problem. A first category is focused on a post-recognition often called *lazy interpretation* [68], i.e. occurring only when the handwritten document is finished. Researches on lazy interpretation can address freeform documents for which the first purpose is to discern the elements or the structure from handwritten notes [43, 90, 91]. These researches also deal with the specific natures of handwritten documents such as mathematical expressions [21, 33, 49, 96], diagrams [13, 20, 34, 43, 44, 90, 95], etc.

On the contrary, the second category of research concerns the pen-based interactive composition of the document. The aim is here to design an *eager interpretation*, i.e. occurring while the user is drawing. In this approach the analysis of the user's ink is done on the fly. To design such an interactive pen-based composition of structured documents, information about document composition, i.e. composition rules, structural information, etc. must be modelled. Moreover the performance of the pen-based user interface influences directly the success of the recognition software. This means that it is important to review existing research into Human–Computer Interaction (HCI).[1]

Even if in these two approaches, the problem is to analyze and to interpret the digital ink, the next section shows that the difficulties and the application contexts are not the same.

---

[1] HCI journals: Human–Computer Interaction, ACM Transactions on Computer–Human Interaction, International Journal of Man–Machine Studies, etc.

Lazy Interpretation of Freeform Documents

For lazy interpretation of freeform documents, the document has to be
entirely realized before its recognition so that all the information for its
analysis is available. The document is potentially made of different kinds of
elements, i.e. freeform handwritten notes. The first difficulty is to separate
the ink strokes: text, graphics, table, mathematical formula, etc. The aim is
to be able to group the ink strokes and to send them to the right recognition
system. This 2D segmentation is essential to design a robust interpretation
of the ink even if the only goal is to do an intelligent ink editing (e.g.
deletion, insertion formatting, etc.) without the entire recognition of the
document. Note taking is one of the most interesting pen-based applications
concerned by these researches. Indeed, experiments [91] show that users
prefer not to be constrained by mechanisms to facilitate ink understanding
such as buttons to switch modes or dedicated regions to identify the type of
notes (e.g. text, drawing, etc.). Digital pen is another application context
where lazy interpretation is important to offer to the user an intelligent
editing capacity or the recognition on his desk-computer of the handwritten
documents stored in its digital pen [35].

For distinguishing the nature of the ink strokes that compose freeform
handwritten notes it is necessary to take into account different kinds of
information: characteristics of the strokes but also their relative spatial
and temporal context. Bishop et al. [11] present a method to separate text
from graphics strokes in freeform handwritten notes. They use both intrinsic features of the strokes and information about gaps between them. This
information is modelled by multi-layer perceptrons (MLPs) and then combined with the temporal context using a Hidden Markov Model (HMM)
to represent a sequence of strokes. Shilman et al. [91] present an automatic parsing approach for ink understanding in freeform notes. They
work both on distinguishing text from drawings and on handwritten text
structure analysis to identify words, lines and paragraphs. We can also
mention the works of Jain et al. [43] who use a hierarchical approach to
analyze on-line documents. After the separation of text from drawings,
they exploit a minimum spanning tree based on the distance evaluation
between the drawing strokes to distinguish homogeneous region of tables
or diagrams.

Lazy Interpretation of Specific Kind of Documents

Lazy interpretation of a specific kind of documents is a post-recognition
of the handwritten document knowing its type: text, tables, mathematical
formulas, diagrams, etc. It can also be considered as the second step of the
analysis of a freeform document. After the identification of the different
homogeneous regions, i.e. of the same nature, it is possible to develop a
specific recognition approach to do an interpretation of each region.

When the nature of a document is known, the interpretation involved in the post-recognition often closely depends on it. Many approaches are inspired by off-line document analysis techniques that can be quite easily adapted to this context. Lazy interpretation of an on-line document have some advantages in comparison to the off-line document interpretation: there is no low level segmentation problems specific to the image analysis, i.e. basic strokes segmentation. On-line ink strokes are easily identified by a sequence of points recorded between a pen-down and a pen-up event. Moreover, it is possible to access to the temporal ordering of the points and of the strokes. This additional information provides important knowledge to analysis the ink.

To date, researches focus mostly on three specific applications: handwritten text segmentation, hand-drawn diagrams or sketches recognition and on-line handwritten mathematical expression recognition.

Text segmentation is a classical problem for off-line [60] and on-line handwritten documents analysis [12, 17, 78, 83, 91]. The aim is to understand the structure of writing, i.e. paragraphs, lines and words. For on-line documents, this process is crucial both to achieve accurate recognition but also to be able to offer user-friendly editing functionalities based on the structure understanding of the writing. Several methods are based on histogram projections [83] or on Hough transform methods [78] inspired by off-line approaches. More recent works focus on real-world notes trying to avoid unrealistic constraints. Blanchard and Artières [12] use probabilistic feature grammars to deal with the combinatory of segmentation hypotheses induced by more poorly structured notes. Shilman et al. [91] develop a multi-pass, bottom up layout analysis to generate a hierarchical clustering of the strokes according to words, lines and blocs.

Diagram, sketch and mathematical formula recognition are typically applications where conventional mouse and keyboard editors are unsatisfactory. The pen-based interfaces offer a user-friendly input to express spatial arrangements between composed objects. Moreover many industrial applications expect to perform diagram entry in the field rather than sketching on paper then transcribing that on a desk-computer. These applications characterize very well the problematic of the interpretation of a structured document: it is a two-dimensional analysis problem where the two main issues are segmentation and symbol recognition which often requires a context to be interpreted.

Segmentation, i.e. grouping process or ink parsing, is often considered as a pre-processing step before the step of symbol recognition. Bottom-up approaches are often used to group progressively ink strokes [34]. Ink parsing can be based on compiler techniques, i.e. grammatically based techniques [13, 89]. They are often inspired by visual or extended positional grammars [20, 89] to absorb 2D segmentation. Close approaches base their clustering on inter-stroke distance modelled by minimum-spanning trees [43]. Particular properties of some hand-sketched diagrams can also be exploited to develop a specific segmentation strategy. Kara et al. [44] present a segmentation process driven by the identification of specific anchorage entities, named "markers". They use the pre-recognition of the arrows in the sketch to delimitate the other groups of strokes.

Symbol recognition is a well-known problem [22]. In the context of online sketch and diagram recognition, the most recent approaches are characterized by two goals: to be able to deal with multi-stroke hand-drawn figures and to be invariant to some aspects of the temporal information such as stroke order. Therefore, many techniques use a rendered image of the strokes to extract features invariant to writing order [44, 90].

In some recent approaches segmentation–recognition problems are combined into a same process. Szummer and Qi [95] present an approach based on conditional random fields to deal jointly with segmentation and recognition of hand-drawn diagrams. They exploit both spatial and temporal context. Shilman et al. [90] integrate also in a same process grouping and recognition steps focusing on spatial context. They use proximity graph model coupled with an AdaBoost symbol recognizer.

Eager Interpretation: Interactive Pen-Based Composition

Lazy recognition is a promising approach to offer an unconstraint understanding of ink. But the difficulties to design an automatic parsing approach coupled with a robust hand-drawn shapes recognition system show that it remains an open problem. Eager recognition constitutes another way to consider on-line structured documents. The idea of this approach is to develop an on-line interactive composition of the document. The system interprets the strokes progressively, directly while the user is composing his document and the results of the analysis are displayed on the screen. Consequently, it is possible to exploit all the possibilities of the pen-based interaction. The human–computer interaction implicitly integrates the user in the recognition process: he can validate or reject the interpretations [56]. As a consequence of this validation, the backtracking of the automatic parsing process is reduced. One drawback of such systems comes from the constraints imposed to the user. For example, in the context of musical score editing, a widely use principle is to constrain the user to another way to compose his document [7,32]: he has to learn a particular alphabet to write musical symbols, and does not compose his document the way he does on paper. The advantage of such an approach is to increase the efficiency of the system because the new alphabet is chosen so as to reduce the possible ambiguities.

In fact, contrary to the lazy recognition approaches where all the information for the analysis of the document is available, in a eager recognition process the system has to deal with partial documents and as a consequence with more ambiguities. Many systems have been developed in order to recognize a given kind of on-line structured documents, such as musical scores [7, 32, 65, 69], mathematical formulas [97, 98], etc. They often rely on hand-coded heuristics and cannot be generalized to any kind of structured document. Yet, it turns out that the needs are quite the same for all these applications: driving the recognition process, taking into account the relative positions and the chronological composition of the document elements and dealing with the interaction with the user. Following this idea, Macé et al. [56] proposed a generic method. By formalizing externally the specific knowledge concerning the composition rules of a document, they can easily design the corresponding pen-based system. This approach presents various advantages: it facilitates and speeds up the development of the application, allowing the programmer to focus, in collaboration with specialists of the domain of the application, on other aspects of pen-based interaction, such as usability and user-friendliness. Moreover, the maintenance of the application is simplified.

7.4.4 Design of Handwriting Input for Small-Size Devices

Input methods for small-size devices such as PDA or smartphones are used to enter text on devices which are equipped with a sensitive screen and a pen. In the case of small-size devices, several constraints must be taken into account. From a hardware point of view, the low resources (memory and CPU speed) and the screen size influence the design process. From a use point of view, the input method must suit the user's skill (mainly novice). The design of the pen-based interface must take into account the capacity of the handwriting recognizer to exploit all its possibilities, to deal with its limitation and to offer adapted functionalities to correct its recognition errors.

Handwriting input methods have already been implemented on digital assistants. We show in the next section that today, researches are conducted both on handwriting recognizer performances and on pen-based interfaces to improve the user acceptability.

Handwriting Recognizer for Small-Size Mobile Devices

The hardware constraints of small-size devices and especially for the new ones such as smartphones, often implied the choice of an isolated character recognition system. Indeed, a handwritten cursive word recognizer would currently be more expensive in term of resources to obtain acceptable response time from a user point of view.

We can identify several generations of handwritten character recognizers. The first generation corresponds to the Graphiti®-like recognizers (Graphiti® 1 and 2). Each character or symbol is obtained with a specific shape written in one or two strokes. This simplifies the recognition process by limiting the confusion errors between several similar character shapes. Consequently the recognizer is more robust and needs less computing and memory resources. The disadvantage is that users have to learn the special way to write each character shape. The input methods using Graphiti-like recognizer are relatively efficient for expert users, but not for novice.

The recent generation of handwritten character recognizers offers a more intuitive entry of character. The shape corresponding to a character is not a specific one. They correspond to the Jot®-like interfaces and more recently to the Vision Object MyScript®, the Decuma OnSpot®, Ericsson [55] and the RESIFCar [4,15] input methods.

Ericsson and RESIFCar handwriting input methods are dedicated to smartphone devices: the first one is based on discrete HMMs and the second one on Fuzzy Inference Systems (FIS) [5]. They have been both optimized to be embedded in smartphone. To embed a handwriting recognition system to a real world application, criteria such as compactness, computing time, modularity, adaptation and optimization capacities are extremely important. These criteria are as much important as the performances in term of recognition rate.

Pen-Based Interfaces for Small-Size Mobile Devices

Several studies [31,46,58,85] show that the first generation of input method based on Graphiti®-like recognizers are indeed slower and more error prone than input virtual keyboard. These input methods offer only a character-by-character input, i.e. only one character can be displayed in the input area. Sears and Arora [85] report results for novice users on realistic task: Graffiti users average only 4.95 wpm (words per minute) and jot users average 7.34 wpm.

The latest handwriting input methods offer new pen-based interfaces to improve usability and then the user acceptability. They allow inputting with the entire word context. It means that the previously written characters are not cleared off from the input area until the user request. In consequence, it becomes easy to edit these characters directly in the input area.

The evolution of these input methods has been induced and/or confirmed by researches in ergonomic psychology [57]. For instance, we can mention the problem of the spatial contiguity respect between the information sources [94]. Indeed, the user must switch his attention between the input area and the application area to check if his characters have been correctly recognized. But the user's working memory is limited. This switch causes a share of attention which is negative for user. Moreover, the number of attention areas and the distance between them influence the performances of an input interface (in terms of words per minute) [57].

The management of the available space to write is also very important to improve the data entry rapidity within a very small writing space. Seni [86] have presented a new concept call "TreadMill Ink" to be able to continuously write on the device screen. The electronic ink input is moved automatically from right to left while it is being entered. In the same way, Bouteruche et al. [15] point out some important principles to take into account to design a small-size pen-based handwriting input interfaces.

Even if recognition engines work better and better, they remain error-prone. Thus the improvement of user-based edition and error correction is essential for acceptance. The latest evolutions of handwriting input methods offer edit gestures to correct, to delete or to make diacritics. They can be considered as "digital ink micro-editor" that should improve the long-term acceptance of these new pen-based input methods [15].

7.5 Conclusion, Open Problems and New Challenges

In the recent years, some progresses and novelties can be noticed in the on-line handwriting acquisition devices from smaller ones (smartphones) to biggest ones (whiteboards) and also interactive pen displays. These new devices have required the design of new human–computer interfaces and also of dedicated recognition systems.

Multi-stage architectures, new recognizers, linguistic post-processing and user adaptation have been proposed to improve the performance of on-line handwriting recognition systems. A first step towards the convergence and complementarities of on-line and off-line handwriting recognition has also been accomplished.

For training and testing on-line handwriting recognition systems, a lot of databases are now available (Unipen, ICROW-2003, SamPDA, Hands-xxx from TUAT, IRONOFF, IAM On-Line). Artificial data generation can be done also by simulators. For example, virtual off-line characters are synthesized from on-line characters [66] or writer-dependent on-line handwriting can be generated [25].

Recently, a renew of interest has occurred concerning the biometric applications of on-line handwriting, namely for writer authentication and signature verification. The domain was also enlarged to pen input interfaces and ink management systems. Moreover, the new idea of on-line construction and understanding of composite documents has emerged. Off-line approach (lazy learning) and on-line approach (eager learning) are still in progress. But the total automatic interpretation of a composite structured document input on-line using a pen-based interface is still an open problem and a challenge.

The replacement of the classic keyboard and mouse devices by pen interfaces for a lot of applications is still in its infancy, but it seems necessary to assume a large success to the mobile and pervasive computing and communicating devices. So, a lot of research work is still needed to reproduce the paper–pen metaphor with the augmented functionalities provided by electronics.

References

1. Alpaydin, E., Kaynak, C., and Alimoglu, F. (2000). Cascading multiple classifiers and representations for optical and pen-based handwritten digit recognition. *Proceedings of the Seventh International Workshop on Frontiers in Hand-Writing Recognition (IWFHR), Amsterdam*, pp. 453–462.
2. Anderson, R. et al. (2004). Experiences with a tablet PC based lecture presentation system in computer science courses. *Proceedings of the 35th SIGCSE Technical Symposium on Computer Science Education*. Norfolk, VA, USA: ACM Press, pp. 56–60.
3. Anderson, R.J., Hoyer, C., Wolfman, S.A., and Anderson, R. (2004). A study of digital ink in lecture presentation. Proceedings of the SIGCHI Conference on Human Factors in Computing Systems. Vienna, Austria: ACM Press, pp. 567–574.
4. Anquetil, E. and Bouchereau, H. (2002). Integration of an on-line handwriting recognition system in a smart phone device. *Sixteenth ICPR International Conference on Pattern Recognition (ICPR'2002)*, pp. 192–195.
5. Anquetil, E. and Lorette, G. (1996). Automatic generation of hierarchical fuzzy classification systems based on explicit fuzzy rules deduced from possibilistic clustering: application to on-line handwritten character recognition. *Sixth Information Proceedings and Management of Uncertainty in Knowledge-Based Systems (IPMU'96)*, pp. 259–264.
6. Anquetil, E. and Lorette, G. (1997). On-line handwriting character recognition system based on hierarchical qualitative fuzzy modeling. *Progress in Handwriting Recognition*. New York: World Scientific, pp. 109–116.
7. Anstice, J., Bell, T., Cockburn, A., and Setchell, M. (1996). The design of a pen-based musical input system. *Proceedings of the Sixth Australian Conference on Computer–Human Interaction (OZCHI 1996)*, pp. 260–267.
8. Artières, T., Marchand, J.M., and Gallinari, P. (2000). Stroke level modeling of on line handwriting trough multi-modal segmental models. *Proceedings of the Seventh International Workshop on Frontiers in Handwriting Recognition, Amsterdam*, pp. 93–102.
9. Bahlmann, C., Haasdonk, B., and Burhardt, H. (2002). On-line handwriting recognition with support vector machines – a kernel approach. *Proceedings of the Eighth International Workshop on Frontiers in Handwriting Recognition (IWFHR), Niagara on the Lake*, pp. 49–54.
10. Berthilsson, R. (2000). Character recognition using shape for curves. *Proceedings of the International Conference on Pattern Recognition*, pp. 2227–2230.
11. Bishop, C.M., Svensen, M., and Hinton, G.E. (2004). Distinguishing text from graphics in on-line handwritten ink. *Ninth Workshop on Frontiers in Handwriting Recognition (IWFHR'04), Tokyo, Japan*, pp. 142–147.
12. Blanchard, J. and Artières, T. (2004). On-line handwritten document segmentation. IWFHR'04: *Proceedings of the Ninth International Workshop on Frontiers in Handwriting Recognition*, pp. 148–153.
13. Blostein, D., Cordy, J.R., and Zanibbi, R. (2002). Applying compiler techniques to diagram recognition. *ICPR'02: Proceeding of the Sixteenth IAPR International Conference on Pattern Recognition*, pp. 123–126.

14. Blostein, D., Cordy, J.R., and Zanibbi, R. (2004). A survey of table recognition: models, observations, transformations, and inferences. *International Journal on Document Analysis and Recognition, 7(1)*, pp. 1–16.
15. Bouteruche, F., Deconde, G., Anquetil, E., and Jamet, E. (2005). Design and evaluation of handwriting input interfaces for small-size mobile devices. *Workshop of HCI'2005: Improving and Assessing Pen-Based Input Techniques, Edinburgh.*
16. Brakensiek, A., Kosmala, A., and Rigoll, G. (2001). Comparing adaptation techniques for on-line handwriting recognition. *Sixth ICDAR*, pp. 486–490.
17. Bruzzone, E. and Coffetti, M. (1999). An algorithm for extracting cursive text lines. *Fifth International Conference on Document Analysis and Recognition (ICDAR'99), Bangalore, India*, pp. 749–752.
18. Bunke, H., Siebenthal, T.V., Yamasaki, T., and Schenkel, M. (1999). On-line handwriting data acquisition using a video camera. *Proceedings of the Fifth International Conference on Document Analysis and Recognition, ICDAR'99, Bangalore*, pp. 573–576.
19. Carbonnel, S. and Anquetil, E. (2004). Lexicon organization and string edit distance learning for lexical post-processing in handwriting recognition. *Ninth International Workshop on Frontiers in Handwriting Recognition (IWFHR 9), Tokyo, Japan*, pp. 462–467.
20. Castagliola, G., Deufemia, V. (2003). Visual language editor based on LR parsing technologies. *IWPT'03: Eighth International Workshop on Parsing Technologies.* Berlin: Springer, pp. 79–90.
21. Chan, K.-F. and Yeung, D.-Y. (2001). PenCalc: a novel application of on-line mathematical expression recognition technology. *ICDAR'01: International Conference on Document Analysis and Recognition*, pp. 774–778.
22. Chhabra, A.K. (1997). Graphic symbol recognition: an overview. In: K. Trombre, A.K. Chhabra (Eds.). Selected Papers from the *Second International Workshop on Graphics Recognition, Algorithms and Systems.* Berlin: Springer, pp. 68–79.
23. Cho, S.-J. et al. (2004). Magic wand: a hand-drawn gesture input device in 3-D space with inertial sensors. *IWFHR'04: Proceedings of the Ninth International Workshop on Frontiers in Handwriting Recognition*, pp. 106–111.
24. Cho, S.-J. and Kim, J. (2003). Bayesian network modeling of Hangul characters for on-line handwriting recognition. *Proceedings of the Seventh International Conference on Document Analysis and Recognition (ICDAR), Edinburgh*, pp. 207–211.
25. Choi, H., Cho, S.J., and Kim, J. (2004). Writer dependent online handwriting generation with Bayesian network. *Proceedings of the Ninth International Workshop on Frontiers in handwriting Recognition (IWFHR), Tokyo*, pp. 130–135.
26. Connell, S.D. and Jain, A.K., (2002). Writer adaptation for online handwriting recognition. *IEEE Transaction on Pattern Analysis and Machine Intelligence, 24(3)*, pp. 329–346.
27. Dziadosz, S., Helfrich, A., Citron, R., and Lund, A. (2005). Designing a user-driven method to improve handwriting recognition on a tablet PC. *Workshop of HCI'2005, Improving and Assessing Pen-Based Input Techniques, Edinburgh.*

28. Ellis, S.E. and Groth, D.P. (2004). A collaborative annotation system for data visualization. *Proceedings of the Working Conference on Advanced Visual Interfaces.* Gallipoli, Italy: ACM Press, pp. 411–414.

29. Faure, C. and Lecolinet, E. (1998). Survey of the state of the art in human language technology. C.R.A. Eds et al. (Eds.). Cambridge: Cambridge University Press, pp. 70–73.

30. Fitzgerald, J., Geiselbrechtinger, F., and Kechadi, T. (2004). Application of fuzzy logic to online recognition of handwritten symbols. *Proceedings of the Ninth International Workshop on Frontiers in Handwriting Recognition, Tokyo,* pp. 395–400.

31. Fleetwood, M.D. et al. (2002). An evaluation of text-entry in palm os – graffiti and the virtual keyboard. *Proceedings of the Human Factors and Ergonomics Society Fourty-Sixth Annual Meeting (HFES'02), Baltimore,* pp. 617–621.

32. Forsberg, A., Dieterich, M., and Zeleznik, R. (1998). The music notepad. *Proceedings of the Eleventh ACM Symposium on User Interface Software and Technology (UIST'98), San Francisco, USA,* pp. 203–210.

33. Garain, U. and Chaudhuri, B.B. (2004). Recognition of online handwritten mathematical expressions. *IEEE Transactions on Systems, Man and Cybernetics – Part B, 34(6),* pp. 2366–2376.

34. Gross, M.D. (1994). Recognizing and *Interpreting Diagrams in Design. Proceedings of the Second Workshop on Advanced Visual Interfaces (AVI'94), Bari,* pp. 88–94.

35. Guimbretière, F. (2003). Paper augmented digital documents. *Proceedings of the Sixteenth Annual ACM Symposium on User Interface Software and Technology.* Vancouver, Canada: ACM Press, pp. 51–60.

36. Guyon, I., Schenkel, M., and Denker, J. (1997). In: H. Bunke (Eds.). *Handbook of Character Recognition and Document Image Analysis.* Singapore: World Scientific, pp. 183–225.

37. Guyon, I. and Warwick, C. (1998). In: C.R.A. Eds et al. (Eds.). *Survey of the State of the Art in Human Language Technology.* Cambridge: Cambridge University Press, pp. 73–77.

38. Hsu, R.C. and Mitchell, W.E. (1997). After 400 years, print is still superior. *Communications of the ACM, 40(10),* pp. 27–28.

39. Htwe, S.M., Higgins, C., Leedham, G., and Yang, M. (2005). Tranliteration of online handwritten Phonetic Pitman's shorthand with the use of a Bayesian network. *Proceedings of the Eighth International Conference on Document Analysis and Recognition (ICDAR), Seoul,* pp. 1090–1094.

40. Jaeger, S. (2000). On the complexity of Cognition. *Proceedings of the Seventh International Workshop on Frontiers in Handwriting Recognition (IWFHR), Amsterdam,* pp. 291–302.

41. Jaeger, S., Liu, C.L., and Nakagawa, M. (2003). The state of the art in Japanese online handwriting recognition compared to techniques in western handwriting recognition. *International Journal on Document and Analysis Recognition, 6(2),* pp. 75–88.

42. Jaeger, S, Manke S, and Waibel, A. (2000). NPEN++: an on-line handwriting recognition system. *Proceedings of the Seventh International Workshop on Frontiers in Handwriting Recognition (IWFHR), Amsterdam,* pp. 249–260.

43. Jain, A.K., Namboodiri, A.M., and Subrahmonia, J. (2001). Structure in on-line documents. *Sixth International Conference on Document Analysis and Recognition (ICDAR'01), Seattle, USA*, pp. 844–848.
44. Kara, L.B. and Stahovich, T.F. (2004). Hierarchical parsing and recognition of hand-sketched diagrams. *Proceedings of the Seventeenth ACM Symposium on User Interface Software and Technology (UIST'04), Santa Fe*, pp. 13–22.
45. Kay, A. and Goldberg, A. (1977). Personal dynamic media. *IEEE Computer, 10(3)*, pp. 31–41.
46. Költringer, T. and Grechenig, T. (2004). Comparing the immediate usability of graffiti 2 and virtual keyboard. *Proceedings of the Eleventh Conference on Human Factors in Computing Systems (CHI'04), Vienna, Austria*, pp. 1175–1178.
47. Lallican, P., Viard-Gaudin, C., and Knerr, S. (2000). From off-line to on-line handwriting recognition. *Proceedings of the Seventh International Workshop on Frontiers in Handwriting Recognition, IWFHR'2000, Amsterdam*, pp. 303–312.
48. Lau, K., Yuen, P., and Tang, Y. (2003). Recovery of writing sequence of static images of handwriting using uwm. *Proceedings of the Seventh International Conference on Document Analysis and Recognition (ICDAR), Edinburgh*, pp. 1123–1127.
49. LaViola, J.J. and Zeleznik, R.C. (2004). MathPad2: a system for the creation and exploration of mathematical sketches. *ACM Transactions on Graphics, 23(3)*, pp. 432–440.
50. Lifchitz, A. and Maire, F. (2000). A fast lexically constrained viterbi algorithm for on-line handwriting recognition. *Proceedings of the Seventh International Workshop on Frontiers in Handwriting Recognition, Amsterdam*, pp. 313–322.
51. Liu, C.L., Jaeger, S., and Nakagawa, M. (2004). Online recognition of chinese characters: the state-of-the-art. *IEEE Transactions on Pattern Analysis and Machine Intelligence, 26(2)*, pp. 198–213.
52. Liu, C.L., Jäger, S., and Nakagawa, M. (2004). Online recognition of Chinese characters: the state-of-the-art. *IEEE Transactions on Pattern Analysis and Machine Intelligence, 26(2)*, pp. 198–213.
53. Long, T. and Jin, L.-W. (2005). Hybrid recognition for one stroke style cursive handwriting characters. *Proceedings of the Eighth International Conference on Document Analysis and Recognition (ICDAR)*, pp. 232–236.
54. Lorette, G. (1999). Handwriting recognition or reading? What is the situation at the dawn of the 3rd millenium? *IJDAR, 2(1)*, pp. 2–12.
55. Loudon, G., Pellijff, O., Zhong-Wei, L., and Hall, H. (2000). A method for handwriting input and correction on smartphones. *Proceedings of the Seventh International Workshop on Frontiers in Handwriting Recognition (IWFHR'00)*, pp. 481–485.
56. Macé, S., Anquetil, E., and Coüasnon, B. (2005). A generic method to design pen-based systems for structured document composition: development of a musical score editor. *Proceedings of the First Workshop on Improving and Assessing Pen-Based Input Techniques, Edinburgh*, pp. 15–22.
57. MacKenzie, I.S. and Soukoreff, R.W. (2002). Text entry for mobile computing: models and methods, theory and practice. *Human–Computer Interaction, 17*, pp. 47–198.

58. MacKenzie, I.S. and Zhang, S.X. (1997). The immediate usability of graffiti. *Proceedings of the Conference on Graphics Interface'97*. Toronto, Ont., Canada: Canadian Information Processing Society, pp. 129–137.

59. Marshall, C., Price, M., Golovchinsky, G., and Schilit, B.N. (1999). Introducing a digital library reading appliance into a reading group. *Proceedings of the Fourth ACM Conference on Digital Libraries*. Berkeley, California, USA: ACM Press, pp. 77–84.

60. Marti, U.V. and Bunke, H. (2001). Text line segmentation and word recognition in a system for general writer independent handwriting recognition. *Sixth International Conference on Document Analysis and Recognition (ICDAR'01), Seattle, USA*, pp. 159–163.

61. Marukatat, S. and Artières, T. (2004). Handling spatial information in on-line handwriting recognition. *Proceedings of the Ninth International Workshop on Frontiers in Handwriting Recognition (IWFHR), Tokyo*, pp. 14–19.

62. Maruyama, K.-I., Maruyama, M., Miyao, H., and Nakano, Y. (2002). Hand-printed Hiragana recognition using support vector machines. *Proceedings of the Eighth International Workshop on Frontiers in Handwriting Recognition (IWFHR), Niagara on the Lake*, pp. 55–60.

63. Matic, N., Guyon, I., Denker, J., and Vapnik, V. (1993). Writer-adaptation for on-line handwritten character recognition. *ICDAR93*, pp. 187–191.

64. Matic, N., Platt, J., and Wang, T. (2002). QuickStroke: an incremental on-line Chinese handwriting recognition system. *Proceedings of the Seventeenth International Conference on Pattern Recognition (ICPR), Quebec*, pp. 435–439.

65. Miyao, H. and Maruyama, M. (2004). An online handwritten music score recognition system. *Proceedings of the Seventeenth International Conference on Pattern Recognition (ICPR'2004)*. Washington, DC, USA: IEEE Computer Society, pp. 461–464.

66. Miyao, H., Maruyama, M., Nakano, Y., and Hananoi, T. (2005). Off-line handwritten character recognition by SVM based on the virtual examples synthesized from on-line characters. *Proceedings of the Eighth International Conference on Document Analysis and Recognition (ICDAR), Seoul*, pp. 494–498.

67. Mouchère, H., Anquetil, E., and Ragot, N. (2005). On-line writer adaptation for handwriting recognition using fuzzy inference systems. *Proceedings of the Eighth International Conference on Document Analysis and Recognition (ICDAR)*. Seoul, Korea: IEEE Computer Society, pp. 1075–1079.

68. Nakagawa, M., Machii, K., Kato, N., and Souya T. (1993). Lazy recognition as a principle of pen interfaces. *Proceedings of the Conference Companion on Human Factors in Computing Systems (INTERACT'93 and CHI'93)*. New York, NY, USA: ACM Press, pp. 89–90.

69. Ng, E., Bell, T., and Cockburn, A. (1998). Improvements to a pen-based musical input system. *Proceedings of the Eighth Australasian Conference on Computer Human Interaction (OZCHI'98)*. Washington, DC, USA: IEEE Computer Society, pp. 178–185.

70. Oh, J.K., et al. (2004). Inertial sensor based recognition of 3-D character gestures with an ensemble of classifiers. *Proceedings of the Ninth International Workshop on Frontiers in Handwriting Recognition (IWFHR'04)*. Washington, DC, USA: IEEE Computer Society, pp. 112–117.

71. Oudot, L., Prevost, L., Moises, A., and Milgram, M. (2004). Self-supervised adaptation for on-line text recognition. *Ninth International Workshop on Frontiers in Handwriting Recognition (IWFHR'04)*, pp. 9–13.

72. Perraud, F., Viard-Gaudin, C., Morin, E., and Lallican, P.-M. (2003). N-gram and N-class models for on line handwriting recognition. *Seventh International Conference on Document Analysis and Recognition (IC-DAR'03)*, pp. 1053–1057.

73. Pitrelli, J.F. and Ratzlaff, E.H. (2000). Quantifying the contribution of language modeling to write-independent on-line handwriting recognition. *Proceedings of the Seventh International Workshop on Frontiers in Handwriting Recognition (IWFHR), Amsterdam*, pp. 383–392.

74. Plamondon, R. (1998). In: R.A. Cole, et al. (Eds.). *Survey of the State of the Art in Human Language Technology.* Cambridge: Cambridge University Press, pp. 77–81.

75. Plamondon, R., Lopresti, D., Schomaker, L. and Srihari, R. (1999). Wiley Encyclopedia of Electrical and Electronics Engineering. Eds WJ (ed) Wiley. pp. 123–146.

76. Plamondon, R. and Srihari, S. (2000). On-line and off-line handwriting recognition: a comprehensive survey. *IEEE Transactions on Pattern Analysis and Machine Intelligence, 22(1)*, pp. 63–84.

77. Prevost, L., Michel-Sendis, C., Moises, A., Oudot, L., and Milgram, M. (2003). Combining model-based and discriminative classifiers: application to handwritten character recognition. *Proceedings of the Seventh International Conference on Document Analysis and Recognition (ICDAR), Edinburgh*, pp. 31–35.

78. Pu, Y. and Shi, Z. (1998). A natural learning algorithm based on Hough transform for text lines extraction in handwritten documents. *Proceedings of the sixth International Workshop on Frontiers in Handwriting Recognition (IWFHR'98), Taejon, Korea*, pp. 637–646.

79. Qiao, Y., Nishhizra, M., and Yasuhara, M. (2005). A novel approach to recover writing order from single stroke offline handwritten images. *Proceedings of the Eighth International Conference on Document Analysis and Recognition (ICDAR), Seoul*, pp. 227–231.

80. Quiniou, S., Anquetil, E., and Carbonnel, S. (2005). Statistical language models for on-line handwritten sentence recognition. *Proceedings of the Eighth International Conference on Document Analysis and Recognition (ICDAR'05), Seoul, Korea*, pp. 516–520.

81. Ragot, N. and Anquetil, E. (2003). A generic hybrid classifier based on hiearchical fuzzy modeling: experiments on on-line handwritten character recognition. *Proceedings of the Seventh International Conference on Document Analysis and Recognition (ICDAR), Edinburgh*, pp. 963–967.

82. Ramachandran, S. and Kashi, R. (2003). An architecture for ink annotations on web documents. *Seventh International Conference on Document Analysis and Recognition (ICDAR'03)*, p. 256.

83. Ratzlaff, E.H. (2000). Inter-line distance estimation and text line extraction for unconstrained online handwriting. *Seventh International Workshop on Frontiers in Handwriting Recognition (IWFHR'00), Amsterdam, The Netherland*, pp. 33–42.

84. Rousseau, L., Anquetil, E., and Camillerapp, J. (2005). Recovery of a drawing order from off-line isolated letters dedicated to online recognition. *Proceedings of the Eighth International Conference on Document Analysis and Recognition (ICDAR), Seoul*, pp. 1121–1125.

85. Sears, A. and Arora, R. (2002). Data entry for mobile devices: an empirical comparison of novice performance with Jot and Graffiti. *Interacting with Computers, 14*, pp. 413–433.

86. Seni, G. (2002). TreadMill Ink – enabling continuous pen input on small devices. *Proceedings of the Eighth International Workshop on Frontiers in Handwriting Recognition (IWFHR'02), Ontario, Canada*, pp. 215–220.

87. Seni, G., Kripasundar, V., and Srihari, R.K. (1996). Generalizing edit distance to incorporate domain information: handwritten text recognition as a case study. *Pattern Recognition, 29*, pp. 405–414.

88. Seni, G., Srihari, R.K., and Nasrabadi, N. (1996). Large vocabulary recognition of on-line handwritten cursive words. *IEEE Transactions on PAMI, 18(7)*, pp. 757–762.

89. Shilman, M., Pasula, H., Russell, S., and Newton, R. (2002). Statistical visual language models for ink parsing. *AAAI Spring Symposium*, pp. 126–132.

90. Shilman, M., Viola, P., and Chellapilla, K. (2004). Recognition and grouping of handwritten text in diagrams and equations. *Ninth International Workshop on Frontiers in Handwriting Recognition (IWFHR'04), Tokyo, Japan*, pp. 569–574.

91. Shilman, M., Wei, Z., Raghupathy, S., Simard, P., and Jones, D. (2003). Discerning structure from freeform handwritten notes. *Seventh International Conference on Document Analysis and Recognition (ICDAR'03), Edinburgh, Scotland*, pp. 60–65.

92. Sternby, J. and Friberg, C. (2005). The recognition graph-language independent adaptable on-line cursive script recognition. *Proceedings of the Eighth International Conference on Document Analysis and Recognition (ICDAR)*, pp. 14–18.

93. Subrahmonia, J. (2000). Similarity measures for writer clustering. *Proceedings of the Seventh International Workshop on Frontiers in Handwriting Recognition (IWFHR), Amsterdam*, pp. 541–546.

94. Sweller, J. and Chandler, P. (1991). Evidence for cognitive load theory. *Cognition and Instruction, 8*, pp. 351–362.

95. Szummer, M. and Qi, Y. (2004). Contextual recognition of hand-drawn shapes with conditional random fields. *Proceedings of the Ninth International Workshop on Frontiers in Handwriting Recognition (IWFHR'04), Tokyo, Japan*, pp. 32–37.

96. Tapia, E. and Rojas, R. (2003). Recognition of on-line handwritten mathematical expressions using a minimum spanning tree construction and symbol dominance. *Proceedings of the Fifth IAPR International Workshop on Graphics Recognition (GREC'03), Barcelona, Catalonia, Spain*, pp. 329–340.

97. Thimbleby, W. (2004). A novel pen-based calculator and its evaluation. *Proceedings of the Third Nordic Conference on Human–Computer Interaction (NordiCHI'04)*. Tampere, Finland: ACM Press, pp. 445–448.

98. Toyozumi, K., Mori, K., Suenaga, Y., and Suzuki, T. (2001). A system for real-time recognition of handwritten mathematical formulas. *Proceedings of the Sixth International Conference on Document Analysis and Recognition (ICDAR'01), Seattle, WA, USA*, pp. 1059–1064.

99. Velek, O., Jaeger, S., and Nakagawa, M. (2002). A new warping technique for normalizing likelihood of multiple classifiers and its effectiveness in combined on-line/off-line Japanese character recognition. *Proceedings of the Eighth International Workshop on Frontiers in Handwriting Recognition (IWFHR), Niagara on the Lake*, pp. 177–182.

100. Vinciarelli, A. (2003). Combining online and offline handwriting recognition. *Proceedings of the Seventh International Conference on Document Analysis and Recognition (ICDAR), Edinburgh*, pp. 844–848.
101. Vuori, V. (2002). Adaptive Methods for On-Line Recognition of Isolated Handwritten Characters. Helsinki University of Technology.
102. Vuurpijl, L. and Schomaker, L. (2000). Two-stage character classification: a combined approach of clustering and support vector classifiers. *Proceedings of the Seventh International Workshop on Frontiers in Handwriting Recognition (IWFHR), Amsterdam*, pp. 423–432.
103. Zheng, Y., Li, H., and Doermann, D. (2004). Machine printed text and handwriting identification in noisy document images. *IEEE Transactions on Pattern Analysis and Machine Intelligence, 26(3)*, pp. 337–353.
104. Zheng, Y., Li, H., and Doermann, D. (2002). The segmentation and identification of handwriting in noisy document images. *Proceedings of the Fifth International Workshop on Document Analysis Systems (DAS'02)*. London, UK: Springer-Verlag, pp. 95–105.

8

Off-Line Roman Cursive Handwriting Recognition

Horst Bunke and Tamás Varga

8.1 Introduction

Automatic handwriting recognition has been a subject of research for more than 40 years [84]. On the one hand, the reading of human handwriting by machine has been considered an interesting and intellectually challenging problem in its own right. To approach, or even surpass, the performance of humans in text recognition has been a major driving force behind many research activities. On the other hand, the field has been quite important from the commercial and application-oriented point of view. Automatic address reading [88], bank cheque processing [43], and recognition of text filled in by hand on forms [25, 102, 105] have been major challenges in automatic handwriting recognition research. Moreover, handwritten data have often been used to validate and test the performance of new pattern classification methods.

Since the beginning of the 1990s, a significant growth of activities in handwriting recognition research has been observed. There is no doubt that enormous progress has taken place in this area. For example, for the tasks of handwritten address reading and amount recognition on bank cheques, commercial systems have become available [26]. Nevertheless, there is a clear need to further develop the field. All successful applications, for example, address and cheque reading, work in narrow domains with limited vocabularies, where task-specific knowledge and constraints are available. Examples are the relation between zip code and city name in address reading, or the redundancy of courtesy and legal amount on a cheque. However, when it comes to general word or sentence recognition where no constraints exist and one is faced with a large, possibly open lexicon, the state of the art is quite limited and recognition rates are rather low. Yet the problem of unconstrained word and sentence recognition is important in a number of future applications, for example, the transcription of personal notes, faxes and letters, or the electronic conversion of historical handwritten archives in the context of the creation of digital libraries [4].

The field of handwriting recognition can be divided into on-line and off-line recognition. In the current chapter, we focus our attention on off-line recognition and consider only roman script. On-line handwriting recognition is the topic of Chapters 6 and 7, and for scripts other than roman see Chapters 3–5 and 10 in this book. Recent surveys on roman script recognition are [8, 72, 89, 96].

This chapter is organized as follows. In Section 8.2, the state of the art in roman cursive handwriting recognition is reviewed, including pre-processing of document images, and recognition of isolated characters or digits, individual words and unconstrained text. A few emerging topics such as databases for handwriting recognition, synthetic training data and multiple classifier systems are discussed in Section 8.3. Finally, Section 8.4 provides some conclusions and an outlook for future work.

8.2 Methodology

Roman cursive handwriting recognition can be divided into the tasks of recognizing isolated characters or digits, individual words and unconstrained text consisting of a sequence of an a priori unknown number of words. Recognition of isolated characters and digits is by far the simplest problem for which mature solutions have become available. The other two problems, word and word sequence recognition, are considerably more difficult and are still subject to research. In this section, we first review methods of text image pre-processing and normalization that are commonly found in any of the three tasks mentioned above. Subsequently, the recognition of isolated characters and digits, individual words and sequences of words is discussed.

8.2.1 Document Image Pre-processing

In the off-line mode an image of the handwriting to be recognized is captured by a sensor, for example, a scanner or a camera. Traditionally, the first processing step consists in converting the grey-level image acquired by the sensor to a binary image. A number of algorithms for this step are known from the literature (see Chapter 2 of [69], for example). However, with increasing processing speed and memory capacity of modern computers, the direct use of grey-level images is becoming increasingly more popular.

Before or after binarization, images are often filtered to remove noise. Popular methods of noise removal in both binary and grey-level images are based on image filtering theory and mathematical morphology (see [34], for example).

Very often, the paper document is not perfectly aligned with the coordinate system of the scanner. To recover from artefacts of this kind, skew correction methods are applied. Methods for skew angle estimation are based on horizontal projection profiles, the handwriting's contour and other quantities [5, 59, 68].

In many applications, there are no constraints imposed on the writing instrument. Consequently, there is considerable variation in stroke width across different input samples. To normalize the handwriting, thinning or skeletonization methods are often applied. The aim of these methods is to normalize the width of each stroke to one pixel, while maintaining the topology of the patterns under consideration (for details see [90], for example).

A feature that varies from one individual writer to another is the slant of the handwriting. Training a classifier on writing that has not been slant corrected may require significantly more effort and training data. Consequently, slant removal is an operation that is found in almost any handwriting recognition system. Methods for slant estimation are dependent on the considered task. For isolated character and digit recognition, often the angle of the principle axis is used as an estimation [35]. For word or word sequence recognition, it is common to approximate the handwriting's contour by straight line segments and use the average or median direction of these straight segments as an estimate of the slant [10, 98]. An example of slant correction is shown in Figure 8.1.

8.2.2 Recognition of Isolated Characters

The task of isolated character recognition is usually cast as a pattern classification problem, where an unknown input pattern is to be assigned to one out of a number of given classes. Most approaches to isolated character recognition follow the traditional paradigm of pattern recognition. There are three main processing steps carried out in sequential order, namely, pre-processing and normalization, feature extraction and classification. Typical pre-processing and normalization steps have been described in Section 8.2.1.

A large number of features for isolated character recognition and corresponding extraction methods have been proposed in the literature. They

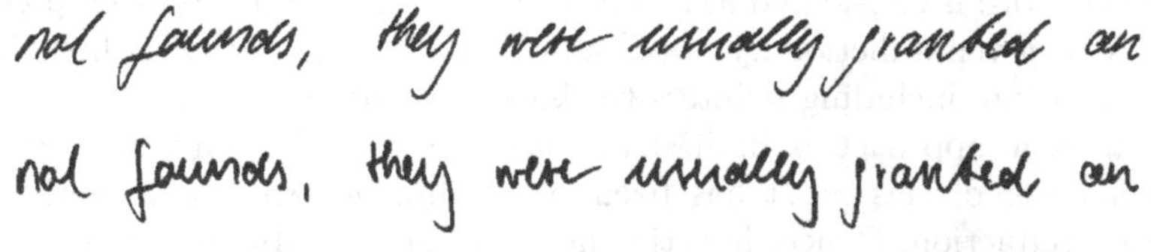

Fig. 8.1. Example of slant correction. The original text line is above, while its slant corrected version is below.

include moments and quantities derived from series expansion (see Chapter 7 in [67]), features based on projection profiles and on the contour [35], as well as structural features such as endpoints, fork points, holes, length, shape or curvature of individual strokes that occur as part of the character under consideration [91]. Also features extracted via principal component analysis from the set of pixels in an image [21] and the raw pixel matrix have been used.

Once a feature vector has been extracted from the image of a handwritten character, it is fed into a classifier. Pattern classification has a long history and almost all generic classifiers that were proposed at some time have been applied to isolated character recognition. Concrete examples include nearest- or k-nearest-neighbour classifier [35], Bayes classifier [81], polynomial classifier [21], neural network [35, 53] and support vector machine [1]. Also structural classifiers that use string or graph representations of the characters to be classified have been proposed (see Chapters 12 and 13 in [67], and [15, 58], for example).

8.2.3 Cursive Word Recognition

One possible approach to word recognition is to segment the given input word into a sequence of characters and then recognize each individual character using one of the methods described in Section 8.2.2. It turns out, however, that the extraction of isolated characters from a word is extremely difficult without knowing the word's identity. Hence one is confronted with a "chicken-and-egg" problem (also known as Sayre's paradox [80]): If the identity of the word were known, its segmentation into individual characters would be feasible. But to know the word's identity, we need to segment it first. To overcome this dilemma, different approaches to word recognition have been proposed. They all try to cope, in the one or the other way, with the segmentation problem. Three prominent examples, known as the holistic, split-and-merge and segmentation-free approach, respectively, are discussed below.

Holistic Methods

Holistic methods have been proposed to completely bypass the difficult problem of segmenting a word into its individual characters. Here the image of the given word is considered as an entity in its whole and it is attempted to classify it, given a dictionary of possible words. For a survey on holistic word recognition, including pointers to the related literature, see [60].

The holistic approach is limited in that it cannot deal properly with a large number of classes. It has been successful, however, as a method for lexicon reduction. Hence, holistic classifiers are suitable to be used in conjunction with one of the two other approaches discussed below.

Segmentation-Based Approaches

Segmentation-based approaches try to segment a given word into smaller entities. However, as it is extremely difficult, if not impossible, to segment a given word into its individual characters without knowing the word's identity, these approaches usually split a word into entities that do not necessarily correspond to exactly one character each, and they consider a number of possible segmentation alternatives at the same time. Typically, an over-segmentation of the given input word is attempted. That is, the image of a character that occurs within a word may be broken into several constituents, also called *graphemes*. At the same time, the segmentation procedure avoids merging two adjacent characters or parts of two adjacent characters, into the same constituent. A large number of heuristics for achieving such kind of segmentation have been reported in the literature. For surveys see [12, 87].

Once the given input word has been transformed, through segmentation, into a sequences of graphemes, $(g_1, g_2, \ldots, g_n)$, all possible combinations of adjacent graphemes, $(g_i, g_{i+1}, \ldots, g_{i+M})$, up to a maximum number M, are considered and fed into a recognizer for isolated characters; $1 \leq i < i + M \leq n$. Typically, it is supposed that the recognizer not only returns an ordered list of class names, but also renders a confidence measure for each class. Once all possible combinations of graphemes have been classified, a search procedure is applied that finds, based on the confidence values returned by the classifier, the best sequence of characters matching the input word image.

HMM-Based Recognition

The third main approach to cursive handwritten word recognition is based on hidden Markov models (HMMs). For all technical details of HMMs we refer the reader to [73]. For a survey of HMMs in cursive handwriting recognition, see [54]. HMMs qualify as a suitable tool for cursive script recognition for a number of reasons. First, they are stochastic models able to cope with noise and shape variations that occur in handwriting. Next, the number of tokens, or feature vectors, representing an unknown word may be of variable length. This is a fundamental requirement in cursive handwriting recognition because the lengths of the individual input words exhibit a great degree of variation. Moreover, using an HMM-based approach, the segmentation problem, which is extremely difficult and error prone, can be avoided. Finally, there are standard algorithms known from the literature for both training and recognition using HMMs.

When using HMMs for a classification problem, an individual HMM is usually constructed for each pattern class. For each sequence of feature vectors extracted from the input pattern, the likelihood that this sequence was produced by a particular HMM can be computed. Eventually, the class with the highest likelihood value is chosen as the recognition result. In word recognition systems with a small vocabulary, it is possible to build an individual HMM for each word. But for large vocabularies, this method is not applicable any longer because of lack of sufficient training data. In this case, HMMs are built on a character basis and character models are concatenated to word models. In this way, the training data are more intensively used [64].

In order to optimize recognition performance, the HMMs have to be fitted to the considered problem. In particular the number of states, the possible transitions and the feature vector probability distributions have to be chosen. Because of the linear, left-to-right direction of handwriting, a linear transition structure is often adopted (i.e. the state transition probabilities are chosen in such a way that a linear left-to-right ordering of the states is imposed). The feature distributions are usually assumed to be Gaussian or mixtures of Gaussians. To adjust the remaining free parameters of an HMM, i.e. the transition probabilities and the parameters of the feature probability distributions, Baum–Welch training, a special version of the EM algorithm is often used [73]. Examples of HMM-based word recognizers can be found in [9, 19, 29, 46, 52, 55, 62, 103].

8.2.4 Cursive Word Sequence Recognition

In its most general form, cursive handwriting recognition requires the transcription of some handwritten text that consists of a sequence of words, for example, a phrase, a sentence or a whole essay, where the text may occupy a line, several lines or a whole page. Similar to the task of word recognition where it has been attempted to segment a word into its constituent characters and then to recognize the individual characters, it has been proposed to segment a line of text into isolated words and then to recognize these words using one of the methods discussed in Section 8.2.3. Various segmentation procedures have been proposed in this context. Many of them are based on analysing the distances between connected components. From the theoretical point of view, the problem can be seen as a classification or clustering task, where a space between two consecutive connected components is to be assigned to the class "within-word" or "between-words". For more details of the segmentation and the corresponding word recognition procedures, see [5, 49, 62, 82].

The problem of segmenting a line of text into words is usually easier than that of a word into its constituent characters. Nevertheless, there are cases where complicated ambiguities arise. Consequently, segmentation-free methods based on HMMs have been proposed for the task of word sequence recognition. The principal idea is to concatenate character models to word models and word models to word sequence models. In this way, the segmentation of a word sequence into individual words is delivered as a by-product of the recognition process, like the segmentation of a word into its constituent characters is delivered as a by-product of HMM-based word recognition. This technique has been successfully used in some systems [64, 98]. The enhancement of an HMM-based recognizer by means of statistical N-gram language models [44, 76] has been described in [64, 97]. Another approach to integrating linguistic knowledge into the recognition process is based on language syntax and syntactic parsing [107].

8.3 Emerging Topics

Many of the methods discussed in Section 8.2 have become state of the art in cursive handwriting recognition. Yet there is still an urgent need to further improve the available recognition technology. In this section we discuss a few topics that have emerged recently.

8.3.1 Databases and Performance Evaluation

The availability of large amounts of data for training and testing is a fundamental prerequisite for building a handwriting recognition system. Furthermore, with an increase in the number of recognition methods becoming available, the comparison and benchmarking of these methods is becoming increasingly important. Consequently, the acquisition of standard databases has become a great concern in the handwriting research community. Since both the collection of the data and the preparation of the ground truth, i.e. the ASCII transcription of the handwritten text, are expensive and time-consuming tasks, it is highly desirable to reuse existing databases as much as possible. This also facilitates the direct comparison of different recognition algorithms.

A survey of existing databases for handwriting recognition research covering the state of the art until about 1996 has been provided in [32]. Databases included in this survey are CEDAR [42], NIST [67] and CEN-PARMI [91]. Moreover, there are databases for the online domain [33] and for Asian characters [78]. A database that contains complete handwritten sentences has been described in [82]. This database has been acquired in the course of developing an HMM-based sentence recognizer. All sentences have been written by the same writer. In [95] a publicly available database is described that contains both on-line and off-line data of handwritten isolated characters, digits and cursive words. A database containing essays written by students is described in [18]. Furthermore, a new database designed to support research on bank cheque processing has been presented in [17].

A fairly large database containing full sentences is the IAM database described in [65]. This database is similar to the one described in [82] in that it is built up from sentences contained in the LOB corpus [45]. However, it is significantly larger than [82] and includes texts from multiple writers.

The current version of the database contains 1539 pages of scanned text produced by 657 writers, including 115,320 instances of handwritten words distributed over 13,353 lines of text. The underlying lexicon includes more than 10,000 different words. Because all texts come from the LOB corpus, which is electronically available, it is possible to automatically generate various kinds of language models. This property makes the database interesting for the development of recognizers that use linguistic knowledge beyond the lexicon level. Originally, the database was designed so as to support the development of a text line recognizer. Consequently, the basic units in the database are complete lines of text. However, a set of segmentation tools have been developed meanwhile that allow splitting a line of text into individual words [65]. Moreover, a novel word segmentation procedure that makes use of the ASCII ground truth has been described in [106]. On a subset of about 3700 lines, this tool achieved a correct word segmentation rate of 98%. A sample page of handwritten text from the IAM database is shown in Figure 8.2

The IAM database was instrumental in the development of a number of handwriting recognition systems at the University of Bern. However, it has also been used by other research groups [6,48,98]. The database is still being enlarged and freely available upon request.[1]

8.3.2 Synthetic Training Data

All methods for handwritten character, word or sentence recognition need to be trained. As a rule of thumb, the larger the training set, the better the recognition performance of the system. This empirical finding has been confirmed in a number of experiments [11,77,86,94]. However, the acquisition of training data is a tedious and expensive process with clear limitations.

In the area of machine-printed character recognition, it was proposed to use synthetic data for training. A number of successful activities in this direction have been reported in the literature. Using a degradation model, Baird successfully constructed a Tibetan OCR system using training data that were initialized with real images but augmented with synthetic variations [2]. Based on the same degradation model, a full-ASCII, 100-typeface classifier was developed using exclusively synthetic training data [20]. A recent review on document image degradation models and their use in synthetic data generation of machine-printed character recognition can be found in [3]. A system for machine-printed Arabic OCR that was trained on synthetic data only is described in [61].

Recently, similar ideas were proposed in the field of handwriting recognition. In [11,66], the synthetic generation of isolated characters from human written samples has been described. Both methods are based on the

---

[1] Please contact the authors at {bunke,varga}@iam.unibe.ch. See also http://www.iam.unibe.ch/~fki/iamDB.

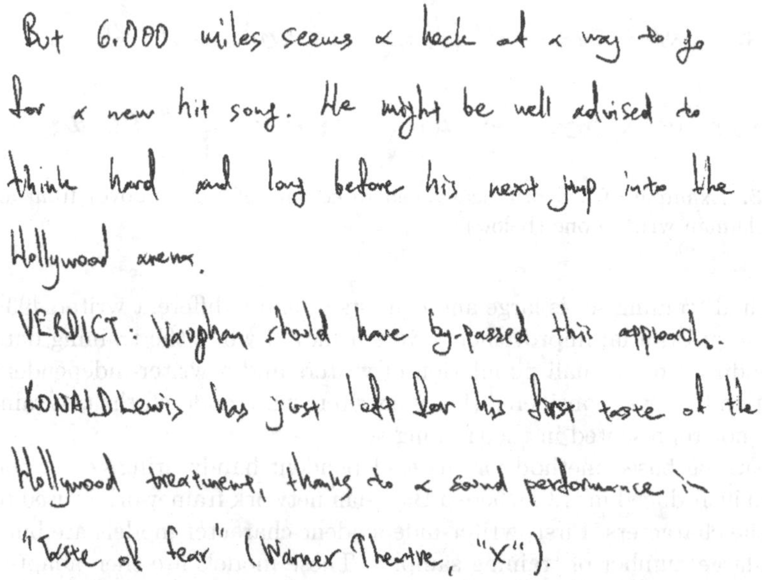

But 6.000 miles seems a heck of a way to go for a new hit song. He might be well advised to think hard and long before his next jump into the Hollywood arena.

VERDICT: Vaughan should have by-passed this approach. RONALD Lewis has just left for his first taste of the Hollywood treatment, thanks to a sound performance in "Taste of fear" (Warner Theatre, "X").

Fig. 8.2. Handwritten text page from the IAM database.

perturbation of character images, and improvements of the recognition rate were achieved when the training set was augmented by such synthetic characters. The generation of synthetic handwritten words and sentences has been described in [31]. The basic idea is to use image templates consisting of n-tuples of characters (with $n = 1, 2, 3$) and to concatenate them to generate words and word sequences from a given ASCII text. A similar approach was adopted in [36]. However, while the aim in [31] was to produce naturally looking handwritten notes from ASCII text for personal communication, the method described in [36] has been tested in conjunction with an HMM-based recognizer for handwritten word sequences. A number of different alternatives in synthetic handwriting generation, with varying degree of complexity, have been explored. Under the most elaborate model, the system trained exclusively on synthetic data reached a recognition rate comparable to that of the same system trained with natural handwriting only.

In [92], a geometrical distortion model for complete lines of handwritten text was proposed. The model is based on a combination of periodic functions that control the strength of geometrical distortion, affecting the slant, width and height of the writing, the shape of the baseline and other parameters. An example of such a synthetically generated line of text can be seen in Figure 8.3. A number of experiments with an HMM-based text line recognizer have been conducted. From these experiments, it can be concluded that the expansion of the natural training set by synthetically generated training data can improve the recognition performance, even if

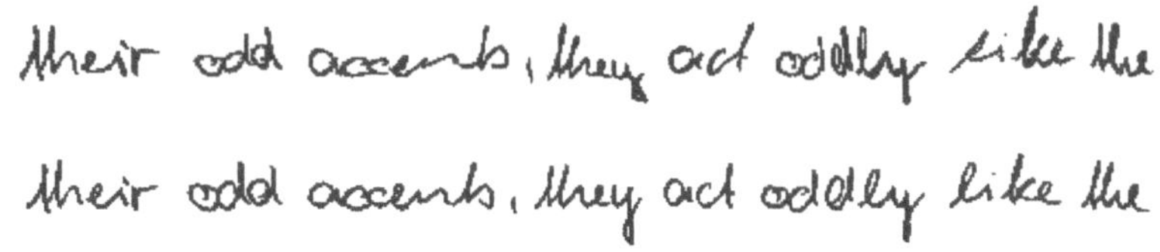

Fig. 8.3. Example of a synthetically generated line of text (above) from an existing human written one (below).

the original training set is large and consists of many different writers [93]. The most substantial improvements were achieved when the training data were produced by a small population of writers and a writer-independent recognition task was considered (i.e. the writers who rendered the test samples are not represented in the training set).

A learning-based method for writer-dependent handwriting generation has been introduced in [13], where a Bayesian network framework is used to model the characters. First, writer-independent character models are built using a large number of training samples. These models are then adapted to a specific writer's writing style to get the writer-dependent character models. For the adaptation, only one training sample per character class is needed. The method was demonstrated on the generation of numeral characters.

However, generating synthetic handwriting does not necessarily require the use of human written texts as a basis. In [56], Korean characters are synthesized from templates of ideal characters, using a handwriting generation model based on [71]. The templates consist of strokes of pre-defined writing order. After the geometrical perturbation of a template, beta curvilinear velocity and pen-lifting profiles are generated for the (overlapping) strokes. Finally, the character is drawn using the generated velocity and pen-lifting profiles. Although the generated characters look natural, they were not used to train a recognizer.

Finally, it has to be noted that the use of synthetic data is not limited to enlarging the training set. It may be meaningful as well to generate synthetic data for extensively testing a system under various conditions. Synthetic data have also been used in the recognition phase, making a classifier insensitive to perturbations that naturally occur in handwriting [35]. Further methods for synthetic handwriting generation have been reported in [83, 99].

8.3.3 Multiple Classifier Systems

Recently, it has been shown that systems incorporating multiple classifiers have the potential of improved classification accuracy over single classifiers in difficult classification tasks [50]. Particularly, in handwriting recognition, the use of multiple classifier systems has been advocated by many authors. Examples include [22, 24, 85].

In order to actually build a multiple classifier system, one needs a number of basic classifiers first. Very often, the design of these basic classifiers is guided by intuition and heuristics. For example, different sets of features and/or different classification algorithms may be used [22]. Sometimes, different sources of information, which are redundant or partly redundant to each other, are exploited, for example, zip code and city name in postal address reading [46], or legal and courtesy amount in bank cheque processing [43, 47]. Recently, a number of procedures for classifier generation, called *ensemble creation methods*, have been proposed in the field of machine learning. They are characterized by the fact that they produce several classifiers out of one base classifier automatically. Prominent examples are Bagging [7], Adaboost [23] and random subspace method [37]. For a summary of these methods see [16]. Applications to the recognition of cursive words are described in [27, 28, 30].

Once a number of classifiers have been generated, an appropriate procedure has to be defined to combine their outputs in order to derive the ensembles' final result. Many methods for classifier combination have been proposed in the literature [75]. They depend on the type of output produced by the individual classifiers. Details can be found in [38, 40, 51, 74].

All classifier combination rules discussed above are not applicable if each classifier of the ensemble outputs a sequence of class names rather than just a single class name. Such a situation typically occurs in word sequence recognition. Because of segmentation errors, it cannot be assumed that the sequences produced by the different classifiers are all of the same length. Therefore, some synchronization mechanism is needed. It has been proposed to use dynamic programming techniques in order to optimally align the individual classifiers' outputs. However, this topic is still under research and only a few solutions have been reported in the literature [63, 100, 104].

8.4 Outlook and Conclusions

The focus of attention in handwriting recognition research has been gradually shifting from isolated character recognition to more complex tasks, such as recognition of words and unconstrained text. Some level of maturity has been reached for isolated characters and digits, but recognition rates in word and word sequence recognition are still rather low. There is no doubt that more research is needed in these areas, particularly as there are some interesting potential applications, examples of which include the automatic reading of personal notes, and the transcription of handwritten archives in the advent of digital libraries.

There is no doubt that many improvements in cursive handwritten word and word sequence recognition are due to the application of HMMs. It is interesting to note that most of the HMM technology that is used in handwriting recognition today has been adopted, without significant modifications except for pre-processing and feature extraction, from speech recognition, although speech is a one-dimensional signal while handwriting is intrinsically two-dimensional. There has been surprisingly little work on developing two-dimensional HMMs or two-dimensional HMM-like stochastic models [14, 70, 79]. A major obstacle in developing such methods is surely their complexity. However, with the steadily increasing power of modern computers and the potential of synthetic training data generation, two-dimensional stochastic models seem a very promising way to improve current handwriting recognition methodology.

The ultimate goal of handwriting recognition is to build machines that can read any text with the same recognition accuracy as humans but at a faster rate [57]. There are many activities currently going on to bring the state of the art closer to that goal. Eventually, however, in order to reach the performance of humans in handwritten text reading, we must aim not only at the *transcription*, but also at the *understanding* of the given text. This includes syntactic and semantic text analysis. Consider, as an analogy, the scenario of a human reader who is faced with the task of transcribing a handwritten text (a) on some subject he or she is familiar with, in his or her native language; (b) on some subject he or she is not familiar with, in his or her native language and (c) in a foreign language he or she does not understand. Clearly, his or her recognition performance will deteriorate as we move from (a) to (b), and from (b) to (c). However, in cursive handwriting recognition (and also in machine printed OCR), we are still at a stage that is comparable to (c). Very few attempts have been reported in the literature to integrate methods from natural language parsing and text understanding into a recognizer [39,41,107]. However, there are such methods available from natural language understanding. Natural language processing techniques and machine translation [76] are very promising to improve the recognition performance of today's handwriting recognition procedures. In addition, they would naturally lead to tools for content-based search and retrieval in the context of handwritten text archives.

Acknowledgment

This work was supported by the Swiss National Science Foundation program "Interactive Multimodal Information Management (IM)2" in the Individual Project "Scene Analysis", as part of NCCR. The present chapter is a revised and updated version of an earlier paper [8].

References

1. Ayat, N.E., Cheriet, M., Remaki, L., and Suen, C.Y. (2001). KMOD – a new support vector machine kernel with moderate decreasing for pattern recognition. *Sixth International Conference on Document Analysis and Recognition, Seattle WA, USA*, pp. 434–438.

2. Baird, H.S. (1992). Document image defect models. In: H.S Baird, H. Bunke, and K. Yamamoto (Eds.). *Structured Document Image Analysis*. New York: Springer, pp. 546–556.

3. Baird, H.S. (2000). The state of the art in document image degradation modeling. *Fourth IAPR Workshop on Document Analysis Systems*, pp. 1–13.

4. Baird, H.S., Govindaraju, V., and Lopresti, D.P. (2004). Document analysis systems for digital libraries: challenges and opportunities. In: S. Marinai and A. Dengel (Eds.). *Lecture Notes in Computer Science*. New York: Springer, Volume 3163, pp. 1–16.

5. Bozinovic, R. and Srihari, S.N. (1989). Off-line cursive script word recognition. *IEEE Transactions on Pattern Analysis and Machine Intelligence, 11(1)*, pp. 68–83.

6. Brakensiek, A., Rottland, J., Kosmala, A., and Rigoll, G. (2000). Off-line handwriting recognition using various hybrid modeling techniques and character n-grams. *Seventh International Workshop on Frontiers in Handwriting Recognition, Amsterdam, The Netherlands*, pp. 343–352.

7. Breiman, L. (1996). Bagging predictors. *Machine Learning, 2*, pp. 123–140.

8. Bunke, H. (2003). Recognition of cursive Roman handwriting – past, present and future. *Seventh International Conference on Document Analysis and Recognition, Edinburgh, Scotland*, Volume 1, pp. 448–459.

9. Bunke, H., Roth, M., and Schukat-Talamazzini, E.G. (1995). Off-line handwriting recognition using hidden Markov models. *Pattern Recognition, 55(1)*, pp. 75–89.

10. Caesar, T., Gloger, J.M., and Mandler, E. (1993). Preprocessing and feature extraction for a handwriting recognition system. *Second International Conference on Document Analysis and Recognition, Tsukuba Science City, Japan*, pp. 408–411.

11. Cano, J., Perez-Cortes, J.-C., Arlandis, J., and Llobet, R. (2002). Training set expansion in handwritten character recognition. In: T. Caelli, A. Amin, R. Duin, M. Kamel, and D. de Ridder (Eds.). *Structural, Syntactic and Statistical Pattern Recognition*. LNCS 2396. New York: Springer, pp. 548–556.

12. Casey, R.G. and Lecolinet, E. (1996). A survey of methods and strategies in character segmentation. *IEEE Transactions on Pattern Analysis and Machine Intelligence, 18*, pp. 690–706.

13. Choi, H., Cho, S.J., and Kim, J.H. (2004). Writer-dependent online handwriting generation with Bayesian networks. *Ninth International Workshop on Frontiers in Handwriting Recognition, Tokyo, Japan*, pp. 130–135.

14. Choisy, A. and Belaid, A. (2002). Cross-learning in analytic word recognition without segmentation. *International Journal on Document Analysis and Recognition, 4*, pp. 281–289.

15. Cordella, L.P., Foggia, P., Sansone, C., and Vento, M. (1997). Subgraph transformation for inexact matching of attributed relational graphs. *Computing, Supplement 12*, pp. 43–52.

16. Dietterich, T.G. (2000). Ensemble methods in machine learning. J. Kittler and F. Roli (Eds.). *First International Workshop on Multiple Classifier Systems*, pp. 1–15.

17. Dimauro, G., Impedovo, S., Modugno, R., and Pirlo, G. (2002). A new database for research on bank-check processing. *Eighth International Workshop on Frontiers in Handwriting Recognition, Niagra-on-the-Lake, Canada*, pp. 524–528.

18. Elliman, D. and Sherkat, N. (2001). A truthing tool for generating a database of cursive words. *Sixth International Conference on Document Analysis and Recognition, Seattle WA, USA*, pp. 1255–1262.
19. Farouz, C., Gilloux, M., and Bertille, J.-M. (1999). Handwritten word recognition with contextual hidden Markov models. In: S.-W. Lee (Ed.). *Advances in Handwriting Recognition*. Singapore: World Scientific, pp. 183–192.
20. Fossey, R. and Baird, H.S. (1991). A 100 font classifier. *First International Conference on Document Analysis and Recognition, St. Malo, France*.
21. Franke, J. (1997). Isolated handprinted digit recognition. In: H. Bunke and P.S.P. Wang (Eds.). *Handbook of Character Recognition and Document Image Analysis*. Singapore: World Scientific, pp. 103–121.
22. Franke, J., Lam, L., Legault, R., Nadal, C., and Suen, C.Y. (1993). Experiments with the CENPARMI database combining different classification approaches. *Third International Workshop on Frontiers in Handwriting Recognition*, pp. 305–311.
23. Freud, Y. and Shapire, R.E. (1997). A decision theoretic generalization of online learning and application to boosting. *Journal on Computer and Systems Sciences, 55*, pp. 119–139.
24. Gader, P.D., Mohamed, M.A., and Keller, J.M. (1996). Fusion of handwritten word classifiers. *Pattern Recognition Letters, 17*, pp. 577–584.
25. Gopisetty, S., Lorie, R., Mao, J., Mohiuddin, M., Sorin, A., and Yair, E. (1996). Automated forms-processing software and services. *IBM Journal of Research and Development, 40(2)*, pp. 211–230.
26. Gorski, N., Anisimov, V., Augustin, E., Baret, O., and Maximor, S. (2001). Industrial bank check processing: the A2iA check reader. *International Journal on Document Analysis and Recognition, 3*, pp. 196–206.
27. Günter, S. and Bunke, H. (2003). Ensembles of classifiers for handwritten word recognition. *International Journal on Document Analysis and Recognition, 5(4)*, pp. 224–232.
28. Günter, S. and Bunke, H. (2004). Handwritten word recognition using classifier ensembles generated from multiple prototypes. *International Journal of Pattern Recognition and Artificial Intelligence, 18(5)*, pp. 957–974.
29. Günter, S. and Bunke, H. (2004). HMM-based handwritten word recognition: on the optimization of the number of states, training iterations and Gaussian components. *Pattern Recognition, 37(10)*, pp. 2069–2079.
30. Günter, S. and Bunke, H. (2004). Multiple classifier systems in off-line handwritten word recognition – on the influence of training set and vocabulary size. *International Journal of Pattern Recognition and Artificial Intelligence, 18(7)*, pp. 1303–1320.
31. Guyon, I. (1996). Handwriting synthesis from handwritten glyphs. *Fifth International Workshop on Frontiers in Handwriting Recognition, Essex, England*, pp. 309–312.
32. Guyon, I., Haralick, R.M., Hull, J.J., and Phillips, I.T. (1997). Data sets for OCR and document image understanding research. In: H. Bunke and P.S.P. Wang (Eds.). *Handbook of Character Recognition and Document Image Analysis*. Singapore: World Scientific, pp. 780–799.
33. Guyon, I., Schomaker, L., Plamondon, R., Liberman, M., and Janet, S. (1994). Unipen project of on-line data exchange and benchmarks. *Twelfth International Conference on Pattern Recognition, Jerusalem, Israel*, pp. 29–33.

34. Ha, T.M. and Bunke, H. (1997). Image processing methods for document image analysis. In: H. Bunke and P.S.P. Wang (Eds.). *Handbook of Character Recognition and Document Image Analysis*. Singapore: World Scientific, Chapter 1, pp. 1–47.

35. Ha, T.M. and Bunke, H. (1997). Off-line handwritten numeral recognition by perturbation method. *IEEE Transactions on Pattern Analysis and Machine Intelligence, 19(5)*, pp. 535–539.

36. Helmers, M. and Bunke, H. (2003). Generation and use of synthetic training data in cursive handwriting recognition. *Proceedings of the First Iberian Conference on Pattern Recognition and Image Analysis.*

37. Ho, T.K. (1998). The random subspace method for constructing decision forests. *IEEE Transactions on Pattern Analysis and Machine Intelligence, 20*, pp. 832–844.

38. Ho, T.K., Hull, J.J., and Srihari, S.N. (1994). Decision combination in multiple classifier systems. *IEEE Transactions on Pattern Analysis and Machine Intelligence, 16*, pp. 66–75.

39. Hong, T. and Hull, J.J. (1993). Text recognition enhancement with a probabilistic lattice chart parser. *International Conference on Document Analysis and Recognition, Tsukuba, Japan*, pp. 222–225.

40. Huang, T. and Suen, C. (1995). Combination of multiple experts for the recognition of unconstrained handwritten numerals. *IEEE Transactions on Pattern Analysis and Machine Intelligence, 17*, pp. 90–94.

41. Hull, J.J. (1992). A hidden Markov model for language syntax in text recognition. *Eleventh Proceedings on International Conference on Pattern Recognition*, Volume B, pp. 124–127.

42. Hull, J.J. (1994). A database for handwritten text recognition research. *IEEE Transactions on Pattern Analysis and Machine Intelligence, 16(5)*, pp. 550–554.

43. Impedovo, S., Wang, P.S.P., and Bunke, H. (Eds.) (1997). *Automatic Bankcheck Processing*. Singapore: World Scientific.

44. Jelinek, F. (1998). *Statistical Aspects of Speech Recognition*. Cambridge, MA: MIT Press.

45. Johansson, S., Leech, G.N., and Goodluck, H. (1978). *Manual of Information to Accompany the Lancaster-Oslo/Bergen Corpus of British English, for Use with Digital Computers*. Oslo: Department of English, University of Oslo.

46. Kaltenmeier, A., Caesar, T., Gloger, J.M., and Mandler, E. (1993). Sophisticated topology of hidden Markov models for cursive script recognition. *Second International Conference on Document Analysis and Recognition, Tsukuba Science City, Japan*, pp. 139–142.

47. Kaufmann, G. and Bunke, H. (2000). Automated reading of check amounts. *Pattern Analysis and Applications, 3*, pp. 132–141.

48. Kavallieratou, E., Fakotakis, N., and Kokkinakis, G. (2002). An unconstrained handwriting recognition system. *International Journal on Document Analysis and Recognition, 4*, pp. 226–242.

49. Kim, G., Govindaraju, V., and Srihari, S.N. (1999). An architecture for handwritten text recognition systems. *International Journal on Document Analysis and Recognition, 2(1)*, pp. 37–44.

50. Roli, F., Kittler, J., and Windeatt, T. (2004). *Multiple Classifier Systems*. LNCS 3077. New York: Springer.

51. Kittler, J., Duin, R., and Hatef, M. (1998). On combining classifiers. *IEEE Transactions on Pattern Analysis and Machine Intelligence, 20*, pp. 226–239.

52. Knerr, S., Augustin, E., Baret, O., and Price, D. (1998). Hidden Markov model based word recognition and its application to legal amount reading from checks. *Computer Vision and Image Understanding, 70*, pp. 404–419.

53. Kressel, U. and Schürmann, J. (1997). Pattern classification techniques based on function approximation. In: H. Bunke and P.S.P. Wang (Eds.). *Handbook of Character Recognition and Document Image Analysis*. World Scientific, pp. 49–78.

54. Kundu, A. (1997). Handwritten word recognition using hidden Markov model. In: H. Bunke and P.S.P. Wang (Eds.). *Handbook of Character Recognition and Document Image Analysis*. Singapore: World Scientific, Chapter 6, pp. 157–182.

55. Kundu, A., He, Y., and Chen, M.-Y. (1998). Alternatives to variable duration HMM in handwriting recognition. *IEEE Transactions on Pattern Analysis and Machine Intelligence, 20*, pp. 1275–1280.

56. Lee, D.-H. and Cho, H.-G. (1998). A new synthesizing method for handwriting Korean scripts. *International Journal of Pattern Recognition and Artificial Intelligence, 12(1)*, pp. 46–61.

57. Lorette, G. (1999). Handwriting recognition or reading? What is the situation at the dawn of the 3rd millennium? *International Journal on Document Analysis and Recognition, 2*, pp. 2–12.

58. Lucas, S. and Amiri, A. (1995). Recognition of chain-coded handwritten character images with scanning n-tuple method. *Electronic Letters, 31*, pp. 2088–2089.

59. Madhvanath, S. and Govindaraju, V. (1999). Local reference lines for handwritten phrase recognition. *Pattern Recognition, 32(12)*, pp. 2021–2028.

60. Madhvanath, S. and Govindaraju, V. (2001). Local reference lines for handwritten phrase recognition. *IEEE Transactions on Pattern Analysis and Machine Intelligence, 23*, pp. 149–164.

61. Maergner, V. and Pechwitz, M. (2001). Synthetic data for arabic OCR system development. *Sixth International Conference on Document Analysis and Recognition, Seattle WA, USA*, pp. 1159–1163.

62. Marti, U.-V. and Bunke, H. (2001). Text line segmentation and word recognition in a system for general writer independent handwriting recognition. *Sixth International Conference on Document Analysis and Recognition, Seattle WA, USA*, pp. 159–163.

63. Marti, U.-V. and Bunke, H. (2001). Use of positional information in sequence alignment for multiple classifier combination. In: J. Kittler and F. Roli (Eds.). *International Workshop on Multiple Classifier Systems*. LNCS 2096. New York: Springer, pp. 388–398.

64. Marti, U.-V. and Bunke, H. (2001). Using a statistical language model to improve the performance of an HMM-based cursive handwriting recognition system. *International Journal of Pattern Recognition and Artificial Intelligence, 15*, pp. 65–90.

65. Marti, U.-V. and Bunke, H. (2002). The IAM-database: an English sentence database for off-line handwriting recognition. *International Journal on Document Analysis and Recognition, 5*, pp. 39–46.

66. Mori, M., Suzuki, A., Siho, A., and Ohtsuka, S. (2000). Generating new samples from handwritten numerals based on point correspondence. *Seventh International Workshop on Frontiers in Handwriting Recognition, Amsterdam, The Netherlands*, , pp. 281–290.

67. Mori, S., Nishida, H., and Yamada, H. (1999). *Optical Character Recognition.* New York: John Wiley and Sons, Inc.

68. Morita, M.E., Facon, J., Bortolozzi, F., Garnes, S., and Sabourin, R. (1999). Mathematical morphology and weighted least squares to correct handwriting baseline skew. *Fifth International Conference on Document Analysis and Recognition, Bangalore, India*, pp. 430–433.

69. O'Gorman, L. and Kasturi, R. (Eds.) (1995). *Document Image Analysis.* New York: IEEE Computer Society Press.

70. Park, H.-S., Sui, B.-K., Moon, J., and Lee, S.-W. (2001). A 2-D HMM method for offline handwritten character recognition. *International Journal of Pattern Recognition and Artificial Intelligence, 15*, pp. 91–105.

71. Plamondon, R. and Guerfali, W. (1998). The generation of handwriting with delta-lognormal synergies. *Biological Cybernetics, 78*, pp. 119–132.

72. Plamondon, R. and Srihari, S. (2000). On-line and off-line handwriting recognition: a comprehensive survey. *IEEE Transactions on Pattern Analysis and Machine Intelligence, 22*, pp. 63–84.

73. Rabiner, L.R. (1989). A tutorial on hidden Markov models and selected applications in speech recognition. *Proceedings of the IEEE, 77(2)*, pp. 257–285.

74. Rahmann, A.F.R., Alam, H., and Fairhurst, M.C. (2002). Multiple classifier combination for character recognition: revisiting the majority voting system and its variations. In: D. Lopresti, J. Hu, and R. Kashi (Eds.). *Fifth International Workshop on Document Analysis Systems.* LNCS 2423. New York: Springer, pp. 167–178.

75. Rahmann, A.F.R. and Fairhurst, M.C. (2000). Multiple expert classification: a new methodology for parallel decision fusion. *International Journal on Document Analysis and Recognition*, pp. 40–55.

76. Rosenfeld, R. (2000). Two decades of statistical language modeling: where do we go from here? *Proceedings of the IEEE, 88*, pp. 1270–1278.

77. Rowley, H.A., Goyal, M., and Bennet, J. (2002). The effect of large training set sizes on online Japanese Kanji and English cursive recognizers. *Eighth International Workshop on Frontiers in Handwriting Recognition, Niagra-on-the-Lake, Canada*, , pp. 36–40.

78. Saito, T., Yamada, H., and Yamamoto, K. (1985). On the data base ETL 9 of handprinted characters in JIS chinese characters and its analysis. *IEICE Transactions, J68-D(4)*, pp. 757–764.

79. Saon, G. (1999). Cursive word recognition using a random field based hidden Markov model. *International Journal of Pattern Recognition and Artificial Intelligence, 1*, pp. 199–208.

80. Sayre, K.M. (1973). Machine recognition of handwritten words: a project report. *Pattern Recognition, 5(3)*, pp. 213–228.

81. Schürmann, J. (1996). *Pattern Classification – A Unified View of Statistical and Neural Approaches.* New York: John Wiley and Sons, Inc.

82. Senior, A.W. and Robinson, A.J. (1998). An off-line cursive handwriting recognition system. *IEEE Transactions on Patten Analysis and Machine Intelligence, 20(3)*, pp. 309–321.

83. Setlur, S. and Govindaraju, V. (1994). Generating manifold samples from a handwritten word. *Pattern Recognition Letters, 15,* 901–905.

84. Simon, J.-C. (1992). Off-line cursive word recognition. *Proceedings of the IEEE, 80(7),* pp. 1150–1161.

85. Sirlantzkis, K., Fairhurst, M.C., and Hoque, M.S. (2001). Genetic algorithm for multiple classifier configuration: a case study in character recognition. In: J. Kittler and F. Roli (Eds.). *Second International Workshop on Multiple Classifier Systems,* pp. 99–108.

86. Smith, S.J. (1994). Handwritten character classification using nearest neighbour in large databases. *IEEE Transactions on Pattern Analysis and Machine Intelligence, 16,* pp. 915–919.

87. Sridar, M. and Kimura, F. (1997). Segmentation-based cursive handwriting recognition. In: H. Bunke and P.S.P. Wang (Eds.). *Handbook of Character Recognition and Document Image Analysis.* Singapore: World Scientific, pp. 123–156.

88. Srihari, S.N. (2000). Handwritten address interpretation: a task of many pattern recognition problems. *International Journal of Pattern Recognition and Artificial Intelligence, 14,* pp. 663–674.

89. Steinherz, T., Rivlin, E., and Intrator, N. (1999). Off-line cursive word recognition – a survey. *International Journal on Document Analysis and Recognition, 2,* pp. 90–110.

90. Suen, C. and Wang, P.S.P. (1994). *Thinning Methodologies for Pattern Recognition.* Singapore: World Scientific.

91. Suen, C.Y., Nadal, C., Legault, R., Mai, T.A., and Lam, L. (1992). Computer recognition of unconstrained handwritten numerals. *Proceedings of the IEEE, 7(80),* pp. 1162–1180.

92. Varga, T. and Bunke, H. (2003). Generation of synthetic training data for an HMM-based handwriting recognition system. *Seventh International Conference on Document Analysis and Recognition, Edinburgh, Scotland,* Volume 1, pp. 618–622.

93. Varga, T. and Bunke, H. (2004). Off-line handwriting recognition using synthetic training data produced by means of a geometrical distortion model. *International Journal of Pattern Recognition and Artificial Intelligence, 18(7),* pp. 1285–1302.

94. Velek, O. and Nakagawa, M. (2002). The impact of large training sets on the recognition rate of off-line Japanese Kanji character classifiers. *Proceedings of the Fifth International Workshop on Document Analysis Systems (DAS 2002),* pp. 106–109.

95. Viard-Gaudin, C., Lallican, P.M., Knerr, S., and Binter, P. (1999). The IRESTE on/off (ironoff dual handwriting database). *Fifth International Conference on Document Analysis and Recognition 99, Bangalore, India,* pp. 455–458.

96. Vinciarelli, A. (2002). A survey on off-line cursive word recognition. *Pattern Recognition, 35,* pp. 1433–1446.

97. Vinciarelli, A., Bengio, S., and Bunke, H. (2004). Offline recognition of unconstrained handwritten texts using HMMs and statistical language models. *IEEE Transactions PAMI, 26,* pp. 709–720.

98. Vinciarelli, A. and Luettin, J. (2000). Off-line cursive script recognition based on continuous density HMM. *Seventh International Workshop*

on Frontiers in Handwriting Recognition, Amsterdam, The Netherlands, pp. 493–498.

99. Wang, J., Wu, C., Xu, Y.-Q., Shum, H.-Y., and Ji, L. (2002). Learning-based cursive handwriting synthesis. *Eighth International Workshop on Frontiers in Handwriting Recognition, Niagra-on-the-Lake, Canada*, pp. 157–162.

100. Wang, W., Brakensiek, A., and Rigoll, G. (2002). Combination of multiple classifiers for handwritten word recognition. *Eighth International Workshop on Frontiers in Handwriting Recognition, Niagra-on-the-Lake, Canada*, pp. 117–122.

101. Wilkinson, R.A., Geist, J., Janet, S., Grother, P.J., Burges, C.J.C., Creecy, R., Hammond, B., Hull, J.J., Larsen, N.W., Vogl, T.P., and Wilson, C.L. (1992). *The First Census Optical Character Recognition Systems Conference #NISTIR 4912*. Gaithersburg, MD: The US Bureau of Census and the National Institute of Standards and Technology.

102. Xi, D. and Lee, S.-W. (2005). Extraction of reference lines and items from form document images with complicated background. *Pattern Recognition, 38(2)*, pp. 289–305.

103. El Yacoubi, A., Gilloux, M., Sabourin, R., and Suen, C. (1999). An HMM-based approach for off-line unconstrained handwritten word modeling and recognition. *IEEE Transactions on Pattern Analysis and Machine Intelligence, 21*, pp. 752–760.

104. Ye, X., Cheriet, M., and Suen, C.Y. (2001). A framework for combining numeric string recognizers. *Sixth International Conference on Document Analysis and Recognition, Seattle, WA, USA*, pp. 716–720.

105. Ye, X., Cheriet, M., and Suen, C.Y. (2001). A generic method of cleaning and enhancing handwritten data from business forms. *International Journal on Document Analysis and Recognition, 4*, pp. 84–96.

106. Zimmermann, M. and Bunke, H. (2002). Automatic segmentation of the IAM off-line handwritten English text database. *Sixteenth International Conference on Pattern Recognition, Quebec, Canada*, Volume 4, pp. 35–39.

107. Zimmermann, M., Chappelier, J.-C., and Bunke, H. (2003). Parsing n-best lists of handwritten sentences. *Seventh International Conference on Document Analysis and Recognition, Edinburgh, Scotland*, Volume 1, pp. 572–576.

Robustness Design of Industrial Strength Recognition Systems

Hiromichi Fujisawa

9.1 Characterization of Robustness

There are a few research works on robustness of OCRs for machine-printed documents [28]. An interesting work to be noted is Baird's document image defect model [2]. The types of defects in machine-printed document images were studied and a quantitative defect model was devised. To estimate the parameters of the model, "calibration" methods were studied. More importantly, it can be used to generate synthetic degraded document images with control parameters [22]. By using such synthetic images, it is hoped that we are able to evaluate the robustness of an existing OCR, and to train the OCR for such degraded images more systematically.

Another work to be mentioned is by Nartker and Taghva, who showed how OCRs from different vendors performed on documents with different qualities [1,35]. They classified 2200 pages of machine-printed English document images into five groups (G1–G5) depending on their image quality measured in terms of the page-wise recognition accuracy (correct recognition rate). Figure 9.1 shows the result of their experiments in terms of recognition accuracy of eight OCRs for five groups of document images [1]. Then, they found that the lower the accuracy for G1 is, the steeper the performance degradation curves are. It meant that the difference between good and bad OCRs is amplification of the error rate for low quality documents.

These works give some insights into how to evaluate the robustness. So, we try to apply the same approach to a more complex recognition system like a postal address recognition system. Figure 9.2 shows how the profiles of read rates[1] of a postal address recognition system look like.

---

[1] Here, "read rate" refers to the accept rate of the recognition system. It is often used for postal address recognition systems, where the error rates are kept around 1%.

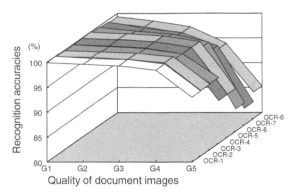

Fig. 9.1. Recognition accuracies of eight OCRs for five datasets of different image qualities. (The graph reproduced from the data shown in [35].)

The profiles shown there are for three different kinds of postal mails, i.e. bulk mail (BK), machine-printed mail (MP) and handwritten mail (HW). The x-axis represents the datasets of postal images numbered so that the corresponding read rates come into decreasing order. Actually, there are three separate sets of datasets corresponding to the kind of mails.

The former discussion on the robustness, saying that the steeper the performance degradation curve, the less robust the recognition system, suggests to measure the robustness in terms of the gradient of the curves. For simplicity, we may calculate the standard deviation (SD) of the plots of read rates instead of the gradient. So we have calculated the average and SD of the read rates for BK, MP and HW mails shown in Figure 9.2. The pairs of average and SD of these read rates are (0.86, 0.10), (0.82, 0.05) and (0.64, 0.06), respectively. When we compare the SDs so calculated, we may conclude that the system is most robust for MP mails, because the MP's standard deviation 0.05 is the smallest. However, it is counterintuitive, because BK has the highest read rate 0.86. Here we need some more discussion.

In the above discussion, the concept of "degradation" requires information about the origin, specifying "from where", to be complete in the meaning. This means that the primary performance measure of pattern recognition systems should be any representative performance such as the performance in the normal operations (or average performance measure), and the robustness is a *secondary* performance measure representing the dispersion of the performance fluctuation influenced by PIFs. Industrial strength recognition systems require not only higher average performance, but also smaller performance fluctuations.

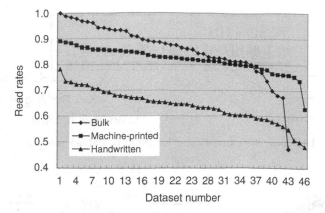

Fig. 9.2. Profiles of recognition rates for bulk, machine-printed and handwritten mails (data from 1999). There were three series of datasets, each of which was rearranged independently so that the read rates come into decreasing order.

9.2 Complex Recognition System: Postal Address Recognition

Japanese Postal Address Recognition. To make the following sections smooth to read, this section minimally introduces a Japanese postal address recognition system, which will be the basis of the chapter.

Postal address recognition is one of the toughest applications of document analysis and recognition along with bank check recognition [7, 27, 30–33]. The task of recognizing postal addresses on the surface of mailpieces (i.e. postcards and envelopes) is a very complex one, and requires multiple recognition algorithms working in a good orchestration [30]. It is especially so for Japanese addresses as described below.

Figure 9.3 shows a standard expression of Japanese postal addresses. It consists of three-plus-four (seven) digit postal code starting with a T-like shape symbol, a Kanji (Chinese character) string showing prefecture name, city name and town name and a three-field address number (e.g. "1-2-3"), followed by optional information of a building number (e.g. "A") and a room number (e.g. "405"). The whole information is referred to as "full-address".

Here, the three-field address number specifies a spatial unit of a house or building, being different from a street number in western countries, which is one dimensional. The first field number designates one of the areas in the town concerned. Usually, a town consists of several areas. Then, each area consists of blocks that are minimal spatial units surrounded by streets. The second field number designates a block in an area. Finally, each block

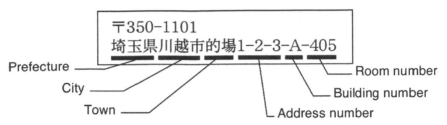

Fig. 9.3. Structure of the Japanese postal address.

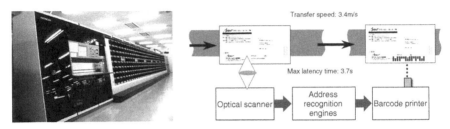

Fig. 9.4. Mail Sorting Machine (Hitachi, 1999) and dataflow.

consists of smallest spatial units of houses or buildings, which are designated by the third field number.

The seven-digit postal code and Kanji part of the address expression are almost equivalent with some exceptions. There are approximately 110,000 valid codes in Japan. The recognition result of full-address is represented in terms of a variable length code, referred to as address code, which consists of 7 digits representing a postal code followed by an address number, a building number and a room number. In this example, the address code is "35011011-2-3-A-405". This is an internal representation of an address point used in the postal automation system. There are about 40 million address points in Japan.

New-type mail sorting machines introduced since 1998 in major Japanese post offices read the postcard and envelope's surfaces, and recognize not only a postal code but also a Kanji address phrase plus an address number, which identifies a house or building. Further, the machines also read a building number and a room number in the case of buildings or apartments. With the identified address point information, the machines can now automate carrier-route sequence sorting.

The mail sorting machine developed by Hitachi, shown in Figure 9.4, can process 30,000 to 50,000 mailpieces per hour depending on the operational mode. The mailpieces on the deck are picked up one by one automatically

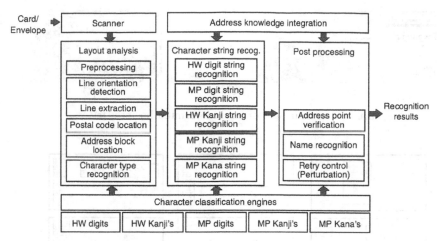

Fig. 9.5. Functional block diagram of a Japanese postal address recognition engine (HW: handwriting, MP: machine printing).

and transferred by the belt mechanism at the speed of 3.4 m/s. A high-speed scanner captures the images of the running mailpieces and sends the captured images to the postal address recognition system composed of more than 20 computers. A control processor dispatches the recognition tasks to available computers running in parallel. Recognition must be ended before the corresponding mailpiece comes to the barcode printer station on the path, where the recognition result in terms of an address code is sprayed in invisible ink. The time limit of recognition is 3.7 s. The mailpiece images that could not be recognized in time and that were rejected are sent to Video Coding System where human operators video-code them.

The postal address recognition engine is actually a software program running on PC servers. The recognition engine consists of many recognition components as shown in Figure 9.5. As shown, the components consist of layout analysis for address block location, character string recognition, character classification engines, address knowledge integration and post processing. The details will be described in Section 9.3.

9.3 Performance Influencing Factors

Postal addresses of Japanese letters have a lot of freedom on the way of printing/writing in practice, resulting in many Performance Influencing Factors (PIFs). They are explained for each recognition component in the following.

Layout Analysis. Identification of postal code and address blocks is the task [3, 33, 38, 39]. As shown in Figure 9.5, it consists of preprocessing of connected component analysis of a binary image, character line orientation

Fig. 9.6. Example images of machine-printed business letters.

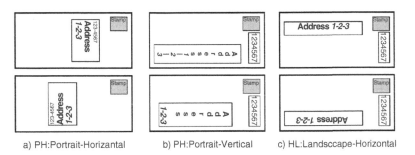

a) PH:Portrait-Horizantal   b) PH:Portrait-Vertical   c) HL:Landsccape-Horizontal

Fig. 9.7. Six layout types of address block. (Digit string "1234567" represents a 7-digit postal code, and character string "Address 1-2-3" represents an address phrase and address number.)

detection, character line extraction, postal code location, address block location and character type recognition.

Regarding PIFs, first of all, there are a lot of background printings such as advertisements (Figure 9.6). Instead of removing the background patterns, character like patterns are searched and attempted to form character line candidates. However, some background pattern is a complex texture that causes a problem in connected component analysis because too many components require excessive time and memory (Figure 9.6(c)).

Address line orientation is multiform as shown in Figure 9.7 and difficult to identify [18]. Although there is an official guideline for the address writing and printing, its existence is not well known by people, resulting in such irregular layouts as shown in Figure 9.7.

Another problem is the noises around an address block, such as the shadow noises from a plastic address block window as shown in Figure 9.8. These noises interfere with character line extraction. Still another problem is extra digit strings that are sometimes printed near the address lines or postal code (Figure 9.8), which could be confused with a postal code or an address number.

Character String Recognition. As a pattern recognition system, this is one of the most important components. Here, character string recognition accomplishes the following tasks:

Fig. 9.8. Shadow noises from a plastic window and an extra digit string near the postal code.

- Postal code recognition
- Address phrase recognition
- Address number recognition
- Building/room number recognition
- Recipient name recognition (Postprocessing)

As shown in Figure 9.3, an address phrase is a Kanji string representing a prefecture name, city name and town name, followed by an address number, which is further followed by building number and a room number. The address number of the Japanese addressing system has three fields of numbers as described above. Recognition of address number plus building/room number is complicated because expressions of the address number have so many variants as shown in Figure 9.9. The layout is also multiform and the numbers are sometimes in Kanji.

Before we talk about the PIFs, there are methodological and architectural difficulties in here. They are about how to conquer the complexity. The questions are how to recognize words which are not separated by space; how to segment touching and separated characters; how to connect phrase recognition and address number recognition; how to cope with the layout variations in address number expressions, and how to integrate a priori knowledge about address expressions and possible address formats.

Character string recognition can be accomplished by integrating the three tasks of character segmentation, character recognition and address interpretation (see for example [4, 16, 19, 23, 26]). Therefore the PIFs relate to these three tasks. They are touching characters, multiple-component characters [17], (touching) underlines, omission of a prefecture name, incomplete address expression, obsolete address expression and variations not covered by the linguistic model being used. An example of incomplete address expression is an address image overlaid by a cancellation stamp (Figure 9.10). When a cancellation stamp hides a city name for example, the address should be recognized because postal code recognition may help provide information on city and town.

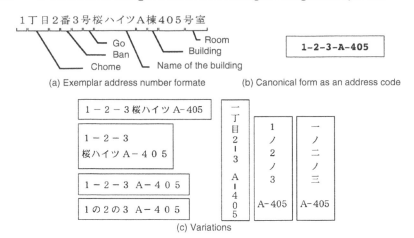

(a) Exemplar address number formate

(b) Canonical form as an address code

(c) Variations

Fig. 9.9. Various address number formats. All examples in (c) represent the same address point as (b).

Fig. 9.10. Cancellation stamp hiding a part of address line.

(a) Normal pen   (b) Felt pen   (c) Brush

Fig. 9.11. Different kinds of writing instruments.

Character Classification Engines. Difficulties exist related to the huge Kanji set, multiple scripts, the variations in writing instrument (Figure 9.11), writing style, typeface, character size, type size, printing quality and so on.

As shown in Figure 9.5, we use five character classification engines, namely those for machine-printed Kanji, handwritten Kanji, machine-printed digit, handwritten digit and machine-printed Kana. Although the Kanji classifier can recognize about 4000 characters including alphabets, digits and Kana's, the specialized character classification engines give better recognition performances. It means that the address block location component must detect the character type of the extracted address line images from out of those five.

The character recognition methods are rather well studied historically [10,13,20,34]. However, it is not well studied how to reject (or give a lower score to) noncharacter patterns. But it is desirable that a character classifier gives a lower score to a mis-segmented pattern (noncharacter pattern) to make segmentation–recognition integration successful. In the case of address phrase recognition, the integration of linguistic information is possible in addition to segmentation–recognition integration, and it can offset this classifier's weakness. In the case of digit string recognition, however, classifier's resistance to noncharacters is important because such additional information is not available [24].

Address Phrase Interpretation. There are three kinds of a priori knowledge to be utilized in the character string recognition.

- Linguistic knowledge about addresses: Lexical entities (words) and syntax (hierarchical relations among words).
- Address points: There are about 40 million address points in Japan, much less than the numbers that can be covered by the address code space.
- Recipient names (residents and companies) related to address points.
- Relations between 7-digit postal codes and town names: The number of valid codes is approximately 110,000 only.

The PIFs for address phrase interpretation include incompleteness and errors in the address database, and variations in address expressions that cannot be represented in the linguistic model being used. For example, a model based on context-free grammar is more flexible than a model using the TRIE structure [16]. The address system used in Kyoto in Japan has peculiarity that requires a context-free grammar to produce every variation.

Post Processing. Actually, post processing relies on the knowledge sources already mentioned above. It receives multiple candidates of identified address points together with corresponding scores as a result of character string recognition. It also receives a "partial" result, which has "unknown" in some of the address fields; for example, a partial result is "35011011-2-"? rather than a full address of "35011011-2-3". When the result is competing multiple candidates or a partial result, the system can retrieve possible recipients names from the address database, and recipient name recognition can choose the right address point. When the result is a total rejection, the retry control module is activated and it requests the whole recognition engine once again to work on a perturbed image only if the remaining time is greater than an expected (average) recognition time. Perturbation will be explained later.

The PIFs for postprocessing are those for address knowledge integration plus those for recipient name recognition which is again character string recognition with name candidates as constraints. So, the PIFs of character string recognition also apply here.

PIFs of Postal Address Recognition. The performance influencing factors of postal address recognition are listed in Table 9.1 with slightly different classification.

9.4 Robustness Design Principles

As shown in Table 9.1, there are many PIFs. When we can understand a problem correctly, the next question is what is the right approach to take to improve the robustness. We think there exist "robustness design principles" that can be applied throughout. These principles literally guide the course of development.

Six Principles. In experiencing the development of an address recognition system, which lasted for five years, we could rely on the following six principles, although some of them are interrelated each other.

- Hypothesis-Driven Principle
- Deferred Decision Principle
- Multiple-Hypothesis Principle
- Information Integration Principle
- Multiple-Solutions Principle
- Perturbation Principle

In the following sections, each principle will be paraphrased and explained.

Hypothesis-Driven Principle: *"When the problem solving process has a dilemma inside, make a hypothesis to break the dilemma link."*

An example that needs this principle is address block location. To locate the address block, we need to have the line candidates. To do so, we need to know the line orientation. To know it, we need to have line candidates. Here is a dilemma. Therefore, we make two hypotheses of horizontal and vertical orientations and then extract line candidates. Furthermore, line extraction requires parameters (thresholds) related to the character size, but this again requires us to have line information. Therefore, we make two hypotheses of machine-printed and handwritten cases. Actually, we need to hypothesize the character orientations as well.

In this way, the address block location method we developed hypothesizes six types as shown below, and it evaluates the resulting candidates using the Bayesian rule [18]. Some of the types are shown in Figure 9.7.

- P-PH: Printed portrait horizontal
- P-PV: Printed portrait vertical
- P-LH: Printed landscape horizontal

Table 9.1. Performance influencing factors of postal address recognition

Recognition component	Performance influencing factors
Optical scanning	Low quality printing
	Address written in a dark ink on a dark coloured envelope
	Plastic address window causing reflection
Binarization and image coding	Low contrast image
	Non-uniform contrast
	Faint/dark printing
	Complex background texture
Address block location	Interfering background patterns such as ads
	Cancellation stamp overlay
	Character sizes
	Printing/writing orientations
	Mixture of different orientations
	Irregular address block locations
	Similar address block of a sender
	Shadow of a plastic window
	Non-square handwritten address block
	Irrelevant number string close to postal code
Address line segmentation	Character size variation
	Handwritten character lines overlapping each other
	Handwritten character lines touching each other
	Mixture of different writing orientations
	Shadow of plastic window
	Skewed letter images
Character segmentation	Touching characters
	Broken characters
	Non-uniform handwritten character size
	Zero-character-space printing
	Underlines
Character recognition	Multiple scripts
	Low quality character image
	Writing style variation
	Peculiar writing
	Writing instrument
	Extremely small characters
	Mixture of writing and printing
Character string recognition/address phrase interpretation	Address expression variations
	Abbreviated address expression
	Incomplete address expression
	Address line hidden by window
	Address line hidden by cancellation stamp
	Extra punctuation
	Wrong address
	Obsolete address

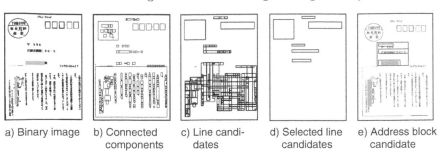

| a) Binary image | b) Connected components | c) Line candidates | d) Selected line candidates | e) Address block candidate |

Fig. 9.12. Address block location process.

- H-PH: Handwritten portrait horizontal
- H-PV: Handwritten portrait vertical
- H-LH: Handwritten landscape horizontal

The evaluation is made based on the confidence value defined as an a posteriori probability of the corresponding hypothesis after observing the evidence. The evidence is the set of feature values of (1) averages of height and width of character lines, (2) variances of height and width of character lines, (3) area of address-block candidate and (4) position of the candidate.

Graphical explanation of the address block location process is shown in Figure 9.12. First, the type of the letter is identified as "postcard" based on the measured size information. Then, connected component analysis is applied to this input binary image, and line candidates are extracted based on the horizontal and vertical hypotheses. In the case of a postcard, existence of a message area is hypothesized and, if it is the case, the message area is disregarded. In this example, the lower half had a character line-like structure and it was determined as a message area. And then, the upper half was analysed to extract character lines that would form an address block.

Deferred Decision Principle: *"Don't decide when it is uncertain. Leave it to other specialists."*

When we cannot make a decision reliably and leave it to the next person, it is important to give him multiple choices. Therefore, this principle almost always comes with the next principle, i.e. Multiple-Hypothesis Principle. These two principles are the same thing looked at from a different angle.

Multiple-Hypothesis Principle: *"Give options when it is uncertain."*

Usually, pattern recognition consists of sequential steps of sublevel pattern recognition problems. Principally important work by Fu on sequential pattern recognition using dynamic programming is well known, and can be a basis for more complex, modern problems [8]. As a matter of fact, the postal address recognition system being discussed consists of many sublevel pattern recognition problems:

- Line orientation detection
- Character size (large/small) detection

- Character line extraction
- Address block identification
- Character type (machine-printed/handwritten) identification
- Script (Kanji/Kana) identification
- Character orientation (0°, 90°, 180°, 270°) identification
- Character segmentation
- Character classification
- Word recognition
- Phrase interpretation
- Address number recognition
- Building/room number recognition
- Recipient name recognition
- Final decision making (accept/reject/retry)

It means that it cannot be a simple concatenation of a series of top-choice decisions. The number of such decisions goes well above 30 if segmentation and recognition decisions are counted for each character. Then, it is interesting to note that 0.9 to the power of 30 is 0.0424, while 0.99 to the power of 30 is 0.740. This means that the total recognition rate will be 74% when the accuracy of 30 decisions is 0.99. To attain this, each recognition component must generate multiple answers (i.e. hypotheses) and send them to the following recognition components. We may attain the success rate of 0.99, for example, if we can produce K hypotheses at each stage. Therefore, the Multiple Hypothesis Principle requests the system to propagate the multiple hypotheses throughout the recognition components, making a hierarchical tree of hypotheses to search for the optimum solution.

The next question is how to make a search in a tree of hypotheses for the optimum solution. The search time is a big concern here, however. Among the usable search methods of Beam Search, Hill Climbing Search and Best First Search [37], we may use basically the Hill Climbing Search, which can reach a solution in a shortest time. To boost the recognition accuracy, however, we can apply Beam Search at the final stages. The control of the number of branches (multiple hypotheses), K, is very important to trade off the total accuracy and total recognition time. Usually, each component generates scores for hypotheses, and they are compared with two kinds of thresholds, i.e. absolute and relative thresholds, to determine which hypotheses we retain. These parameters need to be determined carefully to attain the highest recognition accuracy within a limited recognition time.

To show the effectiveness of this approach, we show an example of the relationship between the total recognition rate and the number of address block hypotheses in Figure 9.13. There are similar curves for other decision processes.

Information Integration Principle: There are three kinds of information integration. Among those, Types 1 and 2 are "process" integration,

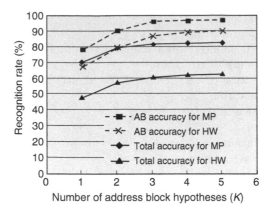

Fig. 9.13. Relationship between the total recognition rate and the number of address block hypotheses (AB: address block; MP: machine-printing, HW: Handwriting).

while Type 3 is literally "information" integration. They can be paraphrased as follows.

Type 1: *"Solve a problem by multiple different experts as a team."*
Type 2: *"Solve a problem by multiple same-field experts as a team."*
Type 3: *"Solve a problem by utilizing as much information as available."*

Type 1 integration has the following examples:

• Segmentation–Recognition Integration
• Recognition–Interpretation Integration
• Segmentation–Recognition–Interpretation Integration

Type 1A: Segmentation–Recognition Integration. An early work on segmentation–recognition integration was to solve a problem of handwritten touching digit recognition [9]. The segmentation component carries out hypothetical presegmentation and generates a network of segmentation hypotheses. In this presegmentation, large connected components are considered to be touching characters, and are separated into two patterns at the hypothetical touching positions. When the estimation of the touching position is ambiguous, multiple positions are hypothesized. Of course, when the "touching" is not completely sure, the non-touching case is also hypothesized. Then, the recognition component recognizes the presegmented patterns assigned to the edges of the segmentation hypothesis network, and the optimal path with the maximum score (or minimum cost) is searched for [24]. Because the difficulty in segmentation of handwritten touching characters was obvious, this integration was a natural consequence.

Type 1B: Recognition–Interpretation Integration. Integrated are a recognition process and a linguistic postprocessing. When Kanji characters are written in well-separated boxes and segmentation is reliable, this approach is effective and efficient. A Finite State Automaton scheme can be used to search a Kanji recognition lattice for valid words in a lexicon. Heuristics is available to speed up the search even for huge lexicons [25]. Because the lattice gives the candidate characters, only those words that start with those candidate characters are searched for. In the case of Japanese, because there is no space between words, every position of the character string is assumed to be a start of a word when the lattice search is carried out. Then the result is again a lattice of word candidates, from which a valid word string is searched for.

Type 1C: Segmentation–Recognition–Interpretation Integration. Integrated here are the three processes of segmentation, recognition and linguistic processing. The approach called lexicon-driven recognition has been successfully used for handwritten check amount recognition and postal address recognition [5,19,21,23]. In this approach, linguistic constraints are utilized in the search of the best segmentation path as shown in Figure 9.14. This approach is especially economical in the sense of speeding up the interpretation process. Character recognition (pattern classification) is carried out only for the presegmented patterns under evaluation, and only against the candidate character classes that meet the linguistic constraints. This feature is very attractive because the number of Kanji classes is more than 4000, and because the segmentation hypothesis network in reality is much more complex than shown in Figure 9.14.

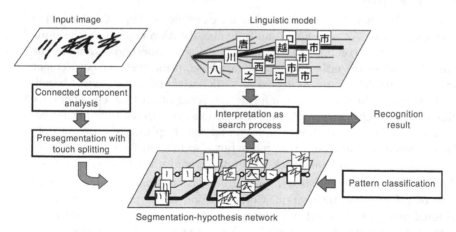

Fig. 9.14. Segmentation–Recognition–Interpretation Integration with TRIE linguistic model. The same architecture can also be applied for context-free grammar models.

A successful application in Japanese handwritten address phrase recognition is given in [23]. The developed method identifies an address from among a lexicon containing 111,349 address phrases that cover address names and main post offices around the country by using a beam search strategy. The recognition rate is over 80% with about 1% error.

Regarding the linguistic model, we can use the TRIE structure and the context-free grammar. The TRIE's effectiveness is manifested in the application to Japanese address phrase recognition as described above. However, it is somewhat limited to the phrases with simple syntax. For example, if a phrase can begin with any of several words, then the TRIE model for the resulting phrases needs repetition. Such a complexity happens when there are word variations, omissions of words and subphrase variations. In such cases, the TRIE approach requires more memory space and more time to search, even if it is possible. The context-free grammar approach solves this problem by implementing it in terms of recursive transition network [16].

It is interesting to note that the information integration scheme as shown in Figure 9.14 can be well compared to the Simon's view on human problem solving in "semantically rich domains" [29]:

> The structure of the problem rather than the organization of memory steers the problem-solving search. When it is solving problems in semantically rich domains, a large part of the problem-solving search takes place in long-term memory and is guided by information discovered in that memory

In this analogy, the linguistic model and the segmentation-hypothesis network correspond to LTM (long-term memory) and STM (short-term memory), respectively.

Type 2: Classifier Combination. It is an example of Type 2 information integration [14]. We may apply multiple classification engines to the same input, and then combine the results. The known methods combine the classification results either at the abstract level, rank level or measurement level. Known schemes are voting based, rank based and measurement based.

It is hoped in this kind of information integration that classifiers are different in several ways: different recognition algorithms, different implementation, different training samples and so on. Expectations are not only for improvements in recognition rates, but also in reduction in error rates. Applications such as bank check recognition require very low error rates.

Type 3: Corroboration-Based Information Integration. This is the third type of Information Integration. Corroboration is the process to find additional evidence. It is different from classifier combination in that more than one input fields are recognized for better recognition performance. In a sense, this is a Recognition–Recognition Integration scheme. One of the good examples is bank check recognition where a legal amount and a courtesy amount are recognized and combined to heighten the recognition reliability [15]. Another is postal code recognition, where postal code recognition and address phrase recognition are conducted in parallel or in serial [23]. In the case of the Japanese postal system, seven-digit postal codes correspond to one or a few towns.

Still another example is to recognize a recipient name to reduce the ambiguity and to identify the address point reliably. When address number recognition gives multiple candidate address points due to some ambiguity, or when room number recognition fails, we can still use the partial recognition result and extract address point candidates. Then, by consulting a directory, we can list up the candidate recipient names, and identify a unique one by recognizing the recipient name image. Actually, recipient name recognition is necessary anyway, when the recognized address point is such a place that there is more than one recipient. For example, a large business building has many tenants, requiring recognition of a recipient name, e.g. a name of a company, although this is not the case of corroboration.

Corroboration-Based Information Integration can be used in several ways. One is to reduce the error rate, resulting in more reliable recognition. Bank check recognition is of this kind. Another is to increase the recognition (accept) rate. This is applied in postal address recognition effectively. However, the final choice of the two objectives is at discretion of users, and it depends on the optimization criteria applied at a higher level. An experiment shows the effectiveness of recipient address recognition as in Figure 9.15, where the recognition rate is more valued.

Multiple-Solution Principle: The paraphrased meaning is *"When the problem is difficult, call more specialists."*

There are many image level problems in postal address recognition, which include problems of characters touching each other, underlines touching characters, shadow noises from a plastic window (Figure 9.8), a cancellation stamp covering address characters, and so on. These require special problem solving mechanisms. Multiple-Solution Principle here is to recommend to provide more than one solution to solve each of these, possibly complementary or very different approaches.

For example, as for touching characters, one solution is to try to separate the pattern as explained before [9], and another solution can be to make a character classifier recognize touching patterns as a whole. A classifier

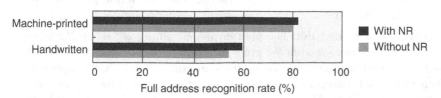

Fig. 9.15. Effectiveness of name recognition (NR) in a postal address recognition system.

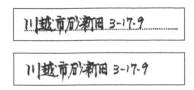

Fig. 9.16. Address handwriting with underline (dotted line) and its removed version.

can be trained to recognize touching two digits by just feeding frequently touching character pairs in the training process. In the case of digits, the number of such pairs is not so big compared with the size of Kanji classes. A small adaptation however is necessary for the classifier to output two-digit class labels in such a case.

Underlines and window shadows are of interest to discuss in that they help recognition, while causing problems. Japanese handwritten addresses are often written on the underlines (sometimes dotted lines), which are preprinted on an envelope (Figure 9.16). Therefore, the underlines are a good cue to locate an address block. The multiple-solution approach here is to detect the underlines and to eliminate thin lines and dotted lines. The window shadow case is similar. Shadow line images are often noisy. Therefore we take two approaches of dilation and erosion. By applying dilation, we expect to be able to detect the frame structure of a window; and we apply erosion to try to treat shadow patterns as noises and to eliminate them. The same approach is applicable to the noisy image of a cancellation stamp. A circular stamp pattern is searched first in the probable area. If it fails, a dilation operation is applied to the same area and a circular pattern is searched. If it fails again, an erosion operation is applied instead in an attempt to remove the noisy patterns.

These two different solutions implemented as recognition components make two branches in the hypothesis tree described in the section of Multiple Hypothesis Principle. These two branches are followed one by one in search of a verifiable address recognition result. By using Hill Climbing, the first recognition result verified terminates the whole recognition process. In this way, to provide complementary solutions is a reasonable approach. When interference is weak, we try to eliminate it; on the other hand, when the interference is intense, we try to extract the interfering patterns and utilize that information.

Perturbation Principle: The paraphrased meaning is *"When the problem is difficult, try to modify the problem slightly."* Historically, it has been used for a rather long time since 1980s in commercial OCRs especially when they used a structural pattern recognition method for handwritten character recognition. When an input pattern could not be recognized due to topological differences, slight changes in the pattern or in recognition parameters were made and the recognition was retried.

Recently, the perturbation approach is studied more scientifically [12]. Transformations are applied to an input image to generate slightly "perturbed" patterns, assuming these new patterns still belong to the same class as the original one. The same recognition engine is applied to recognize these patterns and then, the recognition results are combined. Logically, there can be many ways of doing combination. Transformations to be applied here include the morphological operations such as dilation (thickening) and erosion (thinning), and geometrical transformations such as rotation, slant (horizontal/vertical), perspective and shrink transformations.

A perturbation method has been successfully applied in postal address recognition systems. One way to do is to apply a transformation to a rejected input image and to retry the whole recognition process. In practice, due to the recognition time limitation, only one or two cycles of perturbation can be applied, but it is known that more than 10% points is improved. Another experiment that allowed many kinds of transformations and longer computation time showed that recognition rates for machine-printed and handwritten postal addresses could be well over 40% for rejected mailpieces.

There are two practical concerns, however; i.e. computational cost and additional chances of errors. Regarding the first, when the computer performances improve year by year following Moore's Law, this approach seems very promising to pursue further. However, regarding the errors, a detailed care is necessary to minimize the additional ones. Without the care, it has been observed that the error rate for the perturbation cycles is higher than the first round of normal recognition.

9.5 Robustness Strategy for Implementation

In developing pattern recognition systems, there need to be a higher-order consideration as a methodology on how to implement individual recognition components and algorithms. It is almost impossible to design the whole recognition system in detail in advance and then build it. Almost always, we meet new unknown problems in new applications. Therefore, the developmental process goes step-by-step by checking the validity and analysing the problems for the next step. It goes like a spiral [36].

Cycles of Robustness Implementation Process. Logically, the first step of robustness implementation is to identify the performance influencing factors (PIFs). It is to know the "enemies", or to know what kinds of difficulties the real world casts. So, knowing the PIFs is the most important thing to start with.

However, we can identify difficulties only after we have a recognition system or a simulator. Application of the developed recognition system teaches us the PIFs. So, what we do is to perform simulation experiments on a huge dataset of real samples. A field test of several months duration of a prototype system is preferable to collect a sufficient number of samples covering all difficult cases. The more complex the recognition system becomes, the more PIFs we have, meaning the more samples we need.

In reality, we need to make cycles of the following steps:

- Acquire (more) sample images and groundtruthing
- Develop a (better/additional) recognition method and algorithms
- Implement the method and algorithms into simulation software
- Test and evaluate the method and algorithms
- Analyse errors and rejections
- Identify (additional) performance influencing factors
- Make a plan of the next cycle including that of additional sample acquisition and approaches to attack the identified factors
- Repeat the above steps until the performance is satisfactory

In these cycles, additional sample acquisition is one of the keys to make the whole process efficient and successful. As discussed later in the context of acceleration datasets, it is so because it is practically impossible to acquire all samples that are problematic to the recognizer at once, and it is also because groundtruthing of a huge sample dataset that could cover every difficult problem would be so costly. This discussion relates to *active learning* or *learning with queries*, which is a hot research topic in machine learning [6].

The cycles of this process become more complicated when we need to solve several problems in parallel for efficiency. Postal address recognition discussed so far is such a system. Therefore, project management is another big issue although it is out of the scope of this chapter. It is discussed in [11] for example.

Identifying Performance Influencing Factors. Performance influencing factors are obtained as a result of understanding the problematic phenomena. To understand the phenomena, we should follow the steps:

- Inspect visually and identify the part of the image concerned
- Identify the recognition component(s) that failed
- Identify the fault(s) in the component(s)/algorithm(s)
- Identify a pattern recognition design principle to remedy the fault(s)
- Describe verbally the problem concerned
- Gather more similar samples
- Try new algorithms against the extended samples and analyse the result

The most important in here is to find a "pattern recognition" problem and the corresponding design principle under consideration. Of course, we are not interested in programming bugs neither parameters optimization in this discussion. We should solve them anyway. Understanding of the underlying problems by seeing through the superficial phenomena is important. Only by doing so, we can expect the recognition system become "robust" in a real sense. We would like to be able to create "build-in-robustness" rather than patches of temporary expedients, and to apply the learned principles to other applications. The first part of this chapter has discussed this issue.

Sample Databases to Support the Development Process. As mentioned earlier, the samples that cover the performance influencing factors are the key for the success. Collection is a laborious task and requires repetitive process, however. The width and the depth of variations in the required samples vary depending on the progress of the development and on the problems the recognition system meets. Usually, "difficult problems" require more samples. Four kinds of datasets (databases) are required:

- Validation datasets
- Training datasets
- Test datasets
- Acceleration datasets

The validation datasets are for selecting an approach, architecture and algorithm from their alternatives, while the training datasets are for tuning the parameters of recognition components. Those datasets need to be devised so that each recognition component can use them effectively. For example, there should be datasets for algorithms of address block location, address line segmentation, character string recognition and so on.

The test datasets, which should not be used for training, are for evaluating the recognition performance as a whole. It is recommended to separate the test dataset into multiple datasets. It is not only convenient for experiments but also essential to evaluate the profile of recognition performances. In the case of postal address recognition, mailpieces to be sorted have different properties depending on the sorting operations, equivalently on the operational time. For example, they carry out delivery sequence sorting in very early mornings, outward dispatch sorting in daytime, and bulk mail (business mail) sorting in the afternoon. Mailpiece images in each working time have different characteristics. Therefore sample images from different time domains can form separate datasets. The same thing can be applied to the seasons and areas, because there are seasonal changes and local changes as well.

The acceleration datasets play a major role in the robustness implementation process. They are the datasets of "live images" that have been rejected by the recognizer under test, where the "live images" are samples captured during the system operations. By using these problematic images for algorithm improvements, the cost of groundtruthing, analysing and identifying major performance influencing factors can be minimized. This strategy is parallel to that in active learning, where additional samples are acquired and most informative samples are selected for the additional classifier training [6].

Basic Strategy for the Improvements. In building up the recognition system, control of errors and rejections demands attention. Although the error and the rejection can be traded each other in general, we should note that it is very difficult to convert an erroneous result into a correct one by a single improvement step. Therefore, the basic principle is to try to exterminate the errors first. The most effective way to do so is to set the absolute threshold high enough to turn the error into rejection.

In the following, we discuss the strategy more concretely. To do so, we classify the final recognition result into the following seven classes:

- C: Correct
- R1: Rejections due to competing candidates with a permissible score
- R2: Rejections due to a low score
- R3: Rejections due to no candidates
- E1: Error with the right candidate competing
- E2: Error with the right candidate with a low score
- E3: Error without the right candidate

With these classifications and labels, we may discuss the improvement plans more explicitly.

When we have E1 or R1, the absolute score value of the top choice is good enough, or within a permissible range by definition, but there are competing candidates. In these cases, the plan is to change threshold parameters to convert the E1 case into R1, and/or to train classifiers further to convert R1 to C. When we have E2 or R2, the plan is usually to train classifiers because we have the right candidate with a low score. However, when we have E3 or R3, there must be something wrong somewhere, possibly in early stages, because no right candidate is raised. Then, we need to seek the problems and make a plan to convert E3 and R3 at least to R1. In either case of errors, the threshold values (absolute/relative) should be reviewed to turn the errors into rejections.

In the case of "semantically rich domains" like postal address recognition, we are able to keep the errors low, and we can have many R2 and R3 rejections instead. If we succeed to put us into this situation, the improvement process may proceed in a positive way. Figure 9.17 is an example of read rate improvement curves. The read rates were measured in field experiments for a four-month period of our postal address recognition project.

In this figure, two types of moving average, Moving Ave 1 and Moving Ave 2, were calculated. They are 5-day moving averages of two hypothetical mixtures of bulk mail (BK), machine-printed mail (MP) and handwritten mail (HW). The first type is a mixture of 0% of BK, 60% of MP and 40% of HW. The second is that of 30% of BK, 50% of MP and 20% of HW.

As shown, the improvement was not so much straightforward that the recognition performance curves fluctuated while they globally went up.

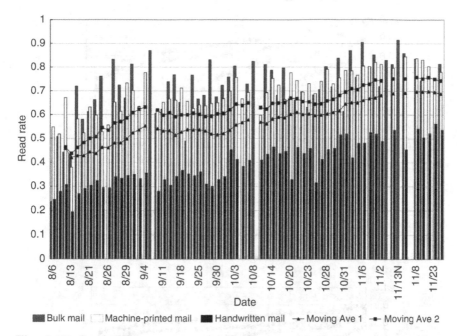

Fig. 9.17. Read rate improvement curves measured in field experiments (data from 1997).

This fact is a reflection of the complexity of the technical difficulties. In the period of these four months, we identified more than 100 problems, and made about 100 "improvements" in the algorithms and 30 software version-ups. Often times, read rate improvements could not be confirmed by a single field experiment, although they were confirmed by acceleration datasets. We had to wait for the field experiments of several days to confirm the read rate improvements.

Robustness Implementation in a Real Project. In the final section, we would like to show a real example of robustness implementation. Figure 9.18 to Figure 9.20 show the read rate profiles of four versions of our postal address recognition system against the test datasets of bulk mail (BK), machine-printed mail (MP) and handwritten mail (HW), respectively. The version numbers in those figures are temporary just to discriminate them here. Recognition software versions of V1 thru V4 are from October 1997, November 1997, March 1998, and June 1999, respectively. Figure 9.21 shows the average read rates and standard deviations of read rates of these four versions in a different dimension.

From these graphs, we can see that the average read rates were dramatically improved, and that the robustness was improved generally. There were cases where robustness did not improve, however. Still, we may conclude

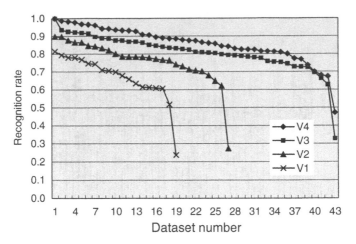

Fig. 9.18. Read rate profiles against the bulk mail test datasets.

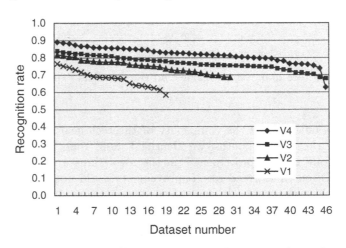

Fig. 9.19. Read rate profiles against the machine-printed test datasets.

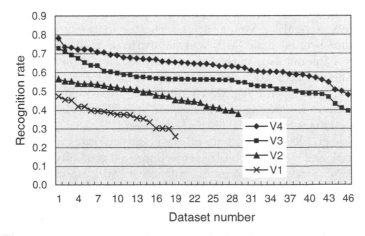

Fig. 9.20. Read rate profiles against the handwritten test datasets.

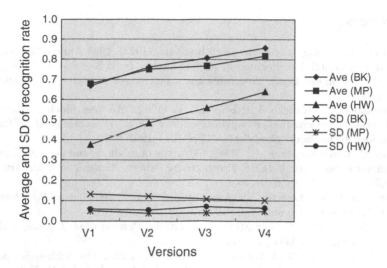

Fig. 9.21. Long-range read rate improvements in terms of average read rates and standard deviations of read rates. Version numbers are temporary just to discriminate. V1: October 1997, V2: November 1997, V3: March 1998, V4: June 1999.

that the improvement process using the acceleration datasets is effective to realize industrial strength recognition systems.

9.6 Conclusions

In this chapter, we have presented the principles to be applied to develop complex pattern recognition systems such as a postal address recognition system. The principles presented are especially to make the system more robust. It was attempted to discuss the robustness centrally, and the design principles for robustness. To be stressed finally is that robustness can be attained only by comprehensive approaches.

Acknowledgments

The author would like to acknowledge with many thanks that development of the postal address recognition system cited in this chapter was done by many colleagues at Central Research Laboratory and at Mechatronics Division of Hitachi at that time. The author is also grateful to Prof. George Nagy, Rensselaer Polytechnic Institute, and Prof. Bidyut Baran Chaudhuri, Indian Statistical Institute, for their invaluable suggestions and comments for the work and for this chapter.

References

1. UNLV: Information Science Research Institute. (1993). 1993 Annual Report.
2. Baird, H.S. (1992). Document image defect models. In: H.S. Baird, H. Bunke, and K. Yamamoto (Eds.). *Structured Document Image Analysis*. New York: Springer.
3. Bashomatsu, T., Kaneko, I., Nishijima, Y. (1992). Address block location and format identification of japanese address OCR. *Proceedings of USPS Advanced Technologies Conference 5*, pp. 1283–1293.
4. Casey, R.G. and Lecolinet, E. (1996). A survey of methods and strategies in character segmentation. *IEEE Transactions Pattern Analysis and Machine Intelligence, 18(7)*, pp. 690–706.
5. Chen, C.H. (1995). Lexicon-driven word recognition. *Proceedings of the Third ICDAR, Montreal, Canada*, pp. 919–922.
6. Duda, R.O., Hart, P.E., and Stork, D.G. (2001). *Pattern Classification*, 2nd ed. New York: John Wiley & Sons.
7. Filatov, A., Nikitin, V., Volgunin, A., Zelinsky P. (1999). The AddressScript recognition system for handwritten envelops. In: S.-W. Lee and Y. Nakano (Eds.). *Document Analysis Systems: Theory and Practice*. New York: Springer, pp. 157–171.
8. Fu, K.S., Chien, Y.T., and Cardillo, G.P. (1967). A dynamic programming approach to sequential pattern recognition. *IEEE Transactions on Electronic Computers, EC16*, pp. 313–326.
9. Fujisawa, H., Nakano, Y., and Kurino, K. (1992). Segmentation methods for character recognition: from segmentation to document structure analysis. *Proceedings of IEEE, 80(7)*, 1079–1092.
10. Fujisawa, H.and Liu, C.-L. (2003). Directional pattern matching for character recognition revisited. *Proceedings of the Seventh ICDAR, Edinburgh, Scotland*, pp. 794–798.
11. Fujisawa, H. and Sako, H. (2003). Balance between optimistic planning and pessimistic planning in a mission critical project. *Proceedings of IEMC2003, Albany, NY*, pp. 605–609.
12. Ha, T.M. and Bunke, H. (1997). Off-line, handwritten numeral recognition by perturbation. *IEEE Transactions on Pattern Analysis and Machine Intelligence, 19(5)*, pp. 535–539.
13. Hamamoto, Y., Uchimura, S., Masamizu, K., and Tomita, S. (1995). Recognition of handprinted Chinese characters using Gabor features. *Proceedings of the Third ICDAR, Montreal, Canada*, pp. 819–823.
14. Ho, T.K., Hull, J.J., and Srihari, S.N. (1994). Decision combination in multiple classifier systems. *IEEE Transactions on Pattern Analysis and Machine Intelligence, 16(1)*, pp. 66–75.
15. Houle, G.F., Aragon, D.B., Smith, R.W., Shridhar, M., and Kimura, F. (1996). A MultiLayered corroboration-based check reader. *Proceedings IAPR Workshop on Document Analysis Systems, Malvern, USA*, pp. 495–546.
16. Ikeda, H., Furukawa, N., Koga, M., Sako, H., and Fujisawa, H. (2000). A context-free grammar-based language model for document understanding. *Proceedings of DAS2000, Rio de Janeiro, Brazil*, pp. 135–146.
17. Kagehiro, T., Koga, M., Sako, H., and Fujisawa, H. (1998). Segmentation of handwritten kanji numerals integrating peripheral information by bayesian

rule. *Proceedings of IAPR Workshop on Machine Vision Applications, Chiba, Japan*, pp. 439–442.

18. Kagehiro, T., Koga, M., Sako, H., and Fujisawa, H. (2004). Address-block extraction by Bayesian rule. *Proceedings of ICPR2004, 2*, pp. 582–585.

19. Kimura, F., Sridhar, M., and Chen, Z. (1993). Improvements of Lexicon-directed algorithm for recognition of unconstrained hand-written words. *Proceedings of the Second ICDAR, Tsukuba, Japan*, pp. 18–22.

20. Kimura, F., Takashina, K., Tsuruoka, S., and Miyake, Y. (1987). Modified quadratic discriminant functions and the application to Chinese character recognition. *IEEE Transactions on Pattern Analysis and Machine Intelligence, 9(1)*, pp. 149–153.

21. Koga, M., Mine, R., Sako, H., and Fujisawa, H. (1999). Lexical search approach for character-string recognition. Document analysis systems: theory and practice. In: S.-W. Lee and Y. Nakano (Eds.). New York: Springer, pp. 115–129.

22. Li, Y., Lopresti, D., Nagy, G., and Tomkins, A. (1996). Validation of image defect models for optical character recognition. *IEEE Transactions Pattern Analysis and Machine Intelligence, 18(2)*, pp. 99–108.

23. Liu, C.-L., Koga, M., and Fujisawa, H. (2002). Lexicon-driven segmentation and recognition of handwritten character strings for Japanese address reading. *IEEE Transactions on Pattern Analysis and Machine Intelligence, 24(11)*, pp. 1425–1437.

24. Liu, C.-L., Sako, H., and Fujisawa, H. (2004). Effects of classifier structures and training regimes on integrated segmentation and recognition of handwritten numeral strings. *IEEE Transactions on Pattern Analysis and Machine Intelligence, 26(11)*, pp. 1395–1407.

25. Marukawa, K., Koga, M., Shima, Y., and Fujisawa, H. (1991). An error correction algorithm for handwritten Chinese character address recognition. *Proceedings of the First ICDAR, Saint-Malo, France*, pp. 916–924.

26. Ogata, H., Ueda, Y., Marukawa, K., Sako, H., and Fujisawa, H. (1999). A method for street number matching in Japanese address recognition. *Proceedings of the Fifth ICDAR, Bangalore, India*, pp. 321–324.

27. Palumbo, P.W., Srihari, S.N., Soh, J., Sridhar, R., and Demjanenko, V. (1992). Postal address block location in real time. *IEEE Computer, 25(7)*, pp. 34–42.

28. Pavlidis, T. (1983). Effects of distortions on the recognition rate of a structural OCR system. *Proceedings of Computer Vision and Pattern Recognition, Washington, DC*, pp. 303–309.

29. Simon, H.A. (1998). The sciences of the artificial, 3rd ed. Cambridge, MA: The MIT Press.

30. Srihari, S.N. (1992). High-performance reading machines. *Proceedings of the IEEE, 80(7)*, pp. 1120–1132.

31. Srihari, S.N., Govindaraju, V., and Shekhawat, A. (1993). Interpretation of handwritten addresses in US mailstream. *Proceedings of the Second ICDAR, Tsukuba, Japan*, pp. 291–294.

32. Srihari, S.N., Shin, Y.-C., Ramanaprasad, V., and Lee, D.-S. (1995). Name and address block reader system for tax form processing. *Proceedings of the Third ICDAR, Montreal, Canada*, pp. 5–10.

33. Srihari, S.N., Wang, C.-H., and Palumbo, P.W. (1987). Recognizing address blocks on mail pieces. *AI Magazine, 8(4)*, pp. 25–40.

34. Suen, C.Y., Mori, S., Kim, S.H., and Leung, C.H. (2003). Analysis and recognition of Asian scripts – the state of the art. *Proceedings of the Seventh ICDAR, Edinburgh, Scotland*, pp. 866–878.

35. Taghva, K., Nartker, T., Borsack, J., and Condit, A. (2000). UNLV-ISRI document collection for research in OCR and information retrieval. *Proceedings of IS&T/SPIE Conference Document Recognition and Retrieval VII, San Jose*, pp. 157–164.

36. Tang, H., Augustin, E., Suen, C.Y., Baret, O., and Cheriet, M. (2004). Spiral recognition methodology and its application for recognition of Chinese bank checks. *Proceedings of the Ninth IWFHR, Kokubunji, Japan*, pp. 263–268.

37. Winston, P.H. (1979). *Artificial Intelligence*. Reading, MA: Addison-Wesley, pp. 89–105.

38. Wolf, M. and Niemann, H. (1997). Fast address block location on handwritten and machine printed mail-piece images. *Proceedings of the Fourth ICDAR, Ulm, Germany*, pp. 753–757.

39. Yu, B., Jain, A.K., and Mohiuddin, M. (1997). Address block location on complex mail pieces. *Proceedings of the Fourth ICDAR, Ulm, Germany*, pp. 897–901.

10

Arabic Cheque Processing System: Issues and Future Trends

M. Cheriet, Y. Al-Ohali, N.E. Ayat, and C.Y. Suen

10.1 Introduction

From the administrative point of view, cheque processing involves all tasks a bank officer may perform to process an incoming cheque for a client. This includes: accessing account numbers, verifying names and signatures on the cheque, verifying the date of the cheque, matching the legal amount with the courtesy amount and verifying the credit of the cheque writer. However, from the technical point of view, cheque processing could involve capturing the cheque image, separating the foreground of the cheque from its background, extracting fields of interest and recognizing each of them.

This work employs theories and methodologies from various fields ranging from Natural language processing, Optical Character Recognition to Banking.

The motivation of the work on Cheque processing is not less than the motivation of the entire research in artificial intelligence, which aims to program the computer to carry out tedious routine processes, freeing time and space for humans to perform tasks that require higher levels of intelligence. A major advantage of such study is that it can be easily adjusted to serve more than 20 different countries (all of them use Arabic as their first language). In addition, legal amounts are widely found in documents other than bank cheques (e.g. business sell/purchase forms). Therefore, this study will be applicable to a wide range of applications. Moreover, similar languages (e.g. Urdu, Farisi) which use the same alphabet can benefit from these studies.

The remaining sections provide a description of datasets available for researchers as well as a detailed description of one system that processes legal amounts and one system dedicated for processing of courtesy amounts.

10.2 Datasets

Due to strict banking rules to protect their customers, it is extremely difficult to gain access to real cheques. This led some researchers to perform their research within financial institutions [16]. Such datasets are owned by, controlled and limited to the respected financial institutions. Other researchers like [18], opted to build artificial databases. In [18], about 2600 English cheques, written by 800 writers with pre-set legal amounts, have been collected. Another set of 1900 French cheques from 600 different writers has been collected too. The legal amounts were set for the writers to reflect balanced word distribution.

In the Arabic cheque-processing domain, however, there are real-world datasets that can be used by scientific researchers worldwide. Thus, researchers can test/evaluate their theories and systems in a real world environment. Real data, however, has a number of disadvantages, one must note. First, researchers have no control on the number of samples from each class, as this would be determined by the actual distribution of the classes and by the sampling bias. Another point that some may regard is the exposure of natural carelessness by some people in the society when filling or handling cheques. With this idea in mind, we contributed with a new database that we built in collaboration with Al-Rajihi Bank in Riyad, Saudi Arabia [2]. These datasets include: legal amount dataset (containing 2499 legal amounts), courtesy amount dataset (containing 2499 courtesy amounts and written in Hindi digits), Arabic sub-word dataset (containing 29,498 sub-words within the domain of legal amount) and Indian digit dataset (containing 15,175 digits). In addition, there is a dataset of complete (original) grey level cheques, which can be used for other research purposes (e.g. date processing). Each of the aforementioned datasets is divided into training and testing sets. As real data may include overlapping parts of consecutive words or digits, such cases are explicitly mentioned by the datasets. Figure 10.1 below shows a sample of our Arabic Cheque database.

Fig. 10.1. A sample of the Arabic cheque data.

10.3 Legal Amount Processing

Processing legal amounts is an important step to achieve automated cheque processing systems. Among the attempts to develop a complete legal amount processing system we cite Kaufmann and Bunke [22], who developed a complete system to read legal amounts extracted from German cheques. Statistical features are extracted from each component and are fed to an HMM classifier. Contextual information is used to post process the classification results. The correct legal amount was among the top 10 choices in 88.8% of the cheques.

In this section, we describe how a grammar and sub-word recognition system could be utilized to interpret the legal amount into a numerical value. A detailed example is shown for the various steps in the interpretation process.

10.3.1 Pre-Processing

The input is assumed to be a grey level digitized image of a cheque. Figure 10.2 shows a sample legal amount and all the pre-processing steps applied to it. First, the legal amount is statically segmented from the cheque form. Dynamic thresholding is then applied to binarize the extracted legal amount. Basic filling and thinning operations are applied next to enhance the image of the legal amount.

Baseline is an important factor that affects object orientation and noise removal decisions. We determine the location of the baseline and its thickness using horizontal projections. Slant correction is then applied by computing the density of the baseline in various angles. The minimum slant of the image will produce the maximum baseline density.

It is very common that undesirable objects occur in the extracted legal amount. Such objects include external noise and intrusions (introduced by the cheque writer or bank officers), portions of the upper (or lower) handwritten lines, or portions of the pre-printed text. It is important to remove such objects as they may affect the recognition results. Due to

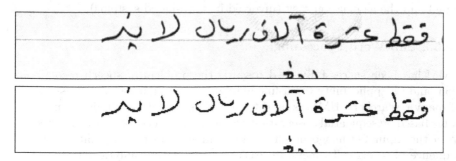

Fig. 10.2. Binarization of the legal amount.

the limited lexicon entries involved in the current application, secondary components (e.g. dots) are not critical in sub-word identification. Noise and secondary components are removed based on the following factors:

(1) Inter-component distances: Small horizontal gaps are normally used to separate handwritten words. Larger gaps are indications of noise or unrelated objects. Dynamic threshold is used to define the term "small gap".

(2) Vertical position of components: Relevant components are normally written near the baseline. Having an object above or below the baseline with significant distance is an indication of unrelated components. Dynamic threshold is used to define the term "significant distance".

(3) Size of each component: Very small or very large objects are clear signs of noisy components. Extreme aspect ratio is another indicator that is used to detect undesirable objects.

(4) Slant: Slant of each component should be close enough to the overall slant of the legal amount.

Different writers have different habits in terms of inter-component distances and letter sizes. Dynamic thresholds are determined based on the mean and standard deviation of the overall components in the legal amount. Location of an object is described in terms of the bounding box and its centre of gravity.

Each connected component is then extracted as a sub-word. Slant correction is applied to each object to correct small slant variations between sub-words. Each sub-word image is assigned a unique position number (index).

10.3.2 Word Versus Sub-Word Processing

An Arabic written word may be composed of one or more connected components, each of which could contain one or more letters. Accordingly, researchers have tackled the problem of Arabic written word recognition based on letter recognition, sub-word recognition or word recognition. The sub-word recognition avoids the segmentation (involved in letter-based systems) and the association task (involved in word-based systems).

10.3.3 Sub-Word Processing

HMM has been successfully used towards the problem of speech recognition, and its applicability to off-line handwriting recognition was the study of many researchers. HMM is used to provide probabilistic similarity measures based on sequential observations. Sequential observations are detected from the input 2D image based on an estimation of the original writing sequence of strokes. To facilitate easier extraction of analytical features, skeletonization is applied to the input sub-word image. Pen-trajectory is

then estimated by finding the most efficient traversal of all edges in the
transformed tree Pen-trajectory is then estimated by finding the most efficient traversal of all points in the skeleton. Vector quantization is then
applied to facilitate efficient use of discrete HMM.

Feature Extraction

The aim of this process is to generate 1D descriptions out of 2D skeletons.
A graph representation of the skeleton is first built and then transformed
to a tree. Tree transformation is simpler and faster than Eulerian and
Hamiltonian graph transformations used in [1] and [21]. Pen-trajectory is
then estimated by finding the most efficient traversal of all edges in the
transformed tree. In the following, we give more details about each of these
steps.

Graph representation is achieved by labelling the skeleton into feature
points and curve segments. Feature points include end points and junction
segments. A junction segment is a cluster of adjacent junction points. The
labelled image is then transformed into a weighted graph G = (V,E) where
the set of vertices V includes all feature points and the set of edges E
includes all curve segments in the skeleton. The weight of each edge is set
equal to the length (in pixels) of its corresponding curve segment. This
representation requires many fewer vertices and therefore less amount of
resources, than the one applied in [1]. Pen trajectory can then be estimated
by a proper traversal of all edges (segment) in G.

Each segment is then represented by a sequence of Freeman chain codes.
Linear approximation is applied next to extract a shorter and less sensitive
description of the chain code list. The approximation process may result in
breaking some segments into several strokes based on direction variations.
It may also allow points from consecutive segments to be merged into one
stroke. This minimizes the effect of unnecessary junctions. Each stroke
is then represented by two values: length and direction. Stroke length is
normalized to the length of the original skeleton.

Vector Quantization

To facilitate effective application of discrete HMM, observation vectors are
mapped into a pre-defined set of values (codebook). A codebook of 170
entries is used to map each pair of direction and length values to a single
observation value. The size of the codebook was experimentally computed.

Clustering

Clustering is needed to reduce within-class variations in human handwriting. The goal of this process is to partition each class into clusters that share
similar feature vectors. Each class is then represented by a single HMM
model. Clustering is performed on the extracted sequence of features.

The number of clusters per class is computed in two steps. First, ISO-DATA algorithm is used to approximate the proper number of clusters for each class using unified threshold values. After that, the number of clusters for each class is manually estimated, based on ISODATA approximation and on the prior knowledge of the variations of each sub-word. The total number of clusters used was 150, representing 67 different classes.

Classification

A left-to-right HMM is used to model each cluster. The model of a cluster ω_i, is noted λ_i (N_i, π_i, A_i, B_i) where N_i represents the number of states, π_i is the initial probability at each state, A_i is the matrix of transition probabilities and B_i is the emission probabilities (the priori probabilities). The number of possible observations, M, is shared for all models. The number of states in each model is defined in relation to the number of letters within each sub-word, and therefore is unique for all models of the same class. This is used to account for the variability in width and structural complexities of different sub-words. Models are trained using the Baum–Welch algorithm. Each model is trained only to feature vectors that belong to it. Therefore, each model learns to produce high probability to similar inputs, but does not learn to produce low probabilities to different inputs. This is known as the maximum likelihood (ML) learning criterion.

Performance

Detail results of the combined classifiers are shown in Table 10.1. While the above results are not ideal for a practical industrial system, they highlight the strengths of both models in solving this problem, and expose them to further improvements.

The results shown in this chapter reflect the complexity of the recognition problem under consideration, and the difficulty of the samples used in this study. Table 10.2 shows the results of the current study as compared to others found in the literature. The table shows impressive results from [27] and [23] considering the lexicon sizes involved in their studies. However, it is important to consider the type of data (domain and quality) used to test each of the presented systems. While the domain of each study is normally stated, the quality of the data is not always reported in detail.

Table 10.1. Performance of the combined recognition system

Data set	Top 1 (%)	Top 3 (%)	Top 5 (%)	Top 10 (%)
Training	85.74	90.69	95.52	99.87
Validation	76.36	82.74	89.33	95.37
Testing	73.53	81.50	88.19	94.36

Table 10.2. Recognition results compared with other systems in the literature

Reference	Lexicon size	Top 1 (%)	Top 10 (%)	Top 20 (%)
Current study	67	73.53	94.36	97.70
[15]	198	65.05	90.83	95.00
[27]	232	81.60	94.90	
[18]	30	86.70	99.90	
[23]	100	84.60		99.00
[8]	28	89.65		

Error Analysis

Throughout the evaluation process, we encountered various sources of errors in the analytical model. Following is a chronologically sorted list of these sources, with some examples.

(1) Difficult handwriting or severe noise on the cheque document (Figure 10.3). We estimate that this type of error caused 20% of all errors encountered in the validation set. This type of error is the most difficult to overcome, because it affects the source of the image, which makes correct classification merely remotely visible. As a result, the correct class is mostly far away from the top choice of the classifier. On average, the correct class is estimated to be the top 11th choice of the classifier in such cases. Rejection control could be used to detect and avoid this type of error.

(2) The extraction and/or binarization steps. Extraction of the legal amount from the cheque image could leave out significant parts of some sub-words. The same could result from the binarization process. In addition, the binarization step could cut a sub-word image into two or more pieces. These errors represent about 20% of all errors in the validation set. The effect on the classifier depends on the significance of the damage caused to the sub-word. On average, the classifier puts images affected by this type of error at the top 10th choice.

(3) Imperfect skeletonization (Figure 10.4). As perfect skeletonization is not visible, imperfect skeletons could affect the sequence of strokes

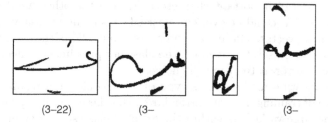

(3–22)   (3–   (3–

Fig. 10.3. Samples of errors caused by difficult handwriting. The correct class number (code) is shown below each image.

Image with its skeleton

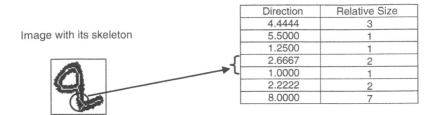

Direction	Relative Size
4.4444	3
5.5000	1
1.2500	1
2.6667	2
1.0000	1
2.2222	2
8.0000	7

Fig. 10.4. An error caused by the skeletonization module.

Feature Vector

Image with its skeleton

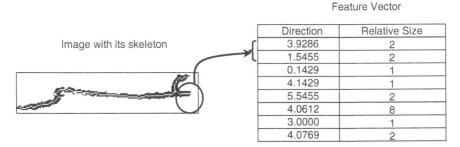

Direction	Relative Size
3.9286	2
1.5455	2
0.1429	1
4.1429	1
5.5455	2
4.0612	8
3.0000	1
4.0769	2

Fig. 10.5. An error caused by the feature extraction module.

used to characterize the input image. This type represents around 8% of the total errors on the validation set. On average, the classifier puts images affected by this type of error at the top 9th choice.

(4) The feature extraction module (Figure 10.5). This type of error is not very frequent, and is mainly due to errors in selecting the starting point. Interchangeable feature points (end points & junction points) could be traced in the wrong direction, creating a reversed portion in the feature vector. This error represents about 4% of the total errors on the validation set. On average, the classifier puts images affected by this type of error at the top 12th choice.

(5) The linear approximation process. This process is used to map the sequence of pixels into line segments. Due to the static thresholds used for this purpose, some significant shape variations could be overlooked causing a loss of important characteristics. On the other hand, some minor variations could be over emphasized causing unnecessary change in the feature vector. This error represents about 24% of the total errors on the validation set. On average, the classifier puts images affected by this type of error at the top 6th choice.

(6) The classification module. This type of error could be a result of the small size of training data of particular classes, large similarity between classes or large variations within the affected classes. This error represents about 24% of the total errors on the validation set. On average,

the classifier puts images affected by this type of error at the top 3rd choice.

10.3.4 Legal Amount Interpretation

Given an ordered list of sub-word images, the sub-word recognizer is invoked to provide a list of candidate sub-word codes for each sub-word image. Table 10.3 shows the sequence of sub-word extracted from an input legal amount. Table 10.4 shows the top 10 choices for each sub-word in Table 10.3. Legal amount (LA) interpretation intends to translate proper sequences of sub-word codes into their equivalent numerical values. LA interpretation is achieved at two levels: local and global. At the local level, we aim to detect a possible word from successive sub-word combinations. A word is encountered in a given position p if all its composing sub-words are found in a sequence that ends at p. This is easily performed using a dictionary lookup procedure. Due to the fact that some words share sub-words, the sequence of words may not be unique (e.g. at a given position p, sub-word w_1 could stand alone as a complete word, or could be concatenated with the preceding sub-word at p–1 to form another word w_2). In such cases, all possible words are passed to the global level. For each word, starting and ending positions are passed, along with the word's probability, to the global interpretation level to determine the best combination of words.

The search complexity in the first level is fairly limited due to the fact that the maximum number of consecutive sub-words that may compose a single word is found to be 4 (for the current vocabulary). This search procedure would then be performed 4kn, where k is a constant defined in relation to the dictionary size, and n is the number of sub-words in the extracted legal amount. Thus the complexity of this level is of $O(n)$.

The global level tries to find a complete and correct legal amount out of the list of all possible words. A correct legal amount should satisfy two conditions:

(1) It should make use of each sub-word exactly once. That is not to ignore any sub-word in the legal amount, and not to use any sub-word more than once.
(2) A correct legal amount should follow the grammatical rules of the Arabic language.

Table 10.3. The sequence of sub-words segmented from an input LA image

11	10	9	8	7	6	5	4	3	2	1	Position ←
ﻣ	ﺪ	ﻭ	ﻟ	✓	ﻒ	ﻟﺍ	ﺍ	ﻪ	ﺴﻤ	ﻬﺌﺎ	Segmented sub-word

Table 10.4. Results from the sub-word classifier – Top 10 choices for each sub-word in Table 10.3. (The correct choices are shaded)

11	10	9	8	7	6	5	4	3	2	1	Position ←
ﻻ	و	ﻻ	ﻒ	ﻟ	ﻐﻳ	ﺷﺎ	ﻟ	ة	ﻋﺸ	ﻓﻘﻂ	1
ﺑ	ﻻ	ﻟ	ﻟﺑ	ﺑ	ﻟ	ﻟﻒ	ا	ﺛﻧﻳﺔ	ﻒ	ﺑﻣﺎ	2
ﺛﻋﺔ	ﻒ	ﺑ	ﻛﺗﺎ	ﻻ	ﺑ	ﺛﻋﺔ	ﻻ	ﺛﻋﺔ	ﻻ	ﻟﻒ	3
ﻐﺑﺮ	ﻐﺑﺮ	ﻐﻳ	ﺛﻋﺔ	و	ﻒ	ﻟﻔ	و	ﻟﻔ	ﻓﺳﻮ	ﻟﻔ	4
ﻟﻠﻣ	ﺑ	ﺛﻋﺔ	ﻻ	ة	ﺛﻋﺔ	ﺑ	ﻟﻔ	ﻒ	ﻓﻳﺳﺔ	ﺿﺑﺎ	5
ﺣﺑﻪ	ﺛﻋﺔ	ﻐﺑﺮ	و	ﻐﺑﺮ	ﻐﺑﺮ	ﻟ	ﻐﺑﺮ	ﻓﻳﺳﺔ	ﻟﻠﻣ	ﻻ	6
ﻒ	ﻟ	ﻟﺑ	ﻟ	ﺑ	ﻛﺗﺎ	ﻻ	ﻟﺑ	ﻟ	ﻟﻔ	ﺑ	7
ﻟﺑ	ﻟ	ﻟﻔ	ﻐﺑﺮ	ﻟﻔ	ﻟﺑ	ﻓﻘﻂ	ﻟ	ﺗﻣﺳﺔ	ﺛﻋﺔ	ﻓﻳﺳﺔ	8
ﻟﺣﺑ	ﻋﺸ	ﺻﺑﻪ	ا	ﺣﺑﻪ	ﺛﻮ	ﻐﺑﺮ	ﺑ	ﻋﺸ	و	ﺳﻣﺑﺎ	9
ﻟ	ﻟﺣﺑ	ﻟﻠﻣ	ﺑ	ﺛﻋﺔ	ﻟﻔ	ﺣﺑﻪ	ﺑ	و	ﻐﺑﺮ	ﺷﺎ	10

These two conditions form the evaluation criteria of the global level. Details of grammar rules are out of the scope of this article but can be found in [2].

To simplify the application of grammatical rules, all words that do not change the numerical value of LA (e.g. the word "only") are removed from the word list. If such words appear in the first position of the legal amount, LA is considered correct even if it ignores the first position. The same can be said about the last position.

Depth first search is applied next to find all correct syntactic trees that satisfy the above two conditions. Numerical values for each complete tree is computed based on predefined correspondence between grammatical terms and mathematical operations ("+" and "*" operations).

10.4 Courtesy Amount Processing

The images of Indian digits are extracted from courtesy amounts (see Figure 10.6 for few samples), which are submitted to a preliminary pre-processing for the bank check background removal and the digit stroke

Fig. 10.6. Few samples of Arabic courtesy amounts.

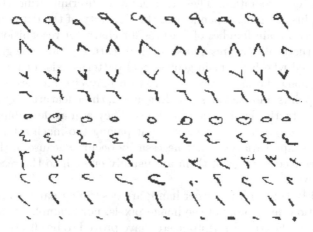

Fig. 10.7. A sample of Indian digits.

extraction. Each of the images has a corresponding literal amount image, which may allow matching further results at a verification level.

The Indian digits are used in many countries of the middle-east and western Asia. Due to the lack of databases, few OCR systems process these kinds of digit images. The Indian digits based numbers are decimal coded, thus having 10 classes. Figure 10.7 shows a representative sample of the database.

10.4.1 Pre-Processing

In order to the images of courtesy amount to be recognized, some reprocessing steps are considered. Indeed, we first clean the images by removing existing dummy strokes using few heuristic rules. The image capturing and thresholding causes some stroke imperfections. In order to cope with the opened occlusions and to preserve the original morphological patterns; a thickening of the stroke is done. Then a filtering phase allows smoothing the stroke contour.

For the image baseline to be corrected, we do a normalization procedure based on Madvanahath algorithm which searches for the horizontal inertia axis of the image [26]. In order to correct the vertical inclination of the amount stroke, we chose to use the histogram-based method. That is, we search for the inclination that provides the most picked histogram [17]. We deal with non-touching digits. Segmenting the digit strokes is done using a run-length following of the outer contours.

10.4.2 Features Extraction and Representation

In the literature, several researchers have proposed dedicated primitives for optical character recognition. Their efficiency in discriminating the digit patterns are plus or minus dependent of the difficulty of the data on hand.

There are two main families of features for character recognition: morphological (structural) features and statistical features. Morphological features usually tell whether certain geometrical patterns exist or not within the image. Among the most used patterns we may cite buckles, concavities, extreme points, intersections, etc. In general, these features were firstly used to feed syntactic classification methods. They aim at describing character shapes in an abstract manner without paying too much attention to the irrelevant shape variations that necessarily occur. Because of their robustness, a reduced number of them are usually enough to the recognizer to generalize well.

Statistical features, on the other hand, are describing patterns through local information descriptors of the image pixels. For example, zoning, invariant moments, Fourier descriptors, etc. have proved to be effective methods of statistical features extraction. Morphological and statistical features are complementary in a way that they describe two distinct properties of the image stroke.

To characterize the digit images, we set a feature vector combining statistics about the contour pixels' directions, the smoothness of the contour pixels and a set of morphological clues. This would be thought as a "fine-in-coarse" recognition through the statistical local descriptors (fine recognition) and structural patterns (coarse recognition). We describe below the used set of primitives.

Morphological Features

Local information such as that embedded within the contour pixels (freeman directions, Fourier descriptors, etc.) is not efficient enough to describe the whole characteristics of existing stroke patterns. In the other hand, morphological patterns have proved to be robust primitives for noisy character images recognition.

Thus, we considered a first subset of primitives based on some structural characteristics of the digit stroke patterns proposed by Cheriet et al. in [11] and Strathy et al. in [33] for the segmentation of handwritten words.

Even though not used as we do, few works has already proposed to exploit geometrical patterns in the feature extraction procedure as did in [12, 19, 20, 25].

A Valley region   A Mountain region   A Hole region

Fig. 10.8. The set of structural patterns considered for the Indian digit characterization.

Fig. 10.9. Indian digits with structural.

In our context, we note that among the Indian digit classes five of them contain some simple geometrical patterns that are rather discriminating. That is, classes "V", "Λ", "O", "٩" and "Γ" contain, respectively, a valley pattern, a mountain pattern, a buckle pattern, a buckle pattern and two valley patterns (Figures 10.8 and 10.9).

Feature Representation

We were faced to several possible representations for the digit images using the morphological patterns described above. One particular representation is to indicate whether or not a specific structural pattern exists within the digit stroke. That is, a four variable Boolean vector is needed. Another powerful method is to use the extracted patterns along with a mesh grid representation that accounts for counting the number of pixels pertaining to each of the morphological patterns and falling in each grid zone. We thus obtain a vector of pixels' frequencies with a dimensionality equal to the number of zones in the mesh grid per the number of structural patterns. In our context, we used a 4 × 4 mesh grid that yield a 64 entries vector.

Statistical Features

In order to capture local features of the digit stroke, we exploit the information embedded within the contour pixels. So we consider statistical primitives based on the calculation of freeman directions and curvatures of the pixels' stroke contour. The contour-based chain code is calculated by a run-length scanning of the image [33]. A prior smoothing of the contour is carried out by averaging the freeman directions with a 5 length neighbourhood window. From the resulting contour is computed the pixels' associated curvatures which amount to the computation of freeman directions' second

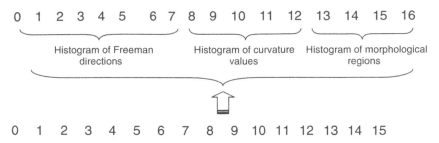

Fig. 10.10. Feature vector representation.

derivatives. Along with the 8 standard freeman directions, we use five magnitudes for the curvature sampling yielding a 13 entries vector superposing an histogram of freeman directions and curvature magnitudes. When considering the zoning grid, we end up with a $(8 + 5 + 4) * 16 = 272$ feature values (Figure 10.10). Normalized values are finally obtained by considering a percentage of the total number of pixels of contour in each zone of the grid.

10.4.3 Experiments

The INDCENPARMI database contains two corpora of Indian digit images. A training dedicated corpus of 4682 images and a testing dedicated set of 1939 images. Once the features are extracted and saved, we proceed to build the classifiers. On that task, neural networks have proved to be, and still is an efficient classification method for OCR systems since many years ago. Many other powerful methods have emerged recently, among them, support vector machines are certainly the most adapted to such applications. Indeed, during the last decade, many pattern recognition problems have been tackled using support vector machines. For instance, Cortes et al., Scholkopf et al. and Burges et al. applied the SVM for optical character recognition [13,14,32]. Blanz et al. used the SVM to recognize some scenes of two-dimensional object views [10]. Schmidt et al. used the classifier as a part of a speaker recognition system [31]. Osuna et al. studied its performance on a face recognition task [30]. Many other applications such as gender classification, data mining, stock action prediction, etc. have also emerged. In many cases, the SVM outperforms most of state of the art classifiers.

Neural Network-Based System

We have used an MLP variant neural network classifier with one hidden layer, 272 entries and 10 class outputs. The MLP weights are initialized randomly regarding a Gaussian distribution and normalized with respect

Table 10.5. TrR: training recognition rate; TsR: testing recognition rate

Class	.	١	٢	٣	٤	٥	٦	٧	٨	٩	.
TrR	99.1	98.0	99.7	100	98.4	99.7	98.1	100	99.3	99.1	86.4
TsR	96.8	92.1	96.9	97.6	92.2	99.4	97.2	94.1	94.9	95.9	84.6

Table 10.6. TrR: training recognition rate; TsR: testing recognition rate

Class	.	١	٢	٣	٤	٥	٦	٧	٨	٩
TrR	99.9	98.5	99.7	100	99.4	100	99.4	100	100	99.1
TsR	98.3	92.6	95.3	96.4	92.2	98.8	97.2	91.8	94.9	93.8

to the fan-in of the neurons. The activation function of the hidden and output neurons is a hyperbolic tangent.

We did several manipulations with different settings. With a rejection threshold equal to zero, we obtained a recognition rate of 95.87% on the testing set with an error rate of 2.71%. We report in Table 10.5 the corresponding recognition rates per class. The most confused cases are between the digit class 0 and the comer class which is due to their great similarity. Hence it seems more appropriate to exploit contextual information within the courtesy amount to locate the position of the analysed stroke so we can differentiate between those classes. We retrained the neural network when considering only the digit classes omitting the comer. So the best recognition rate on the testing set is 96.69%. The error and rejections rates are, respectively, 1.99% and 1.21%. Table 10.6 reports the corresponding recognition rates per class.

The SVM-Based System

The SVM is a binary classifier. That is, it only considers two-class data problems. For multi-class data, unlike monolithic classifiers such as MLP or RBF networks, it is necessary to share the decision process among multiple classifiers and to combine their votes in order to predict the observation's class membership. Given a problem of M classes, in the one-against-all strategy, we need to consider M distinct SVM classifiers, whereas in the one-against-one strategy w need $M(M-1)/2$ SVM classifiers deal with. Considering individual couples of classes in the one-against-one strategy produces simpler frontiers with low support vector number as a result of the smaller tackled sub-problems. In order to yield a class membership, we gather all the votes from the 45 resulting classifiers and apply a majority vote scheme. Given the vote magnitude f_{ij} of the classifier (i,j), the class membership is issued as $c = \arg\max\limits_{i} \sum\limits_{j=0, j\neq i}^{9} [\hat{f}_{ij}]_*$, where $\hat{f}_{ij}$ is equal to the raw SVM output f_{ij} normalized through the margin value. The Heaviside

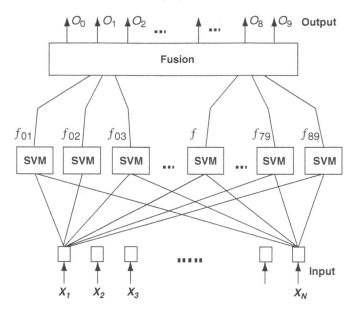

Fig. 10.11. Architecture of the SVM-based system.

Table 10.7. Some state of the art kernels

Kernel	Expression
Linear	$K(x, y) = x.y$
RBF	$K(x, y) = \exp(-\gamma^2 \|x - y\|^2)$
Polynomial	$K(x, y) = (a\,x.y + b)^d$
KMOD	$K(x, y) = a(\exp(\gamma^2/(\|x - y\|^2 + \sigma^2)) - 1)$
Sigmoïd	$K(x, y) = \tanh(a\,x.y + b)$

operator $[\ ]_*$ acts as an activation function which may take smoother forms as noticed by Moreira et al. [29]. Figure 10.11 shows an overall view of the one-against-one-based architecture.

However, the SVM embeds tuning parameters that control the training setting as the kernel parameters and the trade off variable C. Such parameters have a regularization effect the training process and since their values are not trained, they may diminish the overall performance of the classifier if not well chosen. Table 10.7 presents some state of the art kernels.

To do so, we proceed to a series of experiments in order to optimize the classification system and select the best model parameters. So, we choose a predefined interval of values for the parameters to be tuned within. The obtained results are testing error rates after combining the 45 SVM classifiers (for classifying only digit classes) with respect to a one-against-one strategy. The errors on the training set are often nil, so we just omitted reporting them.

Table 10.8. Testing error rates with a polynomial kernel with d = 2 and C = 100

(a,b)	PWC1	PWC4	PWC5	OPWC
(0.1,0.1)	2.24	2.18	3.04	2.18
(0.1,0.5)	2.18	2.13	2.98	2.24
(0.1,1)	2.29	2.24	3.14	2.34
(0.1,5)	2.45	2.29	3.89	2.45
(0.1,10)	2.61	2.50	4.64	2.72
(0.5,0.1)	2.24	2.18	5.17	2.24
(0.5,0.5)	2.24	2.18	5.22	2.24
(0.5,1)	2.24	2.18	5.22	2.24
(0.5,5)	2.29	2.24	5.12	2.34
(0.5,10)	2.34	2.29	5.38	2.34
(1,0.1)	2.24	2.18	5.44	2.24
(1,0.5)	2.24	2.18	5.44	2.24
(1,1)	2.24	2.18	5.44	2.24
(1,5)	2.18	2.13	5.49	2.24
(1,10)	2.29	2.24	5.81	2.34
(5,0.1)	2.24	2.18	6.02	2.24
(5,0.5)	2.24	2.18	6.02	2.24
(5,1)	2.24	2.18	6.02	2.24
(5,5)	2.24	2.18	6.08	2.18
(5,10)	2.24	2.18	6.13	2.24
(10,0.1)	2.24	2.18	6.19	2.24
(10,0.5)	2.24	2.18	6.13	2.24
(10,1)	2.24	2.18	6.13	2.24
(10,5)	2.24	2.18	6.13	2.24
(10,10)	2.24	2.18	6.08	2.18

Tables 10.8 and 10.9 show the testing error rates with a polynomial kernel of degrees 2 and 3, respectively, and C = 100. The variables a and b in the table are, respectively, the multiplicative and additive parameters of the polynomial kernel; whereas PWC1, PWC4, PWC5 and OPWC represent pairwise voting schemes as proposed by [28] and [24] and used by [9]. Tables 10.10 and 10.11 report testing error rates and number of support vectors resulted with respectively KMOD and RBF kernels for C = 100.

10.4.4 Discussion

A decision system for the classification of handwritten non-touching Indian digits is described. It includes a feature extraction module and a classification module. The used characteristics are based on coding some morphological patterns through the use of histograms of belonging pixels, and few contour based statistical features.

Two classification models are experimented. A neural network classifier and an SVM based system. The former is a multi-layer perceptron whereas

Table 10.9. Testing error rates with a polynomial kernel with d = 3 and C = 100

(a,b)	PWC1	PWC4	PWC5	OPWC
(0.1,0.1)	2.02	*1.92*	4.16	2.45
(0.1,0.5)	2.08	1.97	4.42	2.29
(0.1,1)	2.18	2.08	4.58	2.29
(0.1,5)	2.34	2.29	5.22	2.24
(0.1,10)	2.45	2.29	5.65	2.40
(0.5,0.1)	2.02	*1.92*	5.54	2.45
(0.5,0.5)	2.02	*1.92*	5.54	2.45
(0.5,1)	2.02	*1.92*	5.65	2.40
(0.5,5)	2.18	2.08	5.92	2.29
(0.5,10)	2.24	2.18	6.08	2.29
(1,0.1)	2.02	*1.92*	5.65	2.45
(1,0.5)	2.02	*1.92*	5.70	2.45
(1,1)	2.02	*1.92*	5.76	2.45
(1,5)	2.08	1.97	6.13	2.29
(1,10)	2.18	2.08	6.08	2.29
(5,0.1)	2.02	*1.92*	5.76	2.50
(5,0.5)	2.02	*1.92*	5.76	2.45
(5,1)	2.02	*1.92*	5.76	2.45
(5,5)	2.02	*1.92*	5.92	2.45
(5,10)	2.02	*1.92*	6.02	2.40
(10,0.1)	2.02	*1.92*	5.76	2.50
(10,0.5)	2.02	*1.92*	5.76	2.50
(10,1)	2.02	*1.92*	5.76	2.45
(10,5)	2.02	*1.92*	5.81	2.45
(10,10)	2.02	*1.92*	5.92	2.45

the latter is a multiple classifier system which combine 45 SVM trained with respect to the one-against-one strategy. The best error rate is obtained with the SVM-based system that yields 1.92% with no rejection.

The used kernels yield approximately the same performance i.e. 1.92% except the polynomial kernel of degree 2 which lacks expressivity to produce complex enough frontiers. Nevertheless, it is worth noting that performance is better than obtained with the neural network-based system (1.98% of error and 1.21% of reject). However, in term of complexity, experiments confirm the fact that highly non-linear kernels such as KMOD tend to produce complex models with many support vectors (see Table 10.5). Finally, the relative insensibility (in term of SV number) versus kernels is mainly due to the features which are noiseless are robust.

10.5 Conclusion and Future Perspective

The goal of this article is to describe the need and challenges of Arabic cheque processing. A substantial amount of effort has been paid

Table 10.10. Testing error rates and SV number with KMOD kernel and $C = 100$

(γ, σ)	SV	PWC1	PWC4	PWC5	OPWC
(0.1,1)	414	3.46	3.46	3.46	4.64
(0.1,4)	89	*1.92*	*1.92*	*1.92*	2.08
(0.1,5)	72	1.97	1.97	1.97	2.08
(0.1,6)	63	1.97	1.97	1.97	2.13
(0.1,10)	46	2.18	2.24	2.24	2.18
(0.5,1)	438	3.68	3.68	3.68	4.90
(0.5,4)	89	*1.92*	*1.92*	*1.92*	2.08
(0.5,5)	72	1.97	1.97	1.97	2.08
(0.5,6)	63	1.97	1.97	1.97	2.13
(0.5,10)	46	2.13	2.02	2.02	2.24
(1,1)	520	4.64	4.64	4.64	6.40
(1,4)	90	*1.92*	*1.92*	*1.92*	2.08
(1,5)	73	1.97	1.97	1.97	2.08
(1,6)	63	1.97	1.97	1.97	2.13
(1,10)	46	2.08	1.97	1.97	2.24

Table 10.11. Testing error rates and SV number with RBF kernel and $C = 100$

Γ	SV	PWC1	PWC4	PWC5	OPWC
0.05	38	2.35	2.24	2.24	2.40
0.10	41	2.29	2.19	2.19	2.35
0.15	49	2.03	2.03	2.03	2.19
0.20	60	1.97	1.97	2.03	2.08
0.25	77	*1.92*	*1.92*	*1.92*	2.08
0.30	103	1.97	1.97	1.97	2.13
0.35	144	2.13	2.13	2.13	2.24
0.40	210	2.08	2.08	2.08	2.67
0.45	298	2.61	2.61	2.61	3.68
0.50	401	4.22	4.22	4.22	5.92

towards building Arabic cheque databases, a very important infrastructure to develop and compare pattern recognition systems for the Arabic-based cheque-processing systems. Furthermore, we have covered a number of issues including relevant datasets, legal amount cognition and courtesy amount recognition.

The research work in this topic is far from over. Future work could concentrate on the following items:

System improvements in terms of feature extraction and/or classification methods.

System integration:

- Implement the complete legal amount recognition system given an improved sub-word classification rate.

- Define and implement a criterion to combine the results of the legal and courtesy amount recognition systems.
- Develop a complete system to extract and process both the legal and the courtesy amounts.

Public research society:

- Get the databases approved by all parties and ready for publications.
- Find ways to increase the training and testing data.
- Collaborate with the industry to perform on-line test of the complete system.

References

1. Abouhaibah, I. (1998). Recognition of off-line cursive handwriting. *Computer Vision and Image Understanding, 71(1)*, pp. 19–38.
2. Al Ohali, Y. (2002). *Handwritten Word Recognition: Application to Arabic Cheque Processing*. Ph.D. Thesis, Concordia University, Montreal, Canada.
3. Al-Badr, B. and Mahmoud, S. (1995). Survey and bibliography of Arabic optical text recognition. *Signal Processing, 41*, pp. 49–77.
4. Allen, J. (1995). *Natural Language Understanding*. Menlo Park, CA: The Benjamin/Cummings Publishing Company, Inc.
5. Alohali, Y., Cheriet, M., and Suen, C.Y. (2000). Databases for recognition of handwritten Arabic cheques. *Proceedings of the Seventh IWFHR, Amsterdam, The Netherlands*, pp. 601–606.
6. Alshebeili, S., Nabawi, A., and Mohmoud, S. (1997). Arabic character recognition using 1-D slices of the character spectrum. *Signal Processing, 56*, pp. 59–75.
7. Al-Yousefi, H. and Upda, S. (1990). Recognition of handwritten Arabic characters via segmentation. *Arab Gulf Journal for Scientific Research, 8*, pp. 49–59.
8. Amin, A. (2000). Recognition of printed Arabic text based on global features and decision tree learning techniques. *Pattern Recognition, 33*, pp. 1309–1323.
9. Ayat, N.E. (2003). Automatic model selection for support vectors machines: application to the recognition of handwritten digits. PhD thesis. Montreal, Canada: ETS, Université du Québec.
10. Blanz, V., Scholkopf, B., Bulthoff, H.H., Burges, C., Vapnik, V., and Vetter, T. (1996). Comparison of view-based object recognition algorithms using realistic 3d models. *ICANN*, pp. 251–256.
11. Cheriet, M. and Suen, C.Y. (1993). Extraction of key letters for cursive script recognition. *Pattern Recognition Letters, 14*, pp. 1009–1017.
12. Chim, Y., Kassim, A., and Ibrahim, Y. (1998). Dual classifier system for hand printed alphanumeric character recognition. *Pattern Analysis & Applications, 1*, pp. 155–162.

13. Chris, J.C.B. and Schölkopf, B. (1997). Improving the accuracy and speed of support vector machines. In: M.C. Mozer, M.I. Jordan, and T. Petsche (Eds.). *Advances in Neural Information Processing Systems.* CAmbridge, MA: The MIT Press, Volume 9, p. 375.

14. Cortes, C. and Vapnik, V. (1995). Support-vector networks. *Machine Learning, 20(3),* pp. 273–297.

15. Dehghan, M., Faez, K., Ahmadi, M., and Shridhar, M. (2001). Handwritten Farsi (Arabic) word recognition: a holistic approach using discrete HMM. *Pattern Recognition, 34,* pp. 1057–1065.

16. Gilloux, M. and Leroux, M. (1993). Recognition of cursive script amounts on postal cheques. *European Conference. Dedicated to Postal Technologies. Nantes, France,* pp. 705–712.

17. Guillevic, D. (1995). Unconstrained handwriting recognition applied to the processing of bank cheques. PhD thesis. Montreal, Quebec, Canada: Concordia University.

18. Guillevic, D. and Suen, C.Y. (1998). Recognition of legal amounts on bank cheques. *Pattern Analysis and Applications, 1,* pp. 28–41.

19. Heutte, L., Paquet, T., Moreau, J., Lecourtier, Y., and Olivier, C. (1998). A structural/statistical feature based vector for handwritten character recognition. *Pattern Recognition Letters, 19,* pp. 629–641.

20. Il-Seok, Oh. and Suen, C.Y. (1998). Distance features for neural network-based recognition of handwritten characters. *IJDAR,* pp. 73–88.

21. Kato, Y. and Yasuhara, M. (2000). Recovery of drawing order from single-stroke handwritten images. *IEEE Transactions on PAMI, 22(9),* pp. 938–949.

22. Kaufmann, G. and Bunke, H. (2000). Automatic reading of cheque amounts. *Pattern Analysis & Applications, 3,* pp. 132–141.

23. Kim, G. and Goveindaraju, V. (1997). A lexicon driven approach to handwritten word recognition for real time applications. *IEEE Transactions on PAMI, 19(4),* pp. 366–379.

24. Li, Z., Tang, S., and Yan, S. (2002). Pattern recognition with support vector machines. *Lecture Notes in Computer Science, chapter Multi-Class SVM Classifier Based on Pairwise Coupling.* Berlin, Heidelberg: Springer, Volume 2388, pp. 321–333.

25. Loncaric, S. (1998). A survey of shape analysis techniques. *Pattern Recognition, 31(8),* pp. 983–1001.

26. Madhvanath, S. and Govindaraju, V. (1992). Using *Holistic Features in Handwritten Word Recognition.* United States Postal Service (USPS), Volume 1, pp. 183–198.

27. Miled, H., Cheriet, M., and Olivier, C. (1998). Multi-level Arabic handwritten words recognition. *Proceedings of Advances in Pattern Recognition, Sydney, Australia,* pp. 944–951.

28. Miled, H., Olivier, C., Cheriet, M., and Lecourtier, Y. (1997). Coupling observation/letter for a Markovian modelisation applied to the recognition of Arabic handwriting. *ICDAR,* pp. 580–583.

29. Moreira, M. and Mayoraz, E. (1998). Improved pairwise coupling classification with correcting classifiers. IDIAP-RR 09, IDIAP, 1997. *Proceedings of the Tenth European Conference on Machine Learning.*

30. Osuna, E., Freund, R., and Girosi, F. (1997). Training Support Vector Machines: An Application to Face Detection. In Proceedings of the IEEE

Conference on Computer Vision and Pattern Recognition, Puerto Rico, pp. 130–136.

31. Schmidt, M.S. (1996). Identifying speakers with support vector networks. Proceedings of the 28th Symposium on the Interface (INTERFACE-96). Sydney, Australia, July 1996.

32. Scholkopf, B. (1997). Support vector learning. PhD thesis. Berlin, Germany: Universität Berlin.

33. Strathy, N.W. (1993). Master thesis. Montreal, Canada: Concordia University.

11

OCR of Printed Mathematical Expressions

Utpal Garain and Bidyut B. Chaudhuri

11.1 Introduction

Automatic recognition of mathematical expressions (hereafter, referred as expressions) is one of the challenging pattern recognition problems of significant practical importance. Such a recognition task is required while converting printed scientific documents into electronic form or to aid the visually impaired persons in reading scientific documents.

This chapter discusses the key issues involved in the development of a system for recognition of printed documents containing expressions. In fact, studies on this topic date back to 1960s when Anderson [1] proposed a syntax-directed scheme for recognition of hand-printed expressions. Several studies have been reported so far and surveyed in [4, 5, 13].

However, the present discussion starts with showing limitations of existing optical character recognition (OCR) systems in converting scientific papers into corresponding electronic form. Figure 11.1 demonstrates one such example obtained from a popular OCR system, namely ABBYY Fine Reader 6.0.[1] The limitation arises because such a system fails to recognize expressions that often appear in scientific documents.

Instead of developing new OCR systems for scientific documents, we put emphasis on upgrading the existing ones by additional processing modules for expressions in documents. Since the presence of expressions disturbs typical OCR system (not trained for expression recognition), the identification and extraction of expression zones, therefore, could be the first step in this module. It permits an existing OCR engine to process the normal text portion as usual, whereas the extracted expressions can be tackled by a system specially designed for expression recognition.

---

[1] www.abbyy.com.

Let $\widehat{\mathfrak{g}} = \mathfrak{g}[t, t^{-1}] \oplus \mathbb{C}c$ be the affinization of $\mathfrak{g}$, where c is a central element, and where the Lie bracket is given by

$$[xt^n, yt^m] = [x, y]t^{n+m} + n\delta_{n,-m}(x, y)c.$$

The algebra $\widehat{\mathfrak{g}}$ is naturally equipped with a $\widehat{Q} = Q \oplus \mathbb{Z}\delta$-grading, where

$$\widehat{\mathfrak{g}}[\alpha + l\delta] = \mathfrak{g}[\alpha]t^l, \qquad \widehat{\mathfrak{g}}[0] = \mathfrak{h} \oplus \mathbb{C}c, \qquad \widehat{\mathfrak{g}}[l\delta] = \mathfrak{h}t^l.$$

We extend the Cartan form to $\widehat{Q}$ by setting $(\delta, \alpha) = 0$ for all $\alpha \in \widehat{Q}$. The root system of $\widehat{\mathfrak{g}}$ is $\widehat{\Delta} = \mathbb{Z}^*\delta \cup \{\Delta + \mathbb{Z}\delta\}$. We say that a root $\alpha \in \widehat{\Delta}$ is *real* if $(\alpha, \alpha) = 2$ and *imaginary* if $(\alpha, \alpha) \leq 0$.

(a)

Lefg $= Q/I, t]j ©Cc$ be the affinization of g, where c is a central element, and where the Lie bracket is given by

$$[xt^n, yt^m] = (x,y)t^{n+m} + n\delta_{n,-m}(x,y)c.$$

The algebra $\widehat{g}$ is naturally equipped with a $Q = Q ©Z5$-grading, where

$$f[a + IS] = Q[a]t', \qquad f[0] = fj © Cc, \qquad ?[/\$] = Ij^*.$$

We extend the Cartan form to Q by setting $(5, a) = 0$ for all $a e Q$. The root system off is $A = Z^*5 U \{A + Z<5\}$. We say that a root « 6 A is *rea/* if $(a, a) = 2$ and *imaginary* if $(a, a) < 0$.

(b)

Fig. 11.1. OCR output of scientific documents: an example (a) image (b) recognition results.

Mathematical expressions typically appear in documents, either as (a) displayed (isolated) expressions or (b) expressions embedded into (i.e. mixed with) the text lines. As far as automatic identification of expressions is concerned, displayed and embedded expressions impose different level of complexities. The displayed ones are typed in separate lines and exhibit several image-level features that distinguish them from normal text lines. On the other hand, embedded expressions are generally small expression fragments, which are difficult to isolate from the text portion mixed with expressions. These issues have been discussed in Section 11.3.

Once expressions in a document are identified, recognition of them involves two major components namely (i) symbol recognition and (ii) structure interpretation. Symbol recognition is difficult because a large character set (roman letters, Arabic digits, Greek letters, Operator symbols, etc.) with a variety of typefaces (regular, italic, bold), and a large number of different font sizes may be used to generate the expressions. Moreover, certain symbols (e.g. *integration, summation, product, brackets,* etc.) are elastic in nature and have a wide range of possible scales.

Interpretation of structure is particularly another non-trivial problem due to the subtle use of space that often defines the relationship among symbols. For instance, unlike plain text (which is written linearly from left to right), symbols in an expression can be written above, below, and one nested inside another. Therefore, understanding of the spatial relationship among symbols is crucial to the interpretation of structure of an expression. This means that even if all the characters are correctly recognized, there still remains the non-trivial problem of interpreting the two-dimensional structure of an expression. Moreover, several symbols (e.g. *horizontal line*, *dot*, etc.) have multiple meanings depending on the context and such ambiguous role of symbols makes the interpretation task more difficult.

Work on an expression recognition system needs another problem to be addressed, namely quantitative evaluation of the system. Evaluation of such a system is non-trivial since recognition scheme involves two major stages: symbol recognition and structural analysis. The stages are tightly coupled and therefore, if evaluation in one stage is done independent of the other, then it may not reflect true performance of the system. Moreover, error in the symbol recognition stage affects the structure analysis result. This calls for an integrated evaluation mechanism for judging the performance of a system dealing with expression recognition.

The rest of this chapter is organized as follows. Identification of expression zones in a document is discussed in Section 11.2. Section 11.3 presents several methods for recognition of expression symbols. Geometric interpretation of structure of expressions is presented in Section 11.4. Section 11.5 deals with the issues related to performance evaluation of an expression recognition system. Need for generation of standard benchmarked data for a set of scientific documents is outlined and availability of such data is mentioned in Section 11.5. Section 11.6 concludes with outlines of the aspects requiring further research attention in future.

11.2 Identification of Expressions in Document Images

Since embedded and displayed expressions are of different complexities, separate techniques have so far been proposed for identification of embedded and displayed expressions. Some reviews are provided in the next section (Figure 11.2).

11.2.1 Techniques for Identification of Expression Zones

Studies dealing with identification of expression zones are few in number. Most of the previous works assume that expressions are available in isolated form. Among the existing techniques, method proposed by Lee and Wang [29] labels text lines in a document as either *TEXT* (to denote normal text) or *EXP* (to denote displayed expression) based on two properties

Let t_{A_1} and t_{A_2} denote the access times of M_1 and M_2, respectively, relative to the CPU. The average time t_A for the CPU to access a word in the memory system is given by the equation

$$t_A = Ht_{A_1} + (1 - H)t_{A_2} \qquad (5.3)$$

In most two-level hierarchies, a request for a word not in main memory causes a block of information containing the requested word to be transferred to main memory. When the block transfer has been completed, the requested word is accessed in main memory. The time t_B required for the block transfer is called the *block-replacement*, or *block-transfer*, time. Hence we have $t_{A_2} = t_B + t_{A_1}$. Substituting into Eq. (5.3) yields

$$t_A = t_{A_1} + (1 - H)t_B \qquad (5.4)$$

Block transfer requires a relatively slow IO operation; therefore t_B is usually much greater then t_{A_1}. Hence $t_{A_2} \gg t_{A_1}$ and $t_{A_2} \approx t_B$.

Fig. 11.2. A sample page containing *embedded* as well as *displayed* expressions.

(i) isolated expressions are taller compared to the normal text lines and (ii) the line spaces above and below them are larger than those between text lines that contain no mathematical expressions.

The technique [29] for locating embedded expressions initially recognizes characters in a text line from left to right direction and then converts them to a stream of tokens. A token is decided to belong to an embedded expression according to some basic expression forms which considers presence of special mathematical symbols (e.g. horizontal line, summation, product, etc.), scripting or matrix structures. Symbols that are adjacent to the above tokens are heuristically attached to form an embedded expression.

Fateman [12] presented a three-pass algorithm that initially recognizes all connected components in a scanned document and separates them into two bags, math and text. The text bag contains all roman letters, italic numbers and the math bag includes punctuations, special symbols, italic letters, roman digits and other marks (e.g. horizontal lines, dots). Next, components in the math bag are grouped into zones according to their proximity. Symbols that are left ungrouped and appeared to be too far from other math symbols are moved to the text bag. Symbols in the text bag are similarly joined up into groups according to proximity. Text words (hopefully include words like "sin", etc.) that are relatively isolated from other text but within any previously identified math zone are moved to the math bag. Manual intervention is employed to review the segmentation result to correct errors, if any.

The method proposed by Inoue [24] isolates expressions contained in Japanese scientific document by assuming that the OCR recognizes Japanese characters with high confidence, whereas expression symbols are either rejected or recognized (rather misrecognized) with low confidence.

In another approach, Toumit [37] locate embedded expressions by finding special symbols like "=", "+", "<", ">", etc. and some specific context propagation from these symbols is done. For example, for parenthesis and brackets, symbols between them are checked; for horizontal bars, symbols above and below them are investigated, etc.

Later on, Kacem [26] proposed a two-pass scheme that does not put much emphasis on symbol recognition. Initially, expressions are separated from the text lines using a primary labelling which uses fuzzy logic based model to identify some mathematical symbols. Later on, a secondary labelling uses some heuristics to reinforce the results of the primary labelling and locates super- and subscripts inside the text. An evaluation strategy has been presented to judge the expression extraction technique and a success rate of about 93% has been reported on a combined test set of 300 displayed and embedded expressions. A similar technique is used in [34] to locate mathematical expressions in printed documents.

Recently, Chowdhury et al. [10] proposed a recognition-free approach that exploits the usual spatial distribution of the black pixels in math zones. Experimental results show that the method works well for segmenting displayed expression. In another recognition-free technique reported by Jin [25], embedded expressions are extracted based on the detection of two-dimensional structures. However, the authors of [10, 25] concluded that the extraction of embedded expressions is quite difficult without doing character recognition.

11.2.2 Ways to Improve Identification Results

On reviewing the existing methods, it is understood that identification of displayed expressions does not pose much difficulty compared to the task of locating embedded expressions. We also have experienced this while designing an expression recognition system [8]. There the module for detection of displayed expressions initially considers several image level features to suspect text lines containing isolated expressions. Some of these features are (i) wider white space above and below an expression line, (ii) height of the expression line, (iii) non-linear arrangement of symbols in an expressions, etc. Presence of one or more frequently occurring mathematical symbols has been checked to validate the identification results.

These features are formulated to give values in [0,1]. For example, feature representing white space property is defined as $f_{ws} = 1 - e^{(-\frac{r}{r_\mu})}$ where r denotes the average of the white space (measured in number pixel rows) above and below a text line and r_μ denotes the mean of the white space between two consecutive text lines. In case of the first line, only the line below it is considered to measure r (similarly, for the last text line its preceding line is considered).

Similarly, scatteredness of symbols inside a displayed expression is measured as, $f_{ms} = 1 - e^{-\sigma_y}$ where σ_y denotes the standard deviation among the y-coordinates of the lower-most pixels of the symbols (i.e. connected components) of a text line. Feature related to height of a line containing displayed expression is formulated as $f_{mh} = 1 - e^{(-\frac{h}{h_\mu})}$ where h is the height of a text line in terms of pixel rows and h_μ is the mean of all h-**values**. The feature, f_{mo}, keeps track of the occurrence of a few mathematical operator symbols that often appear in expressions. In our experiment [8], only 13 operators are considered for computation of f_{mo} that is defined as $f_{mo} = 1 - \exp\left\{-K \sum_{i=1}^{K} p_i\right\}$ where K denotes the number of operators identified in a text line and p_i denotes the probability of occurrence of the ith symbol.

Next, these features are computed on line level and then integrated (linearly/non-linearly) to produce a single score for individual line. Based on these scores, lines containing displayed expressions are selected.

However, these features are not sufficient (some are relevant at all) in case of embedded expressions. On the other hand, we did explore some aspects that seem interesting for this purpose. For example, if commercial OCRs are invoked to recognize pages containing expressions, OCR output shows interesting patterns:

- Sentences without expressions are recognized with almost no error.
- Also, high recognition accuracy is obtained for normal text words in sentences with expressions.
- Some of the expression symbols (e.g. roman letters, digits, symbols like "+", "−", "=", punctuation marks, etc.) are often recognized properly. However, for majority of these symbols, the OCRs, on recognition, associate suspicion marks with them to indicate that either these symbols in isolation (excepting characters like "a", etc.) do not form any valid word (e.g. isolated characters, characters with scripts, words like "sin", "log", etc.) or to reveal poor OCR confidence during their recognition (sometimes due to italic or bold characters).
- Other expression symbols (mostly Greek letters, majority of mathematical operators, special symbols, etc.) are either rejected (signalled by some special symbol) or mis-recognized with a suspicion mark.

Another interesting linguistic property is also observed. Let us divide sentences in scientific documents into two categories namely, sentences with and without expressions. Next, if word level n-grams are computed for these two categories then word n-gram based category profiles markedly differ from one another. This linguistic property can be used in spotting lines containing embedded expressions.

This technique has been explored in one of our studies [19]. It is experimented with about 4000 sentences appearing in scientific documents. More than 3000 sentences (number of sentences without any expressions: 2655 and number of sentences with embedded expressions: 870) were used to generate word n-gram based category profile. Later on, a test involving 877 sentences showed that on an average in 95% cases these category profiles can distinguish a sentence with expression fragments from the one that does not contain any expression.

11.3 Recognition of Expression Symbols

Symbol recognition in mathematical expressions is difficult because there is a large character set (roman letters, Greek letters, operator symbols, etc.) with a variety of font styles (regular, bold, italic) and a range of font sizes (scripts, limit expressions, etc.). Certain symbols have a wide range of possible scales (e.g. brackets, parentheses, symbols like "$\int$", "$\sum$", "$\prod$", "$\cup$", etc.). Symbols also vary substantially in their shape characteristics. Therefore, recognition of mathematical symbols is considered as an important pattern recognition problem.

Review of existing studies shows that the studies dealing with recognition of symbols are a few. Most of the published papers have put emphasis on analysis of two-dimensional structures appearing in expressions. In several experiments, an error-free symbol recognition is assumed before formulating any method for structure analysis. In a controlled research environment, it is possible to bypass the symbol-recognition step and concentrate on structure analysis phase. However, design of a symbol-recognition module is essential to realize a complete expression recognition system.

11.3.1 Existing Methods for Symbol Recognition

The approaches proposed in previous studies on recognition of printed mathematical symbols can be broadly classified into two categories namely, (i) template matching and (ii) feature extraction and classification. Okamoto et al. [33] followed template matching approach where two sets of dictionaries for normal and script type symbols are maintained. Symbols are normalized to the predefined size prior to classification. Based on this method, an accuracy of 98.96% has been reported.

Fateman et al. [13, 14] proposed another template matching technique where a symbol template is represented by a vector of features. Bounding box of grey-level character image is divided into 5×5-rectangular grids and percentage of grey values in each grid is computed. The feature vector is made up of this set of grey-values along with two more data items, the height-to-width ratio and the absolute height in pixels of the bounding box. During classification of symbols, the authors used a Euclidean metric to define the distance between characters.

Lee and Lee [28] adopted a feature extraction based classification scheme where 13 features are utilized to represent each symbol. Next, a coarse classification algorithm is applied to reduce the number of candidates. For each input symbol, the character with the highest similarity is selected as the candidate symbol. The recognition accuracy reported in [28] is 84.80%.

The method presented by Lee and Wang [29] initially divides the symbol set into three classes based on the aspect ratio of bounding box of symbols. For recognizing a symbol within a class, the symbol image is divided into 4×4 non-uniform blocks and a four-dimensional direction feature vector is computed from each image block. It gives a 64-dimensional feature vector representation for each symbol. The authors achieved an accuracy of 96.18%. Ha et al. [22] also adopted a feature extraction based approach, but their classification is done through neural network.

Suzuki et al. [36] designed a recognition engine that tries to distinguish 564 symbol categories. The number of classes is so large because the authors considered several categories for a single character to tackle font and style variation. For instance, six categories have been considered for the character "B" to take care of its *regular, italic, bold, calligraphic*, etc. versions. A three-step coarse-to-fine classification strategy has been employed for recognition of symbols. The features like aspect ratio, crossing counts, as well as directional, peripheral and mesh features have been used for classification of symbols. Experiments conducted on a set of 476 scientific pages showed an accuracy of 95.18% for recognition of expression symbols.

11.3.2 Ways to Improve Symbol Recognition Accuracy

It is noted that symbol recognition accuracy is often lowered due to presence of touching characters in expressions. In many occasions, the adjacent characters in expressions touch each other in the scanned image and presence of such touching characters causes recognition errors. This is because the expression is typically segmented by connectivity analysis that considers touching characters as a single unit, which the recognition engine cannot properly tackle.

The main reasons of getting touching characters are (i) poor printing technology, (ii) inferior paper quality, (iii) photocopied documents, (iv) digitization errors, etc. Expressions contained in documents printed in ancient times impose a serious problem due to touching characters. Figure 11.3 shows a small set of touching characters found in printed expressions.

Lee and Wang [29] analysed the reasons behind the error in recognizing expression symbols and found that depending on document quality 12–28%

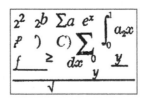

Fig. 11.3. Some touching characters found in mathematical expressions.

errors (out of all types of recognition errors) are due to touching characters. Suzuki et al. [36] also found nearly 2% touching character images
in their database of 11,194 expressions. Therefore, addition of extra module for processing of touching characters is needed to improve the symbol
recognition accuracy.

So far, only a few studies have addressed the issue of segmentation and
recognition of touching characters appearing in expressions. Lee and Lee
[28] proposed a dynamic programming algorithm where the segmentation
is performed on a one-dimensional sequence of curve segments representing
a connected component. The approach presented by Okamoto et al. [34] is
based on the projection profiles of a given binary image of a pair of touching
characters and minimal points of the blurred image obtained by applying
the Gaussian kernel to the original image. This segmentation method is
restricted for cases where only two characters touch each other.

Very recently, Nomura et al. [31] proposed an approach for detection
as well as segmentation of touching characters in expressions. In their approach, touching characters are detected by looking at the deviation of the
feature values (computed on an image of touching characters) from the
standard feature values pre-computed for isolated characters. The segmentation is achieved by comparing a touching character image with a set of
images synthesized from two single character images. Here also touching
of only two characters is assumed. Since the number of ways by which two
single characters touch each other is quite large, synthesis of all possible
touching character images and comparison of a given image with all of these
synthesized images is computationally not very much attractive. Moreover,
such a scheme may fail to tackle variations in size, style and typefaces used
to print expressions.

Segmentation of Touching Symbols: Considering the limitations of the previous approach we proposed a different technique described in one of our
recent papers [17]. Since the number of touching characters is limited in
an expression, no separate module for detection of touching characters is
implemented in our system. Rather, any pattern rejected by the recognizer
is initially suspected as touching character and segmentation is attempted
for its recognition.

Several features contributing towards finding the cut-positions are identified. Selection of features is dictated by some observations like: (1) Though
an image of touching characters mostly contains two characters, three or
more characters touching each other are not rare. In our database [16], we
found that among 2853 images of 6144 touching characters images consisting of 2, 3, and 4 characters are 2501 (87.66%), 266 (9.32%), 86 (3.02%),
respectively. (2) Adjacent characters may touch each other in horizontal,
vertical or diagonal directions. (3) If black runs (or crossing counts) are
computed along the touching direction, a single run is, in general, encountered at the touching position. (4) The thickness of black blob at the

touching position is usually small compared to the thickness of other parts. (5) The character parts generate uncommon (quite a few in number) stroke patterns above and below the touching points.

These observations are captured through computation of a few features. For example, one feature i.e. $f_{ic} = c^{-1}$ is formulated to obtain inverse crossing-count, where c is the crossing-count (number of white to black transitions) computed for an object (column, row, etc.). On the other hand, the vertical thickness of the black blob at the touching point is always small compared to the thickness of the other character parts, so another feature is formulated as $f_{mt} = 1 - e^{\frac{w_\mu}{t}}$, where t is the number of black pixels encountered in one scan and w_μ is the mean thickness of the character strokes.

Other two features concentrate on finding shape patterns above and below the touching blobs. Features are computed along four directions (vertical, horizontal and two diagonals namely, $+45°$ and $-45°$). In each direction, features are evaluated for each scan (e.g. each column for vertical direction; similarly, rows are considered as objects for horizontal direction, etc.). Next, the feature values in each scan are combined to give a scalar, which is used as a prediction for that scan to be a cut-candidate for separation of touching characters. The method does not assume anything about the number of characters that may be present in a touching character image.

Use of Multiple Classifier System: As mentioned earlier, the symbols appearing in mathematical expressions are quite large in number and show wide variety in shape, size and style. Symbols like dot, comma, colon, etc. are small in size and they have little shape signature. Symbols like equal to, plus, minus, fraction bar, vertical bar, greater than, less than, brackets, etc. are not much complex in shape and recognition of such strokes is not very difficult. On the other hand, symbols like roman and Greek letters, etc. involve relatively complex stroke patterns and recognition of these symbols needs some amount of extra effort.

Based on these observations, a multiple classifier system is proposed [18] for recognition of symbols. A group of four classifiers of different capabilities are arranged hierarchically in two levels as shown in Figure 11.4. The classifier used at the top level employs stroke-based classification technique to recognize symbols having high occurrence frequencies. Symbols not recognized at the first level are passed to the second level that employs a combination of three classifiers. The classifiers placed at this level make use of different feature descriptors namely, run-number or crossing-counts, density of black pixels and wavelet decomposition. Different combination techniques have been attempted to integrate the second level classifiers to achieve high recognition accuracy.

From this study, it is experienced that a single classifier is not capable enough to tackle the shape, size, style variations observed in expression symbols. Rather, a set of classifiers each working on subset of symbols

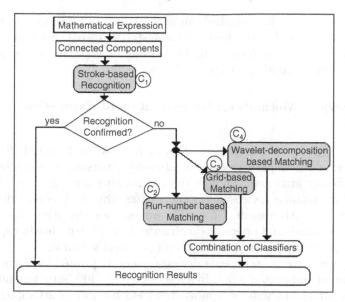

Fig. 11.4. Multiple classifier system.

can achieve better recognition accuracy provided they are combined in a suitable way. For example, in Figure 11.4 the classifiers show different performance in our experiment [15, 18]. Classifier C_1 gives 98.3% accuracy, whereas, classifiers C_2, C_3 and C_4 give accuracies 88.1%, 85.8% and 90.5%, respectively, when tested in isolation. However, logistic regression method (i.e. logistic regression) combining C_2, C_3 and C_4 gives accuracy about 93.77%.

11.4 Interpretation of Expression Structure

The geometric structure of an expression can be significantly more complex than that of normal text lines. For example, plain text is written linearly from left to right, but mathematical symbols are written above, below and one inside another. The spatial relationship among symbols is crucial to the interpretation of the expression. This means that even if all the characters are correctly recognized, there still remains the non-trivial problem of interpreting the two-dimensional structure of an expression. Ambiguities arise in areas like (1) *The semantic role of symbols*: Several symbols (e.g. *horizontal line*, *dot*, etc.) have multiple meaning depending on the context; (2) *Relative symbol proximity and position*: Expression symbols use spatial relationship to indicate the logical relationship among them. For instance, structures like *superscript, subscript, implied multiplication, matrix*, etc. are indicated implicitly by the geometric layout of operands.

Several researchers have studied this problem and various approaches to solve this are reviewed next. However, these studies reveal that additional research is needed for automatic understanding of mathematical expressions to achieve acceptable accuracy.

11.4.1 Previous Methods on Interpretation of Expression Symbols

One of the earliest contributions in this area is by Anderson [1, 2]. His syntax-directed technique is essentially a top-down parsing approach based on a co-ordinate grammar. Though the partitioning strategy used there does not show satisfactory results in many cases, this work is regarded as a pioneering one. Afterwards, Chang [7] proposes an algorithm based on operator precedence and operator dominance, but did not clearly explain the algorithm as well as its performance in practical scenario.

Among other studies, some consider expressions in printed form whereas others assume handwritten input. In a few cases (e.g. [40]), structure analysis in both printed as well as handwritten data have been attempted by a single approach. In 1989, Chou [9] presented a stochastic context-free grammar to understand two-dimensional (2D) structure of expressions. A 2D probabilistic version of Cocke–Younger–Kasami parsing algorithm is proposed to find the most likely parse of the observed image. However, very little is discussed about the construction of the training set and the experimental results. Among other related approaches, Hull [23] computed probabilities by which two sub-expressions are in a particular relationship. The algorithm attempts to enumerate all possibilities by using an A-star search and prunes away the unlikely ones. Later on, Miller and Viola [30] tried to limit the number of potentially valid interpretations by decomposing the expressions into a sequence of compatible convex regions.

Twaakyondo and Okamoto [38] presented a technique that uses notational conventions in typing expressions. Structure of an expression is analysed by *projection-profile cutting* and a top-down strategy is used to analyse the horizontal and vertical relation between sub-expressions. To analyse nested structure such as subscripts, superscripts, etc., a bottom-up strategy is invoked that begin with the smaller symbols. The authors also provided an automatic approach [38] for evaluating their method. An accuracy of 98.04% is reported for recognition of 4701 elementary expression structures like *scripts, limit, fraction*, etc.

Lee and Lee [28] uses a procedure-oriented bottom-up approach to translate a 2D expression into a 1D character string. Initially, smaller symbol groups are formed around seven special mathematical symbols (i.e. "$\sum$", "π", *fraction*, etc.) which may deviate from the typographic centre of an expression. Next, symbol groups are ordered from left to right based on their centre y-coordinates. Matrices are handled separately [29]. The authors consider 105 expressions for training and 50 expressions for testing.

An error rate of about 2% is reported but the approach for computing the error rate is not presented.

Fateman et al. [3,14] described a *recursive decent* parser where an additional stage (called *linearization*) is used in between lexical analysis and the conventional parsing. In the *linearization* phase, adjacency relations among the tokens are detected. Several data-dependent heuristics are used. The experiments put emphasis on parsing of integrals. In another study [22], Ha et al. outlined a system that uses a recursive X–Y decomposition to understand the geometric layout of an expression.

Toumit et al. [37] assigned different priority levels to symbols in order to present a tree representation of the input expression. An alternative approach based on graph representation of an expression image is proposed by Grbavec and Blostein [21]. Nodes in the graph represent symbols or sub-expressions and edges represent relationship between the sub-expressions. Later on, Lavirotte and Pottier [27] used context-sensitive graph grammar technique which attempts to add context in the graph-rewriting rules for replacing one sub-graph by another.

Eto and Suzuki [11] proposed a concept of virtual link network to recognize expression structures. The proposed technique was tested using 123 expressions, of which 110 are properly recognized. The same was incorporated in [36] and experiment conducted on a larger dataset containing 12,493 expressions reported a structure recognition accuracy of 89.6%.

Garcia and Couasnon [20] proposed a generic method, DMOS (Description and MOdification of Segmentation) for recognition of musical scores, tables, forms, etc. The proposed method was tested using 60 formulae but details of the test results were not available. More recently, Zanibbi [40] described an algorithm consisting of multiple passes for (1) constructing a baseline structure tree describing the 2D arrangement of symbols, (2) grouping tokens comprised of multiple symbols and (3) arranging symbols in an operator tree which describes the order and scope of operations in the input expressions. Experiment using 73 expressions of UW-III database [35] showed a recognition (at expression level) accuracy of 38% (at most). However, the authors presented an in-depth analysis of the performance of their proposed method for structure analysis.

11.4.2 Further Research on Interpretation of Expression Structure

Studying the expression corpus [16], we noted a number of structural properties inherent in these expressions. Use of these properties make reconstruction algorithm more robust. A few such properties are mentioned below.

Bounding box of a symbol: For a symbol s, we define its bounding box $B(s)$ to be the smallest upright rectangle enclosing the symbol. We denote

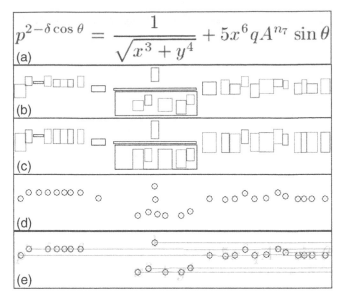

Fig. 11.5. Detection of horizontal lines and symbols' L-values: (a) expression image, (b) bounding boxes for expression symbols, (c) extended bounding boxes for symbols, (d) symbol centres and (e) horizontal lines (excluding the *HEES* symbols).

it by a four-tuple $(xl,\ xr,\ yt,\ yb)$, where $(xl,\ yt)$ and $(xr,\ yb)$ represent the top-most left corner and the bottom-most right corners of B, respectively. Figure 11.5(b) shows bounding boxes for symbols of expression in (a). We define the height (yh) and width (xw) of a symbol by $yh = yb - yt + 1$ and $xw = xr - xl + 1$.

Enclosing Zone (EZ), Extended Bounding box (EB) and Centre (C) of a Symbol: Characters like roman letters, Greek symbols, etc. exhibit three zones in a text line. Let *enclosing zone* (EZ) refers to all the three zones and is **represented** by a pair of y-coordinates (eyt, eyb), eyt and eyb are being the y-coordinates of the top and bottom rows of the zone, respectively. If the symbols "A", "a" and "p" occur within the same EZ, then usually "A" and "a" will have yb-values very close to each other, but the yt-values will vary. Similarly, for symbols 'a' and 'p', yt-values are close but not the yb-values. We normalize EZ by assuming that an EZ starts at $yt = 0$ and ends at $yb = 1$. With respect to a normalized EZ, values of $(yt,\ yb)$-pair for all symbols are computed. However, there are some symbols (*elastic symbols* as discussed next), which are treated as exceptions for computing their EZ.

    Once $EZ(s) = (eyt, eyb)$ is obtained for a symbol (s), its extended bounding box (EB) is computed as $EB = (xl, xr, eyt, eyb)$. For different classes of symbols, the rules for estimating EB from B (bounding box) are formulated from the rules for normalizing EZ. Figure 11.5(c) shows the extended bounding boxes for symbols of expression in (a).

The centre of a symbol s is given by the y-centre of its $EB(s)$ and is computed as the arithmetic mean of the eyt and eyb values. Let EB (xl, xr, eyt, eyb) denote the extended bounding box for the symbol, s. Therefore, centre of s, $C(s)$ is given by $C(s) = (eyt + eyb)/2$. Figure 11.5(d) shows the centre positions for expression symbols in (a).

Elastic Symbols: There are some symbols that vary in size in different context. For example, horizontal lines may appear in expression in different lengths. Some other elastic symbols appear for *sum, integration, arrows, brackets*, etc. For all these symbols, $eyt = yt$, $eyb = yb$ and $C = (yt + yb)/2$. Among these symbols, certain symbols are horizontally elongated and denoted as *HEES* (horizontally elongated elastic symbol) symbols. An elastic symbol is identified as *HEES* if its aspect ratio (i.e. xw/yh) is more than a pre-defined threshold whose value is more than 1.

Level (L) of a Symbol: Computation of symbol L-values initially requires determination of horizontal lines on which symbols are arranged in an expression and identification of one of the lines as the dominant baseline [40] of the expression. The algorithm for finding symbol L-values initially sorts the symbols in ascending order of their centres (C-values). Then symbols having nearly the same C-values are grouped together to have the same L-values. This grouping starts with the first symbol and with $L = 0$. L-value increases for subsequent groups. Symbols labelled *HEES* are ignored for assigning any L-value.

Symbols of same L-values define a horizontal line (HL) in the expression. Let l be the number of such lines, $HL_1, HL_2, \ldots, HL_l$, where HL_i is defined by its member symbols having $L = i$. This l basically determines the geometric complexity (GC) of an expression. Centre of an HL ($C(HL)$) is computed as an average of its members' centre values. Figure 11.5(e) shows the HLs found for expressions in (a). Next, symbols detected as *HEES* are added to different HLs. An *HEES* is added to an HL by looking at their positional proximity.

Once all the symbols are arranged in different HLs, dominant baseline is selected as the HL that contains the left-most expression symbol. L-values of the symbols belong to this HL line is re-assigned to 0 and L-values of other symbols are changed with respect to this new HL_0. L-values of the symbols belonging to the HL just above this line (i.e. the new HL_0) are assigned to 1 and similarly, L-values of the symbols belonging to the HL just below the dominant baseline are assigned to -1. In this way, L-values increases above and decreases below the dominant baseline.

Reduction Ratio: Consider an expression A^A. The size (characterized by the height) of symbol reduces from the base level to the script (superscript or subscript) level. The ratio by which the height of a symbol (say, s) decreases from the base level to script level will be called the *reduction ratio* of that symbol *s*, and denoted by $RR(s)$. In general, the *reduction ratio* of a symbol *s* is defined as, (height of *s* as super/subscript) $\div$ (height of *s* as base).

The RR-values of different symbols have been studied and the mean and standard deviation were found to be 0.60222 and 0.0237, respectively. Thus, the 3Σ-limit for RR-values is given by the interval (0.53109, 0.67335) and all the observed RR-values to lie in this interval. In other words, there is a reduction in height of a symbol by at least 32% (approx.) and at most 47% (approx.) at the script (super/sub) level with respect to its height at base level. This feature helps us to determine a *script* relation between a pair of symbols (or symbol groups) deferring in their *L*-values.

Space Between Symbols: The average space between two symbols, occurring in the same line, side by side, was measured as percentage of the height of their (normalized) enclosing zone (EZ). This measure is denoted by *sp* and shows a mean and variance of 0.05392 and 0.00050, respectively. This measure is used to identify function words (e.g. *sin*, *log*, *lim*, etc.) in expressions.

Expression Reconstruction: Let *S* be the set of pre-processed symbols (i.e. each symbol is tagged with its identity, bounding box info (B), enclosing zone (EZ), extended bounding box (EB), centre (C), level (L-value), etc.). The symbols *S* are sorted in ascending order of their *xl* values. Next, expression structure is interpreted and coded into a *TeX* string as follows.

Initially, the expression image is divided into *n* vertical stripes (called *vStripe*) based on the white space between horizontally adjacent symbols. Figure 11.6(a) shows the *vStripes* for the image in Figure 11.5(a), where $n = 19$. Next, symbols under each *vStripe* are further segmented into horizontal stripes (called *hStripe*) based on the white space between vertically adjacent symbols. This vertical and horizontal segmentation continues until each stripe contains a single symbol or no further segmentation is possible. For the former case *TeX* equivalent of the symbol is returned and in the later case, further processing is invoked. For example, the *vStripe*, V_9 of Figure 11.6(a) is partitioned into three *hStripes* (see Figure 11.6(b)), of which both $H_{9,1}$ and $H_{9,2}$ contain a single symbol. In case of $H_{9,3}$, no further segmentation is possible. In such cases, the largest (based on bounding box area) symbol (i.e. *square root* symbol) is separated (see Figure 11.6(c)) and further segmentation is invoked recursively on the rest of the symbols (see Figure 11.6(d)).

Once segmentation is over for all symbols, merging of symbols takes place. Merging of two/more symbols is guided by a context-free grammar similar to one in [2]. The statistics computed before are used to determine which grammar rule to be applied. For example, application of rule related to *scripts* makes use of information like extended bounding box (EB), reduction ratio (RR), etc. Rule pertaining to *fraction* uses *L*-values of symbols.

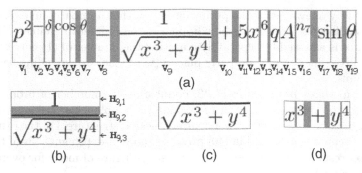

Fig. 11.6. Structural analysis of an expression image: vertical and horizontal segmentation.

Experiment with the database described in [16] shows that out of 5560 expressions 4348 are properly reconstructed giving an accuracy of 78.2%. Error analysis reveals that error increasing with the increase of geometric complexity of the expressions. However, this way of measuring accuracy is not judicious because placement error for a single symbol makes recognition of an expression incorrect. Therefore, a more reasonable performance measure is presented in the next section where a performance index is computed to provide a more meaningful evaluation of accuracy for interpretation of expression structures.

11.5 Performance Evaluation

The quantitative evaluation of expression recognition results is a difficult task, since recognition scheme involves two major stages: symbol recognition and structural analysis. The stages are tightly coupled and therefore, if evaluation in one stage is done independent of the other, then it may not reflect true performance of the system. Errors in the symbol recognition stage affect the structure analysis results. This calls for an integrated evaluation mechanism for judging the performance of system dealing with expression recognition.

Chan and Yeung [6] proposed an integrated performance measure consisting of two independent measures: one for recognition of symbols and another for recognition of operators. These two measures are combined with equal weights. The proposed evaluation is based on manual effort. Later on, Okamoto et al. [32] have presented an automatic approach for evaluating their structure analysis method. They attempted to evaluate the performance by checking whether each typical structure such as scripts, limits, fractions, roots, and matrices, is recognized correctly. In their approach, expressions against which a system is evaluated are groundtruthed into MathML format. More recently, Zanibbi et al. [40] presented another automatic way of evaluating the performance. In that approach, an expression is visualized as a set of symbols appearing on different baselines. The performance is assessed by separately counting the number of (1) correctly recognized baselines and (2) properly placed (w.r.t. the corresponding baseline) symbols.

As the methods proposed in [6, 32] count only the number of properly recognized structures, an error in recognizing a simple structure gets the same weight as that of an error in a complex nested structure. On the other hand, the technique proposed in [40] presents more in-depth analysis of the recognition results, but does not provide a single figure of merit for overall performance evaluation.

11.5.1 Basic Requirements for Performance Evaluation

For evaluating the performance of an expression recognition system, at first, we need a corpus of scientific documents on which the system will be tested. Unavailability of a suitable corpus of expressions has prompted the researchers to define their own data set for testing their algorithms. As a result, replication of experiments and comparison of performance among different methods has become a difficult task.

Therefore, a database of expression images is needed that would facilitate research in automatic evaluation of expressions. The only relevant database available so far is the University of Washington English/Technical Document Database III (UW-III) [35]. However, the database is mainly constructed for general OCR (optical character recognition) research and contains 25 groundtruthed (into TeX) document pages containing about 100 expressions. Therefore, it does not seem to be a representative corpus for the respective research. Another drawback of this data set is that groundtruthing of expressions into TeX only does not support an in-depth analysis of recognition performance [6, 32, 40].

Recently, Uchida et al. [39] developed a database of a large collection of mathematical documents and analysed from several viewpoints for the development of practical OCR for mathematical and other scientific documents. The database contains 690,000 manually ground-truthed characters and available in public domain. The result of their analysis shows the difficulties of recognizing mathematical documents and at the same time, suggests several promising directions to overcome them.

Development of a Corpus of Scientific Documents: In one of our projects [15] we took up this problem and attempted to generate a database of printed scientific documents. The proposed database contains 400 document images containing 2459 displayed and 3101 embedded expression fragments. Both real (297 pages) and synthetic (generated by TeX or Microsoft Word) documents (103 pages) are present in the data set. Real documents are collected from (1) books of various branches of science,

(2) science journals, (3) proceedings of technical conferences, (4) question papers (College/University level examination), etc.

Synthetic documents are selected from sources that are available in Microsoft Word or TeX format. Several electronically available journals, conference proceedings, Internet sites related to various science subjects were considered for this purpose. A few pages were selected from the technical articles published by the members of our research unit. Several factors like (1) frequency of expressions in pages, (2) variations in typeset, (3) aging effect and other degradations, etc. influence the choice of materials.

Groundtruthing of Scientific Documents: The article in [16] describes the groundtruth format in details. Groundtruthing is done at the page level. However, it is assumed that page segmentation is done and only text parts (along with expressions) are labelled for Groundtruthing. Both embedded and displayed expressions are considered. For a given page, embedded expressions are truthed into .emb file whereas displayed expressions are stored in .dis file. Embedded expressions are recorded along with the sentence containing it. A sentence is said to have one or more embedded expressions if it would need the use of *math mode* had the sentence been prepared using *TeX*. On the other hand, displayed expressions are coded in isolation.

MathML format is followed to code the expressions. Some additional tags are used to encode bounding box information that pinpoints the expression zones in a page. Geometric complexity of an expression is coded and it is defined as the number of horizontal lines (on which expression symbols are arranged) found in the expression. For individual symbols, MathML tags are extended to include information like symbols' bounding box, type styles and *level* values. For example, if t is an identifier used in the expression, its MathML representation (i.e. $<$mi$>$ t $<$/mi$>$\$) is extended as follows:

```
<mi>
 <level> ... </level>
 <style> ... </style>
 <truth > ... </truth>
</mi>
```

The *level* indicates symbol L-values (discussed in Section 11.4.2). The *style* indicates the type style (n: normal, b: bold, i: italic, bi: bold-italic) of the symbol. The identity of the symbol is given within the $<$truth$>$ $<$/truth$>$ tag pairs. Some sample images and their corresponding groundtruth can be found at the following site: **http://www.isical.ac. in/~utpal**.

Validation of the Truthed Data: While generating the truthed data, manual intervention was involved at several stages and therefore, prone to contain errors. On the other hand, for different purposes like performance evaluation etc., it is important to have the truthed data free from errors. Therefore, we took some attempt in this direction.

Initially, some tools are developed to generate an upper level description of the page content from the ground-truthed data. This description is manually compared with the original page content. The elements that undergo checking are (1) expression itself (when MathML description is converted into two-dimensional layout), (2) expression positions, (3) their geometric complexity and (4) expression symbols are checked for their type style, level and identity. Bounding box for individual symbols are also checked for displayed expressions. Any error detected during this checking is corrected in the corresponding ground-truthed files.

We do consider the above validation check as the first level task and it is yet to finish for all the pages. Our plan is to check the truthed data (say, T) is to be manually checked and corrected by two different groups in isolation to produce two versions of the same truthed data namely, T_1 and T_2. Later on, T_1 and T_2 are to be compared by automatic file comparison utilities like cmp, diff, etc. Differences are to be marked and corrected to produce the final version of the truthed data.

11.5.2 Performance Evaluation Strategy

We formulate a performance evaluation strategy for expression recognition using the Groundtruthing format as discussed before. The recognition result for an expression (printed or handwritten) is compared with the groundtruth corresponding to that expression. If they do not match, then the result is not correct. This matching can be done by comparing two document object model[2] (DOM) trees, one generated from the groundtruth data for the expression and another generated from the recognition output for that expression. Let G_D be the DOM tree obtained from the ground-truthed data for an expression E and R_D be the DOM tree corresponds to the recognition result for E. A comparison between G_D and R_D detects the errors for recognition of E.

Since matching of two trees is itself a long-standing subject of research,[3] we at present do not explore much in this area (rather we treat this issue for our specific purpose as a future research problem). In our current approach, matching of two DOM trees is centred on the leaf-nodes only and parsing proceeds in a left to right order. At first, the left-most leaf node of G_D is picked up and corresponding leaf node in R_D is matched. Matching considers (1) identities (symbols) of the nodes and (2) the paths found from the leaf-nodes to the root-nodes in two trees. A mis-match in the first

---

[2] http://www.w3schools.com/dom/ and for further reference see http://www.w3.org/TR/MathML2/chapter8.html.

[3] We would like to refer to a recent article on this topic: Philip Bille, "Tree Edit Distance, Alignment Distance and Inclusion", available at "citeseer.ist.psu.edu/bille03tree.html".

case reports a symbol recognition error, whereas mis-match in the second case indicates symbol placement error.

Leaf-nodes generating mis-matches are marked in G_D as it represents the groundtruth. Manual intervention is required because the above DOM-matching approach identifies the symbols suffering from placement errors but at the same time it may mark certain other symbols which truly speaking do not suffer from placement errors. Actually, this matching method pinpoints the structures (i.e. group of symbols that impose a 2D structure like scripts, etc.) for which the arrangements of some constituent symbols are incorrect.

Errors originating from two sources (1) symbol recognition errors and (2) errors in structure interpretation. Symbol recognition errors is easily computed as

$$S_e = \frac{\text{No. of wrongly recognized symbols}}{\text{Total no. of symbols}} \tag{11.1}$$

For computation of structure recognition errors, the symbols with improper placement are identified. In our method, the erroneous arrangement of a symbol (s) is penalized by a factor $\frac{1}{|i|+1}$, where i is the level of the symbol, s.

It may be noted that in case of computing structure recognition error only spatial arrangements are important. For example, no structure recognition error is reported if x^m is recognized as x^{rn}. This is so because such symbol classification errors are accounted for by computing symbol recognition accuracy. In the foregoing example, structure recognition error is detected only if identification of *superscript* structure fails.

For any test expression, let S_t be the total number of symbols, S_e be number of symbols recognized incorrectly, R_i be the number of symbols in the ith level, and O_i be the number of ith level symbols for which incorrect arrangement analysis is encountered. Now, the performance index (γ) is defined as

$$\gamma = 1 - \frac{S_e + \sum_i O_i \times \frac{1}{|i|+1}}{S_t + \sum_i R_i \times \frac{1}{|i|+1}} \tag{11.2}$$

Assuming a test set (T_s) contains Z expressions, γ_k is computed for all $k = 1, 2, \ldots, N$ and to rate the overall system performance, an average γ_{avg} is computed as:

$$\gamma_{avg} = \frac{1}{Z} \sum_k \gamma_k \tag{11.3}$$

11.6 Conclusion and Future Research

Major steps needed for OCR of scientific documents have been discussed. The state of the art and different approaches available for implementation of each step are outlined. Several schemes to achieve further improvement have been presented from our research experience. A new format for groundtruthing of scientific documents has been outlined and a performance index based on this groundtruthing format has been presented to evaluate an expression recognition system.

In spite of good amount of research effort as described in this chapter, commercial OCR systems are still not process expression with acceptable accuracy. Possible reason could be (1) most of the studies have dealt with isolated expressions and therefore, problems to deal with a whole page containing expressions have not been studied well and (2) non-availability of a representative dataset on which a proposed method can be tested to judge its confidence while working in real situation instead of being tested on limited dataset.

Recent research efforts are motivated by these needs. For example, the research group led by Prof. M. Suzuki has put a ground-truthed database along with their software in the Internet[4] so that the resources are available in the public domain. We too have made our groundtruthing method available[5] for public comments. These efforts will simulate interaction among the peer research groups.

Apart from these, we view that further research is needed in at least two areas (1) identification of expression zones in document images and (2) a unified method for performance evaluation of expression recognition systems. In fact, number of studies in these two areas is quite less. In Sections. 11.2 and 11.5, we have tried to discuss these issues. A robust approach that locates expressions in document images will enable the existing OCR systems to be enhanced to process scientific documents with better accuracy. On the other hand, a uniform performance evaluation method is very much needed to evaluate recognition results.

References

1. Anderson, R.H. (1968). Syntax-directed recognition of hand-printed two-dimensional mathematics. Doctoral dissertation. Department of Engineering and Applied Physics, Harvard University.
2. Anderson, R.H. (1977). Two-dimensional mathematical notations. In: K.S. Fu, (Ed.). *Syntactic Pattern Recognition Applications.* New York: Springer, pp. 147–177.
3. Berman, B.P. and Fateman, R.J. (1994). Optical character recognition for typeset mathematics. *ACM Proceedings of International Symposium on Symbolic and Algebraic Computation (ISSAC), Oxford, UK*, pp. 348–353.
4. Blostein, D. and Grbavec, A. (1997). Recognition of mathematical notation. In: H. Bunke and P.S.P. Wang (Eds.). *Handbook of Character Recognition and Document Image Analysis.* Singapore: World Scientific, pp. 557–582.

---

[4] http://www.inftyproject.org/en/index.html.
[5] http://www.isical.ac.in/~utpal (for the link called "Resources").

5. Chan, K.-F. and Yeung, D.-Y. (2000). Mathematical expression recognition: a survey. *International Journal on Document Analysis and Recognition, 3,* pp. 3–15.

6. Chan, K.-F. and Yeung, D.-Y. (2001). Error detection, error correction and performance evaluation in on-line mathematical expression recognition. *Pattern Recognition, 34,* pp. 1671–1684.

7. Chang, S.-K. (1970). A method for the structural analysis of two-dimensional mathematical expressions. *Information Sciences, 2,* pp. 253–272.

8. Chaudhuri, B.B. and Garain, U. (2000). An approach for recognition and interpretation of mathematical expressions in printed document. *Pattern Analysis and Applications, 3,* pp. 120–131.

9. Chou, P.A. (1989). Recognition of equations using a two-dimensional stochastic context-free grammar. *Proceedings of the SPIE, Visual Communication and Image Processing IV, 1199,* pp. 852–863.

10. Chowdhury, S.P., Mandal, S., Das, A.K., and Chanda, B. (2003). Automated segmentation of math-zones from document images. *Proceedings of the Seventh International Conference Document Analysis and Recognition (ICDAR), Edinburgh, Scotland,* pp. 755–759.

11. Eto, Y. and Suzuki, M. (2001). Mathematical formula recognition using virtual link network. *Proceedings of the Sixth International Conference Document Analysis and Recognition (ICDAR), Seattle, USA,* pp. 762–767.

12. Fateman, R.J. (1999). How to find mathematics on a scanned page. *Proceedings of the SPIE, San Jose, California, USA, 3967,* pp. 98–109.

13. Fateman, R.J. and Tokuyasu, T. (1996). Progress in recognizing typeset mathematics. *Proceedings of the SPIE, San Jose, California, USA, 2660,* pp. 7–50.

14. Fateman, R.J., Tokuyasu, T., Berman, B.P., and Mitchell, N. (1996). Optical character recognition and parsing of typeset mathematics. *Journal of Visual Communication and Image Representation, 7,* pp. 2–15.

15. Garain, U. (2005). Recognition of printed and handwritten mathematical expressions. PhD thesis. Indian Statistical Institute.

16. Garain, U. and Chaudhuri, B.B. (2005). A corpus for OCR of printed mathematical expressions. *International Journal of Document Analysis and Recognition (IJDAR), 7(4),* pp. 241–259.

17. Garain, U. and Chaudhuri, B.B. (2005). Segmentation of touching symbols for OCR of printed mathematical expressions: an approach based on multifactorial analysis. *Proceedings of the Eighth International Conference on Document Analysis and Recognition (ICDAR), Seoul, Korea, I,* pp. 177–181.

18. Garain, U., Chaudhuri, B.B., and Ghosh, R.P. (2004). A multiple classifier system for recognition of printed mathematical symbols. *The Seventeenth International Conference on Pattern Recognition (ICPR), Cambridge, UK,* pp. 380–383.

19. Garain, U., Chaudhuri, B.B., and Ray Chaudhuri, A. (2004). Identification of embedded mathematical expressions in scanned documents. *Seventeenth International Conference on Pattern Recognition (ICPR), Cambridge, UK,* pp. 384–387.

20. Garcia, P. and Couasnon, B. (2002). Using a generic document recognition method for mathematical formulae recognition. In: D. Blostein and Y.-B. Kwon (Eds.). *Proceedings of International Workshop on Graphics Recognition (GREC) LNCS.* Berlin, Heidelberg: Springer, 2390, pp. 236–244.

21. Grbavec, A. and Blostein, D. (1995). Mathematics recognition using graph rewriting. *Proceedings of the Third International Conference on Document Analysis and Recognition (ICDAR), Montreal, Canada*, pp. 417–421.

22. Ha, J., Haralick, R.M., and Phillips, I.T. (1995). Understanding mathematical expressions from document images. *Proceedings of the Third International Conference on Document Analysis and Recognition (ICDAR), Montreal, Canada*, pp. 956–959.

23. Hull, J.F. (1996). Recognition of mathematics using a two-dimensional trainable context-free grammar. Master's thesis. Department of Electrical Engineering and Computer Science, Massachusetts Institute of Technology.

24. Inoue, K., Miyazaki, R., and Suzuki, M. (1998). Optical recognition of printed mathematical documents. *Proceedings of Asian Technology Conference in Mathematics (ATCM)*. New York: Springer, pp. 280–289.

25. Jin, J., Han, X., and Wang, Q. (2003). Mathematical formulas extraction. *Proceedings of the Seventh International Conference Document Analysis and Recognition (ICDAR), Edinburgh, Scotland*, pp. 1138–1141.

26. Kacem, A., Belaid, A., Ben Ahmed, M. (2001). Automatic extraction of printed mathematical formulas using fuzzy logic and propagation of context. *International Journal on Document Analysis and Recognition (IJDAR), 4*, pp. 97–108.

27. Lavirotte, S. and Pottier, L. (1997). Optical formula recognition. *Proceedings of the Fourth International Conference on Document Analysis and Recognition (ICDAR), Ulm, Germany*, pp. 357–361.

28. Lee, H.J. and Lee, M.C. (1994). Understanding mathematical expressions using procedure-oriented transformation. *Pattern Recognition, 27*, pp. 447–457.

29. Lee, H.J. and Wang, J.-S. (1997). Design of a mathematical expression understanding system. *Pattern Recognition Letters, 18*, pp. 289–298.

30. Miller, E.G. and Viola, P.A. (1998). Ambiguity and constraint in mathematical expression recognition. *Proceedings of the National Conference of Artificial Intelligence. American Association of Artificial Intelligence, Madison, Wisconsin*, pp. 784–791.

31. Nomura, A., Michishita, K., Uchida, S., and Suzuki, M. (2003). Detection and segmentation of touching characters in mathematical expressions. *Proceedings of the Seventh International Conference Document Analysis and Recognition (ICDAR), Edinburgh, Scotland*, pp. 126–130.

32. Okamoto, M., Imai, H., and Takagi, K. (2001). Performance evaluation of a robust method for mathematical expression recognition. *Proceedings of the Sixth International Conference Document Analysis and Recognition (ICDAR), Seattle, USA*, pp. 121–128.

33. Okamoto, M. and Miyazawa, A. (1992). An experimental implementation of document recognition system for papers containing mathematical expressions. In: H.S. Baird, H. Bunke, and Yamamoto (Eds.). *Structured Document Image Analysis*. New York: Springer, pp. 36–53.

34. Okamoto, M., Sakaguchi, S., and Suzuki, T. (1998). Segmentation of touching characters in formulae. *Proceedings of the Third IAPR Workshop on Document Analysis Systems (DAS), Nagano, Japan*, pp. 283–289.

35. Phillips, I. (1998). Methodologies for using UW databases for OCR and image understanding systems. *Document Recognition V, Proceedings of the SPIE, San Jose, CA, USA, 3305*, pp. 112–127.

36. Suzuki, M., Tamari, F., and Fukuda, R. (2003). INFTY – an integrated OCR system for mathematical documents. In: S. Uchida and T. Kanahori (Eds.). *Proceedings of ACM Symposium on Document Engineering (DocEng), Grenoble, France*, pp. 95–104.
37. Toumit, J.-Y., Garcia-Salicetti, S., and Emptoz, H. (1999). A hierarchical and recursive model of mathematical expressions for automatic reading of mathematical documents. *Proceedings of the Fifth International Conference Document Analysis and Recognition (ICDAR), Bangalore, India*, pp. 119–122.
38. Twaakyondo, H.M. and Okamoto, M. (1995). Structure analysis and recognition of mathematical expressions. *Proceedings of the Third International Conference on Document Analysis and Recognition (ICDAR), Montreal, Canada*, pp. 430–437.
39. Uchida, S., Nomura, A., and Suzuki, M. (2005). Quantitative analysis of mathematical documents. *International Journal on Document Analysis and Recognition (IJDAR), 7(4)*, pp. 211–218.
40. Zanibbi, R., Blostein, D., and Cordy, J.R. (2002). Recognizing mathematical expressions using tree transformation. *IEEE Transactions on Pattern Analysis and Machine Intelligence, 24*, pp. 1455–1467.

The State of the Art of Document Image Degradation Modelling

Henry S. Baird

12.1 Introduction

This chapter reviews the literature and the scientific and engineering state of the art of models of document-image degradation. Images of paper documents are almost inevitably degraded in the course of printing, photocopying, faxing, scanning, and the like. This loss of quality, even when it appears negligible to human eyes, can cause an abrupt drop in accuracy by the present generation of text recognition (OCR) systems. This fragility of OCR systems due to low-image quality is well known by serious users as well as OCR engineers and has been illustrated compellingly in large-scale experiments carried out at the Information Science Research Institute of the University of Nevada ([55] through [53]). In addition, there is growing evidence that significant improvement in accuracy on recalcitrant image pattern recognition problems now depends as much on the size and representativeness of training sets as on choice of features and classification algorithms. To mention only one example, a US National Institute of Standards and Technology (NIST) competition on hand-printed digits [67] had a surprising outcome: the competitor with the highest accuracy ignored the training set offered by NIST, using instead its own, much larger, set; furthermore, in spite of widely divergent algorithms, most of the competitors who used the same training set were tightly clustered in accuracy; and, one of the most promising attacks relied on perhaps the oldest and simplest of algorithms, nearest-neighbour classification [58].

These observations suggest that large improvements in accuracy may be achievable through – and perhaps *only* through – deeper scientific understanding of image quality and the representativeness of image data sets. Such a research programme may be expected to assist engineers by allowing them to measure image quality, control the effects of variation in quality, and construct classifiers automatically to meet given accuracy goals.

This survey is organized as follows. First, I describe those degradations that appear to be most important in document image analysis. Then, I summarize the recent history of image quality measurement relevant to documents. I describe the degradation models that have been proposed, together with methods for estimating their parameters. I give examples of four types of applications of these models: for the automatic construction of classifiers, in the testing of systems, the provision of public-domain image databases, and in theoretical investigations. Finally, I list open problems.

This integrates and updates much material that appeared separately as [8–10]. An earlier version was presented as an invited unpublished plenary address at the IAPR Workshop on Document Analysis Systems in Rio de Janeiro in 1999.

12.2 Document Image Degradations

By "degradations" (or, "defects") I mean every sort of less-than-ideal properties of real document images, e.g. coarsening due to low digitizing resolution, ink/toner drop-outs and smears, thinning and thickening, geometric deformations, etc.

These are all departures from an ideal version of the page image, which, in the domain of machine-printed textual documents, is usually unambiguously well defined. In fact such a page's contents can usually be considered not as an explicit image but as a symbolic representation of an implicit image, in which printing symbols (characters) occur only as references to ideal prototype images in a given library of typeface artwork, together with instructions for their idealized placement (translation, scaling, etc.) on the page surface. In practice, this idealized symbolic version exists concretely, expressed in PostScript, troff or similar low-level page description or typesetting languages. But it should not be assumed that the printing apparatus is always a modern computer-driven typesetting machine. And, in many cases, the symbolic layout description may never have been written down: but it is enough for the present purposes that it could have been.

Once the sizes and locations of all symbols and other artwork have been specified, then it makes sense to speak of the ideal image of the page (or text-block, text line, symbol, etc.). Since the document image degradation model literature focuses almost exclusively on images of high-contrast (essentially monochromatic, black and white) machine-printed pages, I will assume that the idealized input image is bi-level, a two-colouring of the real plane, and thus at an effectively infinite spatial sampling rate.

The defective images resulting from printing and imaging are also commonly bi-level images with a finite spatial sampling rate (often the same, as I will generally assume, along both axes of a conventional X–Y coordinate system, in units of square pixels per inch). The coarsening that results from finite spatial sampling is of course considered to be an image defect.

It is worth noting a few general characteristics of image defects:

- Defects are determined by the physics of the apparatus used in printing and imaging; by "apparatus" I mean to include some human actions, as for example when a page is manually placed on a flatbed scanner.
- Images may result from more than one stage of printing and imaging.
- Some aspects of the physics are uncontrollable, and so must be modelled as random events and analysed statistically.

The physics may of course have both 'global' and 'local' effects. The entire page image is affected by geometric deformations such as non-zero "skew"(rotation). Only a single character image may be affected by ink drop out. Isolated pixels be individually affected by thermal sensor noise. Thus defects can occur per page, per symbol and per pixel – and at other levels of the document hierarchy, such as text blocks and text lines. But not all defects can be associated with the symbolic layout: for example, paper grain and ink non-uniformity produce defects larger than a pixel but smaller than a symbol. Thus, defects occur over a range of scales, and some – but not all – can be associated with logical parts of the document. These are important considerations in the design of the model, and they are likely to vary with the application.

There is far less agreement, of course, about the details of the physics of printing and imaging. Clearly, there is a great diversity of mechanisms, which include:

- defocusing;
- binarization (e.g. fixed and adaptive thresholding);
- paper positioning variations (skew, translation, etc.);
- flaking and poor adhesion generally of ink/toner to paper;
- low print contrast;
- non-uniform illumination;
- pixel sensor sensitivity variations;
- typesetting imperfections (pasted-up layouts, slipped type);
- abrasion, smudging and creasing of the paper surface;
- spatter, scatter and spreading of ink/toner;
- vibration and other non-uniform equipment motion;
- noise in electronic components (both additive and multiplicative);
- irregular pixel sensor placement (e.g. not lying on a perfectly square grid);
- finite spatial sampling rate;
- non-flat paper surface (e.g. curling and warping);
- non-rectilinear camera positioning (e.g. perspective distortion).

Although this list is certainly incomplete, it includes all causes that have been treated quantitatively in the literature to date.

Many images result from multiple stages of printing and imaging. Also, "printing" and "imaging" do not exhaust the possibilities: image compression and transmission (as in FAX) create important classes of defects. Future technologies will no doubt cause defects that are difficult now to imagine.

12.3 The Measurement of Image Quality

In this section I briefly review the state of the art of the recent literature, technical and professional activities, standards and products that are relevant to the document image degradation models. I emphasize monochrome and bi-level images, and neglect colour.

To the best of my knowledge, no comprehensive quantitative study of image defects in printing and imaging has been published. Book-length surveys of a wide range of printing technology, both pre-computer and computer-based, are available (e.g. [45, 51, 60]), but image defects are not a principal theme, and are rarely discussed quantitatively. Reference [42] surveys recent optical scanner technology. Reference [59] gives a thorough review of the basic physics of electronic imaging systems, including a helpful chapter on the formation of images of printed documents. In a discussion on "dot size change", the author offers this useful generalization: "many of these stages [of printing and imaging] can be characterized as analog image transfer [involving defocusing] followed by a sharp threshold process".

Technical meetings that attract papers on this subject include (a) the annual conference of the Society for Imaging Science and Technology, sponsored by [29]; (b) the annual Congress on Non-impact Printing Technologies, sponsored by [29]; (c) the annual Electronic Imaging Science and Technology Symposium, co-sponsored by [29, 62]; and of course (d) this meeting. The proceedings of these conferences occasionally contain descriptions of methods for measuring image quality.

The American National Standards Institute [4] sub-committee X3A1, in addition to its work on OCR-A and OCR-B typefaces (X3.17–1981, X3.49–1982, X3.93M–1981, X3.111–1986), has developed standards for ink (X3.86–1980), paper quality (X3.62–1979) and print quality (X3.99–1983).

The barcode industry has been somewhat more attentive to print quality standards than the OCR industry. ANSI subcommittee X3A1, together with committee MH10.8 on Materials Handling, jointly developed a barcode print quality guideline (X3.182–1990). According to its authors [13], it was the first attempt quantitatively to "enable accurate prediction of symbol performance in a reading environment". It focuses on two-element (bar and space), one-dimensional bar codes. It describes methods for measuring properties of the analog one-dimensional scan reflectance profile such as minimum and maximum reflectance, symbol contrast, edge determination and "defects". "Defects" is defined as the non-uniformity of reflectance within an element relative to overall contrast. The numerical measures can

be combined and converted to one of five symbol "grades". This standard
has been rapidly accepted worldwide as the technical basis for most modern
barcode designs. Although it is specialized in methods for one-dimensional
readout, I recommend it as an excellent guide to the measurement of high-
contrast document images. X3A1 is presently working on guidelines for the
evaluation of barcode reader performance.

ANSI committee X9B is developing standards on image capture, with
special attention to the quality of printed bank cheques necessary to permit
OCR of fields including handwritten courtesy amounts. In addition, they
have inherited the MICR standards from X3A1. The ANSI committee for
Graphic Arts Technology Standards [47] is working on a standard for the
use of densitometers.

The American Society for Testing and Materials [5] has published methods for evaluating business imager quality (committee F5, especially
methods F335, F875, F360) and paper quality (committee D6, especially
methods F1125, F807, F1351, F1319). These include the measurement of
large area density and background for a variety of modern office copiers,
and the susceptibility of paper to smudging, creasing and abrasion (which
affect ink and toner scatter and flaking).

The Association for Information and Image Management [2] develops
standards, terminology and tools (including test targets), for evaluating
image quality, among other issues. Specially relevant here are standards
on recommended practice for quality control of scanners (MS 44) and a
tutorial on image resolution (TR 26).

Test target images are widely used to measure document scanner characteristics, notably resolution, thresholding and contrast ratio [1, 2]. Two
of the most commonly used are (a) the US Air Force 1951 Test Chart
(MIL–STD–150–A), for measuring resolving power of optical systems and
imaging materials and (b) the IEEE Facsimile Test Chart. Applied Image,
Inc. [1] supplies several test targets specialized to OCR (Applied Scanner
test charts 1, 2 and 3). Standardized test target patterns have tended to
reflect the lowest common denominator of industrial practice, and do not
support complex evaluations such as distinguishing the effects of point-
spread function size from the effects of binarization threshold.

A wide variety of densitometers, for measuring point reflectance of paper documents, are commercially available. Aside from these, only a few
methods for image characterization have been used widely enough to sus-
tain a market. Specialized devices to measure the "print contrast ratio"
have been available for some time (082A [20], PCM–II [44]); this is the
quantity $(R_w - R_b)/R_w$, where R_w is the reflectance of a large white spot
(typically 0.25-inch radius), and R_b is the reflectance of a small black spot
(typically 8-mil radius). The default binarization threshold of document
scanners is often specified in units of print contrast ratio, typically as a
value in the range [0.5, 0.7]. These devices are also able to measure point
reflectance, dimensions of symbols, voids and ink spatter.

More versatile products for evaluating image quality have recently appeared [20,54]. They typically consist of a PC, proprietary software and a specially calibrated monochrome grey-level document scanner, able automatically to measure print contrast, point reflectance and layout properties such as the accurate placement of the outlines of fields. Specialized software permits testing of OCR-B images of known size for compliance with standards: this involves semi-automatic superimposition of ideal symbol prototypes on the image, and estimation of symbol height and width and stroke thickness. At present, these products do not support the estimation of point-spread function, thresholding or pixel sensitivity variations; neither do they analyse test target images.

Test methods for evaluating paper quality (opacity, specular gloss, etc.) are available from [64].

It is common practice in industrial laboratories to develop application-dependent methods for measuring and controlling image defects; these methods and their associated devices, software and test target images are often abandoned at the project's end [14, 25, 38, 66]. Thus, although many systematic quantitative studies of defects in printing and imaging equipment have been carried out, most have been narrowly specialized, and few have been published.

12.4 Document Image Degradation Models

This discussion of document image degradation models is prefaced by a brief account of the central technical issues governing their design. Then, briefly, two models are described, one based on the physics of printing and imaging, and the other based on surface statistics of image distributions. For both of these, I summarize methods that have been proposed for estimating their free parameters in order to fit the models to real image populations.

12.4.1 Methodological Issues

The central technical questions to ask about a proposed model are:

- *Parametrization.* Is the model expressible as an explicit computable function of a small, fixed number of numerical parameters? (If not, then it is hard to see how it can be used effectively to solve engineering problems.)
- *Randomization.* Which of the model's effects are intrinsically random? Can their distributions be parametrized (as above)? If so, the parameters of their distributions can be included among the parameters of the model.

- *Validation.* For any given defective image for which an ideal prototype is known, what is the probability that there exists some values of
  the model parameters that, applied to the ideal prototype, will dupli-
  cate the defective image? Since realistic models are likely to be probabilistic, the answer to this question must be probabilistic also.
- *Parameter estimation.* For any given population of defective images
  with known ideal prototypes, can a distribution on the model parameters be inferred that closely fits the real distribution?

Two generic approaches can be distinguished when specifying models.
The first is to model the physics of the apparatus in detail. The completeness of such models can then be justified in part by pointing to the physics.
Certainly this can lead to accurate models, but they may be unnecessarily
specific and complicated. The second approach is more empirical: propose
the simplest model that merely "saves the appearances", that is, that is
able to generate duplicates of real defective images. Such models cannot be
justified by appeals to physics and must rest on purely statistical measures
of completeness. Models of both types have been proposed.

12.4.2 A Physics-Based Model

A single-stage parametric model of per-symbol and per-pixel defects, modelled on the physics of printing and imaging, was proposed in [8] and refined
in [9]. The model parameters include:

- `size`: the nominal text size of the output (units of points);
- `resn`: "resolution", the output spatial sampling rate (pixels/inch);
- `skew`: rotation (degrees);
- `xscl, yscl`: multiplicative scaling factors (horizontally and vertically);
- `xoff, yoff`: translation offsets (output pixels);
- `jitt`: jitter, the distribution of per-pixel discrepancies of the pixel sensor
  centres from an ideal square grid: vector offsets (x,y) are chosen for each
  pixel, each component independently (the standard error of a normal
  distribution with zero mean, in units of output pixels):
- `blur`: defocusing, modelled as a Gaussian point-spread function (psf)
  centred at the pixel sensor centre (the standard error of the psf kernel
  in units of output pixels);
- `sens`: sensitivity, the distribution of per-pixel additive noise (the standard error of a normal distribution with zero mean, in units of intensity);
- `thrs`: the binarization threshold (in units of intensity, where 0.0 represents white and 1.0 black).

When the model is simulated, the parameters take effect in the order given
above: the ideal input image is first rotated, scaled and translated; then
the output resolution and per-pixel jitter determine the centres of each

pixel sensor; for each pixel sensor the blurring kernel is applied, giving an analogue intensity value to which per-pixel sensitivity noise is added; finally, each pixel's intensity is thresholded, giving the output image. In practice the values of these parameters are chosen pseudo-randomly, for each symbol, from first-order parametric distributions determined by mean and variance values specified by the user.

The input to the pseudo-random generator is an "ideal" black-and-white image at high resolution: in practice, scalable outline descriptions purchased from typeface manufacturers are used. The pseudo-random number generator is an implementation of the mathematics in [70], whose seed, during long runs, is occasionally reset with low-order bits of the CPU fine-grain timer.

Note that, for all the parameters, new values are chosen randomly for each symbol – thus I call them per-symbol parameters. But, two of these values – pixel sensor sensitivity and jitter – are themselves per-pixel parameters controlling randomization of each pixel. Thus, the values of the per-symbol parameters are subject to direct control (by specifying a constant distribution), but the values of the per-pixel parameters are subject to only indirect control. This has important consequences for Monte Carlo parameter estimation.

12.4.3 A Statistics-Based Model

Reference [31] proposes a model of document imaging that includes both global (perspective and non-linear illumination) and local (speckle, blur, jitter and threshold) effects. The order of application of the model is similar to that described above. The optical distortion process is modelled morphologically rather than by appeal to the physics of blurring and binarization.

12.4.4 Estimation of Model Parameters

All of the proposed models possess numerous free parameters that must be chosen to fit them to real image populations. Where the printing and scanning apparatus is itself available to be tested, special image patterns ("test targets") can be useful. In other circumstances, we must rely on images not specially designed for the purpose – such as images of machine-printed text in known typefaces – to drive the estimation process.

12.4.5 Estimation Using Images of Test Targets

There appears to be no commercially available test targets for the estimation of these model parameters:

- affine deformations (skew, shear, magnification, etc.);
- size of point-spread function kernel;
- threshold;
- pixel sensitivity variations.

In [9] a conceptual design of test targets, including sector star targets (e.g. [1], target MT–17), for these parameters was given.

Barney Smith has carried out a thorough analysis ([61] through [16]) of the effectiveness of sector star and other test targets in estimating the operating parameters of scanner systems. Using models of the scanning process and specially designed bi-level test targets, four methods of estimating parameters were developed. One of these estimates the displacement of a scanned edge and the other three estimate the scanner's point spread function (PSF) width and binarization threshold by analysis of particular features of the images of the test targets. These methods were tested systematically using both real and synthetic images. The resulting estimates are close to those implied by analysis of grey-level images. The parameters that were estimated were used to generate synthetic character images that "in most cases bear a strong resemblance" to real images acquired on the same equipment.

12.4.6 Estimation Using Images of Text

If we do not have access to the printing and imaging apparatus, we must attempt to estimate the parameters by a computation on a set of images, some of whose properties may be known.

If the documents are Manhattan textual layouts, it is well known then both skew and shear can often be measured to a small fraction of a degree, by a variety of algorithms (cf. [6]).

If the typeface and text size are known, then it may be possible to estimate many of the remaining parameters. Reference [9] describes some preliminary experiments with *black-box* parameter-estimation, in which the defect model is treated as a black box that can be affected only by varying the model parameters and observing the output defective image.

Attempts to exactly match a given target image with pseudo-randomly generated images proved to be futile due to the vast number of distinct images generated. By averaging over a set of "good" (but not identical) matches, estimation succeeds within a reasonable amount of computation, when only one parameter is varied at a time. More realistically, *all* parameters were then treated as unknown during estimation: large-scale runs (requiring 1.8 CPU hours for each set of parameters) were successful in estimating `skew`, `xscl` and `yscl` accurately and repeatably; the other parameters were less tractable.

Kanungo's Method

Kanungo [35] proposed a statistical bootstrapping method for rejecting the hypothesis that two image sets (say, one real, the other synthetic) were drawn from the same unknown distribution. In the context of parametrized degradation models, the rate at which Kanungo's method rejects the hypothesis can be analysed as a function of a model parameter, thereby providing a technique for estimating model parameters: experiments have shown [32–34] it to work reliably and efficiently in the estimation of some (not yet all) parameters of both the [8] and [31] models. In addition, it seems to have promise as a method for comparing two competing models: exploration of this remains an important open issue.

In [11], the slightest changes in document image quality that can be distinguished reliably and fully automatically by Kanungo's method were measured. For six parameters of the [8] model, remarkably fine discriminations are possible, often subtler than are evident to visual inspection. And, as few as 25 reference images are sufficient for this purpose. These results suggest that Kanungo's method is sufficiently sensitive to a wide range of physics-based image degradations to serve as an engineering foundation for many image-quality estimation and OCR engineering purposes.

Barney Smith's Methods

Barney Smith and her colleagues have investigated a family of methods for inferring parameters of models from images of characters. In [17] through [69], they show that corners and especially acute angles in character images provide enough information to make precise estimates of the parameters controlling convolution (blurring) followed by thresholding.

12.4.7 Validation of Models

Effective and well-founded methods for validating these models remain a somewhat vexed issue. In addition to Kanungo's [35] statistical bootstrapping method that attempts to measure how similar sets of synthetic images are to sets of real images under image metrics, Li et al. have proposed [39] that a model is validated *not* when the images 'match', but when "the OCR errors induced by the model are indistinguishable from the errors encountered when using real scanned documents". To this end, they compare confusion matrices for synthetic and real images.

12.5 Applications of Models

Applications of these models have taken many forms. Perhaps their widest impact is in the generation of synthetic data sets used in training classifiers for document image recognition systems. They have also been used to carry out large-scale systematic tests of systems. Public-domain software and image databases have been published. Finally, they have permitted a new class of experimental studies of image recognition systems using very large-scale simulation. The following sections give some representative examples of such applications. A comprehensive survey of applications has not yet been attempted, here or elsewhere.

12.5.1 Conditions for Connectivity and So Forth

Pavlidis [48] investigated conditions under which the connectivity and shape of bi-level patterns are preserved under image degradations resulting from digitization: he formulated a "compatibility condition" restricting the maximum size and boundary curvature of foreground and background connected components, as a function of the sampling rate.

12.5.2 Effects on Recognition Accuracy

The earliest publication known to me that examines the effects of image quality on OCR accuracy is Pavlidis' ground-breaking paper [49] describing systematic tests over a range of page image quality achieved manually by varying type size, copying repeatedly, etc.

Lopresti et al. [40] investigated the effects of random-phase spatial sampling on the optical character recognition. They carried out an exhaustive case analysis for one-dimensional patterns and used large-scale experiments to characterize more complex, two-dimensional patterns, including printed and scanned characters. They conclude that spatial sampling rate and error, alone, account for much of the image variability seen in practice.

12.5.3 Constructing Classifiers

In an early experiment [8], a Tibetan OCR system was constructed using training data that were initialized with real images but augmented by synthetic variations. Perhaps the first large-scale use of these models to help construct an industrial-strength classifier was [12], in which a full-ASCII, 100-typeface classifier was built using synthetic data only (and tested, with good results, on real images). In a series of similar trials, synthetic data have been used [43] to construct pre-classification decision trees with bounded error (which also worked well in practice). Reference [26] discusses an application of image defect generators in the automatic construction of "perfect metrics" (distance functions from an image to a class of images), for use in classifiers exhibiting both high accuracy and excellent reject behaviour.

Similar methodology, applied within the document image decoding paradigm [37], has recently permitted the fully automatic construction of high-performance text-line recognizers that maintain high accuracy even under extreme image degradations [57]. It appears to be feasible often to select [56] the most accurate recognizer automatically from a large set of pre-trained recognizers, and so obviate document-specific training – indeed *any* training on real images.

12.5.4 Testing OCR Systems

Reference [30] describes experiments with synthesized images of complete pages of text, using a model of near-ideal printing and imaging, in support of an effort to measure baseline performance of commercial OCR page readers. Further application of this methodology supported the first reported attempts [15] to predict OCR accuracy using automatically measurable image features that are correlated with image quality. Studies of this sort have continued, e.g. [21,63], but the accuracy of the predictions has, so far, been too low to permit fully automatic process adjustments yielding more than marginal improvements in accuracy across a wide range of documents.

12.6 Public-Domain Software and Image Databases

Software implementing the model of [31] has been made available as part of the "English Document Database CD-ROM" [50] designed by The Intelligent Systems Laboratory of the Department of Electrical Engineering, University of Washington, Seattle, WA.

Image defect models and their associated generators permit a new kind of standard image database that is explicitly parametrized, alleviating some drawbacks of existing databases. The first publicly available database of this kind, the "Bell Labs image defect model database, version 0", was designed for publication in the CD-ROM mentioned above. The database contains 8,565,750 bi-level images, each labelled with ground truth. The images are of isolated machine-printed characters distorted pseudo-randomly using the image defect model of [8]. It is designed to assist research into a variety of topics, including (a) measurement of classifier performance; (b) characterization of document image quality and (c) construction of high-performance classifiers. The ground truth of each image specifies which symbol it is and its typeface, type size, image defect model parameters and true baseline location. Each model parameter ranges over a small set of values, and the cross-product of these ranges has been exhaustively generated, to permit the design of systematically fair experiments operating on a wide variety of subsets of the database.

No more than a third of the images are "easy": that is, only slightly or moderately distorted, and so readily recognizable by most commercial OCR machines. A large number – perhaps a fifth – are "impossible": that is, distorted so extremely that they cannot be recognized by even the best modern experimental OCR algorithms. The rest of the images are distributed, by small steps in parameter space, across the interesting boundary separating easy from impossible.

12.6.1 Simulation Studies

Large-scale simulations [27] using generative models permit empirical exploration of important open questions concerning realistic image pattern recognition problems. Consider a given defect model, applied to a given ideal prototype image, as a stochastic source of an indefinitely long sequence of defective images. This induces a probability distribution on the space of all discrete bi-level images. It should be clear that many questions of practical interest about the performance of classifiers can be stated as quantitative properties of these distributions. Unfortunately, in most cases of practical importance, it is not feasible, with our present analytical methods and computer algorithms, to describe these distributions explicitly. The difficulties do not all arise from the complexities of defect models: many are grounded in the arbitrary nature of the prototype images, which are analytically intractable artefacts of human history and culture.

One interesting question is whether or not the Bayes error of a given problem is non-zero, and whether it can be estimated within tight bounds. This question, posed for a two-class discrimination problem ("e"/"c" in fax-quality images), has been answered: it is now computationally feasible to estimate the Bayes error of such concrete, realistic image recognition problems, within tight bounds.

Another question is whether or not, given an indefinitely large volume of training data, dissimilar classification methodologies will achieve the same accuracy asymptotically. In an experiment on three different trainable classification technologies, all of them capable of increasing their "capacity" (VC-dimension) indefinitely, it has been shown that all three asymptotically approach a classification accuracy that is statistically indistinguishable one from another. Extensions of these experiments to a wider range of classification technologies are an urgent open issue.

Also, it is natural to wonder under what circumstances is classification accuracy a smooth monotonic function of degradation parameters. For the physics-based model of [8] and for classifiers over the ASCII symbol set, it has been shown that this is the case for most of the parameters. Thus it is possible to map a "domain of competency" of the classifier in degradation parameter space, and furthermore it has been shown in small-scale experiments that this domain may be used to select training regimens that improve accuracy at the margins of acceptable performance.

12.7 Open Problems

Many unsolved problems, both theoretical and practical, remain.

We seem to be approaching a day when researchers and engineers can choose among several realistic, carefully validated mathematical models of image defects, together with software implementations in the form of pseudo-random defect generators. In particular, although we have made considerable progress in the last decade, we still feel a need for:

- a theoretical framework for validating models that provides a rigorous foundation for objective, empirical and computable criteria for demonstrating the completeness of models, and for comparing competing models;
- algorithms for estimating distributions on all of their model parameters to fit real image populations closely;
- public-domain, portable and fast model-simulation software capable of generating images at the character, word, text-line and page level.

We should also extend our methods to cope with grey-level and colour document images.

Further progress on these open problems will, I believe, prove to be critical to progress on a broad array of problems arising in theoretical studies and engineering practice.

12.7.1 Uses of Synthetic Data

Synthetic data are increasingly being used, along with or instead of real data, in training and testing of recognition systems. This practice has provoked a debate among engineers, which was reflected in a panel discussion [23] organized at the 5th ICDAR in September 1999. Six panel members, including the present author, spoke to the question "under what circumstances is it advisable to use synthetic data?"

Here is my summary of the – sometimes light-hearted – points that were made:

- The classifier who is trained on the most data wins.
- It doesn't matter how much real data you train on: it's never enough.
- Training only on real data feels safe – after all, almost everyone does it – but it isn't.
- Real data are corrupting: they are so expensive that we reuse them, repeatedly, with unprincipled abandon.
- Synthetic data are selfless: they are born only to be used once and then thrown away.
- Everyone should feel free to train on any data he/she chooses, real or synthetic or both.
- Training only on synthetic data is courageous, today – and perhaps foolhardy – but one day it will be wise.
- Training on a mixture of real and synthetic data may be, today, the safest – but we don't know the right proportions.
- Training on mislabelled data is asking for trouble. Training on correctly labelled data of low image quality is just as dangerous.

- We don't know how to separate helpful from unhelpful training data, whether real or synthetic.
- It might help to generate synthetic training data that complement real data by a process of interpolation between real samples.
- It might hurt to generate synthetic training data by "amplifying" (extrapolating from) real data.
- Testing on synthetic data to claim good performance is unprincipled.
- Testing on synthetic data to identify weaknesses is virtuous.
- Some models are more equal than others, but it remains a mystery which is which.
- Truth is stranger than fiction. And the document image degradation model research area will live forever, since we will never agree on the models.

Acknowledgments

This research topic was introduced to me by Theo Pavlidis **[Pav83]. Much of this work is joint with Tin Kam Ho, Tapas Kanungo, and Prateek Sarkar. I am also indebted to George Nagy, Bob Haralick, Theo Pavlidis, Elisa H. Barney Smith, David Ittner and Dan Lopresti for many stimulating discussions on these subjects. I wish to thank Larry Spitz for providing references **[Mal83], **[Edi87], and **[MS88]; he and Perry Stoll helped me re-implement my model at PARC. I have also benefited from the advice of David Albrecht, Roland Aubey, Chuck Biss, Robert Bloss, Michael Bruno, Ken Church, Allan Gilligan, Robert Gruber, Fred Higgins, Brian Johannesson, Mary Kastner, Robert Lettenberger, Bob Loce, Roger Morton, Del Oddy, Pat Pavlik, Gil Porter, Bud Rightler, Frank Romano, Paul Ross, Timothy Tredwell and Luc Vincent. Any omissions or misstatements are, of course, mine.

References

1. Applied Image, Inc., 1653 East Main St, Rochester, NY 14609.
2. Association for Information and Image Management, 1100 Wayne Avenue, Silver Spring, MD 20910. (Formerly the National Micrographics Association.)
3. AIM USA, 634 Alpha Drive, Pittsburgh, PA 15238–2802. (Trade association for automatic identification and keyless data entry technologies.)
4. American National Standards Institute, 11 W 42 St, New York City, NY 10036.
5. American Society for Testing and Materials, 1916 Race Street, Philadelphia, PA 19103.
6. Baird, H.S. (1987). The skew angle of printed documents. *Proceedings of the 1987 Conference of the Society of Photographic Scientists and Engineers, Rochester, New York, May 20–21, 1987.*

7. Baird, H.S. (1988). Feature identification for hybrid structural/statistical pattern classification. *Computer Vision, Graphics, and Image Processing, 42(3)*, pp. 318–333.

8. Baird, H.S. (1990). Document image defect models. *Proceedings of the IAPR Workshop on Syntactic and Structural Pattern Recognition, Murray Hill, NJ, June 13–15, 1990*. Reprinted in H.S. Baird, H. Bunke, and K. Yamamoto (Eds.), *Structured Document Image Analysis*, Springer: New York, pp. 546–556, 1992.

9. Baird, H.S. (1993). Calibration of document image defect models. *Proceedings, Second Annual Symposium on Document Analysis and Information Retrieval, Caesar's Palace Hotel, Las Vegas, Nevada, April 26–28, 1993*, pp. 1–16.

10. Baird, H.S. (1993). Document image defect models and their uses. *Proceedings, Second International Conference on Document Analysis and Recognition, Tsukuba Science City, Japan, October 20–22, 1993*, pp. 62–67.

11. Baird, H.S. (1999). Document image quality: making fine discriminations. *Proceedings of IAPR 1999 International Conference on Document Analysis and Recognition, Bangalore, India, September 20–22, 1999.*

12. Baird, H.S. and Fossey, R. (1991). A 100–font classifier. *Proceedings of IAPR First ICDAR, St. Malo, France, September 30–October 2, 1991.*

13. Charles, E. and Biss, PSC, Inc., 770 Basket Road, P.O. Box 448, Webster, NY 14580–0448. (Chair, ANSI X3A1.3 Working Group on Image Quality.)

14. Bloss, R. (1993). Personal communication, UNISYS, 41100 Plymouth Rd, Plymouth, MI 48170, March 1993.

15. Blando, L., Kanai, J., and Nartker, T.A. (1995). Prediction of OCR accuracy using simple image features. *Proceedings of IAPR International Conference on Document Analysis and Recognition, Montreal, Canada*, pp. 319–322.

16. Barney Smith, E.H. (2001). Scanner parameter estimation using bilevel scans of star charts. *Proceedings of IAPR International Conference on Document Analysis and Recognition, Seattle, WA*, pp. 1164–1168.

17. Barney Smith, E.H. (2001). Estimating scanning characteristics from corners in bilevel images. *Proceedings of IS&T/SPIE Conference on Document Recognition and Retrieval VIII, Volume 4307, San Jose, CA, January 2001*, pp. 176–183.

18. Barney Smith, E.H. (1998). Optical Scanner Characterization Methods Using Bilevel Scans. Ph.D. dissertation. Rennselaer, Troy, NY: ECSE Department, December 1998. (Thesis advisor: G. Nagy.)

19. Buntine, W. (1992). Learning classification trees. *Statistics and Computing, 2*, pp. 63–73.

20. Clearwave Electronics, 8701 Buffalo Avenue, Niagara Falls, NY 14304.

21. Cannon, M., Kelly, P., Iyengar, S.S., and Brener, N. (1997). An automated system for numerically rating document image quality. *Proceedings of IS&T/SPIE Conference on Document Recognition IV, San Jose, CA, January 12–13, 1997*, pp. 161–167.

22. Casey, R.G. and Nagy, G. (1984). Decision tree design using a probabilistic model. *IEEE Transactions on Information Theory, 30(1)*, pp. 94–99.

23. Dennis, S. and Phillips, I. (1999). Ground truthing: real or synthetic data – a panel discussion. *Fifth International Conference on Document Analysis and Recognition, Bangalore, India, September 20–22, 1999.*

24. Edinger, J.R., Jr. (1987). The image analyzer—a tool for the evaluation of electrophotographic text quality. *Journal of Imaging Science, 31(4)*, pp. 177–183.
25. Allan Gilligan (1993). Personal communication. West Long Branch, NJ: AT&T Bell Laboratories.
26. Ho, T.K. and Baird, H.S. (1993). Perfect metrics. *Proceedings of IAPR Second ICDAR, Tsukuba, Japan, October 20–22, 1993.*
27. Ho, T.K. and Baird, H.S. (1992). Large-scale simulation studies in image pattern recognition. *IEEE Transactions on PAMI, 19(10)*, pp. 1067–1079.
28. *Proceedings of the IEEE*, Special Issue on OCR, July 1992.
29. Society for Imaging Science and Technology, 7003 Kilworth Lane, Springfield, VA 22151.
30. Jenkins, F. (1993). The Use of Synthesized Images to Evaluate the Performance of OCR Devices and Algorithms. Master's Thesis. Las Vegas: University of Nevada.
31. Kanungo, T. Haralick, R.M., and Phillips, I. (1993). Global and local document degradation models. *Proceedings of IAPR Second ICDAR, Tsukuba, Japan, October 20–22, 1993.*
32. Kanungo, T., Haralick, R.M., Baird, H.S., Stuetzle, W., and Madigan, D. (1994). Document degradation models: parameter estimation and model validation. *Proceedings of International Workshop on Machine Vision Applications, Kawasaki, Japan, December 13–15, 1994.*
33. Kanungo, T., Haralick, R.M., and Baird, H.S. (1995). Validation and estimation of document degradation models. *Proceedings, Fourth Annual Symposium on Document Analysis and Information Retrieval, Las Vegas, Nevada, April 24–26, 1995*, pp. 217–225.
34. Kanungo, T., Haralick, R.M., and Baird, H.S. (1995). Power functions and their use in selecting distance functions for document degradation model validation. *Proceedings of IAPR Third International Conference on Document Analysis & Recognition, Montreal, Canada, August 14–16, 1995.*
35. Kanungo, T. (1996). Document degradation models and methodology for degradation model validation. Ph.D. dissertation. Department of Electrical Engineering, University of Washington [Supervisor: Prof. R.M. Haralick].
36. Knuth, D.E. (1986). *Computer Modern Typefaces*. Reading, MA: Addison Wesley.
37. Kopec, G. and Chou, P. (1994). Document image decoding using Markov source models. *IEEE Transactions on PAMI, 16*, pp. 602–617.
38. Robert Loce. (1993). Personal communication. Xerox Webster Research Center, 800 Phillips Road, Webster, NY 14580.
39. Li, Y., Lopresti, D., Nagy, G., and Tompkins, A. (1996). Validation of image defect models for optical character recognition. *IEEE Transactions on PAMI, 18(2)*, pp. 99–107.
40. Lopresti, D., Zhou, J., Nagy, G., and Sarkar, P. (1995). Spatial sampling effects in optical character recognition. *Proceedings of Second IAPR International Conference on Document Analysis and Recognition, Montreal, Canada.*
41. Maltz, M. (1983). Light scattering in xerographic images. *Journal of Applied Photographic Engineering, 9(3)*, pp. 83–89.
42. Marshall, G.F. (Ed.) (1991). *Optical Scanning.* New York: Marcel Dekker.
43. Mallows, C.L. and Baird, H.S. (1997). The evolution of a problem. *Statistica Sinica, 7(1)*, pp. 211–220. Special issue in honor of H. Robbins.

44. Macbeth Corp., P.O. Box 230, Newburgh, NY 12551–0230.

45. McLean, R. (1988). *The Thames and Hudson Manual of Typography*. London: Thames and Hudson.

46. Maltz, M. and Szczepanik, J. (1988). MTF analysis of xerographic development and transfer. *Journal of Imaging Science, 32(1)*, pp. 11–15.

47. National Printing Equipment and Supply Association, 1899 Preston White Drive, Reston, VA 22091.

48. Pavlidis, T. (1982). *Algorithms for Graphics and Image Processing*. Rockville, MD: Computer Science Press.

49. Pavlidis, T. (1983). Effects of distortions on the recognition rate of a structural OCR system. *Proceedings of IEEE Computer Vision and Pattern Recognition Conference (CVPR'83), Washington, DC*, June 21–23, 1983, pp. 303–309.

50. Phillip, I.T., Chen, S., Ha, J., and Haralick, R.M. (1993). English document database design and implementation methodology. *Proceedings, Second Annual Symposium on Document Analysis and Information Retrieval, Caesar's Palace Hotel, Las Vegas, Nevada, April 26–28, 1993*, pp. 65–104.

51. Phillips, A. (1968). *Computer Peripherals and Typesetting*. London: Her Majesty's Stationery Office.

52. Porter, G. (1993). Personal communication, Xerox Webster Research Center, 800 Phillips Road, Webster, NY 14580.

53. Rice, S.V., Nagy, G., and Nartker, T.A. (1999). OCR: *An Illustrated Guide to the Frontier*. Dordrecht: Kluwer, 1999.

54. RDM Corp., 608 Weber St N., Waterloo, Ontario N2V 1K4, Canada.

55. Rice, S.V., Kanai, J., and Nartker, T.A. (1992). A report on the accuracy of ocr devices, ISRI Technical Report TR–92-02, University of Nevada Las Vegas, Las Vegas, Nevada, 1992.

56. Sarkar, P. and Baird, H.S. (2004). Decoder banks: versatility, automation, and high accuracy without supervised training. *Proceedings of IAPR Seventeenth International Conference on Pattern Recognition, Cambridge, UK, August 23–26, 2004*, Volume II, pp. 646–649.

57. Sarkar, P., Baird, H.S., and Zhang, Q. (2003). Training on severely degraded text-line images. *Proceedings of IAPR Seventh International Conference on Document Analysis and Recognition, Edinburgh, Scotland, August 3–6, 2003*.

58. Sabourin, M., Mitiche, A., Thomas, D., and Nagy, G. (1993). Hand-printed digit recognition using nearest neighbour classifiers. *Proceedings of the Second Annual Symposium on Document Analysis and Information Retrieval, Caesar's Palace Hotel, Las Vegas, Nevada, April 26–28, 1993*, pp. 397–409.

59. Schreiber, W.F. (1986). *Fundamentals of Electronic Imaging Systems*. Berlin: Springer.

60. Seybold, J.W. (1984). *The World of Digital Typesetting*. Seybold Publications, P.O. Box 644, Media, PA 19063, 1984.

61. Barney Smith, E.H. (1998). Optical scanner characterization methods using bilevel scans, Ph.D. dissertation. Computer and Systems Engineering Department, Rennselaer Polytechnic Institute [Supervisor: Prof. G. Nagy].

62. Society of Photo-Optical Instrumentation Engineers, 1000 20th St, Bellingham, Washington, 98225.

63. Summers, K. (2003). Document image improvement for OCR as a classification problem. *Proceedings of IS&T/SPIE Conference on Document Recognition and Retrieval X, Santa Clara, CA, January 22–24, 2003*, SPIE Volume 5010, pp. 73–83.
64. TAPPI, 15 Technology Parkway South, Norcross, GA 30092.
65. Kanungo, T., Haralick, R.M., and Phillips, I. (1993). Global and local document degradation models, Submitted to *IAPR Second International Conference on Document Analysis and Recognition, Tsukuba, Japan, 1993.*
66. Tredwell, T. (1993). Personal communication, Head, Imaging Electronics Lab, Eastman Kodak Research Labs, Rochester, NY, March, 1993.
67. Wilkenson, R.A., et al. (1992). The first census optical character recognition systems conference. NIST Internal Report, Gaithersburg, Maryland, 1992.
68. Wang, Q.R. and Suen, C.Y. (1987). Large tree classifier with heuristic search and global training. *IEEE Transactions on PAMI, 9(1)*, pp. 91–102.
69. Yam, H.S. and Barney Smith, E.H. (2003). Estimating degradation model parameters from character images. *Proceedings of IAPR International Conference on Document Analysis and Recognition (ICDAR'03), Edinburgh, Scotland, August 3–6, 2003.*
70. Zeirler, N. (1969). Primitive trinomials whose degree is a mersenne exponent. *Inf. Control.*

13

Advances in Graphics Recognition

Josep Lladós

13.1 Introduction

Traditionally, the field of document image analysis (DIA) has been defined as a combined sub-discipline of image processing and pattern recognition that proposes theory and practice to the automatic recovery, starting from images of digitized documents, of the syntactic and semantic information that was used to generate them. We can classify documents in terms of three criteria, namely the format, the document contents and the input mode. Considering the format, documents are no longer static, physical entities, but we are moving from paper-based (scanned images of document pages) to electronic documents (e-mails, web pages, DXF, PDF, etc.). Documents can also be classified in terms of the type of information they are conveying. Nagy in his review on document image analysis [1] stated two document categories, namely *mostly text* and *mostly graphics* documents. OCR is at the heart of any system to process mostly-text documents. For those documents, the process also aims at segmenting the layout in paragraphs, columns, lines, words, etc. Examples of mostly-graphics documents include engineering drawings, maps, architectural plans, music scores, schematic diagrams, tables and charts. In such disciplines, graphics are the main way to express information and interact with the machine. It is well known the expression "one picture is worth a thousand words". We can also classify documents in terms of the input mode to create them (*off-line* or *on-line*). On-line documents involve a kind of digital pen interface. In this chapter, we focus on mostly-graphics documents. *Graphics recognition* (GR) can be defined as a branch of document analysis that focuses on the recovery of graphical information in documents. Graphics and text documents are not disjoint categories. Although being considered graphic documents, most of them also can contain textual items, so OCR-related processes and graphics recognition ones sometimes are collaborative tasks. *Graphics* or *graphical information* is a broad concept. In a logical level, graphics combine primitives that generally are lines, regions or simple shapes. In a functional or semantic level, graphical information consists of a set of compound objects that, in terms of domain-dependent knowledge, have a particular meaning in the context where they appear.

Graphics recognition, as document analysis, is essentially an engineering discipline. Therefore, from a more general point of view, it can be seen as a component in the document engineering lifecycle. Because of that, graphics recognition systems are usually problem or application oriented. Thus a wide variety of pattern recognition and image processing techniques are used as components in graphics recognition systems. Figure 13.1 is an attempt to summarize the major concepts involved in the graphics recognition domain in a coherent component chart. From the methodological point of view, three levels are involved in the processing of a graphical document, namely the *early*, the *structure* and the *semantic* processing, respectively.

Early-level processing can be organized in two sub-categories. First, *image filtering*, i.e. pixel-based processes for noise removal, binarization, or image enhancement. In general, the above pixel-oriented methods are not exclusive to the graphics recognition domain but common among all the document image Analysis areas. A good overview of such techniques can be seen in [2]. The second sub-category consists of the set of tasks devoted to *primitive segmentation*. In the GR domain, a primitive is considered to be a straight segment, an arc, a loop, or a solid region, i.e. graphical tokens that are combined to form graphical entities. We can notice that most of graphic documents consist in line-drawing structures. Because of that, primitive extraction in GR can usually involve a vectorization process. Other primitives than straight segments are also considered in some GR systems. Arc detection is a particular topic of interest [3,4]. Solid regions are another frequent type of primitives. Typical examples are notes in musical score recognition, text or small symbols in map-to-GIS conversion systems. Different criteria such as connected components, colour, area, etc. can be used to segment them. In other cases, the segmentation is also guided by domain-dependent rules as for example when notes are separated from staff lines in musical scores.

As Dori also discussed [5], GR systems have two additional levels directly related to structure (how graphical entities are constructed) and function (what they do or what they mean in the context where they appear). In other words, a syntactic level where the recognition involves locating the graphic entities in the document and classifying them into the various classes by their shape and context, and a semantic level where, using domain-dependent information, a meaning is assigned to the syntactically recognized entities. Syntactic processing includes several tasks related to the classification of graphical entities. Symbol recognition is the main activity. Signatures compactly represent symbol classes mainly for indexing purposes. A particular signature representation, formulated in terms of the perceptual grouping paradigm, allows to extract salient patterns with weak prior models and also to represent them compactly. In an on-line framework the syntactic level analyses relationships among strokes to recognize compound objects. The goal of the semantic level is to understand the document according to its function and using domain-dependent knowledge.

In addition to the above-defined three stages, as Figure 13.1 shows, other concerns are involved in a GR framework global. We discuss on three issues, namely interfacing, architectures and meta-data modelling, and benchmarking.

The role of the user in the graphics recognition cycle is also an important concern. The user intervention in a GR process should not be seen as negative, but as a natural issue. A recognition and understanding process may need feedback from the user to set particular parameters, validate decisions taken from the system when there is uncertainty or just interact with the system to edit the document or drive the process. The input mode influences the interfacing approach to be considered. While scanning a paper-based document is the classical input mode, the advent of new digital pen devices makes sketching interfaces, i.e. on-line input, a growing interest. The user interaction by means of pen strokes is a powerful tool to draw new graphic documents, digitally augment paper documents or edit documents by sketchy gestures. GR systems based on digital pen devices can take advantage of dynamic information as speed, pressure or order of strokes. Thus, sketching interfaces make closer the domains of GR and HCI (human–computer interaction).

The definition of flexible GR architectures and platforms that allow to assemble components and algorithms is still a challenge. Most of the existing GR platforms are highly domain oriented. A generic GR platform would require a mechanism to combine components and a way to integrate domain knowledge. In addition, a generic architecture requires a meta-data model to represent any graphical document. Some interesting approaches in the literature focus on the definition of generic GR architectures [6–8].

As in other pattern recognition domains, in GR too benchmarking plays an important role. There is a need of building suitable databases and performance evaluation protocols to be used as common ground truth for comparing the performance of the proposed systems. This has motivated a number of GR contests that have provided benchmarking databases [3, 4, 9–12].

In this chapter we update the state of the art in graphics recognition. We especially focus on work arising from the main DIA and GR forums, namely IJDAR, ICDAR and, in particular, the Graphics Recognition Workshop Series [13–17]. The chapter is organized according to the major research concerns stated above and shown in Figure 13.1. Thus, after overviewing the application scenarios of GR in Section 13.2, we focus our attention in early processing algorithms (Section 13.3), symbol recognition (Section 13.4), architectures and platforms for GR (Section 13.5), on-line GR (Section 13.6),

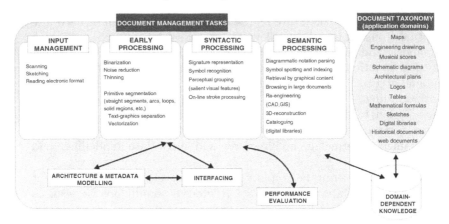

Fig. 13.1. The graphics recognition domain and applications.

and performance evaluation (Section 13.7). An illustrative application example is described in Section 13.8. We conclude by describing the emerging interests among GR community in Section 13.9.

13.2 Application Scenarios

A number of application domains can be identified within the graphics recognition field. Although they share a number of methodological issues, the importance of the domain-dependent knowledge has resulted in each sub-field to develop its particular variations. Let us shortly overview the most representative domains.

Electrical and logic circuit diagrams. It is one of the early application domains of GR [18–23]. Due to their standardized notation, electronic schematics offer the advantage that symbols can be easily segmented prior to their classification. Since symbols can be associated to loop structures, their segmentation is based on the removal of rectilinear connections between loops.

Maps. Map-to-GIS conversion continues attracting the interest of the GR community. We can distinguish between three map categories. First, cadastral city maps [24–26], where the recognition consists in detecting polygonal shapes and hatched patterns, representing parcels. OCR processes complete the meaning of regions with related annotations. A second sub-domain are utility maps [27–29]. They are usually binary images consisting of lines and small symbols composed of geometric basic primitives (squares, circles, arrowheads, etc.). The methods proposed to recognize utility maps are usually very domain dependent. Finally, geographic maps [30–33] are probably the most difficult class of documents of this domain. In this kind of maps, the graphical entities are associated with line objects that usually represent isolines and roads and, on the other hand, small symbols whose meaning is given by a legend. In this kind of maps colour information plays an important role [34]. Thus, a layer segmentation process is usually performed in terms of colour quantization. Line objects are characterized by regular structures that can be represented by a linear grammar. The detection of symbols usually is legend driven and performed by statistical pattern recognition approaches. The meaning of each prototype symbol is also captured by an OCR procedure.

Engineering drawings. A number of graphics recognition systems in the field of engineering drawings can also be stated [35–38]. In such a field, the concept of a symbol is slightly different. While in electronic diagrams or maps a symbol is a graphical entity with a well-defined prototype pattern, in engineering drawings symbols have weakly defined patterns. Engineering drawings can be seen as the assembly of low-level primitives such as arcs and straight lines, dashed lines, cross-hatched and solid areas. The recognition of these low-level primitives combined with domain-dependent knowledge gives meaning to the document and allows it to be converted to a CAD format. Thus, a hatched area combined with a semi-circle could represent a screw, but a similar hatched area in another part of the same document could represent a section of a solid part. A triangular solid area connected to a straight line can be understood as a dimension according to a particular syntactic rule. In summary, graphical entities in engineering drawings usually represent mechanical parts, they are very domain dependent and even document dependent, and the automatic recognition cannot be made fully automatic and requires special interactive techniques and domain-dependent knowledge.

Architectural drawings. A growing number of methods have been proposed for recognizing architectural drawings for conversion to CAD environments and subsequent actions as edition or 3D visualization [39–43]. A particular focus of attention has been made on hand-drawn sketches. Two major symbol structures can be categorized in architectural drawings; prototype-based symbols, e.g. doors or windows; and texture-based symbols consisting of hatching or tiling patterns to represent walls or stairs. The main difficulty of architectural drawings is that symbol segmentation cannot be performed prior to the recognition. Due to this fact, recognition has to be performed by searching throughout all the input documents and, hence it is a computationally hard process. Indexing mechanisms are then required to reduce the search space.

Musical scores. The recognition of musical scores takes advantage of the standardized notation of this domain. This fact has resulted in the development of a set of very specific techniques, only applicable to this family of documents. A number of contributions can be found [7, 44–47] and they organize the interpretation process in three stages. First, the extraction of staff lines that allows the segmentation of individual symbols and can be performed by projection or run analysis techniques. Second, the recognition of individual notes that, since there is a finite set of standard symbols, are robustly recognized by neural networks or feature vector distances. The third stage is the interpretation of the whole musical score that usually is formulated in terms of graph grammars.

Logo recognition. Logos and trademarks are examples of graphical symbols. From the point of view of the application, their recognition differs from the other domains in the following way. While in the above domains the recognition of symbols is a step in a diagram-understanding process, logo recognition is usually performed for document classification or retrieval by content from document databases [48–52]. Due to the unrestricted variety of instances, logo recognition systems are usually based on extracting signatures from the image in terms of contour codification, invariant moments, connected component labelling, etc. and match the unknown logo with the database models using different types of distance or neural networks. Since logos often combine text and graphics, the recognition in some cases also includes OCR processes.

Table and chart recognition. Tables and charts [53, 54] are structured graphical entities that can be seen as particular expressions of visual languages. Since they have a particular syntax, a bi-dimensional grammar is a valid model to represent them. Since table cells and chart components contain textual information, OCR tasks are also involved in the recognition.

Sketching interfaces. As computer systems become more sophisticated, alternative input modalities and interface technologies are emerging. Sketching interfaces can be considered as a new generation of HCI, where the user can work with the computer in a *natural* way, expressing ideas by freehand drawings. GR is the technology that supports this family of applications, providing tools to recognize sketch elements. A sketching or calligraphic interface allows to input commands in a PDA, or to design mechanical parts or architectural plans in a CAD framework. In such applications, the recognition is done on-line, and it basically consists in the recognition of individual strokes and grouping them and matching against models. The recognition of primitive strokes combines spatio-temporal information, and techniques such as string matching or HMM are usually used. An interesting work on sketching interfaces was done by Gross and Do [55]. They use 2D diagrammatic reasoning to analyse structured drawings in a variety of application domains. In Section 13.6 we further study this family of applications.

13.3 Early Processing

We refer to early processing of the set of tasks performed directly to the input data to prepare it for further analysis and interpretation. We have considered two sub-tasks, namely *image filtering* or just pre-processing in other literature, and *primitive segmentation*. When document images come from an optical capture, scanner or camera, pixel-level processes are usually applied. Such processing includes thresholding to reduce grey-scale or colour image to a binary image, noise filtering to reduce extraneous data, image enhancement to contrast the objects to be analysed or thinning and region segmentation to enable the subsequent detection of primitives. Since the current document analysis systems not only work from raw image inputs, but also electronic documents (pdf, dxf, xml formats) or on-line data acquired from digital pen devices, the above processes are not always needed. Since pixel-level processes for DIA are mature techniques, we do not further analyse them in this chapter. The reader is referred to [2] for a review.

When dealing with primitive extraction tasks in GR, vectorization comes to mind. The classic problem of vectorization, i.e. raster-to-vector conversion, is still here. Many solutions have been proposed, either from academia and industry, and it seems to be a mature problem. However, the GR community has not yet reached robust and stable methods. It is not clear what vectorization ought to be, or ought to output. Actually, it is not an isolated step and its goodness depends on the pursued goal of the whole system. For that reason, commercial vectorization systems provide a set of parameters that can be set by the user, or customized in terms of document categories. Tombre et al. [56] discussed some qualitative elements that should be taken into account in the different steps of a vectorization method. From a methodological point of view, vectorization consists in a kind of polygonal approximation of the medial axis of line images. Ramer algorithm [57] inspires a number of polygonal approximation algorithms underlying vectorization processes. Several families of methods exist to compute the medial axis. The most popular is to compute the skeleton of the line-drawing image by a thinning or ridge operator [58–60]. These approaches tend to displace the junction points and to be sensitive to image irregularities. Another family of methods is based on line following or line contour matching [61]. These methods are more precise in junction finding but their performance decreases in complex images. Finally, sparse-pixels approaches is considered to be a third family of methods [62, 63]. These approaches do not analyse all the image pixels but detect vectors by analysing key points in terms of local neighbouring configuration.

Vectorization approaches often involve methods to detect other primitives that straight segments, but curve ones. A primitive that has particular interest in the literature is circular arcs. Outstanding contributions come from Elliman [64] and the Qgar group [65, 66]. Other types of primitives appear in graphical documents. Loops are primitives that focus on the detection of symbols in some types of line drawings [20, 23, 67]. Finally, connected components with particular attributes of compactness and size are also usually used [27, 45]. This last type of primitives leads us to refer to the classical problem of text–graphics separation. Graphical documents often contain text annotations (names of streets in maps, dimensions in engineering drawings, beat in musical scores) that must be segmented and send to an OCR module. Text can be segmented looking for small connected components following a regular path. However, text is sometimes connected to graphics. A classical reference to solve it is the algorithm of Fletcher and Kasturi [68, 69].

13.4 Symbol Recognition and Indexing

Symbol recognition is at the heart of most GR systems. Drawings, maps and diagrams, seen as communication channels, use domain-dependent graphic notations. The automatic interpretation of graphic documents requires processes able to recognize the corresponding alphabet of symbols. In a very general perspective, a symbol can be defined as a meaningful graphical entity in the context of a specific application domain. Thus, a symbol can be a simple 2D binary shape composed of line segments (engineering, electronics, utility maps, architecture), a combination of line segments and solid shapes (musical scores), complex grey level or colour shapes (logos), silhouettes (geographic symbols), etc. In [70] we reviewed the state of the art of symbol recognition. From the methodological point of view, since symbol recognition is a particular application of pattern recognition, either structural or statistical approaches are proposed. Among all the approaches found in the literature, it is difficult to find a general and robust method covering different domains with a well-established and evaluated performance. Authors tend to develop ad hoc techniques that are difficult to be re-used in other domains. Graph-based approaches are usually used when symbols consist of line structures, while grammars are suitable for recognizing symbols or combinations of symbols arranged according to a kind of diagrammatic notation or language like music [46], dimensions [71] or logic diagrams [72]. On the other hand, statistical-based methods seem more useful when symbols are small entities [27] or have heterogeneous components like logos [50]. Moreover, there is no way to compare different methods operating in the same domain or to validate the performance of any approach with a significant set of symbols and drawings.

Let us also briefly review some open issues and challenges in the symbol recognition problem. Some of them are not specific to symbol recognition but general to GR. A first issue, as discussed in Section 13.5, is the need of general methods and data representations for symbol recognition. Domain-dependent methods exist but their performance strongly decreases when we try to generalize. Desirable properties of general methods and representations are extensibility, scalability, robustness to noise and distortion and low computational complexity. On the other hand, whereas there are well-known methods for the recognition of isolated symbols, a further work is required for localizing, extracting and recognizing symbols in their context. In some contexts, segmentation is easy, for example in logic diagrams that consist of loop-like symbols joined by connection lines. However, in other domains when symbols appear embedded in the drawing, the segmentation must be done while the recognition is performed. Another challenge is the study and further work on different issues regarding performance evaluation and benchmarking databases. We further discuss it in Section 13.7. An important concern of symbol recognition, related to performance evaluation, is the scalability, i.e. how a performant symbol recognition method degrades with a growing number of prototypes. Most methods are just tested with databases of a few number of prototypes, but real applications manage sets of hundreds of prototypes. Since the recognition performance tends to degrade with large databases, the robustness against scalability is strongly required to be studied.

Indexing and retrieval by graphical content is a particular application of symbol recognition. New challenges arise when it comes to dealing with large databases of technical documents. Usually, new designs re-use data from previous projects or component libraries. Locating such components is sometimes a slow task that requires a visual examination. Symbol spotting and indexing provide solutions to that problem [73–75].

The use of *signatures* is useful for indexing purposes. A signature is a compact representation for a shape and in the field of GR allows an efficient localization and recognition of symbols. Shape signatures have been proposed at image level. Doermann [76] reviewed different signatures to encode shapes in logo and map symbol recognition. More recently, Tabbone et al. [77] proposed F-signatures, a special kind of histograms of forces, for architectural symbol spotting. Signature have also been proposed at graphical entity level. Vectorial signatures [78] provide descriptions on vectorial data based on spatial relations among segments. The Perceptual Organization framework can also be used to formulate symbol signatures in terms of *proximity, continuation* and *parallelism* of primitives [79]. In [80] we described different grammatical models at different levels of complexity as signatures of bi-dimensional repetitive structures.

13.5 Architectures and Meta-data Modelling

The construction of generic and flexible systems able to tackle the analysis of graphical documents from heterogeneous domains is still a challenge. A number of high-performance GR systems exist, not only in academic domains but also as industrial applications. However, most of such systems are highly domain dependent. There is no reason to reinvent the wheel for each application. It is better to combine basic tools and parametrize them according to a domain-dependent knowledge, building workflows to solve particular scenarios. From our point of view, a generic framework should consider the following issues:

- *A component-oriented architecture.* A component implements a unique single DIA algorithm. A repository should allow to incrementally add new components. Components should be validated before being incorporated to the platform. They should work in a collaborative way to solve a given GR problem.
- *A meta-data definition.* Document representations are heterogeneous. Blostein et al. [81] studied different ones distinguishing between *internal* and *external* representations. A number of tools and standards, such as XML, or scalable vector graphics (SVG) are emerging that can provide more powerful technical capabilities for defining formal meta-models of documents. In addition XML-based representations allow to make internal and external representations compatible, represent heterogeneous documents, integrate semantic knowledge and be a standard for data manipulation and communication.
- *A workflow construction mechanism.* It would allow to "instantiate" the generic architecture to a particular scenario. Thus, components should be connected to generate a document processing workflow customized according to the user request. For example, in a music score recognition framework, connecting the following components: binarization, line detection (for staff lines), connected component labelling, symbol recognition and OCR. Not only pipeline processes should be considered, but different collaboration strategies among components and also feedback mechanisms (sketchy gestures for example) are suitable.
- *A way to integrate semantic knowledge.* Components are indeed content extraction units, but to understand a document it is necessary to use domain-dependent semantic knowledge. For example, a bi-dimensional grammar in the music recognition framework stated above, could be used to define rules of "valid" scores. The design of generic platforms requires the conception of semantic-based systems to acquire, organize, share and use the knowledge embedded in documents. The field of data mining, applied to document engineering offers a robust methodological basis to perform tasks such as descriptive modelling (clustering and segmentation), classification, discovering patterns and rules or retrieval by content applied to document sources and databases.
- *A ground-truth space.* A generic platform should include a repository of benchmarking data and performance evaluation criteria that allow to validate new components to be integrated in the platform. This space would also allow one to benchmark different workflow versions for a particular scenario.

In the literature, some attempts to propose generic architectures can be found. Let us review some of them. The DocMining framework [82] has a plug-in oriented architecture that permits the integration of heterogeneous software components. An XML-based document meta-model allows using the document structure as knowledge container (it stores the processing parameters and results at different execution stages). The third major concept of DocMining is a scenario definition component that allows the user to define workflows in terms of component parameters, links among them and objects to be manipulated. Scenarios can become new components. Edelweiss [83] is a Web-based cooperative document understanding framework. It consists of the following elements: Jobs are elementary document processing operations. eDocuments are XML-based structured text documents that describe jobs and the data produced by them. Repositories provide hierarchical storage and retrieval mechanisms for eDocument collections. Schedulers are processing units that can load an eDocument from a repository, execute some of its jobs and save it back on the repository. DMOS [7] is a grammatical formalism for segmentation of structured documents. It uses a language to do a graphical, syntactical and semantical description of a document. A parser performs the recognition process operating with a given document description. Case examples are provided for music notations, math formulae and tables. Pridmore et al. [8] studied the possibility of applying knowledge engineering approaches to produce line-drawing interpretation systems. They studied models of expertise that describe the knowledge, inference and control structures that may be used to perform instances of particular classes of task in a particular application.

13.6 On-Line Graphics Recognition and Sketching Interfaces

Graphics are a good way for expressing ideas. They are more than just a complement of text. In this chapter we have stated different domains where, according to a particular diagrammatic notation, graphics allow to communicate information. On-line input of drawings by a tablet or a digital pen in HCI is a mode of natural, perceptual and direct interaction. It allows not only to input graphic objects to the system, but to process them in real time and, hence to give instant feedback to the user. A sketch is a line-drawing image consisting of a set of hand-drawn strokes drawn by a person using an input framework. Thus, by *sketching* or *calligraphic interface* we designate those applications consisting in the use of digital-pen inputs for creation or edition of handwritten text, diagrams or drawings. A *digital pen* is like a simple ballpoint pen but uses an electronic head instead of ink. We refer to *digital ink*, the chain of points obtained by a trajectory of a pen movement during touching a dynamic input device. Devices as PDAs or TabletPCs incorporate such a kind of digital-pen input protocols. Interesting applications of digital-pen protocols are freehand drawing for early design stages in engineering, biometrics (signature verification), query by sketch in image database retrieval, or augmenting and editing documents.

In a recent review, Liu [84] considered three levels in a general architecture of an on-line GR system. The first level recognizes primitives while the user is drawing freehand strokes. The second level recognizes composite objects, i.e. combines primitives corresponding to consecutive strokes using information on their spatial arrangement and classifies them in terms of a given set of symbol models. Finally, the third level uses semantics related to the domain to interpret the drawing and beautify and re-display it. It is worth telling, concerning the semantic level, that recognized on-line graphic objects can be classified in two categories: freehand symbols and gestures. While the former are elements of a diagram vocabulary and give meaning to the drawing itself, the latter have an *interaction* meaning and have associated actions to modify the diagram. From a methodological point of view, on-line sketch processing, especially in the primitive-level extraction, has the added value of using dynamic information. It allows to use curvature, speed or pressure information of strokes. Davis in [85] illustrated how to locate dominant points in strokes to produce low-level geometric descriptions by looking for points along the stroke having maximum curvature and minimum speed.

A number of illustrative on-line graphics recognition applications can be found in the literature. Most of them consists in sketching interfaces. SILK (*Sketching Interfaces Like Krazy*) [86] allows to design a GUI. The system recognizes the widgets and other interface elements as the designer draws them. It also allows to interact with the system by gestures and also to build storyboards. Gestures and primitive strokes are recognized by a statistical classifier. Widgets are recognized in terms of the primitive classification and spatial relationships among them. Jorge et al. have used different types of grammars as adjacency grammars [87] or fuzzy relational grammars [88] to recognize sketched shapes. They apply it to different scenarios as JavaSketchIT, which is a tool for GUI design. ASSIST (*A Shrewd Sketch Interpretation and Simulation Tool*) [85] works in a mechanical engineering domain. It recognizes mechanical objects that are beautified, and the interpretation step performs a mechanical simulation. Leclercq et al. [89] propose a multi-agent system for interpreting architectural sketches. A collaboration strategy is performed between agents that recognize different types of plan components. Sketching is also useful in CAD/CAM frameworks to re-construct 3D models from 2D wire-frame sketches. Piquer [90] uses an optimization approach for hypothesis validation on faces, edges and vertices. Symmetries are used as a visual cue that improves the interpretation. Another useful application of sketching interfaces is as a visual programming and diagrammatic reasoning tool. Tahuti [91] is a system for recognizing UML diagrams that generates code for RationalRose. Finally, sketches are also used for retrieval by shape content [92, 93]. A particular application of indexing by sketches is *SmartSketch Pad* [94] that has been designed for PDAs.

13.7 Performance Evaluation

A pervasive request among the GR community is the generation of evaluation studies for assessing and comparing the accuracy, robustness and performance of various GR methods and algorithms in some systematic and standard way. Usually, the algorithms are only evaluated by the subjective criteria of their own developers, and based on qualitative evaluation reported by human perception. Liu and Dori [95] distinguished three components to evaluate the performance of GR algorithms. First, the design of a sound ground truth covering a wide range of possible cases and degrees of distortion. Second, a matching method to compare the ground truth with the results of the algorithm. Finally, the formulation of a metric to measure the "goodness" of the algorithm. The GR community has fostered in the last years the activities around benchmarking, performance evaluation, reference ground-truthed data sets, etc. A number of contests have been held in GREC Workshop series for dashed line detection [9], vectorization [10, 11], arc detection [3, 4] and symbol recognition [12].

It is not easy to measure the precision of vectorial representations. What does a good vectorization is expected to produce? Is it better to have well-positioned vectors although ground-truth ones are split into several vectors in the vectorization result, or to have the same number of vectors than the ground truth, regardless their attributes? Phillips and Chhabra [96] defined a benchmarking protocol for raster-to-vector conversion systems. Using that protocol, they compared three commercial vectorization packages. The benchmarking was also used in GREC contests [10, 11]. They consider seven graphical entities, namely text blocs and dashed and solid straight lines, arcs and circles. An accuracy measure is defined for matches between detected graphical entities and ground-truth ones. Their approach to measure the performance of a vectorization system is to formulate the accuracy in terms of the required edit effort to correct the mistakes made by the system. To do so, empirical weights are assigned to edit operations between graphical primitives (n to m mappings, false positives and false negatives).

Liu and Dori in [97] proposed another performance evaluation protocol for line detection algorithms that was used in the arc detection contests [3, 4]. The proposed performance evaluation indices followed shape preservation criteria and were defined at pixel level (overlapping distance between ground-truth pixels and image pixels) and vector level (endpoints, location offset, line width, geometry and line style). Either synthesized or scanned test images were used with different types of noise and distortion.

It is not an easy task to define a benchmarking for symbol recognition. It should include a high number of symbol classes from different domains to evaluate the generality and scalability of methods; test images should contain symbols with different kinds and degrees of distortion; non-segmented instances of the symbols are also required to test segmentation ability. From the point of view of metrics, indices should be developed to measure issues such as recognition accuracy, computation time, degradation of performance with increasing degrees of distortion, degradation of performance with increasing number of symbols, generality, etc. The first contest in binary symbol recognition was held in ICPR 2000 [98]. The dataset consisted of 25 electrical symbols with small rotation angles, scaled at different sizes and with three types of noise: quantization error, replacement noise and salt-and-pepper noise. Performance measures include misdetection, false alarm and precision of location and scale detection. In the contest of GREC 2003 [12], 50 symbol classes from the fields of electronics and architecture were used. All the symbols consisted of line structures. The benchmark contained both raw and vectorial data. Test data were generated from ideal symbol models considering the following interests: affine transformations; statistical degradation, i.e. adding noise to bitmap data, and statistical distortion for vectorial data; scalability and computation time. This contest was a starting point towards the construction of a collaborative benchmarking platform for symbol recognition.

To conclude this section, let us refer to a recent study provided by Lopresti and Nagy [99] on ground-truthing graphical documents. They identified a number of issues that must be solved to develop automated GR systems: what is the best data format; either to represent input and truth data? In OCR evaluation, ASCII is a standard format; but when dealing with graphics, information for benchmarking is more complex and no standard exists that is able to represent all desired evaluation features. There is an intrinsic ambiguity in ground-truthing graphical documents. Vectorization is an example, we have discussed it before. In some cases, different ground-truth options would be required. The training of users is also a key issue because the users only produce the ground truths (compiling data from different users).

13.8 An Application Scenario: Interpretation of Architectural Sketches

As an example of the application of GR techniques, we briefly overview our work on the recognition of sketched architectural floor plans [43]. This scenario is thought as a tool to assist an architect in the early design phase of a new project. In this stage, an architect uses it to convert ideas to sketches. Actually, the system presented in this chapter is part of a more general platform that aims to get a 3D view of a building from a sketched floor plan. Then the architect can navigate into the building using a virtual reality environment. Our proposed system combines the following elements: first, a sketch-based interface paradigm to draw architectural floor plans or to interactively edit existing ones by adding new elements. Second, an attributed graph structure to represent the documents. And third, a set of descriptor extraction modules and domain-dependent knowledge to recognize building elements (graphic symbols) as walls, doors, windows, etc. The main components of the system are symbol recognition algorithms used to recognize building elements of the sketch and also gestures to edit it. Recognition is done at pixel level and at vectorial level, depending on the class of symbols to be recognized. At pixel level, circular zoning and Zernike moments classifiers are used. At vectorial level, we use structural (graph matching) and syntactic (adjacency grammars) techniques.

The input of the system can be done by means of a scanner device or a digital pen device. The application also allows the option of interacting with the system by adding new symbols or by means of gestures. In Figure 13.2(a), we can see the sketchy input of the system, as it can be seen that the symbols have distortion, which makes recognition difficult. Figure 13.2(b) shows the output after the recognition process. In Figure 13.2(c) and (d), we can see how the user interacts with the system by means of a gesture *rotate*, and the result after recognizing the gesture and performing the corresponding action.

13.9 Conclusions: Sketching the Future

In this chapter we have reviewed the domain of graphics recognition. The first conclusion is that GR is a mature field. The first applications to recognize graphic diagrams date back to ten years. The field has progressed in this period, both from a scientific and an industrial points of view. However, there are a number of open issues and emerging challenges that mould the future of the field.

The area has moved a little bit away from pure recognition and retroconversion purposes to other paradigms such as indexing, retrieval and spotting. The classical goal was to develop fully automatic systems that are able to close the loop between paper and electronic formats, i.e. convert scanned pages of graphic documents to electronic formats compatible with CAD or GIS platforms. Now, the concept *document* has a broader sense and also the workflows where it participates have new needs. Digital libraries of graphic-rich documents exist, and the user has to retrieve documents containing a particular graphical entity (for example an engineer or an architect wanting to re-use old projects instead of starting from scratch). Other scenarios deal with large documents, and the user wants to spot a given symbol for navigating and edit purposes.

The role of the user in the document management has an increasing significance. Whereas classical systems were designed as fully automatic and the user was only asked to set up some parameters, the new platforms do

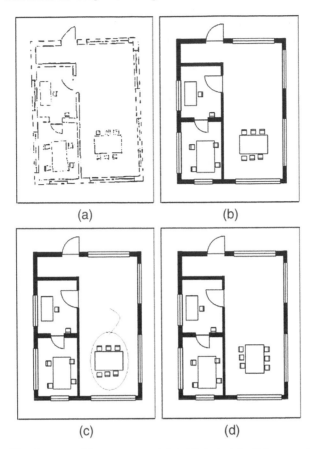

(a)　　　　　　　　　　(b)

(c)　　　　　　　　　　(d)

Fig. 13.2. Sketch recognition process: (a) initial sketch, (b) recognized entities, (c) gesture *rotate* and (d) final result after recognizing the gesture.

not see the user intervention as negative but a natural issue. A confirmation of this trend is the use of sketching interfaces. Applications based on freehand drawing by a digital pen device are increasingly more widespread.

The definition of graphics recognition architectures and document representation standards is also a challenge. There is a need of general, component-based and collaborative platforms that can be customized to particular scenarios. The inclusion of domain-dependent knowledge in such architectures and data models is required. It probably requires interdisciplinarity when designing GR platforms. As an example, some engineers working on map recognition face the fact that they had a few feedback from cartographers.

People tend to validate their algorithms using their own data. Robust and stable ground truths and performance evaluation protocols are required not only to compare systems in a competitive way, but also to share information and know the state of the art of the field. The IAPR Technical Committee on Graphics Recognition (IAPR-TC10) is promoting different initiatives to develop and collect such benchmarks. In this chapter, some GR contests have been described.

The traditional areas of graphics recognition are still there. Vectorization is a mature problem, however *new* methods are proposed. The unanswered question about what vectorization method is to be chosen still remains. What do we really expect from a vectorization package? Symbol recognition continues playing a central role. A lot of methods exist in the literature with high recognition scores. The recognition of symbols without a previous segmentation but embedded in their context requires further research efforts. Some people in this field wonder if progress should be measured in years or in decades.

Finally, there are emerging applications where GR can play an important role, probably not by working alone but in collaboration with close fields within document analysis (OCR, either printed or handwritten, or page layout analysis) or other such as data mining or human–computer interaction. Examples of Web document analysis, digital libraries or the analysis and recognition of historical documents contain graphical information. These last two fields have strong relations because there are a lot of historical archives to be converted to a digital format. This conversion requires the extraction of descriptors and indices for future indexing.

Acknowledgment

This work has been partially supported by the Spanish project CICYT TIC2003-09291 and Catalan project CeRTAP PVPC.

References

1. Nagy, G. (2000). Twenty years of document image analysis in PAMI. *IEEE Transactions on Pattern Analysis and Machine Intelligence, 22*, pp. 38–62
2. O'Gorman, L., Kasturi, R., (Eds.) (1997). *Document Image Analysis.* Silver Springer MD: IEEE Computer Society Press (1997)
3. Liu, W., Zhai, J., and Dori, D. (2002). Extended summary of the arc segmentation contest. In: D. Blostein and Y. Kwon (Eds.). *Graphics Recognition: Algorithms and Applications.* Berlin: Springer, Volume 2390 of LNCS, pp. 343–349.
4. Liu, W. (2004). Report of the arc segmentation contest. In: J. Lladós and Y.B. Kwon (Eds.). *Graphics Recognition: Recent Advances and Perspectives.* Berlin: Springer, Volume 3088 of LNCS, pp. 364–367.

5. Dori, D. (2000). Syntactic and semantic graphics recognition: the role of the object-process methodology. In: A. Chhabra and D. Dori (Eds.). *Graphics Recognition: Algorithms and Systems.* Berlin : Springer, Volume 1941 of LNCS, pp. 277–287.

6. Clavier, E., Masini, G., Delalandre, M., Rigamonti, M., Tombre, K., and Gardes, J. (2003). DocMining: a cooperative platform for heterogeneous document interpretation according to user-defined scenarios. *Proceedings of Fifth IAPR Workshop on Graphics Recognition, Barcelona, Spain,* pp. 21–32.

7. Couasnon, B. (2001). DMOS: a generic document recognition method, application to an automatic generator of musical scores, mathematical formulae and table structures recognition systems. *Proceedings of Sixth International Conference on Document Analysis and Recognition, Seattle, USA,* pp. 215–220.

8. Pridmore, T., Darwish, A., and Elliman, D. (2002). Interpreting line drawing images: a knowledge level perspective. In: D. Blostein and Y. Kwon (Eds.). *Graphics Recognition: Algorithms and Applications.* Berlin: Springer, Volume 2390 of LNCS, pp. 245–255.

9. Chhabra, A. and Phillips, I. (1996). The first international graphics recognition contest – dashed line recognition competition. In: R. Kasturi and K. Tombre (Eds.). *Graphics Recognition: Methods and Applications.* Berlin: Springer, Volume 1072 LNCS, pp. 270–300.

10. Chhabra, A. and Phillips, I. (1998). The second international graphics recognition contest – raster to vector conversion: a report. In: K. Tombre and A. Chhabra (Eds.). *Graphics Recognition: Algorithms and Systems.* Berlin: Springer,Volume 1389 LNCS, pp. 390–410.

11. Chhabra, A. and Philips, I. (2000). Performance evaluation of line drawing recognition systems. *Proceedings of Fifteenth International Conference on Pattern Recognition, Barcelona, Spain, 4,* pp. 864–869.

12. Valveny, E. and Dosch, P. (2004). Symbol recognition contest: a synthesis. In: J. Lladós and Y.B. Kwon (Eds.). *Graphics Recognition: Recent Advances and Perspectives.* Berlin: Springer, Volume 3088 LNCS, pp. 368–386.

13. Kasturi, R. and Tombre, K. (Eds.) (1996). *Graphics Recognition – Methods and Applications.* Volume 1072 of LNCS. Berlin: Springer.

14. Tombre, K. and Chhabra, A.K., (Eds.) (1998). *Graphics Recognition - Algorithms and Systems.* Berlin: Springer, Volume 1389 of Lecture Notes in Computer Science.

15. Chhabra, A. and Dori, D. (Eds.) (2000). *Graphics Recognition – Recent Advances.* Berlin: Springer, Volume 1941 of LNCS.

16. Blostein, D. and Kwon, Y. (Eds.) (2002). *Graphics Recognition – Algorithms and Applications.* Berlin: Springer, Volume 2390 of LNCS.

17. Lladós, J. and Kwon, Y. (Eds.). *Graphics Recognition – Recent Advances and Perspectives.* Berlin: Springer, Volume 3088 of LNCS.

18. Groen, F., Sanderson, A., and Schlag, F. (1985). Symbol recognition in electrical diagrams using probabilistic graph matching. *Pattern Recognition Letters 3,* pp. 343–350.

19. Habacha, A. (1991). Structural recognition of disturbed symbols using discrete relaxation. *Proceedings of the First International Conference on Document Analysis and Recognition, Saint Malo, France,* pp. 170–178.

20. Kim, S., Suh, J., and Kim, J. (1993). Recognition of logic diagrams by identifying loops and rectilinear polylines. *Proceedings of the Second IAPR International Conference on Document Analysis and Recognition, ICDAR'93, Tsukuba, Japan*, pp. 349–352.

21. Kuner, P. and Ueberreiter, B. (1988). Pattern recognition by graph matching. Combinatorial versus continuous optimization. *International Journal of Pattern Recognition and Artificial Intelligence, 2*, pp. 527–542.

22. Lee, S. (1992). Recognizing hand-written electrical circuit symbols with attributed graph matching. In: H. Baird, H. Bunke, and K. Yamamoto (Eds.). *Structured Document Analysis*. Berlin: Springer, pp. 340–358.

23. Okazaki, A., Kondo, T., Mori, K., Tsunekawa, S., and Kawamoto, E. (1988). An automatic circuit diagram reader with loop-structure-based symbol recognition. *IEEE Transactions on PAMI, 10*, pp. 331–341.

24. Antoine, D., Collin, S., and Tombre, K. (1999). Analysis of technical documents: the REDRAW system. In: H. Baird, H. Bunke, and K. Yamamoto (Eds.). *Structured Document Image Analysis*. Berlin: Springer, pp. 385–402.

25. Boatto, L., Consorti, V., Del Buono, M., Di Zenzo, S., Eramo, V., Espossito, A., Melcarne, F., Meucci, M., Morelli, A., Mosciatti, M., Scarci, S., and Tucci, M. (1992). An interpretation system for land register maps. *Computer, 25*, pp. 25–33.

26. Madej, D. (1991). An intelligent map-to-CAD conversion system. *Proceedings of First. International Conference on Document Analysis and Recognition, Saint Malo, France*, pp. 602–610.

27. Adam, S., Ogier, J., Cariou, C., Gardes, J., Mullot, R., and Lecourtier, Y. (2000). Combination of invariant pattern recognition primitives on technical documents. In: A. Chhabra, D. Dori (Eds.). *Graphics Recognition – Recent Advances*. Berlin: Springer, Volume 1941 of LNCS, pp. 238–245.

28. Arias, J., Lai, C., Surya, S., Kasturi, R., and Chhabra, A. (1995). Interpretation of telephone system manhole drawings. *PRL, 16*, pp. 355–369.

29. Hartog, J., Kate, T., and Gerbrands, J. (1996). Knowledge-based segmentation for automatic map interpretation. In: R. Kasturi, K. Tombre (Eds.). *Graphics Recognition: Methods and Applications*. Berlin: Springer, Volume 1072 of LNCS.

30. De Stefano, C., Tortorella, F., and Vento, M. (1995). An entropy based method for extracting robust binary templates. *Machine Vision and Applications, 8*, pp. 173–178.

31. Myers, G., Mulgaonkar, P., Chen, C., DeCurtins, J., and Chen, E. (1996). Verification-based approach for automated text and feature extraction from raster-scanned maps. In: R. Kasturi, K. Tombre (Eds.). *Graphics Recognition: Methods and Applications*. Berlin: Springer, pp. 190–203.

32. Reiher, E., Li, Y., Donne, V., Lalonde, M., Hayne, C., and Zhu, C. (1996). A system for efficient and robust map symbol recognition. *Proceedings of the Thirteenth IAPR International Conference on Pattern Recognition, Viena, Austria*, Volume 3, pp. 783–787.

33. Samet, H. and Soffer, A. (1996). Marco: map retrieval by content. *IEEE Transactions on PAMI, 18*, pp. 783–797.

34. Levachkine, S., Velázquez, A., Alexandrov, V., and Kharinov, M. (2002). Semantic analysis and recognition of raster-scanned color cartographic images. In: D. Blostein, Y. Kwon (Eds.). *Graphics Recognition: Algorithms and Applications*. Berlin: Springer, Volume 2390 of LNCS, pp. 178–189.

35. Joseph, S. and Pridmore, T. (1992). Knowledge-directed interpretation of mechanical engineering drawings. *IEEE Transactions on PAMI, 14*, pp. 928–940.
36. Vaxiviere, P. and Tombe, K. (1992). Celesstin: CAD conversion of mechanical drawings. *Computer, 25*, pp. 46–54.
37. Tombre, K. and Dori, D. (1997). Interpretation of engineering drawings. In: H. Bunke, P. Wang (Eds.). *Handbook of Character Recognition and Document Image Analysis*. Singapore: World Scientific, pp. 457–484.
38. Boose, M., Shema, D., and Baum, L. (2004). Automatic generation of layered illustrated parts drawings for advanced technical data systems. In: J. Lladós, Y.B. Kwon (Eds.). *Graphics Recognition: Recent Advances and Perspectives*. Berlin: Springer, Volume 3088 of LNCS, pp. 109–115.
39. Ah-Soon, C. and Tombre, K. (2001). Architectural symbol recognition using a network of constraints. *Pattern Recognition Letters, 22*, pp. 231–248.
40. Aoki, Y., Shio, A., Arai, H., and Odaka, K. (1996). A prototype system for interpreting hand-sketched floor plans. *Proceedings of the Thirteenth International Conference on Pattern Recognition, Vienna, Austria*, pp. 747–751.
41. Leclercq, P. (2004). Absent sketch interface in architectural engineering. In: J. Lladós and Y.B. Kwon (Eds.). *Graphics Recognition: Recent Advances and Perspectives*. Berlin: Springer, Volume 3088 of LNCS, pp. 351–362.
42. Park, Y. and Kwon, Y. (2002). An effective vector extraction method on architectural imaging using drawing characteristics. In: D. Blostein, Y. Kwon (Eds.). *Graphics Recognition: Algorithms and Applications*. Berlin: Springer, Volume 2390 of LNCS, pp. 299–309.
43. Sánchez, G., Valveny, E., Lladós, J., Mas, J., and Lozano, N. (2004). A platform to extract knowledge from graphic documents. Application to an architectural sketch understanding scenario. In: S. Marinai, A. Dengel (Eds.). *Document Analysis Systems VI*. Berlin: Springer, Volume 3163 of LNCS, pp. 349–365.
44. Blostein, D. and Baird, H. (1992). A critical survey of music image analysis. In: H. Baird, H. Bunke, K. Yamamoto (Eds.). *Structured Document Image Analysis*. Berlin: Springer, pp. 405–434.
45. Ng, K. (2002). Music manuscript tracing. In: D. Blostein, Y. Kwon (Eds.). *Graphics Recognition: Algorithms and Applications*. Berlin: Springer, Volume 2390 of LNCS, pp. 330–342.
46. Fahmy, H. and Blonstein, D. (1993). A graph grammar programming style for recognition of music notation. *Machine Vision and Applications, 6*, pp. 83–99.
47. Yadid-Pecht, O., Gerner, M., Dvir, L., Brutman, E., and Shimony, U. (1996). Recognition of handwritten musical notes by a modified neocognitron. *Machine Vision and Applications, 9*, pp. 65–72.
48. Chang, M. and Chen, S. (2001). Deformed trademark retrieval based on 2d pseudo-hidden Markov model. *Pattern Recognition, 34*, pp. 953–967.
49. Cortelazzo, G., Mian, G., Vezzi, G., and Zamperoni, P. (1994). Trademark shapes description by string matching techniques. *Pattern Recognition, 27*, pp. 1005–1018.
50. Doermann, D., Rivlin, E., and Weiss, I. (1996). Applying algebraic and differential invariants for logo recognition. *Machine Vision and Applications, 9*, pp. 73–86.

51. Francesconi, E., Frasconi, P., Gori, M., Mariani, S., Sheng, J., Soda, G., and Sperduti, A. (1998). Logo recognition by recursive neural networks. In: K. Tombre and A. Chhabra (Eds.). *Graphics Recognition – Algorithms and Systems*. Berlin: Springer, Volume 1389 of LNCS.

52. Soffer, A. and Samet, H. (1998). Using negative shape features for logo similarity matching. *Proceedings of the Fourteenth International Conference on Pattern Recognition, 1*, pp. 571–573.

53. Zanibbi, R., Blostein, D., and Cordy, J. (2004). A survey of table recognition. *International Journal on Document Analysis and Recognition, 7*, pp. 1–16.

54. Gross, M. (1996). The electronic cocktail napkin – working with diagrams. *Design Studies,17*, pp. 53–69.

55. Gross, M. and Do, E. (2000). Drawing on the back of an envelope: a framework for interacting with application programs by freehand drawing. *Computers and Graphics, 24*, pp. 835–849.

56. Tombre, K., Ah-Soon, C., Dosch, P., Masini, G., and Tabbone, S. (2000). Stable and robust vectorization: how to make the right choices. In: A. Chhabra, D. Dori (Eds.). *Graphics Recognition: Recent Advances*. Berlin: Springer, Volume 1941 of LNCS, pp. 3–18.

57. Ramer, U. (1972). An iterative procedure for the polygonal approximation of planar curves. *Computer Graphics and Image Processing, 1*, pp. 244–256.

58. Ablameyko, S., Bereishik, V., and Paramonova, N. (1994). Vectorization and representation of largesize 2-D line-drawing images. *Journal of Visual Communication and Image Representation, 5*, pp. 245–254.

59. Nagasamy, V. and Langrana, N. (1990). Engineering drawing processing and vectorisation system. *Computer Vision, Graphics and Image Processing, 49*, pp. 379–397.

60. Hilaire, X. and Tombre, K. (2002). Improving the accuracy of skeleton-based vectorization. In: D. Blostein, Y. Kwon, (Eds.). *Graphics Recognition: Algorithms and Applications*. Berlin: Springer, Volume 2390 of LNCS, pp. 273–288.

61. Han, C. and Fan, K. (1994). Skeleton generation of engineering drawings via contour matching. *Pattern Recognition, 27*, pp. 261–275.

62. Dori, D. and Liu, W. (1999). Sparse pixel vectorization: an algorithm and its performance evaluation. *IEEE Transactions on PAMI, 21*, pp. 202–215.

63. Elliman, D. (2000). A really useful vectorization algorithm. In: A. Chhabra and D. Dori (Eds.). *Graphics Recognition: Algorithms and Systems*. Berlin: Springer, Volume 1941 of LNCS, pp. 19–27.

64. Elliman, D. (2002). TIF2VEC, an algorithm for arc segmentation in engineering drawings. In: D. Blostein and Y. Kwon (Eds.). *Graphics Recognition: Algorithms and Applications*. Berlin: Springer, Volume 2390 of LNCS, pp. 351–358.

65. Dosch, P., Masini, G., and Tombre, K. (2000). Improving arc detection in graphics recognition. *Proceedings of the Fifteenth International Conference on Pattern Recognition, Barcelona, Spain, 2*, pp. 243–246.

66. Hilaire, X. (2002). RANVEC and the arc segmentation contest. In: D. Blostein and Y. Kwon (Eds.). *Graphics Recognition: Algorithms and Applications*. Berlin: Springer, Volume 2390 of LNCS, pp. 359–364.

67. Lladós, J., Martí, E., and Villanueva, J. (2001). Symbol recognition by error-tolerant subgraph matching between region adjacency graphs. *IEEE Transactions on Pattern Analysis and Machine Intelligence, 23*, pp. 1137–1143.

68. Fletcher, L. and Kasturi, R. (1988). A robust algorithm for text string separation from mixed text/graphics images. *IEEE Transactions on Pattern Analysis and Machine Intelligence, 10*, pp. 910–918.

69. Tombre, K., Tabbone, S., Pelissier, L., and Dosch, P. (2002). Document analysis and world wide web. In: D. Lopresti, J. Hu, and R. Kashi (Eds.). *Document Analysis Systems V.* Berlin: Springer, Volume 2423 of LNCS, pp. 200–211.

70. Lladós, J., Valveny, E., Sánchez, G., and Martí, E. (2002). Symbol recognition: current advances and perspectives. In: D. Blostein and Y. Kwon (Eds.). *Graphics Recognition: Algorithms and Applications.* Berlin: Springer, Volume 2390 of LNCS, pp. 104–127.

71. Collin, S. and Colnet, D. (1994). Syntactic analysis of technical drawing dimensions. *International Journal of Pattern Recognition and Artificial Intelligence, 8*, pp. 1131–1148.

72. Bunke, H. (1982). Attributed programmed graph grammars and their application to schematic diagram interpretation. *IEEE Transactions on PAMI, 4*, pp. 574–582.

73. Tombre, K. and Lamiroy, B. (2003). Graphics recognition from re-engineering to retrieval. *Proceedings of Seventh International Conference on Document Analysis and Recognition*, Edinburgh, Scotland, pp. 148–155.

74. Muller, S. and Rigoll, G. (2000). Engineering drawing database retrieval using statistical pattern spotting techniques. In: A. Chhabra and D. Dori (Eds.). *Graphics Recognition: Recent Advances.* Berlin: Springer, Volume 1941 of LNCS, pp. 246–255.

75. Fonseca, M. and Jorge, J. (2003). Towards content-based retrieval of technical drawings through highdimensional indexing. *Computers and Graphics, 27*, pp. 61–69.

76. Doermann, D. (1998). The indexing and retrieval of document images: a survey. Technical Report CS-TR-3876, University of Maryland.

77. Tabbone, S., Wendling, L., and Tombre, K. (2003). Matching of graphical symbols in line-drawing images using angular signature information. *International Journal on Document Analysis and Recognition, 6*, pp. 115–125.

78. Dosch, P. and Lladós, J. (2003). Vectorial signatures for symbol discrimination. *Proceedings of Fifth IAPR Workshop on Graphics Recognition, Barcelona, Spain.*

79. Lorenz, O. and Monagan, G. (1995). Automatic indexing for storage and retrieval of line drawings. *Storage and Retrieval for Image and Video Databases (SPIE)*, pp. 216–227.

80. Sánchez, G. and Lladós, J. (2004). Syntactic models to represent perceptually regular repetitive patterns in graphic documents. In: J. Lladós and Y.B. Kwon (Eds.). *Graphics Recognition: Recent Advances and Perspectives.* Berlin: Springer, Volume 3088 of LNCS, pp. 166–175.

81. Blostein, D., Zanibbi, R., Nagy, G., and Harrap, R. (2003). Document representations. *Proceedings of Fifth IAPR Workshop on Graphics Recognition, Barcelona, Spain*, pp. 3–20.

82. Clavier, E., Masini, G., Delalandre, M., Rigamonti, M., Tombre, K., and Gardes, J. (2004). DocMining: a cooperative platform for heterogeneous document interpretation according to user-defined scenarios. In: J. Lladós and Y.B. Kwon (Eds.). *Graphics Recognition: Recent Advances and Perspectives.* Berlin: Springer, Volume 3088 of LNCS, pp. 13–24.

83. Roussel, N., Hitz, O., and Ingold, R. (2001). Web-based cooperative document understanding. *Proceedings of Sixth International Conference on Document Analysis and Recognition, Seattle, USA*, pp. 368–373.

84. Liu, W. (2004). On-line graphics recognition: state-of-the-art. In: J. Lladós and Y.B. Kwon (Eds.). *Graphics Recognition: Recent Advances and Perspectives*. Berlin: Springer, Volume 3088 of LNCS, pp. 291–304.

85. Davis, R. (2002). Understanding in design: overview of work at the mit lab. *2002 AAAI Spring Symposium Sketch Understanding*.

86. Landay, J. and Myers, B. (2001). Sketching interfaces: toward more human interface design. *IEEE Computer, 34*, pp. 56–64.

87. Jorge, J. and Glinert, E. (1995). Online parsing of visual languages using adjacency grammars. *Proceedings of the Eleventh International IEEE Symposium on Visual Languages*, pp. 250–257.

88. Caetano, A., Goulart, N., Fonseca, M., and Jorge, J. (2002). Javasketchit: issues in sketching the look of user interfaces. *2002 AAAI Spring Symposium Sketch Understanding*.

89. Juchmes, R., Leclercq, P., and Azar, S. (2004). A multi-agent system for the interpretation of architectural sketches. *Proceedings of Eurographics Workshop on Sketch-Based Interfaces and Modeling, Grenoble, France*.

90. Piquer, A. (2003). Percepción Artificial de Dibujos Lineales. PhD thesis, Universitat Jaume I.

91. Hammond, T. and Davis, R. (2002). Tahuti: a geometrical sketch recognition system for uml class diagrams. *2002 AAAI Spring Symposium Sketch Understanding*.

92. Fonseca, M. (2004). Sketch-based retrieval in large sets of drawings. PhD thesis, Instituto Superior Técnico, Technical University of Lisbon.

93. Rigoll, G. and Muller, S. (2000). Graphics-based retrieval of color image databases using hand-drawn query sketches. In: A. Chhabra and D. Dori (Eds.). *Graphics Recognition: Algorithms and Systems*. Berlin: Springer, Volume 1941 of LNCS, pp. 256–265.

94. Liu, W., Xiangyu, J., and Zhengxing, S.: (2002). Sketch-based user interface for inputting graphic objects on small screen device. In: D. Blostein and Y. Kwon (Eds.). *Graphics Recognition: Algorithms and Applications*. Berlin: Springer, Volume 2390 of LNCS, pp. 67–80.

95. Liu, W. and Dori, D. (1998). A proposed scheme for performance evaluation of graphics/text separation algorithms. In: K. Tombre and A. Chhabra (Eds.). *Graphics Recognition: Algorithms and Systems*. Berlin: Springer, Volume 1389 of LNCS, pp. 359–371.

96. Phillips, I. and Chhabra, A. (1999). Empirical performance evaluation of graphics recognition systems. *IEEE Transactions on PAMI, 21*, pp. 849–870.

97. Liu, W. and Dori, D. (1997). A protocol for performance evaluation of line detection algorithms. *Machine Vision and Applications, 9*, pp. 240–250.

98. Aksoy, S., Ye, M., Schauf, M., Song, M., Wang, Y., Haralick, R., Parker, J., Pivovarov, J., Royko, D., Sun, C., and Farneboock, G. (2000). Algorithm performance contest. *Proceedings of the Fifteenth International Conference on Pattern Recognition, Barcelona, Spain*, Volume 4, pp. 870–876.

99. Lopresti, D. and Nagy, G. (2002). Issues in ground-truthing graphic documents. In: D. Blostein and Y. Kwon (Eds.). *Graphics Recognition: Algorithms and Applications*. Berlin: Springer, Volume 2390 of LNCS, pp. 46–66.

14

An Introduction to Super-Resolution Text

Céline Mancas-Thillou and Majid Mirmehdi

14.1 Introduction

The quest for high-resolution images or image sequences from a cheap and small acquisition system is a challenge rooted deeply in both hardware and software. While hardware advances in leaps and bounds in terms of more powerful yet smaller footprint processors, sensors and memory, the progress of software and appropriate algorithms requires longer-term research and development.

Due to the increased use of embedded low-resolution imaging devices, such as handheld PDAs and mobile phones, coupled with the need to extract information accurately and quickly, super-resolution (SR)-based techniques are fast becoming a focus of research in the field of text recognition. SR processes the information from one (or more) low-resolution (LR), possibly noisy and blurred, image(s) of a scene to produce a higher resolution image (or sequence). A typical application scenario may be the use of a mobile phone camera to capture one or more lines of text on an advertising poster while on a metro train. The result may be a shaky low-resolution image sequence. This could possibly be sent to a server for transformation into text or be done on the fly on the phone if (one day) enabled. Other applications that may require SR text pre-processing include a tourist translation assistant or a text-to-speech transformation for the visually impaired.

Classical image restoration algorithms resulting in a single output image from a single degraded image are sometimes referred to as *single-input single-output (SISO) super-resolution*. Even though some may disagree with such a categorization, high-resolution (HR) information missing in a single LR image can be recovered by training models to learn piecewise correspondences between LR and possible HR information to form an SR image.

A possible application of SISO super-resolution is for face resolution enhancement to add details and enable to zoom-in in the image.

Most SR algorithms deal with the integration of multiple LR frames to estimate a higher resolution image. The most common term of reference for multiple frame super-resolution found in the literature is *multiple-input single-output (MISO)* or *static super-resolution*. An example application area is in licence plate recognition from a video stream to increase the alphanumeric recognition rates.

A recent focus of SR research relates to *dynamic super-resolution*, which is aimed at reconstructing a high-quality set of images from low-quality frames, often referred to as *multiple-input multiple-output (MIMO) super-resolution*. This approach is also known as *video-to-video super-resolution*. For example, applications can be found in video enhancement captured by surveillance cameras to increase the general visibility and acuity of a recorded criminal event.

Figure 14.1 illustrates the three methods outlined above. SR methods can be found in a multifarious range of imaging applications, such as remote sensing, microscopy and medical imaging, astronomical and space imaging, surveillance and forensic imaging and many more. (For more details on general super-resolution and its applications, the reader is referred to [1].) In this chapter the focus is on the application area of text analysis: how can SR be used in the generation of higher quality text images that can be more accurately interpreted by in-house or off-the-shelf OCR software? We concentrate on MISO or static SR methods since this is the most appropriate area of SR likely to have immediate impact in terms of multiple input frames from a mobile device, e.g. capturing information from a business card, a restaurant menu or a map with printed text.

Most articles dealing with SR text consider cropped sequences of detected text areas [2–4]. As SR techniques can be computationally expensive, then processing regions of interest only is both cost saving and allows the algorithm to focus more towards local properties. In this chapter, we do not

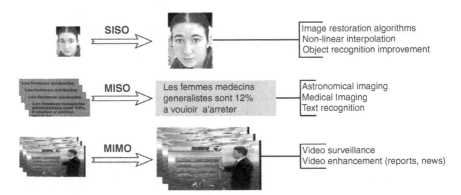

Fig. 14.1. Categories of super-resolution and some example applications.

deal with the specific process of locating the text and assume the region of interest is either already detected and/or spans the entire given image. For works dealing with the automatic location of text, the reader is referred to works such as [5–8].

In the rest of this chapter, we deal with the general SR inverse problem theory and then focus on the different stages involved in obtaining SR, including motion estimation, warping, interpolation and deblurring. In particular we examine the application of these stages to text SR. Finally, a case study application using an embedded low-resolution camera is presented.

14.2 Super-Resolution: An Analytical Model

Text analysis has been popular for over three decades, from character recognition to layout decomposition, exercised after scanner-based acquisition. With the emergence of mobile devices, new text interpretation challenges have arisen particularly in natural scene images. Text in such scenes suffers from different degradations, including uneven lighting, optical and motion blur, low resolution, geometric distortion, sensor noise and complex backgrounds. Fortunately, by using multiple frames of a video sequence and static SR techniques, most of these degradations can be minimized or even suppressed, e.g. one can enhance the resolution of the image by recovering the high frequencies corrupted by the optical system. For example, in character recognition, text fonts are assumed to have sufficient resolution to be reliably recognized by OCR. For document images, 300 dpi is plenty for satisfactory recognition and that means characters can occupy an area as large as 40×40 pixels. However, in video frames, a resolution of 320×240 is very common and therefore text may well be rendered no larger than 10×10 pixels, hence the enhancement of spatial resolution becomes important.[1]

The SR problem is usually modelled as the reversal of a degradation process. This is an example of an inverse problem where the source information (SR image) is estimated from the observed data (LR images). Solving an inverse problem generally requires first constructing a forward model. Most imaging devices can be described as a camera lens and aperture that produce blurred images of the scene contaminated by additional noise from various sources: quantization errors, sensor measurement or model errors. Then, for an SR image x of size $M \times N$ and a set of K LR images y_k, the observation model can be expressed as:

$$y_k = DB_kW_kx + n_k \qquad (14.1)$$

where W_k is an $M \times N$ warp matrix that maps the HR image coordinates to the LR coordinates and represents the motion that occurs during image

---

[1] These numbers are based on the assumption that the acquisition device is at a sensible, realistic distance from the text.

acquisition, B_k is an $M \times N$ blur matrix caused by the optical system, the relative motion during the acquisition period and the point spread function (PSF) of the LR sensor, D is the decimation matrix of size $(M \times N)^2/(L \times P)$, where L and P are the subsampling factors in the horizontal and vertical directions, respectively, and finally n_k is the associated noise. Usually D and y_k are known and are inputs in the SR algorithm. Using columnwise reordering and by stacking the frame equations, (14.1) can be rewritten as:

$$y = Hx + n \tag{14.2}$$

where H represents all the degradations, i.e. $H = DB_kW_k$ for all k. Super-resolution is a computationally intensive problem that involves several thousand unknowns. For example, super-resolving a sequence of just 50×50 pixel LR frames into a 200×200 SR image by a factor of 4 in each direction involves $40,000$ unknown pixels. As mentioned above, SR is an inverse problem and is ill-conditioned due to the obvious lack of LR frames and the additional noise. Therefore matrix H is under-determined and regularization techniques may have to be used to overcome this problem in the image super-resolution process.

14.3 MISO Super-Resolution: A Closer Look

Super-resolution algorithms require several processing stages, from motion estimation through reconstruction to deblurring, possibly involving regularization along the way. An overview is shown in Figure 14.2. These stages can be implemented consecutively or simultaneously depending on the reconstruction methods chosen (we come across examples of these later).

14.3.1 Motion Estimation and Registration

An important key to successful super-resolution is the existence of change between frames, e.g. by motion in the scene or through ego motion. For example for scene motion, consider a fixed camera video surveillance scenario monitoring cars for licence plate recognition; low-resolution and low-quality image sequences arising due to weather conditions and changing illumination can be enhanced to increase the chance of character recognition.

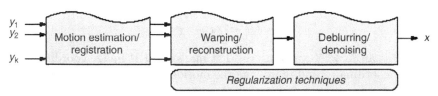

Fig. 14.2. General scheme for super-resolution.

On the other hand, an example of camera motion would be a handheld camera-enabled PDA capturing a text document for a short period. The difference between the frames arising through hand jitter would result in a suitable set of frames for super-resolution. We use this very type of image capture process in the case study in Section 14.4.

Motion estimation is then the first step in SR techniques and motion parameters are found through some form of registration, i.e. the relative translations, rotations and other transformations that define an accurate point-to-point correspondence between images in the input sequence. Usually, each frame is registered to a reference one (most commonly the first) to be able to warp all frames into a single higher resolution image in the reconstruction stage. An alternative would be to register each frame against its preceding frame, but consecutive temporal errors can accrue leading to inaccurate results.

An error in motion estimation induces a direct degradation of the resulting SR image and if too many errors are present, it is generally better to interpolate one of the LR images (i.e. perform SISO) than to create an SR one from several images. The artefacts caused by a misaligned image are visually much more disturbing to the human eye than the blurring effect from interpolation! Nevertheless, we see later on how to deal with a limited number of motion estimation outliers. Clearly, the performance of motion estimation techniques is highly dependent on the complexity of the actual motion and the model used to represent it. Motion estimation techniques can be categorized in many different ways. We look at the progress and the methods proposed so far in the area of SR text analysis, gravitating around the motion models used. This is briefly illustrated in Figure 14.3.

The two-parameter translational model is often enough to reasonably represent scene motion in many different applications, not least one where a handheld device is used for a short period to capture some text. Indeed according to [9], the model approximates well the motion contained in

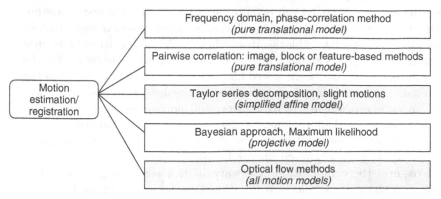

Fig. 14.3. Possible techniques for SR text analysis (with those not yet applied in grey).

image sequences where the scene is still and the camera is moving. Moreover, for sufficiently high frame rates most motion models can, at least locally, be approximated by this simple and low-cost model. However, the assumption of a pure translational model is not always valid and can result in significantly degraded performance. Then, a regularization technique or a deblurring process must be applied to constrain or correct motion estimation errors (or a higher order motion model employed).

Correlation is the main path to a solution in the translational model and both frequency and spatial domain-based variations have been applied in text-related applications. The main advantages in using correlation in the frequency domain are fast computation and illumination-invariance in phase space.

Phase correlation is a well-known method in frequency domain analysis and was applied by [2] for text SR. The main steps in phase correlation are based on the shifting property of the Fourier transform [10]. Hence, if the motion vector is assumed to be only the translation $(\Delta x, \Delta y)$ between two frames, then

$$f_{t+1}(x, y) \approx f_t(x - \Delta x, y - \Delta y) \tag{14.3}$$

for frames at times t and $t + 1$. After applying the Fourier transform:

$$F_{t+1}(u, v) \approx F_t(u, v) \exp^{-2\pi j(u\Delta x + v\Delta y)} \tag{14.4}$$

Then the cross-power spectrum CPS of F_t and F_{t+1} can be defined as:

$$CPS = \frac{F_t(u, v)F_{t+1}^*(u, v)}{|F_t(u, v)F_{t+1}^*(u, v)|} \approx \exp^{-2\pi j(u\Delta x + v\Delta y)} \tag{14.5}$$

where F_{t+1}^* is the complex conjugate of F_{t+1}. The maximum of the Fourier inverse of CPS is then at $(\Delta x, \Delta y)$.

In the spatial domain, Donaldson and Myers [3] used pairwise correlation over the whole image with quadratic interpolation and a least-squares fit to determine the translation vector for each observed LR frame. Li and Doermann [11] performed sub-pixel registration by first bilinearly interpolating frames and then by using correlation minimizing sum of square differences (SSD) between text blocks. In another application, a driver assistance system, Fletcher and Zelinski [12] used feature-based registration for the recognition of road signs, e.g. speed limits. First, signs were detected as the dominant circles in a sequence using the fast symmetry transform. Then, the circles were the features to register, and normalized cross-correlation was performed on them to compute the translational motion vectors.

The affine motion model assumes planar surfaces and an orthographic projection. It is clearly more involved than the pure translational model and requires the computation of a warp matrix accounting for rotation, scale and shear as well as a translational vector term. Interestingly no solicitation of this model can be found in application to text SR within a MISO framework. This is rather surprising given that text capture at a close distance, where images in a sequence would mostly differ by translation and rotation, is an ideal scenario for applying the affine motion model. Li and Doermann [11] in fact mention that the general 6-parameter affine model should be used in their text analysis application, but resort to a pure translational model due to the difficulty in obtaining a sufficient set of corresponding points to compute the affine parameters. They applied the translational model to multiple frames to enhance overlaid movie credits that move up the screen or ticker text that moves across the screen. In Section 14.4 we present a case study based on a simplified affine motion model with the parameters obtained using Taylor series decomposition.

For rigid scenes, the 8-parameter projective model provides the most precise parameters to account for all possible camera motions. Capel [13] applied this model for text SR. He first computed interest point features to sub-pixel accuracy using the Harris corner detection algorithm [14]. Then using RANSAC [15] to deal with outliers, a maximum likelihood estimator was used to compute the homography matrix between successive frames. Shimizu et al. [4] computed motion estimates between each frame pair by assuming that the consecutive frames exhibit only small pure translational motion differences. To reconstruct all the frames into an SR image, motion estimation parameters have to be estimated against a single reference LR image. Hence, simultaneous 8-parameter projective estimation using an 8D hyperplane and parabola fitting was then performed to refine the initial motion parameter estimates. Some results of this method are presented in Section 14.3.5.

Optical flow is another motion estimation approach not yet applied to text super-resolution. No doubt researchers in the field will turn their attention to it soon especially as increasing computational power will be able to deal with such an intensive technique, particularly for more complex motion models.

In summary, there are few SR techniques in which motion estimation is dealt with in-depth and most works concentrate on reconstruction and regularization. If necessary, motion registration parameters are assumed to be known or integrated as errors from an additive Gaussian noise process.

At the extreme end, highly complex, non-rigid, non-planar motions are very difficult to investigate and can occur in text analysis; an example is for text that appears on a curled page or on a moving person's loose t-shirt. Such examples need very special treatment and are beyond the scope of this chapter.

14.3.2 Warping and Reconstruction

The stage after motion estimation comprises in some way of bringing together all the input LR images into a coordinate frame that reconstructs an SR output. There are several methods that divide the reconstruction process into "grid mapping and interpolation" or "interpolation

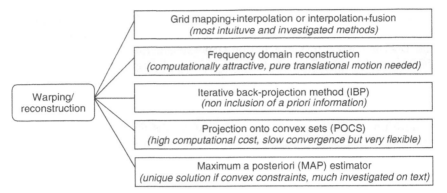

Fig. 14.4. Possible techniques for reconstruction in SR text analysis (with those not yet applied in grey).

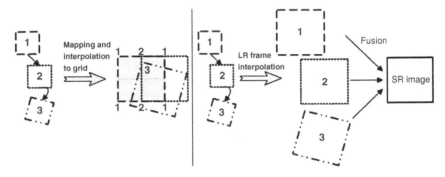

Fig. 14.5. Left: grid mapping and interpolation, right: interpolation and fusion.

and fusion". There are also other methods that simultaneously reconstruct and deblur. Figure 14.4 illustrates some of these techniques that we review particularly in relation to text analysis.

Grid Mapping and Interpolation: This is the most intuitive reconstruction process involving mapping onto a higher resolution grid followed by bilinear or higher order interpolation; first motion estimation parameters are applied to map LR pixel values into the SR sampling grid. This is shown in the left of Figure 14.5 with three LR frames where the second frame is a translation of the first and the third frame is a translated and rotated version of the first. For pure translational motion, this algorithm is often called *shift-and-add*. Nevertheless, some pixels are unknown or missing because of a lack of LR frames and have to be interpolated to build and refine the reconstruction. The advantage of grid mapping and interpolation is in its low computational cost making real-time applications possible. On the other hand, only the same blur and noise for all LR frames can be assumed, which reduces the overall performance.

Interpolation and Fusion: Warping, using the motion estimation parameters, is applied between each independent LR frame and the first instead of mapping to a SR grid as in the previous scheme. Then, linear or nonlinear interpolation methods are performed to increase the resolution of each LR frame separately. Finally, a fusion between all the resolved frames results in an SR image at the resolution of the interpolated LR frames. This is shown in the right of Figure 14.5. Depending on the fusion method, not all frames contribute to reconstruct pixels in the SR image. In the particular example of median fusion, only one of the LR frames is used for each reconstructed pixel. Therefore, motion estimation outliers, salt and pepper noise, etc. are discarded in the reconstruction process. Farsiu et al. [9] recommend the median for this purpose. For text enhancement in digital video, Li and Doermann [11] use bilinear interpolation followed by averaging of the interpolated frames. In order to be invariant against illumination changes, Chiang and Boult [16] fuse only the edges of each warped text frame into a reference-interpolated image with a median filter.

Interpolation and fusion is fast and robust to outliers but it can result in the appearance of some artificial effects in the super-resolved image due to the nature of the fusion process.

Frequency-Domain Reconstruction: This particular form of reconstruction is very often the continuation of frequency-domain motion estimation in the case of pure translational model assumption. It was first derived by Tsai and Huang [17] and was the first implemented SR reconstruction method, also called *alias-removal* reconstruction. Assuming that LR images are under-sampled, the translations between them allow an up-sampled SR image to be built based on the shifting property of the Fourier transform and the aliasing relationship between the continuous Fourier transform of an original SR image and the discrete Fourier transform of observed LR images [1]. Several extensions [18, 19] were then proposed to enlarge the initial conditions of Tsai and Huang, which were integer-shift translation only. Frequency-domain reconstruction has never been implemented in an SR text application. The major advantage is its simplicity but only global translational models can be considered.

Iterative Back-Projection (IBP): IBP reconstruction was first introduced by Irani and Peleg [20] and has found much use in mainstream SR reconstruction. Given the knowledge of the imaging process (PSF model and blur parameters amongst others) relating the scene to the observed image sequence, it becomes possible to simulate the output of the imaging system with the estimate of the original scene. The simulated images may then be compared with the observed data and a residual difference error found. Next the process is repeated iteratively to minimize this error. Thus this technique comprises two steps: simulation of the observed images and back-projection of the error using an adequate kernel to correct the estimate of the original scene. Several works, such as [21], run comparisons against this method using text images; however, they are for demonstration only and are not specifically designed for text. IBP methods have no unique solution due to the ill-posed nature of the inverse problem. In fact, minimizing the error does not necessarily imply a reasonable solution and a convergent iteration does not necessarily converge to a unique solution.

Projection Onto Convex Sets (POCS): The POCS method describes an alternative iterative approach but with more flexibility to include prior knowledge about the solution into the reconstruction process. Convex constraint sets have first to be defined to delimit the feasible solution space for SR restoration containing all LR images. Constraints can be various but have to represent data in the best way to yield desirable characteristics of the solution. For example, one constraint could be to enable only a range of pixel values. Other more complex constraints can be defined depending on the objectives and the application. The solution space of the SR restoration problem is the intersection of all the constraint sets. This method was initially proposed by Stark and Oskoui [22] and then extended by Patti et al. [23].

POCS can be considered as a generalization of the IBP method and has never been investigated in SR text. It has several disadvantages such as the non-uniqueness of the solution, slow convergence and high computational cost, but provides the flexibility to enable the inclusion of a priori information.

Maximum A Posteriori estimator (MAP): The MAP approach provides a flexible and convenient way to model a priori knowledge to constrain the solution. Usually, Bayesian methods are used when the probability density function (pdf) of the original image can be established. Given the K LR frames y_k, and using the Bayes theorem, the MAP estimator of the SR image x maximizes the a posteriori pdf $P(x|y_k)$, i.e.:

$$x_{MAP} = \arg\max_x P(x|y_k) = \arg\max_x \frac{P(y_k|x)P(x)}{P(y_k)} \qquad (14.6)$$

The maximum is independent of y_k and only the numerator need be considered.

MAP reconstruction in SR text has seen in-depth investigation by Capel and Zisserman [21] and Donaldson and Myers [3]. Capel and Zisserman [21] used an image gradient penalty defined by the Huber function as a prior model. This encourages local smoothness while preserving any step edge sharpness. Donaldson and Myers [3] used the same Huber gradient penalty function with an additional prior probability distribution based on the bimodal characteristic of text.

Maximum likelihood (ML) estimation, a simple case of MAP estimation with no prior term, was also applied to SR reconstruction in [21]. A subjective comparison of the IBP, the ML estimator and the MAP estimator reconstruction techniques is shown in Figure 14.6. The MAP

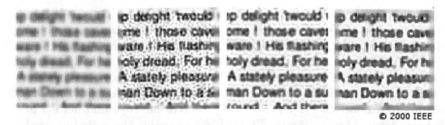

Fig. 14.6. Comparison of different reconstruction methods using an upsampling factor of 2: from left to right: one LR frame, ML estimator-based reconstructed image, IBP reconstructed image, MAP estimator-based reconstructed image. (Reproduced with kind permission from [21].)

estimator with the Huber penalty prior term provides slightly smoother results. Robustness and flexibility in degradation model estimation and a priori knowledge of the solution are the main benefits of the MAP estimator approach to the ill-posed SR problem. On the other hand, the main disadvantages are the high computational costs and the complexity of implementation.

Assuming that the noise process is Gaussian white noise and a convex prior model, MAP estimation ensures the uniqueness of the solution. Elad and Feuer [24] proposed a general hybrid SR image reconstruction that combines the advantages of MAP and POCS. Hence, all a priori knowledge is put together and this ensures a single optimal solution (unlike the POCS-only approach).

14.3.3 Regularization Techniques

Regularization techniques can either be used during the reconstruction process or the deblurring and denoizing step as shown in Figure 14.2. We describe both of these possibilities in this section.

Super-resolution image reconstruction is an ill-posed problem because of a recurrent lack of LR images and ill-determined blur operators. To stabilize the problem and find a relevant solution, it is necessary to incorporate further information about the desired solution and this is the main purpose of regularization. Using (14.2), a regularization cost function $\Lambda(x)$ can be added such that:

$$\sum_{k=1}^{K} \|y_k - Hx\| + \lambda\Lambda(x) \tag{14.7}$$

where λ is the regularization parameter for balancing the first term against the regularization term. The choice of x is then obtained by minimizing (14.7).

An optimal regularization parameter must be chosen carefully and there are various methods for its selection [25]. Tikhonov regularization (Λ_T) and total variation (TV) regularization (Λ_{TV}) are popular techniques for this purpose expressed as $\Lambda_T(x) = \|\Gamma x\|_2^2$ where Γ is usually a high-pass operator and $\Lambda_{TV}(x) = \|\nabla x\|_1$ where ∇ is the gradient operator, respectively. Tikhonov regularization is based on the assumption of smooth and continuous image regions while TV is not and preserves the edge information in the reconstructed image. Hence, TV is of late becoming the more preferred regularization method for denoizing and deblurring to reach a stabilized solution in SR reconstruction.

Regularization methods are very complementary to the MAP estimator as the cost function can be seen as a priori information. Capel and Zisserman [21] implemented both of the cost functions above in their MAP reconstruction process. Farsiu et al. [26] compared various reconstruction techniques, among which were grid mapping and cubic spline interpolation, Tikhonov regularization and bilateral TV regularization (extension of TV regularization). The latter approach was found to perform best with lesser smoothing effects as shown in Figure 14.7.

To obtain acceptable results in complex images, a regularization technique is often required during the reconstruction process but not all reconstruction methods can include spatial a priori information, e.g. frequency domain reconstruction methods.

The second main use of regularization techniques is for denoizing and deblurring and can be applied on single images as well. The process is the same: for a blurred and noisy image, a regularization technique can be performed to recover the original data from the degraded one as an inverse process. Moreover, if the high-pass operator Γ in the Tikhonov cost function is the identity matrix, then the method is the well-known inverse Wiener filtering.

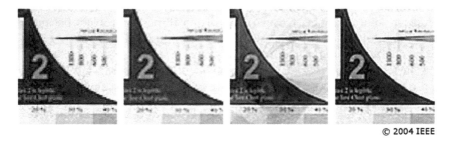

Fig. 14.7. Comparison of different enhancement methods: from left to right: one of 20 LR frames, grid mapping and cubic spline interpolation, Tikhonov regularization, bilateral TV regularization. (Reproduced with kind permission from [9].)

14.3.4 Deblurring and Denoizing

Causes of blur are the optical system, relative motion during the acquisition stage and the PSF of the sensor as well as from interpolation and registration errors. Noise can come from salt-and-pepper noise in the LR images as well as from misregistration outliers. SR algorithms generally include an independent post-processing step to deblur and denoise the final image. Usually, standard deconvolution algorithms, such as Wiener deblurring or blind deconvolution, are applied. Nevertheless, if the PSF is unknown and the LR images are strongly motion blurred, a robust estimation of the PSF and the direction of the motion blur must first be performed before applying deblurring methods such as in [27].

If the blur estimation is accurate enough, efficient deblurring can occur simultaneously during reconstruction. Recovering an image with an estimated PSF is a mathematically ill-posed problem; that is why regularization techniques described previously are used to solve it. However, knowledge of the blurring process is the best route to the cure and blur identification is sometimes included in the reconstruction procedure and refined iteratively. Chan and Wong [28] proposed blind deconvolution based on TV regularization by iteration. In another example, Chiang and Boult [16] performed local blur estimation by modelling a blurred edge with a step edge and a Gaussian blur kernel. During the reconstruction process, the unknown standard deviation of the kernel was estimated iteratively with the edges extracted previously. Hence, edge pixels were re-estimated using the edge model. The purpose was then to fuse the edge information into a reference interpolated image to overcome illumination sensitivity.

Denoizing can be approached via classical post-processing routes, for example after all LR frames are warped and interpolated separately, image fusion can be applied at each pixel position across the available frames. Additionally, noise removal can be implemented, e.g. Zhao et al. [29] used a trimmed mean while Farsiu et al. [9] applied a median filter.

14.3.5 Colour Super-Resolution Text

Colour remains a ripe area for investigation in general SR, let alone for the text SR application. The most common solutions apply monochrome SR algorithms to each of the colour channels independently or simply the luminance channel only [20]. An interesting work in the text SR area is that of Shimizu et al. [4] who proposed a reconstruction step that took into account colour information by demosaicing. After motion estimation from non-demosaiced LR frames, extended IBP reconstruction was used, reinforced by the evaluation of the difference between the simulated LR frames and the original LR frames (see IBP description in Section 14.3.2). Hence, Bayer sampling was used instead of classical down-sampling. An example of their sharper, less blurred results is shown in Figure 14.8.

Fig. 14.8. Results from Shimizu et al.'s [4] SR algorithm on natural scene text–left to right: one video frame, classical demosaicing with resolution enhancement by bi-cubic interpolation, and direct colour-based demosaicing SR image. (Reproduced with kind permission from [4].)

14.4 Case Study: SURETEXT – Camera-Based SR Text

As mentioned earlier in this chapter, recent advances in hardware and sensor technologies have led to handheld camera-enabled devices such as PDAs or smartphones giving rise to new potential applications, such as handy text OCR. In this case study, we present an experimental approach to reconstructing a higher resolution image, from the low-resolution frames obtained from a PDA device, by applying a novel super-resolution technique with the aim of getting a better response from standard off-the-shelf OCR software.

The data consist of short greyscale video sequences of text documents (e.g. advertisements, newspapers, book covers) captured with a camera-enabled PDA at 320×240 resolution. The scene motion was induced by simply holding the device over the document (with a quivering hand) for a short period of around 5–7 s at approximatively 5 fps, resulting in 25–35 frames per sequence. The scenes were mainly composed of nearly uniform backgrounds. No a priori knowledge of parameters such as camera sensor noise, PSF, etc. was used. Hence, the approach is independent of camera models.

The method described here enhances the classical SR approach by complementing it with high-frequency information extracted from the LR frames using an unsharp masking filter called *the Teager filter*. The classical SR approach can be said to consist of the stages shown in the upper row in Figure 14.9. The lower row shows the added Teager filtering process. Motion parameters are estimated for the LR frames using Taylor decomposition, followed by a simple RANSAC-based step to discard obvious outlier frames. The frames are then warped on to a high-resolution grid and bilinearly interpolated to obtain a preliminary SR result. The original frames (except the outliers) are then put through the Teager filter to generate a high-pass set of frames that are also warped and interpolated for a secondary SR result. The two resulting SR images are then fused, and median denoising is applied to smooth artefacts due to the reconstruction process to obtain the final SR image. We call this method *SURETEXT* (SUper-Resolution Enhanced TEXT) and the entire process is outlined next.

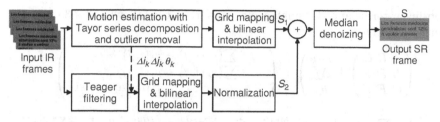

Fig. 14.9. Schema of SURETEXT.

14.4.1 Motion Estimation Using the Taylor Series

For motion estimation we apply Taylor series decomposition as presented in [30] who used it to register frames to correct atmospheric blur in images obtained by satellite. This approach fits very well to text capture with a quivering hand since a shaking hand can produce slight random motions and the approximation computed by Taylor series decomposition can be suitable due to the small motion amplitudes involved. Initially a pure translational model was used but this led to too many (small) misregistration errors to adequately and reasonably correct afterwards. A significant improvement was noticed when stepping up to a 3-parameter affine motion model (Δi_k, Δj_k, for horizontal and vertical translation, and θ_k for rotation). Given K frames with $k = 1, \ldots, K$, the motion between a frame y_k and the first frame y_1 can be written as:

$$y_k(i,j) = y_1(i \cos \theta_k - j \sin \theta_k + \Delta i_k, j \cos \theta_k + i \sin \theta_k + \Delta j_k) \quad (14.8)$$

Replacing the sin and cos terms by their first-order Taylor series expansion:

$$y_k(i,j) \approx y_1(i + \Delta i_k - j\theta_k - i\frac{\theta_k^2}{2}, j + \Delta j_k + i\theta_k - j\frac{\theta_k^2}{2}) \quad (14.9)$$

This can be approximated using its own first-order Taylor series expansion:

$$y_k(i,j) \approx y_1(i,j) + (\Delta i_k - j\theta_k - i\frac{\theta_k^2}{2})\frac{\partial y_1}{\partial i} + (\Delta j_k + i\theta_k - j\frac{\theta_k^2}{2})\frac{\partial y_1}{\partial j} \quad (14.10)$$

The optimum motion parameter set $\mathbf{m}_k = (\Delta i_k, \Delta j_k, \theta_k)$ can then be estimated by solving this least-squares problem:

$$\underset{\Delta i_k, \Delta j_k, \theta_k}{\arg \min} \sum_{i,j} [y_1(i,j) + (\Delta i_k - j\theta_k - i\frac{\theta_k^2}{2})\frac{\partial y_1}{\partial i} + (\Delta j_k + i\theta_k - j\frac{\theta_k^2}{2})\frac{\partial y_1}{\partial j} - y_k(i,j)]^2$$

$$(14.11)$$

To find $\mathbf{m}_k$, the minimum can be computed by obtaining the derivative with respect to Δi_k, Δj_k and θ_k and setting it to zero. Neglecting the non-linear terms and the small coefficients, then the following 3×3 system must be resolved:

$$
\begin{pmatrix} A & B & C \\ B & D & E \\ C & E & F \end{pmatrix} \begin{pmatrix} \Delta i_k \\ \Delta j_k \\ \theta_k \end{pmatrix} = \begin{pmatrix} \sum (y_k(i,j) - y_1(i,j)) \frac{\partial y_1}{\partial i} \\ \sum (y_k(i,j) - y_1(i,j)) \frac{\partial y_1}{\partial j} \\ \sum (y_k(i,j) - y_1(i,j)) (i \frac{\partial y_1}{\partial j} - j \frac{\partial y_1}{\partial i}) \end{pmatrix}
$$

with $A = \sum \frac{\partial y_1}{\partial i}^2$, $B = \sum \frac{\partial y_1}{\partial i} \frac{\partial y_1}{\partial j}$, $C = \sum (i \frac{\partial y_1}{\partial j} - j \frac{\partial y_1}{\partial i}) \frac{\partial y_1}{\partial i}$, $D = \sum \frac{\partial y_1}{\partial j}^2$, $E = \sum (i \frac{\partial y_1}{\partial j} - j \frac{\partial y_1}{\partial i}) \frac{\partial y_1}{\partial j}$, $F = \sum (i \frac{\partial y_1}{\partial j} - j \frac{\partial y_1}{\partial i})^2$. After the motion estimation stage in SURETEXT, outlier frames corresponding to incorrect motion estimates are removed (see Section 14.4.3). This allows the warping and bilinear interpolation (by a factor of 4) of the remaining N LR images to obtain an initial SR image S_1 as:

$$
S_1 = \mathcal{I} \left(\sum_{k=1}^{N} W_{\mathbf{m}_k} y_k \right) \tag{14.12}
$$

where $W_{\mathbf{m}_k}$ is the warp matrix for each LR frame y_k using motion estimation parameter set $\mathbf{m}_k$ and $\mathcal{I}$ is the interpolation function.

14.4.2 Unsharp Masking Using the Teager Filter

SURETEXT attempts to recover the high frequencies in the LR images such that the relevant high frequencies such as character/background borders can be highlighted but impulsive perturbations cannot. Non-linear quadratic unsharp masking filters can satisfy these requirements. For example, the 2D Teager filter, which is a class of quadratic Volterra filters [31], can be used to perform mean-weighted high-pass filtering with relatively few operations. Using the set of N corresponding original frames, Teager filtering is performed to obtain $y_k^\tau, (k = 1, ..., N)$ as the set of filtered images. For example, for any image y:

$$
y^\tau(i,j) = 3y^2(i,j) - \frac{1}{2} y(i+1, j+1) y(i-1, j-1)
$$

$$
- \frac{1}{2} y(i+1, j-1) y(i-1, j+1) - y(i+1, j) y(i-1, j)
$$

$$
- y(i, j+1) y(i, j-1) \tag{14.13}
$$

This filter enables us to highlight character edges and suppress noise. The shape of the Teager filter is shown in Figure 14.10 along with an example image and its Teager filtered output. Next, the frames can be warped using the same corresponding motion parameters $\mathbf{m}_k$ to reconstruct a secondary SR image S_τ:

$$
S_\tau = \mathcal{I} \left(\sum_{k=1}^{N} W_{\mathbf{m}_k} y_k^\tau \right) \tag{14.14}
$$

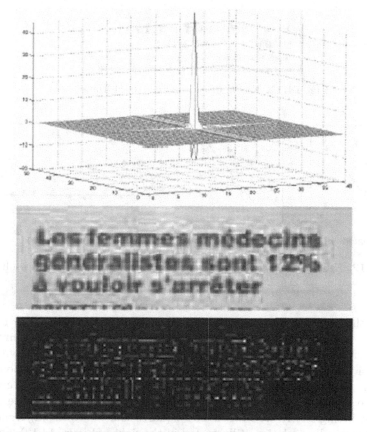

Fig. 14.10. Left: Visualization of the 2D Teager filter, right top: initial LR image, right bottom: Teager-filtered output.

This is then normalized to provide:

$$S_2(i,j) = \frac{S_\tau(i,j) - min(S_\tau)}{max(S_\tau) - min(S_\tau)} \qquad (14.15)$$

Also see the lower row in Figure 14.9. The final SR output image S is then:

$$S = med(S_1 + S_2) \qquad (14.16)$$

where *med* is median denoizing applied after fusion of the motion corrected representation with the motion-corrected high-frequency content.

14.4.3 Outlier Frame Removal

During motion estimation between frames errors occur if a text line is incorrectly registered with a neighbouring one. A frame corresponding to incorrectly estimated parameters in $\mathbf{m}_k$ should therefore be dropped

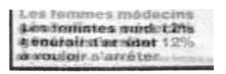

Fig. 14.11. Fusion of two misregistered frames.

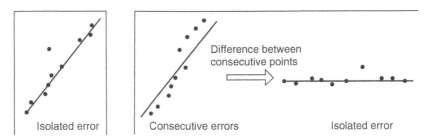

Fig. 14.12. Left: an isolated Δj_k error, right: consecutive Δj_k errors result in wrong estimation, so Δj_k *differences* must be examined.

from further analysis. In this set of experiments, it was found that Δi_k or θ_k rarely caused any errors, whereas misregistrations frequently occurred on the vertical translations Δj_k leading to results such as that shown in Figure 14.11. The left example in Figure 14.12 shows a plot of Δj_k points in which an outlier value can be rejected after linear regression. However, there may be consecutive sets of outlier frames; hence outliers can be detected by fitting a RANSAC-based least squares solution to the *differences* between vertical translations (illustrated in the right of Figure 14.12). Outlier frame rejection not only reduces the number of frames processed, but most importantly removes the need to apply regularization techniques during or after the reconstruction process. Note, this can easily be performed in SURETEXT on all parameters in $\mathbf{m}_k$.

14.4.4 Median Denoizing

In Figure 14.13 a zoomed view of a text document is presented to emphasize the importance and effect of (a) Teager filtering and (b) the median denoizing stages. The second image shows a pure interpolation of the original frame. The third shows the interpolation result of all the frames in the sequence and hence is the result of $med(S_1)$ only. The fourth image is the result of $(S_1 + S_2)$ illustrating significant improvement when the Teager processing pipeline shown in Figure 14.9 is employed. Median denoizing becomes necessary as the reconstruction result $(S_1 + S_2)$ alone is not smooth enough with errors arising from all the earlier stages of motion registration, warping and interpolation. The resulting artefacts are objectionable to the human eye and would affect OCR. A 3×3 neighbourhood median filter

Fig. 14.13. From left to right: original LR frame, bilinear interpolation applied on one LR frame, SR output without using Teager-filtered frames (S_1), SURE-TEXT without the denoizing stage ($S_1 + S_2$) and the complete SURETEXT method.

Fig. 14.14. First row: left: classical approach ($med(S_1)$), right: Teager-filtered frames after median fusion with an interpolated original frame. Second row: the result from SURETEXT.

was applied in all text images in this work. The last image in Figure 14.13 shows the final result obtained from (14.16).

14.4.5 Experiments and Results

The impact of Teager filtering can be further emphasized as follows. The top-left image in Figure 14.14 shows the results of a classical MISO approach (the same as just the top row of the schema in Figure 14.9, i.e. $med(S_1)$ only). In comparison, the top-right image shows Teager filtering of a set of LR frames fused together and then combined with an interpolated original frame, similar to the edge enhancement concept suggested in [16]. The bottom image shows the result of SURETEXT, which exhibits more sharpness and readability.

In Figure 14.15 the result of SURETEXT is compared to the method in Li and Doermann [11] in which a simple translational model was used for text enhancement. Bearing in mind that [11]'s method was developed for text primarily moving in vertical and horizontal directions, this comparison nevertheless shows that the use of an affine model is minimally necessary in the type of applications referred to in this chapter. The registration errors in the left image of Figure 14.15 make it very difficult for interpretation by OCR analysis.

Figures 14.16 and 14.17 present more text images with and without the Teager stage to highlight the usefulness of this filter. In the zoomed examples in Figure 14.17, while OCR of all the SR images will recognize the characters in both methods, note the difference in quality however after Otsu binarization where the SURETEXT produces a much sharper and better defined set of characters with Teager filtering than without.

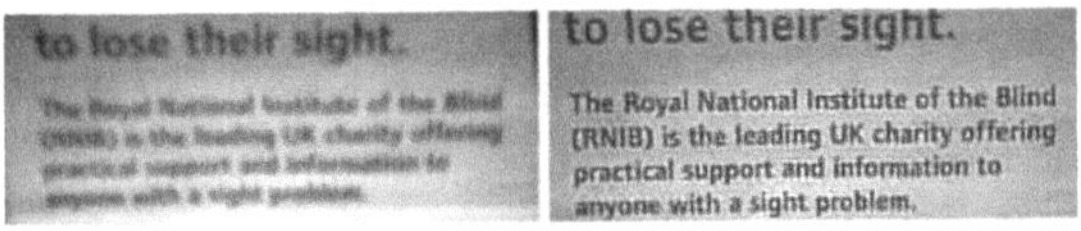

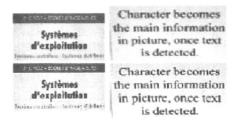

Fig. 14.15. Left: SR image obtained with the algorithm in [11], right: our method.

Fig. 14.16. SR using the classical approach (top) and the proposed method (bottom).

Fig. 14.17. Two zoomed in SR results comparing the classical approach and the proposed method and their binarized images.

Table 14.1. Comparative OCR accuracy rates

Method	1	2	3	4	5	6	7	Avg.
C	48.1%	75.2%	95.1%	66.6%	75.0%	72.7%	72.5%	72.1%
L	78.8%	94.3%	100.0%	83.3%	79.5%	81.8%	88.8%	86.7%
S	78.8%	92.9%	100.0%	91.6%	86.4%	90.9%	93.8%	90.6%

The Teager filter is very good as a quadratic, unsharp masking filter. Other similar filters such as the rational filter of Ramponi [32] may also be capable of achieving similar results.

Finally, percentage recognition rates based on several natural scene text video sequences are shown in Table 14.1 for comparison of the classical approach in general super-resolution (C), a framework the same as SURETEXT but with a standard Laplacian unsharp masking filter (L) and SURETEXT, as proposed here, with the Teager filter (S). The results demonstrate much better performance by SURETEXT at 90.6% accuracy on average, computed on the number of correctly recognized characters, showing unsharp masking to be clearly an important additional step to generating an SR image while also being less sensitive to noise than a standard unsharp masking filter such as the Laplacian.

14.5 Conclusions

Of course in any introductory discourse most concepts can only be presented within limited depth. This introduction to super-resolution text is no exception. (For further details on the possible methods and the novel works in this area so far, the reader is referred to the rich review and investigative papers provided in the References section of this chapter). The SURETEXT method in the case study is typical of a general approach to SR text in which frame sequences must at first be adequately registered and subsequently enhanced to increase the rate of character recognition. Methods such as SURETEXT must not be computationally expensive to fit into PDA and mobile-phone devices; however such limitations are expected to be overcome as advances in hardware and software continue to surpass expectations.

Acknowledgment

The first author was partly funded by Ministére de la Region wallonne in Belgium and by a mobility grant from FNRS to work at the University of Bristol.

References

1. Park, S.C., Park, M.K., and Moon, G.K. (2003). Super-resolution image reconstruction: a technical overview. *IEEE Signal Processing Magazine, 3,* pp. 21–36.
2. Zandifar, A., Duraiswami, R., Chahine, A., and Davis, L.S. (2002). A video-based interface to textual information for the visually impaired. *Proceedings of ICMI,* pp. 325–330.
3. Donaldson, K. and Myers, G.K. (2005). Bayesian super-resolution of text in video with a text-specific bimodal prior. *Int. J. Document Analysis and Recognition.* Vol. 7, No. 2–3, pp. 159–167.
4. Shimizu, M., Yano, T., and Okutomi, M. (2004). Super-resolution under image deformation. *IEEE Proceedings of the International Conference on Pattern Recognition,* pp. 586–589.
5. Liang, J., Doermann, D., and Li, H. (2005). Camera-based analysis of text and documents: a survey. *Int. J. Document Analysis and Recognition.* Vol. 7, No. 2–3, pp. 84–104.
6. Clark, P. and Mirmehdi, M. (2002). Recognising text in real scenes. *International Journal of Document Analysis and Recognition, 4,* pp. 243–257.
7. Mirmehdi, M., Clark, P., and Lam, J. (2003). A non-contact method of capturing low-resolution text for OCR. *Pattern Analysis and Applications, 1,* pp. 12–22.
8. Myers, G.K., Bolles, R.C., Luong, Q.-T., Herson, J.A., and Aradhye, H.B. (2005). Rectification and recognition of text in 3-D scenes. *Int. J. Document Analysis and Recognition.* Vol. 7, No. 2–3, pp. 147–158.

9. Farsiu, S., Robinson, D., Elad, M., and Milanfar, P. (2004). Advances and challenges in super-resolution. *International Journal of Imaging Systems and Technology, 2*, pp. 47–57.
10. Kuglin, C. and Hines, D. (1975). The phase correlation image alignment method. *Proceedings of International Conference Cybernetics Society,* 163–165.
11. Li, H. and Doermann, D. (1999). Text enhancement in digital video using multiple frame integration. *Proceedings of the ACM International Conference on Multimedia,* pp. 19–22.
12. Fletcher, L. and Zelinsky, A. (2004). Super-resolving signs for classification. *Proceedings of Australasian Conference on Robotics and Automation,Australia.*
13. Capel, D.P. (2001). Image mosaicing and super-resolution. PhD thesis.
14. Harris, C.J. and Stephens, M. (1988). A combined corner and edge detector. *Proceedings of the Fourth Alvey Vision Conference, UK,* pp. 147–151.
15. Fischler, M. and Bolles, R. (1981). Random sample consensus: a paradigm for model fitting applications to image analysis and automated cartography. *Communications of ACM,* pp. 381–395.
16. Chiang, M.-C. and Boult, T.E. (1997). Local blur estimation and super-resolution. *Proceedings of IEEE Computer Vision and Pattern Recognition,* pp. 821–826.
17. Tsai, R.Y. and Huang, T.S. (1984). Multiple frame image restoration and registration. *Advances in Computer Vision and Image Processing,* pp. 317–339.
18. Tekalp, A. (1995). *Digital Video Processing.* Englewood Cliffs, NJ: Prentice-Hall.
19. Kim, S., Bose, N., and Valenzuela, H. (1990). Recursive reconstruction of high resolution image from noisy undersampled multiframes. *IEEE Transactions on Acoustics, Speech and Signal Processing, 6,* pp. 1013–1027.
20. Irani, M. and Peleg, S. (1991). Improving resolution by image registration. *CVGIP: Graphical Models and Image Processing,* pp. 231–239.
21. Capel, D. and Zisserman, A. (2000). Super-resolution enhancement of text image sequences. *Proceedings of ICPR,* pp. 1600–1605.
22. Stark, H. and Oskoui, P. (1989). High resolution image recovery from image-plane arrays, using convex projections. *Journal of Optical Society of America,* pp. 1715–1726.
23. Patti, A.J., Sezan, M.I., and Tekalp, A.M. (1997). Superresolution video reconstruction with arbitrary sampling lattices and non-zero aperture time. *IEEE Transactions on Image Processing, 8,* pp. 1064–1076.
24. Elad, M. and Feuer, A. (1997). Restoration of a single superresolution image from several blurred, noisy, and undersampled measured images. *IEEE Transactions on Image Processing, 12,* pp. 1646–1658.
25. Kilmer, M.E and O'Leary, D.P. (2001). Choosing reguralization parameters in iterative methods for Iill-posed problems. *SIAM Journal on Matrix Analysis Applications, 4,* 1204–1221.
26. Farsiu, S., Robinson, M.D., Elad, M., and Milanfar, P. (2004). Fast and robust multiframe super-resolution. *IEEE Transactions on Image Processing, 10,* pp. 1327–1344.
27. Rav-Acha, A. and Peleg, S. (2005). Two motion-blurred images are better than one. *Pattern Recognition Letters,* pp. 311–317.

28. Chan, T.F. and Wong, C.K. (1998). Total variation blind deconvolution. *IEEE Transactions on Image Processing, 3*, pp. 370–375.
29. Zhao, W., Sawhney, H., Hansen, M., and Samarasekera, S. (2002). Super-fusion: a super-resolution method based on fusion. *Proceedings of ICPR*, pp. 269–272.
30. Keren, D., Peleg, S., and Brada, R. (1988). Image sequence enhancement using sub-pixel displacements. *Proceedings on CVPR*, pp. 742–746.
31. Mitra, S.K. and Sicuranza, G.L. (2001). *Nonlinear Image Processing*. New York: Academic Press.
32. Ramponi, G. (1996). The rational filter for image smoothing. *IEEE Signal Processing Letters, 3*, pp. 63–65.

15

Meta-Data Extraction from Bibliographic Documents for the Digital Library

A. Belaïd and D. Besagni

15.1 Introduction

The digital library (DL) [19] has become an increasingly common tool for everyone, a trend accentuated by the success of the Web and the easy access to every kind of information. Among the most important DL projects [17], we can mention "Project Gutenberg", the oldest producer of free electronic books [21], the "Million Book Project" [22], and more recently Google announced its intention to digitize the book collections from several famous universities (Michigan, Harvard, Stanford, Oxford) and from the New York Public Library [20].

The DL provides information located in one specific place to anyone, anywhere in the world, as long as the information can be retrieved. Contrary to the Web at large, the DL offers a more organized access to selected information that is often validated, filtered and structured. With this trend, documents not registered in electronic form will risk becoming invisible. It is the Google effect: "if it isn't in Google then it doesn't exist!". This electronic registration is not sufficient enough to define a DL: the document itself must be in electronic form, which does not mean it is machine readable.

A good DL is not only a good document retrieval system but the content must be at the same time accessible as well by the machines than by the users responding to their multiple needs. There are different aspects revealing the DL qualities relative to the:

(a) *Content:* The more structured a document is, the more useful it is. Added to this, the quality of the meta-data accompanying the document is essential.
(b) *Organization:* The more standardized a format is, the more usable and durable the document is.

(c) *Updating and patrimony valorization:* The main problem is not in the feeding of new digital document but in importing digital documents from other DLs, or in adding patrimonial non-electronic documents.

(d) *Use:* The DL function does not stop with the document consultation, but the more options the better.

Since all the documents are not specifically generated to enter a DL, we need cost-effective tools such as OCR, retro-conversion, hypertextualization and meta-data extraction techniques. There again the content defines the approach. Depending on the expected quality, these techniques will need more (or less) adaptation and depth.

At the DL level, independent of the origin of the document (electronic or not), it is obvious that the most important elements in terms of organization and structure are the meta-data and the hyperlinks. Although the hyperlinks, made popular by the Web, are the "icing on the cake" because they improve the navigation functionalities, the meta-data are more basic, even indispensable, because they include for example the catalogue.

Although some problems remain [9], we have now a generation of OCRs capable of extracting the content with a good quality close to 100%, the research tends towards systems dedicated to structure extraction. This structure, generally of an editorial or logical nature, obviously constitutes a first step towards meta-data generation.

As the documents in general are described in a DL by at least their descriptive meta-data, a straightforward use of a DL can be done by correspondence between the terms outlined in bibliographic documents (like bibliographic references, citations, cards, tables of contents, etc.) and the DL meta-data. Depending on the structure finesse of documents in DL and the precision of the outlined terms (which in our case are roughly recognized by OCR) the meta-data recognition can be considered as a "mapping problem" between the real meta-data and the recognized terms. Proper mapping of the bibliographic reference with its actual content within a DL is a challenging task of research [3].

15.2 The Users' Needs

Considering the DL as a very structured document repository that is well organized and continuously updated, we can envisage its use for some important requests similar to which they are done on the Web. But contrary to the Web, the use of bibliographical data may offer more possibilities in the use of common DL services such as:

- *Information retrieval:* This is related to a simple DL consulting. The major need of DL is to retrieve the actual document from DL based on approximated bibliographic terms (roughly recognized by OCR or provided by the user). This corresponds to about 70% of the real DL activities where the users (such as researchers, students, etc.) are always requesting the DLs to get actual content from secondary documents (bibliographic documents). Here the impact of a misrecognition is low since the search is limited to document consulting.

- *Technological watch:* The goal of technology watch is to exploit all available information that can give indicators about the environment of any firm or organization. Among the information that are at hand, bibliographic references are an interesting source of data for such a study. The contribution of bibliographic references is of course immediate if they are in electronic and structured form, bringing out rapidly the elements directly exploitable with the techniques of bibliometric analysis. But often, this bibliographic information is not available in electronic form, thus turning the analysis of information into a time-consuming task. Then comes the problem of retro-converting the information from documents on various media that is a research field in itself. Here, we make the hypothesis that the more the information is repeated by different authors, the more it is important. The search of importance can be initiated by the analysis of local DL. Here, the impact of a misrecognition is average since we will pass beside significant novelties that can momentarily affect the development of the company. This minor incidence can be hurdled by frequently repeating the watch procedure.

- *Research piloting and evaluation:* It indicates the importance of evaluation principles as well as issues related to the preparation. The more spread approaches have privileged technical parameters leading to the document fabrication and diffusion. The foundation of the Institute for Scientific Information (ISI) in the 1960s at Philadelphia (USA) by Eugene Garfield was instrumental in turning the citation into a unit of measure. At first, used only as a tool for information retrieval, the citation has become an important criterion because it allows distinguishing among different publications from those that received the approbation of the scientific community. By the same token, the citation is also used to appraise scientific journals especially with the impact factor calculated as the average number of citations a paper receives over a period of 2 years. Here, the impact of a misrecognition may be high, since we can affect the prestige of an individual or an institution by misrepresenting their scientific output.

According to the needs, documents should be structured in such a way that they will be available from a DL in an easy manner.

15.3 Bibliographic Elements as Descriptive Meta-Data

For a long time, librarians redacted bibliographical records or indexes to describe the available documents. To refer to the computer lingo, these

Table 15.1. Meta-data typology

Type	Purposes	Examples	Implementations
Descriptive or intellectual	Describe and identify information objects and resources	– Unique identifier (URL, access number, ISBN) – Physical attributes (media, size, etc.) – Bibliographical attributes (title, authors, language, keywords, etc.)	– PURL, MARC – Dublin Core – Controlled vocabularies as thesaurus
Structural	– Facilitate navigation and display of information objects – Give data on the internal structure of the information objects as page, section, chapter, index and ToC – Describe the relationships between materials (e.g. picture B is inserted in manuscript A) – Link connected files and scripts (e.g. file A is the JPEG image of archive file B)	Structuring tags	– SGML – XML – Encoded Archival Description (EAD) – MOA2, Structural Meta-data Elements Electronic Binding (Ebind)
Administrative	– Facilitate the management and treatment of electronic collections – Include technical data on creation and quality control – Include right management, access control and required use conditions	Technical data as scanner type and model, resolution, bit size, colorimetric space, file format, compression, owner, copyright date, use limitations, licence information, conservation consigns, etc.	MOA2, Administrative Meta-data Elements National Library of Australia, Preservation Meta-data for Digital Collections CEDARS

records constitute data that serve to describe other data (e.g. book contents): they are called *meta-data*. We can encode some essential information about the documents in a clear fashion: title, author, date of publication, keywords, etc. Table 15.1 lists the several categories of meta-data used in DL as reported in [23].

As the descriptive meta-data are mandatory, their constitution is necessary for all types of documents.

□   For raster image, it is mostly done manually even if some information (e.g. bibliographical record) can be imported from a specific database.

□   For simple text (ASCII, Unicode), some elements (e.g. author, page, etc.) can sometimes be deduced by analysing the text layout. For example, a centred nominal sentence in the beginning of the text can be interpreted as a title; a short text justified on the left and preceded by a number can be considered as a section title, under condition that this style is somewhat redundant in the text. On the other hand, as long as we have a text, we can apply automatic indexing techniques to extract keywords.

□   For structured text (e.g. all the structural elements are tagged), all the descriptive meta-data are directly extractable. If the structure is well identified for the text class, then the automatic DIA techniques can be applied to mark-up this structure.

Document image analysis (DIA) can also be employed in the structural meta-data extraction. For the internal structure, its contribution is similar to the one used for descriptive meta-data. For the relationship between documents, DIA techniques can be used in some cases to find such links. For example, different entries of a table of content (ToC) can be related to each separate document. In the case of citations in a scholarly work, a link can be generated at first between the body of the text and the bibliography section, as well as a second link between the citing document and the cited document.

15.4 Meta-Data Extraction in Bibliographic Documents

Here, the structure granularity is relatively fine, reduced to some words and symbols. The punctuation plays an important role in its structure, which is a source of problem if the recognition process is not efficient enough. Figure 15.1 shows three different kinds of bibliographic documents. We can notice the poverty of the text and the fact that the punctuation and the typographic style can be used as syntactic clues to separate the different fields.

Coming back to the classical DIA schema, the system steps will be oriented more towards word detection than text recognition. This phenomenon will be explained in the following.

15.5 General Overview of the Work

Fig. 15.2 illustrates the general overview of the mapping procedure. This schema is composed of three main elements (1) the object document (e.g.

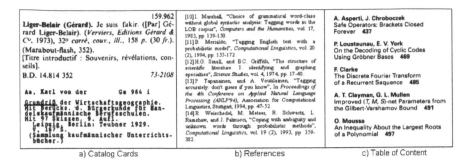

a) Catalog Cards   b) References   c) Table of Content

Fig. 15.1. Examples of bibliographic elements.

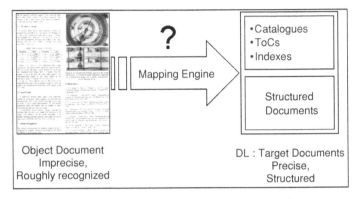

Fig. 15.2. Overview of the mapping procedure.

document containing the keywords for searching, such as bibliographic references), (2) the search engine and (3) the target document (e.g. the documents to be retrieved from the DL) described below. This schema poses the real question for which the paper will give some answers: "how to make the link between the extracted terms in secondary documents and the corresponding documents in a DL which have been differently and soundly structured?"

- *Object document:* contains some related information to the target document to retrieve the document from the DL properly. Considering the secondary documents, this information may contain author names, title, conference name, editor, etc. or other information regarding the date of publication, etc.
- *Target document:* corresponds to the DL and contains at the same time illustrative documents like catalogues, ToCs and indexes, and structured documents.
- *Mapping Engine:* is a query interpreter that allows us to map the terms with document meta-data and to find the closer document answering the query. The result accuracy is a strong tributary of the query precision and by consequence of the terms recognition accuracy.

In the following, we try to instantiate this schema relative to the three needs.

15.6 Bibliographic Element Recognition for Library Management

Here we favour the meta-data like those proposed by Dublin Core (author name, date, conference title, editor, etc.) because we want to satisfy some easy bibliometric needs. The question often asked is: "I structure my document and I'd like that my colleague will retrieve it very quickly". This is also the attitude of some librarians offering a helpful tool for scientists to access very quickly their collections by giving some keywords.

15.6.1 Catalogue Retro-Conversion

Several library programmes that have been launched in the 1990s in Europe placed emphasis on the enhancement and harmonization of machine-readable bibliographies and catalogues in Europe, thus contributing to the efficiency of libraries and improving resource sharing between them. Among the projects proposed, FACIT and MORE [18] were requested to determine the feasibility of converting older card catalogues into modern OPAC[1] using scanning, OCR, and automatic formatting into a bibliographic format, such as UNIMARC.[2]

Object Document

The object document corresponds to the data as produced by OCR and arranged in XML. Character extraction is based on the use of commercially available OCR packages in the lower or middle price range. A combination procedure is applied on three OCRs looking for a substantial improvement of individual performances which are minimal on this kind of material. We have used Myers's algorithm, based on an optimal dynamic programming matching [16]. The result is represented in XML where elements correspond to the text words and attributes are related to their topographical and lexical properties.

Target Document

The target document is related to the UNIMARC format, which is a generalization of MARC (acronym for Machine Readable Catalogue or Cataloguing). Initially, UNIMARC was used for the exchange of records

---

[1] On line Public Access Catalogue.
[2] Universal Machine-Readable Cataloguing.

on magnetic tape, but has since been adapted for use in a variety of exchange and processing environments. The fields, which is identified by three-character numeric tags, are arranged in functional blocks. These blocks organize the data according to their function in a traditional catalogue record. In the table below, fields 0–1 hold the coded data, while fields 2–8 contain the bibliographic data:

Block	Example
0 – Identification block	010 International Standard Book Number
1 – Coded information block	101 Language of the work
2 – Descriptive information block	205 Edition statement
3 – Notes block	336 Type of computer file note
4 – Linking entry block	452 Edition in a different medium
5 – Related title block	516 Spine title
6 – Subject analysis block	676 Dewey Decimal Classification
7 – Intellectual responsibility block	700 Personal name – primary intellectual responsibility
8 – International use block	801 Originating source
9 – Reserved for local use	

In addition to the 9 block, any other tag containing a 9 is available for local implementation. The fields defined by UNIMARC provide for different kinds and levels of information. This can be shown by looking at a typical record in the UNIMARC format. Figure 15.3 illustrates the UNIMARC conversion on one example.

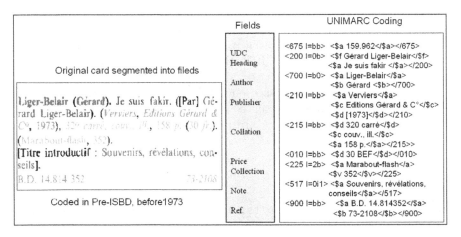

Fig. 15.3. Example of bibliographic card (left-hand side) and its UNIMARC representation (right-hand side).

The target document is represented by a model, which is formally described by a context-free grammar. The format of a production rule is as follows:

TERM ::=	CONSTRUCTOR SUBORDINATE_OBJECTS[QUALIFIER]|
	CONSTANT | TERMINAL
CONSTRUCTOR ::=	TD-SEQ | LR-SEQ | SEQ | AGGREGATE | CHOICE | IMPORT

The constructor describes the element arrangement among sequence (SEQ) (TD for top-down, LR for left–right) and AGGREGATE. The constructor "IMPORT" is used to inherit for the term some or the total description of another existent and similar term. As in XML DTDs, quantifiers such as "optional" (?), "repetitive" (+) or "optional–repetitive" (*) are used to specify the terms' occurrences. Furthermore, because of the weakness of the physical structure and the multitude of choices represented in the model, some attributes, given by the library, are added to the previous description. These attributes are associated to each rule in the following format. The following example describes the term "TITLE" as a logical sequence of two objects: PROPER-TITLE and REST-OF-TITLE where the style is not italic (may be bold or standard), which is located at the beginning of the line (BEGLINE) and whose separator is a comma.

TITLE ::=	SEQ PROPER-TITLE REST-OF-TITLE
STYLE	-ITALIC
POSITION	BEGLINE
SEP	COMMA

In the following table, the optional object PARTICULE (whose weight is A) is more important than LCAP (whose weight is G). This specification is logical since an optional object normally helps in reinforcing the possible presence of a term more than an object that is always present.

ZPB ::=	SEQ LCAP RP PARTICULE?
WEIGHT	PARTICULE A LCAP G

In the following, the production rule describes a choice between two terms neither of which should contain any of the strings in the lexicon Abn (expressed by the attribute Clex). There are two actions that will be activated during the rule analysis. The first one indicates verifying before the rule analysis that the search zone does not contain the string "fr.". In the event of the hypothesis being verified, the second function is executed to create a UNIMARC tag before restituting the result in the required format.

FIP ::=	CHO FIP1 IPA
CLEX	-ABN
ACTION	+VERIFYSTRINGINFIELD(FR.,FALSE) RESTITUTE(215,BB)

Research Engine

The research engine corresponds to a syntactic analyser whose role is to structure the input data according to the model description. The structure recognition is preceded by Index recognition (e.g. author names or title terms existing at the end of the catalogue). Then, structural analysis operates by hypothesis verification. Weights associated to the attributes contribute to the hypothesis ranking and strategy ordering during the analysis. The UNIMARC code is generated thanks to some special remedial functions, prepared by the librarians and establishing the different translation rules. These functions, associated with some terms in the model, try to establish the correspondence between the real structure and the recognized structure. The objective of this approach is to introduce qualitative "reasoning" as a function of the recognition evaluation. This evaluation allows (1) the reduction of errors and ambiguities due to faulty data OCR errors, data not fitting the model specification, etc.), (2) taking into account what is important to recognize, the qualitative evaluation of the obtained solutions and (3) the isolation and separation of doubtful areas (Figure 15.4).

ToC Recognition for Electronic Consulting of Scientific Papers

Tables of Content (ToC) are the most synthetic meta-data and most introductory with the contents. They provide rapid indicators on the main document components. Their automatic identification may help to a rapid document organization and consulting in digital library.

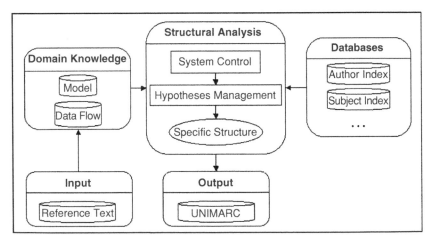

Fig. 15.4. System overview of card recognition.

Object Document

A textual ToC is a document composed of one header, a list of sections, article references and footnotes (see Figure 15.1). An article reference is made of an article title, a list of authors and a page number, written in one, two or three separate columns. Article references may have high or low complicated structure, but must be separated from each other. Sections corresponding to session names are given to a group of papers. Although the structure is straightforward, some peculiarities can introduce ambiguities during recognition. For example (1) the titles can contain author names, (2) the author names can be confused with common nouns, (3) the fields can follow each other and their separation is done by a random punctuation and (4) the successive articles can follow without a real distinctive sign, only the context or the semantics can help.

An automatic processing of ToC needs to recognize the content and to structure it in order to recover the article fields. For content recognition, OCRs are often used and an XML file is always generated highlighting the terms and their typographical and lexical attributes.

Document Target

The document target is usually very simple, corresponding to gathering of two or three fields. The difficulty comes from matching authors' names when their syntax can change from one document to another. For example, the first name can be given in full, the middle initial or a hyphen can be missing.

Mapping Engine

The mapping engine corresponds to two operations: ToC recognition and article searching in the database from the fields recognized in the ToC.
Few ToC recognizers have been proposed in the literature. On the one hand, Takasu et al. [4, 5] proposed a system named CyberMagazine, based on image segmentation into blocks and syntactic analysis of their contents. The article recognition combines the use of decision tree classification and a syntactic analysis using a matrix grammar. On the other hand, Story and O'Gorman [8,13] proposed a method that combines OCR techniques and image processing.

We proposed a method based on text coding that in turn is based on Part of Speech tagging (PoS) [2]. The idea of this method, employed in language processing and text indexing, is to reassemble nouns in nominal syntagmas (syntactic element) representing the same information (see Figure 15.5). The nouns are given by a specific morphological tagging. This method can be applied in ToC recognition for article field identification by reassembling in the same syntagma "Title" or "Author",

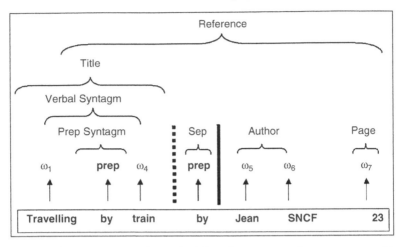

Fig. 15.5. Syntagm extraction principle, where ω_1: words, prep: proposition.

words having similar tags. The process of tagging consists of three stages: tokenization, morphological analysis, and syntactical grouping and disambiguation. The tokenizer isolates each textual term and separates numerical chains from alphabetic terms. The morphological analyser contains a transducer lexicon. It produces all the legitimate tags for words that appear in the lexicon. If a word is not in the lexicon, a guesser is consulted. The guesser employs another finite-state transducer that examines the context and decides to assign the token to "Title" or to "Author" depending on prefixes, inflectional information and productive endings that it finds.

As an application of ToC recognition system, to the best of our knowledge, Calliope [2] is the most straightforward application used for article consulting. Calliope allows the management of distributed scientific documentary resources (related to computer science and applied mathematics) through Internet, composed of papers or electronic documents circulating among a community of researchers.

Calliope operating principles include (1) consultation via navigation of a list of scientific journals (about 650 titles) as well as their corresponding tables of contents, (2) consultation of new tables of contents, further to a weekly updating of the server, (3) a personalized subscription by electronic mail, to electronic tables of contents of selected journals; the user will thereby receive the contents of the latest published issue. At any time, the user is able to consult his list of subscriptions, cancel some or other or subscribe to new journals and (4) the search by word (title of article or journal, or author's name).

As illustrated in Figure 15.6, Calliope is based on Rank Xerox XDOD (Xerox Document On Demand) software for scanning, and DocuWEB, the

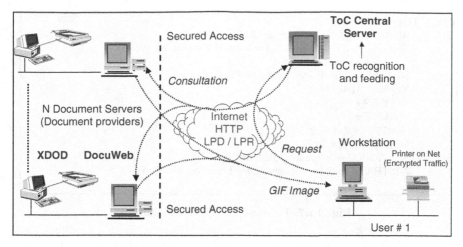

Fig. 15.6. The scientific paper server: Calliope.

XDOD WEB server, for display and printing of articles. The images of scanned documents are stored and managed on several servers of documents, not necessarily near the scanning sites. The electronic tables of contents supplied by OCR-DIA are reformatted in HTML before being integrated into the Calliope WEB server.

15.7 Bibliographic Reference Structure in Technological Watch

The technological watch based on bibliographic references consists in analysing the citations at the end of scientific papers or on the Web and in deducing interesting information in terms of new topics, famous authors and good conferences. The investigation is more oriented towards the search of stability of selected elements alone and always within the same context, than to the exhaustive recognition of all the reference. The syntactic methods, as shown before, are not adapted. Parmentier [7] proposed an AI-based approach for bibliographic term extractions. The approach is based on a conceptual model.

15.7.1 Object Document

Bibliographic references correspond to the citations at the end of scientific papers. They are extracted from existing databases or searched on the Web. The basic format can be the one used in BibTeX, but the real structure can change according to the writer and the editor.

The model is determined from a reference database in BibTeX format (see Figure 15.7) and from the printed file of this database, using LaTeX.

```
@ARTICLE { joseph92a,
        AUTHOR = { S.  H.  Joseph and T.  P.  Pridmore } ,
        TITLE = { Knowledge-Directed Interpretation of Mechanical
            Engineering Drawings} ,
        JOURNAL = { IEEE Transaction on PAMT } ,
        YEAR = { 1992 } ,
        NUMBER = { 9 } ,
        VOLUME = { 14 } ,
         PAGES = { 211 - - 222 } ,
        MONTH = { september } ,
        KEYWORDS = {segmentation, forms } ,
        ABSTRACT = {The approach is based on item extraction }
}
```

Fig. 15.7. Reference in BibTeX format.

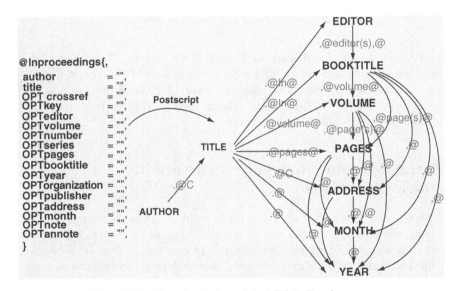

Fig. 15.8. The physical model of BibTeX references.

In order to have at our disposal all the possible optional fields, we generate automatically an artificial base using a BibTeX reference structure where field contents are replaced by field names. This reference has been used for the model construction. Each reference is then formatted in Postscript by BibTeX/LaTeX and converted into XML. Then, all that is needed is to search for the field contents in order to locate them and deduce the separators. Fig. 15.8 represents the result of the application of LaTeX in plain printing style on the artificial reference of Fig. 15.7. It can be noticed that some fields are missed such as "editor" and "number".

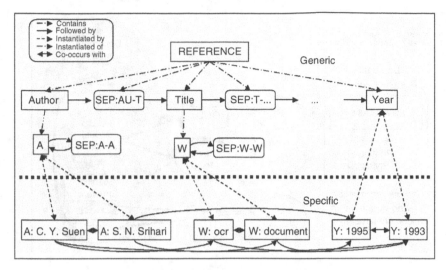

Fig. 15.9. The concept model.

15.7.2 Target Document

We used a concept network in order to represent the generic structure. The concept network is composed of nodes and links. Nodes are divided into two categories: generic, corresponding to the structure components; and specific, dealing with examples contained in the database. The links represent the conceptual proximity of the nodes (e.g. author and co-authors in the AUTHOR field, VOLUME and NUMBER, words in the TITLE, etc.). Fig. 15.9 gives a global view of an example of such concept network.

15.7.3 Retrieval Engine

As the model is more conceptual than syntactic, translating a less rigorous manner of structure produced by humans, the analysis approach is based on the extraction and the validation of terms. Fields are validated by studying the coherence of each term with its neighbours in the same field and with terms in the other fields. The system architecture is drawn from the work of Hofstadter and Mitchell [6, 14] on emergent systems. In this system, knowledge is represented by a slip net, and evolves dynamically during the treatment in order to adapt the architecture to the given problem. The evolution is managed by a mechanism of propagation of activation pointing out the more pertinent concepts. These concepts (called "emerged") lead to the execution of specific agents.

Belaïd and David showed in [1] how information retrieval techniques can be used at the same time to enhance the recognition process and to speed up the document retrieval. Fig. 15.10 illustrates this principle. From the document structures, an object-oriented database (OOD) is generated.

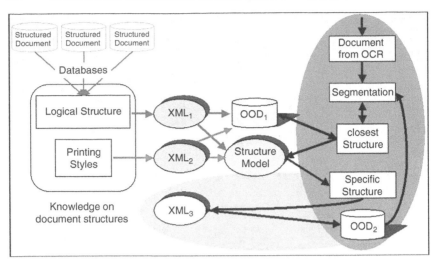

Fig. 15.10. IRS techniques for DIA and document retrieval. XML1,2 are the normalized structure obtained from the databases and XML3 corresponds to the specific structure. OOD2 is the intermediate database for recognition.

OOD allows the implementation of the concept of class from which object instances can be created. The OOD query method developed is what we call *classification* with *constraints*. The method used is by attaching a set of instructions to each marker. The end doc marker invokes the document instance method for the generation of inverse list for each attribute that can be used for request formulation and for calculus of indicators.

Given an attribute, the inverse list, for that attribute, gives the objects in which the given value is assigned to the attribute. He has adopted the approach that consists in transforming the logical and physical structures into their XML equivalents.

15.8 Citation Analysis in Research Piloting and Evaluation

15.8.1 Impact Factors

The measure of impact factors in bibliometrics is also operated on the bibliographic references present at the end of a scientific publication (article, conference, book, etc.) that refer to the work of an author cited in the body of the text. The difference between "citation" and "reference" is just a difference of perspective: for the citing author, it is a "reference" to the cited author; for the cited author, it is a "citation" by the citing author.

The Institute for Scientific and Technical Information (INIST) of the French National Center for Scientific Research (CNRS) has begun an experiment to digitize these bibliographic references especially because of the interest of citations in bibliometrics and/or scientometrics. In order to analyse the scientific production with objective indicators, the measurement of that production was soon reduced to either scientific (articles, conferences, reports, etc.) or technological (patents) publications. The first obvious indicator was the number of publications, but soon the citations were preferred because they have the advantage of representing an endorsement by the scientific community at large. That indicator gives a measure of the impact of a study, a laboratory or even a country in a particular scientific domain. Likewise, by analysing citations from journal to journal, their impact can be assessed. It is the impact factor that is defined and supplied by the *Journal of Citation Reports* (JCR) from ISI.

Another use for citations is the analysis of relationships within a scientific community by a co-occurrence analysis of those citations. The main method: co-citations analysis developed by Small [10] measures the likeliness of cited documents by the number of documents citing them together. A clustering of these co-citations allows identifying islands within the mainstream scientific literature that defines the research fronts. That co-citation analysis can also be used by authors instead of documents.

At the present time, all these citations are supplied by a single database which is the Science Citation Index (SCI) from ISI. Therefore, biases exist, especially:

- only journal articles are treated (neglecting conference proceedings, reports, doctoral dissertations, etc.);
- it strongly favours publications in English in general and USA in particular;
- some domains as physical sciences are better covered than others like engineering, and some domains are altogether neglected as humanities.

The interest of our work is to propose a method that allows INIST to fill part of these shortcomings. We are especially looking for:

- Adding links between citing and cited documents to the bibliographic records of INIST's own databases PASCAL and FRANCIS for the purpose of information retrieval.
- Supplying citations for scientific journals and domains not considered by ISI.

15.8.2 Methodology

Object Document

Contrary to what is described in Section 15.7, the bibliographic references used in this experiment come from actual articles from scientific (i.e. pharmaceutical) journals. After recognizing by OCR, all the references from the same article are in an XML file with each reference individualized. However, the different parts of those references (authors, title, journal, date, etc.) are not identified. The character set used in the data files is ISO Latin-1 (standard ISO 8859-1). The other alphabetic characters not belonging to that character set are represented as character entities as defined in the SGML/XML standards, i.e. "Ş" for the character "Ş".

The problems we encountered while trying to segment the bibliographical references are of several orders:

- □ *Problems due to the digitization:* non-recognized characters, badly recognized characters (e.g. the uppercase letter **D** that sometimes gives the uppercase letter **I** followed by a right parenthesis) or missing characters (mostly punctuation marks).
- □ *Problems due to the heterogeneity of the data:* the structure of a reference depends on the type of the cited document and on the origin of the citing article since the model of the citation depends on the journal where the article is published. Although on this last point, it must be said that all the journals do not enforce their own rules with the same rigour and that the form of the references may vary from one article to the other in the same issue of some journals;
- □ *Other problems:* one must add the typing errors, the omissions and sometime the presence of notes that have nothing to do with bibliographic references.

Target Document

For the time being, we try to identify the different fields of references from journal articles because they are more frequent (at least in the chosen domain) and are the usual subject of citation analysis. Although we use a bottom-up data-driven method, we have some generic model of the structure of a reference, e.g. when given, author names are at the beginning of the reference or the date of publication can only be in one of three positions: after the authors or the journal title or the page numbers.

Also helpful is the fact that an author will respect the form of a reference type within a given article. Therefore, not only can we check the validity of the segmentation, we can also create a model for each set of references to correct and validate the final result.

Mapping Engine

In the literature, we identified a work done at the NEC Research Institute as part of the CiteSeer system [15]. The Autonomous Citation Indexing (ACI) uses a top-down methodology applying heuristics to parse citations. This approach employs some invariants considering that the fields of a citation have relatively uniform syntax, position and composition. It uses trends in syntactic relationships between fields to predict where a desired field exists if at all.

Even though this method is reported to be accurate, its functioning is not described enough explicitly to measure its efficiency on OCR output.

Similar works have been done in the field of mathematics to link together retro-converted articles in specialized databases looking for known patterns of author names, invariants and journal titles from a predefined list [11, 12].

Conversely, we prefer not to do the retro-conversion of bibliographic references in a top-down way guided by a structure generic model. From one document to the other, the structure of the citations shows a great variability, too important to reuse the same model. So we propose a bottom-up data-driven methodology. It is based on locally studying the common structure of all the references written in the same bibliographic document and adapting accordingly the heuristic rules. The methodology of retro-conversion of bibliographic references is based on exploiting two essential particularities: regularity of the structure and redundancy in the same document.

The proposed approach is also based on part-of-speech tagging as used for ToCs. However, since the citations have a more complete structure than the ToC articles, the structure analysis is more investigated in this case. The different lists we use came from electronic resources from INIST like the Pascal database for author names, journal titles and country names and from electronic dictionaries for English and French words as well as prepositions.

That analysis is done by studying the regularity and the redundancy of specific elements of the text or by grouping some elements together (Figure 15.11). In the first case, we define qualitatively or quantitatively the chosen element, i.e. the date of publication, for each reference in function of its type but also in function of its position and of the characteristics of the elements, words or punctuation marks, surrounding it. The regularity and the frequency of these characteristics on the whole set of references from the same article allow us to locate and tag that element in most of the references. In the second case, the search is done by gathering words from the text in function of some rules:

Reduction rules	IT + IT => IT
	IT + PU- + IT => IT
Forming rules	IT + PN => AU
	IT + PU, + PN => AU
Extending rules	AU + CC + AU => AU
	AU + EA => AU
Agglutination rules	UN + AU => AU
	UN + PU, + AU => AU
Mixed rules	NU + PU- + NU => PG
	AN + PU- + AN => PG

Fig. 15.11. Typology of grouping rules with some simple examples.

- *Reduction rules:* These rules are used to group consecutive identical tags. For example, the grouping of two initials (**IT**) from an author's name or two proper names (**PN**) while taking into account the type of punctuation marks (**PU**) that may be present in such a context.

- *Forming rules:* These rules are used to initiate the beginning of a field by associating tags that are complementary in their description. For example, the association of the name and the initials in the formation of an author's name (**AU**).

- *Extending rules:* These rules are used to concatenate sub-fields recognized independently. For example, an author and the expression "*et al.*" (**EA**), which confirms the field "**AU**" or the expansion of the article title from an initial core composed of three common nouns by adding nouns, connectors (**CC**) and prepositions to let the field grow as much as possible.

- *Agglutination rules:* These rules are used to allow the unknown terms (**UN**) to be absorbed if the conditions are right. For example, between two author names, an unknown term should be absorbed.

- *Mixed rules:* These rules are used to combine a set of grouping rules to detect potential candidates before using regularity to select the best amongst them. It is notably the case with page numbers (**PG**) that can be made of numbers (**NU**) and/or alphanumeric strings (**AN**).

At the end of that process, each term or group of terms gets a new tag that gives a more explicit identification of the field to which it belongs. But that kind of analysis shows some limits, so the next step consists in exploiting what has been well recognized to create a model of how the different fields of the reference are supposed to be joined together (inter-field model) and how some of them (e.g. authors, journal title) are structured (intra-field model). Then, both models are used in turn to complete and to correct the faulty references. As shown in Figure 15.12, the model extracted in Figure 15.13, is used to extend the title field up to the right parenthesis and to deduce the journal title from its position.

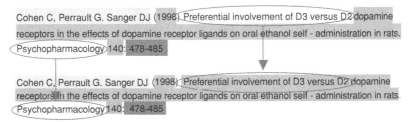

Fig. 15.12. Example of inter-field correction.

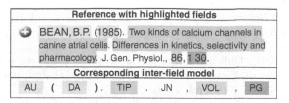

Fig. 15.13. Inter-field modelling.

15.9 Conclusion

As the digital libraries grow more complex and more numerous, there is a need for methods of meta-data extraction to improve information retrieval and navigability within the database. Such methods can also add new usage to existing DLs as extracting information from bibliographic references for bibliometric analyses. The methods described here can not only be improved, but must also be considered as part of an iterative process. The more information you extract, the more possibilities you have to refine the whole process: e.g. collecting the different models for a bibliographic references help find the correct model for a set of references, which is too small or contains too many errors for the statistical analysis to be efficient.

References

1. Belaïd, A. and David, A. (1999). The use of information retrieval tools in automatic document modelling and recognition. *Workshop on Document Layout Interpretation and its Applications, Bangalore, India*, pp. 522–526.
2. Belaïd, A. (2001). Recognition of table of contents for electronic library consulting. *International Journal on Document Analysis and Recognition, 4*, pp. 35–45.
3. Belaïd, A. (1998). Retrospective document conversion: application to the library domain. *International Journal on Document Analysis and Recognition, 1*, pp. 125–146.
4. Takasu, A., Satoh, S., and Katsura, E. (1994). A document understanding method for database construction of an electronic library. *International Conference on Pattern Recognition*, pp. 463–466.
5. Takasu, A., Satoh, S., and Katsura, E. (1995). A rule learning method for academic document image processing. *International Conference on Document Analysis and Recognition, ICDAR'95, I*, pp. 239–242.
6. Hofstadter, D.R. and Mitchell, M. (1992). The Copycat Project: a model of mental fluidity and analogy-making. In: J. Barnden and K. Holyoak (Eds.). *Advances in Connectionist and Neural Computation Theory*. London: Lawrence Erlbaum Associates, Volume 2, pp. 31–113.
7. Parmentier, F. and Belaïd, A. (1997). Logical structure recognition of scientific bibliographic references. *International Conference on Document Analysis and Recognition (ICDAR), Vienna, Austria*, pp. 1072–1076.

8. Story, G.A., O'Gorman, L., Fox, D., Levy Schaper, L., and Jagadish, H.V. (1992). The right pages image-based electronic library for alerting and browsing. *Computer, 25(9)*, pp. 17–26.

9. Baird, H.S. (2004). Difficult and urgent open problems in document image analysis for libraries. *First International Workshop on Digital Image Analysis for Libraries (DIAL 2004)*, pp. 25–32.

10. Small, H.G. and Griffith, B.C. (1974). The structure of scientific literature. I: identifying and graphing specialties. *Science Studies, 4*, pp. 17–40.

11. Dennis, K., Michler, G.O., Schneider, G., and Suzuki, M. (2003). Automatic reference linking in digital libraries. *Workshop on Document Image Analysis and Retrieval (DIAR'03), Madison, Wisconsin.* http://www.exp-math.uniessen.de/algebra/retrodig/digili b2.pdf.

12. Kratzer, K. (2002). Automatic reference linking by means of MR lookup. *Workshop on Linking and Searching in Distributed Digital Libraries, Ann Arbor, Michigan, March 18–20, 2002.* http://www.exp-math.uni-essen.de/algebra/veranstaltungen/kratzer.pdf.

13. O'Gorman, L. (1992). Image and document processing techniques for the right pages electronic library system. *International Conference on Pattern Recognition, 2*, pp. 260–263.

14. Mitchell, M. (1993). *Analogy-Making as Perception: A Computer Model.* Cambridge, MA: MIT Press.

15. Lawrence, S., Giles, C.L., and Bollacker, K. (1999). Digital libraries and autonomous citation indexing. *IEEE Computer, 32(6)*, pp. 67–71.

16. Miller, W. and Myers, E.W. (1985). A file comparison program. *Software, Practice and Experience, 15(11)*, pp. 1025–1040.

17. http://en.wikipedia.org/wiki/List_of_digital_library_projects.

18. http://www.cordis.lu/libraries/en/projects.html.

19. http://www.dlib.org/metrics/public/papers/dig-lib-scope.html.

20. http://www.google.com/googleblog/2004/12/all-booked-up.html.

21. http://www.gutenberg.org.

22. http://www.library.cmu.edu/Libraries/MBP_FAQ.html.

23. http://www.library.cornell.edu/preservation/tutorial/metadata/table5-1.html.

Document Information Retrieval

Stefan Klink, Koichi Kise, Andreas Dengel, Markus Junker,
and Stefan Agne

16.1 Introduction

Due to the widespread use of ubiquitous electronic tools like laptops, PDAs
and digital cameras for the acquisition, production and archiving of documents, more and more information exists in electronic form. The ease with
which documents are produced and shared in the World Wide Web has led
to a potentiation of information reachable by each user. This has created a
growing demand of adaptive and intelligent access to relevant information.

A study of the International Data Corporation (IDS) shows that the
capacity of data in enterprise networks will increase from 3200 petabytes
in the year 2002 up to 54,000 petabytes and growing in the year 2004.
Cleverdon estimates that the number of new publications in the most important scientific journals will be 400,000 per year [1]. Storing this mass of
information is a problem, but searching specific information is a challenge
that has become an even greater object of public concern. These tremen-
dous masses of data make it very difficult for a user to find the "needle in
the haystack" and nearly impossible to find and flip through all relevant
documents and images. Because a human can no longer gain an overview
over all information, the risk of missing important data or of getting lost
in the haystack is very high.

The task of document information retrieval is to retrieve relevant documents in response to a query that describes a user's information need.
Its basic operation is to measure the similarity between a document and a
query. Documents with high similarity are presented to the user as the result of retrieval. Although this research field has several decades of history,
there still exist some open problems.

The rest of this chapter is organized as follows. In Section 16.2 we
give an overview of the vector-space model and basic techniques commonly

utilized in document retrieval. In Section 16.3 three innovative applications are introduced that make use of these techniques.

16.2 Document Retrieval Based on the Vector-Space Model

Throughout the previous few decades of information retrieval science, many models have been invented and a huge amount of variations have been tested. In the field of document retrieval, only a few are established. The most popular retrieval model is the vector-space model (VSM) introduced by Salton [2–4].

16.2.1 Identification of Index Terms

The fundamental unit of an automatic statistical indexing is a word. Each word of a document can be seen as a discriminative feature between the current document and all other documents in the document collection. This feature can be quantified and could also be negative.

During the late 1950s, Luhn showed that the most discriminative words are those that occur with a relatively average frequency within a document collection [5]. If a word – e.g. a pronoun or preposition – occurs very often, then it cannot characterize the content of a document. On the other hand, words occurring very rarely in documents are also rarely used in a user's query. These observations are the foundation of frequency-based techniques for automatic term extraction methods.

Nowadays, it is common not to extract single words according to their frequency but to simply extract all words of the documents and then assign them a frequency-based weight. Words with high frequency will get weights near zero. Due to memory restrictions, they will probably not be included in the index, or they will be skipped over entirely in the case that a *stop word list* is employed. Such a list contains functional words like "with", "also", "can", "the", etc. Furthermore, this list may contain words with no discriminative meaning or words that are given by the semantic of the document collection – e.g. 'computer' or 'program' in a collection of computer science documents.

Another linguistic problem is that the same meaning of a word can be represented by several similar but not identical words – e.g. "sofa" vs. "couch". In the same manner, singular and plural of nouns are often different. This is a significant problem for matching functions that use just the exact occurrence of query terms within the documents.

Several techniques have been proposed to avoid this problem. They are mostly based on a mapping of words to a set of descriptors for word families. Such methods that identify variants of word forms are also known as *conflation methods*. A widely used morphological approach is *word stemming*, also known as *suffix stripping*. It is based on a rule-based removal of derivative and declined word suffixes and reduces each word to its stem, which is not necessarily a complete word as used in a document. Of course, a list of word endings is not able to follow a set of grammatical rules. Therefore, it is not possible to implement a system with 100% accuracy. But for some languages, such as English or German, an algorithm developed by Porter is a suitable method for word stemming [6–8].

Approaches to identify variants of word forms are not just based on cutting off the suffix. A more general approach for combining words makes use of the comparison of two words based on the number of *n-grams*, which means sub-strings with *n* characters occurring in both words. This approach is able to identify words as related independent to a certain prefix or suffix [9].

Lewis and Spärck Jones showed that the removal of stop words and word stemming is mainly used to reach two problematical aims: discrimination and normalization [10]. On the one hand, documents must be discriminative to be able to find a specific document out of the collection. On the other hand, documents must be normalized so that a comparison of the user query with the documents is successful and query term are compared on the concept level and not on the exact character level.

The selection of algorithms for word stemming is one of the factors that influence the trade-off between the two aspects above. Indexing will be always just sub-optimal. Kupiec elucidates this fact with a reference to the book and film title *Gone With the Wind* [11]. With standard indexing algorithms, this will be reduced to "go wind". Another example that shows the problem even better is the word "trainers" (sport shoes), which will be reduced to "train" (railway).

The effects of word stemming are fundamental and pervade the complete retrieval process from the beginning (indexing) up to the satisfaction of the user need (query result). The problems shown here occur all over and are often discussed. But over-normalization and sub-optimal discrimination are just two main problems during automatic indexing. Further approaches tackle the problem of how to handle spelling, inappropriate hyphenation and the occurrence of alphanumerical words such as "2005".

In general during the balancing act of indexing, the profit from normalization is higher than the loss from discrimination methods.

16.2.2 The Simple Vector-Space Model

In this section we explain the vector-space model, which is the basis of our work. Essential parts of this model are the representation of documents and queries, a scheme for weighting terms and an appropriate metric for calculating the similarity between a query and a document.

Representation of Documents and Queries

The task of traditional document retrieval is to retrieve documents that are relevant to a given query from a fixed set of documents – i.e. a document database. A common way to deal with documents, as well as queries, is to represent them using a set of index terms (simply called *terms*) and ignore their positions in documents and queries. Terms are determined based on words of documents in the database. In the following, t_i ($1 \leq i \leq m$) and d_j ($1 \leq j \leq n$) represent a term and a document in the database, respectively, where m is the number of terms and n is the number of documents. In the VSM, a document is represented as an m-dimensional vector

$$d_j = (w_{ij}, \dots, w_{mj})^T \tag{16.1}$$

where T indicates the transpose and w_{ij} is the weight of a term t_i in a document d_j. A query is likewise represented as

$$q = (w_{iq}, \dots, w_{mq})^T \tag{16.2}$$

where w_{iq} is the weight of a term t_i in a query q.

Weighting Schemes

The weighting of these terms is the most important factor for the performance of an IR system in the vector-space model. The development of a good weighting scheme is more an art than a science; in the last three decades of literature, several thousands of weighting schemes have been introduced and tested, especially in the SMART project [12]. Although Salton had experimented with term weights in the 1960s, most of the methods have been introduced in the 1970s through the late 1990s [13].

An overview of the earlier methods is given in [14] and in [15]. Salton, Allen and Buckley summarized in 1988 the results of 20 years' development of term weighting schemes in the SMART system [16]. More than 1800 different combinations of term weighting factors were tested experimentally and 287 of them were clearly seen as different. Fuhr and Buckley [17] introduced a weighting scheme that is based on a linear combination of several weighting factors. The INQUERY system developed in the late 1980s uses a similar linear combination for calculating the term weights [18]. The start of the TREC conferences in 1992 gave a new impulse to the development of new weighting schemes.

In our work, we use the most distributed weighting scheme. The standard normalized *tf idf* of the SMART system is defined as

$$w_{ij} = tf_{ij} \cdot idf_i, \tag{16.3}$$

where tf_{ij} is the weight calculated using the frequency of the term t_i occurring in document d_j, and idf_i is the weight calculated using the inverse of the document frequency [19].

Similarity Measurements

The result of the retrieval is represented as a list of documents ranked according to their similarity to the query. The selection of a similarity function is a further central problem having decisive effects on the performance of an IR system. A detailed overview of similarity functions can be found in [20].

A common similarity function in text-based IR systems is the cosine metric, which is also used in the SMART system and in our approach. For this metric, the similarity $sim(d_j, q)$ between a document d_j and a query q is measured by the standard cosine of the angle between the document vector d_j and the query vector q:

$$sim(d_j, q) = \frac{d_j^T \cdot q}{\| d \| \cdot \| q \|},$$

(16.4)

where $\| * \|$ is the Euclidean norm of a vector.

16.2.3 Relevance Feedback

Because the retrieval techniques discussed in this work belong to the family of relevance feedback techniques, this section gives a short overview of relevance feedback techniques first and our approaches are introduced later.

Taxonomy of Relevance Feedback Techniques

A common way of searching information is to start with a short initial query and to reformulate it again and again until satisfying results are returned. To do this, a lot of effort and time has to be invested by the user.

The main idea of relevance feedback techniques is to ask the user to provide evaluations or *relevance feedback* on the documents retrieved from the query. This feedback is then used for subsequently improving the retrieval effectiveness in order to shorten the way to more satisfying results.

The feedback is given by marking just the relevant documents in the result list or more specifically by marking the relevant and the irrelevant documents. The marking itself can be boolean (marked or not) or within a given scale in more advanced systems.

In general, relevance feedback techniques are not restricted to specific retrieval models and can be utilized without a document assessment function that is responsible for the ranking of the retrieved documents.

In literature, many different strategies are described and many implementations have been tested. Figure 16.1 shows how the two main strategies for relevance information are utilized: (1) the user's search query is reformulated, and (2) documents of the collection are changed.

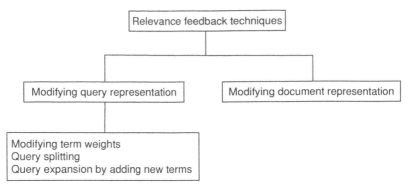

Fig. 16.1. A taxonomy of relevance feedback techniques.

Both approaches have their pros and cons. Approaches that reformulate the search query only influence the current search and do not affect further queries from the same or other users. On the other hand, approaches that change the documents within the collection possibly do not affect the current search.

Especially of interest is the way in which the query is reformulated because the approach described in this work also tries to answer this question.

In general, all introduced approaches in the following sections reach improvements after some number of iterations.

Changing the Document Collection

Information retrieval methods that change documents within the collection are also known as *document transformation methods* [21] or *user-oriented clustering* [22, 23].

The hope of information retrieval in the vector-space model lies in the fact that the vector of a document relevant to the user's query is located near to that of the query. Document transformation (DT) approaches aim to improve those cases where this is not accomplished by moving the document vectors relevant to the query to the direction of the query. Those vectors that are irrelevant are moved further away.

When moving the document vectors (either closer to or away from the query vector), close attention must be paid so that each single movement is very small. The main reason for this is that the assessment of a particular user is not necessarily in agreement with those of other users.

DT methods were first described in the late 1960s by the SMART team [12, 24]. It is one of the strategies that is easy and efficient enough to be part of big search engines. Although these approaches were introduced early on, they achieved little attention and were only tested in a restricted way. Twenty years later, Salton identifies the main reason for this negligence [25, p. 326]:

Document-space modification methods are difficult to evaluate in the laboratory, where no users are available to dynamically control the space modifications by submitting queries.

In literature, several algorithms for DT can be found. Some examples are given in [21]:

$$D = (1 - \alpha)D + \alpha \frac{\| D \|}{\| Q \|} Q \tag{16.5}$$

$$D = D + \beta Q \tag{16.6}$$

$$D = D_{original} + D_{learned}, \quad \text{whereas} \tag{16.7}$$

$$D_{learned} = \begin{cases} D_{learned} + \beta \, Q & \text{if } \| D_{learned} \| < l; \\ (1 - \alpha) \, D_{learned} + \alpha \frac{\| D_{learned} \|}{\| Q \|} Q & \text{otherwise.} \end{cases}$$

Here Q is the user query, D is the relevant document and l is a threshold.

The strategy in (16.5) ensures that the length of the document vector stays constant. Brauen [12] and Savoy et al. [26] have shown that this strategy is able to improve the retrieval results on small- and mid-sized document collections.

The strategy in (16.6) is the most simple, but it performs well on a low quantity (less than 2000) of queries [21]: terms of Q are weighted with β and then added to the document vector D. It should be noted that this method of summation causes the length of the document to grow without limitation.

Both strategies are sensitive to a supersaturation. If many queries are assigned to a relevant document, then the effect of the initial document terms is decreased with the growing amount of queries and the effect of the query terms dominates. This document saturation is a serious problem in search engines that utilize variants of these formulae.

The strategy in (16.7) was developed to solve this problem. With a growing number of queries (document length), the effect of queries is decreasing.

In general, DT techniques have been shown to improve retrieval performance over small- and medium-sized collections [12, 26]. There was no winner among the strategies that have been tried; different strategies perform best on different collections [26].

One notable and important difference between the DT methods and the methods modifying the query described next is that only the first ones leave permanent effects on a system.

Reformulation of the Query

As opposed to DT methods that try to move relevant documents nearer to their appropriate queries, methods for reformulating the query try to solve the retrieval problem from the other side. They try to reformulate the initial user query in a way that the query moves nearer to the relevant documents.

Three basic approaches to improve the retrieval results are known in literature: (1) methods that modify weights of the query terms, (2) methods for query splitting and (3) methods for query expansion by adding new terms. The approach in Section 16.3.1 used in our work belongs to the latter group, which is most important.

Modification of Term Weights

Methods for modifying weights of query terms do not add any terms to the initial query but merely increase or decrease the available weights with the help of the feedback information. The main problem of this approach is that no additional information (i.e. new terms) is placed in the query.

Query Splitting

In some cases, relevance feedback techniques supply only unsatisfying re- sults – e.g. documents marked as relevant are not homogeneous, meaning that they do not have a single topic in common and do not form a common cluster in the vector space. Another problem is irrelevant documents that lie near (or in between) relevant documents. In this case, the initial query vector will be moved also to these irrelevant documents by the feedback.

To discover these cases, a common method is to cluster the documents marked as relevant and therewith to analyse if the documents share a topic and if they are homogeneous in the vector space. If the relevant documents are separable into several distinct clusters, then the initial query is split appropriately into the same number of sub-queries. The term weights are adjusted according to the document clusters [23].

Query Expansion

The third and in general most distributed group of methods for modifying the user query is the expansion of the query by adding new terms. These new terms are directly chosen with the help of user feedback after the presentation of the retrieved document. The selected terms (documents) are added to the initial query with appropriate weights.

Experimental results have shown that positive feedback – i.e. mark- ing only relevant documents – is better than using positive and negative feedback in general. The reason is that documents within the relevant set are positioned more homogeneously in the vector space than those in the negative set.

Rocchio Relevance Feedback

Rocchio [27] suggested a method for relevance feedback that uses average vectors (centroids) for each set of relevant and irrelevant documents. The new query is formed as a weighted sum of the initial query and the centroid vectors. Formally, the Rocchio relevance feedback is defined as follows:

Let q be the initial query, n_1 the number of relevant documents and n_2 the number of irrelevant documents. Then the new query q' is formed by:

$$q' = q + \frac{1}{n_1} \sum_{relevant} \frac{D_i}{\| D_i \|} - \frac{1}{n_2} \sum_{non-relevant} \frac{D_i}{\| D_i \|}. \quad (16.8)$$

An important characteristic of this method is that new terms are added to the initial query and the former term weights are adjusted. Salton and Buckley [28] have tested a mass of variants of this linear vector modification. They asserted that this technique needs only a low calculation effort and in general it achieves good results. But they also observed that the performance varies over different document collections. Furthermore, they stated that these techniques have bigger gains in cases with poor initial queries compared to cases where the initial query provides very good results.

Pseudo-Relevance Feedback

The Rocchio relevance feedback of the previous section supplies good results but it has a crucial disadvantage: it needs user feedback. This is very hard to get in real IR systems because few users are willing to do the job of assessing documents.

One idea to simulate this explicit user feedback is to rely on the performance of the IR system and to assume that the top n_1 documents in the ranked document list are relevant. These are used as positive feedback for the relevance feedback method.

In contrast to the Rocchio relevance feedback, no negative feedback is considered. It may be possible to assume that the bottom n_2 documents are irrelevant and use them as negative feedback. But this variation is uncommon and generally leads to poorer results.

Like the Rocchio relevance feedback, the pseudo-relevance feedback works in three steps: (1) The initial query is given to the system and the relevant documents are determined. (2) In contrast to Rocchio relevance feedback, these relevant documents are not presented to the user for marking, but rather the n most similar documents are selected automatically to reformulate the query by adding all (or just certain) terms of these documents to the query. (3) The reformulated query is given to the system and the relevant documents are presented to the user.

An interesting variation of the pseudo-relevance feedback is described in Kise et al. [29]: Let E be a set of relevant document vectors for expansion given by

$$E = \left\{ d_j^+ \Big| \frac{sim(d_j^+, q)}{\max_{1 \leq i \leq N} sim(d_i^+, q)} \geq \theta \right\}, \quad (16.9)$$

where q is the original query vector, d_j^+ a document vector relevant to the query and θ a similarity threshold. The sum d_s of these relevant document vectors,

$$d_s = \sum_{d_j^+ \in E} d_j^+,\qquad (16.10)$$

can be considered as enriched information about the original query.[1] With this, the expanded query vector q' is obtained by

$$q' = \frac{q}{\| q \|} + \beta \frac{d_s}{\| d_s \|},\qquad (16.11)$$

where β is a parameter for controlling the weight of the newly incorporated terms. Finally, the documents are ranked again according to the similarity $sim(d_j, q')$ to the expanded query.

This variation has two parameters: (1) the weighting parameter β, which defines how great the influence of the relevant documents is vs. the initial query and (2) the similarity threshold θ, which defines how many documents are used as positive feedback.

As opposed to the previously described approach, which defines a fixed amount of positive documents (n_1), the threshold θ describes only "how relevant" the documents must be in order to be used as positive feedback. Thus the number of documents used is dynamic and individual, depending on the document collection and on the current query. If many documents are similar to the initial query, then the document set E used for the expansion of the query is very large. But assuming the same θ, if only one document is sufficiently similar to the given query, then E contains only this single document.

16.2.4 Passage Retrieval

This section describes another important variant of the vector-space model called *passage retrieval*. It is closely related to the applications described in Sections 16.3.2 and 16.3.3.

Passage retrieval is a task where the goal is not to retrieve not whole documents but rather small snippets of text or *passages* relevant to the user's query. This technique has advantages over the standard vector-space model when documents consist of multiple topics. The standard vector-space model can be easily disturbed by the multi-topicality because the document vector is defined for the whole document. On the other hand, passage retrieval is less affected by this problem, since it is capable of retrieving relevant passages in documents. Another advantage of passage retrieval is that it is capable of segmenting relevant parts that interest

---

[1] Remark that the sum d_s is a single vector.

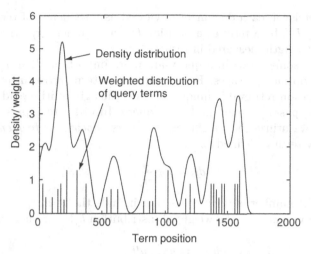

Fig. 16.2. Density distribution.

the user; it is unnecessary for the user to find where to read in retrieved documents.

In general, passages used in passage retrieval can be classified into three types: discourse, semantic and window passages [30]. Discourse passages are defined based on discourse units such as sentences and paragraphs. Semantic passages are obtained by segmenting text at the points where a topic of text changes. Window passages are determined based on the number of terms.

We have proposed a method called *density distributions* (DD) [29, 31, 32], which is based on window passages. A notion of density distributions was first introduced to locate explanations of a word in text [33] and applied to passage retrieval by some of the authors. Comparison of various windows for document retrieval and other tasks can be found in [34, 35].

An important idea of DD is the assumption that parts of documents with a particularly dense distribution of query terms are relevant to said query. Figure 16.2 shows an example of a density distribution. The horizontal axis indicates the positions of terms in a document. A weighted distribution of query terms in the document is shown as spikes on the figure; their height indicates the weight of a term. The density distribution shown in the figure is obtained by smoothing the spikes with a window function. The details are as follows.

Let us first introduce symbols used for explanations. The task of passage retrieval is to retrieve passages from a fixed set of documents or a document collection. In order to deal with documents as well as queries, both are represented using a set of terms. Let t_i $(1 \leq i \leq m)$ and d_j $(1 \leq j \leq n)$ be a term and a document in the database, respectively, where m is the number of different terms and n the number of documents in the database.

In passage retrieval, each document is viewed as a sequence of terms. Let $a_j(l)$ $(1 \leq l \leq L_j)$ be a term at a position l in a document d_j, where L_j is the document length measured in terms.

In general, some terms in a query are more important than others for locating appropriate passages. For example, the term *retrieval* in papers about information retrieval is ubiquitous and thus gives little evidence for distinguishing passages relevant to the query. In order to represent such information, we utilize the weight called *inverse document frequency idf_i*, which for any term t_i defined as

$$idf_i = \log \frac{n}{n_i}, \tag{16.12}$$

where n_i is the number of documents that include the term t_i.

Using the weight idf_i, the weighted distribution $b_j(l)$ of query terms is defined as

$$b_j(l) = w_{iq} \cdot idf_i, \tag{16.13}$$

where $a_j(l) = t_i$ and w_{iq} is the weight of a term t_i in a query. The weight w_{iq} is defined based on the frequency f_{iq} of the term t_i in the query as

$$w_{iq} = \log(f_{iq} + 1) \tag{16.14}$$

Smoothing of $b_j(l)$ enables us to obtain the density distribution $dd_j(l)$ for a document d_j:

$$dd_j(l) = \sum_{x=-W/2}^{W/2} f(x)\, b_j(l-x), \tag{16.15}$$

where $f(x)$ is a window function with a window size W. We employ the Hanning window function, whose shape is shown in Figure 16.3, and is defined by

$$f(x) = \begin{cases} \frac{1}{2}(1 + \cos 2\pi \frac{x}{W}) & \text{if } |x| \leq W/2; \\ 0 & \text{otherwise.} \end{cases} \tag{16.16}$$

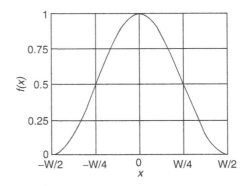

Fig. 16.3. Hanning window function.

16.3 Applications

In following section we propose three document retrieval methods based on the techniques described above: a collaborative information retrieval approach, a question-answering system and the recently developed document image question-answering system called *IQAS*.

16.3.1 Collaborative Information Retrieval

In this section, some central aspects of collaborative information retrieval in general are discussed and our approach for learning term-based concepts and query expansion techniques is introduced.

No Memory in Ad Hoc Search

A shortcoming of the ad hoc IR systems currently being used is their lack of any memory and their inability to learn. All information from a previous user or a previous query of the same user are gone immediately after the presentation of the list of relevant documents. Even systems with relevance feedback (see Section 16.2.3) do not learn. They only integrate the most recently given feedback information with the current query. All information about previous feedback is not stored and is unavailable for future queries, unless the feedback is explicitly coded within the new query.

Basic Idea of Collaborative Information Retrieval

To overcome this imperfection, we are using in our work an approach called *collaborative information retrieval* (CIR) [36–40]. This approach learns with the help of feedback information of *all* previous users (and also previous queries of the current user) to improve the retrieval performance with a lasting effect.

Generally, for satisfying the user's information needs, it is necessary to traverse a complex search process with many decisions and deliberations to achieve an optimal query. On the way from the initial query to a satisfying set of documents the user must invest a lot of effort and time that is lost in a common ad hoc IR system after the sending of the query. If another user (or the same user in the future) is searching for the same information, then they must invest the same time and effort again. In the case of complex search processes, it is virtually impossible to reconstruct all decisions and query reformulations in the same way. The users will not find the needed information (again) and will give up the search.

The idea of CIR is to store all information obtained during a search process in a repository and to use this information for future queries. A later user with similar information needs can profit from this automatically acquired wisdom on several ways:

- The current search process will be shortened and focussed on the desired topic.
- The retrieval performance of the IR system will be improved with the help of acquired wisdom of other users.

Restricted Scenario

This work is based on standard document collections (e.g. TREC [41]) to ensure comparability with standard retrieval methods described in literature. However, a shortcoming of these collections is that they do not contain any search processes as described above. They only contain a set of documents, a set of queries and the appropriate and relevant documents to each query (see also (16.17)). Due to this shortcoming, a restricted scenario is used for this work. The scenario has the following characteristics:

No complex search processes: The standard document collections only contain a set of documents, a set of user queries, and, for each query, a list of relevant documents.

No personalization: The scenario assumes one single, global user querying the IR system. No differentiation of several users, group profiles or personalization hierarchies are taken into consideration. (See [42] for further information about this topic.)

No user judgement: The user queries are qualitatively not differentiated and there is no judgement or assessment of the user or user queries.

No reflection over time: The queries are absolutely independent and no reflections or changes over time are made. An example problem that is not considered is the following: a user is initially searching for some publications to get an overview of a current problem. In the meantime, he is learning more and more about the topic and the next time he looks for more "deeper" documents and specific information, even though he is formulating the same query.

Global relevance feedback: The approaches shown here are based on global relevance feedback and learn with the complete learning set of queries, in contrast to ordinary local feedback that is used in every step within the search process to generate the new query. In our approach, the global feedback is used to directly form the new query in one single step.

Figure 16.4 illustrates the scenario used in this work. The user query q is transformed to the improved query q' with the help of relevance feedback information that is provided by the document collection.

A set of relevant documents is assigned to each query. Relevance information r_k for a query q_k is represented by an N-dimensional vector:

$$r_k = (r_{1k}, r_{2k}, \ldots, r_{Nk})^T, \quad 1 \leq k \leq L, \tag{16.17}$$

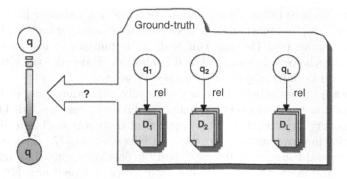

Fig. 16.4. Restricted scenario of the CIR with TREC collections.

where

$$r_{jk} = \begin{cases} 1 \text{ if document } j \text{ is relevant to query } k; \\ 0 \text{ otherwise.} \end{cases} \qquad (16.18)$$

Here N is the number of documents and L the number of test queries in the collection. $()^T$ is the transpose of a matrix or a vector.

Central Aspects of Query-Expansion Techniques

The crucial point in query expansion is the question, "Which terms (or phrases) should be included in the query formulation?" If the query formulation is to be expanded by additional terms, there are two problems that are to be solved:

- How are these terms selected?
- How are the parameters estimated for these terms?

For the selection task, three different strategies have been proposed:

Dependent terms: Here, terms that are dependent on the query terms are selected. For this purpose, the similarity between all terms of the document collection has to be computed first [43].

Feedback terms: From the documents that have been judged by the user, the most significant terms (according to a measure that considers the distribution of a term within relevant and non-relevant documents) are added to the query formulation [19]. Clear improvements are reported in [19] and more recently in [44].

Interactive selection: By means of one of the methods mentioned before, a list of candidate terms is computed and presented to the user. The user then makes the final decision as to which terms are to be included in the query [3].

Many terms used in human communication are ambiguous or have several meanings [43], but most ambiguities are resolved automatically without noticing the ambiguity. The way this is done by humans is still an open problem in psychological research, but it is almost certain that the context in which a term occurs plays a central role [45, 46].

Historically, most attempts at automatically expanding queries have failed to improve the retrieval effectiveness, and it was often concluded that automatic query expansion based on statistical data was unable to bring a substantial improvement in the retrieval effectiveness [47]. This could be due to several reasons. Term-based query expansion approaches mostly rely upon hand-made thesauri or just plain co-occurrence data [48, 49]. They do not use learning technologies for the query terms. On the other hand, those that use learning technologies (neural networks, support vector machines, etc.) are query based. This means these systems learn concepts (or additional terms) for the complete query.

The vital advantage of using term-based concepts and not learning the complete query is that other users can profit from the learned concepts. A statistical evaluation of log files has shown that the probability that a searcher uses exactly the same query as a previous searcher is much lower than the probability that parts of a query (phrases or terms) occur in other queries. So, even if a web searcher never uses a given search term, the probability that some other searcher has used it is very high, and the former can therefore profit from the learned concept.

Learning Term-based Concepts

A problem of the standard VSM is that a query is often too short to rank documents appropriately. To cope with this problem, one approach is to enrich the original query with terms that occur in the documents of the collection.

Our method uses feedback information and information globally available from previous queries. Feedback information in our environment is available within the ground truth data provided by the test document collections. The ground truth provides relevance information – i.e. for each query, a list of relevant documents exists.

In contrast to traditional pseudo-relevance feedback methods where the top j-ranked documents are assumed to be relevant and their terms incorporated into the expanded query, we use a different technique to compute relevant documents [38]. The approach is divided into two phases, as shown in Figure 16.5:

- The *learning phase* for each term works as follows
  1. Select old queries in which the specific query term occurs.
  2. From these selected old queries, get the sets of relevant documents from the ground truth data.

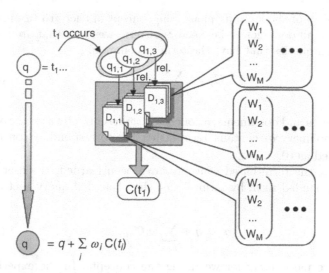

Fig. 16.5. Strategy of learning term-based concepts.

3. From each set of relevant documents, compute a new document vector and use these document vectors to build the term concept.

- The *expansion phase* for each term is then performed as documented in literature
  1. Select the appropriate concept of the current term.
  2. Use a weighting scheme to enrich the new query with the concept.

For the formal description of the learning phase, we need the following definitions:

- $D = d_1, \ldots, d_N$ is the set of all documents.
- $Q = q_1, \ldots, q_L$ is the set of all known queries.
- $q_k = (w_{1k}, \ldots, w_{ik}, \ldots, w_{Mk})^T$ is represented within the vector-space model. For each term of the query, the appropriate weight w_{ik} is between 0 and 1.
- $R^+(q_k) = \{d_j \in D \mid r_{ij} = 1\}$ is the set of all documents relevant to the query q_k (see also (16.18)).

Now, the first step of the learning phase collects all queries having the ith term in common:[2]

$$Q_i = \{q_k \in Q \mid w_{ik} \neq 0\}. \tag{16.19}$$

Step two collects all documents that are relevant to these collected queries:

$$D_{ik} = \{\, d_j \mid d_j \in R^+(q_k) \wedge q_k \in Q \,\}. \tag{16.20}$$

---

[2] If the ith term does not occur in any query q_k, then the set Q_i is empty.

In the last step of the learning phase, the concept of each ith term is built as the sum of all documents (i.e. vectors of term weights) that are relevant to the known queries that have the term in common:

$$\mathbf{C}_i = \sum_{d_j \in \mathbf{D}_{ik}} d_j. \tag{16.21}$$

As with queries and documents, a concept is represented by a vector of term weights. If no query q_k contains term i, then the corresponding concept $\mathbf{C}_i$ is represented as $(0, \ldots, 0)^T$.

Now that the term-based concepts have been learned, the user query q can be expanded term by term. Thus, the expanded query vector q' is obtained by

$$q' = q + \sum_{i=1}^{M} \omega_i \mathbf{C}_i, \tag{16.22}$$

where ω_i are parameters for weighting the concepts. In the experiments described below, ω_i is globally set to 1.

Before applying the expanded query, it is normalized by

$$q'' = \frac{q'}{\|q'\|}. \tag{16.23}$$

For this approach, the complete documents (all term weights w_{ij} of the relevant documents) are summed up and added to the query. Although in literature it is reported that using just the top-ranked terms is sufficient or sometimes better, experiments with this approach on the TREC collections have shown that the more words used to learn the concepts, the better the results. So the decision was made to always use the complete documents and not merely some (top-ranked) terms.

If no ground truth of relevant documents is available, (pseudo-)relevance feedback techniques can be used and the concepts are learned by adding terms from the retrieved relevant documents.

The advantage of the document transformation approach – leaving permanent effects on a system – also holds for learned concepts.

16.3.2 Question-Answering System

Next we show an important application of passage retrieval called *question-answering* (QA). The task of QA is to find a text portion that contains an answer to a given query. A typical interaction between a user and a QA system might go as follows:

User: What is the population of Japan?

System: ...Ministry said last month Japanese population was 122.74 million at...

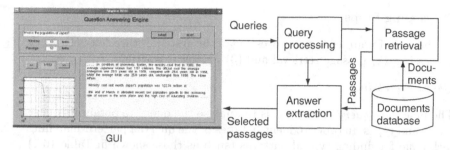

Fig. 16.6. Question answering system.

In order to realize this scenario, it is necessary to apply a method of finding passages that include answers to the question. This is why the QA task is an important application area of passage retrieval.

Overview of the System

Figure 16.6 illustrates an overview of the proposed QA system [50]. The system employs three steps of processing: query processing, passage retrieval and answer extraction. The outline of processing is as follows. First, the system takes as input a natural-language query from a user through the GUI. Next, the query is sent to query processing for extracting query terms and finding the types of the query. The extracted query terms are sent to passage retrieval for retrieving passages from documents in the database. Retrieved passages are then transferred to the answer extraction component for examining whether or not they include entities required by the query. Lastly, filtered passages are sorted according to their scores, and the top-ranking passage is displayed on the GUI.

Types of Queries and Terms

An important point specific to the QA task is in the query processing and the answer extraction: some "types" are assigned to terms as well as to queries for the purpose of selecting appropriate passages. These types are employed for clarifying the following points:

- What does a query ask about? (types of queries)
- Which terms can be a part of an answer to the query? (types of terms)

We currently use the types shown in Table 16.1 for both queries and terms. Note that more than one type can be assigned to a term as well as to a query, while some terms and queries have no type whatsoever. In the case that a query has a type, passages that contain the terms of the same type can be possible answers.

Processing Steps

As shown in Figure 16.6, the processing of the system is threefold: (1) query processing, (2) passage retrieval and (3) answer extraction.

Query Processing

The first step, *query processing*, is to analyse the query to obtain its query terms and types. In order to identify types of the query, a pattern-matching technique for finding typical patterns (such as those shown in Table 16.1) is applied. In parallel, stemming and stopword elimination are applied to the query to obtain query terms. Extracted query terms are utilized to find relevant passages at the next step.

Passage Retrieval

We employ the passage retrieval method of density distributions described in Section 16.2.4. The outline of processing is as follows. First, density distributions such as in Figure 16.2 are calculated for all documents. Passages are then extracted based on every peak in the density distributions. For example, in the density distribution shown in Figure 16.7, there are two peaks, P_1 and P_2. For each peak, a passage with fixed width (P_w) is extracted by taking the position of a peak as a centre of the passage. Each passage has its score defined as the density of its peak. In Figure 16.7, S_1 and S_2 are the scores. Finally, passages extracted from all density distributions are ranked according to their scores. Note that we do not take

Table 16.1. Types of queries and terms

Type	Examples of queries	Examples of terms
Money	How much money...?	$10
Time	How long...?	10:00, a.m., p.m.
Month	What time of year...?	Jan., December
Number	How far...?	10,000, 0.5
Name	Who...?	Bush

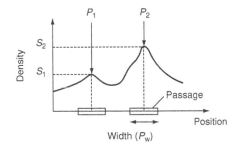

Fig. 16.7. Passages extracted from a density distribution.

account of types of queries and terms in extracting passages. At this step, passages are obtained based solely on the density of terms in the query.

Answer Extraction

This step is to filter out inappropriate passages using the types. The filtering strategy is simple: if types are assigned to a query, passages that include at least one term of one of the types are retained, but passages without such terms are removed from the ranked list of passages.

16.3.3 Document Image Retrieval

Question-Answering for Document Images

All of the methods described so far are for electronic documents. However, it is not enough for us to deal only with electronic documents, at least because of the following two reasons. First, we now have a huge number of document images in various databases and digital libraries. For example, the journal *Communications of the ACM* in the ACM digital library [51] consists of 80% document images and 20% electronic documents. Another reason is that mobile devices with digital cameras are now coming into common use. The resolution of such cameras has been rapidly improved in recent years.[3] Some users have started using them not only for imaging faces and scenes, but also for taking digital copies of documents, because it is much more convenient than writing a memo or finding a photocopier.[4] This indicates that not only legacy documents but also new documents continue to be stored as document images.

In order to utilize such document images, establishing a way of retrieving them is required. As described in the previous section, it would be good to implement a question-answer system for document images for improving the usability of retrieval. From this viewpoint, we have developed a QA system for document images called *IQAS*[5] (Document **I**mage **Q**uestion **A**nswering **S**ystem) [52].

Figure 16.8 illustrates the graphical user interface of IQAS. In this figure, the part relevant to the query is highlighted. The user can magnify the retrieved part in the page. If it does not contain the answer, the user can obtain the next page.

---

[3] Early in 2005, a camera phone with the resolution of seven megapixels was released. The size of captured images is equivalent to the size of images obtained by scanning a sheet of A4 paper at 270 dpi.

[4] In Japan, "digital shoplifting" – i.e. making pictures of books and magazines in bookstores with mobile camera phones – has become a subject of economic concern.

[5] The pronunciation of the term IQAS is close to the Japanese word *ikasu*, which can mean either *to exploit* or *cool*.

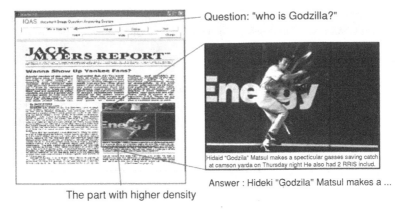

Fig. 16.8. Graphical user interface.

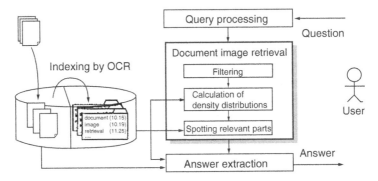

Fig. 16.9. System configuration.

Figure 16.9 shows the system configuration of IQAS that follows the configuration shown in the previous section except for the "document image retrieval" part. In the step of document image retrieval, we utilize a passage retrieval technique based on the density distributions extended for dealing with two-dimensional images.

Document Image Retrieval in IQAS

As shown in Figure 16.9, the step of document image retrieval consists of three smaller steps: (1) filtering, (2) calculating density distributions and (3) identifying relevant parts. In the following, the details of each step are explained after a brief introduction of indexing of document images and query processing.

Indexing

Since document images are two-dimensional entities, it is necessary to extend the indexing scheme to be capable of dealing with two-dimensionality.

In our indexing scheme, document images are viewed as two-dimensional distributions of terms.

The outline of indexing is as follows. First, all words and their bounding boxes are extracted from page images with the help of OCR. Second, stemming and stopword elimination are applied to the extracted words. The resultant words are called *terms* and stored with the centres of their bounding boxes.

Query Processing

The task of query processing is shared by the QA system for electronic documents. Suppose we have a query, "Where is the Baseball Hall of Fame?". The query type is "location" and the query terms are "baseball", "hall", and "fame". Note that only the extraction of query terms is relevant to the task of document image retrieval. In the following, the sequence of extracted query terms is called *the query* and represented as $q = (q_1, \ldots, q_r)$, where q_i is called a query term and i indicates the order of occurrence in the query. For the above example, $q = $ (baseball, hall, fame).

Filtering

Filtering is first applied to ease the burden of the next step, which is relatively time consuming. The task here is to select N_v pages that are likely to include the answer to the query. For this purpose, we utilize the simple vector-space model (VSM). Pages are sorted according to similarity, and the top N_v pages are selected and delivered to the next step.

Calculation of Density Distributions

This step calculates density distributions of the query q for each selected page. Density distributions of the query are defined based on those of each query term q_i. Let $T_i^{(p)}(x, y)$ be a weighted distribution of a term $q_i(= t_k)$ in a selected page p defined by

$$T_i^{(p)}(x, y) = \begin{cases} idf_k & \text{if } q_i(= t_k) \text{ occurs at } (x, y), \\ 0 & \text{otherwise}, \end{cases} \tag{16.24}$$

where (x, y) is the centre of the bounding box of a term. A density distribution $D_i^{(p)}(x, y)$ is a weighted distribution of q_i smoothed by a window $W(x, y)$:

$$D_i^{(p)}(x, y) = \sum_{u=-M_x/2}^{M_x/2} \sum_{v=-M_y/2}^{M_y/2} W(x - u, y - v) T_i^{(p)}(u, v). \tag{16.25}$$

As a window function, we utilize a pyramidal function with the window widths M_x (the horizontal width) and M_y (the vertical width) shown in Figure 16.10.

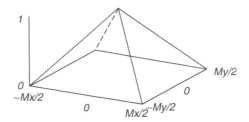

Fig. 16.10. Window function.

A way to define the density distributions of the whole query is to sum up $D_i^{(p)}$ for all q_i, as described in Section 16.2.4. However, this sometimes causes a problem of insufficient discrimination power in the case of document image retrieval: irrelevant parts are erroneously retrieved due to the effect of frequent terms. Therefore, in order to improve the discrimination power, we introduce a notion of N-grams in calculating the distributions. To be precise, we consider the smaller number of successive query terms. For example, the density distribution obtained by r–1 successive query terms is defined by

$$C_{r-1}^{(p)}(x,y) = \prod_{i=1}^{r-1} D_i^{(p)}(x,y) + \prod_{i=2}^{r} D_i^{(p)}(x,y), \qquad (16.26)$$

where r is the number of query terms. For the general case of k successive query terms, the density distribution is defined by

$$C_k^{(p)}(x,y) = \sum_{j=0}^{r-k} \prod_{i=j+1}^{j+k} D_i^{(p)}(x,y). \qquad (16.27)$$

In the proposed method, the density distribution of the whole query for a page p is defined as the weighted sum of the combinations from all the r terms down to s successive terms:

$$D^{(p)}(x,y) = \sum_{k=s}^{r} \alpha_k C_k^{(p)}(x,y), \qquad (16.28)$$

where the parameter s and the weight α_k are experimentally determined.

Identifying Relevant Parts

Based on the density distribution of (16.28), parts that are likely to include the answer are located on page images. First, page images are ranked according to their score of the maximum density:

$$s^{(p)} = \max_{x,y} D^{(p)}(x,y). \qquad (16.29)$$

Then, the top-ranked page is presented to the user through the GUI shown in Figure 16.8.

16.4 Summary and Conclusion

In this chapter, we have given an overview of the vector-space model and basic techniques commonly utilized in document information retrieval. Relevance feedback techniques rely on user feedback regarding the relevance of retrieved documents, whereas passage retrieval is based on the assumption that not the document as a whole but rather specific passages are relevant to a query if they contain terms of the query with high density.

Collaborative information retrieval systems are document retrieval systems that adapt to the user's needs by transferring search knowledge from one user to others. For this, our new query expansion method is learning term-based concepts from previous queries and their relevant documents. In contrast to other relevance feedback and query expansion methods, the query is expanded by adding those terms that are similar to the *concept* of individual query terms, rather than selecting terms that are similar to the complete query or that are similar to single query terms.

For question answering, the passage retrieval method is applied for finding very short snippets of documents that contain an answer to a given query.

In order to use the passage retrieval method as a tool of intelligent access to documents, the following points should be further considered. First, the window size appropriate for analysing documents should be determined automatically. Second, sophisticated learning techniques must be incorporated in order to avoid manual adjustment of processing parameters, including expressions for the type identification in the QA task.

Retrieving document images is still an active research topic and has become increasingly an object of public concern. For finding relevant images or parts thereof, question-answering and passage retrieval techniques are combined for improving the usability of retrieval.

The issues described in this chapter will be subjects of our future research.

References

1. Cleverdon, C.W. (1984). Optimizing convenient online access to bibliographic databases. *Information Services and Use, 4*, pp. 37–47.
2. Salton, G. (1971). *The SMART Retrieval System – Experiments in Automatic Document Processing*. Englewood Cliffs, NJ: Prentice-Hall, Inc.
3. Baeza-Yates, R. and Ribeiro-Neto, B. (1999). *Modern Information Retrieval*. Reading, MA: Addison-Wesley.
4. Ferber, R. (2003). *Information Retrieval – Suchmodelle und Data-Mining-Verfahren für Textsammlungen und das Web*. Germany: dpunkt.verlag.
5. Luhn, H.P. (1958). The automatic creation of literature abstracts. *IBM Journal of Research and Development, 2*, pp. 159–165.

6. Porter, M.F. (1980). An algorithm for suffix stripping. *Program, 14*, pp. 130–137.

7. Porter, M.F. (2005). http://www.tartarus.org/_martin/PorterStemmer/.

8. Porter, M.F. (2005). A small string processing language for creating stemmers. http://snowball.tartarus.org.

9. Porter, M.F. (1983). Information retrieval at the Sedgwick Museum. *Information Technology: Research and Development, 2*, pp. 169–186.

10. Lewis, D.D. and Spärck Jones, K. (1993). Natural language processing for information retrieval. *Technical Report 307, University of Cambridge Computer Laboratory.*

11. Kupiec, J., Kimber, D., and Balasubramanian, V. (1994). Speech-based retrieval using semantic co-occurrence filtering. *Proceedings of the Human Language Technology (HLT) Conference, US Advanced Projects Research Agency (ARPA)*, pp. 373–377.

12. Brauen, T.L. (1971). *Document Vector Modification.* Englewood Cliffs, NJ: Prentice Hall, pp. 456–484.

13. Salton, G. and Lesk, M. (1968). Computer evaluation of indexing and text processing. *Journal of the ACM, 15*, pp. 8–36.

14. Belkin, N.J. and Croft, W.B. (1987). Retrieval techniques. *Annual Review of Information Science and Technology, 22*, pp. 109–145.

15. Harman, D.K. (1992). *Ranking Algorithms.* Upper Saddle River, NJ: Prentice Hall, pp. 363–392.

16. Salton, G., Allen, J., and Buckley, C. (1988). Term-weighting approaches in automatic text retrieval. *Information Processing & Management, 24*, pp. 513–523.

17. Fuhr, N. and Buckley, C. (1991). A probabilistic learning approach for document indexing. *ACM Transactions on Information Systems, 9*, pp. 223–248.

18. Turtle, H.R. and Croft, W.B. (1991). Evaluation of an inference network-based retrieval model. *ACM Transactions on Information Systems, 9*, pp. 187–222.

19. Rocchio, J.J. *Relevance Feedback in Information Retrieval.* Englewood Cliffs, NJ: Prentice Hall, pp. 313–323.

20. Wilson, R. and Martinez, T.R. (1997). Improved heterogeneous distance functions. *Journal of Artificial Intelligence Research, 6*, pp. 1–34.

21. Kemp, C. and Ramamohanarao, K. (2002). Long-term learning for web search enginges. In: T. Elomaa, H. Mannila, and H. Toivonen (Eds.). *Proceedings of the Sixth European Conference of Principles of Data Mining and Knowledge Discovery (PKKD2002).* Lecture Notes in Artificial Intelligence 2431, Helsinki, Finland, Springer, pp. 263–274.

22. Bhuyan, J.N., Deogun, J.S., and Raghavan, V.V. (1997). An adaptive information retrival system based on user-oriented clustering. *ACM Transaction on Information Systems.*

23. Gudivada, V.N., Raghavan, V.V., Grosky, W.I., and Kasanagottu, R. (1997). Information retrieval on the World Wide Web. *IEEE Internet Computing, 1.*

24. Friedman, S.R., Maceyak, J.A., and Weiss, S.F. (1971). *A Relevance Feedback System Based on Document Transformations.* Englewood Cliffs, NJ: Prentice Hall, pp. 447–455.

25. Salton, G. (1989). *Automatic Text Processing: the Transformation, Analysis, and Retrieval of Information by Computer.* Reading, MA: Addison-Wesley.

26. Savoy, J. and Vrajitoru, D. (1996). Evaluation of learning schemes used in information retrieval. *Technical Report CR-I-95-02, Faculty of Sciences, University of Neuchâtel.*

27. Rocchio, J.J. (1966). Document retrieval systems – optimization and evaluation. Ph.D. thesis. Cambridge, MA: Harvard Computational Laboratory.

28. Salton, G. and Buckley, C. (1990). Improving retrieval performance by relevance feedback. *Journal of the ASIS, 41*, pp. 288–297.

29. Kise, K., Junker, M., Dengel, A., and Matsumoto, K. (2001). Passage-based document retrieval as a tool for text mining with user's information needs. In: K.P. Jantke, A. Shinohara (Eds.). *Discovery Science.* Lecture Notes in Computer Science. Princeton, NJ: Springer, Volume 2226, pp. 155–169.

30. Callan, J.P. (1994). Passage-level evidence in document retrieval. In: W.B. Croft, C.J. Rijsbergen (Eds.). *SIGIR.* New York: ACM/Springer, pp. 302–310.

31. Kise, K., Mizuno, H., Yamaguchi, M., and Matsumoto, K. (1999). On the use of density distribution of keywords for automated generation of hypertext links from arbitrary parts of documents. *ICDAR*, pp. 301–304.

32. Kise, K., Junker, M., Dengel, A., and Matsumoto, K. (2001). Experimental evaluation of passage-based document retrieval. *ICDAR.* Silver Spring, MD: IEEE Computer Society, pp. 592–596.

33. Kurohashi, S., Shiraki, N., and Nagao, M. (1997). A method for detecting important descriptions of a word based on its density distribution in text. *Transactions of Information Processing Society of Japan, 38*, pp. 845–853 (In Japanese).

34. Kretser, O. and Moffat, A. (1999). Effective document presentation with a locality-based similarity heuristic. *SIGIR.* New York: ACM, pp. 113–120.

35. Kozima, H. and Furugori, T. (1994). Segmenting narrative text into coherent scenes. *Literary and Linguistic Computing, 9*, pp. 13–19.

36. Hust, A., Klink, S., Junker, M., and Dengel, A. (2003). Towards collaborative information retrieval: three approaches. *Text Mining*, pp. 97–112.

37. Klink, S. (2004). Improving document transformation techniques with collaborative learned term-based concepts. *Reading and Learning*, pp. 281–305.

38. Klink, S., Hust, A., and Junker, M. (2002). TCL – an approach for learning meanings of queries in information retrieval systems. *Content Management – Digitale Inhalte als Bausteine einer vernetzten Welt*, pp. 15–25.

39. Klink, S., Hust, A., Junker, M., and Dengel, A. (2002). Collaborative learning of term-based concepts for automatic query expansion. *Proceedings of the 13th European Conference on Machine Learning (ECML 2002).* Lecture Notes in Artificial Intelligence. Helsinki, Finland: Springer, Volume 2430, pp. 195–206.

40. Klink, S., Hust, A., Junker, M., and Dengel, A. (2002). Improving document retrieval by automatic query expansion using collaborative learning of term-based concepts. *Proceedings of the Fifth International Workshop on Document Analysis Systems (DAS 2002).* Lecture Notes in Computer Science. Princeton, NJ: Springer, Volume 2423, pp. 376–387.

41. Text REtrieval conference (TREC). (2005). http://trec.nist.gov/.

42. Klink, S. (2001). Query reformulation with collaborative concept-based expansion. *Proceedings of the First International Workshop on Web Document Analysis (WDA 2001), Seattle, Washington, USA*, pp. 19–22.

43. Pirkola, A. (1999). Studies on Linguistic Problems and Methods in Text Retrieval: The Effects of Anaphor and Ellipsis Resolution in Proximity Searching, and Translation and Query Structuring Methods in Cross-Language Retrieval. Doctoral dissertation. Finland: Department of Information Science, University of Tampere.

44. Jansen, B.J., Spink, A., and Saracevic, T. (2000). Real life, real users, and real needs: a study and analysis of user queries on the web. *Information Processing and Management, 36*, pp. 207–227.

45. Schütze, H. (1998). Automatic word sense discrimination. *Computational Linguistics, 24*, pp. 97–123.

46. Oh, J.H. and Choi, K.S. (2002). Word sense disambiguation using static and dynamic sense vectors. *Proceedings of the 19th International Conference on Computational Linguistics, Taipei, Taiwan.*

47. Peat, H.J. and Willet, P. (1991). The limitations of term cooccurrence data for query expansion in document retrieval systems. *Journal of the American Society of Information Systems, 42*, pp. 378–383.

48. Chen, J.N. and Chang, J.S. (1998). A concept-based adaptive approach to word sense disambiguation. *Proceedings of 36th Annual Meeting of the Association for Computational Linguistics and 17th International Conference on Computational Linguistics.* Los Altos, CA: Morgan Kaufmann, Volume 1, pp. 237–243.

49. Guthriee, J.A., Guthrie, L., Aidinejad, H., and Wilks, Y. (1991). Subject-dependent cooccurrence and word sense disambiguation. *Proceedings of 29th Annual Meeting of the Association for Computational Linguistics,* pp. 146–152.

50. Kise, K., Junker, M., Dengel, A., and Matusmoto, K. (2004). Passage retrieval based on density distributions of terms and its applications to document retrieval and question answering. *Reading and Learning, Adaptive Content Recognition.* Lecture Notes in Computer Science. Springer, Volume 2956, pp. 306–327.

51. The ACM ditigal library. (2005). http://www.acm.org/dl/.

52. Kise, K., Fukushima, S., and Matsumoto, K. (2004). Document image retrieval in a question answering system for document images. *Proceedings of the Sixth International Workshop on Document Analysis Systems (DAS 2004).* Lecture Notes in Computer Science. Springer, Volume 3163, pp. 521–532.

Biometric and Forensic Aspects of Digital Document Processing

Sargur N. Srihari, Chen Huang, Harish Srinivasan, and Vivek Shah

17.1 Introduction

The field of forensic document examination (FDE) is concerned with issues such as whether the writer of a questioned document, say a ransom note, is the same as the known writer of sample documents, whether a signature is genuine or is a forgery, etc. The basis of the use of handwriting as evidence is its individuality, i.e. every person's writing is different, or every person's signature is unique.

More recently, researchers in biometrics have been developing automated means for authenticating a person, i.e. verifying whether a person is indeed who he/she claims to be. The commonly considered modalities for biometrics are fingerprints, iris, hand prints, voice, gait, etc. Since handwriting is a characteristic that is potentially unique to each individual and since it can be captured non-invasively, handwriting and signatures can also be useful as biometrics.

The field of FDE is much broader than the examination of handwriting and signatures. For instance, the examination of inks, typed and printed manuscripts is also in the purview of FDE. The area of commonality between forensics and biometrics is the examination of handwriting and signature by automated methods. It is this area of intersection that is addressed in this chapter.

Forensic examination has been largely based on manual examination by the expert to discern writing habits and other characteristics. Automated methods for handwriting examination are only recently being developed and introduced to the FDE community. Automated signature verification has a longer history although much of the work has been in the on-line case. The use of handwriting and signatures in biometrics is still more recent. Since handwriting is a behavioural characteristic, in contrast to biological characteristics such as fingerprints, handwriting is possibly useful to biometrics only when used in conjunction with other modalities.

17.1.1 Individuality of Handwriting

Writer identification has a long history perhaps dating to the origins of handwriting itself. Classic forensic handwriting examination is primarily based upon the knowledge and experience of the forensic expert.

The individuality of handwriting has been a contentious issue in the courts. There are several rulings in the United States courts that are concerned with the admissibility of handwriting as evidence. The central ruling on this issue is the supreme court case of Daubert *versus* Merrell Dow Pharmaceuticals, which required that any expert evidence to be admitted has to have a scientific basis. Whether a theory or methodology has a scientific basis has many philosophical implications, e.g. whether it is falsifiable. Four specific criteria to determine whether there exists a scientific basis for an expertise were proposed as follows: (i) experimentation, (ii) error rates, (iii) peer review of the methods and (iv) general acceptance.

Since many types of evidence used by the courts, e.g. fingerprints and handwriting, did not have support in all four measures, research was only recently undertaken to fill the gaps. The individuality of handwriting was studied recently leading to a characterization of the individuality of handwriting when there were sufficient amount of data available [1].

Due to the subjective nature of expert decisions, traditional methods are being supplemented by computerized semi-automatic and interactive systems. Such systems allow for large-scale testing so that error rates can be determined. The choice of the test sets is relevant, e.g. testing on data from twins or other cohort types would pose a more challenging test than when they are collected otherwise.

17.1.2 Organization of Chapter

Section 17.2 describes image pre-processing operations and interactive user interfaces for FDE. Section 17.3 describes discriminating elements, also known as *features* or *characteristics,* that are useful for writer/signature discrimination. Section 17.4 describes a statistical model for writer verification. This model is also applicable to signature verification and other biometric modalities such as voice and fingerprints. Section 17.5 describes an approach to signature verification that includes performance in terms of false acceptance rates and false rejection rates. The concluding remarks in Section 17.6 indicate the future of handwriting in forensics and biometrics.

17.2 Image Pre-processing and Interactive Tools

A computer system for retrieving a small set of documents from a large set, known as the Forensic Information System for Handwriting, or the FISH system [2], has been developed by German law enforcement. Also motivated by the forensic application, a handwritten document management system, known as CEDAR-FOX [3], has been developed for handwritten document analysis, identification, verification and document retrieval. As a document management system for forensic analysis, CEDAR-FOX provides user three major functionalities. First, it can be used as a document analysis system. Second, it can be used for creating a digital library for forensic handwritten documents, and third it can be used as a database management system for document retrieval and writer identification. The CEDAR-FOX system is used as a case study in the rest of this chapter.

As an interactive document analysis system, a graphic interface is provided. It can scan or load a handwritten document image. The system will first automatically extract features based on document image processing and recognition. The user can then use tools provided to perform document examination and extract document metrics. These tools include image selection, image enhancement, contour display, etc.

17.2.1 Region of Interest (ROI) Selection

A document image may include many text or graphical objects. In a complex document there could be combinations of machine-printed (or typed) paragraphs, tables, accompanying annotations, logos and signatures. The user often needs to specify a local region of most interest. A cropping tool is provided so that the user can scissor-out a region of interest (ROI) from the original document and then do all the analysis based on the selected ROI.

In addition, forensic document examiners use writing characteristic pertaining to certain characters or glyphs in comparing documents. For example, one of the features they often look for is the lower loop in characters "g" and "y". Thus identification and recognition of document components, including those belonging to the same character category, are always necessary and important. Besides automatic identification and recognition for isolated handwritten characters, the system also provides a useful tool for document examiners to easily crop out certain character images manually. Then, a set of features will be computed for the cropped characters for comparison. Figure 17.1 shows a screenshot of manually defined characters. The upper image shows a letter image "g" manually selected from each of two documents below.

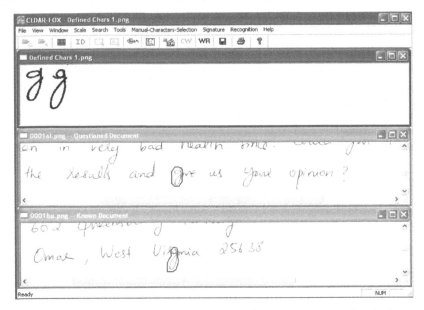

Fig. 17.1. Manually defined characters selected using an interactive device, e.g. mouse.

17.2.2 Image Pre-processing

Several tools for pre-processing the image need to be available for the purpose of preparing the image for analysis, either for further automatic processing or for human visual examination. Some of these, viz. thresholding, ruled-line removal, contour display and stroke thickening are described here.

Thresholding

Thresholding is to convert a grey-scale image into binary by determining a value for grey-scale (or threshold) below which the pixel can be considered to belong to the writing and above which to the background. The operation is useful to separate the foreground layer of the image, i.e. the writing, from the background layer, i.e. the paper. The system includes several types of thresholding algorithms, e.g. global thresholding – when the background is uniform as in the case of a cleanly written sheet of paper, adaptive thresholding – when the contrast varies. Figure 17.2 shows the result of a thresholding operation.

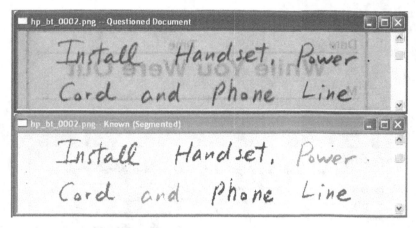

Fig. 17.2. Thresholding a grey-scale image into a binary image followed by line-and- word segmentation.

Segmentation

Once the foreground image is obtained, the writing can then be segmented, or scissored, into lines and words of text. Figure 17.2 shows the segmented lines and words also.

Underline Removal

The use of ruled-line paper is common in handwritten documents. Words and phrases are also sometimes underlined. If the document was written using rule-lined paper, an "underline removal" operation will erase the underlines automatically. Figure 17.3 shows a screen-shot of underline removal operation.

Contour Display

For the purpose of visual examination by a document examiner, displaying the detailed inner and outer contours of each stroke is useful. Figure 17.4 shows such a contour display.

Stroke Thickening

This operation takes faint lines and thickens them for visibility, which is shown in Figure 17.5.

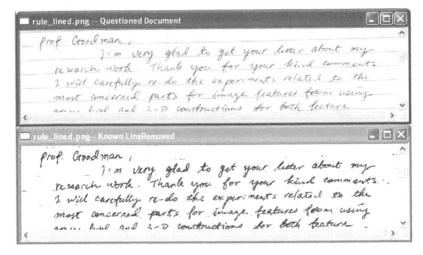

Fig. 17.3. Removal of ruled lines.

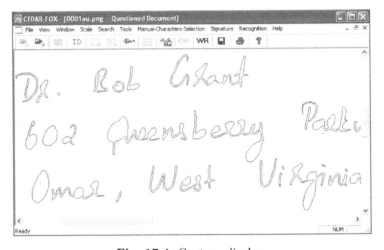

Fig. 17.4. Contour display.

17.3 Discriminating Elements and Their Similarities

Discriminating elements are characteristics of handwriting useful for writer discrimination. There are many discriminating elements for FDE, e.g. there are 21 classes of discriminating elements [4]. In order to match elements between two documents, the presence of the elements is first recognized in each document. Matching is performed between the same elements in each document.

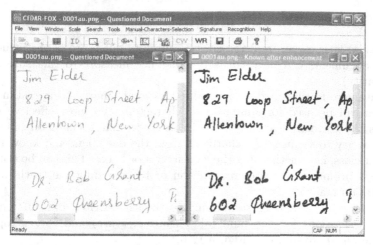

Fig. 17.5. Stroke thickening to enhance visibility.

Features that capture the global characteristics of the writer's individual writing habit and style can be regarded as macro-features and those that capture finer details at the character level as micro-features. For instance, macro-features are grey-scale based (entropy of the distribution of grey-scale values in the document the threshold needed to separate foreground from background (discussed in Section 17.2.2), and the number of black pixels in the document after thresholding), contour based (external and internal contours), slope based (horizontal, positive, vertical and negative), stroke-width, slant and height. Details of these features are described in [1].

Micro-features are attributes that describe the shapes of individual characters. A set of micro-features that capture the finest variations in the contour, intermediate stroke information and larger concavities and enclosed regions, e.g. [1] are derived from the scanned image of a character. These features are obtained from the character image by first imposing a 4×4 grid on it. From this grid, a 512-bit feature vector is determined as follows. Gradient (G) features, which are obtained using an image gradient (or derivative) operator, measure the magnitude of change in a 3×3 neighbourhood of each pixel. For each grid cell, by counting statistics of 12 gradients, there are $4 \times 4 \times 12 = 192$ gradient features. Structural (S) features capture certain patterns, i.e. mini-strokes, embedded in the gradient map. A set of 12 rules is applied to each pixel – to capture lines, diagonal rising and corners – yielding 192 structural features. Concavity (C) features, which capture global and topological features, e.g. bays and holes, are $4 \times 4 \times 8 = 128$ in number. These features were previously used in character recognition [5], word recognition [6] and writer identification [1]. The concept of micro-features can also be expanded to pairs of characters and other glyphs.

17.3.1 Similarity

Since macro-features are real valued, the absolute difference of the values for two documents can be used as the distance measure (or measure of dissimilarity).

Since micro-features are binary valued, several binary string distance measures can be used for similarity of characters, the most effective of which is the correlation measure [7]. In order to match characters, it is first necessary to segment the character from the document and know its character class, i.e. whether it is the character a or b, etc. This can be done either by automatic character recognition or by providing the truth and segmentation manually.

Similarity histograms corresponding to the same-writer and different-writer distributions for the numeral 3 (micro-feature) and for entropy (macro-feature) are shown in Figure 17.6.

17.4 Writer Verification

Writer verification is the task of determining whether two handwriting samples were written by the same or by different writers. In contrast, the task of writer identification is to determine for a questioned document as to which individual, with known handwriting, it belongs to. Identification can be accomplished by repeated verification against each known individual. However, a higher accuracy identification method can be devised by taking advantage of the differences among the known writers.

This section describes a statistical model of the task of verification that has three salient components: (i) parametric modelling of probability densities of feature dissimilarities, conditioned on being from the same or

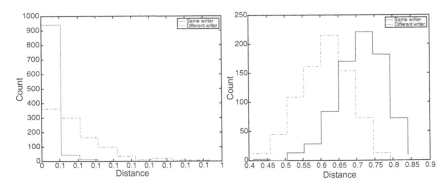

Fig. 17.6. Histograms of dissimilarity between pairs of handwriting samples for same and different writers for: (a) entropy, which is a macro-feature, and (b) numeral 3, which is characterized by micro-features.

different writer, (ii) design of the statistical classifier and (iii) computing the strength of evidence. Each of the components of the model is described in the following sections.

17.4.1 Parametric Models

The distributions of distances (or dissimilarities) conditioned on being from the same or different writer are useful to determine whether a given pair of samples belongs to the same writer or not. In the case of similarities that are continuous-valued, it is useful to model them as parametric densities, since it only involves storing the distribution parameters. Several choices exist for the parametric forms of the densities, e.g. Gaussian or other exponential distributions such as the gamma distribution.

Assuming that the similarity data can be acceptably represented by Gaussian or gamma distributions, the probability density functions of distances conditioned upon the same-writer and different-writer categories for a single feature x have the parametric forms $p_s(x) \sim N(\mu_s, \sigma_s^2)$, $p_d(x) \sim N(\mu_d, \sigma_d^2)$ for the Gaussian case, and $p_s(x) \sim Gam(a_s, b_s)$, $p_d(x) \sim Gam(a_d, b_d)$ for the gamma case. These parameters are estimated using maximum likelihood estimates. The Gaussian and gamma density functions are as follows:

$$Gaussian : p(x) = \frac{1}{(2\pi)^{1/2}\sigma} \exp^{-\frac{1}{2}(\frac{x-\mu}{\sigma})^2} \qquad (17.1)$$

$$Gamma : p(x) = \frac{x^{a-1}\exp^{(-x/b)}}{(\Gamma(a)).b^a} \qquad (17.2)$$

Conditional parametric pdfs for the numeral 3 (micro-feature) and for entropy (macro-feature) are shown in Figure 17.7.

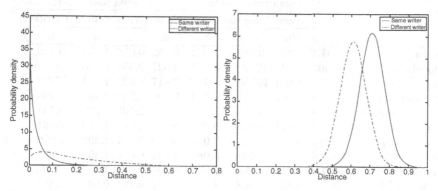

Fig. 17.7. Parametric pdfs for: (a) distances along the entropy feature, which are modelled by gamma distributions and (b) distances between pairs of numeral 3s, which are modelled by Gaussian distributions.

The Kullback Leibler (KL) divergence test was performed for each of the features to estimate whether it is better to model them as Gaussian or as gamma distributions. The gamma distribution is possibly the better model since distances are positive-valued, whereas the Gaussian assigns non-zero probabilities to negative values of distances. Table 17.1 gives the KL test result values, in bits, for each macro-feature. A training set size of 1000 samples was chosen for each of the same and different writers. The test set size was 500 for each. As can be seen, the gamma values are consistently lower than that of the Gaussian values, thereby indicating that the gamma is a better fit.

Table 17.1. KL test results for the 12 macro-features

Macro-feature	Same writer		Different writer	
	Gamma	Normal	Gamma	Normal
Entropy	0.133	0.921	0.047	0.458
Threshold	3.714	4.756	2.435	3.882
No. of black pixels	1.464	2.314	2.151	2.510
External contours	2.421	3.517	2.297	2.584
Internal contours	2.962	3.373	2.353	2.745
Horizontal slope	0.050	0.650	0.052	0.532
Positive slope	0.388	1.333	0.173	0.315
Vertical slope	0.064	0.664	0.054	0.400
Negative slope	0.423	1.385	0.113	0.457
Stroke width	3.462	6.252	3.901	4.894
Average slant	0.392	1.359	0.210	0.362
Average height	3.649	4.405	2.558	2.910

Table 17.2. Gaussian and gamma parameters for the 12 macro-features

Feature	Gaussian parameters				Gamma parameters			
	Same writer		Different writer		Same writer		Different writer	
	Mean	Std	Mean	Std	a	b	a	b
Entropy	0.0379	0.044	0.189	0.162	0.752	0.050	1.355	0.139
Threshold	1.603	2.025	12.581	35.430	0.627	2.559	0.126	99.779
No. of black pixels	22761	28971	107061	89729	0.617	36875	1.424	75204
External contours	1.828	2.965	9.135	7.703	0.380	4.810	1.406	6.496
Internal contours	2.626	2.348	5.830	5.144	1.251	2.100	1.285	4.538
Horizontal slope	0.013	0.014	0.072	0.066	0.930	0.014	1.179	0.061
Positive slope	0.014	0.023	0.112	0.081	0.392	0.037	1.890	0.059
Vertical slope	0.016	0.016	0.101	0.083	1.041	0.015	1.492	0.068
Negative slope	0.008	0.013	0.060	0.050	0.381	0.021	1.416	0.042
Stroke width	0.235	0.431	0.968	1.185	0.297	0.791	0.667	1.451
Average slant	1.730	2.674	12.402	8.955	0.419	4.133	1.918	6.465
Average height	1.809	1.920	8.458	7.147	0.888	2.037	1.400	6.039

Table 17.3. Comparison of error rates for each macro-feature when distances are modelled using gamma and Gaussian distributions

Macro-feature	Same writer		Different writer	
	Gamma	Normal	Gamma	Normal
Entropy	21.30	13.00	23.20	38.40
Threshold	2.60	2.60	53.40	60.00
No. of black pixels	22.19	9.80	22.40	39.60
External contours	30.10	6.20	18.60	46.80
Internal contours	28.30	8.80	33.00	56.60
Horizontal slope	13.44	5.40	25.20	34.40
Positive slope	10.59	3.60	16.80	31.20
Vertical slope	11.60	5.60	23.20	31.60
Negative slope	14.46	3.00	23.10	37.00
Stroke width	23.20	23.20	0.00	31.60
Average slant	9.97	3.00	18.60	31.40
Average height	17.43	5.00	22.40	40.80

The parameters of the distributions of the macro-feature distances (for a training set of size 1000) are given in Table 17.2.

The likelihood ratio (LR) summarizes the statement of the comparison process. The LR values for a given x (where x is the random variable) is obtained as $p_s(x)/p_d(x)$. The log-likelihood ratio (LLR), obtained by taking the logarithm of LR, is more useful since LR values tend to be very large (or small). The error rates (percent misclassification) obtained from a classifier based on the LLR (evaluated for each macro feature, using a test size of 500) are given in Table 17.3. The average error rate is lower for gamma over Gaussian although for one of the two classes (same writer) the Gaussian does better.

17.4.2 Design of Classifier

Since the document is characterized by more than one feature, we need a method of combining the feature values. We assume that the writing elements are statistically independent. Although this is strictly incorrect, the assumption has a certain robustness in that it is not an overfitting of the data. The resulting classifier, also known as the naive Bayes classifier, has yielded good results in machine learning. Moreover, in the earliest FDE literature, there is reference to multiplying the probabilities of handwriting elements (e.g. [8]).

Each of the two likelihoods that the given pair of documents were either written by the same or different individuals can be expressed, assuming statistical independence of the features as follows. For each writing element, $e_i, i = 1, \ldots, c$, where c is the number of writing elements considered, we compute the distance $d_i(j, k)$ between the jth occurrence of e_i in the first

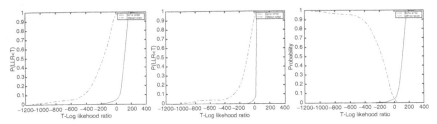

Fig. 17.8. CDF of LLRs for same and different writer populations (a) 12 macro- and 62 micro features, (b) 12 macro- and 8 micro-features, (c) CDF of LLRs for same-writer population and inverse CDF for different writer population.

document and the kth occurrence of e_i in the second document for that writing element. We estimate the likelihoods as

$$L_s = \prod_{i=1}^{c} \prod_j \prod_k p_s(d_i(j,k)) \qquad (17.3)$$

$$L_d = \prod_{i=1}^{c} \prod_j \prod_k p_d(d_i(j,k)) \qquad (17.4)$$

The log-likelihood ratio (LLR) in this case has the form

$$LLR = \sum_{i=1}^{c} \sum_j \sum_k [\ln p_s(d_i(j,k)) - \ln p_d(d_i(j,k))] \qquad (17.5)$$

The two cumulative distributions of LLRs corresponding to same and different writer samples are shown in Figure 17.8(a) and (b). It is observed that as the number of features considered decreases the separation between the two curves also decreases. The separation gives an indication of the separability between classes. The more the separation, the easier it is to classify.

For macro-features that are discrete, distances are modelled with a probability table. For macro-features that are continuous-valued, they are modelled as gamma distributions. The list of features and the distributions they are modelled by is given in Table 17.4. The list of macro-features modelled as gamma and their parameters are given in Table 17.5.

The distributions of micro-feature distances are also modelled as gamma distributions.

Performance with Twins Data Set

In many areas of forensics, it is traditional to evaluate performance on a set of twins. This is because they presumably pose higher similarities than a general population.

Table 17.4. Statistical models for for macro- and micro-features

Feature	Type of distribution	Modelled using
Entropy	Continuous	Gamma
Threshold	Discrete	Probability table
Black pixels	Continuous	Gamma
Exterior contours	Discrete	Probability table
Interior contour	Discrete	Probability table
Horizontal slope	Continuous	Gamma
Positive slope	Continuous	Gamma
Vertical Slope	Continuous	Gamma
Negative slope	Continuous	Gamma
Stroke width	Discrete	Probability table
Avg. slant	Discrete	Probability table
Avg. height	Continuous	Gamma
Avg. word gap	Continuous	Gamma
Micro-features (0–9,A–Z,a–z)	Continuous	Gamma

Table 17.5. Gamma parameters for continuous macro-features

Feature	Shape parameter		Scale parameter	
	Different writer	Same writer	Different writer	Same writer
Entropy	2.3585	2.7967	0.0179	0.0149
Black pixels	1.4838	1.7143	3520	1736.6
Horizontal slope	1.6041	1.2237	0.0444	0.0199
Positive slope	1.8346	0.9005	0.0569	0.0187
Vertical slope	1.8138	1.5775	0.0523	0.0150
Negative slope	1.3219	0.9506	0.0426	0.0100
Avg. height	1.5134	1.3562	5.2860	2.0184
Avg. word gap	2.9363	3.4487	0.0372	0.0128

Automatic writer verification was performed on a data set consisting of handwriting samples obtained from more than two hundred pairs of twins. This was done for both micro- and macro-features using both the gamma and Gaussian parametric models. It was found that gamma performed better (94.7%) than Gaussian (93.5%) for macro-features but did not improve the results for micro-features. This was more evident in the case of non-twins than twins. Considering just the macro-features, we were able to get 94.7% accuracy for samples of non-twins. A similar test was also done on the twin data set and it was found that gamma and Gaussian error rate are similar. Table 17.6 gives the error rate for twins and non-twins for each of the macro-features. The system was trained using 1500 same and 1500 different writer samples of different content.

Table 17.6. Macro-feature performance with twins and non-twins sample pairs

Features under consideration	Same writer Different content (SD) %		Different writer Different content (DD) %		Average error rate SD+DD %	
	Twins	Non-twins	Twins	Non-twins	Twins	Non-twins
Entropy	45.7	34.7	40.1	45.6	42.9	40.0
Threshold	18.0	21.4	36.9	33.7	27.5	27.6
Black pixels	32.8	30.0	41.8	35.6	37.3	32.8
Exterior contours	22.9	30.0	49.1	41.6	36.0	35.8
Interior contour	35.5	32.5	44.3	43.8	39.9	38.1
Horizontal slope	20.2	23.8	42.1	27.3	31.2	25.5
Positive slope	13.6	13.2	35.5	23.6	24.6	18.4
Vertical slope	17.5	16.5	41.4	24.0	29.5	20.2
Negative slope	14.5	14.9	38.9	28.4	26.7	21.6
Stroke width	31.9	31.3	41.1	36.5	36.5	33.9
Avg. slant	15.6	12.0	36.7	23.0	26.2	17.5
Avg. height	24.8	27.8	45.7	37.7	35.3	32.7
Avg. word gap	22.4	19.8	38.4	29.1	30.4	24.4

17.4.3 Evaluating the Strength of Evidence

In order to present the result in the form of the strength of evidence [9], it is useful to represent the LLR scores on a scale ranging from -1 to 1 (-1 representing a confident different writer case and 1 representing a confident same writer case). It would be inappropriate to state all results with $LLR > 0$ as same writer and all results with $LLR < 0$ as different writer. Instead of using binary decisions, a range of interpreted results is always better and more practical from the QDE point of view. Based on the Tippet plot [10] (inverse CDF plot) and the CDF plot, we develop a scheme for calibrating the LLR scores. The CDF and inverse CDF for same and different writer LLRs (considering 12 macro-features and 62 micro-features) is shown in Figure 17.8(c).

In the case of characters, the number of matches is variable resulting in multiple instances of each feature. Since the number of features is unbound, it is necessary to do some averaging to bound the value. Assume a set of m features (macro-features and 62 characters 0–9, a–z, A–Z represented by micro-features). If for the ith feature we get $k_i LLR$ values, $LLR_{i1}, LLR_{i2}, . LLR_{ik_i}$ then their average is

$$LLR_{ave}(i) = \frac{1}{k_i} \sum_{j=1}^{k_i} LLR_{ij} \qquad (17.6)$$

For each feature i, the CDF and inverse CDF for same and different writers are obtained from the distribution of $LLR_{ave}(i)$. For the same writer case, we obtain $P_{same_i}(LLR < LLR_{ave}(i))$ from the CDF of same writer LLR for that feature. For the different writer case, we obtain $P_{diff_i}(LLR > LLR_{ave}(i))$ from the inverse CDF of different writer LLR for that feature.

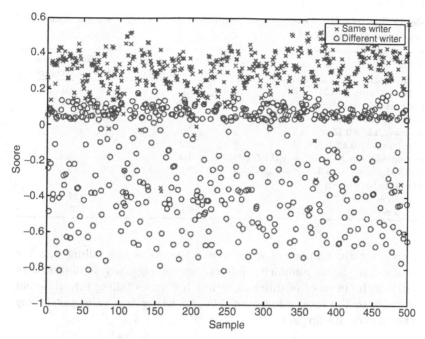

Fig. 17.9. Scatter plots of scores obtained for same and different writer test set after calibration.

Assuming m features are available, we compute the geometric means

$$P1 = \prod_{j=1}^{m}(P_{same_j})^{1/m} \quad and \quad P2 = \prod_{j=1}^{m}(P_{diff_j})^{1/m} \qquad (17.7)$$

to make the calibration independent of the number of features present. Finally, we compute the calibration score as $Score = P1 - P2$.

The values of $Score$ is always between -1 and 1. QD examiners use nine categories of opinion: identify, highly probable, probable, indicative did, no conclusion, indicative did not, probably did not, highly probable did not and eliminate. The scatter plots of scores obtained are shown in Figure 17.9 for 500 for same and 500 different writer cases. Observing the histograms of scores for same and different writers, the score range is divided into nine zones.

Table 17.7 summarizes the results of the calibration on the test set. The first four zones are same writer zones, the fifth is "no-conclusion" zone and the last four zones are different writer zones. Based on the zones obtained, 2.2% of same writer and 4.8% of different writer test cases fell into the "no-conclusion" zone. Same writer accuracy obtained was 94.6%, while different writer accuracy is 97.6%. Same writer accuracy is obtained as the ratio of the number of same writer test cases falling into same writer

Table 17.7. Strength of evidence calibration of LLR values (for the test set of 500 same and 500 different)

Category	Same writer (% in each category)	Different writer (% in each category)
Identified as same (>0.5)	2.0	0.0
Highly probable same (>0.35 & <0.5)	34.6	0.0
Probably did (>0.2 & <0.35)	48.8	0.0
Indications did (>0.15 & <0.2)	7.2	2.2
No conclusion (>0.12 & <0.15)	2.2	4.8
Indications did not (>-0.05 & <0.12)	3.6	45.4
Probably did not (>-0.3 & <-0.05)	0.6	12.6
Highly probable did not (>-0.65 & <-0.3)	1.0	27.8
Identified as different (<-0.65)	0.0	7.2

zones to the total number of same writer test cases not falling into the "no-conclusion" zone. Similarly, different writer accuracy is obtained as the ratio of the number of different writer test cases falling into different writer zones to the total number of different writer test cases not falling into the "no-conclusion" zone.

17.4.4 Summary of Writer Verification

A statistical model for a handwriting verification has been described. First, a set of characteristics from the questioned and known documents are extracted and their corresponding differences are recorded. The likelihoods for the two classes are computed assuming statistical independence of the distances, where the conditional probabilities for the differences are estimated using parametric probability densities that are either Gaussian or gamma. The log-likelihood ratio (LLR) of same and different writer are computed for decision making. Cumulative distributions of the LLRs are used to calibrate the LLR values so as to present the strength of evidence.

Using a specific set of characteristics with the model, same-writer accuracy was 94.6% and different-writer accuracy was 97.6%. Overall accuracy was 96.1% with only 3.5% of test cases falling into the "no-conclusion" zone.

17.5 Signature Verification

Automatic verification of signatures from scanned paper documents has many applications such as authentication of bank cheques, questioned document examination, biometrics, etc. On-line, or dynamic, signature verification systems have been reported with high success rates [11]. However, off-line or static research is relatively unexplored – the difference can be attributed to the lack of temporal information, the range of intra-personal variation in the scanned image, etc.

Methods have been described for both writer-dependent (WD) and writer-independent (WI) signature verification. WD models extract features from genuine signatures of a specific writer and are trained for that writer. The questioned signature is compared against the model for that writer. This is the standard approach to signature verification [12]. Based on a writer-independent approach to determining whether two handwritten documents – not just signatures – were written by the same person or not [1], a writer independent (WI) signature verification method was proposed in [13]. In the WI model, the probability distributions of within-writer and between-writer similarities, over all writers, are computed in the training phase. These distributions are used to determine the likelihood of whether a questioned signature is authentic.

17.5.1 Learning Strategies

Signature verification is a problem that can be approached using machine learning techniques. A set of samples of signatures, D, can be prepared with the help of several individuals. The parameters derived from such a set can be used in determining whether an arbitrary pair of signatures, e.g. a questioned signature and a genuine signature, match or not. One can also learn from samples of a specific individual and use only these parameters (or model) in matching for that individual.

These two learning strategies are: writer independent (WI) and writer dependent (WD), as shown in Figure 17.10. In WI learning, D_g and D_f are the training data sets of genuine and forged signatures from several writers. A model S is trained from pairs of samples (genuine-genuine and genuine-forgery) from D_g and D_f. Given a questioned signature Q and a set K of genuine signatures for individual w, S is used to determine whether Q is accepted as genuine. In WD learning, only the genuines for individual w, i.e. the set K, is used to determine the model S, which is then used to determine whether Q is accepted as genuine.

17.5.2 Signature Test-Bed

A database of off-line signatures was prepared as a test bed. Each of 55 individuals contributed 24 signatures, thereby creating 1320 genuine signatures. Some were asked to forge three other writers' signatures, eight times per subject, thus creating 1320 forgeries. One example of each of 55 genuines are shown in Figure 17.11. Ten examples of genuines of one subject (subject no. 21) and 10 forgeries of that subject are shown in Figure 17.12.

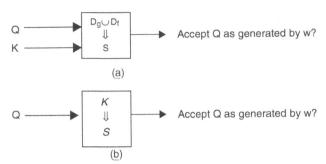

(a)

(b)

Fig. 17.10. Verification models: (a) writer independent: a questioned (Q) is matched against a set of genuines K using a model S derived from genuines and forgeries of other writers and (b) writer dependent: a model for an individual is determined using only K.

Fig. 17.11. Genuine signature samples.

Fig. 17.12. Samples for one writer: (a) genuines and (b) forgeries.

Image Preprocessing

Each signature was scanned at 300-dpi grey scale and binarized using a grey-scale histogram. Salt-and-pepper noise was removed by median filtering. Slant normalization was performed by extracting the axis of least

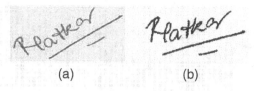

(a)   (b)

Fig. 17.13. Pre-processing: (a) original (b) final.

inertia and rotating the curve until this axis coincides with the horizontal axis [14]. Given an $M \times N$ image, $G = (u_k, v_k) = (x_{(i,j)}, y_{(i,j)} | x_{(i,j)} \neq 0, y_{(i,j)} \neq 0)$. Let S be the size of G, and let $\overline{u} = \frac{1}{S} \sum_k u_k$ and $\overline{v} = \frac{1}{S} \sum_k v_k$ be the coordinates of the centre of mass of the signature. The orientation of the axis of least inertia is given by that of the least eigenvector of the 2×2 matrix $I = \begin{pmatrix} \overline{u^2} & \overline{uv} \\ \overline{uv} & \overline{v^2} \end{pmatrix}$, where $\overline{u^2} = \frac{1}{S} \sum_k (u_k - \overline{u})^2$, $\overline{v^2} = \frac{1}{S} \sum_k (v_k - \overline{v})^2$ and $\overline{uv} = \frac{1}{S} \sum_k (u_k - \overline{u})(v_k - \overline{v})$ are the second-order moments of the signature [15]. The result of binarization and slant normalization of a grey-scale image is shown in Figure 17.13.

Feature Extraction

Features for static signature verification can be one of three types [16, 17]: (i) *global*: extracted from every pixel that lie within a rectangle circumscribing the signature, including image gradient analysis [18] , series expansions [19], etc. (ii) *statistical*: derived from the distribution of pixels of a signature, e.g. statistics of high grey-level pixels to identify pseudo-dynamic characteristics [20], (iii) *geometrical and topological*: e.g. local correspondence of stroke segments to trace signatures [21], feature tracks and stroke positions [16], etc. A combination of all three types of features was used in a writer-independent (WI) signature verification system [13, 22]. These features, expanded from the GSC features of characters (see Section 17.3), were used here.

The average size of all reference signature images was chosen as the reference size to which all signatures were resized. The image is divided into a 4×8 grid from which a 1024-bit GSC feature vector is determined (Figure 17.14). Gradient (G) features measure the magnitude of change in a 3×3 neighbourhood of each pixel. For each grid cell, by counting statistics of 12 gradients, there are $4 \times 8 \times 12 = 384$ gradient features. Structural (S) features capture certain patterns, i.e. mini-strokes, embedded in the gradient map. A set of 12 rules is applied to each pixel – to capture lines, diagonal rising and corners – yielding 384 structural features. Concavity (C) features, which capture global and topological features, e.g. bays and holes, are $4 \times 8 \times 8 = 256$ in number.

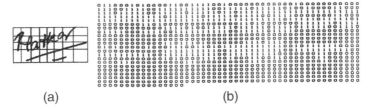

(a)   (b)

Fig. 17.14. Features: (a) variable grid and (b) feature vector.

Distance Measure

A method of measuring the similarity or distance between two signatures in feature space is essential for classification. The correlation distance performed best for GSC binary features [23], which is defined for two binary vectors X and Y, as follows:

$$d(X,Y) = \frac{1}{2} - \frac{s_{11}s_{00} - s_{10}s_{01}}{2((s_{10} + s_{11})(s_{01} + s_{00})(s_{11} + s_{01})(s_{00} + s_{10}))^{1/2}} \quad (17.8)$$

where s_{ij} represents the number of corresponding bits of X and Y that have values i and j. Both the WI-DS and WD-DT methods described below use $d(X,Y)$ as the distance measure.

17.5.3 Writer-Independent Verification

The objective is to determine whether pair (K, Q) belongs to the same individual, where Q is a questioned signature and K is a set of known signatures for that individual. Two WI classification methods, distance statistics [1] and naive Bayes, are presented below.

Distance Statistics (DS) Method

The verification approach of [1] is based on two distributions of distances $d(X,Y)$: genuine–genuine and genuine–forgery pairs. The distributions are denoted as P_g and P_f, respectively. The means and variances of $d(X,Y)$ where both X and Y are genuine, and X is genuine and Y is a forgery are shown in Figure 17.15, where the number of writers varies from 10 to 55. Here, 16 and genuines 16 forgeries were randomly chosen from each subject. For each n, there are two values corresponding to the mean and variance of $n \times C_2^{16}$ pairs of same writer (or genuine–genuine pair) distances and $n \times 16^2$ pairs of different writer (or genuine–forgery pair) distances. The values are close to constant with $\mu_g = 0.24$ and $\mu_f = 0.28$ with corresponding variances $\sigma_g = 0.055$ and $\sigma_f = 0.05$. Given a questioned signature Q and a single known signature K, the probabilities of $d(K, Q)$

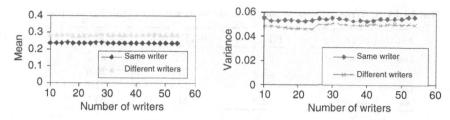

Fig. 17.15. Statistics of genuine–genuine and genuine–forgery distances.

are: $P(genuine|Q) = P_g(d(K,Q))$ and $P(forged|Q) = P_f(d(K,Q))$. Q is accepted as genuine if the genuine probability exceeds the forgery probability. Normal distributions are assumed for genuine–genuine distances and genuine–forgery distances.

Generalization to n genuines: when there are n genuine signatures available, i.e. $|K| > 1$, given a questioned signature Q,

$$P(genuine|Q) = \prod_{j=1}^{n} P_g(d(K_j, Q)) \tag{17.9}$$

$$P(forged|Q) = \prod_{j=1}^{n} P_f(d(K_j, Q)) \tag{17.10}$$

Naive Bayes (NB) Method

Rather than determining the distributions of distances between two feature vectors, each pair of corresponding bits in the questioned and known feature vectors can be treated as random variables. The pairs corresponding to different positions in the feature vector are considered to be independent and identically distributed, which is the naive Bayes (NB) assumption. Let feature vectors $X = \{x_1, x_2, \ldots, x_n\}$ and $Y = \{y_1, y_2, \ldots, y_n\}$. The probabilities of ith same-value bits in a genuine–genuine pair and a genuine–forgery pair are computed using:

$$P_{s,x_i=y_i} = \frac{|(X,Y)|x_i = y_i, X, Y \in D_g|}{|(X,Y)|X, Y \in D_g|} \tag{17.11}$$

$$P_{s,x_i \neq y_i} = \frac{|(X,Y)|x_i \neq y_i, X, Y \in D_g|}{|(X,Y)|X, Y \in D_g|} \tag{17.12}$$

$$P_{d,x_i=y_i} = \frac{|(X,Y)|x_i = y_i, X \in D_g, Y \in D_f|}{|(X,Y)|X \in D_g, Y \in D_f|} \tag{17.13}$$

$$P_{d,x_i \neq y_i} = \frac{|(X,Y)|x_i \neq y_i, X \in D_g, Y \in D_f|}{|(X,Y)|X \in D_g, Y \in D_f|} \tag{17.14}$$

Table 17.8. Writer-independent methods with 1 and 16 training samples

Methods (n)	FRR (%)	FAR (%)	AER (%)
Distance stats(1)	27.6	27.8	27.7
Naive Bayes(1)	27.2	26.0	26.6
Distance stats(16)	21.3	22.1	21.7
Naive Bayes(16)	22.9	24.1	23.5

where D_g and D_f are the training sets of genuine and forged signatures. Knowing the probabilities of the values of the bit pair for each feature, given (K, Q), the overall genuine–genuine and genuine–forgery probabilities are calculated as the product of the probabilities for all feature pairs, i.e.,

$$P(genuine|Q) = P_s(K, Q) = \prod_{i=1}^{1024} P_{s,k_i=q_i}^{k_i \otimes q_i} P_{s,k_i \neq q_i}^{k_i \oplus q_i} \qquad (17.15)$$

$$P(forged|Q) = P_d(K, Q) = \prod_{i=1}^{1024} P_{d,k_i=q_i}^{k_i \otimes q_i} P_{d,k_i \neq q_i}^{k_i \oplus q_i} \qquad (17.16)$$

They are compared to determine whether they are from the same writer or not. Generalization to n genuines is as follows:

$$P(genuine|Q) = \prod_{j=1}^{n} P_s(K_j, Q) \qquad (17.17)$$

$$P(forged|Q) = \prod_{j=1}^{n} P_d(K_j, Q) \qquad (17.18)$$

Performance

The two writer-independent methods were evaluated using the test bed. False reject rate (FRR), false accept rate (FAR) and average error rate (AER = (FRR + FAR)/2) were determined. To calculate probabilities 16 genuines and 16 forgeries from each subject were randomly chosen as the training set and the rest are used as test set. FRR, FAR and AER of two methods are shown in Table 17.8.

In Table 17.8, the probabilities with 16 training samples were calculated as follows. The probabilities in WI-DS are the products of 16 distance probabilities. For WI-NB, the probabilities are products over individual probabilities for each feature and over sixteen known samples. The WI-DS and WI-NB were evaluated with 16 genuines in training compared to one in section 17.5.3. Instead of original distance probabilities in WI-DS and feature probabilities in WI-NB, the product of 16 distance probabilities in WI-DS or the product of feature probabilities in WI-NB was used.

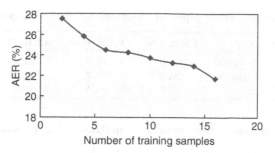

Fig. 17.16. Average error rate of writer-independent distance statistics method.

With both methods performance increases with more training genuines. For training, n genuines were randomly chosen. The test set consisted of 8 genuines from the rest and 24 forgeries. WI-DS has the best performance. Figure 17.16 shows performance improvement of WI-DS with n.

17.5.4 Writer-Dependent Verification

Assuming that there exist sufficient training genuines, a machine of S is learned only from the training data for a specific individual. Four classification methods were considered: distance threshold (which is the standard method used of biometrics), distance statistics, naive Bayes and SVM. Two sub-formulations are considered: one-class where forgeries for the individual are unavailable, and two-class where genuines and forgeries are available.

Training with Genuines Only

Distance Threshold (DT): The DT method is the common signature verification model. The first step is to enrol genuines K as reference signatures. The distance $d(X, Y)$ is computed for each pair (X, Y) in K to determine the threshold $thres = max\{d(X, Y) | X, Y \in K\}$. Given a questioned signature Q, the average of $\{d(Q, Y) | Y \in K\}$, denoted as $dist$, is computed. If $dist < thres$, then Q is accepted as a genuine; and rejected otherwise.

Distance Statistics (DS): Here the genuine–genuine distance distribution is obtained only from K, i.e. the mean and variance of P_g are determined from $\{d(X, Y) | X, Y \in K\}$. The genuine–forgery distance distribution P_f is from D_g and D_f as in WI-DS.

Naive Bayes (NB): Let $X = \{x_1, x_2, ..., x_n\}$, where $X \in K$. Two distributions are computed from K: Given a test signature $Q = \{q_1, q_2, ..., q_n\}$, the likelihood, $P(genuine|Q) = \prod_{i=1}^{n} P_{s, x_i = q_i}$. A common optimal threshold $thres$ for the likelihoods is trained for all writers. Q is accepted as a genuine if $P(genuine|Q) \geq thres$.

Experimental results for three methods, with a training set size of 16, are shown in Table 17.9. Here, the distance threshold performs best.

Table 17.9. One-class writer-dependent methods (trained with genuines only)

Methods (n)	FRR (%)	FAR (%)	AER (%)
Distance threshold	22.5	19.5	21.5
Distance statistics	23.0	21.7	22.4
Naive Bayes	25.9	24.1	25.0

Table 17.10. Two-class writer-dependent methods (with 16 genuines and 5 forgeries)

Methods (n)	FRR (%)	FAR (%)	AER (%)
Distance Statistics	17.6	20.7	19.2
Naive Bayes	9.95	13.0	11.45
SVM	8.5	10.1	9.3

Training with Genuines and Forgeries

Forgeries were included in training in the following experiments. In WD-DT, since the threshold is determined only by genuines, it is unchanged. However, in WD-DS, instead of gathering genuine–forgery distance distribution from all writers, such distribution is generated directly from the genuine–forgery pairs for the individual. Similarly in WD-NB, 0 and 1 distributions of each feature in forgeries are generated from the feature vectors in the forgery set.

In a support vector machine (SVM) [24, 25], hyperplanes are determined by support vectors instead of training samples. Due to unbalanced training datasets, instead of finding equal size maximal margin on both sizes of optimal hyperplanes, margins are dynamically adjusted according to sample sizes. With more positive samples than negative ones, different penalty parameters are used to balance weights. Given training vectors $x_i \in R^n, i = 1, ..., l$, in two classes, and a vector $y \in R^l$ such that $y_i \in \{1, -1\}$, the formation in [26] solves the classification problem for unbalanced data.

For each writer, 16 genuines were randomly selected from the genuine set and 5 forgeries selected from the forgery set by one forger. The other 8 genuines and 16 forgeries by other forgers constitute the test set. Table 17.10 presents the classification results showing that SVM outperforms others.

17.5.5 Summary of Signature Verification

Several learning strategies for signature verification were evaluated using a high-dimensional feature space that captures both local geometric information as well as stroke information. In the writer-independent case, the newly introduced distance statistics method outperformed classical distance threshold and naive Bayes approaches. In the writer-dependent case, distance threshold performed best with distance statistics being close. The distance statistics method has the advantage that it can be used when few training examples, even one, are available, and it generates a match likelihood rather than a distance score.

17.6 Concluding Remarks

The use of automated methods in writer verification and identification is in its early stages. The use of handwriting and signatures in biometrics is at an even earlier stage. The early results indicate their potential for use in both biometrics and forensics.

Writer identification has significant potential since high accuracies can be obtained as larger samples of handwriting, e.g. line, paragraph, page, etc. are available. In the case of signatures, the same high accuracies that can be obtained in the on-line case cannot be expected in the off-line case. Also, it can be argued that since the amount of writing available in a signature is limited, compared with a paragraph of writing, its accuracies will be lower. However, the signature is known to be deliberately individualistic – and therefore has a strong potential as a biometric.

The entire field of off-line handwriting processing by computer is in its infancy although much success has been achieved in constrained domains such as postal address reading and bank cheque reading. As recognition techniques improve the methods of writer verification will also improve, particularly since recognition is frequently the first step in verification. Improvement of recognition will in turn depend upon the ability to exploit contextual knowledge.

References

1. Srihari, S.N., Cha, S., Arora, H., and Lee, S. (2002). Individuality of handwriting. *Journal of Forensic Sciences, 47(4)*, pp. 856–872.
2. Franke, K., Schomaker, L., Vuurpijl, L., and Giesler, S. (2003). Fish-new: a common ground for computer-based forensic writer identification. *Proceedings of the Third European Academy of Forensic Science Triennial Meeting, Istanbul, Turkey*, p. 84.
3. Srihari, S.N., Zhang, B., Tomai, C., Lee, S., Shi, Z., and Shin, Y.C. (2003). A system for hand-writing matching and recognition. *Proceedings of the Symposium on Document Image Understanding Technology (SDIUT), Greenbelt, MD*.
4. Huber, R. and Headrick, A. (1999). *Handwriting Identification: Facts and Fundamentals*. Boca Raton, FL: CRC Press.

5. Srikantan, G., Lam, S., and Srihari, S.N. (1996). Gradient-based contour encoding for character recognition. *Pattern Recognition, 7*, pp. 1147–1160.
6. Zhang, B. and Srihari, S.N. (2003). Analysis of handwriting individuality using handwritten words. *Proceedings of the Seventh International Conference on Document Analysis and Recognition, Edinburgh, Scotland.*
7. Zhang, B., Srihari, S.N., and Lee, S.-J. (2003). Individuality of handwritten characters. *Proceedings of the Seventh International Conference on Document Analysis and Recognition (ICDAR)*, pp. 1086–1090.
8. Osborn, A.S. (1029). *Questioned Documents.* London: Nelson Hall Pub.
9. Champod, C. (1999). The inference of identity of source: theory and practice. *The First International Conference on Forensic Human Identification in the Millennium, London, UK, October 1999*, pp. 24–26.
10. Tippett, C.F., Emerson, V.J., Fereday, M.J., Lawton, F., and Lampert, S.M. (1968). The evidential value of the comparison of paint flakes from sources other than vehicles. *Journal of Forensic Sciences Society, 8*, pp. 61–65.
11. Plamondon, R. and Srihari, S.N. (2000). On-line and off-line handwriting recognition: a comprehensive survey. *IEEE Transactions on Pattern Analysis and Machine Intelligence, 22(1)*, pp. 63–84.
12. Plamondon, R. and Lorette, G. (2000). On-line and off-line handwriting recognition: a comprehensive survey. *IEEE Transactions on Pattern Analysis and Machine Intelligence, 22(1)*, pp. 63–84.
13. Kalera, M.K., Zhang, B., and Srihari, S.N. (2003). Off-line signature verification and identification using distance statistics. *Proceedings of the International Graphonomics Society Conference, Scottsdale, AZ*, pp. 228–232.
14. Horn, B. (1986). Robot Vision. Cambridge, MA: MIT Press.
15. Munich, M.E. and Perona, P. (2003). Visual identification by signature tracking. *IEEE Transactions on Pattern Analysis and Machine Intelligence, 25(2)*, pp. 200–217.
16. Fang, B., Leung, C.H., Tang, Y.Y., Tse, K.W., Kwok, P.C.K., and Wong, Y.K. (2003). Off-line signature verification by the tracking of feature and stroke positions. *Pattern Recognition, 36*, pp. 91–101.
17. Lee, S. and Pan, J.C. (1992). Off-line tracing and representation of signatures. *IEEE Transactions on Systems, Man and Cybernetics, 22*, pp. 755–771.
18. Sabourin, R. and Plamondon, R. (1986). Preprocessing of handwritten signatures from image gradient analysis. *Proceedings of the Eighth International Conference on Pattern Recognition*, pp. 576–579.
19. Lin, C.C. and Chellappa, R. (1997). Classification of partial 2-d shapes using fourier descriptors. *IEEE Transactions on Pattern Analysis and Machine Intelligence, 9*, pp. 696–690.
20. Ammar, M., Yoshido, Y., and Fukumura, T. (1986). A new effective approach for off-line verification of signatures by using pressure features. *Proceedings of the Eighth International Conference on Pattern Recognition*, pp. 566–569.
21. Guo, J.K., Doermann, D., and Rosenfeld, A. (1997). Local correspondence for detecting random forgeries. *Proceedings of the International Conference on Document Analysis and Recognition*, pp. 319–323.
22. Xu, A., Kalera, M.K., and Srihari, S.N. (2004). Learning strategies and classification methods for off-line signature verification. *Proceedings of the Ninth International Workshop on Frontiers in Handwriting Recognition*, pp. 161–166.

23. Zhang, B. and Srihari, S. (2003). Binary vector dissimilarity measures for handwriting identification. *Proceedings of SPIE, Document Recognition and Retrieval X*, pp. 155–166.

24. Joachims, T. (1998). Text categorization with support vector machines: learning with many relevant features. *Proceedings of the European Conference on Machine Learning*, pp. 137–142.

25. Osuna, E., Freund, R., and Girosi, F. (1997). Support vector machines: training and applications. Technical Report AIM-1602. MIT.

26. Boser, B., Guyon, I., and Vapnik, V. (1992). A training algorithm for optimal margin classifiers. *Proceedings of the Fifth Annual Workshop on Computational Learning Theory*.

18

Web Document Analysis

Apostolos Antonacopoulos and Jianying Hu

18.1 Introduction

The Web has now become a very popular information repository where content providers and end-users routinely publish and access, respectively, documents on-line. The availability and extent of this vast and varied information gives rise to the need for automated content analysis. Such content analysis is crucial for applications such as information extraction, web mining, summarization, content re-purposing for mobile and multi-modal access and web security.

There are two broad categories of web documents, those that are intended and designed as web services and those that are created as web publications, where visual appearance (to human users) is critical. The development of XML and the new initiatives on the Semantic Web aim to improve the machine-readability of web documents. This semantic tagging makes content analysis rather straightforward for the documents that conform to such standards. However, while such conformance is generally true for the former type of documents, it is far less common in the latter (web publications). This fact is unlikely to change as web publications are produced by a multitude of the widest variety of authors (practically anyone can create web documents and publish them on their website). It is, therefore, correspondingly unlikely that the challenges for content analysis will diminish significantly.

The emerging issues pose new challenges (and opportunities) for Document Analysis, in a number of traditional as well as new areas. This chapter presents an overview of a number of diverse and interdisciplinary areas that reflect current research directions. The following section discusses the broad fundamental topics of web content extraction, repurposing and mining. Section 18.3 focusses on issues related to images (and their content) encountered in web documents. Finally, the complementary areas (to analysis) of web document modelling and annotation are discussed in Section 18.4, before the chapter concludes with Section 18.5.

18.2 Web Content Extraction, Repurposing and Mining

Web content extraction refers to the process of identifying and retrieving any specific information from a web page. It goes beyond traditional information extraction which focusses on text analysis using Natural Language Processing techniques [30] and aims to make use of the structural information embedded in the markup language. On the one hand, web pages are always encoded in a markup language such as HTML or XHTML which could potentially contain rich structural information. On the other hand, for many web pages, particularly those created as on-line publication, markup tags are primarily used to create a specific display and thus do not directly correspond to any semantics or formal relations. Thus web documents are often referred to as "semi-structured" documents, and much effort in web content extraction has been focussed on inferring semantics from the markup tags.

One of the earliest works in this area was a wrapper induction system developed in 1997 [24]. The system generates extraction rules using a designated set of HTML tags as delimiters for document head, tail and data tuples for specific content such as weather or restaurant. Since then, much effort has been made by various researchers to develop wrapper induction systems that can accommodate more variations in formatting (e.g. [14, 19, 30, 31]). One limitation of this line of systems is that they all treat a marked up document as a sequence and thus the analysis is inherently local, making it difficult to infer structural relations between items places far apart in the text stream.

In order to take advantage of document structures at higher levels, researchers started analysing the HTML parse tree, or directly the DOM tree of a web document [1, 11, 13, 29, 33]. While the DOM tree provides a much more global view of the document structure, it is still insufficient because there are often multiple ways of arranging different markup tags to achieve the same appearance. As a result, a visually regular document may be highly irregular in its DOM structure, or multiple structural patterns of the DOM tree may correspond to the same visual pattern. Cohen et al. identified the problem and used pre-processing to normalize some of the common variations [11]. Others used features designed to directly infer visual characteristics of documents. Wang and Hu developed layout features to measure the visual coherence among potential table cells [45]. Yang et al. introduced visual similarity measures based on attributes such as size and colour of various DOM objects [46]. Because the rendering of a web document is highly device dependent, how to reliably infer visual structure from its DOM structure remains a challenge.

One type of document structure that has attracted particular interest is the table. As a compact and efficient way to present relational information, tables are used frequently in web documents. Since tables are inherently concise as well as information rich, the automatic understanding of tables is central to web content extraction. The processes of table understanding in web documents include table detection, functional and structural analysis and finally table interpretation. Table detection is necessitated by the fact that the <table> tag and its associated group of tags (<tr>, <td>, etc.) are very often used not only for relational information display but also to create any type of multiple-column layout to facilitate easy viewing, thus their presence alone does not necessarily indicate the presence of a true relational table. Wang et al. defined *genuine* tables to be document entities where a two-dimensional grid is semantically significant in conveying the logical relations among the cells [45]. Conversely, *non-genuine* tables are document entities where <table> tags are used as a mechanism for grouping contents into clusters for easy viewing only. Figure 18.1 gives a few examples of both genuine and non-genuine tables on a single web page.

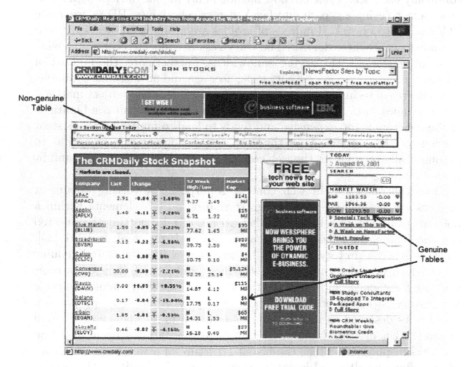

Fig. 18.1. Examples of genuine and non-genuine tables on a web page.

Penn et al. used a simple set of rules specifically designed to identify genuine tables appearing in news front pages [33]. Wang and Hu proposed a machine learning based method to detect genuine tables in generic web pages using a combination of layout, content type and linguistic features [45]. Cohen et al. proposed a wrapper induction system exploiting multiple document representations including a token sequence, a DOM tree as well as derived views of visual characteristics such as the size and font of rendered text and geometric analysis of tabular information [11]. They applied this wrapper system to the problem of table detection in generic web pages. Yoshida et al. focussed on the problems of table structure analysis and content interpretation assuming genuine tables are already detected [47]. They identified and trained classifiers for nine common types of table layout. Once the layout type of a table is identified, corresponding attribute–value pairs are extracted. They then used such automatically extracted pairs to train an ontology which can then be used to automatically extract similar attribute-value pairs from non-table structures such as a list.

An area closely associated with web content extraction is web content repurposing. Web documents have traditionally been designed for display on large computer screens. However, in recent years we have witnessed a rapid increase in the types of devices used to access the web. The range of commonly used access devices now include many mobile devices with small or no screen (using a speech interface) such as cell phones, PDAs, wearable PCs and set-top boxes. Hundreds of profiles are available for accessing web documents using these devices. These devices are connected through a wide range of networks with varying bandwidths. Furthermore, the number of different usage scenarios – activity type, user age and profile, time available, user's degree of technical savvy and prior knowledge of the subject matter – also continues to increase. Handcrafting web content for all combinations of these factors is too expensive and tends to lead to multiple, inconsistent versions of the content. Thus the goal of web content repurposing is to automatically re-engineer the web content designed for one scenario and fit it another [39].

Two central issues in web content repurposing involving document analysis are the analysis and categorization of various elements within a document for content selection, and strategies of reformatting the selected content. The earliest work in this area was by Penn et al. in 2001 [33]. They designed a prototype system to extract new link items and genuine table, which were determined to be the most content rich items on a news web site front page, and reformat them in a hierarchical manner suitable for delivery to a text only mobile phone display. Alam et al. proposed a set of rules designed to identify and re-author lists for display on a small screen [1]. Chen et al. developed a web page adaptation scheme based on two-level display [10]. First, the layout structure of a web page is analyse of identifying smaller and logically related unites. If identified, the page is re-authored with thumb-nail representations providing a global view as well as index into sub-pages at the second level. For pages that cannot be split logically, auto-positioning and scrolling-by-block are provided as an alternative to assist browsing. Chen et al. proposed using a specialized binary tree called DRESS (Document REpresentation for Scalable Structure) as a scalable representation of web documents to facilitate dynamic adaptation of content based on display and bandwidth requirements [9].

Web content has rapidly become increasingly multi-media and many recent papers have started to look at image or video elements in the context of a web document. Addressing the issue that many documents available on-line are in page image form (e.g. PDF) which by itself provides no markup information for reformatting, Breuel et al. proposed a novel method to segment a document image into atomic fragments (e.g. word images), which can then be "reflowed" onto a display device of arbitrary size and aspect ratio [7]. Kasik focussed on issues involved in the effective partitioning and display of technical drawings and descriptive geometry, which are two types of graphical images frequently used by industrial companies such as Boeing [23]. Hu and Bagga proposed a system for functionally categorizing images found in web documents [16]. They argued that for content repurposing applications it is more important to categorize an image based on what it is used for (e.g. Story, Commercial, Heading, Icon, etc.) rather than what is in the image. As the first step towards an automatic functionality based image categorization system, they designed an algorithm to automatically identify news and preview images using a combination of image-based features and linguistic features extracted from the surrounding text.

Another area related to web content extraction is web content mining. In this context the structural information extracted from a web document is used to enrich the features or similarity measures that are used to compare different web pages for the purpose of either searching for unknown patterns or classification into known classes. Schenker et al. proposed representing a web document as a graph and extended the traditional vector-based clustering framework to a graph-based k-mean clustering algorithm [37]. Lopresti and Wilfong designed a novel probing-based method to efficiently compute the similarity between graphs representing different web pages [27]. Shih and Karger designed a machine learning framework to classify a web link based on its location in the URL hierarchy as well as layout placement on the referring page [38]. They demonstrated promising results using this technique for ad blocking and page recommendation.

18.3 Web Image Analysis

In terms of images (especially in terms of their function and nature), there are important distinctions between web documents and traditional documents. A web document is rendered visually on a browser screen as a collection of parametrically formatted objects (e.g. encoded text) and images. As there are rather limiting constraints on what can be achieved by the former, images may be used not only for their illustrative value (as in traditional documents) but also for achieving particular layout effects.

First, in the worst case (no semantic value), is the example of small transparent images used sometimes to achieve specific spacing between objects. Second, of slightly higher semantic value, are items such as bullets, borders, separators, etc. used not only for decorative but also for delimiting document entities. Third, is the more interesting case of (usually semantically important) text that exists in image form. This is text that is only visible when the corresponding image that contains it is viewed. Finally, there can be images in web documents much as there are illustrations (e.g. photographs, graphics, etc.) in traditional documents. This section focusses on the analysis of the latter two instances – text in image form and general images.

Text in image form results (in almost all cases) from the desire of the web document author to present the text with an effect that is not possible using standard markup language features. This text is usually created with a graphics software tool, the necessary effects are applied (to it and its background) and the result is saved in image format (e.g. JPEG, GIF, etc.). It is interesting to note that it is, more often than not, text of high indexing value (such as titles and headings) that receives this treatment (authors create it in a way that "stands out" from the surrounding text).

There is an increasing need to extract and recognize text in image form for the following reasons. First, current search engine technology ignores such text when indexing (text in images is simply inaccessible to current tools). Second, for a number of web document analysis applications (including content repurposing, summarization, voice browsing, etc.) it is necessary to have access to the full text of the document in a uniform machine readable form. Finally, despite the existence of means for alternative textual descriptions of images (e.g. the ALT tag), web authors do not ensure the existence or consistency of these descriptions (a number of studies [2,21,28] has shown that as many as 56% of the ALT tag description are either incorrect or simply do not exist).

The extraction and recognition of text in web images is a substantially more complex problem than the one faced by OCR in traditional documents. There is usually not enough information in the image (72 dpi resolution, about 5–7 pt text size [28]) and various image artefacts are present due to colour quantization and lossy compression.

A relatively small number of approaches have been proposed so far to address this problem. Naturally, most methods produce good results for relatively simple images, but fail when more complex images are encountered. This can be due to some methods' requirement for the existence of only a very small number of colours in the image (they do not work on full-colour – e.g. JPEG – images). Some methods also assume a practically constant and uniform colour for text [4,28] and fail when this is not the case. While

Fig. 18.2. An example of text in image form, showing some of the difficulties in recognition.

this performance may be sufficient for targeted applications [34], in the general case, there are many situations where gradient or multi-colour text is present. The situation where dithered colours are present (especially in GIF images) has received some attention [28, 48] but such colours can only be found in a relative small number of Web images. Furthermore, the background may also be complex (in terms of colour) so that the assumption that it is the largest area of (almost) uniform colour in the image [18] does not necessarily hold. Attempts have been made to deal with the complexity of situations encountered in web images by exploiting factors of human perception of colour differences (when identifying distinct objects) [3, 22] among other features in order to extract the text. Despite good progress, though, the extraction and recognition of text in web images remains a difficult open problem (Figure 18.2).

An interesting application area that has exploited the very difficulty of automated text extraction and recognition in web images is that of Human Interactive Proofs (HIPs) [5]. The idea is to use the fact that most human users can recognize text in web images that is specifically rendered in circumstances that current automated methods cannot recognize, to be able to verify that a human (not a software process) is interacting with a web service. This can help prevent large scale automated misuse (e.g. compromise of transmitted information, spam or illegal distribution of copyrighted material) by denying automated (bogus) registration for email and chatroom accounts, for instance. In this type of particular reading-based HIPs users are simply asked to enter the text they see in the image. Verification or not of the fact they are human rests on whether the text matches to the text that the server uses to generate the HIP challenge. Examples of reading-based HIP challenges can be seen in Figure 18.3. Part (a) uses a string of random characters (does not exist in a dictionary) which are deformed and have various line segments overlaid (from *www.yahoo.com*). Part (b), an *ESP-TEXT* challenge from *www.captcha.net*, is an existing web image (text in image form) which is slightly distorted to make it even more difficult to automatically recognize (the fact that text in image form is used as a HIP challenge emphasises the difficulty in recognizing such text

(a)

(b)

(c)

Fig. 18.3. Examples of reading-based HIP challenges.

as explained earlier in this section). Finally, part (c) is a *Gimpy* challenge (from *www.captcha.net*) which uses English words, distorted and overlapping, superimposed on on-uniform gradient colour background.

Finally, in terms of general images (photographs, graphics, etc.) in web documents, there is a significant need for categorization and retrieval. Although this appears to be a quite similar problem as in the case of the same application for databases, the vast and open (uncontrolled and effectively unbound) nature of the web poses additional challenges. For instance, it is practically impossible to index all images on the web based on a consistent set of keywords (metadata) or image features. Consequently, image retrieval methods that rely on the presence of the above characteristics (metadata or image features) will not work on the web. It could be argued that images can be analysed and features extracted on the fly during each search, however this would be a prohibitively time-consuming endeavour.

It can be observed, however, that images to be retrieved are contained in web documents along with contextual information (mostly in the form of text). To narrow down the search domain an initial search can be performed based on the document text using an established search engine. A more detailed search can be performed on the resulting document set. Studies on assessing the effectiveness of image retrieval based on certain text present on the containing document (HTML tag text, image filename, caption, etc.) have been conducted and as a result a relevance model for web mage search has been proposed [40]. A search framework based on perceptual features [25] also incorporates image features to help the user to progressively arrive at the desired image.

18.4 Web Document Modelling and Annotation

Compared to the traditional paper medium, documents on the web enjoy almost unlimited possibilities of enrichment. Some of the most rapidly evolving aspects of web documents are multi-media content, multi-modal interaction, and active collaboration and dynamic annotation and authoring. There has been increasing demand for research on issues raised by these new possibilities, and new research forums have sprung up in response (i.e. [17,41]). In previous sections we have reviewed various research activities on analysing multi-media content on the web. The other side of this challenge is how to effectively create documents with multi-media content. Because of the diversity of the media objects involved (text, image, audio, video and animation), complex models and tools are necessary to integrate them into a single, coherent document. Roisin et al. proposed a multi-media document modelling framework that integrates media description models to define, locate, describe and group media objects and temporal and spatial models to organize these objects in time and space [42,44]. Ossenbruggen et al. advocates a formal multi-media formatting vocabulary in order to provide for multi-media presentations equivalent functionality available for text transformations [43]. They argue that such a vocabulary is necessary to combine the ability to style XML-based multi-media presentation such as SMIL and the ability to generate multi-media presentations using document transformations such as provided by XSLT.

The World Wide Web provides a natural medium for sharing, thus collaborative editing is another important aspect of web authoring. Early developments of the web focussed on the browsing aspect of the shared environment, with tools for browsing free and easy to use, while tools for document creation and particularly collaborative authoring limited and expensive, often requiring sophisticated technical expertise to use. More recently, many web editing tools have been developed to address some of these issues. Weblogs [6] are tools for easy editing and publishing of personal diaries. Various annotation tools such as CritLink [20] enable users to comment generic WWW pages and add annotations that can be inserted into the original document. For collaborative editing, Wikis [26] provide mechanisms for shared writing as well as browsing, allowing users to access and edit any page of the site. The limitation of Wikis is that they only allow editing of documents residing in a wiki site. WebDAV [15] is an HTTP extension that allows users to collaboratively edit and manage files on remote web servers. More recently, Di Iorio et al. proposed a system called XanaWord, which provides a collaborative editing environment by integrating MS Internet Explorer as the navigation browser and MS Word as the content editor [12].

In recent years there has been a shift of web access from the desk top to various mobile devices such as PDAs, tablet PCs and mobile phones. This increasingly ubiquitous nature of web content dictates the need for novel multi-modal interfaces, particularly, pen-based and voice-based interfaces. For many hand-held devices, pen input (electronic ink) is the most natural mechanism for making annotations or entering and editing notations directly on the screen. Kashi et al. presented a preliminary system for ink annotation that includes three basic components: (1) ink capture and rendering, (2) ink understanding, which recognizes and associates ink with underlying document and (3) the storage and retrieval of ink annotations [35]. In situations which require hands-free interaction (e.g. driving in a car), voice becomes the only possible mode of communication with the web. One of the earliest works on voice browsing was a system called PhoneBrowser developed by Brown et al. [8], which is a speaker-independent voice enabled proxy server that provides automatic voice description of a web page and automatically activates the hyperlink titles by voice command. Much research effort has been devoted to this subject since then and the two most recent directions are represented by two papers published in WWW2004. The first, by Narayan et al. focusses on developing a software framework for multi-modal web interaction management that supports mixed-initiative dialogs between users and websites [32]. The second, by Ramakrisnan et al. focusses on creating audio browsable content from web documents along the lines first proposed by Brown et al. but with more advanced structural and semantic analysis [36].

18.5 Concluding Remarks

This chapter has presented a broad overview of web document analysis. Emerging issues from the fact that the web is now an established publication medium have given rise to the need for content analysis in a number of applications. Current research has been discussed in view of this need and other closely related problems. It is evident that several of the issues discussed are quite challenging and, as the field of web document analysis is in its infancy, will provide significant scope for future research.

References

1. Alam, H., Hartono, R., and Rahman, A.F.R. (2004). Extraction and management of content from HTML documents. In: A. Antonacopoulos and J. Hu (Eds.). *Web Document Analysis: Challenges and Opportunities.* Singapore: World Scientific, pp. 95–112.
2. Antonacopoulos, A., Karatzas, D., and Ortiz Lopez, J. (2001). Accessing textual information embedded in internet images. *Proceedings of SPIE Internet Imaging II, San Jose, USA*, pp. 198–205.
3. Antonacopoulos, A. and Karatzas, D. (2002). Fuzzy segmentation of characters in Web images based on human colour perception. In: D. Lopresti, J. Hu, and R. Kashi (Eds.). *Document Analysis Systems V.* London: Springer, LNCS 2423, pp. 295–306.
4. Antonacopoulos, A. and Delporte, F. (1999). Automated interpretation of visual representations: extracting textual information from WWW images. In: R. Paton and I. Neilson (Eds.). *Visual Representations and Interpretations.* London: Springer.
5. Baird, H.S. and Popat, K. (2004). Web security and document image analysis. In: A. Antonacopoulos and J. Hu (Eds.). *Web Document Analysis: Challenges and Opportunities.* Singapore: World Scientific.

6. Blood, R. Weblogs: a history and perspective. http://www.rebeccablood.net/essays/weblog_history.html.

7. Breuel, T.M., Janssen, W.C., Popat, K., and Baird, H.S. (2004). Reflowable document images. In: A. Antonacopoulos and J. Hu (Eds.). *Web Document Analysis: Challenges and Opportunities*. Singapore: World Scientific.

8. Brown, M.K., Glinski, S.C., and Schmult, B.C. (2001). Web page analysis for voice browsing. *Proceedings of the First International Workshop on Web Document Analysis (WDA2001), Seattle, USA*.

9. Chen, L.Q., Xie, X., Ma, W.Y., and Zhang, H.J. (2003). Dress: a slicing tree based web page representation for various display sizes. *WWW2003 (poster), Budapest, Hungary*.

10. Chen, Y., Ma, W., and Zhang, H.J. (2003). Detecting web page structure for adaptive viewing on small form-factor devices. *WWW2003, Budapest, Hungary*.

11. Cohen, W.W., Hurst, M., and Jensen, L.S. (2004). A wrapper induction system for complex documents and its application to tabular data on the web. In: A. Antonacopoulos and J. Hu (Eds.). *Web Document Analysis: Challenges and Opportunities*. Singapore: World Scientific, pp. 155–178.

12. Di Iorio, A. and Vitali, F. (2003). A xanalogical collaborative editing environment. In: A. Antonacopoulos and J. Hu (Eds.). *Second International Workshop on Web Document Analysis (WDA2003)*.

13. Gupta, S., Kaiser, G., Neistadt, D., and Grimm, P. (2003). Dom based content extraction of html documents. *WWW2003, Budapest, Hungary*.

14. Hsu, C. and Dung, M. (1998). Generating finite-state transducers for semi-structured data extraction from the web. *Journal of Information Systems, 23*, pp. 521–538.

15. http://www.webdav.org.

16. Hu, J. and Bagga, A. (2004). Functional categorization of images in web documents. *IEEE Multimedia Special Issue on Content Repurposing*.

17. International workshop on web document analysis. http://www.csc.liv.ac.uk/{~wda2001~wda2003}.

18. Jain, A.K. and Yu, B. (1998). Automatic text location in images and video frames. *Pattern Recognition, 31(12)*, pp. 2055–2076.

19. Ashish, N. and Knoblock, C. (1997). Wrapper generation for semi-structured internet sources. *Proceedings of PODS/SIGMOD'97*.

20. Yee, K.P. CritLink: Public Web Annotation. http://zesty.ca/crit.

21. Kanungo, T., Lee, C.H., and Bradford, R. (2001). What fraction of images on the web contain text? *Proceedings of the First International Workshop on Web Document Analysis (WDA2001), Seattle, USA*, pp. 43–46.

22. Karatzas, D. and Antonacopoulos, A. (2004). Text extraction from web images based on a split-and-merge segmentation method using colour perception. *Proceedings of the Seventeenth International Conference on Pattern Recognition (ICPR2004), Cambridge, UK*. Silver Spring, MD: IEEE-CS Press, pp. 634–637.

23. Kasik, D.J. (2004). Strategies for consistent image partitioning. *IEEE Multimedia Special Issue on Content Repurposing*.

24. Kushmerick, N., Weld, D. and Doorenbos, R. (1997). Wrapper induction for information extraction. *Proceedings of the Fifteenth International Conference on Artificial Intelligence*, pp. 729–735.

25. Lai, W.C., Chang, E.Y., and Cheng, K.T. (2004). An anatomy of a large-scale image search engine. In: A. Antonacopoulos and J. Hu (Eds.). *Web Document Analysis: Challenges and Opportunities.* Singapore: World Scientific.

26. Leuf, B. and Cummingham, W. (2001). *The Wiki way.* New York: Addison-Wesley.

27. Lopresti, D. and Wilfong, G. (2004). Applications of graph probing to web document analysis. In: A. Antonacopoulos and J. Hu (Eds.). *Web Document Analysis: Challenges and Opportunities.* Singapore: World Scientific.

28. Lopresti, D. and Zhou, J. (2000). Locating and recognizing text in WWW images. *Information Retrieval, 2(2/3),* pp. 177–206.

29. Mukherjee, S., Yang, G., Tan, W., and Ramakrishnan, I.V. (2003). Automatic discovery of semantic structures in html documents. *Proceedings of the Seventh International Conference on Document Analysis and Recognition (ICDAR2003), Edinburgh, Scotland.*

30. Muslea, I. (1999). Extracting patterns for information extraction tasks: a survey. *AAAI-99 Workshop on Machine Learning for Information Extraction.*

31. Nanno, T., Saito, S., and Okumura, M. (2003). Structuring web pages based on repetition of elements. In: A. Antonacopoulos and J. Hu (Eds.). *Second International Workshop on Web Document Analysis (WDA2003).*

32. Narayan, M., Williams, C., Perugini, S., and Ramakrishnan, N. (2004). Staging transformations for multimodal web interaction management. *WWW2004. New York, USA,* pp. 212–223.

33. Penn, G., Hu, J., Luo, H., and McDonald, R. (2001). Flexible web document analysis for delivery to narrow-bandwidth devices. *Proceedings of the Sixth International Conference on Document Analysis and Recognition (ICDAR01), Seattle, WA, USA,* pp. 1074–1078.

34. Perantonis, S.J., Gatos, B., and Maragos, V. (2003). A novel Web image processing algorithm for text area identification that helps commercial OCR engines to improve their Web image recognition efficiency. *Proceedings of the Second International Workshop on Web Document Analysis (WDA2003), Edinburgh, Scotland,* pp. 61–64.

35. Ramachandran, S. and Kashi, R. (2003). An architecture for ink annotations on web documents. *Proceedings of the Seventh International Conference on Document Analysis and Recognition (ICDAR2003), Edinburgh, Scotland.*

36. Ramakrishnan, I.V., Stent, A., and Yang, G. (2004). Hearsay: enabling audio browsing on hypertext content. *WWW2004, New York, USA,* pp. 80–89.

37. Schenker, Last, M., Bunke, H., and Kandel, A. (2004). Clustering of web documents using a graph model. In: A. Antonacopoulos and J. Hu (Eds.). *Web Document Analysis: Challenges and Opportunities.* Singapore: World Scientific.

38. Shih, L.K. and Karger, D.R. (2004). Using URLs and table layout for web classification tasks. *WWW2004, New York, USA,* pp. 193–202.

39. Singh, G. (2004). Content repurposing. *IEEE Multimedia Special Issue on Content Repurposing.*

40. Tao, C. and Munson, E.V. (2003). A relevance model for web image search. *Proceedings of the Second International Workshop on Web Document Analysis (WDA2003), Edinburgh, Scotland,* pp. 58–60.

41. The ACM Symposium on Document Engineering. http://www. documentengineering.org.

42. Thuong, T.T. and Roisin, C. (2004). Structured media for authoring multimedia documents. In: A. Antonacopoulos and J. Hu (Eds.). *Web Document Analysis: Challenges and Opportunities*. Singapore: World Scientific.

43. van Ossenbruggen, J., Rutledge, L., and Hardman, L. (2003). Towards a multimedia formatting vocabulary. *WWW2003, Budapest, Hungary*.

44. Villard, L., Roisin, C., and Layaida, N. (2000). An XML based multimedia document processing model for content adaptation. *Digital Documents and Electronic Publishing Conference (DDEP00)*, pp. 1–12.

45. Wang, Y. and Hu, J. (2002). A machine learning based approach for table detection on the web. *WWW2002, Honolulu, Hawaii, USA*.

46. Yang, Y., Chen, Y., and Zhang, H.J. (2004). HTML page analysis based on visual cues. In: A. Antonacopoulos and J. Hu (Eds.). *Web Document Analysis: Challenges and Opportunities*. Singapore: World Scientific.

47. Yoshida, M., Torisawa, K., and Tsujii, J. (2004). Extracting attributes and their values from web pages. In: A. Antonacopoulos and J. Hu (Eds.). *Web Document Analysis: Challenges and Opportunities*. Singapore: World Scientific.

48. Zhou, J., Lopresti, D., and Tasdizen, T. (1998). Finding text in color images. *Proceedings of the IS&T/SPIE Symposium on Electronic Imaging, San Jose, California*, pp. 130–140.

Semantic Structure Analysis of Web Documents

Rupesh R. Mehta, Harish Karnick, and Pabitra Mitra

19.1 Introduction

Today the web has become the largest information source for a large section of the world population. The web contains documents that are highly volatile, distributed and heterogeneous. The content of a web page is usually much more diverse when compared with traditional plain-text documents and may encompass multiple regions/segments with unrelated topics. Currently, most information retrieval systems on the web considers a web page as the smallest and indivisible unit. However, often it is not appropriate to represent a whole web page as a single semantic entity as web documents are heterogeneous and contain multiple topics that are not necessarily related to each other. Moreover, for the purpose of browsing and publication, non-content materials, such as navigation bars, decoration items, interaction forms, copyrights and contact information, are usually embedded in web pages. Considering the web page not as an individable unit but as having an underlying semantic structure with topically coherent segments as atoms, relevant and wealth of information contents on the web page (excluding noisy and irrelevant contents) can be found out and a better performance of web information retrieval systems can be achieved.

Many web applications can exploit the semantic structure of web documents to its benefit. For example, in query expansion system, relevant words are added to the query to increase the information content. The quality of expansion terms is highly affected by top-ranked documents. Two major negative factors for query expansion systems are noisy content and multiple topics embedded in the document. With the use of semantic structure of a web page, semantically homogeneous web page segments can be easily obtained. As the term correlation within a segment will be much higher than those in other parts of web page, high-quality expansion terms can be extracted from the segments and used to make more specific and relevant query. This helps in improving the information retrieval performance. Recently, link analysis has received more importance. Generally, web pages are treated as single semantic and hence all links in a web page get equal importance. Traditionally, all the links in a web page are treated equally. The basic assumption of link analysis in information retrieval systems is that multiple citations from a single web page are likely to cite semantically related web pages, i.e. if there is a link between two pages, there is some relationship between the two whole pages. In short, the relevance of a web page is a reasonable indicator of the relevance of its neighbours. But in most cases, a link from page X to page Y indicates that there might be some relationship between a certain part of page X (containing the link) and a certain part of page Y but not necessarily between the whole web pages X and Y. Also, it has been shown that the main reason for topic drift problem in the HITS (hyperlink induced topic search) algorithm [1, 2] is existence of a large amount of noisy information. The same observation can be made from recent works on topic distillation [3, 4] and focused crawling [5]. However, these works are based on a DOM (document object model) tree of the web page that does not have sufficient power to semantically segment the web page. Furthermore, due to the small size of screen of handheld devices, it is better to show the list of categories to which web page belongs and later display user-interested segment only, rather than the whole web page. This efficient browsing of large web pages on small handheld devices also necessitates semantic analysis of web pages [6].

19.2 Related Work

Document passage (segment) retrieval is a research topic with a long history in the information retrieval (IR) community that addresses the shortcomings of whole-document ranking. Previous work reveals that it is sometimes beneficial to apply retrieval algorithms to portions of a document, particularly when documents contain multiple drifting subjects or have varying lengths [7, 8].

In traditional passage retrieval, passages can be categorized mainly into three classes: discourse, semantic and window. Discourse passages rely on the logical structure of the documents marked by punctuation, such as sentences, paragraphs and sections [7–9]. Semantic passages rely on semantic structure of document to partition it into topics or sub-topics [8, 10, 11], whereas windows-based passage retrieval approach partition the document based on the fixed number of words (per passage) [7, 12, 13].

We cannot directly adopt these plain-text document passage retrieval techniques for partitioning web pages. Some research [14] on web page segmentation and its applications has been done using traditional passage retrieval methods, but the results are not encouraging. This indicates that traditional passages might not be appropriate in web context, and that we need to take advantage of other characteristics of web documents. Few characteristics of web pages (which plain-text documents do not possess) are given as below:

1. *Two-Dimensional Logical Structure.* Web pages have a 2D view and a more sophisticated internal content structure. Each region of a web page could have relationships with regions from up to four directions and contain or be contained in some other regions. A semantic structure exists for most web pages and can be used to enhance performance of information retrieval tasks.
2. *Visual Layout Presentation.* To facilitate browsing and attract attention, web pages usually contain plenty of visual information in the tags and properties in HTML. Typical visual hints include lines, images, blank areas, colours, fonts, etc. Visual cues are very helpful in detecting semantic regions in a web page.

Some approaches rely on the DOM, since it provides a hierarchical structure for every web page. Some useful tags or tag types are used to identify blocks [15,16], including $\langle P_i \rangle$, $\langle TABLE \rangle$, $\langle UL \rangle$, $\langle H1 \rangle$, $\langle H6 \rangle$, etc. Some others also consider extra information such as content [17] and link [4]. Some simple experiments have been performed on web information retrieval to take advantage of the DOM structure [18], but little improvement is obtained. The main reason behind negligible improvement may be that DOM is still a kind of linear structure and is usually unable to represent the semantic structure of a web page. From this perspective, DOM-based blocks are, in some sense, similar to traditional discourse passages.

A function-based object model (FOM) of a web page has been proposed by Chen [19] for content understanding and adaptation. Every undividable element in the tag tree is called *a basic object* and can be grouped into a composite object. A function type can be defined for each object, and it helps to build a hierarchical structure for the page. However, the grouping rules and the functions are hard to define accurately, and thus make the whole tree-constructing process very inflexible.

The VIPS (vision-based page segmentation) algorithm assumes that visual layout structure of a web page is faithful to the semantic partitioning of the web page. It also utilizes the fact that semantically related contents are often grouped together and the entire page is divided into different regions using implicit or explicit visual separators such as images, lines, font sizes, blank areas, etc. VIPS iteratively uses the DOM tree structure and visual cues in a web page for block extraction, separator detection and content structure generation. Based on this visual segmentation, each node of a VIPS tree is assigned a DoC (degree of coherence) value (ranging from 1 to 10) to indicate how coherent the content within a block is. A higher DoC value signifies that a segment is more homogeneous. This approach gives better page segmentation than the other mentioned approaches.

Two major problems with this approach are:

- Web page segmentation depends on a pre-defined DoC value. But, sometimes some web pages need further segmentation, whereas for some web pages, due to visual cues' richness, semantically coherent segments are obtained. Segments formed by using a higher DoC value are small sized and due to very little information available in a segment, it may result in poor information retrieval, also sometimes, part of a web page, unnecessarily gets further segmented, though it is semantically more homogeneous.

- This approach is based on the assumption that semantically related contents are often grouped together. But often, semantically related content is distributed across the web page bad authoring or sorting of segments or blocks based on some key. For example, a faculty page is often sorted using a person's name as a key. So, it is possible that a segment of professors having the same area of interest is dispersed across the web page.

Basically, the decision of degree of coherency (DoC) of a segment based on only visual information is not a good idea as visual information on the web page varies from author to author. The content of the web page should also be considered.

19.3 Semantic Structure of Web Documents

The semantic structure of a web page consists of a tree containing blocks, where blocks can be basic objects or set of objects. Here, basic object is defined as leaf node in a tree, which cannot be decomposed further.

Similar to the basic model of vision-based content structure [20], the model for semantic structure for web page is described below: A web page W is represented as a quadruple W = {O, S, M, C}. $O = \{W_1, W_2, W_3, ..., W_n\}$ is a finite set of blocks. All these blocks are non-overlapping. Each block can be viewed as a sub-web page that has a similar semantic structure as W. Separator is horizontal or vertical line that does not cross any visual block. $S = \{S_1, S_2, S_3, ..., S_n\}$ is a finite set of separators. Each separator is assigned some weight based on the amount of visual information it has. M is the relation between every two blocks in O and can be expressed as: $M = OXO \Rightarrow SU\{NULL\}$. For example, if $M(O_i, O_j) \neq NULL$ indicates that O_i and O_j are two objects exactly separated by separator $M(O_i, O_j)$. $C = \{C_1, C_2, ..., C_n\}$ is a finite set of categories to which a block belongs. It helps in automatic web page updation, semantic web mining, small handheld devices to list the categories, the web page belongs to.

Figure 19.1 shows an example of semantic structure for a Google News page of "Sci/Tech" category. It shows an example page and its semantic

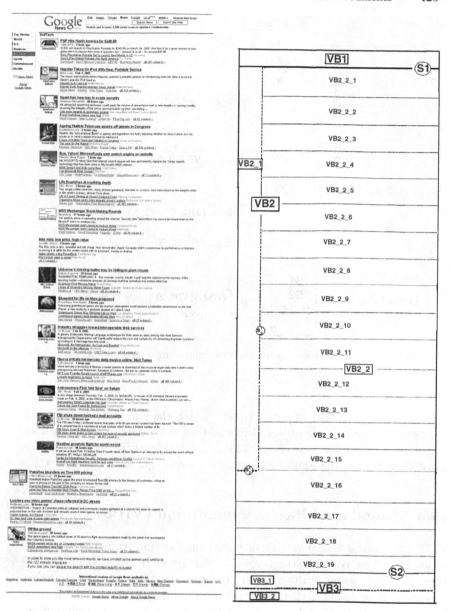

Fig. 19.1. An example page and its semantic structure.

structure. At the first level, the original web page has three blocks, VB1–VB3, and two separators, S1 and S2, as specified in Figure 19.2. Further sub-semantic structure for each sub web page can be constructed in a similar way. For example, VB2 has two offspring objects and two separators. It can further be analysed as shown in Figure 19.2. The "C" field of semantic

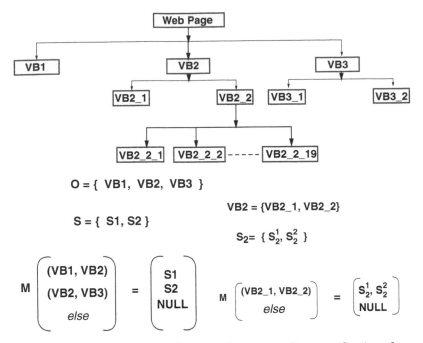

Fig. 19.2. The example page layout and corresponding specification of semantic structure.

structure contains a list of categories to which the current sub-web page belongs. Here, each basic object (leaf node) of the semantic structure tree represents a single semantic entity. This semantic structure of a web page is more likely to give the exact semantics of a web page.

19.4 Vision-based Page Segmentation (VIPS)

VIPS [21] utilizes visual wealth of visual information available with web pages to output content structure of a web page. It is based on the assumption that semantically related contents are often grouped together and implicit or explicit visual separators like images, line-breaking tags, font sizes, background colours, etc. divide the web page into different regions that are not semantically close. It uses the DOM structure and visual information for block extraction, separator detection and content structure generation.

The page segmentation process is shown in Figure 19.3. First, the DOM structure and visual information, such as position, background colour, font size, font weight, etc. are obtained from a web browser. Then, from the root node, the visual block extraction process is started to extract visual blocks at the current level from the DOM tree based on visual cues. Using some

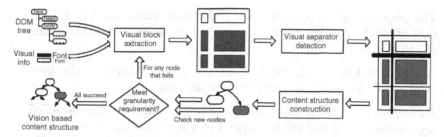

Fig. 19.3. Vision-based page segmentation.

heuristic rules, every DOM node is checked to judge whether it forms a single block or not. If not, its children will be processed in the same way. When all blocks of the current level are extracted, they are put into a pool. Visual separators among these blocks are identified, and the weight of a separator is set based on properties of its neighbouring blocks. After constructing the layout hierarchy of the current level, each newly produced visual block is checked to see whether or not it meets the granularity requirement. If it does not, this block is further partitioned. After all blocks are processed, the final vision-based content structure for the web page is output.

19.4.1 Visual Block Extraction

In this phase, all visual blocks contained in current sub-tree of a web page are obtained and their DoC value is set according to their intra-visual differences. The visual block extraction algorithm is shown as Algorithm 19.1.

The judgement about further division of DOM node is taken based on the following considerations:

- *The properties of the DOM node itself.* Examples: The HTML tag of this node, the background colour of this node, the size and shape of the block corresponding to this DOM node.

Algorithm DivideDOMTree
Input: pNode, nLevel
Output: Pool of visual blocks
if *Dividable(pNode, nLevel)* == *TRUE* then
    for *Each Child of pNode* **do**
        Call DivideDOMTree recursively with pNode = child and nLevel = nLevel+1 as an input parameters.
    end
end
else
    Put the sub-tree (pNode) into the pool as a block.
end

Algorithm 19.1. Visual block extraction algorithm.

- *The properties of the children of the DOM node.* Examples: The HTML tags of children nodes, background colour of children and size of the children.

Based on WWW HTML specification 4.01, the DOM node is classified into two categories: inline node and line-break node:

- *Inline Node.* The DOM node with inline text HTML tags that affect the appearance of text and can be applied to a string of characters without introducing a line break. Such tags include ⟨B⟩, ⟨BIG⟩, ⟨EM⟩, ⟨FONT⟩, ⟨I⟩, ⟨STRONG⟩, ⟨U⟩, etc.
- *Line-break Node.* The node with tag other than inline text tags.

Based on the appearance of the node in the browser and the properties of child nodes, some definitions are given below:

- *Valid node.* A node that can be seen through the browser. The node's width and height are not equal to zero.
- *Text node.* The DOM node corresponding to free text that does not have an HTML tag.
- *Virtual text node (recursive definition).*
  1. Inline node with only text node children is a virtual text node.
  2. Inline node with only text node and virtual text node children is a virtual text node.

Some important cues that are used to produce heuristic rules in algorithm are:

- *Tag cue*
  - Tags such as ⟨HR⟩ are often used to separate different topics from a visual perspective. Therefore, it is preferable to divide a DOM node if it contains these tags.
  - If an inline node has a child that is a line-break node, this inline node is subjected to division.
- *Colour cue.* A DOM node is divided if its background colour is different from any one of its children. At the same time, the child node with different background colour will not be divided in this round.
- *Text cue.* If most of the children of a DOM node are text nodes or virtual text nodes, it is preferably not divided.
- *Size cue.* A relative size threshold (the node size compared with the size of the whole page or sub-page) is pre-defined for different tags (the threshold varies with the DOM nodes having different HTML tags). If the relative size of the node is smaller than the threshold, we prefer not to divide the node.

Based on these cues, heuristic rules are produced to judge if a node should be divided. If a node should not be divided, a block is extracted and the DoC value is set for this block.

According to the above definitions, the following text cue- and size cue-based heuristic rules are used to further enhance the block extraction process:

- A node will be dropped if it has no valid child.
- If a node has only one valid child and this child is not a text node, then trace into the child.
- If all the children of a node are text nodes or virtual text nodes, then set the DoC 1.
- If the node's size is 3 times greater than all his children's total size, divide it.
- If the node's child is a text node or virtual text node and the node's width or height is smaller than a threshold, set the DoC 0.8.
- Split the node that has more than two successive ⟨BR⟩ children. (It means there is space in the middle, may be two different topics).

In addition, some tags, such as ⟨TABLE⟩, ⟨TBODY⟩, ⟨TR⟩, ⟨TD⟩, ⟨P⟩, ⟨UL⟩ and ⟨LI⟩, are very important and common in web page and are more likely to form a content coherent sub-tree. Some special routines in algorithm are defined to handle these tags and thresholds are set for these tags in the above rules.

19.4.2 Visual Separator Detection

In this algorithm, a pool of visual blocks is maintained. Initially it is empty. Each visual block detected in visual block extraction algorithm is kept in the pool according to the rules described in Algorithm 19.2.

Visual Separator Detection Algorithm
Initialize the separator list. The list starts with only one separator (Pbe, Pee), whose start pixel and end pixel correspond to the borders of the pool.
for *Each block in the pool* **do**
  | The relation of the block with each separator is evaluated as:
  | **if** *The block is contained in the separator* **then**
  | | Split the separator.
  | **end**
  | **if** *The block crosses with the separator* **then**
  | | Update the separator's parameters.
  | **end**
  | **if** *The block covers the separator* **then**
  | | Remove the separator.
  | **end**
end
Remove the four separators that stand at the border of the pool.

Algorithm 19.2. Visual separator detection algorithm.

Setting Weights for Separators

Separators are used to distinguish blocks with different semantics, so the weight of a separator can be assigned based on the semantic difference between its neighbouring blocks. The following rules are used to weight each separator:

- The more the distance between blocks on different side of the separator, the greater the weight.
- If a visual separator is at the same position as some tags such as ⟨HR⟩, its weight is made higher.
- If font properties such as font size and font weight differ clearly on the two sides of the separator, the weight is increased. Moreover, the weight will be increased if font size before adding the separator is smaller than that after adding the separator.
- If background colours are different on two sides of the separator, the weight will be increased.
- When the structures of the blocks beside the separator are very similar (e.g. both are text), the weight of the separator will be decreased.

19.4.3 Content Structure Construction

After separators are detected and their weights set, the content structure can be constructed. The construction process starts by merging blocks with the lowest separators' weight separators to form new virtual blocks. This process iterates till separators with maximum weights are met. The DoC of each new block is also set by methods similar to those described in Section 19.4.1. After that, each leaf node is checked to see whether it meets the granularity requirement. For every node that fails, we go to the visual block extraction phase again to further construct the sub content structure within that node. If all the nodes meet the requirement, the iterative process is stopped and the vision-based content structure for the whole page is obtained. The common requirement for DoC is that DoC > PDoC, if PDoC is pre-defined.

In summary, the VIPS algorithm takes advantage of visual cues to obtain the vision-based content structure of a web page and thus successfully bridges the gap between the DOM structure and the semantic structure. The page is partitioned based on visual separators and structured as a hierarchy closely related to how a user would browse the page. Content-related parts could be grouped together to some extent even if they are in different branches of the DOM tree. VIPS is efficient, since it traces down the DOM structure for visual block extraction and does not analyse every basic DOM node, the algorithm is totally top-down.

19.5 Determining Topic Coherency of Web Page Segments

The content homogeneity of a sub-web page can be determined from its degree of belongingness to different categories in a topic hierarchy. The open directory project (ODP) [22] topic hierarchy is considered for this purpose. The ODP is the largest, most comprehensive human-edited directory of the Web. It is constructed and maintained by a vast, global community of volunteer editors. The degree of belongingness to a category is measured in terms of the "posterior" probability of classifying a segment into the category using a pre-trained naive Bayes classifier (NBC) [23]. If the probability is above certain Threshold Th ($= 0.4$, say) for some category, the segment is considered as belonging to that category. The working of naive Bayes classifier (NBC) works as follows

- The basic principle of NBC is to use the joint probabilities of words and categories to estimate the probabilities of categories given a document. The NBC applies to learning tasks where each instance x is described by a conjunction of attribute values and where the target function f(x) can take on any value from some finite set V. A set of training examples of target function and a new instance is presented, described by the tuple of attribute values $< a_1, a_2, a_3, ..., a_n >$. The learner is asked to predict the target value or classification for this new instance.
- The NBC is trained on the web documents belonging to each category of ODP, considering document terms as attributes. This trained NBC is used to classify a given instance of a (sub) web page. In our case, given an instance of a (sub) web page, NBC returns a set of categories containing probability values that give the probability that the (sub) web page belongs to the corresponding category (only values above specific threshold are considered). Naive Bayes classifier formula is given as:

$$V_{NB} = argmax_{v_j \in V} P(v_j) \prod_i P(a_i|v_j)$$

where V_{NB} denotes the set of target values output by the NBC. $argmax$ is a function returning all target values above a certain Threshold, Th. $P(a_i|v_j)$ a probability that attribute a_i belongs to class v_j.

The primary reasons for using this method instead of a vector-space cosine similarity approach are as follows:

- Page segments are usually of short length and the vector-space model is not a good representation of their semantic content.
- By using a trained classifier, one exploits the statistical properties of the training corpus in the coherency determination process.

It may be noted that purely content-based document segmentation without considering any markup structure has been a well-studied problem in information retrieval. For web documents, only content-based classification gives poor results.

19.6 Extracting Semantic Structure by Integrating Visual and Content Information

The integrated algorithm [24] uses both visual and content information of a web page to obtain semantically more meaningful blocks. It uses VIPS algorithm to take full advantage of visual information available on a web page and pre-trained naive Bayes classifier to check the content homogeneity of (sub) web page. The basic idea is to use visual information to obtain web page segments and content information to decide the homogeneity of those segments. The approach works as: initially, content structure of a web page is obtained by using method described in VIPS algorithm. The basic blocks (leaf nodes) of content structure tree are extracted and checked for semantic coherency using pre-trained NBC. Any basic block belonging to more than one category implies that it is not semantically coherent as yet, and hence needs further segmentation. For such blocks only, the VIPS method is applied recursively with higher DoC to get finer, more semantically related segments. At the end of this process, either each basic block of content structure tree belongs to exactly one category or the number of words in that block (basic) is less than some threshold, i.e. that block cannot be further segmented. Later, basic blocks belonging to similar category are merged together to form a single semantic, basic block. The output of this whole process is semantic structure tree containing more homogeneous basic blocks belonging to a single category. This process is divided into two phases.

19.6.1 Split Phase

In this phase, a finer content structure of a web page is obtained using pre-trained NBC and VIPS approach. Use of VIPS approach in this phase takes full advantage of visual structure layout of a (sub) web page, whereas pre-trained NBC helps to check the semantic similarity of a (sub) web page (Algorithm 19.3). The algorithm works as:

Initially, the VIPS algorithm (with lesser DoC value) is used to have initial content structure tree of a web page. The basic blocks of content structure are examined for intra-content homogeneity using pre-trained NBC. Only those basic blocks whose content are not homogeneous, i.e. basic blocks belonging to more than one category are considered as a further candidate for segmentation. The content tree generation process is repeated for those blocks. The initial content structure tree is modified by replacing such basic blocks with newly generated content structure tree (of

---

Split Phase Algorithm
Input: Web Document, ParentNode, pDoC
Output: Intermediate Semantic Structure Tree
Content Structure Tree = **VIPS (document, pDoC)**
if *Parent ≠ NULL* then
| Add Content Structure Tree as a node to Parent.
end
for *Each leaf node in the Content Structure Tree* do
| Compute the probability of node belonging to each listed category
| (from ODP), using pre-trained NBC.
| if *There are more than one category to which probability of a node*
| *belonging to them is above certain Threshold and Node has Word*
| *Count ≥ Minimum Word Threshold* then
| | Apply Split Phase Algorithm recursively with current node as
| | document, parent Node of current node as ParentNode, and
| | pDoC = pDoC + 1;
| end
| else
| | if *Node belong to single category* then
| | | No further Segmentation of Node.
| | | Assign that category name to nodes meta-data field.
| | end
| | else
| | | if *Node still belongs to more than one category* then
| | | | No further Segmentation of Node.
| | | | Assign "Mixed" as category name to the nodes meta-data
| | | | field.
| | | end
| | end
| end
end

Algorithm 19.3. Algorithm to check semantic similarity.

that basic block). This process stops when each basic block of modified content structure tree belongs to exactly one category or the number of words in that basic block is less than a pre-defined threshold. Along with the other visual meta-data (like height, width of the block, font size, etc.), categoryList, C (list of categories to which that node belongs) is added to each node of content structure tree to form an intermediate semantic structure tree of a web page. This phase helps in getting finer, semantically more homogeneous segments at leaf level of semantic structure tree.

19.6.2 Merge Phase

The output of a split phase is an intermediate semantic structure tree of a web page, in which each basic block (leaf segment) belongs to exactly one category. This structure may contain few basic blocks that belong to the same category. The category information of each basic block is obtained from categoryList field of a semantic structure of that block. In this phase, All basic blocks having same categoryList (belonging to exactly one and same category) are merged together to form a new semantic block with same categoryList field. All merged basic blocks are removed from intermediate semantic structure tree, and a newly formed block is added as a basic block in the semantic structure tree. The parent of this newly formed block is the least common ancestor of all merged basic blocks.

In this way, all basic blocks belonging to similar category, i.e. having content homogeneity are merged together and finally modified semantic structure tree is outputted. This phase helps in combining semantically related contents that are distributed across the web page.

Although VIPS algorithm does (sub) web page segmentation, and form a content structure tree, the height of resultant semantic structure tree is determined by the content homogeneity of a (sub) web page, rather than visual information available on (sub) web page. Content information of a web page using pre-trained NBC helps to remove listed drawbacks of VIPS algorithm, increasing intra-segment content similarity. Also, categoryList is added to the semantic structure of a web page, which may be helpful in automatic web page adaptation, semantic web mining, etc. Most of the time, it has been observed that applying the above-mentioned approach on a web page, all leaf nodes of semantic structure tree, belonging to multiple topic and containing number of words less than certain threshold, are nodes containing noisy, navigational information that is of no use in information retrieval systems.

19.7 Advantages of the Integrated Approach

There are several advantages of proposed approach over other existing page segmentation algorithms, some of them are listed below:

1. It represents distributed but semantically related contents as a single semantic.
2. It gives better semantic structure of web documents compared to other approaches as it takes full advantage of both visual layout and content information available on the web page.
3. The semantic structure of web page described above contains each node's category information that can be useful in many applications.
4. To some extent, it helps to filter out noisy, navigational information that in turn helps in improving performance of many information retrieval, information extraction systems.

19.8 Conclusions and Discussion

Extracting semantic structure of web documents is an important step in improved information retrieval and extraction process. We have discussed some of the popular methods for semantic analysis of web documents. A novel method for extracting the semantic structure of web pages using visual and content information is presented. In this semantic structure extraction algorithm, topic coherency determines the granularity of the individual segments and in turn the height of semantic tree. Semantically related segments may be distributed across the web page intentionally or unintentionally. This approach treats physically distributed but semantically homogeneous blocks as a single semantic unit.

Incorporating topic hierarchy in the semantic structure tree of a web page would make it more amenable to semantic web mining. This semantic analysis of a web page can be useful in enhancing the performance of various web applications like information retrieval, information extraction, automatic web page adaptation and small handheld device applications. Also, most of the time, it has been observed that leaf nodes of semantic structure tree belonging to more than one category and containing number of words less than some threshold, carry noisy and navigation information that is of no use for information retrieval system. Up to a large extent, this approach helps in automatically filtering out noisy, navigational information.

References

1. Bharat, K. and Henzinger, M.R. (1998). Improved algorithms for topic distillation in a hyperlinked environment. *Proceedings of SIGIR-98, Twenty-first ACM International Conference on Research and Development in Information Retrieval, Melbourne, Australia*, pp. 104–111.
2. Kleinberg, J.M. (1999). Authoritative sources in a hyperlinked environment. *Journal of the ACM, 46*, pp. 604–632.
3. Chakrabarti, S. (2001). Integrating the document object model with hyperlinks for enhanced topic distillation and information extraction. *World Wide Web*, pp. 211–220.
4. Chakrabarti, S., Joshi, M., and Tawde, V. (2001). Enhanced topic distillation using text, markup tags, and hyperlinks. *Research and Development in Information Retrieval*, pp. 208–216.
5. Chakrabarti, S., Punera, K., and Subramanyam, M. (2002). Accelerated focused crawling through online relevance feedback. *WWW'02: Proceedings of the Eleventh International Conference on World Wide Web*. New York, NY: ACM Press, pp. 148–159.
6. Kaasinen, E., Aaltonen, M., Kolari, J., Melakoski, S., and Laakko, T. (2000). Two approaches to bringing internet services to wap devices. *Computer Networks, 33*, pp. 231–246.
7. Callan, J. (1994). Passage-level evidence in document retrieval. In: Croft, W.B., van Rijsbergen, C. (Eds.): *Proceedings of the Seventeenth Annual International ACM SIGIR Conference on Research and Development in Information Retrieval*. Dublin, Ireland: Spring, pp. 302–310.
8. Salton, G., Allan, J., and Buckley, C. (1993). Approaches to passage retrieval in full text information systems. *Proceedings of the 16th Annual International*

ACM SIGIR Conference on Research and Development in Information Retrieval, pp. 49–58.

9. Wilkinson, R. (1994). Effective retrieval of structured documents. *Research and Development in Information Retrieval*, pp. 311–317.

10. Hearst, M. (1994). Multi-paragraph segmentation of expository text. *Thirty-second Annual Meeting of the Association for Computational Linguistics*. Las Cruces, New Mexico: New Mexico State University, pp. 9–16.

11. Ponte, J.M. and Croft, W.B. (1997). Text segmentation by topic. *European Conference on Digital Libraries*, pp. 113–125.

12. Kaszkiel, M. and Zobel, J. (2001). Effective ranking with arbitrary passages. *Journal of the American Society of Information Science, 52*, pp. 344–364.

13. Zobel, J., Moffat, A., Wilkinson, R., and Sacks-Davis, R. (1995). Efficient retrieval of partial documents. *TREC-2: Proceedings of the Second Conference on Text Retrieval Conference*. Elmsford, NY: Pergamon Press, pp. 361–377.

14. Kwok, K.L., Grunfeld, L., Dinstl, N., and Chan, M. (2000). Trec-9 cross language, web and question-answering track experiments using pircs. *TREC*.

15. Lin, S.H. and Ho, J.M. (2002). Discovering informative content blocks from web documents. *KDD'02: Proceedings of the Eighth ACM SIGKDD International Conference on Knowledge Discovery and Data Mining*. New York, NY: ACM Press, pp. 588–593.

16. Wong, W. and Fu, A. (2000). Finding structure and characteristics of web documents for classification. *ACM SIGMOD Workshop on Research Issues in Data Mining and Knowledge Discovery*, pp. 96–105.

17. Embley, D., Jiang, S., and Ng, Y. (1999). Record-Boundary Discovery In Web Documents.

18. Crivellari, F. and Melucci, M. (2001). Web document retrieval using passage retrieval, connectivity information, and automatic link weighting. *TREC-9: Proceedings of the Ninth Text Retrieval Conference*.

19. Chen, J., Zhou, B., Shi, J., Zhang, H., and Fengwu, Q. (2001). Function-based object model towards website adaptation. *World Wide Web*, pp. 587–596.

20. Cai, D., Yu, S., Wen, J.R., and Ma, W.Y. (2003). Vips: a vision-based page segmentation algorithm. Microsoft Technical Report, MSR-TR-2003-79.

21. Cai, D., Yu, S., Wen, J.R., and Ma, W.Y. (2003). Extracting content structure for web pages based on visual representation. *Proceedings of the Fifth Asia Pacific Web Conference, Xi'an, China*.

22. ODP. Open directory project. http://dmoz.org/.

23. Mitchell, T. (1997). *Machine Learning*. New York: McGraw-Hill.

24. Mehta, R.R., Mitra, P., and Karnick, H. (2005). Extracting semantic structure of web documents using content and visual information. *WWW'05: Proceedings of the Fourteenth International Conference World Wide Web*, pp. 928–929.

Bank Cheque Data Mining: Integrated Cheque Recognition Technologies

Nikolai Gorski

20.1 Introduction

Recently, one can observe new trends in bank cheque processing. Earlier, the customers (who are banks and other financial institutions) were mainly interested in automation of reading the cheque amount. Nowadays, there are more and more demands on deeper analysis of cheque content. They originated from general political and economical situation in the world: banks try to prevent money laundering, reduce losses from fraud cheques or even detect potential terrorists among their clients.

When processing a cheque, a bank is interested to read automatically as much information from the document as possible. Besides the cheque amount, this can include the date of cheque issue, the beneficiary name, the payer's address and signature, code line(s), etc. This poses new tasks for developers of document analysis systems. They should be able to process and understand a cheque as an integral document with many loosely structured information fields, some of which are mandatory and others are optional.

Many papers on bank cheque processing have been published recently [2, 4, 6–15]. Most of them are devoted to amount recognition as the most actual task for cheque industry. In this paper we also touch it, but mainly concentrate attention on new-coming tasks and describe approaches to their solution by the example of A2iA CheckReader recognition system.

Section 20.2 outlines cheque processing task definitions and demands to their automation. Section 20.3 describes in detail recognition technologies for one of the most important cheque fields: payee name (including results post-processing with user-defined dictionaries). Location, extraction and understanding of this field on both cursive handwritten and machine-printed documents are discussed. Section 20.4 briefly presents recognition of other cheque fields, such as date, payee address and name, and a code

line. It also discusses experimental and exploitation results of the A2iA
CheckReader system achieved on bank cheques originated from different
countries.

20.2 Challenges of the Cheque Processing Industry

20.2.1 What to Read?

In many countries, the bank cheque is one of the most popular ways of
payment. The financial institutions receive daily hundreds of millions of
paper cheques and other payment documents, from which miscellaneous
data should be read, converted into electronic form and send on for further analysis. Reading and keying these data to a great extent remains a
manual job performed by human operators. Replacing them by automatic
reading systems is the greatest challenge of cheque processing industry. An
important question is what should be read from a bank cheque?

Traditionally, banks were interested in three pieces of information:
amount to be paid, account to be debited with this amount and account
to be credited.

In most countries, information of debit account is coded in a special
field (so called *code line*) pre-printed on each cheque with magnetic ink –
see Figure 20.1. In the USA, the use of code lines on cheques was introduced
in 1956, being the first step towards automated cheque processing. Special
MICR scanners can read magnetic code lines with high accuracy, so the
information they contain (e.g. payer account number, issue bank, etc.) need
not be manually keyed for a great majority of cheques.

The credit account number is normally known from the payee – a person
or an organization who deposits the cheque at his bank. The payee is identified by his name indicated in the cheque (Figure 20.1), while his account
number is frequently present in a separate document – deposit ticket – associated with the cheque. The credit account number also comes in electronic
form keyed by a clerk of payee's bank at the moment of depositing.

Thus, the first information to be automatically read from the cheque
is the amount to be paid. Normally, it exists in two forms: literal (legal
amount) and numeric (courtesy amount), both being subject to read and
cross-validate each other for higher reliability. These amounts can be handwritten or machine-printed, typical fraction of machine-printed variants
being around 20% of the total number of items in the document flow.

Other important information fields of a cheque are the date and the
payer's signature. In some countries (e.g. Canada, Ireland, Italy), a cheque
becomes payable only from its date, which might be far in future from the
current date. In these countries, reading the cheque date is a mandatory
operation, which should be automated together with amount reading. As
for the payer's signature, in practice, banks do verify it only on cheques

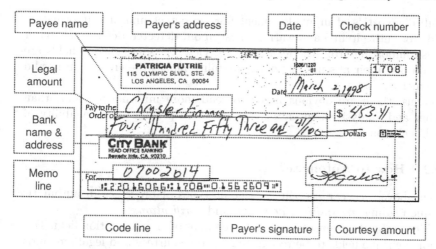

Fig. 20.1. Most important information fields of a US bank cheque.

with relatively big amounts, because it is quite costly to accomplish this operation for all cheques. Nevertheless, signature verification remains a good part of manual work, which needs to be automated.

New trends in cheque processing originate from realities of our anxious life. First, financial institutions are highly interested in further reducing the cost of cheque processing. Besides automation of traditional manual operations, this includes reducing of indirect losses, first of all from cheque frauds. According to the US National Check Fraud Center, cheque fraud and counterfeiting are among the fastest-growing problems affecting the financial system. They produce estimated annual losses of $10 billion. To detect frauds, it is necessary to analyse many cheque fields and features in common, and this, in turn, demands an ability to read more information than it was several years ago.

Second, the governments increase efforts in preventing money laundering and reduction threats of terrorist attacks. New laws force banks to control more closely their transactions, thoroughly check their clients and trace who pays to whom and how much. The banks can receive lists of persons or companies under investigation whose names should be detected among payers or beneficiaries. For this, they have to read in cheques such fields as payee name, payer's address, the name and address of the issuing bank. So, in this case information from a cheque should be analysed in common with the external data like address books, name dictionaries, etc.

Third, massive automation of cheque processing raises its own problems, such as document image quality and usability. Digital copies of paper originals should be fully consistent and readable to serve as legal subjects of automatic reading; otherwise, the whole process could become useless. To prevent this, a cheque processing system should be able to perform a full diagnostics of input document flow to detect unusable information fields (or entire items) and warn its host about detected defects. The later is also important from the legal point of view. As some cheque fields are mandatory, their absence or poor readability makes the cheque an invalid document.

Thus, there are obvious needs to read more information fields than earlier and analyse these data in common, to provide high reliability of final decisions.

20.2.2 How to Automate?

From above, one can see three different types of processes in automatic cheque reading: *recognition, detection* and *verification.*

The *recognition process* targets the content of an information field. Traditional cheque fields to be recognized are the courtesy and legal amounts; in certain countries it is also the cheque date. New demands include recognition of the payee name, payer's name and address, the issue bank name. Sometimes, a code line also needs to be recognized, because not every cheque scanner is supplied with a MICR reader. This is true, for instance, for ATMs and cash machines, which are able to automatically deposit cheques and dispense banknotes.

Automated recognition process should replace manual information keying. In reality, this is true only to a certain extent, because automatic reading systems still have lower reading abilities than human beings. However, it is possible to reduce a part of manual work by processing automatically those items (documents, fields, etc.), which the system reads with the same error level as an operator. Suppose, an operator keys items with 1% errors (a typical value for keying cheque amounts). Then the system, which reads 80% of items and makes among read items the same 1% errors, will do exactly 80% of operator's job. So, two principal characteristics of a recognition process are the *read rate* (READ) and the *substitution rate* (SUBS):

$$\text{READ} = 100\% \ ^* \ (\# \text{ of automatically read items/total } \# \text{ of items})$$

$$\text{SUBS} = 100\% \ ^* \ (\# \text{ of incorrectly read items}/\# \text{ of read items})$$

Note, that substitution is related to the number of items read by the system, and not to the total number of items. When a human operator is replaced with an automatic reading system, it is the SUBS adjusted equal to that of an operator. Then the READ value reflects a labour economy. Sometimes, it is also called the "killing rate" of a system, as it shows a percentage of documents processed fully automatically and never seen by humans.

Another characteristic similar to the read rate, but measured only on the correctly read items, is the *recognition rate* (REC):

$$\text{REC} = 100\% \ ^* \ (\# \text{ of correctly read items/total } \# \text{ of items})$$

READ and REC have a close meaning, but different domain of use: commercial people prefer to speak about READ (as it is connected with labour saving), while the scientific community more often uses REC, as it presents recognition ability of an algorithm or a system.

The *detection process* targets an item with a certain property or of a certain type (for example, cheques of a particular payee). Typically, such items are very rare, their fraction being much lower than the total number of items in the flow. Traditional detection task is finding cheques without payer's signature – these cheques are not valid. New demands include detection of absence of any mandatory cheque fields; detection of payee and/or payer names belonging to certain people; detection of fraud cheques in the cheque flow, etc.

While recognition-type processes usually have well organized but non-automated prototypes in cheque processing industry, detection processes are somewhat new and frequently do not have manual analogues. So, their implementation supposes creation of new industrial procedures, rather than replacing existing human operators by computers. As much work as possible should be performed automatically, and only a very small part demanded be done manually. In such a process, all items are analysed by an automatic system, which selects a set of suspicious items – potential detection targets. Only these items are subjects of human inspection. For example, 1% of cheques can be selected as potentially invalid items. After manual verification, half of them can be found as valid; the other half being really invalid should be rejected as non-payable cheques.

Efficiency of a detection process can be characterized by two complementary values: the *detection rate* (DET) and the *suspect rate* (SUSP):

DET = 100% * (# of detected target items/total # of target items)

SUSP = 100% * (# of suspicious items (potential targets)/total # of items)

The lower the suspect rate, the lower is the cost of the detection process, because the volume of a manual work decreases. The higher is detection rate, the higher is the revenue from the process implementation. The process is profitable when its revenue from detected targets is greater than its cost determined by the suspect rate. So, the process might be efficient even if it has not a very high detection rate, which can be achieved, for instance, by selective processing of items in the flow. For example, DET = 50% of cheque frauds might bring higher savings than the cost of manual inspection of suspicious items at SUSP = 1%.

The *verification process* is complementary to that of detection: while detection process finds "bad" items, verification targets at "good" ones. Again, the fraction of "bad" items is supposed to be tiny in the item flow. Verification is somehow similar to a quality control: all items are investigated, most of them are accepted, but some are rejected. An example of a traditional verification process is the payee name verification while cheque depositing. New demands include verification of payer's signature and document image quality verification.

As detection, verification processes frequently do not have manual analogues and their implementation supposes creation of new automated processing where most of the work should be done automatically, and the rest needs manual processing. An automated system should analyse all items and pass only the good ones. Items rejected by the system are potential invalids – they are verified manually. Typical goal of a verification process is to pass only "good" items with a guaranteed (and very low) level of "bad" items among them. This needs total processing of every item in the flow, which might be very expensive. Totality of the process and demanded very low level of missed "bad" items are two important differences of a verification process from a detection one.

For example, all cheques go to automatic image quality control. In this process 98% passes the control, and 2% are rejected as suspicious. After manual inspection, most of suspicious cheques are also verified, however, some documents with unreadable or corrupted information fields are considered non-payable.

Efficiency of a verification process can be measured by the same parameters as for detection one: the detection rate (DET) and the suspect rate (SUSP). The cost of a verification process is proportional to the fraction of suspicious items (SUSP), which have to be processed manually. In cheque processing applications, verification processes are rarely profitable, because most of them are mandatory. For example, recently, US Check 21 standard has obliged verification of cheque image quality in all applications, which use digital copies of paper documents.

Table 20.1 summarizes properties of three process types described in this section.

Table 20.1. Summary of main automated processes in cheque processing applications

Process	Typical tasks	Typical demanded rates	Automatic work (%)	Manual work (%)
Recognition	Amount recognition, date recognition, payee name recognition	READ = 50–80% SUBS = 1–3%	READ	100-READ
Detection	Cheque fraud detection, invalid cheque detection	DET = 50–90% SUSP < 2%	100-SUSP	SUSP
Verification	Image quality verification, signature verification	DET = 90–99% SUSP < 5%	100-SUSP	SUSP

20.3 Payee Name Recognition

Most of cheque recognition papers are devoted to recognition of courtesy and legal amounts in cheque images [4, 7, 8, 10, 12–14]. We have also presented our technology in this domain in several papers [1, 6, 11]. Since that time the geography of cheque amount applications has been greatly enlarged (see Section 20.4.1), but the technology itself remained basically the same. So in this section we consider another technology that aims at recognition of the payee name field.

20.3.1 Field Location and Extraction

One of the most difficult tasks in bank cheque data analysis is the proper location of information fields. Despite numerous standards and regulations defining how a cheque should look like and what it should contain, bank clients have enough freedom to design their own cheques with different layouts, miscellaneous pictures, exotic fonts, etc. Thus, a bank cheque is a typical loosely structured document: getting a cheque you can be sure that certain information fields are present in it, but you never know where these fields are really placed.

For example, in US business cheques issued by corporate clients, the payee name can be found nearly anywhere in the left part of the cheque image (see Figure 20.2). It can be placed on a separate text-line below or above the legal amount, or present in a payee address block, or even sealed by a rubber stamp.

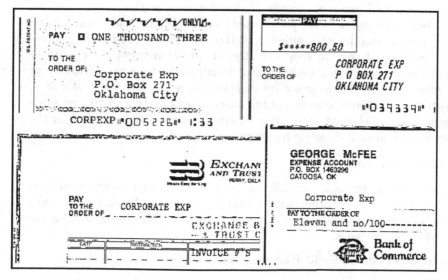

Fig. 20.2. Four examples of payee name positioning in business cheques.

There are not many features, which help to locate a payee name. For business cheques they are:

- Key-words "pay to the order of" or "to the order of" in the vicinity of the name.
- A paragraph of several left-aligned text-lines – possible payee address block that contains the payee name, or possible "pay to the order of" paragraph.
- Possible underline of the payee name text-line.
- Possible long text-lines (legal amount) above or below the name.

We use all these features in the payee name location process. As soon as a business cheque comes into processing, all machine-printed text-lines in its left part are located and then their mutual positions are analysed to form the set of possible payee name candidate locations. Each location is characterized by the set of quantitative features that are used to train a neural network (NN) estimating the posterior probability of every candidate to be the true payee name. The candidate with the maximum probability is then taken for further analysis. In case the candidate location contains several text-lines, only the first one is considered a potential payee name. On an average, this enables to reach 90–99% correct locations of the payee name field. After cleaning the noise and side objects (e.g. underlines), the image of the payee name is sent for recognition.

In case of personal cheques, payee name position is more stable than in business ones. Usually, the name is located opposite to the pre-printed currency sign (the courtesy amount marker) and underlined. It can also be preceded by the key-phrase "pay to the order of" – see Figure 20.1. More than 95% personal cheques are handwritten, so the task is to find a handwritten text-line in the pre-defined location. In this case we extract the payee name zone by its position, and then remove all pre-printed objects of the cheque layout to keep only the handwritten text-line. The latter operation is quite delicate and difficult to adjust, because handwritten text is often very similar to other information fields. So there is a danger of both under- and over-cleaning of the payee name field. Figure 20.3 presents several name fields extracted from cheque images. Slant correction of the extracted images is done for handwritten fields at this step.

20.3.2 Field Recognition

Recognition technologies are different for handwritten and machine-printed fields. Machine-printed fields are recognized character-by-character, while handwritten fields (both hand-printed and cursive) are recognized on the word or phrase basis.

Machine-Printed Field Recognition

First, text-line is segmented into potential characters. Segmentation takes place "in parallel" with character recognition: every potential character image goes to an OCR, which estimates its score. Segmentations with higher

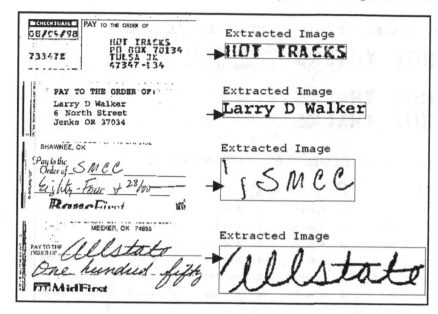

Fig. 20.3. Location and extraction of the payee name field.

scores are selected and form the preliminary character set. Then preliminary characters are split and/or merged depending on their sizes, scores and general properties of a text-line such as font regularity and font discontinuity. Finally, several character segmentation options are formed, each having its own probability (Figure 20.4). For example, in the Figure 20.4 the first character may be presented by a single box (correctly containing an "H") or by two boxes (erroneously containing two "I"s).

Once characters are recognized, the payee name candidates are stochastically generated by combining character classes with their probabilities, probabilities of character segmentation options and word segmentation options (Figure 20.5).

At the next step, payee name candidate list is generated from word candidates the same way as word candidates were generated from character recognition results. With this, raw recognition of the field is finished. Note, at this moment the correct candidate for the above example is only at second position in the list:

1. HOT IRACKS = 0.32520
2. HOT TRACKS = 0.13726
3. HDT IRACKS = 0.05914

Finally, the obtained raw list is filtered with a dictionary of possible payee names or with a dictionary of possible words, if they are available. The dictionary of words can be internal for the system, while the name dictionary is usually supplied by a customer. Of course, it can cover only

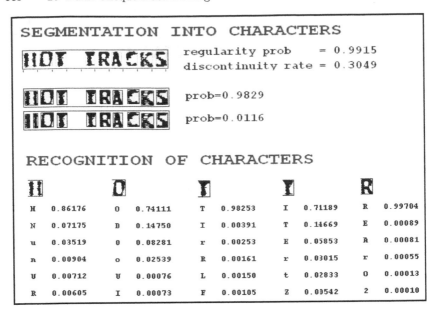

Fig. 20.4. Character segmentation and recognition of a machine-printed field.

RECOGNITION OF OBJECTS

HOT		IRACKS	
HOT	0.70393	IRACKS	0.46203
HDT	0.12869	TRACKS	0.19516
NOT	0.06594	IRAEKS	0.08058
UOT	0.03453	IRASKS	0.07104
NDT	0.01205	IRACES	0.06104
IIOT	0.00838	ERACKS	0.03797

Fig. 20.5. Word segmentation and recognition of a machine-printed field.

a part of the set of possible names. Dictionary post-processing greatly improves recognition results, as it can be seen from Table 20.2. This topic is discussed also in Section 20.3.3.

Handwritten Field Recognition

Recognition of handwritten fields is based on Hidden Markov Models (HMMs). First, the extracted field image is segmented into graphemes

Table 20.2. Payee name recognition with and without dictionary fully covering the set of recognized names

REC(%) SUBS(%)	Machine-printed without dictionary (REC, %)	Machine-printed with dictionary (REC, %)	Handwritten with dictionary (REC, %)
1	–	90.1	70.2
2	17.8	91.0	74.9
5	60.8	91.1	79.5
10	87.9	–	82.2

Fig. 20.6. Handwritten payee name recognition with a dictionary.

which are supposed to be smaller entities than letters. In Figure 20.6 graphemes are displayed with alternate colours. Then graphemes are classified with a neural network to go from pixel representation to a feature representation, each grapheme being associated with a class probability vector. Obtained sequence of vectors is used to match with HMM models of dictionary words (phrases). Word models can be "static" trained in advance for the most frequent words like numerals, or "dynamic" built when necessary from letter models. The best-matching models form the list of possible answers, each answer being associated with its probability. In the example of Figure 20.6, the correct answer is obtained at first position in the list. Detailed description of this technology can be found in [1, 3].

It is important, that word/phrase models should be build prior to the beginning of the recognition. Thus, unlike the machine-printed text, the handwritten text can be recognized only when the dictionary of possible words/phrases is provided to the recognizer. For the payee name recognition this means that the customer who wants to use the system should either supply a dictionary of possible names or allow the use of a generic dictionary of most frequent names, which of course could be incomplete.

Table 20.2 below demonstrates recognition results of the payee name field separately for machine-printed (business) cheques and personal (handwritten) cheques taken from a real document flow. The ceiling of recognition rate at 91% is mainly explained by field location problems and partly by presence of over-lighted cheque images where the name is hardly can be read.

20.3.3 Semantic Processing

Alias Problem

One of the difficulties in name recognition is so-called alias problem. Aliases are different forms of a word (in particular, a name), which have identical semantic meaning. Examples of possible name aliases are:

- Reduced or abbreviated form(s) of the prototype name (California Gas → CA Gas)
- The prototype name with suffix or prefix words (AmEx → AmEx Co).
- The prototype name with inserted/omitted non-important words (ATT → AT and T).
- Misspelled name, which however can be identified with the prototype (Johannes → Johanes).
- Permutated words in the name (United States Treasury → Treasury of the United States).

Typical information fields where aliases can be found are payee-, payer- or addressee-names in cheques. Also, aliases are often appearing in dictionaries, which are used for post-processing recognition results. In this case, the name in the recognized document can be different from any its aliases in the dictionary. Presence of aliases leads to several problems:

- The correctly recognized name is rejected or gets a low score because the dictionary does not contain this name, having contained however its aliases. This reduces the recognition rate and increases rejections.
- The correctly recognized name is accepted, but considered as an error, because the recognition result does not match the desired truth name which is expressed by an alias.
- The correctly recognized name is rejected because the dictionary contains neither this name nor its aliases.

Two instruments named *alias detector* and *alias generator* have been developed to take into account presence of possible aliases in the name field and overcome the above problems.

Alias Detector

The alias detector evaluates the probability that two input names are aliases. It is based on a neural network trained to distinguish aliases from non-aliases. Input features of this NN are the answers of seven heuristic

Table 20.3. Detection of payee name aliases at different detection thresholds

Detection threshold	Detected non-aliases (%)	False-detected non-aliases (%)	Detected aliases (%)	Missed aliases (%)
0.5	99.7	0.3	97.4	2.6
0.8	99.8	0.2	94.3	5.7
0.9	99.89	0.11	90.9	9.1
0.95	99.95	0.05	85.6	14.4

primitive detectors, each of which is specialized in detecting aliases of a certain type:

- Primitive detectors 1 and 2 cheque possible word permutations in the name, as well as letter permutations.
- Primitive detectors 3 and 4 detect aliases originating from mis-spellings and typing errors.
- Primitive detector 5 and 6 find out and cheques reduced or abbreviated words in the compared names.
- Primitive detector 7 compares names after removing non-important words, articles and suffix words.

All primitive detectors are functions returning a score from 0 to 1. These scores are features for the NN-based alias detector. Training of this NN has been performed on the manually annotated data of 2000 dictionaries of real payee names as they were read and keyed by human operators.

From the annotated material, approximately 2,000,000 name pairs were generated, 20,000 (1%) being pairs of real aliases. All pairs of real aliases and 10% non-alias pairs were used for training the alias detector. Quality of the obtained detector is characterized by figures presented in Table 20.3.

Thus, at the probability threshold 0.95, approximately 86% of aliases are successfully detected with an error rate 0.05%, i.e. 5 non-aliases is erroneously detected as aliases among 10,000 name pairs (in average). Such an error rate is negligible compare to the usual error rate of recognition engines, so alias probability level 0.95 was chosen as decision threshold of the alias detector.

Despite the fact that annotated material has been taken from data of a particular site, alias detector is not site-specific, as its all primitive detectors are not site-dependent. We successfully use it for any Anglo-Saxon material of personal or company names. Some experiments even demonstrated that it is applicable also for names from non-English speaking countries, e.g. France.

Alias Generator

The task of the alias generator is to produce the list of most probable aliases of a given name. The core of the alias generator is a name thesaurus. It consists of nests, each nest representing aliases of one name along with their frequencies. The thesaurus was filled with data from 20,000 name dictionaries containing about 700,000 real names as they appeared in the cheque flow. The thesaurus filling consisted of four steps:

1. *Creation of the name frequency list* (approximately 300,000 entries).
2. *Primary thesaurus filling.* Each name from 20,000 most frequent names is considered as a nest. With the alias detector, it is compared with all existing nests and either is added to the most similar nest, or forms a new nest. The most frequent names cover about 45% of name data.
3. *Compression of nests.* For each nest, most frequent names, words, and abbreviations are remembered. This information forms a canonical representation of a nest. Based on the canonical representation, the list of most frequent aliases is generated for each nest. This list is truncated when the cumulative frequency of its members covers 98% of all possible aliases. Typically, such a list contains 5–15 members.
4. *Secondary thesaurus filling.* Reminded names are compared with the lists of generated aliases in all nests and possibly added to the closest nest.

The filled thesaurus covers approximately 60% of names from processed dictionaries. After filling, it is used for alias generation. Given an input name, the generator determines the most probable thesaurus nest to which the input name belongs. If such a nest is found, the list of most probable aliases is returned as a result. Optionally, this list can be truncated or enlarged depending on the desired number or frequency of generated aliases.

It should be noted, that the thesaurus is filled with data from a particular set of dictionaries. Fortunately, names presented in these dictionaries were of a great variability – input cheques came from different states and different companies. So, hypothetically this thesaurus can be used not only for a particular site, but also for other similar applications. However, it is surely country-specific.

Implementation of Alias Recognition Techniques

There are several ways to improve recognition results with the alias detector and the alias generator:

1. The number of recognition candidates in the output list is reduced by aggregating all aliases of each name. The idea behind this is to get a more "contrast" list where each name is represented by a single entry. This is important both for cursive- and machine-printed name recognition, making the list shorter and candidate scores more objective.
2. The name dictionary is extended with the thesaurus and alias generator by the most frequent names absent in the dictionary and most frequent aliases of dictionary entries in a hope to cover more forms of recognized

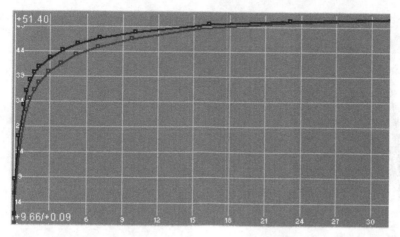

Fig. 20.7. Alias detector used for shrinking the output candidate list (upper curve) vs. the base recognition engine (lower curve). The X-axis represents recognition rate and Y-axis represents substitution rate.

names. This is more important for recognition of cursive names, as it is sensitive to the set of input models.

3. A more objective result evaluation procedure compares recognition results with truth data taking into account alias presence.

Figure 20.7 demonstrates the influence of alias detector used for shrinking the output list. As can be seen, this essentially improves recognition rate in the domain of relatively low substitutions. A low recognition rate (∼51%) is explained by the fact that nearly half of recognized names were not covered by the input dictionary provided by the customer in this application.

After extending input dictionary with most frequent names obtained with the alias generator, further result improvement was obtained (Figure 20.8).

The last experiment demonstrates efficiency of the alias detector in non-US application – payee name recognition on UK cheques (Figure 20.9). In this case the detector was used both for shrinking the output candidate list and objective evaluation of recognition results. Alias generator was not used in this case, as it is applicable only to US payee names.

20.4 Cheque Mining with A2iA CheckReader™

20.4.1 Amount Recognition

A2iA CheckReader™ was primarily designed to replace human operators in automated payment systems, i.e. to read amounts of bank cheques

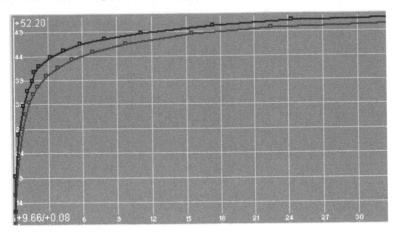

Fig. 20.8. Alias detector and alias generator used together (upper curve) vs. the base recognition engine (lower curve). X-axis represents recognition rate, Y-axis represents substitution rate.

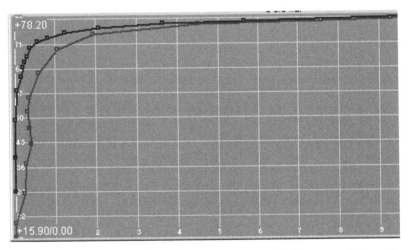

Fig. 20.9. Payee name recognition on UK cheques with alias recognition technology (upper curve) and without it (lower curve). The X-axis represents recognition rate and Y-axis represents substitution rate.

and associated documents [6, 11]. Besides cheques themselves, a real document flow contains other items, such as deposit tickets, debit and credit forms, money orders, cash tickets, etc. As cheques, these items also contain amounts to be recognized. Normally, all payment documents are scanned in a common stream and should be processed in a similar way. Thus, the main task of the system in this application is detection and recognition of amounts on all documents of the flow.

Table 20.4. Cheque amount recognition results of country-specific CheckReader versions

Country-specific version	Recognized LA language(s)	REC (%) at SUBS=1%	REC (%) at SUBS=2%	Maximum REC (%)
Australia	English	79	83	89
Belgium	n/a	91	93	94.5
Brazil	Portuguese	52	60	75
Canada	English and French	75	79	85
France	French	70	76	82
Germany	n/a	65	71	80
Hong Kong	English and Chinese	63	70	80
Ireland	English	81	86	89.5
Italy	Italian	65	72	80
Mexico	Spanish	55	59	71
Malaysia	English	57	62	72
New Caledonia	French	55	62	72
Portugal	Portuguese	68	74	85
Singapore	English	71	76	83
Thailand	n/a	42	50	63
UK	English	80	84	88
US	English	79	82	87

Since 1994, 17 country-specific versions of the system have been developed, most of them providing recognition and cross-validation of courtesy amount (CA) and legal amount (LA). Recent developments included recognition of handwritten Chinese hieroglyphic amounts on Hong Kong cheques [16] and cursive Italian LA frequently written without word spaces. Table 20.4 summarizes amount recognition results at different substitution levels. In most of real applications, customers either chose substitution level between 1 and 1.5%, or use maximum recognition. Results of Table 20.4 should be considered with care, as they are site-specific. From site to site, the rates can easily vary within 5% margins mainly depending on the quality of input cheque images.

20.4.2 Recognition of Other Cheque Fields

Gradually, CheckReader enlarges the variety of recognized field types. The demand of new field recognition usually originates from a single customer, and then the new functionality added to the system is spread among other customers and frequently extended to other countries. For example, cheque date recognition developed first for Canada is now available for six country versions, and payee name recognition – for three countries.

Table 20.5. Recognition results of CheckReader versions. Each cell presents values REC (%)/SUBS (%) for corresponding country version and field type

Country	Date	Payee name (with dict.)	Payer address (without dict.)	Code line
Canada	60/3	–	–	94/1
France	39/3	71/1	Max 55	98/1
Italy	42/3	–	–	73/1
Ireland	52/3	–	–	85/1
UK	55/3	78/1	–	96/1
US	65/3	82/1	max 58	85/1

Technology of cheque field recognition is similar to that described in Section 20.3. The first step consists of field location in the cheque image with subsequent extraction of machine-printed or handwritten text-lines to be recognized. Further steps are different for fields with well-separated characters (machine- or hand-printed) and fields with touching characters (unconstrained handwriting or pure cursive).

Well-separated fields are segmented into characters that are recognized by OCRs. Word and phrase options are then stochastically generated from character recognition results forming the raw candidate list of possible field contents. In case of available semantic or linguistic information, the raw list is post-processed or filtered with a dictionary to improve the result.

Unconstrained or cursive fields are segmented into graphemes and recognized with HMMs. In this case presence of linguistic or semantic information is mandatory; mainly it is used to prepare properly the set of models to which the recognized field is matched.

The concluding step is decision making. It is similar for all field types. It consists of evaluating the probability that the obtained recognition result is correct. Normally, a specially trained NN is used to fulfil this operation (see [5] for more detailed description of the technology). If the obtained decision probability is higher than a pre-defined threshold, the recognition result is accepted; otherwise, it is rejected. Table 20.5 summarizes CheckReader results for non-amount field recognition.

20.4.3 Detection and Verification Tasks

Recently, CheckReader has acquired functionalities to accomplish new types of cheque processing tasks. They are: detection of invalid cheques, cheque fraud detection, detection of names from "black lists" and name verification.

Invalid Cheque Detection

In every country, there are regulations specifying the set of features that a valid cheque should possess. Mainly they concern presence or filling of

Table 20.6. Invalid cheque detection by CheckReader versions

Country	DET (%) at SUSP=1%	DET (%) at SUSP=2%	DET (%) at SUSP=5%
Canada	50	68	81
France	45	65	92
US	65	76	85

Table 20.7. Fraud cheque detection by the CheckReader-US

DET (%)	79.5	92.4	95.9	97.8
SUSP (%)	0.5	1	2	5

certain information fields in the cheque. For example, both courtesy and legal amounts should be indicated; payee name should be present as well as the payer's address; the cheque should be signed by the payer.

To answer a question whether a cheque is valid or not, CheckReader is trained to locate all mandatory fields in the cheque image and detect whether each of them is filled or remains empty. If at least one detector reports emptiness of a mandatory field, the cheque is considered suspicious and sent to the suspect basket. Suspicious cheques are evaluated by a neural net, which is trained to distinguish invalid cheques from valid ones. This network returns a cheque invalidity probability. When it is higher than a decision threshold, the cheque goes to manual inspection to confirm its invalidity. Table 20.7 presents invalid cheque detection results achieved by the CheckReader. Test data included 3000 valid and several hundred invalid cheques of different types for every country version. Most invalid cheques for the test were selected while visual inspection of real documents and some were prepared manually.

Detection of Cheque Frauds

Another important functionality is fraudulent cheques detection. Cheque frauds become a serious problem causing sensible losses in payment systems, especially in US where many people do not have their own bank accounts and can get cash at the moment of cheque depositing.

To detect cheque frauds in the cheque flow, CheckReader has an ability to compare each input cheque with reference cheque(s) of the payer. Of course, every payer who wants to protect his cheques from counterfeits should supply at least one valid cheque and all mandatory fields properly filled as a reference. The payer's account number indicated in the code-line identifies the reference.

Twelve various fraud detectors are used to compare a new incoming cheque with the existing reference(s). Each detector verifies a certain feature, which can indicate a possible fraud. In particular, detectors analyse geometry of cheque layout; positions of pre-printed markers, logos and key-words; positions of cheque information fields. Other detectors analyse payer's handwriting (in case of a handwritten cheque). There are also detectors to find hidden cross-correlations between the content of the reference(s) and the investigated cheques. Results of all detectors are integrated and fraud probability of the analysed cheque is evaluated. If it is higher than a given threshold, the cheque is considered a potential fraud and goes to manual verification.

Table 20.7 presents experimental results of fraud detection obtained on a data set of 5780 documents. One third of the set were fraud cheques manually simulated from real ones. Probably frauds were not enough sophisticated, as demonstrated detection rate is rather high.

Name Detection and Verification

A number of cheque processing applications are concentrated around payee and payer's name analysis. Besides ordinary name recognition described in Section 20.2, they include detection and verification of special names. In both of these applications, the system is supplied with a dictionary of names, which should be found in the cheque.

Name detection is a search process, when the system is supplied with a so-called "black list" of wanted people (e.g. terrorists, criminals, etc.). Then every name recognized in the cheque is matched with names from the black list and if matching occurs, the cheque goes to a special basket of items to be manually inspected.

The difference from the ordinary name recognition is in the percentage of cheque names covered by the dictionary: in case of usual recognition dictionary coverage varies from 30 to 100%, while in detection tasks it is essentially lower than 1%. To adapt CheckReader to this task we tuned decision-making module to detect demanded fraction of "black" names. Table 20.8 present detection results for payee and payer names. Results for payer name are higher because this name is always machine-printed, while payee name is handwritten in 60–80% of cheques.

Name verification is one of the ways to prevent cheque frauds. In this case, the bank issuing the cheque supplies it with a special record, duplicating the payee name. When such a cheque is deposited, its payee name is verified with the recorded name coming to the depositor by an alternative information channel. Mismatch of two names signals that the cheque is a potential fraud. Despite its seeming simplicity, this task is one of the most difficult, because (as every verification task) it demands analysis of every cheque and a very high acceptance rate. Therefore, both name location and recognition rates should be good enough; otherwise, too many cheques would be rejected and the fraction of manual work becomes too big. Fortunately, all cheques in this application are machine-printed.

To solve this task, CheckReader uses the payee recognition process described in Section 20.2, i.e. makes full name recognition without dictionary.

Table 20.8. "Black" name detection by the CheckReader-US

Field type	DET (%) at SUSP=1%	DET (%) at SUSP=2%	DET (%) at SUSP=5%
Payee name	78	80.5	84
Payer name	92	93.5	94

Table 20.9. Payee name verification by the CheckReader-US

DET (%)	90	92	93.5	95
SUSP (%)	1	2	5	10

Then, the obtained candidate list is compared with the recorded name, which plays the role of a dictionary with a single entry. A special decision module has been developed to reach demanded performances of the verification process. The achieved results are present in Table 20.9.

20.5 Conclusions

We have presented integrated technologies of bank cheque processing, which aim to extract and use all available information from the cheque image. Three types of processes were considered: recognition (of the cheque amount, date, payee name, payer address, code line), detection (of the signature, "black" payee names, frauds) and verification (of the payee name). Implementation of developed technologies in the A2iA CheckReader™ demonstrates that a recognition system is able to reach the level of automation at 60–80% in recognition processes and 90–99% in detection and verification processes, thus greatly reducing manual work in banking industry.

References

1. Augustin, E., Baret, O., Price, D., and Knerr, S. (1998). Legal amount recognition on French bank checks using a neural network-hidden Markov model hybrid. In: S.-W. Lee (Ed). *Advances in Handwriting Recognition.* Singapore: World Scientific, pp. 81–90.
2. In: Impedovo, S., Wang, P., and Bunke, H. (Eds) (1997). *Automatic Bankcheck Processing.* Singapore: World Scientific.
3. Dupre, X. and Augustin, E. (2004). Hidden Markov models for couples of letters applied to handwriting recognition. *Proceedings of the Seventeenth International Conference on Pattern Recognition, Cambridge, UK,* pp. 618–621.
4. Dzuba, G., Filatov, A., Gershuny, D., Kil, I., and Nikitin, V. (1997). Check amount recognition based on the cross validation of courtesy and legal

amount fields. *International Journal of Pattern Recognition and Artificial Intelligence, 11(4)*, 639–655.

5. Gorski, N. (1997). Optimizing error-reject trade-off in recognition systems. *Proceedings of the Fourth International Conference on Document Analysis and Recognition. Ulm, Germany*, pp. 1092–1096.

6. Gorski, N., Anisimov, V., Augustin, E., Baret, O., and Maximov, S. (2001). Industrial bank check processing: A2iA check reader. *International Journal of Document Analysis and Recognition, (3)4*, 196–206.

7. Greco, N., Impedovo, D., Lucchese, M., Salzo, A., and Sarcinella, L. (2003). Bank-check processing system: modifications due to the new European currency. *Proceedings of the Seventh International Conference on Document Analysis and Recognition, Edinburgh, Scotland*, pp. 343–348.

8. Guillevic, D. and Suen, C.Y. (1995). Cursive script recognition applied to the processing of bank checks. *Proceedings of the Third International Conference on Document Analysis and Recognition. Montreal, Canada*, pp. 11–14.

9. Kaufmann, G. and Bunke, H. (1999). Error localization and correction in check processing. In: S.-W. Lee (Ed.). *Advances in Handwriting Recognition*. Singapore: World Scientific, pp. 111–120.

10. Kelland, S. and Wesolkovski, S. (1999). A comparison of research and production architectures for check reading. *Proceedings of the Fifth International Conference on Document Analysis and Recognition, Bangalore, India*, pp. 99–102.

11. Knerr, S., Anisimov, V., Baret, O., Gorski, N., Price. D., and Simon, J.-C. (1997). The A2iA intercheque system: courtesy amount and legal amount recognition for French checks. *International Journal of Pattern Recognition and Artificial Intelligence, 11(4)*, pp. 505–547.

12. Lethelier, E., Leroux, M., and Gilloux, M. (1995). An automatic reading system for handwritten numeral amounts on French checks. *Proceedings of the Third International Conference on Document Analysis and Recognition, Montreal, Canada*, pp. 92–96.

13. Di Lecce, V., Dimauro, A., Guerriero, A., Impedovo, S., Pirlo, G., and Salzo, A. (2000). A new hybrid approach for legal amount recognition. *Proceedings of the Seventh International Workshop on Frontiers in Handwriting Recognition, Amsterdam, The Netherlands*, pp. 199–208.

14. Oliveira, L., Sabourin, R., Bortolozzi, F., and Suen, C.Y. (2001). A modular system to recognize numerical amounts on Brazilian bank checks. *Proceedings of the Sixth International Conference on Document Analysis and Recognition, Seattle, USA*, pp. 389–394.

15. Shetty, S., Shridhar, M., and Houle, G. (2000). Background elimination in bank checks using greyscale morphology. *Proceedings of the Seventh International Workshop on Frontiers in Handwriting Recognition, Amsterdam, The Netherlands*, pp. 83–91.

16. Tang, H., Augustin, E., Suen, C.Y., Baret, O., and Cheriet, M. (2004). Recognition of unconstrained legal amounts handwritten on Chinese bank checks. *Proceedings of the Seventeenth International Conference on Pattern Recognition, Cambridge, UK*, pp. 610–613.

Index